FAMILY
MATTERS

Family Matters: An Introduction to Family Sociology in Canada, Third Edition
Barbara A. Mitchell

First published in 2017 by
Canadian Scholars, an imprint of CSP Books Inc.
425 Adelaide Street West, Suite 200
Toronto, Ontario
M5V 3C1

www.canadianscholars.ca

Library and Archives Canada Cataloguing in Publication

Mitchell, Barbara A. (Barbara Ann), 1961-, author
        Family matters : an introduction to family sociology in Canada / Barbara A. Mitchell. —
Third edition.

Includes bibliographical references and index.
Issued in print and electronic formats.
ISBN 978-1-77338-021-6 (softcover).--ISBN 978-1-77338-022-3 (PDF).--
ISBN 978-1-77338-023-0 (EPUB)

        1. Family--Canada--Textbooks. 2. Textbooks. I. Title.

HQ560.M58 2017   306.850971   C2017-906632-3
                                                                 C2017-906633-1

Cover and text design by Elisabeth Springate
Typesetting by Brad Horning

Printed and bound in Canada by Webcom

FAMILY MATTERS

An Introduction
to Family Sociology
in Canada

THIRD EDITION

Barbara A. Mitchell

CANADIAN SCHOLARS

Toronto | Vancouver

Contents

PART I: UNDERSTANDING CONTINUITY, DIVERSITY, IN-EQUALITY, AND SOCIAL CHANGE IN FAMILIES

Chapter 14: Trying to Make Ends Meet: Family Poverty, Living on the Margins, and Financial Struggle   365

Chapter 15: Families in Crisis: Family Violence, Abuse, and Stress   392

Chapter 16: Families and the State: Family Policy in an Era of Globalization and Economic Uncertainty   421

List of Boxes, Tables, and Figures

CHAPTER 4

CHAPTER 5

CHAPTER 6

CHAPTER 7

CHAPTER 11

CHAPTER 12

CHAPTER 16

Preface

The first family-focused course that I took was in high school, at London Central Secondary School in Ontario during my senior year. And from that time onward, I was hooked! In this class, we learned about different family structures and forms, as well as family life in foreign places and fascinating cultures. This class opened my eyes to a whole new way of seeing the world. Growing up in the 1960s and 1970s in Kitchener, then just outside of Stratford, Ontario, and subsequently London, Ontario, while I finished secondary school, most of my friends and neighbours—in fact almost all of the people I saw in my everyday life and on television—were fairly homogeneous. They tended to be relatively middle class, living in nuclear, heterosexual, biological-parent family structures, and were from British or European backgrounds. It was rare to see deviations from this norm, since "non-traditional" family types such as stepfamilies, single-parent families, cohabiting, mixed-race, and same-sex families were uncommon at the time. Of course these family types certainly did exist, and I had experienced a single-father, adoptive, and stepfamily environment myself.

Beyond my own family and a few others, however, the most common "alternative" family structure that I observed up close was that of my rural Mennonite neighbours during my teenage years. To me, these families seemed markedly exotic and different than others, with their traditional lifestyles, distinctive dress, and highly segregated gender roles. "Older order" families still relied on horse and buggies as a principal means of transportation and lived on large farms with no electricity. Of course, once I got to know these families, in many ways, they were not that much different than my own. Similar to my own parents, these parents also wanted to raise happy, healthy, and productive children in a safe, peaceful, and loving environment.

Once I started post-secondary school at the University of Waterloo in 1981, I continued to pursue my fascination with family studies. Canadian families were also undergoing metamorphosis at the time. These changes prompted theorists and researchers (who were increasingly likely to be female) to question conventional conceptualizations and ways of studying families. Emergent trends such as women's rising labour force participation and college/university enrolment, skyrocketing divorce, and changing immigration patterns were also creating a richer and more complex tapestry of family life—patterns that sparked my interest in wanting to know more about the factors underlying processes of family social change.

Graduate school at the University of Waterloo and McMaster University allowed me to expand on many conventional themes in family sociology. This was mainly due to the encouragement and inspiration so generously offered to me by the many terrific professors at these institutions. And although the curriculum was only beginning to incorporate aging and generational issues, these soon became interests that I developed while working on my Master's and Ph.D. theses. In part, this was the result of the strong influence of social demographers who had begun to document and elucidate the phenomenon of population aging. I also developed a keen interest in life-course issues and gendered processes as I began to appreciate the value in studying families throughout the entire lifespan, rather than at only one point in time. In addition, I realized that good health is not experienced by all families but is integral to positive family functioning and relationships, as well as successful aging.

Since working and teaching as a family sociologist and gerontologist at Simon Fraser University, I have continued with this perspective on families, viewing them from a critical, gendered lens, synthesized with a dynamic life-course approach. I also recognize that aging and health/well-being issues need to receive more than just cursory attention. Indeed, you will see throughout this book that a sociological focus on the changing roles of women and men in families and society is fundamental for understanding a wide variety of issues relevant to our everyday lives, including our health and well-being.

In closing, writing this introductory family textbook—which is suitable for university courses on the family or for anyone wanting to learn more about Canadian family theory and research—has been a way for me to share with you my own personal journey and enthusiasm for family sociology. It has also provided me with the opportunity to contribute to a field that I believe is the most exciting and important substantive area in sociology. Therefore, my greatest hope is not only that you will enjoy reading and learning valuable information presented in this textbook, but that you, too, will become hooked on family sociology.

ACKNOWLEDGEMENTS

Writing a textbook like this one is an enormously time-consuming endeavour that requires patience and dependence on others' expertise, guidance, wisdom, and support. To this end, many people have graciously contributed their time and enthusiasm to bring this project to fruition.

First, I would like to extend a heartfelt appreciation to everyone at Canadian Scholars' Press who assisted with the production of this work. In particular, I am extremely grateful to Megan Mueller, the editorial director of the first edition; the editorial director of the second edition, Lily Bergh; as well as my recent editorial/production managers, Natalie Garriga and Karri Yano. These women have provided me not only with prompt, impeccable editorial assistance during various stages of writing, revising, and polishing the text, but also served as an enormous source of support and encouragement. In short, they should be recognized for their incredible professionalism, collaborative working style, and steadfast enthusiasm. This created a working relationship that was not only very productive but highly enjoyable as well.

I would also like to express my sincere gratitude to all of the reviewers who provided me with constructive and insightful feedback on earlier editions of this manuscript. These reviewers provided me with thought-provoking and highly useful suggestions that improved the quality of this work.

Also, special thanks to Bea Jablonski, a graduate student in the Department of Sociology/Anthropology at Simon Fraser University, for her assistance with updating some of the material in this book and proof-reading, as well as to Melinda Aikin of the Department of Gerontology at Simon Fraser University for some technical assistance with table/figure formatting.

And last, but most importantly, I would like to express appreciation to my own family—from my large, extended family network to my immediate family. These people have taught me innumerable lessons about the importance and meaning of family, regardless of its changing structure or relationship history. In particular, I would like to express my gratitude to my partner, best friend, and colleague, Andrew V. Wister, and my daughter, Kayzia, for their never-ending support. Andrew's keen interest and expertise in family sociology has undoubtedly influenced my writings on family sociology through our endless discussions about family theory and research. Moreover, the various editions of this book could not have been written without their patience, particularly given my excruciatingly long bouts of "hiding out" in the home office. In closing, the support that I have been fortunate enough to receive from these sources reinforces my fundamental belief that, indeed, "family matters."

NEW TO THIS THIRD EDITION

This third edition of the book has undergone a significant renovation since the first edition was published in 2009 and the second edition in 2012. While the overarching conceptual approach, organizational and pedagogical structure, broad thematic areas, and chapter topics remain similar, several key changes were made to this latest version. These revisions involved the creation of a new, separate chapter entirely devoted to Indigenous families in Canada. Material was also considerably expanded on two previous chapters: (1) cross-cultural and global families; and (2) immigration and the changing ethnic mosaic of Canada families. A comprehensive updating of material in existing chapters, including coverage of theoretical and research studies and the latest in student resources (such as the further reading lists and web sites, including Facebook and Twitter sites, if available, that appear at the end of each chapter). The most up-to-date statistical information available on family trends has also been added, as well as widened coverage of selected topical areas. For example, this newest edition provides more detailed discussions of areas including: intersectionality theory and emancipatory/participatory action research methods, the impact of environmental and technological change on families, skip-generation families, LAT relationships (Living Apart Together), consensual non-monogamies and plural partnerships, families dealing with health challenges (e.g., substance abuse and disabilities), and family caregiving as a basic human right.

And finally, more examples from today's news headlines and contemporary family-related events are provided, as well as case studies and examples of situations that you may have experienced in your own lives. These updated revisions are geared toward showing you the usefulness of sociology as an academic discipline and for better understanding our everyday experiences. My greatest hope is that this newest edition will help you to better recognize and appreciate why, and how, families matter and have such great significance for us all.

PART I

UNDERSTANDING CONTINUITY, DIVERSITY, INEQUALITY, AND SOCIAL CHANGE IN FAMILIES

The first part in this book (chapters 1 through 6) focuses on different ways of conceptualizing families and introduces us to broader text themes of continuity, diversity, inequality, and social change. These wider themes will be re-visited and applied to various substantive topics throughout the rest of the book since they are fundamental to family sociology. A central theme is that definitions, meanings, interpretations, and experiences of families are not static or universal and are constantly "under construction." This idea will be critically examined in chapter 1 and chapter 2 when we consider various institutional and ideological practices involved in defining, theorizing, and studying families. In addition, we will learn that shifting conceptualizations of family reflect how families (in whatever shape or form) are products of particular historical, economic, and political conditions and environments, as well as our own personal lived experiences and behaviours. This temporal and contextual perspective illuminates the idea that our shared and diverse experiences in families also change over the course of our lives. Overall, these fundamental notions underlie basic tenets of the life-course perspective and will be detailed in chapter 2, along with a number of other important theoretical and methodological orientations and issues.

Moreover, it will become apparent that, in order to dig beneath the surface of the broad themes of this text, we need to step outside of our own families and our own contemporary society in both time and place. Indeed, the value of situating family lives on anthropological, historical, cross-cultural, and global levels is revealed and elaborated in chapters 3, 4, and 5. This "digging" not only facilitates a better understanding of Canadian family life, but also reveals systemic or root causes of structured sources of inequality that are historically specific or that tie in to wider trends of inequity related to gender, social class, and ethnicity/race. Moreover, we can also critically reflect upon and contemplate how processes of colonization and the Residential School experience have had a devastating impact on "first families" or Indigenous communities in chapter 4.

In chapter 5, we will learn how our changing ethnic mosaic and immigration patterns have dramatically shaped the cultural landscape of Canadian society. It will also become apparent that broader globalization patterns and processes are influencing families worldwide for better and for worse, a theme that will be revisited in subsequent parts of the text. We will also see that amidst and embedded within these processes of globalization, there are incredible socio-demographic, political, and technological transformations that have occurred both outside and in Canadian families. For example, in chapter 6, we will trace evolving and gendered patterns of domestic and labour force participation—work that is fundamental to the making and reproduction of daily family life, as well as to our basic experiences of health and well-being over the life course. Yet despite significant gains made by women and new technological advancements, many inequities persist in the division of paid and unpaid labour in most of the world's economic systems.

CHAPTER 1

Family Matters: An Introduction to the Sociology of Canadian Families

LEARNING OBJECTIVES

In this chapter you will learn that ...

- families are diverse and represent a fundamental aspect of our lives as a key societal institution
- many ideological and institutional practices are involved in defining The Family
- definitions of family are socially constructed and can serve a diversity of interests and purposes
- family life—which is often viewed as a private zone or sphere—cannot easily be separated from the public sphere
- families are reciprocally linked to socio-economic, cultural, political, and technological circumstances
- the apocalyptic idea that the modern family is in decline or is falling apart is nothing new and operates largely to serve personal or political agendas

INTRODUCTION

Reflect for a moment on how your life has been and continues to be influenced by your family background as well as by certain family members such as your mother, father, sibling, or grandparent. Also try to imagine how their lives would be different if you had never been born. In addition, try to envision what life was like for your grandparents, and in what ways it was the same or different than yours. It should come as little surprise to you to realize that our unique family histories have a tremendous impact on our life courses, just as we have an enormous influence on the life courses of our own family. And since most of us live out a large portion of our lives in some sort of family setting, these experiences—both good and bad—inevitably transform and alter our lives forever.

From a life-course perspective—the foundational and guiding theoretical framework of this book—we can also easily see that families cannot be ignored if we want to understand societal and institutional patterns and processes around us, as well as social change. This is because the social relationships we call family are an integral feature and institution of society. In short, a **family** is a microsocial group that reciprocally links and reflects other macro-level institutions of society. In fact, no society has ever existed without some sort of social arrangements that are labelled kinship or familial. Thus, what people do in their families makes a significant difference not only to themselves but also to wider society. For example, if we increasingly choose to have small families, there may be repercussions not only for our own lived experiences in a family, but also for other institutions, such as the educational system and the economy.

Despite the significant impact of family life in all facets of human existence and our own intimate familiarity with some type of family, it will be shown that it is not that simple to identify or define families. It is also not that easy to situate our own personal family experiences within the context of previous family life, or within the context of other people's family lives. This is because our personal family stories unfold within a unique and particular historical time and place, another major tenet underlying the life-course perspective, which will be further discussed in subsequent chapters. This is why a sociological study of families is so important. Could you imagine, for instance, how misguided our theories, research, and social policies would be if we relied only on our own personal observations or "hunches" of what family is and means? Or, if we automatically assumed that family life was better in "the good old days," and that modern-day families are all falling apart? Indeed, family sociology becomes very useful (and critical) in understanding and critically evaluating existing social patterns, as well as in gaining valuable knowledge about Canada and the world that we live in.

In this chapter we will tackle and identify some provocative issues in order to lay the groundwork for subsequent chapters. We begin by asking the question, "What are families?" with the adjacent inquiries "What ideological and institutional practices are involved in defining family?" and "Why do these practices matter to us?" This is followed by a brief overview of selected socio-demographic, cultural, and technological trends in family life.

A basic summary of these patterns also provides an introduction to fundamental concepts, terms, themes, and issues that are pivotal to defining families and a sociological study of Canadian families. Notably, **social demography**, or the scientific study of population, is integral to family sociology, since it addresses social trends in family life such as marriage and divorce, changes in age at marriage and child-bearing, and living arrangements. Highlighting some of these basic family patterns also allows us to consider two sides of an ongoing debate in family sociology, namely the family decline hypothesis, which purports that modern-day families, relative to families of the past, are in trouble and in "crisis." And, as will be shown in this chapter and throughout this book, a critical analysis of this debate also helps us to carefully evaluate how our reflections, definitions, and meanings of family are socially constructed and embedded within ideological and institutional practices.

"WE ARE FAMILY," BUT WHAT ARE FAMILIES?

In the late 1970s, an American musical group called Sister Sledge (comprised of four sisters) became an international sensation with their number-one song "We Are Family." But what is family? What are families? Is a retired childless couple a family? Are same-sex couples with adopted children families? Is your best friend or pet considered one of your family members? Is it appropriate to talk about The Family as if it were an objective homogeneous structure with a finite number of shapes and forms?

As you can tell, defining "family" or "families" is a complicated matter. Previous scholarly definitions (particularly those formulated in the 1940s, 1950s, and 1960s) tended to emphasize that The Family was the basic institution of society and that it was a social and economic unit consisting of two adults of the opposite sex who shared economic resources, sexual intimacy, labour, accommodation, reproduction, and child-rearing (e.g., see Goode, 1963; Murdock, 1949). Similarly, cultural representations of families portrayed The Family as having two parents, one as a breadwinner husband and one as a homemaker wife, as shown in television shows such as "Father Knows Best," "I Love Lucy," and "Leave It to Beaver." These family types were popularized on television in the 1950s and portrayed a family structure that was relatively common during that time, although it was certainly not the norm from a historical perspective (as will become evident later in the book). Indeed, as will be revealed in this text, these definitions and images are certainly at odds with the real lives and historical experiences of most families in Canada and throughout the world.

Most scholars today readily acknowledge that previous definitions and stereotypes of The Family were often idealized and ideologically based. In other words, they reflected a particular **ideology**, which refers to a body of systematic beliefs and ideas (which claim to represent the truth) and that justify or rationalize certain actions or behaviours. Yet, Dorothy Smith (1999) notes that the Standard North American Family (**SNAF**) continues to represent an "ideological code" since it characterizes The Family as a legally married heterosexual couple living in the same household (see box 1.1 for further discussion). SNAF as an ideological code also continues to be foundational to many economic theories of the family, and it creates a text-mediated discourse that is generated in different settings. These family-related texts are found in national and local public discussions on family life (including the mass media), social scientific research in universities and think tanks, government systems of collecting statistics, and policy making in government. These practices extend to and invade other settings (e.g., by providing the terms of policy-talk) since they generate a common ordering ("the normative family") by which other family types are compared and measured.

Box 1.1: The Standard North American Family: SNAF as an Ideological Code

I am using the term ideological code as an analogy to genetic code. Genetic codes are orderings of the chemical constituents of DNS molecules that transmit genetic information to cells, reproducing in the cells the original ordering. By analogy, an ideological code is a schema that replicates its organization in multiple and various sites. I want to make clear that an ideological code in this sense is not a determinate concept or idea, though it can be expressed as such. Nor is it a formula or a definite form of words. Rather it is a constant generator of procedures for selecting syntax, categories, and vocabulary in the writing of texts and the production of talk and for interpreting sentences, written or spoken, ordered by it. An ideological code can generate the same order in widely different settings of talk or writing—in legislative, social scientific, and administrative settings, in popular writing, television advertising, or whatever.

The Standard North American Family (hereafter SNAF) is an ideological code in this sense. It is a conception of The Family as a legally married couple sharing a household. The adult male is in paid employment; his earnings provide the economic basis of the family-household. The adult female may also earn an income, but her responsibility is to the care of husband, household, and children. The adult male and female may be parents (in whatever legal sense) of children also resident in the household. Note the language of typification—"man," "woman"—and the use of the atemporal present. This universalizing of the schema locates its function as ideological code. It is not identifiable with any particular family; it applies to any. A classic enunciation of the code can be found in George Murdock's use of files containing summaries of ethnographic data accumulated by anthropologists from different parts of the world to establish the universality of the nuclear family (Murdock, 1949). The nuclear family is a theorized version of SNAF. Characteristically, Murdock was able to generate its distinctive form even when ethnographic descriptions contradicted it. Even when the nuclear family is not the "prevailing form," it is the "basic unit from which more complex familial forms are compounded." It is "always recognizable" (Murdock, 1949: 2).

Source: Smith, D. 1999. "The Standard North American Family: SNAF as an Ideological Code." In D. Smith, *Writing the Social: Critique, Theory and Investigations* (pp. 157–171). Toronto: University of Toronto Press (p. 159).

Put simply, these texts coordinate multiple sites of representation, are coordinated conceptually, and produce "an internally consistent picture of the world." Moreover, Smith asserts that as active agents, we all enter into and participate in such relations in ordinary and unthinking ways, as these texts are reproduced in our everyday practices of thinking about families and in our own experiences in families. Yet, as we will see later in this chapter and throughout this text, these texts or representations of families are not reflective of reality and the variability that occurs within families, particularly with respect to living arrangements, economic co-operation, and sexual relations.

There are also many religious, legal, or official-based meanings of family, and these classifications may or may not be consistent with public or scholarly definitions. This is because religious organizations are particularly concerned with moral issues and obligations, and that families adhere to the teachings of their faith. Policy makers and government officials, on the other hand, while also ideological, need to establish set criteria as to what constitutes family in order to meet their specific needs. For example, they might need to produce population estimates of the number and types of poor families in a given province. And while these definitions change over time, Statistics Canada (2012), the official census and survey agency for Canada, defines a **census family** quite broadly as:

> A married couple (with or without children of either or both spouses), a couple living common-law (with or without children of either or both partners), or a lone parent of any marital status, with at least one child living in the same dwelling. A couple living common-law may be of opposite sex or same sex. "Children" in a census family includes blood, step-, or adopted sons and daughters (regardless of age or marital status) who are living with their parent(s), as well as grandchildren living with their grandparent(s) but with no parents present.

Moreover, government-based or other official agency–based definitions can vary across domains (e.g., immigration policy vs. marriage laws) and these definitions determine who may receive certain formal and informal rights, entitlements, and benefits. For example, an individual may not be able to immigrate under a family reunification policy if they fall outside given certain requirements. Or, if gay and lesbian couples are not legally considered married, they may not be able to claim the same entitlements as heterosexual married couples. Therefore, far from being an obscure issue of linguistic and philosophical debate, these definitions have very real and very critical consequences. Notably, if certain individuals cannot claim to be part of a family, then they may be ineligible for benefits ranging from housing to health care and sick leave. In addition, those deemed "non-families" may be considered illegitimate, inappropriate, or immoral within the community or in other settings (Newman and Grauerholz, 2002). Thus, the term "family" is not simply a concept, but a minefield of contested values and power relationships (Silva and Smart, 1999).

Our everyday discourse or usage of the word "family" also illuminates how it can conjure up a wide array of meanings. Consider for a moment the slogans of two corporations, The Olive Garden (an Italian restaurant) and Kimpton Hotels, both popular chains

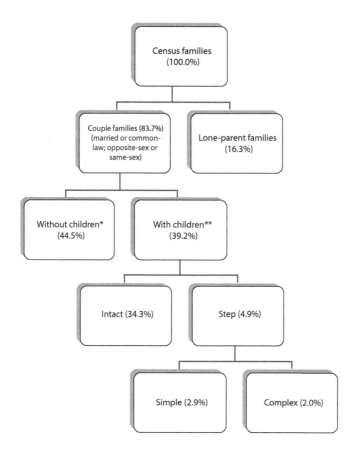

Figure 1.1: Overview of Census Families, 2011

Without children aged 24 and under.

**Without* children aged 24 and under.

Note: Intact = a couple family in which children are the biological and/or adopted children of both members of the family; Step = a couple family in which at least one child is the biological or adopted child of only one partner; Simple Step = a stepfamily in which all children are the biological or adopted children of one and only married spouse/partner and whose birth preceded the current relationship; Complex Step = three possible types (at least one child from both parents and one from only one parent; at least one child of each parent and no children of both parents; at least one child of both parents and at least one child of each parent).

Source: Statistics Canada. 2012. "Portrait of Families and Living Arrangements in Canada: Families, Households and Marital Status, 2011 Census of Population." Catalogue no. 98-312-X2011001. Ottawa: Minister of Industry.

in Canada and the US. The former uses the tag line "When you're here, you're family," while the latter uses "Because pets are family too." In fact, Kimpton Hotels is known not only for its pet-friendly policies, but also for its employee pet-care benefits. All employees receive Pet Assure comprehensive pet benefits programs, such as a special ID and access to veterinary service networks. And while these meanings of family may seem far-fetched to some, many individuals consider their pets to be "part of the family" (see box 1.2).

Box 1.2: Pets: An Integral Part of the Family

More than 50% of Canadian households own pets of some kind. Dogs, cats, birds, and other companion animals are living in more than five million homes. For their owners, these animals are more than pets—they are part of the family.

Each year, Canadian families spend about three billion dollars on their pets. This exceeds consumer spending on children's toys, footwear, eye care, and dental plans.

A recent survey of pet owners revealed that nearly 80% of respondents gave their pets holiday or birthday presents. More than 60% signed their pets' names on cards or letters. A slight majority (51%) gave their pets human names.

While virtually all pet owners talk to their pets, an astounding 94% spoke to their pets as though they were human. One-third of respondents spoke to their pets on the telephone or via the answering machine. More than 90% of pet owners believed their pets were aware of their moods and emotions.

As millions of Canadians already know, pets make wonderful, loving companions. In return for proper care and attention, pets offer unconditional love.

PET OWNERSHIP: IT'S GOOD FOR YOUR HEALTH

Chances are, you'll live longer and feel better if you own a pet.

Medical studies on the human-animal bond reveal that pet owners are more likely to have reduced stress levels, cholesterol levels, and blood pressure levels. They also experience fewer heart attacks than people without pets.

Researchers have found that the mere presence of an animal has a beneficial effect on heart function, and stroking and talking to a pet reduces blood pressure and stress.

Many hospitals and retirement homes engage in animal therapy. This may involve visits from volunteer animals or a pet that is kept at the facility. Seniors with pets are much less lonely than non-pet owners. Consequently, they do not make unnecessary visits to their doctor out of loneliness.

A study of women undergoing stress tests demonstrated that the presence of a dog had a greater effect on lowering blood pressure than the presence of friends.

Companion animals also provide psychological benefits. Pets are sympathetic, supportive, and non-judgmental listeners. Pets provide us with a distraction from our worries; they encourage social interaction and provide a soothing presence.

Source: The Ontario Veterinary Medical Association. n.d. "Choosing a Pet: Benefits of Pet Owner-ship." Retrieved June 5, 2006, from www.ovma.org/pet_owners/ownership_benefits/index.html.

Moreover, many consider **fictive kin** or non-relatives such as friends, neighbours, or co-workers family, despite the popular saying "Blood is thicker than water." These "kin by a fiction," in fact, may exhibit bonds that are even stronger than bonds with blood relatives. A good example of this interpretation of domestic ties and family structure is illustrated in Carol Stack's now classic ethnography of an African-American community, *All Our Kin* (1974), which is discussed from a social constructionist approach (see box 1.3). This approach highlights how "family" is not objectively meaningful, but instead, is constantly "under construction" and mediated by local culture (Holstein and Gubrium, 1999). We also often use the term "family" when we really mean "household," which includes all those sharing a dwelling. Household members, however, may or may not be related by blood, marriage, or adoption. Also, most people consider an aunt or uncle family but probably do not share a household with these relatives.

Box 1.3: What Is Family? Further Thoughts on a Social Constructionist Approach

Holstein and Gubrium (1999) outline their constructionist approach to family studies by considering how fictive kin represent one interpretation of family life. In the following quote, Billy, a young African-American woman living in a Midwestern city, describes the family ties structuring her life:

> Most people kin to me are in this neighbourhood...but I got people in the South, in Chicago, and in Ohio too. I couldn't tell most of their names and most of them aren't really kinfolk to me...Take my father, he's no father to me. I ain't got but one daddy and that's Jason. The one who raised me. My kids' daddies, that's something else, all their daddies's people really take to them—they always doing things and making a fuss about them. We help each other out and that's what kinfolks are all about. (p. 4)

Here, Billy projects family structure and meaning by convincingly articulating a familiar, recognizable vocabulary with features of her day-to-day life in order to construct and convey what it means to be family. She uses language of care and co-operation to establish the parameters of her "family." By actively assigning family status in this way, Billy indicates what persons mean to one another, simultaneously designating their interpersonal rights and obligations. She instructs her listeners in how to interpret and understand the concrete meaning of particular social ties, publicly constituting domestic order in relation to the practical circumstances that compose the life world that she confronts daily.

Source: Holstein, J.A. and J. Gubrium. 1999. "What Is Family? Further Thoughts on a Social Constructionist Approach." In B.H. Settles, S.K. Steinmetz, G.W. Peterson and M.B. Sussman (eds.), *Concepts and Definitions of Family for the 21st Century*. New York: The Haworth Press (p. 6).

Despite the near impossibility of arriving at a single definition of families, The Vanier Institute of the Family (2016: 1) adopts a perspective that embraces Canada's diversity of families. This diversity ranges from cultural and socio-demographic characteristics (e.g., ethno-racial group, Indigenous status, age, gender, and sexual orientation) and geographical location, as well as differences in attitudes, values, health, and subjective well-being of family members. This organization defines "family" as: "Any combination of two or more persons who are bound together over time by ties of mutual consent, birth, and/or adoption or placement and who, together, assume responsibilities for variant combinations of some of the following:

- physical maintenance and care of group members
- addition of new members through procreation or adoption
- socialization of children
- social control of members
- production, consumption, distribution of goods and services
- affective nurturance–love

This definition stresses the primary functions and activities of families, such as providing for the health and well-being of family members, raising children, and sustaining the economy through the production, exchange, and consumption of goods and services. Similarly, McDaniel and Tepperman (2004) observe that there are common elements or processes fundamental to the social groups we call families. First, all close relations usually involve some relational type of attachment, emotional bonding, dependency, or interdependency. These family relations tend to include birth-to-death or long-term commitments, both to one another and to the family per se. This means that there is some degree of familiarity—in fact, one source (The Online Etymology Dictionary, 2016) traces the word family as derived from the Latin word *familia*, which is close to the word *familiar*. Interestingly, this 15th-century word literally translates to "servants of the household." This definition includes all members of the household or property/estate, including servants/slaves, boarders, and lodgers, in addition to all other relatives living in the household.

Overall, a review of various definitions suggests that there can be many relational landscapes since families are not a single entity and can take many forms and structures. Aunts and uncles, for example, can play a significant role in the socialization and raising of nieces and nephews. Families also typically change and expand as we age. For example, as shown in figure 1.2, we can have two (or more) families by the time we reach adulthood—the family that we are born into (our family of orientation), and the family that we create when we marry and have children (our family of procreation).

Second, sexual relations tend to be regulated, such that certain relations are appropriate (e.g., between spouses) whereas others are taboo (e.g., between parent and child). Third, most families exhibit some degree of power imbalance, such as by gender or age, which means that ideally, more powerful family members tend to protect the less powerful family members. Fourth, families tend to guard their members against all

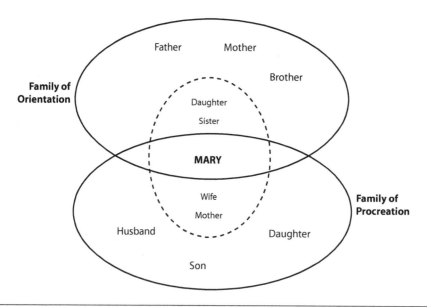

Figure 1.2: Mary's Two Families

Source: Modified from Nett, E.1988. *Canadian Families: Past and Present.* Toronto: Butterworth.

kinds of internal and external danger, although in reality, we know that violence, abuse, exploitation, or neglect can occur. As will be shown in chapter 15, our family may be more dangerous to us than the outside world.

In this textbook, we will use the term "families" in a fairly broad sense to refer to a group of people who have intimate or close social relationships and a shared history together. There are also many acceptable family structures and relationships. And, as Eichler (1988) suggests, it is more realistic and productive to view families in broad terms (rather than as a single entity) and as interacting and varying along several key dimensions. These dimensions include procreation, socialization, sexual relations, residence, economic co-operation, and emotional ties. Within each of these dimensions, various degrees of interaction can be identified. By way of illustration, in the procreative dimension, interaction can range from a couple having children with each other and only with each other, to both having children with other partners and/or having children together, to having no children at all.

Therefore, Eichler reminds us of the importance of always critically reflecting upon definitions of families, as presented both in the past, as well as in the present. She also encourages us to be cognizant of several biases that characterize the sociology of family literature, as will be further elaborated in the next chapter. For example, a monolithic bias results in the tendency to treat the family as a monolithic structure, with an emphasis on uniformity of experiences and universality of structures and functions instead of on a diversity of experiences, structures, and functions. However, as will be shown in chapter 3, there is little evidence to support the idea of "a universal family." Instead, different family

Box 1.4: Relational Landscapes

Oddly enough, aunting and uncling have little clear representation in the public discourse about families. The relationships of aunts and uncles with nieces and nephews are rarely discussed or examined in any comprehensive way. Yet relationships among siblings are among the more resilient, long lasting, and intimate of family ties, and with the introduction of children, the roles of aunt and uncle are added to the bonds linking siblings and their parents or spouses.

Even the terms "aunting" and "uncling" are relatively new; they appeared only recently in the popular and academic literature on families, and then amidst some controversy. Among the early appearances of the terms was an article I wrote and submitted for review to a leading academic journal. The article was published in due time, but not without some spirited exchanges. One of the reviewers questioned the terms "aunting" and "uncling" and lamented over their inclusion in the family lexicon, perhaps thinking they were unnecessary, unusual, or simply dreadful. The story illustrates the invisibility of the family work of aunts and uncles because specific terms to describe what they do are not in common usage. We have heretofore no common terms by which to describe our expectations of aunts and uncles or their typical activities and to differentiate them from the expectations and activities of other family members such as parents or grandparents. Terms such as "aunting" and "uncling" have a clear linguistic parallel with the term "parenting," a word in common usage, but the former still sound foreign to some ears, as they did to the journal reviewer. The gap in our common language is suggestive of how the family positions of aunts and uncles are rarely discussed in any formal way. The family work of aunts and uncles, nieces and nephews is neatly hidden from public view and acknowledgement, although as we shall see, aunts and uncles routinely discuss among themselves and their intimates their relationships with nieces, nephews, and other family members, and their contributions to family work are varied, consequential, and apparently commonplace.

The invisibility of aunts, uncles, nieces, and nephews, as well as relationships among adult siblings more generally in the field of family studies, contrasts sharply with the lived experience of actors who know quite clearly the importance of each to the other. Family members commonly talk among themselves, visit, phone, e-mail, circulate family photos in person or via web sites, and celebrate holidays, birthdays, and anniversaries. In their contacts, they share news and gossip, and all of this occurs across households of grandparents, parents, adult siblings (some of whom are single), and close friends, including coworkers. To be sure, not all families are in frequent communication, but then not all exist in isolated households. One need only recall travel patterns on major North American holidays to confirm this.

Source: Milardo, R.M. 2009. "Relational Landscapes." In R.M. Milardo (ed.), *The Forgotten Kin: Aunts and Uncles* (pp. 1–3). New York: Cambridge University Press (pp. 1–2).

forms—from monogamous to polygamous—are found historically and worldwide. These family forms are reciprocally linked to the economic and political conditions in which families live their daily lives. For example, polygamy, which is a common family form in many parts of the world, can be traced to structural arrangements of economic control and power. A conservative bias, on the other hand, results in the tendency to ignore changes in family life. Instead, Eichler argues that the boundaries of contemporary families need to be recognized as fluid and ever-changing. Notably, in a period of rapid social, technological, and economic change, family lives change and transform such that definitions of family continually need to be re-evaluated.

In summary, many of the issues raised so far beckon us to rethink The Family as an objective condition apart from acts of interpretation, as well as a private zone or entity and as separate from public life. Instead, Gubrium and Holstein (1987) assert that The Family can fruitfully be considered "a way of interpreting, representing, and ordering social relations." The Family's social organization is "not to be discerned through carefully focused attention to its component parts," but instead "is gleaned from the diverse categories and varied contexts in which considerations of family order are raised." Similarly, Fahey (1995: 687) observes that a focus on a simple public/private dichotomy (which is common in sociological practice) points to the "multiple, cross-cutting, context-specific zones of privacy found in social life." Thus, it is recognized that meanings of related family experiences cannot be separated from the interpretations of those studying families (Gubrium and Holstein, 1987). It is therefore useful to adopt descriptive practices that allow for both deviance and normality as categories of domestic definition, regardless of household location or setting. Yet, as will be further shown in the next section, there remains a tendency to produce normative or ideological visions of family life as if The Family were one distinct and immutable structure or form.

"THE SKY IS FALLING": THE FAMILY DECLINE HYPOTHESIS

It is common to hear people idealize the past, when family life was supposedly stable and harmonious, free of conflict, and devoid of serious social problems. As a result, past family life is romanticized, seen through a lens of rose-coloured glasses and assumed to have been simpler, happier, and less stressful. And indeed, we do hear startling statistics on the news and from religious and political leaders about family demise in modern life. This includes aspects such as declining marriage and fertility rates, skyrocketing divorce rates, latchkey children, drugs and gangs, and how the elderly are being abandoned by their children, and we worry that our society is now rejecting marriage and commitment to family relationships. Similarly, in the academic literature, scholars point to these and similar trends that contribute to an acrimonious debate about family life and the future viability of the family.

Dave Popenoe (1996, 1993, 1988), an American family sociologist, has been at the forefront of this debate with the view that the family is deteriorating and is in crisis.

His main argument is that the family as an institution is in unprecedented decline since individuals are in the process of rejecting the bedrock of family functioning: the nuclear family. The rise of alternative family forms (e.g., single-mother families, cohabitation), the absence of fathers in many families (particularly in the United States), and other similar changes are purported to be the main causes of family decline. In his book, *Life Without Father* (1996: 1, 3), for example, he writes:

> And according to a growing body of evidence, this massive erosion of fatherhood contributes mightily to many of the major social problems of our time ... [among them] crime and delinquency; premature sexuality and out-of-wedlock teen births; deteriorating educational achievement; depression, substance abuse, and alienation among teenagers; and the growing number of women and children in poverty.

As a result, he argues that the family is becoming ill suited to serve its two most basic functions: rearing children and providing sustained emotional sustenance to its members. On the other side of this hotly contested debate are those who maintain that "families are no worse than ever before"; these are the **family change perspective** theorists. These proponents argue that what is in decline is our normative idea of what a family is, or rather a particular historical ideological vision of the family. This depiction is usually represented by the prototypical 1950s family previously discussed—a family type in which parents marry for life, children are born inside the marriage, and the mother works inside the home while the father works outside the home to provide for the family (Casper and Bianchi, 2002). Feminist scholars such as Judith Stacey (1996) argue that the family is not in decline but is undergoing metamorphosis as many come to realize that this vision of the traditional family is no longer viable or even desirable.

Moreover, some theorists (e.g., Coontz, 1992; Gee, 2000) argue that family life, even during the 1950s, was never "golden" or stable. Social problems such as poverty, alcoholism, drug addiction, family violence, and incest were prevalent, although often hidden behind closed doors. Also, previous to this time, sickness, disease, and war created very low life expectancy, as shown in figure 1.3. These conditions robbed family members of infants, husbands, wives, and parents at young ages. As a result, the family change perspective highlights change as well as patterns of continuity, showing that the social and personal problems we think of as recent also existed long ago, albeit with different underlying circumstances. For example, we often hear alarming figures for the number of children raised in lone-parent households, yet rates of single parenthood were almost as high in the 1930s (see table 1.1). In 2011, for example, lone-parent families constituted 16.3% of all census families (see figure 1.4), which is only 3% higher than in 1931. However, single-parent families at that time were typically formed when one parent died at a young age or when a father deserted the family because of economic hardship. Today, they are more likely to be created by divorce or by individual choice.

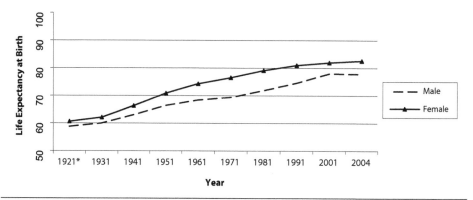

Figure 1.3: Historical Trends in Life Expectancy by Sex, Canada, 1921–2004

*1921 life table excludes Quebec

Sources: Adapted from Novak, M., and L. Campbell. 2001. *Aging and Society: A Canadian Perspective,* 4th ed. Toronto: Nelson Thomson Learning (p. 55); Statistics Canada. 2006. "Deaths." *The Daily* (Dec. 20).

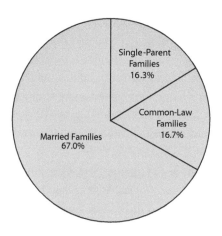

Figure 1.4: Profile of the Canadian Family, 2011 Census, Total Number of Families = 9,389,700

Source: Statistics Canada. 2012. "Portrait of Families and Living Arrangements in Canada: Families, House-holds and Marital Status, 2011 Census of Population." Catalogue no. 98-312-X2011001. Ottawa: Minister of Industry.

Thus, family life has almost always been diverse, as noted by the late Ellen Gee, a promi-nent Canadian family sociologist who is well known for her historical, life-course research on family change (see box 1.5 on page 18). Similarly, Statistics Canada (2012) documents that while today's census families are characterized by diversity, this was also the case for families from 1911 to 1961, albeit for different circumstances (see box 1.6 on page 19).

Table 1.1: Percentage of Lone-Parent Families in Canada, 1931–2011

Year	Percentage
1931	13.4
1941	10.5
1951	9.9
1961	8.4
1971	6.8
1981	6.0
1991	13.0
2001	16.0
2006	15.9
2011	16.3

Sources: Gee, E. M. 2000. "Contemporary Diversities." In N. Mandell and A. Duffy (eds.), *Canadian Families: Diversity, Conflict, and Change*, 2nd ed. (pp. 78–111). Toronto: Harcourt Canada; Statistics Canada. 2003. "Update on Families." *Canadian Social Trends*, Catalogue no. 11-008 (Summer) (pp. 11–13); Statistics Canada. 2007. "2006 Census: Families, Marital Status, Households and Dwelling Characteristics." *The Daily* (September 12); Statistics Canada. 2012. "Fifty Years of Families in Canada: 1961–2011." Catalogue no. 98-312-X201103. Ottawa: Minister of Industry.

Yet, it is also important to recognize that significant changes have occurred in family life and that we need to understand and study these shifts. For example, as a result of declining family sizes, the number of private households has increased and household size has decreased, as shown in figure 1.5. In the early 20th centuries, households contained more children and were quite large and flexible, and could include relatives and boarders on a temporary or longer-term basis. More recently, higher rates of separation and divorce are also likely to produce smaller households after the dissolution of a previously larger one. This change in household size and composition has enormous implications with respect to housing and patterns of consumption within families, for example, and raises a number of issues ranging from environmental impacts to patterns and exchanges of available family and social support.

These observations highlight the necessity of identifying historical benchmarks as well as personal or institutional motives with respect to assessing family change. For example, when we assert that family life was somehow better in the past, how are we defining family and which past are we referring to? Whose interest is being served in holding onto a certain definition or vision of family life? With these questions in mind and in consideration of the **family decline hypothesis** and the family change perspective, we will review some key socio-demographic, cultural, and technological changes in the family in order to critique this debate in greater detail. And while this discussion is only intended to briefly highlight some key patterns and issues, these and other fundamental patterns and processes integral to understanding Canadian family life will be explored in more depth in subsequent chapters.

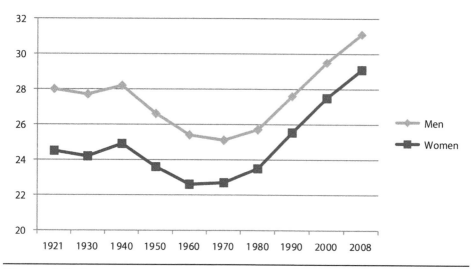

Figure 1.5: Average Age at First Marriage, by Sex, Canada, 1921–2008

Note: Unfortunately, Statistics Canada discontinued publishing average age at first marriage data (in addition to marriage/divorce rates) in 2008 due to budgetary cutbacks. Also, since 2003, the definition of marriage has been changed in some provinces and territories to include the legal union of two persons of the same sex. Age at first marriage for same-sex couples tends be higher than for opposite-sex couples.

Sources: For 1921 to 1987: Statistics Canada. 1992. "Marriage and Conjugal Life in Canada." Catalogue no. 91-534E. Ottawa: Minister of Industry; for 1988 to 1999: Statistics Canada, Demography Division; for 2000 to 2004: Statistics Canada. 2008. CANSIM Table 101-1002-Mean Age and Median Age of Males and Females, by Type of Marriage and Marital Status, Canada, Provinces and Territories. Ottawa: Minister of Industry; and for 2005 to 2008: Statistics Canada. 2011. Canadian Vital Statistics, Marriage Database and Demography Division (Population Estimates). Ottawa: Minister of Industry; and Human Resources and Skills Development Canada, Family Life and Marriage, n.d. Retrieved January 18, 2011, from www4.hrsdc.gc.ca/.3ndic.1t.4r@-eng.jsp?preview=1&iid=78.

Box 1.5: Family Diversity

Family diversity is the norm in Canadian society, past and present. Only for a short period of history—the post-World War II "baby boom" years (circa 1946–62)—did Canadian (and US) families approach uniformity, centred around near-universal marriage and parenthood, family "intactness," and highly differentiated gender roles. This period was anomalous in terms of family life, a time when the gap between "actual" and "ideal" narrowed to an unprecedented degree. This was due, in part, to improved mortality levels (death contributed less to family breakup) and also to substantial economic growth (men's wages alone could support a family). It is also no coincidence that then pre-eminent US sociologist Talcott Parsons, developed his conceptualization of the homogenous modern family model at this time in history...It is very important not to examine today's families in the light of that period; to do so is to overestimate familial change and trends related to diversity.

Source: Gee, E.M. 2000. "Contemporary Diversities." In N. Mandell and A. Duffy (eds.), *Canadian Families: Diversity, Conflict and Change*, 2nd ed. (pp. 78–111). Toronto: Harcourt Canada (p. 81).

Box 1.6: Canadian Families: 1911–1961

While today's census families are characterized by diversity, this was also the case for families in the first half of the 20th century, but often for different reasons.

Widowhood and remarriage following the death of a spouse were more common in the early decades of the 1900s, when there was higher maternal mortality and higher mortality rates overall for infants, children, and adults. There were also many deaths that occurred during the two world wars and the Korean War. In 1921, for example, nearly 1 in 10 children aged 14 and under (8.8%) had experienced the death of at least one parent. As a result, lone-parent families were relatively prevalent in the early decades of the 20th century. These families represented 12.2% of all census families in 1941, a level that was higher than in 1961 (8.4%), near the height of the baby boom, and that was not surpassed again until 1986.

Note: For more information, see Milan, A. 2000. "One Hundred Years of Families." *Canadian Social Trends*, no. 56, Catalogue no. 11-008. Ottawa: Statistics Canada.

Sources: Statistics Canada, Censuses of Population, 1911, 1921, 1931, 1941, 1951 and 1961, as cited in Statistics Canada. 2012. "Portrait of Families and Living Arrangements in Canada: Families, Households and Marital Status, 2011 Census of Population." Catalogue no. 98-312-X2011001. Ottawa: Minister of Industry.

EVALUATING THE FAMILY DECLINE HYPOTHESIS: A BRIEF OVERVIEW OF KEY SOCIO-DEMOGRAPHIC, CULTURAL, AND TECHNOLOGICAL TRENDS IN FAMILY LIFE

Contemporary family life is often deemed in collapse or in crisis based on a number of social behaviours and assumptions. One of these is based on the tendency of young adults to take longer to establish themselves in adult roles and statuses since they are marrying and having children later than ever before (if at all). Therefore, it is assumed that young people are rejecting the institutions of marriage and family. Moreover, it is observed that today's individuals are engaging in a wider array of less permanent living arrangements, such as non-marital cohabitation and returning to live with parents as "boomerang kids." It is also argued that by marrying more than once we have created a hedonistic divorce culture.

Further, many point to the emergence of non-traditional family forms and behaviours due to technological advances such as in the areas of work, medical, digital, and reproductive technologies. And while these technologies make our lives easier and lengthen our life expectancy, some purport that we are living with more chronic illness and stress, with little time left for our families. These technologies are also blamed for undermining certain family communication and social interaction patterns, as witnessed by the privatizing effects of some electronic technologies (e.g., television, computers, cellphones, iPads). They also further contribute to our ability to reject or delay "natural" family-related transitions, for example, through the usage of in-vitro fertilization and surrogate motherhood.

For example, few trends in the family have been as significant as the increase in the prevalence of unmarried cohabitation in Canada, a topic to be further explored in chapter 7. From 1981 to 2011, the proportion of common-law families increased from 5.6% to 16.7% of all census families (Statistics Canada, 2012). Between 2001 and 2006, common-law families showed a particularly high growth rate (an increase of 18.9%), making this the fastest growing family structure in Canada (Statistics Canada, 2007). Moreover, there has been a dramatic increase in cohabitor households with children. These trends have created concern about the impact of cohabitation on marriage and family life, since these unions are viewed as less committed and are found to be more fragile than legal, marital partnerships (Riedmann et al., 2003).

However, many assert that living together before or as an alternative to marriage is not something new. In fact, cohabitation has existed long enough to predate marriage. Until the mid-18th century, the difference between the two statuses was fluid in many countries, such as England (Wu and Schimmele, 2003). It is further argued that the growing popularity of cohabitation does not mean a rejection of marriage or family, since the vast majority of Canadian families are comprised of married parents, as shown in figure 1.4. Moreover, it is asserted that those who choose to cohabit rather than be married are still entering into intimate partnerships that often serve the same functions as marriage, albeit without a marriage certificate. For example, people who choose to live together report that it allows them to pool resources with a loved one, as well as an opportunity to test the waters in order to avoid divorce later on.

Other cohabiting individuals maintain that it is their personal choice and that the state or religious institutions have no business defining or regulating their private lives. In short, they claim that a piece of paper does not guarantee commitment or a lifetime of happiness. Yet others point to some parts of the world like Africa, Latin America, and Sweden, and maintain that not only does cohabitation have a long history in these societies, but that it is widely practised and highly accepted. Thus, it is also argued that as the legal and social distinction between marriage and cohabitation increasingly blur, cohabitation should not be a sign of family demise.

Similarly, the popular media and other commentators have played a large role in the public perception that there has been a large increase in unmarried people, suggesting that society is rejecting the institution of marriage. And statistics do reveal shrinking marriage rates, rising ages of first marriage, and the growth of non-traditional living arrangements (such as cohabitation). Notably, the latest ages of first marriage are now evidenced: In 2008, the average age of first marriage was 29.1 for women and 31.1 for men (Statistics Canada,

2008). If we compare these average ages to the timing of first marriage in previous decades, these age differences are startling indeed! Figure 1.6 shows that in 1960, for instance, the average age of first marriage for women was 23, while it was about 26 for men (Dominion Bureau of Statistics, 1962).

If we take a longer historical view, we can see that average ages of marriage (as well as parenthood) have fluctuated widely. Figure 1.6 also reveals that the average ages of first marriage (for men) were relatively similar in the 1930s compared to recent trends, with only about a two-and-a-half year increase in average age. Moreover, when calculating marital rates, it is important to realize that delayed marriage (since most people eventually marry) is an important contributing factor to lower marital rates. Thus, many argue that the fact that young people are delaying marriage is not a sign of a dwindling commitment to marriage, but rather evidence of a general extension of young adulthood and more carefully planned life-course choices.

Furthermore, as covered in chapter 11, young people are taking longer to establish themselves in adult roles due to changing economic policies, education, and labour market demands. It is also argued that other socio-demographic changes (e.g., increased life expectancy) and alternative family forms provide the opportunity to experience a wider variety of living arrangements and relationship partners, many of which are familistic or family oriented in nature (Mitchell, 2006). Furthermore, historical data again reveal that

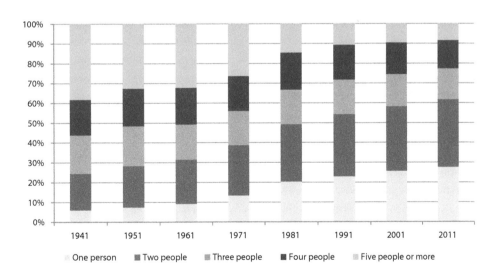

Figure 1.6: Distribution (in Percentages) of Private Households by Number of People, Canada, 1941–2011

Sources: Statistics Canada. 1979. "Canadian Households and Families, 1981 to 2011 Censuses of Population." Catalogue no. 99-753. Ottawa: Minister of Industry. Retrieved June 8, 2016, from www.statcan. gc.ca/pub/11-630-x/11-630-x2015008-eng.htm.

many people chose not to marry in earlier times. The percentage of Canadian women who had never married by ages 45–49, for instance, was exactly the same in 1891 as it was in 2001, at 10% of the population (Mitchell, 2006: 38).

Moreover, we could examine many other socio-demographic trends and provide counter-evidence to every purported claim offered by those in the family decline camp. For example, in the past, there were no problems with the aged because most people never aged. In other words, with low life expectancy, people died relatively young. Thus, we could counter the argument that life was better for the elderly in the past with the compelling fact that, unlike in previous times, grandparents now have the opportunity to live long enough to watch their children (and grandchildren) grow up. From this vantage point, this increased generational overlap of lives could easily be interpreted as creating both new opportunities and challenges for aging families. In addition, many assert that Canadian family life is increasingly diversifying, making family decline arguments untenable. Indeed, current trends paint a portrait of rising cultural and structural variation in family life rather than a linear trend toward one monolithic "troubled" type of family.

Family Doom and Gloom Is Nothing New

It is also fascinating to note that throughout history, social scientists and the general public have always expressed concern over the demise of the family. In the 18th century, for instance, industrialization arose and farming began to decline. This led commentators to report that these changes brought with them "the break in the web of connections between the family and the community; the dispersion of the household group, with the young increasingly inclined to seek their fortune in a new setting; the improvement in the status of women; the erosion of parental authority; and a growing permissiveness in the area of sex," all of which were interpreted as signs of impending family demise (Demos, 1975: 66). In a similar vein, a well-known author writing in the 1920s (Groves, 1928) asserted that marriages were in "extreme collapse," in addition to citing numerous other problems purported to plague families at that time, such as high divorce rates, hedonism, sexual promiscuity, and financial strain.

And by the late 1950s, many religious writers, politicians, educators, and parents were also worried about family decline, given social problems like juvenile delinquency and the emergence of popular culture, which targeted youth. Magazines like *Time*, for instance, ran stories about rampant delinquents in the streets (Liazos, 2004). Many were also concerned that families were being torn apart by the new music of rock 'n roll because it was ruining the moral fabric of communities. When Elvis Presley (known as the King of Rock and Roll) sang "Hound Dog" on the Milton Berle show on June 5, 1956, the official response was that television networks banned filming Presley from the waist down. The intensity of his pelvis-shaking made his teenaged fans scream, and his "vulgarity" and "animalism" were perceived to contribute to promiscuity and already weakening family values. And since that time, every decade has produced a multitude of alarmist concerns about family breakdown. For example, in the 1970s, there was a great deal of concern that family life was eroding as women began to enter the paid labour force in record numbers and divorce rates began to climb.

SUMMARY

Despite the enormous difficulty inherent in defining families, our personal experiences of family constitute a significant influence on our lives, and the family remains a fundamental institution in society. In this chapter, we explored changing and varied meanings of family. In particular, it is recognized that there are many ideological and institutional practices involved in defining families. Against an objective and private image of family life that many of us take for granted, "domestic order can be conceptualized as a working, experiential issue in collective representation, or a socially symbolic reality" (Gubrium and Holstein, 1987: 783). Therefore, the tendency to objectify families and dichotomize the public/private into two separate spheres should be understood as "a flexible cultural image which is put to use in a wide variety of situations which serve a great diversity of purposes and interests" (Fahey, 1995: 687).

Furthermore, a "normative" domestic order generates ideological codes that operate largely outside of our consciousness. As a result, these codes generate texts that are all around us and give substance to a version of The Family that masks the actualities of people's live. The consequences of these everyday practices are obviously enormous since they penetrate a wide variety of settings in largely unthinking ways. As stated by Smith (1999: 171), "ideological codes may have a peculiar and important political force, carrying forward modes of representing the world even among those who overtly resist the representations they generate."

In this chapter we also critically evaluate the family decline hypothesis. This hypothesis purports that modern-day families are troubled and in demise relative to earlier family life, yet this hypothesis is based largely on pessimistic speculation and suggests ideological or personal agendas tied to meanings of family. From a life-course framework, this chapter underscores the importance of situating family life and social change in its relative historical time frame and socio-political location. In particular, it can be socially and politically dangerous and inaccurate to rely on the prototypical 1950s "Leave It to Beaver" family as the benchmark for "traditional" family life. From a longer-range life-course perspective, this nuclear family structure was actually a historical fluke. It is also not a universal norm from an anthropological or cross-cultural lens, a theme to be explored in more detail in chapter 3. Indeed, a critical analysis of the family decline hypothesis using socio-demographic data and other evaluation methods is necessary in order to anchor speculation, hypotheses, and theorizing about families and family change (Casper and Bianchi, 2002).

A closer inspection of the family decline hypothesis also suggests that families—in whatever shape or form—have always struggled with external circumstances and inner conflicts. And, in many ways, families may be better off now than in previous times due to improved life expectancy, economic and technological conditions, and a wider range of choice in family-related behaviour. This is not to say that contemporary families are without their share of problems and complexities, but they are as alive, vibrant, diverse, and socially significant as ever before.

QUESTIONS FOR CRITICAL REFLECTION AND DEBATE

1. Ask several people outside of your class to define family. In what ways do these definitions reflect themes and issues covered in this chapter?
2. Some individuals argue that the "normative" institution of the family is oppressive because it is a private domain characterized by hierarchical relationships and inequality (e.g., such as age and gender-based segregation). Do you agree with this viewpoint?
3. Debate the following: Family decline today is cause for alarm.
4. Provide some specific examples of how ideological codes and practices might operate outside your conscious intention as a student, as well as for a social scientist, or a political or religious leader.
5. To what extent has personal "choice" replaced institutional constraint on young people's family-related decisions, such as when and whom to marry? How might this vary by gender, ethnicity, and social class in Canadian society?
6. Try to predict what Canadian family life will look like in 50 years. For example, do you think that the institution of marriage will be replaced with new forms of family living? How might new technological advancements (e.g., medical, reproductive, electronic media) shape future family life courses?

GLOSSARY

Census family is defined by Statistics Canada as a married or common-law couple (with or without children of either or both spouses/partners) or a lone parent of any marital status, with at least one child living in the same dwelling.

Family is a basic social institution and, in the broadest sense, is a group of people who have intimate social relationships and a shared history together.

Family change perspective assumes that families have always been changing (despite much continuity) and that in some ways, modern-day families may be better than ever.

Family decline hypothesis refers to the idea that families today are in demise or are falling apart and have serious problems.

Fictive kin are non-relatives whose bonds are strong and intimate, such as very close friends.

Ideology is a system of beliefs and ideas that justifies or rationalizes action.

SNAF (**Standard North American Family**) as an ideological code is a conception of The Family as a legally married couple sharing a household. It is a constant generator of procedure for selecting text-mediated discourse (e.g., vocabulary) and can generate the same order in widely different settings.

Social demography emphasizes the scientific study of population from a sociological perspective.

FURTHER READING

Cheal, D. (ed.). 2014. *Canadian Families Today: New Perspectives*, 3rd ed. Don Mills, Ontario: Oxford University Press.
Presents a compilation of original essays on issues and trends affecting Canadian life, with an emphasis on multiple perspectives, inequality, and diversity.

Coontz, S. 1992. *The Way We Never Were: American Families and the Nostalgia Trap*. New York: Basic Books.
Examines two centuries of family life and shatters a series of myths and half-truths that burden contemporary families.

McDaniel, S.A., and L. Tepperman. 2015. *Close Relations: An Introduction to the Sociology of Families*, 5th ed. Toronto: Pearson/Prentice-Hall.
Provides a comprehensive overview of the history, structure, and future of family life in Canada, in addition to making international comparisons.

Skolnick, A.S., and J.H. Skolnick. 2014. *Family in Transition*, 17th ed. New York: Pearson and Allen/Bacon.
This is a very popular reader on American families and intimate relationships that explores myths about family life from a socio-historical and economic perspective.

Treas, J., J. Scott, and M. Richards (eds.). 2014. *The Wiley-Blackwell Companion to the Sociology of Families*. Chichester, Oxford, UK: Wiley Blackwell.
This volume investigates modern-day family relationships, partnering, and parenting against a backdrop of rapid social, economic, cultural, and technological change.

Ward, M. and W. Bélanger. 2015. *The Family Dynamic: Canadian Perspectives*, 6th ed. Toronto: Nelson Canada.
Following a developmental approach, this book serves as a basic, practical introduction to family studies, particularly for those who are interested in finding employment in human services fields.

RELATED WEB SITES

BC Council for Families, established in 1977, is a non-profit society devoted to strengthening, encouraging, and supporting families through information, education, research, and advocacy. It is the relationship affiliate of the Canadian Health Network, and its web site has useful publications and resources for all Canadians, www.bccf.ca.

National Council on Family Relations is a national political and professional organization committed to educating the public about family issues and offers a multitude of resources and links to other family-related sites, www.ncfr.org. Facebook: NCFR

Real Women of Canada provides a good example of a national, conservative organization that views contemporary family life as fragmented. Its mission is to promote equality for homemakers and it emphasizes values congruent with "traditional" family life, www. realwomenofcanada.ca. Facebook: REAL Women of Canada

Sociological Images encourages students to exercise and develop their sociological imaginations with discussions of compelling visuals that span the breadth of sociological inquiry. For family-related images, search for postings under the tag "marriage and family," which has over 350 images in its archives, www.thesocietypages. org/socimages. Also see Facebook: Socimages, Twitter: SocImages, YouTube: www. youtube.com/socimages

Statistics Canada is the official federal government agency that provides statistics and information on many family-related areas such as marriage and marital status, living arrangements, economy, society, and culture, www.statcan.gc.ca.

REFERENCES

Casper, L.M., and S.M. Bianchi. 2002. *Continuity and Change in the American Family.* Thousand Oaks, California: Sage.

Coontz, S. 1992. *The Way We Never Were: American Families and the Nostalgia Trap.* New York: Basic Books.

Demos, J. 1975. "The American Family in Past Time." In A. Skolnick and J. Skolnick (eds.), *Family in Transition*, 2nd ed. Boston: Little, Brown.

Dominion Bureau of Statistics. 1962. *Canada Year Book.* Ottawa: Queen's Printer and Controller of Stationery.

Eichler, M. 1988. *Families in Canada Today: Recent Changes and Their Policy Consequences*, 2nd ed. Toronto: Gage.

Fahey, T. 1995. "Privacy and the Family: Conceptual and Empirical Reflections." *Sociology* 29: 687–702.

Gee, E.M. 2000. "Contemporary Diversities." In N. Mandell and A. Duffy (eds.), *Canadian Families: Diversity, Conflict, and Change*, 2nd ed. (pp. 78–111). Toronto: Harcourt Canada.

Goode, W.J. 1963. *World Revolution and Family Patterns*. Glencoe, Illinois: The Free Press.

Groves, E.R. 1928. *The Marriage Crisis*. New York: Longmans, Green.

Gubrium, J.F., and J.A. Holstein. 1987. "The Private Image: Experiential Location and Method in Family Studies." *Journal of Marriage and the Family* 49: 773–786.

Holstein, J.A., and J.F. Gubrium. 1999. "What Is Family? Further Thoughts on a Social Constructionist Approach." *Marriage and Family Review* 28: 3–20.

Liazos, A. 2004. *Families: Joys, Conflicts, and Change*. Boulder: Paradigm.

McDaniel, S.A., and L. Tepperman. 2004. *Close Relations: An Introduction to the Sociology of Families*, 2nd ed. Toronto: Pearson/Prentice-Hall.

Mitchell, B.A. 2006. *The Boomerang Age: Transitions to Adulthood in Families*. New Brunswick, New Jersey: Aldine-Transaction.

Murdock, G.P. 1949. *Social Structure*. New York: Macmillan.

Newman, D.M., and L. Grauerholz. 2002. *Sociology of Families*, 2nd ed. Thousand Oaks, California: Sage.

Online Etymology Dictionary. 2016. "Family." Retrieved December 27, 2016 from http://www.etymonline.com/index.php?term=family

Popenoe, D. 1988. *Disturbing the Nest: Family Change and Decline in Modern Societies*. New York: Aldine de Gruyter.

Popenoe, D. 1993. "American Family Decline, 1960–1990: A Review and Appraisal." *Journal of Marriage and the Family* 55: 527–555.

Popenoe, D. 1996. *Life Without Father*. New York: Free Press.

Riedmann, A., M. Lamanna, and A. Nelson. 2003. *Marriages and Families*. Scarborough, Ontario: Thomson Nelson.

Silva, E.B., and C. Smart. 1999. "The 'New' Practices and Politics of Family Life." In E.B. Silva and C. Smart (eds.), *The New Family?* (pp. 1–12). London: Sage Publications.

Smith, D. 1999. *Writing the Social: Critique, Theory, and Investigations*. Toronto: University of Toronto Press.

Stacey, J. 1996. *In the Name of the Family: Rethinking Family Values in the Postmodern Age*. Boston: Beacon.

Stack, C. 1974. *All Our Kin*. New York: Harper and Row.

Statistics Canada. 2007. *Family Portrait: Continuity and Change in Canadian Households in 2006, 2006 Census*. Ottawa: Minister of Industry.

Statistics Canada. 2008. "Crude Marriage Rates, All Marriages, Canada, CANSIM Table 101–1004. Ottawa: Minister of Industry.

Statistics Canada. 2012. "Portrait of Families and Living Arrangements in Canada: Families, Households and Marital Status, 2011 Census of Population." Catalogue no. 98-312-X2011001. Ottawa: Minister of Industry.

The Vanier Institute of the Family. 2016. "Definition of Family." Retrieved December 26, 2016, from www.vanierinstitute.ca/defintion-family.

Wu, Z., and C.M. Schimmele. 2003. "Cohabitation." In J.J. Ponzetti (ed.), *The International Encyclopedia of Marriage and Family Relationships,* 2nd ed. (pp. 315–323). New York: MacMillan Reference.

CHAPTER 2

Family Theory and Methods: Windows on Families and Family Research

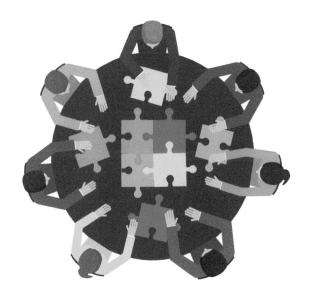

LEARNING OBJECTIVES

In this chapter you will learn that ...

- sociologists use a variety of theories and methods to explain the structure and dynamic of families
- family research is invaluable to human knowledge and understanding
- theory and research depend closely on each other
- there are two equally scientific and complementary methodological approaches to studying families—quantitative and qualitative
- a researcher's choice of theory and methods, as well as his or her own values, biases, and behaviours, can influence the entire research process
- it is important to critically evaluate research in order to make meaningful interpretations

INTRODUCTION

The fascination of sociology lies in the fact that its perspective makes us see in a new light the very world in which we have lived our lives. This also constitutes a transformation of consciousness.

—P.L. Berger, *Invitation to Sociology: A Humanistic Perspective*

What makes some families more prone to poverty and homelessness than others? Why are women more likely to do more housework and child care than men, even when they work full-time outside the home? What makes some children vulnerable to sexual or physical abuse and neglect? To make advancements on these kinds of intellectual and practical questions, researchers operate in two distinct but highly related worlds—the abstract (the world of concepts/ideas) and the concrete (the observable/empirical world). Indeed, scientific **theories** link these two separate domains, and in doing so provide descriptions, summaries, integration, and explanations about what is known from research. Theories also guide subsequent research and practices that will increase our knowledge and further understanding, as well as new sets of solution. For example, if we theorize that children are more likely to be abused when parents lack institutional support and good parenting skills, we can test these ideas in order to improve our social programs targeted at this social problem.

Although a wide variety of terms (e.g., paradigm, conceptual framework, model) indicate the same general ideas as the term "theory," theorizing can be defined as "the process of systematically developing and organizing ideas to explain phenomena, and a theory is the total set of empirically testable, interconnected ideas formulated to explain those phenomena" (Chibucos and Leite, with Weiss, 2005: 1).Thus, research is integral to this process, since if one addresses questions only on a conceptual level, or vice versa—if one deals only with observable information without trying to systematically explain it—then scientific theory development or answers to our social problems will not be found. In this chapter, an overview of main "classical" and emergent sociological theories and conceptual frameworks relevant to families will be outlined. And since research is integral to knowledge building, a brief introduction to family research methods will also be provided.

STRUCTURAL FUNCTIONALISM: FAMILIES AS STABLE AND HARMONIOUS AND "LEAVE IT TO BEAVER"

This perspective can be traced to early attempts by August Comte (1798–1857) and Émile Durkheim (1858–1917), who sought to establish the study of society as a science. It views the family as a social institution that performs essential functions for society to ensure its stability. Society is envisioned as a biological organism, made up of interdependent parts or institutions, such as family, education, religion, and workplace, that enable the larger whole (or society) to function. The best-known and leading proponent of the structural-functionalist perspective was Talcott Parsons (1902–1979), whose ideas were enormously influential during the 1950s and 1960s. He began his career as a biologist, and later taught sociology at Harvard University from 1931 until just before his death. His work was influenced by the earliest functionalistic theorists to focus on the family, particularly British anthropologist Malinowski.

In 1913, Malinowski published the classic work *The Family among the Australian Aborigines*, which drew on 19th-century debates about families and which became the basis for most sociological theories in the first half of the 20th century. His basic argument was that "the family" consisted of a man, a woman, and their children, and that this family was universal. He asserted that this family form could be found in all societies, including diverse European societies and among the Aboriginal groups of Australia. Moreover, he assumed that this universal family was rooted in biological sex differences, which supports the need for a strict gendered division of labour. In addition, he assumed that a major function of the family was to provide a home, to organize sexual reproduction, and to provide nurturance and love to its members.

At Harvard, Parsons and his colleague Bales (1955) applied this theory when they co-wrote *Family, Socialization, and the Interaction Process*. Similar to Malinowski, they maintained that families function best when husbands and fathers carried out and specialized in instrumental roles and mothers carried out expressive roles. This idealization is similar to the nuclear family depicted in the "Leave It to Beaver" television situation comedy, which was produced between 1957 and 1963 (with reruns still shown). In his instrumental role as breadwinner, Mr. Cleaver (the Beav's dad) was hard-working and confident, while Mrs. Cleaver (the Beav's mom) was nurturing and caring in her expressive role as full-time homemaker. Indeed, this ideological view of a woman's role in society was widespread at this time, as illustrated in the depiction of a housewife in a Canadian encyclopedia in 1958.

Families have three primary functions, all of which lend order, stability, or homeostasis to the larger society. First, families must ensure that society has an ongoing supply of new members and be a source of socialization. Thus, the family must control and regulate reproduction, as well as socialize offspring to learn attitudes, beliefs, and values appropriate to their society and culture so that they can function effectively. Second, families need to provide economic support for family members, such as food, clothing, and housing. Third, families need to provide emotional support for family members by offering intimacy, warmth, safety, and protection. This is deemed to be an antidote to the dehumanizing and alienating forces of modern society. In short, this family function provides a useful service to society by offering a "haven in a heartless world" (Lasch, 1977).

SOCIAL CONFLICT, POLITICAL ECONOMY, AND GENDER THEORIZING: INEQUALITY, CLASS, AND POWER RELATIONS AS FUNDAMENTAL FEATURES OF FAMILY LIFE

Functionalist ideas pervaded all aspects of sociological thinking from the 1930s until they were challenged by conflict theorizing in the late 1960s. Rather than stressing order, equilibrium,

R. G. & BATTEN

The housewife accepts her never-ending work, not for its own sake but to keep one corner of a hurried world secure and bright and warm. She encourages the first steps, the first wondering contact with the world. She offers love where there is hurt or pain, and shares the delights that tumble in and fill the house with laughter.

Figure 2.1: The Role of the 1950s Housewife

Source: This photo and caption appeared inside the front cover of the 1958 *Encyclopedia Canadiana; The Encyclopedia of Canada*, Vol. 10. 1958. Ottawa: The Grolier Society of Canada Ltd.

and consensus, conflict theory focuses on power relations and inequality and how political and economic processes affect family life. At a macro level, inequality may be between the family system and the work/employment/economic system, between males and females, between social classes, or between age groups. At the micro level, inequality may occur between certain family members, such as between parent and child, or between daughter-in-law and mother-in-law, or between siblings. Furthermore, conflict is not necessarily viewed as bad or disruptive of social systems and human interactions, since it is seen as an assumed and expected feature of society and human behaviour (Eshleman and Wilson, 2001).

Social conflict theory (including political economy theory, to be discussed later) has its roots in the work of Karl Marx (1818–1883), who studied the transition from feudalism to capitalism as two major classes developed—the bourgeoisie and the proletariat. These two classes were primarily in opposition to each other and interdependent, since the proletariat class was vulnerable to exploitation and alienation under the dominant, ruling bourgeoisie class. Although Marxist analysts have generally given little attention to the study of the family per se, Marx's colleague, Frederick Engels, wrote the first conflict framework of the family. In his book *The Origin of the Family, Private Property, and the State* (1884/1902), Engels traces the relationship between the mode of production and the type of family that exists in society. For example, he argued that the communal family systems of technologically simple societies seemed to be more egalitarian than patriarchal, monogamous families, which were based on private property (Porter, 1987).

Since Marx and Engels were primarily concerned with economic relations, families were primarily viewed as sites for the reproduction of labour power that ultimately benefits the capitalists. Also, domestic labour, which is primarily done in the household, did not fit into standard Marxian concepts such as surplus (or unpaid labour) value. Domestic labour was also seen as a "natural" role for women (Sydie, 1987), though Marx and Engels did regard it as the major source of women's oppression. In their view, only as women became members of the paid labour force could they achieve political and social influence. This would remove gender inequalities in society and produce truly egalitarian marital relationships.

A POLITICAL ECONOMY VIEW OF FAMILY LIFE: THE FAMILY AS A UNIT OF CONSUMPTION

Although not a unified discipline or theory per se, a political economy view of the family is useful for further understanding contemporary family life, since it elaborates on the role of economic processes in shaping society and history. This approach makes extensive use of class analysis in making sense of society and history, particularly in the context of political, cultural, and socio-economic processes. Political economists assume that the dominant class in any society is advantageously placed to exact obedience or compliance from the subordinate classes. This implies a relationship not only between class and ideology, but also between power and ideology—the organized and structured power of a given class. Therefore, there is an element of social control, since dominant groups are able to **manufacture consent**, a term used to denote how the mass media filters information so that the interests of elite groups go unchallenged. Thus, while many of us assume that we willingly engage in certain behaviours as free agents, in reality, this may be only illusory (Côté and Allahar, 1994).

In order to apply some of these ideas to specific aspects of family life, we need to consider how our industrial economy and capitalist mode of production (based on liberal democracy) shape our choices, lifestyles, and behaviours. Family forms are viewed as historically embedded outcomes of global capitalist practices and changes in work patterns and technology (Luxton, 2005), as discussed in box 2.1. This reduces families to units of consumption that foster cultural values of individualism and hedonism rather than collectivist goals. Since capitalists rely on the consumption of commodities (or goods) in order to survive, families must be "encouraged" to consume goods and services, which can extend to education and parenting. For instance, Barkley (2003) argues that we live in a culture that has commodified parenting through a constant barrage of parenting magazines, books, television channels, and programs, yet parents have not voluntarily participated in the process. Indeed, according to Barkley:

Box 2.1: The Effect of the Industrial Economy on Families: A Political Economy Approach

In the modern industrial economy, the responsibility of the family for the material welfare of its members declined with the professionalization of health care and the slow emergence of state care for those in need. The traditional pattern of home births, home remedies, and informal kinship support systems was increasingly replaced by hospitals, clinics, and publicly funded welfare offices. In this sense, the general direction of the 20th century has been toward the building of public institutions to support individual existence (Strong-Boag, 1979; Struthers, 1983). Nonetheless, these institutions do not fully respond to individual needs, and families have maintained an important support role for their members as well as for kin. The processes of social and economic change may have encouraged some sense of individualism, but family and kin still provide an important framework for personal welfare in the late 20th century much as they have since the 17th century.

The instability of the family during the urban growth and industrial development of the mid-nineteenth century caused considerable concern among politicians and other public leaders, who feared that widespread social disorder would result from the rapid pace of social change. These leaders believed that the family was in peril as a social institution, and so they promoted new ideals for family members, especially for women and children, who were most affected by the new modes of production. The major development for children was the establishment of schooling as a dominant experience growing up. For women, the result was a definition of their responsibility that limited them to the home and to the roles of wives and mothers.

Source: Gaffield, C. 1990. "The Social and Economic Origins of Contemporary Families." In M. Baker (eds.), *Families: Changing Trends in Canada* (pp. 23–40). Scarborough, Ontario: McGraw-Hill Ryerson Ltd. (p. 33).

In our post-industrial society, social activity has become commodified; our needs have been absorbed into the marketplace and sold back to us. Most activities related to our children now require the intervention of the marketplace. Sales people and "experts" help us to decide on the right clothes, pets, the timing of talks about sex, the correct bedtime, normal versus abnormal adolescent behaviour, how to monitor television, how to discipline, how to deal with homework, anger, activities, entertainment, computers, sports—the list is endless, and exhausting. (Barkley, 2003: 278)

Moreover, from this perspective, the advertising industry aggressively targets certain social groups of people (e.g., young people) to buy their goods and may, in fact, even appear to embrace the values of oppressed or marginalized groups (e.g., the "gangster" subculture with its identifiable music and clothing). Consequently, capitalist enterprises are able to sell more hip-hop and designer clothing, jewellery, tattoos, and running shoes. Similarly, the fast-food industry bombards us with ads that target children and families since they are able to provide quick and inexpensive meals (albeit with little nutritive value). Added "bonuses" such as free plastic toys also "bully" parents into buying these meals for their children. Overall, a conflict/political economy perspective situates family life and its decision making in the context of political, socio-economic, cultural, and environmental processes.

FEMINIST AND MASCULINITY PERSPECTIVES: GENDER AND THE FAMILY

Similar to the conflict/political economy perspective, there is not "one" unified feminist theory and feminist theoretical perspective. Socialist feminists, for example, tend to analyze the relationship between the processes of capital accumulation and "the reproduction of labour power." Capitalism relies on the existence of workers to supply labour power in addition to unpaid domestic labour (which is mainly performed by women) in order to survive. Radical feminists, on the other hand, tend to emphasize differences between men and women and the ways in which men's power oppresses and controls women and creates unsafe places for women and children (e.g., see Luxton, 2005 for further discussion). Despite considerable variation in theories, five basic themes that appear in feminist approaches can be identified (Osmond and Thorne, 1993; Seccombe and Warner, 2004):

1. Emphasis is placed on the female experience, since social life has traditionally been studied through the gaze of men.
2. Gender is an organizing concept of social theory and is seen as a set of relations imbued with power and inequality.
3. Gender and family relations need to be contextualized in their respective socio-cultural and historical situations and vary by social class, ethnicity, and geographic location.
4. There is not one single unitary definition of "the family."
5. Instead of taking a "value-neutral" orientation, feminists purport that inequality exists and should be eliminated.

Generally, feminist theorists have been very critical of traditional sociological approaches (e.g., Smith, 1974, 1999), especially ones that ignore power and inequality and how this is structured by gender, in addition to other root sources of disadvantage, such as race, ethnicity, social class, sexual orientation, and age. Thus, a feminist perspective recognizes how social interaction, including discourse (i.e., the usage of language and symbols) is socially constructed and mirrors privilege and inequities as depicted in figure 2.2. Feminists also tend to assume that if reality is socially constructed, it can therefore be reconstructed. As a result, feminist theories are designed to uncover the mechanisms by which inequality is maintained so that new mechanisms can be constructed to dismantle it (Seccombe and Warner, 2004). Moreover, it is assumed that around the world, women in developing nations face very different challenges than women in advanced industrialized nations. Therefore, poverty, environmental degradation, sexual exploitation, and starvation can also be key concerns for many feminists.

Since feminism grew into an important social movement during the 1960s, scholars have been researching women in greater depth. However, the theoretical study of men and their various masculine identities is a relatively new field (e.g., see Carrigan, Connell, and Lee, 2002). From this lens, theorists are interested in historical conceptualizations of masculinity and masculine identity and its social construction. Family-related topics of interest might include: men's socialization; men, relationships, and sexuality; men and power/violence; and men and fatherhood. And while masculinity studies can be found in other disciplines (e.g., cultural studies), a sociological perspective typically centres on common Marxist-feminist themes such as power and oppression; the public and the private domain; and social, cultural, and political change (e.g., see Whitehead and Barrett, 2001).

Moreover, there has been a resurgence of work that draws upon an **intersectionality lens** by integrating the complex factors and processes that shape gendered and human lives. As outlined by Hankivsky (2014: 2), "Intersectionality promotes an understanding of human beings as shaped by the integration of different locations (e.g., race/ethnicity, Indigeneity, gender, class, sexuality, geography, age, disability/ability, migration status, religion)." Conceptually, these interactions happen within a context of intertwined structures of power (e.g., laws, policies, media). Therefore, it is argued that our social lives cannot be

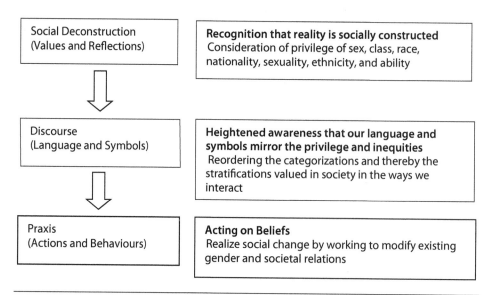

Figure 2.2: Social Interaction from a Feminist Perspective

Source: Ingoldsby, B B., S.R. Smith, and J.E. Miller. 2004. *Exploring Family Theories.* Los Angeles: Roxbury Publishing.

theorized or explained simply by taking into account a single category such as gender, since people's lives are not simply the products of singular factors but are multi-dimensional.

SOCIAL CONSTRUCTIONISM AND THE SYMBOLIC INTERACTION PERSPECTIVE: FAMILIES CREATING THEIR OWN REALITIES

Social constructionism is a sociological theory of knowledge that became prominent in the US with the publication of Berger and Luckman's 1966 book entitled *The Social Construction of Reality*. This sociological theory of knowledge focuses on the idea that social phenomena are created or constructed in particular social and cultural contexts. In other words, what may appear as a "natural" or a singular reality is actually an "invention" or construction reflective of a particular group, culture, or society. Thus, a major consideration is given to uncovering the manner in which individuals, families, or other social groups participate in the creation of their perceived reality, such as in the creation of family rituals and stories, childhood memories, and romantic "ideals" (e.g., see Bulcroft, Smeins, and Bulcroft, 2005).

In contemporary times, social constructionism is viewed as a source of the "postmodern movement" (e.g., the "deconstructing" of asserted knowledge), and has been influential in the field of cultural studies. Its roots can also be traced to other popular sociological theories of the family such as symbolic interactionism. Symbolic interactionism emerged in the United States in the 1920s at the University of Chicago. Based on the work of Charles Horton Cooley (1909) and George Herbert Mead (1934), as well as other influential sociologists during the 1920s and 1930s, the term "symbolic interactionism" was later adopted by Herbert Blumer (1969) to describe the process of interpersonal interaction. Applied to family studies, this perspective emphasizes micro or internal family interactions, and the ongoing action and response of family members to one another. Family interactions are the result of reciprocal acts whereby individuals are acting, negotiating, and responding to one another as minded beings. Interactions occur via symbols, or gestures or words that have shared meaning.

Interpretations and meanings are anchored in actual situations of social interactions, and through interactions, a person develops a sense of self. For example, through primary relationships with "significant others," such as parents or peers, a child acquires a sense of competencies and a feeling of self-worth. A person's self is composed of a socialized component called the "me," plus an "I," which refers to the more spontaneous behaviour that arises out of biological needs and immediate sensations (Mead, 1934).

Therefore, unlike the structural functionalists, who consider the family as a standard structure, these theorists view the family as the creation of its members as they spontaneously interact with one another in joint action. Thus, a family takes on a reality of its own based on subjective meanings and interpretations, role playing, and the interchanges of its members. This reflects the famous Thomas theorem introduced by Thomas and Thomas (1928: 572), which states that, "If people define situations as real, they are real in their consequences." For example, if you interpret the glances and words that your date is exchanging with others at a party as flirtatious, your interpretation of reality could result in a certain outcome, such as jealousy, accusations, and the ultimate breakup of the relationship.

SOCIAL EXCHANGE THEORY: RELATIONSHIPS AND FAMILY LIFE AS "FAIR TRADE"

Similar to symbolic interactionism, social exchange theory is a micro-level theory that focuses on the interaction between individual actors. However, social exchange theory views family life and decision making in terms of costs and benefits. Early proponents include George Homans (1910–1989), who drew from the work of developmental psychology, and Peter Blau (1918–2002), who was heavily influenced by the field of economics. Exchange theorists assume that humans are primarily motivated by self-interest and seek to maximize rewards or profits in relationships while minimizing costs or possible punishments. Humans are also seen as rational beings who consciously calculate relative costs and rewards, although rules and/or the importance of any exchange are variable across people and cultures. Moreover, exchanges are regulated by norms of reciprocity and are characterized by interdependence (Gouldner, 1960).

Although this approach is criticized for its "market relations" type of analysis and failure to address why people hold varying amounts of resources in the first place, it has been used to study topics such as dating, marital satisfaction, divorce, and other relationship patterns. Applied to the area of mate selection, most of us have an idea of how much we are "worth" in terms of our looks, personality, ability, and even possessions. As a result, we expect to get the "best return" for what we provide in relationships at the least cost to ourselves. For example, if we perceive ourselves to be fairly attractive and intelligent, we expect to find a mate who is also smart, good looking, or has some other benefit such as an exceptionally pleasant personality. Further, norms of reciprocity suggest that both partners should perceive some gain or reward from the exchange or interaction. In other words, there should be a sense of balance such that if the exchange results in a net loss for one partner, then the relationship could be in trouble (Seccombe and Warner, 2004).

THE FAMILY DEVELOPMENT PERSPECTIVE: A HYBRID THEORY

Originating in home economics and elaborated by sociologists during the 1930s, the family development approach tries to synthesize the ideas of several approaches into one unified theme (Eshleman and Wilson, 2001). For example, from rural sociologists these sociologists borrowed the concept of stages of the family life cycle, and from child psychologists they used the concepts of developmental needs and tasks. From the structural-functionalist and symbolic interactionist approaches they borrowed the concepts of family functions and sex roles and the idea of the family as a system of interacting actors (Hill and Hansen, 1960).

This perspective proposes that family members accomplish developmental tasks as they move through stages in the family life cycle. Although there are many variations on family life cycle, the best known is that of Evelyn Duvall, who developed an eight-stage model of the family in the 1950s. These stages entail: a married couple with no children; the child-bearing family; the family with preschoolers; the family with school-aged children; the family with adolescents; the family as "launching pad" (e.g., children leaving home); the middle-aged "empty nest" family; and the aging family from retirement to death. Throughout the life span, members' roles, expectations, and relationships change, largely depending upon how they adapt to the presence or absence of child-rearing responsibilities (Duvall, 1957).

Since the 1960s, there has been a great deal of attention given to the analysis of marital satisfaction over the life cycle from this perspective. However, you can probably see many aspects of family life that do not fit neatly into the life cycle approach, such as the refilled "empty nest," which is covered in chapter 11. This approach has also been based on White, middle-class families and has generally ignored diversity such as same-sex households and social change, although it is constantly undergoing reformulation (e.g., see White and Klein, 2002).

EMERGENT FAMILY THEORY: THE LIFE COURSE PERSPECTIVE

Although not considered a formal theory by some, a notable emergent framework in the field of family sociology is the life-course perspective (e.g., see Giele and Elder, 1998). It is also common to conjoin this approach with a modified family developmental one. Both share many similar concepts and complement each other, and together they provide important insights into the ways that families grow and change over time (e.g., see White, Klein, and Martin, 2015).

Typically, a life-course perspective approach draws upon a variety of disciplines in addition to sociology (e.g., social demography, history, economics, and developmental psychology). It is particularly relevant to contemporary trends in family life, given its relevance to population aging and health-related issues. Indeed, it is generally considered the dominant perspective in the field of social gerontology at the present time.

This perspective has its roots in age stratification theory and draws heavily on prominent American sociologist C. Wright Mills's (1959) call for a theoretical orientation that bridges individual biography and history and the intersections of these domains within the social structure. Therefore, this perspective can link macro (history, social structure) elements and the micro (or individual/interpersonal) level (Chappell, Gee, McDonald, and Stones, 2003). The life course of individuals and their families is embedded and shaped by their relative historical, cultural, and geographic location, as well as by factors such as age, gender, family history, socio-economic status, and ethnicity/race. The family is perceived as a micro social group within a macro social context—a "collection of individuals with shared history who interact within ever-changing social contexts" (Bengston and Allen, 1993: 470).

Concerned with lifelong developmental processes in the family, the life course can be defined as trajectories that extend across the life span, such as family or work; and by short-term changes or transitions, such as entering or leaving school, acquiring a full-time job, and the first marriage (Elder, 2000). Transitions are also subject to reversal, such as becoming divorced or returning to the parental home. Age and social time are connected by the concept of normative timing. In other words, societies have expectations or social clocks about the "appropriate" age for people to take on (or exit from) social roles. Some of these expectations are formal (e.g., retirement at age 65), or they may be embedded in wider social and cultural norms (e.g., at what age one should marry).

Another key principle is that individuals and families have differential access to resources (e.g., economic and social), and this can shape the timing and nature of transitional behaviours and other family-related decisions. For example, young adults with fewer resources and supports have less opportunity to delay adult roles and responsibilities. Moreover, family lives are "linked" or lived interdependently, such that the actions of one family member can affect the actions or circumstances of another. Becoming a parent, for instance, creates the counter-transition of grandparenthood, with its new sets of generational roles and responsibilities.

Finally, the timing and nature of transitions and events can result in impacts that are felt as one ages, and can be envisioned as "ripple effects." For example, if a young person drops out of high school, leaves home at a young age, and becomes homeless, this situation can have far-reaching consequences for the rest of his or her life (i.e., poverty and poor health in old age). Thus, this approach emphasizes how cumulative disadvantage (or advantage) can set up a chain reaction of experiences that reverberates across the life course—a social inequality perspective that has valuable utility for creating effective social policy and programs (e.g., see O'Rand, 1996; also see chapter 16).

OTHER WINDOWS ON FAMILIES

It should be recognized that these theories are not the only frames of reference used in family sociology. For example, some sociologists draw upon social ecological theory, a multidisciplinary perspective that integrates a life-course perspective and calls for simultaneously considering family-level variables and contextual variables. It has received considerable attention from theorists and researchers as both a developmental and a historical framework for the study of intergenerational relations, and is often used to study substantive areas such as family violence and elder abuse (see chapter 15 for overview and application). Another popular theory is family systems theory, which bridges family sociology and family therapy. From a family systems perspective, a family is viewed like a machine, with parts or family members that interact in a meaningful way (Chibucos and Leite, with Weiss, 2005). Therefore, problems in families cannot be understood and solved without taking into account the entire family system.

Thus, family sociologists can synthesize theoretical ideas from several sources. For example, they could integrate elements of feminism with queer theory, a theory that questions the use of socially constructed categories of sex/gender. Sociologists can also be influenced by other disciplines, such as biology and psychology, resulting in cross-disciplinary hybrid "windows" on the family (e.g., see chapter 8 for theories on child socialization). Bio-social theory, for example, suggests that biology always interacts with culture in creating certain family forms (Walsh and Gordon, 1995). Alternatively, they may use models or other types of less formal theory, such as the Double ABCX model used in family stress/abuse research, which is covered in more detail in chapter 15. Moreover, by rigorous scientific standards, some of these "theories" would be considered "conceptual frameworks," since they are based on loosely interrelated concepts or are only partially applied to substantive topics (Porter, 1987).

WHICH THEORY IS RIGHT? CRITICALLY EVALUATING FAMILY THEORIES

Students often wonder which theory is the most accurate, given varying (and often conflicting) foci and assumptions about the nature of reality and social life. Indeed, each theory or conceptual framework contains its own set of concepts defined to explain family life efficiently within *its* world view (see table 2.1 for a summary of key concepts), and this influences how researchers ask (and answer) questions about the family. Yet, on a broad level, all theory is a kind of discourse that seeks generalization, as elaborated by Canadian family theorist David Cheal in box 2.2.

Box 2.2: What Is Theory?

Theory is a kind of discourse. It is a set of topics and a way of talking about those topics. Not all discourse is theoretical discourse, however. Theory is the kind of discourse that seeks generalizations. It moves from the particular to the general, and makes statements that apply to a large number of cases under a variety of conditions. The purpose of theory may be to explain, or to construct a narrative, or to summarize knowledge, but the form of argument is always one of generalization. Theory is that discourse which takes particular cases and places them in a context where they can be compared with other cases having similar or different properties.

   The principal means by which generalizations are made in theoretical discourse is through the use of concepts that identify types of objects. Concepts are the heart of any theory, and definitions of concepts therefore rightly receive a great deal of attention in the process of theorizing. A renewal of family theory must include renewed attention to problems of definitions in family studies, including the problem of defining family itself.

   If the goal of theory is generalization, we need to pay attention to the different levels of theory. This involves including in our repertoire of theories those theories which are general in the sense of applying to aspects of society beyond family relations. Concepts such as industrial society and post-industrial society are relevant here, and seem likely to become more important as we try to take account of changes in family life.

Source: Cheal, D. 2005. "Theorizing Family: From the Particular to the General." In V.L. Bengtson et al., *Sourcebook of Family Theory and Research* (pp. 29-31). Thousand Oaks, California: Sage Publications (pp. 29-30).

It should also be remembered that theoretical frameworks have evolved from the efforts of social scientists to understand large-scale social changes taking place in industrializing Europe and North America during the 19th century, yet these theories changed throughout the century in response to differing conceptions and conditions of family life. Thus, the effort of family sociologists to develop tenable explanatory frameworks is constantly being challenged by social and technological change. This is illustrated in the structural-functionalist theorizing that held sway during the 1950s and 1960s, a time in which the heterosexual nuclear family structure with rigid gender roles was more prevalent than it is today. In this way, each perspective represents an "intellectual heritage" that reflects a distinct socio-historical location and has been modified and expanded through the years by many contributors (Porter, 1987). As a result, some theories are now viewed as "outdated" and not reflective of contemporary family life, although some fundamental concepts or tenets may reappear in newer theories. In addition, each perspective has its own relative strengths and limitations, based on its primary emphasis or conception of the phenomenon under study (also see table 2.1). For instance, social exchange theories are commonly critiqued for the assumption that we are rational actors in our decision-making. Children, for instance, do not choose their parents. Also, parents tend not to be motivated by a calculating and optimization of monetary profits in return for the personal sacrifices that they make as parents.

FAMILY RESEARCH METHODS: A BRIEF INTRODUCTION

As previously stated, research and theory are interdependent—research without any underlying theoretical reasoning is simply a string of meaningless bits of information, whereas theory without research is abstract and speculative (Mills, 1959). Fundamentally, there are three basic ways of knowing (see table 2.2) and two basic "ideal types" of conducting research (see figure 2.3).

Deductive and Inductive Approaches

One way of conducting research is by adopting the "traditional" scientific method or **deductive approach**, whereby the researcher begins with a theory and develops hypotheses about what he or she expects to observe. For example, social exchange theory purports that those with more resources in a relationship hold the balance of power. Therefore, we might hypothesize that in a dual-career couple, the partner who earns the higher salary will do less housework, on average. We would then collect data from couples (e.g., on their income, distribution of domestic work) and try to determine if there is support for our hypothesis. Surveys, interviews, and experimental designs would be popular methods of collecting data from this approach, and these data are usually amenable to quantitative analysis (i.e., by statistically analyzing these data using numeric and coded forms).

Alternatively, we might adopt an **inductive approach**, which begins with systematic observations and is often used in **qualitative research**. Typically, these observations help

Table 2.1: How Sociological Theories View Families

Theoretical Perspective	Key Concepts
Structural Functionalism	Order, stability, equilibrium, consensus, harmony, socialization, instrumental/expressive roles
Example: What are some long-term consequences of parental divorce for children?	
Feminist Perspective	Gender inequality, women's subordination, patriarchy, social change
Example: How does women's disproportionate participation in unpaid work affect their economic standing and well-being later in life?	
Symbolic Interactionism	Day-to-day interactions, communication, symbols, subjective meanings, perceptions, definition of the situation, role playing, joint action
Example: :How does religion help families understand and cope with normative and non-normative events?	
Social Exchange Theory	Rewards, costs, profit, reciprocity, expectations, self-interest, humans as rational
Example: Why do abused women stay with their partners?	
Family Development	Expectations, norms, family career, life stages, developmental tasks
Example: How does marital satisfaction change over the life cycle?	
Life Course Approach	Age-related transitions, counter-transitions, social timetables, diversity, linked lives, cumulative advantage and disadvantage
Example: How does the timing of life course transitions during young adulthood affect intergenerational relationships?	
Conflict/Political Economy	Capitalist economy, inequality, class struggle, ideology and illusion, manufacturing consent, social control, production, consumption
Example: How does capitalism influence family patterns of consumption?	

us to move toward more abstract concepts and ideas that contribute to the further development of theory. This approach is favoured by those who do not want to begin their research with predetermined ideas, or is used when a theory on that topic is not explicit or well developed enough to predict certain outcomes. Inductive styles of research are also popular among those who want to collect "quality" data rather than engage in "number crunching." Common approaches to data collection include: in-depth interviews, direct observations or ethnographies, participant observation, archival/document analysis, or case studies.

Let's assume that a social constructionist interested in the study of family rituals (e.g., wedding ceremonies) wants to learn about family traditions in relation to religious practices and behaviours. One possible approach might be to conduct a narrative analysis. **Narrative analysis** is concerned with the knowledge base and stories that people and groups use to give meaning to their experiences. Researchers can examine family

Table 2.2: Three Ways of Knowing Applied to Family Studies

	1. Scientific Approach to Knowing	**2. Interpretive Approach to Knowing**	**3. Critical Approach to Knowing**
View of knowledge:	There are objective truths, processes, or realities to be discovered about families	Truth is subjective, and all knowledge about families is created by interpreting actors engaged in conversations with one another	Truth is defined by those in power, who impose their definition of the situation on others
Values:	Family theories should reflect values on honesty, skepticism, universalism, open communication, and evidence	Family science is values-relevant, and family scientists should become aware of and open about their own values	Family theories are value-laden. Opportunities for change are created only when the values underlying theories are exposed and challenged
Criteria for evaluating family theories:	Good theories should be relationally constructed (e.g., internally consistent, simple, coherent) and empirically relevant (testable, fit well with data)	Good theories should have literary qualities (e.g., elegance, imagination, narrative power). They should be based on data grounded in the experiences of family members	Good theories contextualize phenomena and allow for pluralism. They are emancipatory, prescribe changes, display the theorists' ethical stances, and fit well with the theorists' personal experiences
Goals:	Explanation and prediction	Understanding	Emancipation or empowerment of oppressive peoples and social groups
Scholarly style:	Analytic, causal, deductive or inductive, deterministic or probabilistic, factual, logical, materialistic, structural, observant, quantitative	Artistic, intuitive, phenomenological, postmodern, processual, self-reflective, speculative, symbolic	Constructivist, dialectical, feminist, liberal or radical, postmodern, pluralistic

Source: Adapted from Klein, D.M., and J.M. White. 1996. *Family Theories.* Thousand Oaks, California: Sage Publications (p. 48) and J.M. White, D.M. Klein, and T.F. Martin. 2015. *Family Theories: An Introduction*, 4th ed. Thousand Oaks, California: Sage Publications (pg. 30).

narratives or family stories (which may be different or conflicting) in order to better understand the role of religious background in shaping marital rituals across generations. In this way, one can better understand how family members "author" and "reauthor"

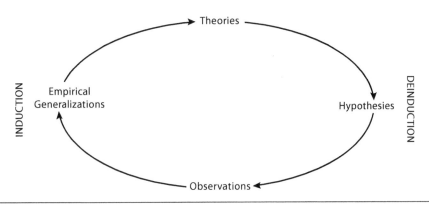

Figure 2.3: The Wheel of Science

Source: Adapted from Wallace, W. 1971. The Logic of Science. New York: Aldine deGruyter.

their own lives in line with alternative and preferred stories of identity and ways of life. This could also be done in order to reveal how family members use religious meanings and symbols to construct experiences and to develop their sense of self as a family over time (Chatters and Taylor, 2005).

Relatedly, we could conduct a **discourse analysis**, which would involve the critical reading of language and texts that make up our social locations. Although sociologists differ enormously in terms of how they define this approach, discourse analysis is generally concerned with the production (and reproduction) of meaning through talk, written texts and visual images and how meanings reproduce power, dominance, and inequality. For example, one might study the documents and resources offered by a web-site organization that is geared toward supporting and providing information to families. Through critical analysis of their on-line content, the researcher might uncover a strong conservative bias and agenda that is implicitly (rather than obviously) biased against gay marriage or single-parenthood. It should also be noted that discourse analysis is sometimes defined less in terms of it being a particular method, but as more of a way of questioning certain assumptions that underlie the way that we "do" methods.

Overall, attention in qualitative research is paid to uncovering and understanding how subjective meanings imbue multiple meanings of reality instead of singular or "objective" realities. Focus is placed on process rather than cause-effect, as well as the daily lived experiences of family members. And while the descriptions of these approaches illustrate two very different styles of reasoning or doing research, in reality, researchers adopting one approach do not always follow these steps in perfect sequence. One might begin with a theory and a set of rigid hypotheses, but then modify this work as the research progresses. Indeed, science depends upon continuous movement between theory and observation (Seccombe and Warner, 2004). Also, qualitative researchers may be interested in quantifying some data, while quantitative researchers may also collect data via open-ended questions, which can contain subjective data. Furthermore, as you have learned in this chapter, there are different styles of doing research under the rubric of either quantitative or qualitative methods, and these methods may be shared with other disciplinary foundations (see figure 2.4 for examples of three types of qualitative methodologies).

Moreover, mixed methodological approaches have become highly popular, since no single methodological orientation can answer all our questions about families. Mixed methods can be used in a single study, which could entail the collection of both quantitative and qualitative data. These studies could be sequential, starting with **quantitative methods** (e.g., statistical analysis of census data) and then using qualitative methods (e.g., case studies) to further probe meanings of emergent themes uncovered in the initial analyses. Alternatively, the study could begin with a qualitative study, or it might combine both methods simultaneously, but at different levels of aggregation (Greenstein, 2006). For example, a researcher could do a statistical analysis of the factors that increase the likelihood of getting divorced, while at the same time conducting in-depth interviews of recently divorced couples.

Participatory Action Research and Anti-Oppressive Practices

Finally, another complementary strategy, rather than a discrete research methodology, is **participatory action research (PAR)**. Its emphasis is on democratic empowerment through

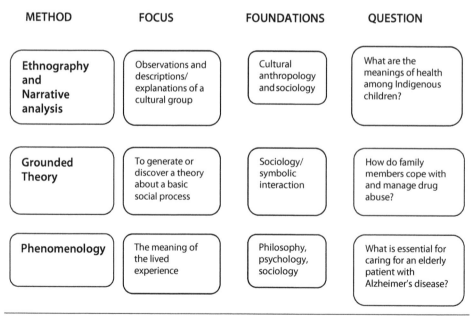

Figure 2.4: Examples of Qualitative Methods

Source: Adapted and modified from Jackson, W. 2003. Methods: Doing Social Research, 3rd ed. Toronto: Prentice-Hall.

participation in the process of research, knowledge production, and social change (Turnbull, Friesen, Ramirez, 1998). The researchers and stakeholders (those who potentially benefit from research results) collaborate in the design and in the conduct of all phases of the research—from designing the research question or problem to be solved, to how the results will be used and disseminated. Although this strategy can present unique challenges for researchers (e.g., cost, time, methodological rigor), many advantages can be gained. For example, family members can become research leaders and advisors. These "insiders" are also in the best position to offer practical solutions to the problems they face in their own communities.

A good PAR applied example is offered by Ginn and Kulig (2015). These researchers wanted to decrease inequities among Indigenous people in Canada due to residual effects of colonization and assimilation (a topic that will be examined in chapter 4) and develop positive strategies for health and healing. For their study, they directly involved seven grandmothers in every phase of the research cycle. Since First Nations grandmothers are known to pass on wisdom and knowledge and create support networks for their families and communities, they were able to effectively assist in the development of innovative strategies for health reform and policy development.

PAR is also highly compatible with other empowerment approaches to research, including **anti-oppressive practices** in the process of inquiry (see box 2.3). Drawing from Indigenous, feminist, and critical race scholarship, this practice emphasizes critical reflexivity in addition to participatory methods. It is maintained that while research can be a powerful tool for social change, it can also be used to suppress ideas, people, and social justice. Therefore, choosing to be an "anti-oppressive" researcher means choosing to do research that challenges dominant ideas about research, and carrying it out in a socially just way (Strega and Brown, 2015).

Box 2.3: The Anti-Oppressive Approach to Knowledge and Research

How do we know what we know? The answer to this epistemological question is key to understanding an anti-oppressive approach to research. From an anti-oppressive perspective, knowledge does not exist "out there" to be discovered. Rather is produced through the interactions of people, and as all people are socially and politically located (in their race, gender, ability, class identities, and so on), with biases, privileges, and differing entitlements, so too is the knowledge that is produced socially located and political. Knowledge is neither neutral nor benign, as it is created within and through power relations between people. Knowledge can be oppressive in how it is constructed and utilized, or it can be a means of resistance and emancipation. Often, it is a complex combination of both.

Recognizing that knowledge is socially constructed means understanding that truth is created, rather than pre-existing and available to be measured and observed.

Therefore, in anti-oppressive research, we do not look to disprove a singular "truth" about the social or political world. We look for meaning, for understanding, for insights that can enable resistance and change. However, anti-oppressive researchers recognize that we live in a culture biased toward positivist research---that is, using natural science principles of counting, quantifying, and measuring claims to social issues. As anti-oppressive researchers, we argue that we must problematize the dominance of positivism, because while counting, measuring, and quantifying can measure inequalities, the complex causes of social injustice remain unexamined.

We contend that, in the present moment, positivism is part of the infrastructure that allows neoliberalism to flourish and the transformation to a knowledge economy to occur. Recognizing knowledge as socially constructed means being politically astute about this context. Knowledge has been turned into a commodity in the new knowledge economy (David and Foray, 2002), and an increasing emphasis on patents, copyrights, and other regulations is restricting the free sharing of knowledge. Knowledge becomes a profitable commodity, and knowledge creation a profit-making endeavour, when knowledge can be made scarce or where access to knowledge can be limited and controlled (AUCC, 2001). Anti-oppressive research resists the commodification of knowledge and instead advocates "democratizing knowledge" by ensuring it is accessible for the common good (Hall, 2011). As anti-oppressive researchers, we set out to construct emancipatory and liberatory knowledge that can be acted on, by, and in the interests of the marginalized and oppressed.

Knowing is not enough, we must apply. Willing is not enough, we must do.

—Goethe

Knowing without doing isn't really knowing.

—Fortune Cookie

Source: Excerpt from Potts, K.L. and L. Brown. 2015. "Becoming an Anti-Oppressive Researcher." In S. Strega and L. Brown (eds.), *Research as Resistance: Revisiting Critical, Indigenous, and Anti-Oppressive Approaches*, 2nd ed. (pp. 17-44). Toronto: Canadian Scholar's Press (pp. 19-20; pg. 32).

Researcher Values, Biases, and Research Ethics

Relatedly, no discussion of research methods would be complete without mentioning the role of researcher values and biases (also see box 2.4) and the topic of research ethics. This is because researchers invariably hold values orientations that are shaped by such factors as their gender, age, ethnic and religious identification, and family history. These values can influence the entire research process, from the choice of theory, the framing of the research question, a preferred style of data collection, and the interpretation and application of findings. For example, if one values the traditional nuclear family as "ideal" for raising children, then one might speculate that deviation from this structure would result in negative outcomes. This is illustrated by the past tendency of functionalist researchers to assume a "deficit" model of the family, whereby single-parent, step-, and same-sex families were automatically expected to produce negative outcomes for children (e.g., low education, poor socio-emotional adjustment). Yet, after decades of research, many problems found in "non-intact" families (as they were commonly conceptualized) are found to be due to a lack of economic or community resources rather than family structure per se.

Therefore, it is crucial for family sociologists to be critical, culturally sensitive, and self-reflective in order to contemplate how their own values influence their work. They also need to consider whether or not they are explicit in their theorizing. Some argue that researchers should strive for transparency so that any implicit theorizing, research design, and reporting of results can be examined in a full and open scholarly debate

Box 2.4: Seven Biases in Family Literature

Canadian family sociologist Margrit Eichler identifies seven biases evident in studies of families. These biases can influence every stage of the research process and the process of understanding changes in structures and processes in family life:

1. A monolithic bias is a tendency to treat the family as a monolithic structure by emphasizing uniformity of experience and universality of structure and function over diversity of experiences, structures, and functions.
2. A conservative bias is an over-romanticized view of the nuclear family in the past, which overlooks problematic aspects of family life throughout history.
3. A sexist bias is an assumption of a natural division of labour between the sexes.
4. Ageist biases are familial interactions that are considered mainly from the perspective of middle-aged adults without considering those of the children or the elderly.
5. A microstructural bias is a tendency to treat families as encapsulated units rather than taking external factors into account.
6. Racist biases are ones that devalue families of culturally or ethnically non-dominant groups.
7. A heterosexist bias is one that assumes a heterosexual family is the only natural unit.

Source: Eichler, M. 1997. *Family Shifts: Families, Policies and Gender Equality.* Toronto: Oxford University Press.

(Bengtson et al., 2005). In this regard, feminist theorists have been particularly upfront in showing that they are value-committed. That is, they are often lauded for their general tendency to acknowledge that they are aware of their values (i.e., gender equality), a reflection of a particular ideological position, and of a belief that research cannot be truly value-free (Chibucos and Leite, with Weiss, 2005). In short, it is important to critically evaluate the sources and positions (explicit and implicit) of research in order to make meaningful interpretations.

Finally, while trying to answer questions about family life, researchers can encounter a number of ethical issues and challenges. How do families feel about being observed? If they know that they are being studied or watched, will they change their behaviour? Would it be morally right to observe their behaviour without telling them? Should participants be forced to answer questions that are highly sensitive in nature and could cause psychological harm? What do we do if we suspect that a family member is being cheated on or abused? Fortunately, these and other concerns over the use of human subjects are now widely discussed, and it is now a routine procedure for researchers to have their research approved by ethical review boards of granting councils and universities.

However, attention to ethical issues is a relatively recent development. It was not until the middle of the 20th century that the government and other agencies became involved in the regulation of research using humans (Seccombe and Warner, 2004). In Canada, a tri-council policy statement (involving medical, social science and humanities, and natural science/engineering councils) on the ethical conduct for research involving humans was established only in 1998. The guiding ethical principles of this policy include respect for human dignity, free and informed consent, privacy and confidentiality, justice and inclusiveness, balancing harm and benefits, minimizing harm, and maximizing benefits.

Prior to the establishment of regulations, there were many studies that generated a great deal of controversy with respect to their violation of these principles. One such example is Laud Humphries' (1975) infamous Tearoom Trade Study, which took place in the mid-1960s. Humphries, a doctoral student in sociology at Washington University, was interested in learning what motivates men who have anonymous sex in public washrooms. He was interested in their personal characteristics, such as their marital status and the nature of their sexual activity. In the first part of his study, he befriended men in public washrooms by acting as a lookout. He also wrote down the licence plate numbers of these men's cars, and then obtained identifying information via a policeman. In the second part of the study, he used this information to contact and interview these men in their homes. However, he disguised himself and purported to be doing a study on health issues. Clearly, he used very deceptive methods, although he justified this work by claiming that it was for the benefit of social knowledge. Many people did not support his position, and a petition was later sent to the president of the university to rescind his degree.

SUMMARY

In this chapter, an overview of key theoretical perspectives used to study families is outlined. These theories are empirically testable, interconnected ideas that explain some phenomena and increase our understanding of family and social life. In other words, theory is an attempt to move beyond the "what" of our observations to the questions of the "why" and "how" of what we have observed (Bengtson et al., 2005). It is also noted that theories do not develop in a vacuum but within a particular social, historical, and political context. There are also many practical impacts of ongoing theoretical explanation. For example, if our empirical results consistently provide support for our theory, then there are many implications for prevention, intervention, or treatment of persistent family problems. Thus, theory should not be viewed as dry or boring. Rather, it should be seen as an exciting opportunity to improve our understanding of a particular aspect of family life by developing conceptual and empirical linkages about what people actually do (and need) in their everyday life (Chibucos and Leite, with Weiss, 2005).

The relationship between theory and research is noted by identifying three ways of knowing and two general orientations to conducting research—deductive and inductive—as well as quantitative and qualitative research methodologies. These methodologies are equally scientific and complementary, and each approach will have its relative strengths and weaknesses in terms of such aspects as generalizability and richness of data. Therefore, it is important for sociologists to choose a research approach that can best describe the human reality they wish to study (Ambert, 2006). Finally, a discussion on methods is incomplete without acknowledgement of the **ethics of research**. In short, ethical issues require ongoing sensitive reflection so that we become good researchers, as well as critical consumers, of family research.

QUESTIONS FOR CRITICAL REFLECTION AND DEBATE

1. Critically reflect on how your own personal experiences and definition of "family" could affect the way that you theorize and research family life.
2. Debate the following: Theory and research should remain value-free.
3. Consider how social context (i.e., one's historical and political location) shapes theory creation and development. Also consider how a theorist's gender, family, and ethnic background might influence the process of theorizing about some aspect of family life.
4. Collect some articles from newspapers or magazines that deal with some aspects of families. To what extent are "the facts" presented? What seems to be missing from these stories that would have allowed you to more accurately assess their accuracy?
5. Imagine that you are a family researcher hired to study a sensitive area of family life (e.g., child abuse, sexual relations). What kinds of strategies might you use to study what goes on behind closed doors? What ethical issues might arise?
6. Critically evaluate the advantages and disadvantages of using the Internet to research family life.

GLOSSARY

Anti-oppressive practices entail a research approach and form of critical thinking that aim to question "truth" and increase emancipation among marginalized groups.

Deductive approach involves the process whereby the researcher begins with a theory, develops hypotheses, and then collects data in order to test the hypotheses.

Discourse analysis is generally concerned with the production (and reproduction) of meaning through talk and texts (written or visual), and with how meanings reproduce power, dominance, and inequality.

Ethics of research extends beyond regulations (i.e., informed consent) to include underlying ethical assumptions and implications related to the entire research process, from initial topic selection to application of findings.

Inductive approach entails beginning with data collection or observation, finding patterns, and developing theoretical understandings based on these patterns.

Intersectionality lens refers to the viewing and understanding of human beings as shaped by the integration of different locations (e.g., race/ethnicity, Indigeneity, gender, class, sexuality, geography, age, disability/ability, migration status, religion) rather than focusing on a singular factor.

Manufacture of consent refers to how elite groups and dominant institutions (e.g., mass media) shape social behaviour in insidious ways rather than through physical coercion.

Narrative analysis is concerned with the knowledge base and stories that people and groups use to give meaning to their experiences.

Participatory action research (PAR) is a collaborate process that actively involves both researchers and stakeholders in all phases of the research in order to solve some problem.

Qualitative research focuses on verbal or subjective descriptions of behaviour, and typically includes in-depth interviews, direct observation, document analysis, or case studies.

Quantitative methods usually entail the gathering of data that can be presented in the form of numbers (e.g., surveys) and are analyzed using statistical techniques.

Theories are perspectives that explain why and how processes and events occur and contain concepts and empirically testable interconnected ideas.

FURTHER READING

Fawcett, M. and D. Watson. 2016. *Learning through Child Observation*, 3rd ed. London: Jessica Kingsley Publishers.
Examines the value of observation and the importance of fully recognizing children holistically. Focuses on the importance of fully recognizing the child's developmental and emotional state as intervening with and within the context of the family and community.

Greenstein, T.N. and S.N. Davis. 2013. *Methods of Family Research*, 3rd ed. Thousand Oaks, California: Sage Publications.
Teaches students basic concepts, quantitative, qualitative, and mixed methods using real-life examples, as well as how to critically "consume" research.

Kohlman, M.H. 2013. *Notions of Family: Intersectional Perspectives*. Bingley, UK: Emerald Publishing.
Presents a new and original framework for understanding gender and the family, featuring both quantitative and qualitative analyses. Focus is on how salient identities, class position, race, sexuality, and other demographic characteristics simultaneously produce the lives of family members.

Lloyd, S.A. Few, K. Allen (eds.). 2009. *Handbook of Feminist Family Studies*. Thousand Oaks, California: Sage Publications.
Outlines feminist theory, methods, and praxis for the field of family studies and includes a variety of perspectives including: racial-ethnic feminisms; postmodern, constructionist, and biosocial views; as well as frameworks for theorizing motherhood.

McHale, S.M., P.R. Amato, and A. Booth. 2013. *Emerging Methods in Family Research*. New York: Springer Publishers.
Details innovative approaches so that researchers can stay current with the diversity and complexities of today's families. Includes not only new frameworks for basic research on families, but also offers examples of their practical use in intervention and policy studies.

Moore, N., A. Slater, L. Stanely, and M. Tamboukou. 2016. *The Archive Project*. New York: Routledge.
Written by four authors with extensive experience in conducting research and creating archives around the world, this book offers a contemporary "state of the field." It shows the different ways in which archival methodology, practice, and theory can be employed.

Strega, S., and L. Brown. 2015. *Research as Resistance: Revisiting Critical, Indigenous, and Anti-Oppressive Approaches*, 2nd ed. Toronto: Canadian Scholars' Press.
Contributes to the recent resurgence of marginalized knowledge in social science research, drawing from Indigenous, feminist, and race scholarship. Also features narrative

research, Foucauldian methods, community action research, queer theory, and insurgent Indigenous research.

White, J.M., D.M. Klein, and T.F. Martin. 2015. *Family Theories*, 4th ed. Thousand Oaks, California: Sage Publications.

This book provides an overview of popular theoretical perspectives used in family studies research—rational choice and social exchange, symbolic interactionism, life-course family developmental, systems theory, conflict and critical, feminist, and ecological perspective framework.

RELATED WEB SITES

Social Science Space is an online social network forum that brings together various social scientists, writers, and bloggers to discuss current issues in social science fields, www. socialsciencespace.com. Facebook: Socialsciencespace, Twitter: socscispace

Sociological Methods and Research is a journal that specializes in new techniques and innovative approaches to recurring research challenges and clarifies existing methods. It is also a member of the Committee on Publication Ethics (COPE), www.journals.sagepub. com/home/smr.

Theory.org focuses on social theory and popular culture and provides commentary on various theorists and articles on topics such as the media, sexuality, identity, and gender roles, www.theory.org.uk. Facebook: Theory.org.uk and Friends, Twitter: davidgauntlett

The Panel on Research Ethics is an advisory panel consisting of Canada's three federal research agencies, CIHR, NSERC and SSHRC. This website focuses on issues relating to the second edition of the *Tri-Council Policy Statement: Ethical Conduct for Research Involving Humans*, www.pre.ethics.gc.ca/eng/index.

REFERENCES

Ambert, A.M. 2006. *Changing Families: Relationships in Context*. Toronto: Pearson Education.

Barkley, J. 2003. "The Politics of Parenting and the Youth Crisis." In L. Samuelson and W. Antony (eds.), *Power and Resistance: Critical Thinking about Canadian Social Issues*, 3rd ed. (pp. 275–292). Blackpoint, Nova Scotia: Fernwood Publishing.

Bengtson, V.L., A.C. Acock, K.R. Allen, P. Dilworth-Anderson, and D.M. Klein. 2005. "Theory and Theorizing in Family Research: Puzzle Building and Puzzle Solving." In V.L. Bengtson et al. (eds.), *Sourcebook of Family Theory and Research* (pp. 3–29). Thousand Oaks, California: Sage Publications.

Bengtson, V.L., and K.R. Allen. 1993. "The Life Course Perspective Applied to Families over Time." In W. Boss, R. Doherty, W. LaRossa, W. Schumm, and S. Steinmetz (eds.), *Sourcebook of Family Theories and Methods: A Contextual Approach* (pp. 469–499). New York: Plenum Press.

Berger, P.L., and T. Luckmann. 1966. *The Social Construction of Reality: A Treatise in Sociology of Knowledge*. Garden City, NY: Doubleday.

Berger, P.L 1973. *Invitation to Sociology: A Humanistic Perspective*. Woodstock: Overlook.

Blumer, H.G. 1969. *Symbolic Interactionism: Perspectives and Method*. Englewood Cliffs: Prentice-Hall.

Bulcroft, R., L. Smeins, and K. Bulcroft. 2005. "Cultural Narratives and Individual Experiences in Relationships." In V.L. Bengtson et al., (eds.), *Sourcebook of Family Theory and Research* (pp. 278–280). Thousand Oaks, California: Sage Publications.

Carrigan, T., B. Connell, and J. Lee. 2002. "Toward a New Sociology of Masculinity." In R. Adams and D. Savran (eds.), *The Masculinity Studies Reader* (pp. 99–118). Oxford: Blackwell Publishers.

Chappell, N., E. Gee, L. McDonald, and M. Stones. 2003. *Aging in Contemporary Canada*. Toronto: Prentice-Hall.

Chatters, L.M., and R.J. Taylor. 2005. "Religion and Families." In V.L. Bengtson et al. (eds.), *Sourcebook of Family Theory and Research* (pp. 517–530). Thousand Oaks, California: Sage Publications.

Cheal, D. 2005. "Theorizing Family: From the Particular to the General." In V.L. Bengtson et al. (eds.), *Sourcebook of Family Theory and Research* (pp. 29–31). Thousand Oaks, California: Sage Publications.

Chibucos, T.R., and R.W. Leite, with D.L. Weiss. 2005. *Readings in Family Theory*. Thousand Oaks, California: Sage Publications.

Cooley, C.H. 1909. *Social Organization*. New York: Scribner's.

Côté, J.E., and A.L. Allahar. 1994. *Generation On Hold: Coming of Age in the Late Twentieth Century*. Toronto: Stoddart.

Duvall, E. 1957. *Family Development*. Philadelphia: Lippincott.

Elder, G.H., Jr. 2000. "The Life Course." In E.F. Borgatta and R.J.V. Montgomery (eds.), *The Encyclopedia of Sociology*, vol. 3 (pp. 939–991). New York: Wiley.

Engels, F. 1902. *The Origin of the Family, Private Property, and the State: In the Light of the Researches of Lewis H. Morgan*. Chicago: Charles H. Kerr & Company.

Eshleman, J.R., and S.J. Wilson. 2001. *The Family*, 3rd Canadian ed. Toronto: Pearson.

Giele, J.Z., and G.H. Elder, Jr. 1998. *Methods of Life Course Research: Qualitative and Quantitative Approaches*. Thousand Oaks, California: Sage Publications.

Ginn, C. S. and J.C. Kulig. 2015. "Participatory Action Research with a Group of Urban First Nations Grandmothers: Decreasing Inequities through Health Promotion." *The International Indigenous Policy Journal* 6, 1–16.

Gouldner, A.W. 1960. "The Norm of Reciprocity: A Preliminary Statement." *American Sociological Review* 25:161–178.

Greenstein, T.N. 2006. *Methods of Family Research*, 2nd ed. Thousand Oaks, California: Sage Publications.

Hankivsky, O. 2014. *Intersectionality 101*. Simon Fraser University, Burnaby, British Columbia: Institute for Intersectionality Research and Policy.

Hill, R., and D.A. Hansen. 1960. "The Identification of Conceptual Frameworks Utilized in Family Study." *Marriage and Family Living* 22:299–311.

Humphries, L. 1975. *Tearoom Trade: Impersonal Sex in Public Places*. New York: Aldine de Gruyter.

Lasch, C. 1977. *Haven in a Heartless World: The Family Besieged*. New York: Norton.

Luxton, M. 2005. "Conceptualizing 'Families': Theoretical Frameworks and Family Research." In M. Baker (ed.), *Families: Changing Trends in Canada*, 5th ed. (pp. 29–51). Toronto: McGraw-Hill Ryerson.

Malinowski, B. 1913. *The Family among the Australian Aborigines: A Sociological Study*. London: University of London Press.

Mead, G.H. 1934. *Mind, Self, and Society*. Chicago: University of Chicago Press.

Mills, C.W. 1959. *The Sociological Imagination*. New York: Oxford University Press.

O'Rand, A.M. 1996. "Precious and the Precocious: Understanding Cumulative Disadvantage and Cumulative Advantage over the Life Course." *The Gerontologist* 36: 230–238.

Osmond, M.W., and B. Thorne. 1993. "Feminist Theories: The Social Construction of Gender in Families and Society." In P.G. Boss, W.J. Doherty, R., LaRossa, W.R. Schumm, and S.K. Steinmetz (eds.), *Sourcebook of Family Theories and Methods: A Contextual Approach* (pp. 591–623). New York: Plenum.

Parsons, T., and R.F. Bales. 1955. *Family, Socialization, and the Interaction Process*. Glencoe, Illinois: Free Press.

Porter, E. 1987. "Conceptual Frameworks for Studying Families." In K. Anderson et al. (eds.), *Family Matters: Sociology and Contemporary Canadian Families* (pp. 41–61). Toronto: Methuen.

Seccombe, K., and R.L. Warner. 2004. *Marriages and Families: Relationships in Social Context*. Toronto: Thomson Wadsworth.

Smith, D. 1974. "Women's Perspectives as a Radical Critique of Sociology." *Sociological Inquiry* 44: 7–1.

Smith, D. 1999. *Writing the Social: Critique, Theory and Investigation*. Toronto: University of Toronto Press.

Strega, S., and L. Brown. 2015. *Research as Resistance: Revisiting Critical, Indigenous, and Anti-Oppressive Approaches*, 2nd ed. Toronto: Canadian Scholars' Press.

Sydie, R. 1987. *Natural Women, Cultured Men: A Feminist Perspective*. Toronto: Methuen.

Thomas, W.I., and D.S. Thomas. 1928. *The Child in America: Behavior Problems and Programs*. New York: Knopf.

Turnbull, A.P., B.J. Friesen, and C. Ramirez. 1998. "Participatory Action Research as a Model for Conducting Family Research." *Research and Practice for Persons with Disabilities* 23, 178–188.

Walsh, A., and R.A. Gordon. 1995. *Biosociology: An Emerging Paradigm*. Westport, Connecticut: Praeger.

White, J.M., and D.M. Klein. 2002. *Family Theories*, 2nd ed. Thousand Oaks, California: Sage Publications.

White, J.M., D.M. Klein, and T.F. Martin. 2015. *Family Theories*, 4th ed. Thousand Oaks, California: Sage Publications.

Whitehead, S.M., and F.J. Barrett (eds.). 2001. *The Masculinities Reader*. Cambridge: Polity Press.

CHAPTER 3

Canadian Families in Historical, Cross-Cultural, and Global Context

LEARNING OBJECTIVES

In this chapter you will learn ...

- that in order to understand contemporary Canadian family life, we need to look backwards in time (or historically), as well as outwards into other societies
- that cross-cultural studies do not support the idea of the "universal family," despite some commonalities
- how everyday family life, family structure, and gender roles are profoundly shaped by cultural, economic, religious, and political systems in all societies
- how worldwide globalization processes, such as the growth of mass commercialization, information technologies, rising power differentials, and population processes influence families
- that a global perspective prompts an understanding of how families from around the world are connected, despite differing family lifestyles

INTRODUCTION

Since the beginning of humankind, families have always existed in some form or an-other. However, this form, in terms of what it looks like, what it does, and how it operates depends on many complex factors. In other words, families do not operate in a vacuum, and it is imperative that we try to understand families within the context of their environments. Moreover, families are not just passive recipients of social structure, or the social, economic, and political forces around them (Leeder, 2004). In a dynamic or reciprocal dance, the family acts and reacts to these social arrangements, and adapts in an ongoing manner that makes it highly flexible and changeable. Consider, for in-stance, how Canadian pioneer families negotiated their lives in the context of their harsh environment compared to contemporary farm families living in Canada, with access to electricity, running water, and the latest in farm machinery. And how might rural Canadian life be different from rural life in an underdeveloped region in the world, such as Africa? Chances are that family life in an underdeveloped or developing part of the world could be at least as challenging as it was for our pioneer families, although it is highly probable that the arms of "modernity" and global capitalism have reached into these populations, as illustrated in figures 3.1 and 3.2

Figure 3.1: McDonald's and Western-Style Fast Food: A "Family Restaurant" in India

Source: Paul Prescott/Shutterstock.com

Figure 3.2: Mothers with AidPod in Tanzania

ColaLife: Piggybacking simple medicines on cola supply chains is used to save lives in underserved rural areas in Africa.

Source: Photo courtesy of ColaLife. Retrieved January 1, 2017, from Ashoka Changemakers: www.changemakers.com/morehealth/entries/colalife.

In order for us to truly comprehend Canadian families, it is necessary to look backwards in time (or historically) as well as outwards—by examining family forms and structures in our past, as well as in societies outside of our own. In the first chapter, one conclusion was that there is much mythology surrounding previous family life, such as the belief that we have somehow lost the "traditional" family, and the related assumption about life in the "good old days." In this chapter, we further develop this theme by considering additional material focused on family lives in the context of place and time, major tenets underlying our guiding life-course theoretical framework. This will be facilitated by integrating some cross-cultural work conducted in the field of **anthropology,** a perspective that is a neighbouring discipline to sociology. Both specialize in the study of human behaviour, although anthropologists (particularly cultural anthropologists) have a particularly strong interest in families in other cultural contexts. A separate chapter on "First Families"—that is, Indigenous Peoples or Aboriginal family life in pre-Confederate Canada—will follow this material. This material should be considered

as complementary and an extension to this chapter, since we will also be covering important historical and anthropological trends and issues relevant to past/previous Canadian
family life. Finally, we will also consider how processes of **globalization**, capitalization,
and economic and population change are affecting families worldwide.

CANADIAN FAMILIES IN HISTORICAL CONTEXT

The pre-industrial economy, which predominated in various parts of Canada up until the 19th century, was organized on the basis of a **family-based economy**. Family
members relied heavily on one another to keep the household running, and homes were
both places of residence and places of work as settlers produced most of their goods and
services in their own homes (Nett, 1988). In 1617, the first French family arrived in
Quebec, and harsh conditions meant that many families struggled to eke out a living.
In New France, rules governing inheritance and marriage protected women's rights and
property. Conversely, in English Canada, common law dictated that men held all power
and property in families so that once women married, they lost all legal status and could
not control property. Slavery also existed in Canada. Notably, from the late 1600s until
the early 1800s, Black slaves were held in Quebec, Nova Scotia, New Brunswick, and
Ontario (Mandell and Momirov, 2005).

By the turn of the 18th century, most Canadian families lived in rural settings in
Quebec, Ontario, and the Maritimes. With these agricultural settlements, populations
stabilized and women's family positions became more traditional. Most of the well-paying
jobs were not available to women or girls, who often lacked specialized training and education (Bradbury, 2005). Apprenticeships were also common among children at an early age
to learn trades and skills. For instance, working-class boys of age 9 or 10 apprenticed in
jobs as carpenters, blacksmiths, accountants, lawyers, or doctors, whereas working-class
girls around the age of 10 often filled domestic contracts, which lasted until they were
married (Mandell and Momirov, 2005). And by the end of the 18th century, many families
began to move west in search of a better life, although life was often very severe for these
pioneering families, as illustrated in the book *Pioneer Girl*.

Pioneer Girl contains a collection of letters, written in 1887 by 14-year-old Maryanne
Caswell. These letters, published first in a newspaper in 1952 and then as a book in 1964,
are an account of the trials Caswell's family faced when they moved from Ontario to the
Prairies to find a better life. In one letter to her grandmother, Caswell describes some of
the harsh realities of her daily life:

> The mosquitoes were terribly vicious as we neared home. Berry became
> unmanageable, broke from me, upsetting and scattering the pots, pails, laundry
> and water barrel. So ended our first of July, 1887. During the night the rain
> came in torrents. The knot-holes of the roof-boards leaked and rivers flowed
> inside and out. Mother, as she frequently had to do, put pots and pans on the

beds to catch the drips. We dared not move the least bit or water is spilt. The quilts take such a long time to dry thoroughly hanging on poles of the garden fence and this hot, golden sun burns and fades them very much.

Small-scale farming was gradually replaced with large-scale commercial agriculture. Employment opportunities also expanded in shops and factories. Factories increased from 2.4 million in 1851 to 5.4 million in 1901 in cities like Montreal, Quebec, and Hamilton. With the shift to industrialization and urbanization, work and family life increasingly became separate spheres, although different family forms occasionally emerged when women, rather than men, took on paid work or earned high-income-generating jobs (see box 3.1 for an example of this in Paris, Ontario, between 1880 and 1950). Femininity became associated with women's domestic and child-rearing work in the home, while masculinity was associated with the world of paid work. Generally, it was considered demeaning for married women to labour for wages, since it was thought to compromise the husband's authority as household head and could be potentially damaging for children's moral and cognitive development (Wilson, 1991).

Box 3.1: The Gender of Breadwinners: Women, Men, and Change in Two Industrial Towns, 1880–1950

In Paris [Ontario], men took on the characteristics of dispensability and irregularity in employment that dual labour market theorists have commonly associated with the secondary sector and with women. Those who stayed on irregular work, who commuted to jobs elsewhere, or who were among the male minority with secure local employment, were members of households where the family income was collectively amassed, not won by a male breadwinner. Similarly, in these households, domestic labour was derived from several sources rather than delegated to a single homemaker. These circumstances evoked some changes in thinking about women's and men's roles and in the practice of domestic gender divisions, but the influence of patriarchal ideology continued to cast women as the primary custodians of kin. In Paris, mill families coped by generally accepting mainstream prescriptions about what was manly and womanly work within the home. To accommodate lifelong female wage work they rather remade the boundary between the household and the market by purchasing goods and services conventionally created within the home. They also reconstrued the borders of the household itself, clubbing together as female kin, sharing houseroom, trading domestic labour, and determining by their own logic of mutual advantage who ought to go to the mill and who might better stay home.

Source: Parr, J. 1990. *The Gender of Breadwinners: Women, Men, and Change in Two Industrial Towns 1880–1950* (pp. 235–235). Toronto: University of Toronto Press.

During the 20th century women gradually gained more political rights, but only after many years of speeches, protests, and legal battles. In Britain, the Married Women's Property Act of 1870 was viewed as a significant milestone for women's rights because it allowed them to control their earnings, their bank accounts, and their property. Similar laws were introduced in most Canadian provinces within the next few years. And although marriage was traditionally a religious contract, it gradually became a legal one that could be broken through divorce proceedings. In 1925, the grounds for divorce became identical for women and men (see table 3.1 for a brief history of key changes governing marriage and divorce in Canada). Yet marital property had to be divided according to certain rules, and one parent was usually granted custody of the children (Baker and Dryden, 1993).

During early industrialization, children under the age of 15 from poor or working-class families often were employed in paid wage labour in order to contribute to the family economy. Often their father had died, was sick, drank, or earned insufficient wages (Bradbury, 1993). Unfortunately, these children were sometimes exposed to dangerous working conditions (see box 3.2). Over time, the changing role of children involved them less and less in work at home and eventually school attendance was required for all. By the end of World War One, with corporate capitalism or full industrialization, the only individual considered to be working was the husband-father. Between the two world wars

Table 3.1: A Brief Chronology of Changes in Laws Governing Marriage and Divorce in Canada

Prior to 1758	No divorce law existed since the Church of England in Upper Canada and the Roman Catholic Church in Lower Canada did not recognize divorce.
1758	New Brunswick allows divorce on the grounds of adultery and desertion.
1787	Nova Scotia allows divorce on the grounds of adultery.
1800–1837	Marriage contract introduced in Western provinces in which a husband agreed to support his family *à la façon du pays* (i.e., according to the custom of the Aboriginal peoples) and to marry as soon as a clergyman was available.
1867	With Confederation, federal Parliament gained exclusive authority in divorce, yet it did allow existing provincial laws in Nova Scotia, New Brunswick, and British Columbia to stand.
1925	Women could now sue for divorce on the same grounds as men (previously, men had to prove adultery, whereas women had to prove adultery and either desertion for two or more years or extreme physical or mental cruelty—now they both had to prove only adultery).
1968	All provinces except Quebec and Newfoundland had divorce laws with adultery basically the sole grounds for divorce.
1985	Law amended to show "no fault" of either partner; waiting period for divorce on grounds of marriage breakdown reduced to one year.

Source: Ward, M. 2002. *The Family Dynamic: A Canadian Perspective*, 3rd ed. Toronto: Nelson Thomson Learning (pp. 227–228).

(1920–1940), a consumer society was born, and families were exposed to a new advertising industry, which created a new awareness and demand for consumer goods. Therefore, the sole wage–earner family came to be seen more in terms of its economic role as a consumer rather than a producer (Nett, 1988).

At the beginning of World War Two, many women began to work in the paid labour market when men left for military service. When they returned, women left their employment due to the widespread belief that it was harmful to children for their mothers to be in the labour force. However, since the 1970s, more and more families with only one income

---

Box 3.2: Working Families: Age, Gender, and Daily Survival in Industrializing Montreal

Most young children's jobs involved long and tedious hours, either repeating monotonous tasks or, as in the case of message boys, continually coming and going or sitting around waiting for errands to run. Hours were the same for children and adults—ten hours or more, six days a week. Lucks and Blackeby were shocked to see young children whose appearance and condition by the afternoon of a hot summer's day was "anything but inviting or desirable"...They had to be at the mills or factories at 6:30 a.m. necessitating their being up from 5:30 to 6 o'clock for their morning meal, some having to walk a distance of half a mile or more to their work. The tobacco of the cigar manufactories and the lead in printing shops exposed them to substances that were health hazards. The commissioners hearing evidence in 1888 were pained to see that working with tobacco had already stunted children's growth and "poisoned" the blood of some of the young witnesses. They appeared "undersized, sallow and listless."

The relationship of these young workers, their parents, and the employer was complex. Parents appear to have endowed the employer with the patriarchal and disciplinary powers usually attributed to a father. Indeed, some employers claimed such powers for themselves. M. Fortier justified beatings in his factory by arguing that children had not been beaten "other than what they have deserved for wrongs they have committed, the same as a parent would punish a child." He and his manager claimed that parents asked them to discipline their children, especially in situations where parental control failed. One boy's mother told him to "use any means in my power to chastise the body as she could not get any good at all out of him." When "apprentices" in his factory failed to turn up on time, he first notified the parents, then "had the child arrested." Employers were apparently using the [Quebec Manufacturing] Act with respect to masters and apprentices against any workers who absented without permission.

Source: Bradbury, B. 1993. *Working Families: Age, Gender, and Daily Survival in Industrializing Montreal.* Toronto: University of Toronto Press (p. 130).

earner have found it difficult to meet the new "needs" that the economy created for families. The feminist movement was also instrumental in creating more equal opportunities for women in education and labour. When compared to the 1950s family, the percentage of two-income workers has skyrocketed. In 2003, 80% of married women were in the paid labour force, whereas it was only 11% in 1951 (Statistics Canada, 2003a), and this upward trend has remained relatively constant since this time. Moreover, family life has increasingly become culturally diversified as immigration patterns changed, a theme that will be further explored in chapter 5.

CANADIAN FAMILIES IN CROSS-CULTURAL CONTEXT: THE MYTH OF THE UNIVERSAL FAMILY

The preceding discussion highlights the fact that Canadian families have taken on many forms and cannot be characterized by one monolithic structure. Similarly, there is no single type of marriage or family pattern that is found exclusively throughout the world. As will be shown in this section, there is widespread diversity in what is socially accepted, tolerated, or even expected. With this in mind, variations in family structure throughout the world will be highlighted, with a focus on marriage structures, patterns of authority, rules of descent, and patterns of residence.

Marriage Patterns

There are four types of marriage: monogamy, polyandry, polygyny, and group marriage. In Western cultures and countries such as China, monogamy is the preferred form of marriage, in which there are only two spouses. In the 21st century, bigamy and sexual relations outside marriage are generally socially or legally frowned upon. However, since divorce and remarriage have become increasingly common, the practice of **serial monogamy**—having more than one sexual partner in sequence—has become more prevalent.

Polygamy or plural marriage is the practice of having more than one husband or wife. There are three forms of polygamy: polygyny, polyandry, and group marriage. Many societies permit polygyny, in which a man can have multiple wives, and it is generally a sign of wealth and power. This practice is found in many cultures, such as in the Middle East, Asia, and Africa, and in some fundamentalist Mormon groups in the United States (e.g., in rural areas among Utah's borders with Arizona and Colorado) and Canada (e.g., Bountiful, British Columbia), and is commonly sanctioned by religion. Polyandry is the practice of having two or more husbands. It is very uncommon, although considered to be the ideal marriage form in societies such as the Toda of India, the Marquesians of the Polynesian Islands, and among some Tibetans. Group marriage is relatively rare and involves the marriage of two or more men to two or more women.

In the West, the choice of a marriage partner is largely voluntary and depends upon the attachment between the partners. In most Western, industrialized societies, the most common reason for marrying is for love, based upon a mutual emotional and/ or physical attraction and the desire to form a lifelong commitment. In other parts of the world, such as many parts of Africa, Asia, and the Middle East, as well as within some cultural groups in Western societies, the choice of mate is deemed too important to be left to the individual and marriage is often arranged, a topic that will be revisited later in the text.

Practices and behaviours with respect to the timing of marriage also vary widely throughout the world, particularly between less developed and more economically developed countries. Some of this variability is shown in table 3.2, which presents the rank-ordered top 20 countries in the world that have the highest percentage of girls married by age 18. This type of marriage is referred to as child marriage, and if present trends continue, 100 million girls are estimated to marry over the next decade, according to the International Centre for Research on Women (2011). This group argues that traditional practices of child marriage are harmful, since they undermine global development efforts focused on creating more educated, healthier, and economically stable populations. Girls living in poor households are more than twice as likely to marry before 18 as girls in higher-income households. Those younger than 15 are also five times more likely to die in childbirth than women in their 20s. Child brides also face a higher risk of contracting HIV because they tend to marry much older men who have had more sex partners. These girls are also more likely to experience domestic violence and signs of sexual abuse and post-traumatic stress such as feelings of hopelessness and severe depression.

Patterns of Authority and Descent

Cross-cultural research establishes that women and men are often treated very differently in many parts of the world. The term *patriarchy*, which translates to "rule of the father," refers to a form of social organization in which the norm or the expectation is that men have a natural right to have authority over women. This pattern of authority is manifested and upheld in a wide variety of social institutions, including educational, religious, legal, and economic institutions. For example, the educational system may enforce unequal or no formal education for girls, and religious institutions may attribute male dominance to God's will. Conversely, a less dominant form of authority is matriarchy, in which the norm is that the power and authority in society should be vested in women. In between these two extremes are egalitarian patterns, in which power and authority are equally present in both men and women. Countries such as Canada, the United States, and some Scandinavian countries are close to, or headed in, this direction, although many vestiges of patriarchy remain (Seccombe and Warner, 2004).

Turning to patterns of descent, contemplate where your last name came from and how property is passed down in your family. There are many ways in which a family's descent or heritage can be traced. Industrial nations usually use a bilateral pattern of

Table 3.2: Child Marriage around the World, 2015

Rank	Country	% Girls Married Before 18
1	Niger	75
2	Chad	68
3	Central African Republic	68
4	Bangladesh	66
5	Guinea	63
6	Mozambique	56
7	Mali	55
8	Burkina Faso	52
9	South Sudan	52
10	Malawi	50
11	Madagascar	48
12	Eritrea	47
13	India	47
14	Somalia	45
15	Sierra Leone	44
16	Zambia	42
17	Dominican Republic	41
18	Nepal	41
19	Nicaragua	41

Note: Data are based on the analysis of the Demographic and Health Survey. Rankings are based on data in which women ages 20–24 reported being married or in a union by age 18.

Source: International Centre for Research on Women. 2015. Retrieved June 30, 2016, from www.icrw. org/child-marriage-facts-and-figures.

descent, whereby descent can be traced through both female and male sides of the family. In Canada, for instance, both of our parents' parents are seen as related to us, as two sets of grandparents. Yet, in many parts of the world we see a patrilineal pattern, in which lineage is usually traced through the man's family line. As a result, minimal connections would be established with your mother's side of the family. We also see traces of this practice in Canada, as reflected in the tendency for our last names to reflect the father's lineage. Moreover, a few societies can be characterized as having matrilineal descent patterns. However, it is not the mirror opposite of the patrilineal pattern, since women often pass on their lineage through male members of the family. In other words, lineage is not the same as power (Seccombe and Warner, 2004).

Patterns of Residence

Another aspect of diversity of family patterns found worldwide is the residential patterns of family members. In industrial societies, the norm is for newly married couples to live separately from either set of parents, known as **neolocal residence,** which means new place in Greek. However, in many parts of the world, patrilocal residence is practised, with the expectation that the son and his wife will live with the husband's father. Matrilocal patterns, which are less common, dictate that the newly married daughter and her husband live with the wife's family.

Extended or joint family living, rather than the nuclear family, is normative throughout many parts of the world. And, with increasing immigration and cultural diversity in Canada, a rising number of families live in multigenerational households, defined as three or more generations living under one roof. This practice remains common in families from countries with a history of extended family living (e.g., India) and is still practiced for cultural, economic, or practical reasons. Finally, there has also been a tendency for young adults (sometimes with partners and/or children) to stay at home longer, or return to the parental home after an initial "launch," in many industrialized countries, a topic explored later in chapter 11. This living arrangement occurs for economic, cultural, or health-related reasons and has become more socially acceptable due to changing times. These family-centred trends run counter to the overall rise in the number of one-person households, especially among young unmarried and widowed females in addition to female-headed households.

Overall, these findings reveal that family forms and structures are highly diverse worldwide. Patterns of marriage, authority, descent, and living arrangements also have very real consequences for the way that we live our family lives. They also reflect whom we should marry, who should have power in the family, the status of family members, and the distribution of resources in families. In addition, they mirror divergent expectations with respect to where and with whom we live.

Myths and Half-Truths: Families Worldwide Are Also Similar

Although families around the world have looked and continue to look different based on these diverse patterns, or based on dress, food, or rituals, basically they share much in common. One of the unifying themes among all families is that they are a source of procreation. In other words, it is within families that children are born and reared, a universal function on which sociologists and anthropologists can agree. However, procreation is more than birthing, and there are dissimilarities when it comes to the context of how births occur and the life chances of those babies and mothers. For example, birthing huts in rural Africa differ from birthing rooms in modern hospitals, and the probability that the mother or baby survive depends on economic conditions of the society and where the family fits into the social stratification system.

Another condition unifying families is that they are primary agents of socialization, a topic to be discussed in greater detail in chapter 8. Moreover, as discussed in chapter 1, families also tend to regulate and legitimate sexual behaviour, and families are also responsible for the care (emotional and economic) provision of their members. And finally, another consistent theme that emerges is that families provide status to their members. Indeed, the family is the place in society where race/ethnicity, class, and gender converge, since it is the locus of intersection of these forces (Leeder, 2004).

WORLDWIDE TRENDS: GLOBALIZATION, CAPITALIZATION, INFORMATION TECHNOLOGIES, AND TRANSNATIONAL FAMILIES

In light of important historical and cross-cultural patterns in family life, let us consider Canadian families within the context of globalization, as well as several salient issues facing families. Globalization refers to the world scale of economic and other market activity facilitated by the expansion of telecommunication technology and the growth of multinational corporations operating throughout the world. Hence, our postindustrial economy is characterized by information technology, paper speculation (the stock market), and the predominance of the service sector. Consequently, national economies are vulnerable to worldwide financial fluctuations more than ever before. This was quite evident in the 2008–2009 recession, which was largely generated by a lack of controls over the paper economy and risky borrowing that originated in the US. (Ambert, 2012).

Globalization is also a vast social field, in which dominant or **hegemonic social groups**, states, interests, and ideologies collide with counter-hegemonic or subordinate social groups. In the past three decades, transnational interactions have intensified significantly, from production systems and financial transfers, to the worldwide dissemination of information and images through the media, or the mass movements of peoples, whether as tourists, migrant workers, or refugees (de Sousa Santos, 2006).

BILL PROUD

"Globalization never did me any harm."

Figure 3.3: A Cartoonist's Depiction of Globalization

Source: Proud, B. 2006. "Globalization." Retrieved January 1, 2017, from Cartoon Stock.com (ID: WPR0063).

Overall, the processes of globalization are multifaceted, with economic, social, political, cultural, religious, and legal dimensions. Globalization also seems to be related to a vast array of transformations across the globe, such as the rise in female employment, delayed family transitions, and rising inequality between rich and poor countries as well as between the rich and the poor in each country. Moreover, globalization is often linked to environmental disasters, ethnic conflicts, international mass migration, the proliferation of civil wars, globally organized crime, terrorism, formal democracy as a political condition for international aid, and so on (de Sousa Santos, 2006).

And while there are many debates with respect to the origin, nature, and meaning of globalization, it appears that the idea of globalization as a linear, homogenizing, and irreversible phenomenon oversimplifies certain patterns and processes (de Sousa Santos, 2006). Moreover, as discussed by Therborn (2014: 15), after globalization, **transnationalism** has become a "buzzword" of our times. However, while globalization typically refers to an economic and mass culture macro perspective, the latter term denotes the microsocial dynamics of human actors crossing and straddling economic and cultural regions, in addition to state boundaries. Nonetheless, despite the global diversity of families and the persistence of worldwide transnational migration (see box 3.3 for a more complete discussion), many processes of globalization are deemed to affect families worldwide. This is because they impel structural and processual changes in families, from their economic opportunities and activities, to the increased need for schooling and education, and changing gender roles. For example, a general rise in education and increased consumerism means that children lose their utilitarian value to families, especially in industrialized countries, a value that had been very obvious in former centuries.

Box 3.3: Transnationalism: Familism and Global Diversity

After globalization, transnationalism has become a buzzword of our times (Portes, 2001; Vertovec, 2009). In contrast to the economic and mass culture macro perspective of the former, the latter focuses on the microsocial dynamics of human actors crossing and straddling economic and cultural regions as well as state boundaries. The size and the novelty of transnationalism had better not be exaggerated by romantic fascination. Worldwide transnational migration today is about the same size as it was a good century ago--when the Americas got its mass population and when crowds of Chinese and Indians fanned out overseas--now and then about 3% of the world population living outside their country of birth (UNFPA, 2911b, p. 66). Largely new are the global care chains--mothers from poorer countries migrating for caring work in richer ones, while somebody else is caring for their children at home (Hachschild, 2000; Yeats, 2012)-- and the East Asian transborder marriage mass markets. For 2005-2009, more than 10% of South Korean marriages were to foreign spouses. Between a fourth and a third of Taiwanese men's marriages were to wives from abroad (Choe, 2011).

Families continue to differ around the world in size, in composition, in sexual regulation and marriage, in patriarchy or male sex-gender-generation power, in stability, in the care for the elderly, and in fertility and patterns of reproduction. Persistent global diversity should also be considered in relation to the ongoing processes of divergence by class in postindustrial societies. Successful industrialization once meant a stabilization and standardization of the Euro-American family (Therborn, 2004, 163ff). Currently, a new postindustrial sociocultural dynamic is driving family patterns apart between classes, through mounting educational and income homogamy and bifurcated paths of prosperity and insecurity. It has received most attention and is perhaps most pronounced in the United States (Murray, 2012; Brooks, 2012; reporting research by Robert Putnam).

From the persistent global diversity of systems of family-sex-gender relations, from transnational migratory familism, and from the growing divergence of family patterns in the postindustrial centre of the world, we may also conclude a persistent, and in comparison with a generation ago probably increasing, importance of the family.

Source: Therborn, G. 2014. "Family Systems of the World: Are they Converging?" In J. Treas, J. Scott, and M. Richards (eds.), *The Wiley Blackwell Companion to the Sociology of Families* (pp. 3–19). New York: John Wiley & Sons, Ltd (pp. 15–16).

Women also begin to gain more social and political power as their roles become less tied to motherhood. As a result, families begin to shrivel in size, extended families become the exception, more women work outside the home, and young people defer marriage and parenthood. And in many parts of the world, these processes also present challenges to families in holding on to their long established cultural traditions and practices (Roopnarine and Gielen, 2005). Exposure to the media, for example, via satellite television and the Internet, exposes families to alternative lifestyles and Western values that often emphasize consumerism and individualism.

Pressing Issues for the World's Families

In addition to meeting the challenges of changing family structures and gender roles, families around the world are also experiencing pressures in their ability to raise their children, care for their elderly, and maintain healthy, close relationships. Issues that are particularly salient at this time include war, terrorism, and armed conflict; poverty and economic instability; migration; and world population growth. With respect to the first pressing concern, as you read this book, all kinds of war, conflict, and terrorist acts are being experienced in many parts of the world. Indeed, the history of humankind is also one of conflict and war, and this horrible reality has dire consequences for societies and families. These events also influence Canadian society; for instance, as refugees flee countries, our young people join the military to fight wars, or individuals experience the psychological trauma of terrorist threats, a topic that will re-visited in chapter 5.

Another pressing challenge facing families worldwide is poverty and economic hardship, a state that negatively experiences every aspect of family daily life and functioning. In Canada, these issues remain a significant social problem (and will be further explored in chapter 14), particularly when we compare poverty rates to those of other industrialized societies such as the Scandinavian countries, which tend to have strong social safety nets.

The World Bank has estimated that there are approximately 1.4 billion people who live on $1.25 a day or less. And while the International Labour Organization revealed stability and improvement in poverty reduction in most countries from the late 1990s through the late 2000s, spikes in unemployment and vulnerable employment occurred following the 2008 global financial crisis. This crisis was precipitated by the bursting of the housing-price bubble and the banking collapse in the United States. It rapidly spread to most of the world and is considered the worst financial crisis since the Great Depression, at least in developed countries. Notably, 34 million people lost their jobs and 64 million more people fell under the $1.25 a day poverty threshold. Millions of workers have also been coping with job losses, prolonged unemployment, reduced working hours, lost or reduced income, and aggravated poverty. To date, the labour markets in many developing countries still remain in crisis, although there are some signs of slow recovery (October, 2011).

Global economic recessions have different effects on men and women depending on which sectors are most affected by the crisis. However, given persistent ascribed gender roles that affect patterns of paid and unpaid work (e.g., women earn only about three-quarters of men's wages in the non-agricultural sector of 56 countries, as cited in Smith, 2006), women are particularly vulnerable to long-lasting negative socio-economic effects. Indeed, there is fear that in the wake of the global economic crisis, the progress made in the past decades in advancing women's position in the world of work is being wiped out (October, 2011).

Although women who were already in disadvantaged positions in the labour market prior to the crisis have generally suffered less in terms of the number of job losses, the overall reduction of employment and income for poor families has serious implications for the reproduction of gender inequities. When the resources and incomes available to poor households are being diminished, women and children are likely to be the worst affected. For example, children drop out of school because parents cannot afford to have them attend, and this has an inter-generational impact on poverty. There is also a gender bias against females in the household in many poor developing countries in that they have less access to education, food, and health provisions relative to males (International Labour Office, 2011).

And with rising poverty, another related trend is the growth of substandard housing (i.e., slums, shantytowns), as well as many related health and well-being issues. Economic hardship and crisis increase infant mortality and malnutrition, with severe long-term costs from stunting (the failure to thrive). Damaging effects can also be found in increases in the numbers of street children, in suicide and crime rates, in abuse and domestic violence, and in ethnic tensions (Human Development Report, 2010).

Another example of a global health concern is the HIV/AIDS epidemic, as illustrated in figure 3.4, with an estimated 36.9 million people worldwide currently living with HIV, and 1.2 million deaths due to AIDS in 2014 (UNAIDS, 2015). And while deaths due to AIDS have fallen (mainly due to access to life-saving drugs and the anti-retroviral program), there are still a staggering number of new cases each year (e.g., 2 million cases were reported in 2014).

The implications for poverty from these staggering numbers are many, ranging from slowing economies to reducing agricultural productivity and thereby contributing to persistent food shortages (Rank and Yadama, 2006). Family structure and relationships are also affected, for example, when grandparents are left to raise grandchildren who are infected with HIV/AIDS after parents have died. Fortunately, many grassroots organizations have formed to assist these families. One noteworthy initiative is the Grandmothers to Grandmothers Campaign (see box 3.4), which was established in Canada to assist African grandmothers.

People living with HIV……..36.7 million (34–39.8 million)
New HIV infections 2015……2.1 million (1.8–2.4 million)
Deaths due to AIDS in 2015….1.1 million (940,000 -2.1.3 million million)

Figure 3.4: Global HIV/AIDS Estimates for Adults and Children, 2015

Source: UNAIDS. 2016. "Global Statistics-2015." UNAIDS *Fact Sheet 2016.* Retrieved June 6, 2016, from www.unaids.org/sites/default/files/media_asset/20150901_FactSheet_2015_en.pdf.

Box 3.4: The Grandmothers to Grandmothers Campaign

"It's quite extraordinary to see the bond that has developed between grandmothers on both sides of the ocean. In a dramatic way, it helps to redefine the chasm between the developed and developing nations. It goes without saying that the chasm exists in the realms of poverty, conflict and disease, but in the realms of sophistication, intelligence and fundamental human decency, nothing separates the African grandmothers from the Canadian grandmothers. They are as one." –Stephen Lewis

The Stephen Lewis Foundation launched the Grandmothers to Grandmothers Campaign in March 2006, in response to the emerging crisis faced by African grandmothers as they struggled to care for millions of children orphaned by AIDS.

What began with only a few groups of committed Canadian grandmothers has since evolved into a dynamic and responsive movement made up of grandmothers working to mobilize support in Canada for Africa's grandmothers.

The campaign currently boasts more than 240 grandmother groups across the country. Many of the groups have organized into regional and national networks in order to support one another's development, fundraising, and advocacy networks.

Funds from the Grandmothers Campaign are used to support African grandmothers with food, health care, school fees and school uniforms for their grandchildren, income-generating programs, counselling, social support, essential shelter, and other necessities. Throughout Africa, grassroots organizations run by and for grandmothers are sharing insights, deepening their expertise, collaborating with other local organizations, and building their capacity to turn the tide of AIDS at the community level.

The Grandmothers to Grandmothers Campaign exists to support the indomitable African grandmothers who are caring for the millions of children who have been orphaned by AIDS. Members of the Grandmothers Campaign share three goals. They work to:

- raise funds to meet the needs of African grandmothers and the children in their care;
- listen to African grandmothers, respect their expertise, and amplify their voices, in order to promote authentic and substantive responses to the pandemic in Africa; and
- build solidarity among African and Canadian grandmothers in order to motivate and sustain the vital work of turning the tide of AIDS in Africa.

Canadian grandmother groups are tremendously active in their communities. They put on concerts, organize card tournaments, sell jewellery, and march on Parliament Hill. They visit countless schools and community organizations. They bake, cook, sew, knit, paint, write, organize cycle tours and walks, and even ride motorcycles—all to raise funds and awareness for grandmothers in sub-Saharan Africa through the Stephen Lewis Foundation.

Source: The Stephen Lewis Foundation. n.d. "About the Campaign." Retrieved June 17, 2011, from www.stephenlewisfoundation.org/get-involved/grandmothers-campaign/about-the-campaign.

Another issue for families worldwide is migration, since it is one means for women and men to try to escape poverty and build a better life. However, many poor migrant workers become deeply indebted to labour recruiters and are trapped in dangerous or oppressive working conditions. In Asia, for instance, many women migrants left their families for a more promising life working in the garment industry, only to experience low wages and job vulnerability. Other unemployed women and children throughout the world have been driven into the human trafficking industry and work as prostitutes on the streets, in brothels, or in massage parlours. Men are also often forced to migrate. For example, a substantial number of Latino farmworkers, many of whom are fathers, migrate to the US and Canada from Mexico and other Central American countries. (Arditti et al., 2014).

Finally, another salient global issue is world population growth and resource sustainability. Recent population statistics show that there are now more than twice as many people alive on Earth as there were as recently as in the 1960s. In 2015 the world population reached 7.3 billion, and this number is expected to reach 8.5 billion by 2030 and 9.7 billion by 2050 (United Nations, 2015). Figure 3.5 provides us with an overview of the population explosion between 1750 and 2150, where it is shown that much of the growth has occurred and will occur in developing regions of Africa, Asia, and Latin America.

Some scientists worry that the human population is growing at a rate that will threaten the planet's future availability and sustainability of essential resources such as land, food, and water. They also warn that this could also create greater social inequality and war as groups vie for scarce resources. Indeed, recent data show that the number of hungry people recently topped one billion and that one in every eight people in the world go to bed hungry every night (MercyCorps, 2015). Indeed, the World Health Organization considers global hunger to be the greatest single threat to global public health. Not surprisingly, 98% of the word's hungry live in developing countries. Moreover, 75% of the world's poorest families don't buy their food, they grow it, but many of these families depend upon their land and livestock for both food and income, leaving them vulnerable to natural disasters such as drought. Drought, the result of climate change and increasingly unpredictable rainfall, has become one of the most common

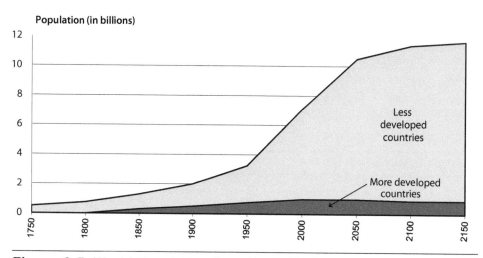

Figure 3.5: World Population Growth, 1750–2150

Source: United Nations. 1998. *United Nations World Populations: The 1998 Revision.* New York: United Nations; and estimates by the Population Reference Bureau. Copyright © 2001 Population Reference Bureau.

causes of food shortages in the world. Relatedly, there are also many concerns about the significant increases in food prices in the past several years, increases that have been particularly devastating to those with only a few dollars a day to spend (MercyCorps, 2015).

However, others suggest that population growth is not a problem because this rate is starting to decline and advancements in technology should increase the availability of food supplies and other basic resources. In other words, it is argued that since the world can easily produce enough food to feed everyone, food shortages should not be a problem. Instead, other factors than population growth per se are to blame, such as harmful economic and political systems, war and conflicts that displace families, and climate change, since the latter increases drought and flooding and disrupts the conditions necessary for producing food. Further, there is also a reciprocal effect in that hunger causes poor health, low levels of energy, and even mental impairment. In a feedback loop, this leads to even greater poverty since it creates a cycle that reduces people's ability to work and learn, thus leading to even greater malnourishment and hunger (World Hunger Organization, 2011).

THE CYCLE OF HUNGER

There are many ways hunger can trap people in a cycle of poverty and need. Here is how it can burden someone for a lifetime, and pass it on to the next generation.

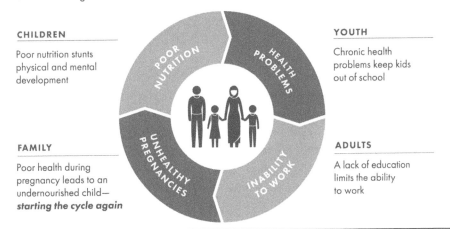

CHILDREN

Poor nutrition stunts physical and mental development

YOUTH

Chronic health problems keep kids out of school

FAMILY

Poor health during pregnancy leads to an undernourished child—
starting the cycle again

ADULTS

A lack of education limits the ability to work

Figure 3.6: Quick Facts: What You Need to Know about Global Hunger

Hunger is more than missing a meal. It's a debilitating crisis that has almost one billion people in its grip. Families struggling with chronic food insecurity, hunger, and malnutrition don't consistently have the food their minds and bodies need to function, which then prevents them from having the resources to improve their lives. It's a perilous cycle that passes hunger from one generation to the next.

Source: "The Cycle of Hunger," courtesy of Mercy Corps.

Despite the complexity of this issue, what is clear is that our world population growth has important implications for families. More families will live in cities, as evidenced by the worldwide trend of families migrating from the countryside to cities. For example, about 1.1 billion people in Asia are expected to move to cities in fewer than 20 years (about 137,000 every day), according to the Asian Development Bank. This rapid urbanization creates a multitude of problems related to housing and space, disease and crime, noxious pollution, overwhelmed infrastructure, and crippling congestion (Bartlett, 2011).

Moreover, we are experiencing an aging of the world's population that is unprecedented in human history. At the beginning of the 21st century, there were 600 million over the age of 60 on the planet, three times the number observed 50 years earlier. With a 2% growth rate per year, this means that there will be more older people than younger people throughout the world by 2050 (United Nations, 2002).

Underlying global **population aging** is a process known as the demographic transition, in which mortality and then fertility decline from higher to lower levels. The role of international migration in changing age structures is far less important than population aging (Lesthaeghe, 2000). Over the last half century, the total fertility rate decreased globally by almost half, from five children per woman to almost three. It is expected to fall to the replacement level (the number of people needed to keep the population at the same size) of 2.1 children per woman over the next half century. These processes reshape the age structure of the population by shifting relative weight from younger to older groups and have consequences for virtually every aspect of family life. Notably, population aging affects family composition, interaction, and functioning; housing; health care; and systems of financial support, as well as overall economic growth and consumer spending.

Moreover, families around the world are at different stages in the aging process (Ingoldsby and Smith, 2006), and will face different life cycle demands and challenges. For example, in the developed regions, it is expected that one-third of the population will be older than 60 years of age by 2050, compared to only 20% in the less developed regions.

Finally, it is noteworthy that a counter-movement has emerged in response to many of the world's pressing challenges. Many social activist groups are found on social media websites and in communities, for instance, that oppose the rise in corporatization, rampant consumerism, waste, pollution, and moral apathy, and the unfair distribution of the world's wealth and natural resources. The Occupy Wall Street movement, which began in New York on September 17, 2011, is a good example of a recent international movement (initiated by a Canadian group called Adbusters) to protest growing economic and social inequality.

Some groups (and families) also engage in activities in an attempt to promote eco-sustainability, which is also deemed to be a significant planetary issue. "Freegans," for example, recognize that in a complex, industrial, mass-production economy driven by profit, abuses of humans, animals, and the earth, problems abound at all levels of production and in just about every product we buy. Thus, a freegan individual or family might avoid buying certain products and engage in such activities as urban foraging or dumpster diving, which is a rummaging technique employed to turn garbage into useful household goods (Freegan.info, 2011). More "typical" family-related activities (with a less radical philosophy) might include the adoption of eco-behaviours within the home in an attempt to "go green" and decrease reliance on the planet's resources. This might include recycling, using fewer packaged or processed foods, reducing dependence on cars, limiting children's use of energy-consumptive entertainment, using bio-degradable cleaning products, and buying locally grown food.

Overall, these commitments to social justice and environmentalism by a relatively small but growing number of Canadian families have obvious implications for daily life. There is also the potential for effects on the division of household labour, gender equity, and marital relationships. For example, a recent study concluded that women generally perform more eco-friendly domestic labour than their husbands, suggesting that (ironically) eco-friendly practices can actually reinforce traditional divisions of general household labour in addition to time spent on household tasks (e.g., see Judkins and Press, 2008).

SUMMARY

A life-course approach to the study of Canadian family life emphasizes the need to travel across temporal, geographic, and cultural boundaries to explore and appreciate the diversity of family life. Indeed, a historical, anthropological and cross-cultural perspective on families shows that they are diverse not only in Canada and throughout the world, but also in family structure, processes, history, and social and environmental contexts (Ingoldsby and Smith, 2006; also see Yu, 2015, for a summary of challenges related to conducting cross-national family research). This existence of multiple family forms forces us to question notions of monogamy, two-parent heterosexual unions, rigid gender roles, and marriage as primordial to family formation. It also prompts us to critically evaluate the idea of one traditional family or the existence of a universal family. Moreover, another major theme is that while families are diverse in structure, they can be similar in basic functioning and values. That is, despite differing cultural traditions and opportunities, virtually all families want to feed, raise, and socialize their children in a peaceful, safe environment and make a living. In short, most families worldwide want to provide love and support to their family members to the best of their ability.

A global perspective on families also illuminates the fact that we are all connected through a world economy. In other words, we all use resources that are produced in other parts of the planet, and what occurs in one part of the world impacts the rest. Families are also all influenced by the global hierarchy and the market system under which this hierarchy operates. This means that there is a pecking order with rules of domination and subordination among people. These rules specify who has access to resources, and who controls, manages, and oppresses other people. It also means that there are many distinctions among people based on their social position, such as age, gender, race/ethnicity, and social class (Leeder, 2004). Thus, although families at first glance may look different from one another, they are all influenced by and influence similar social forces. At this point, it is difficult to predict how processes of globalization, political and economic crises, and other social changes will shape family lives worldwide. However, one thing that's certain is that economic, technological, and other changes will continue to transform family structure, roles, and relationships in significant and far-reaching ways.

QUESTIONS FOR CRITICAL REFLECTION AND DEBATE

1. How can a cross-cultural view of family life reduce ethnocentrism (the tendency for us to see the world only through our own eyes so that we evaluate other cultures based on our own beliefs or ways of doing things)?
2. Debate the following: Regardless of society, power and sexuality have always been linked throughout history, and this determines how families are formed.
3. Choose a cultural group from anywhere in the world (preferably one that is very different from your own) and examine how family life (e.g., structure, rituals, and gender roles) is both different and similar.
4. What criticisms can be made of the manner in which the Western media have portrayed family life in non-Western societies? Does this help or hinder non-Western families? Provide specific examples to illustrate your points.
5. How do war, terrorism, or natural catastrophes in other countries (such as the 2004 tsunami in Southeast Asia) influence Canadian family life?
6. Some futurists maintain that the forces of globalization will eventually result in a common world culture with virtually identical "Stepford" family lifestyles. Do you agree or disagree?

GLOSSARY

Anthropology is the broad study of humankind around the world and throughout time, and is concerned with both the biological and the cultural aspects of humans.

Family-based economy includes all those activities (domestic, economic, and social) that keep a family functioning.

Globalization refers to the world scale of economic and other market activity facilitated by the expansion of telecommunications technology.

Hegemonic social groups are the more powerful groups in society that establish control (cultural, social, and moral) or domination over less powerful groups through consensus or coercion.

Neolocal residence is a couple's household that is established in a new place, apart from their parents.

Polygamy or plural marriage is the practice of having more than one husband or wife, and consists of three forms: polygyny, polyandry, and group marriage.

Population aging occurs primarily as fertility declines and life expectancy increases.

Serial monogamy is a form of monogamy in which participants have only one sexual partner at any one time but have more than one sexual partner in their lifetime.

Transnationalism focuses on the microsocial dynamics of human actors crossing and straddling economic and cultural regions as well as state boundaries.

FURTHER READING

Bradbury, B. 1992.*Canadian Family History: Selected Readings*. Toronto: Copp Clark Pitman. This is a collection of articles on the history of families in Canada from the time of New France to the 1970s. Subjects include gender relations, divorce, legal systems and the state, child labour, and the work roles of men and women.

Buechler, S. and A.M. Hanson (eds.). 2015. *A Political Economy of Women, Water and Global Environmental Change*. New York: Taylor and Francis.
This edited volume explores how a feminist political ecology framework can help us to better understand how rural and urban livelihoods depend on vulnerable rivers, lakes, watersheds, wetlands, and coastal environments.

Comacchio, C.R. 2010. *The Infinite Bonds of Family: Domesticity in Canada, 1850–1940*. Toronto: University of Toronto Press.
This historical overview shows how families have both changed and remained the same through urbanization, industrialization, and war. The many stories of individual families highlight both historical trends and more intimate issues related to race, gender, class, region, and age.

Edgar. S. 2011. *Global Girlfriends: How One Mom Made It Her Business to Help Women in Poverty Worldwide*. New York: St. Martin's Press.
An inspirational story of how one woman used her $2,000 tax return to create a socially conscious business specializing in handmade, fairly traded eco-conscious apparel and items that helped poor women in five continents feed their families and send their children to school.

Kilkey, M., E. Palenga-Mollenbeck, and D. Shepherd. 2016. *Family Life in an Age of Migration and Mobility: Global Perspectives through the Life Course*. UK: Palgrave Macmillan.
This book includes case studies from Europe, India, the Philippines, South Korea, the United States, and Australia. It covers a wide range of topics ranging from mail-order

brides, transnational parenting, reproductive tourism, and elderly migration at different stages of the life course.

Merla, L. 2017. *Transnational Family Solidarity in Local Contexts*. New York: Routledge. This text examines state policies/international regulations in facilitating (or hindering) solidarity across borders. Using a case study of Latin American immigrants in Europe, it focuses on family networks and how they are shaped by such aspects as gendered care and labour market regimes of their home and host societies, and by their access to banking, transport, and communication technologies.

RELATED WEB SITES

Canadian Genealogy Centre facilitates the discovery of Canadian family histories and includes all physical and online genealogical services of Library and Archives Canada, www.collectionscanada.gc.ca/genealogy/index-e.html.

Early Canadiana Online provides many articles and resources on early family life in Canada, www.canadiana.org/ECO.

Freegan.info is an organization that promotes alternative strategies for living based on limited participation in the conventional economy and minimal consumption of resources and is opposed to a society based on materialism and greed, www.freegan.info

MercyCorps is a leading global organization dedicated to helping people overcome adversity. It provides information, resources, and strategies to create secure, productive, and just communities through its adoption of principles adapted from the Universal Declaration of Human Rights, www.mercycorps.org.

United Nations Population Information Network is a centralized community of population institutions organized into global, regional, and national networks. It provides information and articles on many issues facing families worldwide, www.un.org/popin.

REFERENCES

Ambert, A.M. 2012. *Changing Families: Relationships in Context*, 2nd Canadian ed. Toronto: Pearson and Allyn Bacon.

Arditti, J., M. Remington, J. Grzywacz, A. Jaramillo, S. Isom, S. Quandt, and T. Arcury. 2014. "Fathers in the Field: Father Involvement among Latino Migrant Farmworkers." *Journal of Comparative Family Studies* 45, 537–557.

Baker, M., and J. Dryden.1993. *Families in Canadian Society: An Introduction*, 2nd ed. Toronto: McGraw-Hill Ryerson.

Bartlett, L. 2011. "7-Billionth Person Expected This Fall," *The Vancouver Sun*, B5, Wednesday, June 22.

Bradbury, B. 1993. *Working Families: Age, Gender, and Daily Survival in Industrializing Montreal*. Toronto: McClelland & Stewart Inc.

Bradbury. 2005. "Social, Economic, and Cultural Origins of Contemporary Families." In M. Baker (ed.), *Families: Changing Trends in Canada*, 5th ed. (pp. 71–98). Toronto: McGraw-Hill Ryerson.

De Sousa Santos, B. 2006. "Globalization." *Theory, Culture, and Society* 23: 393–399.

Freegan.info. 2016. "What is a Freegan?" Retrieved December 6, 2016, from www.freegan.info.com.

Ingoldsby, B.B., and S.D. Smith. 2006. *Families in Global and Multicultural Perspective*, 2nd ed. Thousand Oaks, California: Sage.

International Labour Office. 2011. *World of Work Report 2010: From One Crisis to the Next?* Geneva: International Institute for Labour Studies.

Judkins, B., and L. Presser. 2008. "Division of Eco-Friendly Household Labour and the Marital Relationship." *Journal of Social and Personal Relationship* 25: 923–941.

Leeder, E.J. 2004. *The Family in Global Perspective: A Gendered Journey*. Thousand Oaks, California: Sage.

Lesthaeghe, R. 2000. "Europe's Demographic Issues: Fertility, Household Formation, and Replacement Migration." IPD Working Paper 2000-6, Interface Demography, VU Brussels.

Mandell, N., and J. Momirov. 2005. "Family Histories." In N. Mandell and A. Duffy (eds.), *Canadian Families: Diversity, Conflict, and Change* (pp. 31–63). Toronto: Thomson Nelson.

MercyCorps. 2015 (March 18). "Quick Facts: What You Need to Know about Global Hunger." Retrieved June 1, 2016, from www.mercycorps.org/articles/quick-facts-what-you-need-know-about-global-hunger.

Modo, I.V.O. 2001. "Migrant Culture and Changing Face of Family Structure in Lesotho." *Journal of Comparative Family Studies* 32: 443–452.

Nett, E.M. 1988.*Canadian Families Past and Present*. Toronto: Butterworths.

Otobe, N. 2011. *Global Economic Crisis, Gender and Employment: The Impact and Policy Response*. International Labour Office, Employment Sector Working Paper No. 74, Geneva, Switzerland.

Rank, M.R., and G.N. Yadama. 2006. "Poverty and Family Policy in Global Context." In B.B. Ingoldsby and S.D. Smith (eds.), *Families in Global and Multicultural Perspective*, 2nd ed. (pp. 379–404). Thousand Oaks, California: Sage.

Roopnarine, J.L., and U.P. Gielen (eds.). 2005. *Families in Global Perspective*. Toronto: Pearson.

Seccombe, K., and R.L. Warner. 2004. *Marriages and Families: Relationships in Social Context*. Toronto: Thomson Wadsworth.

Smith, S.D. 2006. "Global Families." In B.B. Ingoldsby and S.D. Smith (eds.), *Families in Global and Multicultural Perspective*, 2nd ed. (pp. 3–24). Thousand Oak, California: Sage.

Statistics Canada.2003a. *Labour Force Historical Review 2003*. Catalogue no. 71F0004XCb. Ottawa: Statistics Canada.

Therborn, G. 2014. "Family Systems of the World: Are they Converging?" In J. Treas, J. Scott, and M. Richards (eds.), *The Wiley Blackwell Companion to the Sociology of Families* (pp. 3–19). New York: John Wiley & Sons, Ltd.

The International Centre for Research on Women. 2011. *Child Marriage Facts and Figures*, re-trieved June 19, 2011, from www.icrw.org/child-marriage-facts-and figures.

UNAIDS. 2015 (Nov 24). "AIDS by the Numbers 2015." Retrieved June 1, 2016, from www.unaids.org/en/resources/documents/2015/AIDS_by_the_numbers_2015.

United Nations. 2002. *World Population Aging: 1950–2050*. New York: United Nations Departments of Economic and Social Affairs.

United Nations. 2015, July 29. "World Population Projected to Reach 9.7 Billion by 2050." New York: United Nations Department of Economic and Social Affairs, Population Division. Retrieved May 15, 2017, from http://www.un.org/en/development/desa/news/population/2015-report.html.

Wilson, S.J. 1991. *Women, Families and Work*, 3rd ed. Toronto: McGraw-Hill Ryerson.

World Hunger Organization. 2011. *2011 World Hunger and Poverty Facts and Statistics*, retrieved from www.worldhunger.org/articles/Learn/world hunger facts 2002.htm.

Yu, W.-H. 2015. "Placing Families in Context: Challenges for Cross-National Family Research." *Journal of Marriage and the Family* 77: 23–39.

CHAPTER 4

First Families: Indigenous Peoples and Family Life in Pre-Post Confederate Canada

LEARNING OBJECTIVES

In this chapter you will learn that ...

- Indigenous families in Canada have a long and unique history that is characterized by colonization, cultural genocide, and oppression
- Indigenous Peoples have not always had the right to live in a family context of their own choosing as reflected in previous and prevailing government laws and discourse
- the legacy and harms of the Residential School experience continue and have been passed from generation to generation
- despite different historical legacies and cultural traditions, there are similarities and differences between, and within, contemporary Indigenous People and non-Indigenous People families
- slow, but important and promising progress has been made toward improving the well-being and family lives of Indigenous families in this country

INTRODUCTION

Although Canada is often stereotyped as a land of immigrants, more than 500 distinct indigenous peoples originally inhabited what came to be known as the Canada-US geographic border. As European settler societies populated themselves across the continent, colonial (and later, Canadian) governments aggressively attempted to exert power and control over these "first families" and their land to create space for more settlement. Indeed, much of Canada's pre-Confederation history is characterized by colonist ideologies of racial and cultural supremacy among European colonizers. Not surprisingly, this history has created a complicated and ambivalent relationship with Indigenous or First Nation's peoples and their families (Albanese, 2016; Morrison et al., 2014).

In this chapter we will learn that **Indigenous or Aboriginal Peoples**—defined as those persons who report identifying with at least one Aboriginal group (First Nations, Métis or Inuit, and/or those reported Registered or Treaty Indian Status)—have experienced a long-standing history of patronizing, subordination, and marginalization. It should be noted that the terms Indigenous Peoples and Aboriginal Peoples are sometimes used interchangeably throughout this text, although it is acknowledged that some groups or individuals prefer one term over another. In some cases, outright **genocide** marks this history, which can be defined as the deliberate intent or act of killing a particular ethnic or cultural group or nation. Notably, these families have been subjected to racist and aggressive assimilation policies that have prevented them from forming families of their own choosing. These policies continue to have a detrimental impact on the social and economic well-being of Indigenous families, although not all families have been equally affected.

We will begin this chapter by providing some additional historical context on the "first families" that inhabited this land, followed by the identification of some key historical events and assimilation policies. Special attention will be placed on the legacy of the Residential School experience, which was the result of our government trying to aggressively assimilate Indigenous Peoples into dominant culture. In particular, we will consider the effects of these experiences on the lives of these peoples, families, and communities for subsequent generations and contemporary family life.

Another goal of this chapter is to underscore the futility of making assumptions or blanket generalizations about Indigenous families. This kind of labelling contributes to the "othering" and marginalization of racialized groups. This practice also perpetuates and sustains oppressive and discriminatory stereotypes, policies, and pre-dominant colonialist discourses. Therefore, we will conclude this chapter by critically assessing dominant discourses about Indigenous families and how these families today are both similar to, and different than, non-Canadian families. Finally, we will review some important recent efforts that have been made to reconcile previous and ongoing social injustices. This review will include identification of some important gains that have been made, in addition to highlighting some areas that require urgent attention.

A SHORT ANTHROPOLOGICAL HISTORY OF CANADIAN FAMILIES

Hunting and Gathering Families

It is estimated that 99% of human history involved hunting and gathering as the principal means of subsistence. For thousands of years, Canadian hunters and gatherers moved with the seasons following available food supplies (Mandell and Momirov, 2005). Groups comprised of between one and five families hunted and trapped wild game such as caribou, moose, beaver, and bear and also fished, hunted small animals, and gathered wild berries and vegetation (Leacock, 1991). These families travelled light, lived frugally, and seldom recorded any aspects of their lives. Their life expectancy was very short, and they developed shared economies and leadership based on residence, gender, age, and ability (Druke, 1986).

These families exhibited diverse but distinct structures and organizations. For Indigenous families, the family was the basic unit of the community, and their socio-economic and political systems were based on kinship networks, which were large and extensive. Many families were matrilineal, whereby mothers, daughters, and sisters worked together. Hierarchies existed, but Native men considered the work of women to be as important as and equal to that of males. Women and children did most of the harvesting and gathering of fruits, vegetables, and firewood, while men's hunting and fishing often took them far away from home for long periods of time (Mandell and Momirov, 2005). Moreover, both genders had freedom to perform non-traditional work if they displayed a particular talent (Anderson, 2000).

These cultures persisted in Canada well into the 1800s, and were described by colonizing Europeans as among the most highly developed in the world. In the mid-1800s, when the first major wave of White immigrants settled into the Canadian West, they discovered about 30 bands in Quebec and Labrador, and a Native population of 150,000 people harvesting herds of millions of buffalo in the West. Europeans brought the use of plows, irrigation, animal culture, and horsepower. Thus, agriculture is a relatively recent phase in Canadian history, and this allowed for greater productivity, greater population density, and political centralization (Mandell and Momirov, 2005; Nett, 1988).

The European Conquest

In the late 1500s and early 1600s, Jacques Cartier arrived from France, which marked the beginning of settlements in Canada. Over time, French settlers (also known as Acadians) were joined by settlers from the British Isles and Germany. This led to the establishment of trading posts and trade with First Nations families. Over time, Indigenous peoples became dependent on the Europeans, who introduced alcohol to them, as well as other goods such as guns, knives, and axes. Unfortunately, Europeans also brought disease, destruction, and defeat, which dramatically reduced the Indigenous population. Also, diets and lifestyles were dramatically affected, and their life expectancy dropped. Moreover, most Indigenous peoples never accepted some European ideals of unequal spousal relationships, premarital chastity, marital fidelity, male courtship, and male dominance (Mandell and Momirov, 2005). Once the Canadian Confederacy (1867) was established, the Canadian state implemented a policy of "civilizing Indians," an ideology fraught with racist assumptions and marriage regulations.

Indigenous Families under French and British Colonization

As previously mentioned, the Indigenous First Nations were the first families to inhabit what was later to become Canada and numbered about 200,000 when Europeans first "discovered" the Americas in the 1490s. At that time, the most densely populated regions were along the St. Lawrence River and the Great Lakes, as well as in some regions of future British Columbia. These families were primarily hunter-gatherers and horticulturalists that lived in settled villages and engaged in some trade. And as the term "First Nations" suggests, more than 300 nations existed, each possessing unique histories, dialects, languages, cultures, laws, and levels of economic development. Yet, they had common features such as a preference for communal living and the sharing of resources and responsibilities, from child-rearing to food (Ambert, 2012). Indigenous Peoples or Aboriginal families include status (registered) and non-status Indians, Métis, and Inuit, and there is considerable diversity within each of these groups.

In the 1500s, the history of Canadian families began to change when the French established the colony of New France at what is now Quebec City. A nuclear family structure and very high rates of child-bearing caused the population rate to explode. Also, many French male colonists took First Nations women as wives, called *les femmes du pays*, in unions outside of the Church. Many factors influenced family life at this time, such as economic and political forces, as well as the expanding authority of the Roman Catholic Church. The Church developed a gender-specific curriculum, such that girls were taught to be good wives, mothers, and servants of the Church (Nett, 1993).

The British also brought unique family institutions to Canada. During British colonial rule (which lasted until 1867), rapid population growth and industrialization fuelled the emergence of major towns and the development of social stratification with classes of merchants, professionals, artisans, farmers, and labourers (MacDonald, 1990). Most families were nuclear and founded upon the same legal patriarchy as those in England. Although there was no central religious power similar to the Roman Catholic Church in New France, there were several Protestant religious authorities that strongly shaped family life. The Christian notion that fathers and husbands owned property and should be the legal head of their families prevailed, yet women's work played a critical role in the development of British Canada and the expansion of the economy (Errington, 1995).

Contact with both the French and the British brought great changes to Indigenous families. As mentioned in the last chapter, settlers brought disease, such as smallpox and tuberculosis. They also brought alcohol, which created an economic dependency among the Indigenous peoples on the colonizers. The colonists also set out to destroy the Indigenous culture, since they wanted to assimilate these peoples (assimilation is the process by which a group or an individual becomes more like the dominant group with respect to cultural elements) into a Euro-Canadian society.

The Indian Act of 1876 had a very powerful influence on Indigenous families. Those designated "Indians" were relegated to lands set aside for them, which put them on the margins of Canadian society and its economy. This act was also detrimental to status Indian women who married non-status men. Section 12 (1)(b) stated that a woman married to anyone other than an Indian was not entitled to status as an Indian, nor were her children. And if she did marry an Indian man, she then became a member of his band and lost her own band. This patriarchal law contravened the matrilineality of many Indigenous peoples and disrupted family life. For example, if an Indian woman with children lost her status, she would have no place on the reserve if her marriage dissolved because she was no longer an Indian. This loss of community and friends meant that her children would have limited experience of the reserve community and its Native culture (Momirov and Kilbride, 2005).

THE RESIDENTIAL SCHOOL EXPERIENCE

The term **residential schools** refers to an educational system (operating from the 1880s until the closing decades of the 20th century) that was created by the Canadian government and administered by churches. The schools were formally constituted as industrial schools, since they emphasized training in areas such as manual labour in agriculture, lighter industries such as woodworking, or domestic work such as laundry and sewing. Children were boarded in dormitories for most of the year and Indigenous communities had no voice in this practice. A primary goal of these schools was to educate and indoctrinate children into Euro-Canadian and Christian ways of living.

Until fairly recently, much of the Canadian public was not fully aware of this policy, and school curriculum did not typically cover this part of our Canadian history. Speaking from my own personal experience as someone who grew up in Ontario during the 1960s and 1970s, I was completely uninformed about this school system. This lack of knowledge changed when I moved out West and began teaching at the University of British Columbia as a sessional instructor in the early 1990s.

Ironically, at the time I was teaching an upper-division course entitled "Sociology of Education." During one of the classes, one of my very bright and energetic students, Elizabeth Furniss, presented me with me a copy of her recently completed monograph *Victims of Benevolence: Discipline and Death at the Williams Lake Indian Residential School, 1891-1920* (see box 4.2 for excerpt). In this monograph, she presents a study of governmental investigations into the care of students at the Williams Lake Indian Residential School, focusing on the death of a runaway boy in 1902 and the suicide of a young boy in 1920. She also includes many historical photographs and several moving stories about the long-term structural relationship between First Nations and the Canadian government and the tragic consequences it has had for innocent people.

After I read her work and listened to her stories, you can well imagine (and especially since I was the teacher) the various emotions that I experienced in fully learning, for the first time, about this tragic and disturbing part of our Canadian history. As Furniss notes on the back cover of her work, this "conspiracy of silence" was fuelled by the paternalistic assumptions of the Church and the government, who felt they were acting in the students' "best interests." Yet, despite feeling shock, anger, and betrayal, I also felt (and continue to feel) enormous gratitude and appreciation for Furniss's work. Indeed, I will always remember her as a very special student who genuinely and passionately wanted to become a teacher so that she could educate others about an atrocity that was committed by our own government.

Two primary objectives of the residential school system were to remove and isolate children from the influence of their homes, families, traditions, and cultures, and to assimilate them into the dominant culture. These objectives were based on the assumption that Indigenous cultures and spiritual beliefs were inferior and unequal. Not surprisingly, this practice had a drastic impact on almost all Indigenous families. Low self-esteem and self-concept problems arose because children were taught that their own culture was uncivilized and savage (Lafrance and Collins, 2003). Some teachers sought, as it was infamously said, "to kill the Indian in the child." Moreover, taking children away from their parents and communities kept them from their influence and caused parents and children to become strangers to each other (Unger, 1977: 16).

One instrument for social control was the imposition of a European educational system, with the primary intention of solving what was deemed "the Indian problem," without cultural or parental influence (see boxes 4.1 and 4.2 for an example of this rationale provided by a missionary and an adult woman's experience at a residential school). In order to meet this objective, residential schools were built during the 1840s. At their peak, there were 82 residential schools operating in Canada, with the last school closing in 1996 (Assembly of First Nations, 2016).

However, the type of social control exerted over this population entailed a kind of forced (and non-consensual) assimilation that is very different from the types of acculturation and assimilation processes that usually characterize the experiences of immigrants as they move to, and adjust to, a new society. **Acculturation** is the transfer or transmission of values and customs from one cultural group to another, although some original values, traditions, and customs may be retained. Similarly, **assimilation** refers to the process of cultural absorption of a minority group into the main cultural body or society, although there is often the loss of original characteristics such as language, traditions, or self-identity.

Box 4.1: "Children's Best Interests"

Missionaries often placed pressure on the federal government to fund schools for Indigenous children, given that their attempts to convert children were often unsuccessful. Below you will find an excerpt from the year 1878 from the writings of Father McGuckin, of St. Joseph's Mission. McGuckin thought that a residential school would be the solution to the missionaries' problems:

In a few years hence all our boys and girls will speak English, mix with the whites and lose all of their original simplicity. To resist them the temptations that will be placed in their way nothing less than a thorough religious education will suffice. This they will never acquire in their own language. Not as children, for during childhood there is no opportunity so long as they remain with their parents. Not during boyhood or girlhood, for then they are too busy and can be found for a short time in the winter, and often then unwilling to occupy their spare time at religious institutions. Hence, if we will preserve the faith amongst them, and provide them with arms to resist temptation, we must endeavor to get them into school and keep them for a certain number of years.

Source: Furniss, E. 1995. *Victims of Benevolence: Discipline and Death at the Williams Lake Indian Residential School, 1981-1920.* Williams Lake, BC: Cariboo Tribal Council (p. 11).

Box 4.2: The Residential School Experience

An adult woman describes her experience and the reality of punishment as a child in a residential school:

I remember those horrifying years as if it were yesterday. There was one nun, Sister Gilberta, she always passed out the punishment. Every day, she would take me to the bathroom and lock the door. She would then proceed to beat me 30 times on each hand, three times a day, with a strap. She would count to 30, out loud, each time she hit me. It's an awful way to learn to count to 30. My older sister, Grace, learned to count to 50.

I never understood why I had to get those beatings, but at this age of 37, I realize it had to be because I spoke my language. To this day, I can't speak my language very well, but I do understand when I am spoken to in Micmac.

Why was our language and culture such a threat that it had to be taken away from us with such vengeance?

To be taught your language with respect and kindness by your people, then to have the White Man pull it from your heart with meanness and torture. Some people wonder why we are so tough, because we had to, we had no choice.

I have polio and it affected my bladder and as a child, I wet my pants a lot. I received extra beatings for that too.

Once I was thrown across the dorm floor by Sister Gilberta. At the age of six, it seemed far away. I bounced off the wall at the other end of the dorm. I was sore on one side of my body for a few days.

Source: Cited in Schissel, B. and T. Wotherspoon. 2003. *The Legacy of School for Aboriginal People.* Toronto: Oxford University Press (pp. 51–52).

When Indigenous children were placed in these church-run residential schools (primarily Roman Catholic, Anglican, United, and Presbyterian), they were not only taken away from their families and reserves but also stripped of their culture. Forced to take Christian names and forbidden to practise their spiritual beliefs or speak in their mother tongue, the children had their hair cut and their clothes were replaced with uniforms. Many were physically and sexually assaulted, as illustrated in box 4.2, and some tried to commit suicide or run away. Sadly, these children had little contact with their parents, since "the physical isolation of children from their families and communities was a central ingredient in the residential school system" (Furniss, 1995: 14). When these children returned home as young adults, they were expected to recommence "normal family life, now among kin that they had been taught to be ashamed of. One former student stated, 'many of us raised our children the way we were raised at the schools. We disciplined our children with physical force, and we called them stupid, dumb, and lazy. We showed little or no emotion, and we found it hard to say we loved them'" (Timpson, 1995: 535).

Not surprisingly, these residential school experiences decreased the children's capacity to care for their own children later in life and perpetuated a cycle of family breakdown and dysfunction. When many of these young adults formed their own families, usually in economically and socially depressed communities, they themselves experienced the removal of their children through cross-cultural foster placements and adoptions (Albanese, 2016; Trocmé al. 2004). As noted by Das Gupta (2000: 152), "Generations of depression, alcoholism, suicide, and family breakdown are the legacy of such traumatic experiences and are described as the 'residential school syndrome' by native people themselves."

In addition to these issues, many other health-related problems plagued, and continue to plague, Indigenous families. As shown in box 4.3, many highly unethical and illegal nutrition experiments were performed on children at residential schools between 1942 and 1952. Used as "guinea pigs," groups of malnourished children were denied adequate nutrition and dental care. Consequently, children lost their teeth. As adults, many experienced chronic diseases that could be linked back to their poor diets as children.

Today, we recognize that despite the fact that there may have been some good intentions, this policy of assimilation was Eurocentric and racist, and has caused great harm. Yet, it was not until recently that the government openly acknowledged how misguided

Figure 4.1: Red Deer Institute, Circa 1919, and Students at the Blackboard, Red Deer Institute, Circa 1914

Source: United Church of Canada Archives. n.d. "School Images Gallery." *Residential School Archive Project: The Children Remembered.* Retrieved on October 10, 2017, from www.thechildrenremembered.ca/school-images/red-deer-images.

Box 4.3: Canada's Shameful History of Nutrition Research on Residential School Children

THE NEED FOR STRONG MEDICAL ETHICS IN ABORIGINAL HEALTH RESEARCH

While both science and research have very long and detailed histories, the formal history of medical ethics is short. The discipline's foundation arises from the medical atrocities performed in the name of science by a cadre of Nazi doctors during World War II. The actions were so despicable that 20 physicians were put on trial in Nuremberg for violation of the Hippocratic oath and behaviour incompatible with their education and profession. A result of this 1946 trial was the Nuremberg Code of Medical Ethics.

In 2013, Ian Mosby, a food historian and postdoctoral fellow at the University of Guelph (Guelph, Ontario), revealed details of highly unethical nutrition experiments performed on Canadian Aboriginal children at six residential schools between 1942 and 1952—our own medical atrocities. The experiments were performed by the Department of Indian Affairs of Canada under the direction of two physicians: Dr Percy Moore, the Indian Affairs Branch Superintendent of Medical Services, and Dr Frederick Tisdall, a famed nutritionist, a former president of the Canadian Paediatric Society, and one of three paediatricians at the Hospital for Sick Children (Toronto, Ontario) who developed Pablum infant cereal in the 1930s. In these experiments, parents were not informed, nor were consents obtained. Even as children died, the experiments continued. Even after the recommendations from the Nuremberg trial, these experiments continued.

In these experiments, control and treatment groups of malnourished children were denied adequate nutrition. In one experiment, the treatment group received supplements of riboflavin, thiamine and/or ascorbic acid supplements to determine whether these mitigated the problems—they did not. In another, children were given a flour mix containing added thiamine, riboflavin, niacin, and bone meal. Rather than improving nutrition, the supplements made the children more anemic, likely contributing to more deaths and certainly impacting their development. In these experiments, efforts were made to control as many factors as possible, even when they harmed the research subjects. For example, previously available dental care was denied in some settings because the researchers wanted to observe the state of dental caries and gingivitis that resulted from malnutrition.

How could we have let this happen? Why did we not know about this long before now? Why did these experiments not stop when the Nuremberg Code was put forward?

Similar to the US Public Health Service Syphilis Study at Tuskeegee (Alabama)—which, in 1932, began with the "best of intentions" to learn about the natural history of syphilis among black men in hopes of justifying a treatment program for them—Canadian researchers used Aboriginal children in residential schools to learn about malnutrition. The problem with the Tuskeegee study was that the natural history observations continued long after penicillin became available to treat syphilis. In Canada's case, the basics of alleviating malnutrition (adequate food) were well known even before these experiments began. The most striking fact is that both studies were performed among individuals who were already marginalized and vulnerable. No one was looking out for the best interests of these research subjects. They had no voice.

While many changes and improvements have been made in the area of ethical health research since the 1940s, Aboriginal children and youth remain a highly vulnerable population. Extra care must be taken.

Source: MacDonald, N.E., R. Stanwick, and A. Lynk. 2014. "Canada's shameful history of nutrition research on residential school children: The need for strong medical ethics in Aboriginal health research." *Paediatrics & Child Health* 19(2): 64.

this policy was in terms of its intentions and consequences. Indeed, it was not until June 11, 2008, that Prime Minister Stephen Harper offered an official apology, an apology that has been met with mixed reactions.

Moreover, while not a specific government policy, a spinoff of the residential school experience was the **sixties scoop,** a term coined by Johnson (1983), author of *Native Children and the Child Welfare System.*" The sixties scoop refers to a large-scale removal of Indigenous babies and children from their families, usually without parental consent, into the child welfare system and into middle-class, European-Canadian families. Yet, even today, Indigenous children are over-represented in the child welfare system, a system that continues to devalue traditional systems of childrearing and child protection by judging standards of care by dominant Canadian norms and through the use of non-Native foster homes (Muir and Bohr, 2014).

SELECTED CONTEMPORARY FAMILY TRENDS AND ISSUES

Indigenous Families in Canada Today and the Legacy of the Residential School Experience

The Indigenous population has fluctuated over time but rose significantly between 1971 and 2011. Today, people reporting an Aboriginal ethnic identity represent 4.3% of the total population of Canada, with the largest number living in Ontario and British Columbia (Statistics Canada, 2015). The proportion of this population living off reserve has significantly increased over time. By 2016, over 50% of registered Aboriginal Canadians lived off reserves, particularly in industrial areas and cities (Statistics Canada, 2015).

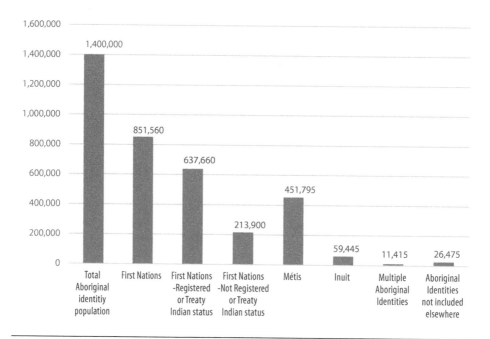

Figure 4.2: Population Counts, by Aboriginal Identity and Registered or Treaty Indian Status, Canada, 2011

Note: Based on National Household Survey Data, 2011. Excludes data for one or more incompletely enu-merated Indian reserves or Indian settlements. The three Aboriginal groups are based on the population reporting a single identity of 'First Nations,' 'Métis,' 'or' 'Inuit.'

Source: Statistics Canada. 2015. "Aboriginal Statistics at a Glance," 2nd edition. Catalogue no. 89-645-x2015001. Ottawa: Minister of Industry (Chart 2).

The Royal Commission on Aboriginal Peoples (2016) has reported on the serious social and economic conditions among many Aboriginal peoples, including low life ex-pectancy, inadequate education, high teenage pregnancy rates, high levels of incarceration, alcohol and substance abuse, overcrowded housing, poverty, and family breakdown. Many Indigenous peoples (regardless of where they live) have difficulty finding employment due to discrimination and lower educational attainment than the general population. Those living in remote, isolated areas are particularly disadvantaged and face significant geo-graphic, socio-economic, and cultural barriers, including access to important programs and services. As a result, health disparities, unsafe housing conditions, and continuing poverty are serious contributors to problems in families (NCCAH, 2011).

Research consistently documents that the Residential School System has affected four generations of survivors who may have transmitted the trauma they experienced to their own children and grandchildren. For example, a history of residential school attendance or having a relative with a residential school attendance is associated with suicide thoughts and attempts, a problem that is particularly prevalent in remote areas (Elias et al., 2012). As a result of these trends, individual and family life can be significantly impacted due to mental health issues, poverty, abuse/violence, relationship quality, and intergenerational relationships.

Skip-Generation Families

One area of concern is family structure, living arrangements, and grandparent-grandchild relations. As shown in figure 4.3, while Aboriginal children are less likely than non-Aboriginal children to live with both parents, they are also more likely to live with their grandparents in a **skip-generation family** (2.7% versus only 0.4%, respectively). A skip-generation family is defined by Statistics Canada as a census family that consists of grandparents and grandchildren without the presence of parents in the home. Grandparents often provide care for grandchildren in response to crisis, such as alcohol and drug addiction or imprisonment of the parents. This can create a number of challenges and vulnerabilities between the generations. Grandparents raising their grandchildren are more likely to be living in poverty and overcrowded conditions and to have a disability or depressive symptoms. As a result, many custodial elders may face substantial financial, emotional, and physical costs, which trickle down to their grandchildren.

On the positive side, care from grandparents can provide continuity among the generations, since it allows Indigenous children to learn traditional ways and receive guidance from their elders. Indeed, elders have traditionally played key roles as wise advisers and keepers of their cultural legacy. This has historically helped to socialize and instruct their grandchildren, since the elders have often played an important role in their physical care (Castellano, 2002; Fuller-Thomson, 2005).

Overall, despite certain challenges, it is important to keep these issues in perspective, since research shows that only a relatively small minority of Aboriginal children are raised by their grandparents, are in foster care, or live with other relatives. As shown in figure 4.3, it is far more likely that Aboriginal children are living in a lone-parent household (34.4% versus 17.4% of non-Aboriginal children).

REDRESSING HISTORICAL INJUSTICES

It is also not uncommon for children to report that they experience positive ties with their families and communities. For instance, a recent study showed that most Inuit living in the North report having "strong" or "very strong" ties with their families, with only a minority reporting that their ties were "weak" or "very weak" (Canadian Council on Learning, 2009).

Another promising movement has been the extent to which Indigenous Peoples have created their own grass-roots organizations and advocacy groups in order to voice their opinions and empower children, youth, women, and families. For example, The Native Women's Association of Canada has released a list of recommendations to help guide the MMIW (Inquiry into Missing and Murdered Indigenous Women and Girls). Another good illustration is the First Nations Child and Family Caring Society, which uses a reconciliation framework that respectfully engages First Nation and non-Indigenous peoples. This national, non-profit organization also provides research, policy, professional development, and networking. It also provides important resources and publicizes important information on landmark rulings (see box 4.5, "Jordan's Principle").

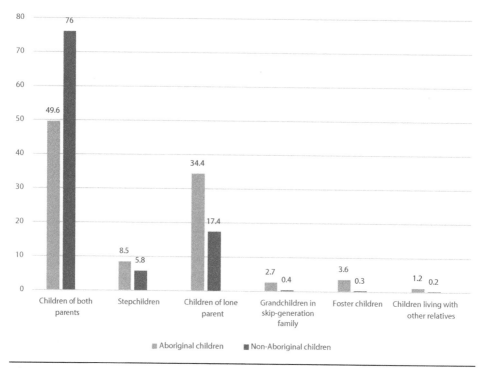

Figure 4.3: Family Composition and Living Arrangements of Aboriginal Children, 2011

Source: Statistics Canada. 2015. "Aboriginal Statistics at a Glance, 2nd edition." Catalogue no. 89-645-x2015001. Ottawa: Minister of Industry (Chart 8).

Box 4.4: Five Recommendations for National MMIW Inquiry: Native Women's Association of Canada

The federal government has wrapped up the cross-country pre-inquiry consultation with families and has announced the inquiry for missing and murdered Indigenous women will be launched by this summer. But there are still many questions about how the government will conduct the inquiry.

The Native Women's Association of Canada (NWAC) has released a list of 22 recommendations to help guide the inquiry, created with the help of indigenous female leaders, family members of missing and murdered Indigenous women, and human rights experts from the United Nations and the Inter-American Commission on Human Rights.

"The road ahead will be grueling, but it is nothing we can't handle if we remain focused and committed to our overarching purpose: bringing justice to our women and girls," NWAC president Dawn Lavell-Harvard stated in a release.

Here are a few themes highlighted in the recommendations:

LED BY INDIGENOUS WOMEN

The report urges that the inquiry be led by Indigenous women, since they are in the best position to speak to the unique experiences of others like them.

Dawn Lavell-Harvard, president of the Native Women's Association of Canada, says Indigenous women must take the lead in the national MMIW inquiry.

"We have a long history of governments, and the mainstream, stepping in and attempting to do for us, and speak for us, which has never led to positive outcomes," Lavell-Harvard told CBC News.

"So even though it seems like a bit of a 'no brainer,' it needs to be absolutely included."

EXAMINE ROOT CAUSES

The group wants the federal government to examine why Indigenous women and girls remain socially and economically disadvantaged, in addition to examining why Indigenous women experience sexualized stereotyping.

"We can't lose sight that this isn't just a race issue, that it is a fact that a particular group is being doubly discriminated against ... because you have the intersection of the racism and the sexism, and the challenge here is about the intersectional violence," said Lavell-Harvard.

CO-OPERATION FROM PROVINCES, POLICE

The group foresees an obstacle in getting full co-operation in the inquiry, writing "that the government of Canada [should] immediately secure participation in the inquiry from the eight provinces and three territories."

Carolyn Bennett, minister of Indigenous and Northern Affairs, has wrapped up the cross-country consultations with families and friends of missing and murdered indigenous women. (Adrian Wyld/Canadian Press)

"If the provinces don't commit to [giving access to] all of their jurisdictional areas ... we're going to have half an inquiry, we're going to have a significant gap," said Lavell-Harvard.

The report also states that there needs to be an effort made to examine past failures of police and judicial systems. And for families that want a case re-examined, a "special mechanism for the independent review of those cases" must be developed.

HUMAN RIGHTS FRAMEWORK

The group also encourages changes to be made to Canada's Indian Act to remove all language that is discriminatory to women—a recommendation repeatedly made by the United Nations Committee on the Elimination of Discrimination Against Women.

"We need to ensure that the national plan that emerges from the inquiry will move us toward fulfilling the rights of Indigenous women and girls and meet the obligations of Canadian governments," Shelagh Day, with the Canadian Feminist Alliance for International Action (FAFIA) stated in a release.

NO TIME FRAME

The federal government has committed two years of funding for the national inquiry, but NWAC believes setting a time limit might prove to be a problem.

The recommendations state that the inquiry must "be independent from government, adequately funded and free from legal, time or funding restrictions."

Source: Cram, S. 2016. "5 Recommendations for National MMIW Inquiry: Native Women's Association of Canada." *CBC News*, February 23. Retrieved February 26, 2016, from www.cbc.ca/news/aboriginal/5-recommendations-for-national-mmiw-inquiry-1.3458993.

Box 4.5: Jordan's Principle

In a landmark ruling in January 2016, the Canadian Human Rights Tribunal found the Canadian government was racially discriminating against 163,000 First Nations children living on reserve. Among the remedies is the full implementation of Jordan's Principle.

Jordan's Principle is a child-first principle named in memory of Jordan River Anderson. Jordan was a First Nations child from Norway House Cree Nation in Manitoba. Born with complex medical needs, Jordan spent more than two years unnecessarily in hospital while the Province of Manitoba and the federal government argued over who should pay for his at-home care. Jordan died in hospital at the age of five, never having spent a day in a family home.

Payment disputes within and between federal and provincial governments over services for First Nations children are not uncommon. First Nations children are frequently left waiting for services they desperately need, or are denied services that are available to other children. This includes services in education, health, child care, recreation, culture, and language. Jordan's Principle calls on the government of first contact to pay for the services and seek reimbursement later so the child does not get tragically caught in the middle of government red tape.

Jordan's Principle was unanimously passed in the House of Commons in 2007, but sadly, the Canadian Paediatric Society reports that neither the federal government nor the provinces or territories have fully implemented it.

Source: First Nation Child & Family Caring Society of Canada. n.d. "Jordan's Principle." Retrieved April 5, 2016, from: wwwhttps://fncaringsociety.com/jordans-principle.

In short, it is important to consider some positive advancements and to recognize that not all families are having significant problems. In other words, it should not be taken for granted that all Indigenous families are poor, suicidal, and have alcohol- or other family-related problems, as is commonly portrayed in public discourse and news media. Indeed, the Osoyoos Indian Band is one of the most prosperous First Nations in Canada, with virtually no unemployment among the band's 520 members. The reserve's impressive school also teaches native heritage and the Okanagan language, and many problems common to other First Nations families have been greatly diminished (MacDonald, 2014). It is also important to consider that many non-Indigenous families also experience social and economic problems and racialization. Moreover, in both rural and urban areas, recent research suggests that Indigenous and non-Indigenous families are becoming increasingly diverse, with more variability in education, income, health, and longevity.

Another positive trend is that colonial discourses, polices, and practices are increasingly being critiqued and deconstructed from a discursive perspective (as illustrated in box 4.6). Moreover, many efforts are being made by the government to redress historical injustices, such as compensation for Residential School survivors and support for commissions, programs, and services that give more direct control to Indigenous peoples. Notably, the Truth and Reconciliation Commission of Canada provided those directly or indirectly affected by the legacy of the Residential School system with an opportunity to share their stories and experiences. Although this Commission officially ended in 2015, a National Centre for the Truth and Reconciliation was established in 2013 (hosted by the University of Manitoba) in order to create a place of learning and dialogue. The centre also provides a permanent and secure home for statements, documents, oral histories, and other archival materials it gathers. Hopefully, this will ensure that former survivors and their families have access to their own history, and that the history and legacy of the Residential School system are preserved and never forgotten.

Box 4.6: What Good We Might Hope For: Thinking about Decolonization and Social Determinants of Health as Solutions to Addictions and Mental Health Challenges

The state of Indigenous people's health, including addictions and mental health, cannot in Canada be extricated from colonial projects. By discursively and directly intervening into the lives of Indigenous peoples, colonial policies and practices have colluded to produce states of poor health in many Indigenous communities. Many of the discursive apparatuses, and their concurrent material interventions, turned on paternalistic logics that colonial states and subjects had at heart the best interest of Indigenous peoples, who were by nature abject and deficient beings often suffering from addictions. Best interests often focused on Indigenous children. When charted into the present day, many of the same interventionist logics appear alive and well in the form of state child "welfare" and child protection legislations. Given that the health and well-being of Indigenous peoples has not markedly improved over time; that Indigenous peoples continue to exhibit some of the worst health profiles of any group in Canada; and given that the state continues to aggressively intervene into Indigenous communities through child protections services, we wonder if part of a health future for Indigenous peoples might reside in significant reconfigurations of state logics concerning what constitutes a child's well-being. This reconfiguration, we suggest, is emergent in efforts to Indigenize and decolonize the literature on the social determinants of health.

What does a discussion of discourse offer to the social determinants literature and to understandings of Indigenous addictions and mental health? We argue in this paper that when applying a social determinants approach to the study of the health of racialized and colonized groups, and particularly to the health of Indigenous peoples, it is imperative to account for the discursive context within with social factors such as education, income, social support networks, healthy child development, and physical environments emerge. We argue that discourses determine health, and in particular that the heterogeneous and yet intersecting practices, institutions, laws, texts, and ideas that constitute discourses of Indigenous deviance and non-Indigenous care and protection have material effects upon the health and well-being of Indigenous peoples in Canada.

These discourses have not only produced and naturalized the conditions that compromise Indigenous peoples' health (such as the dispossession of land, the removal and targeting of children, and a host of other assimilative and coercive practices); the poor health that results from colonial discursivities is used today to justify the continual attack upon Indigenous children through the child welfare system and results in further erosion of the health of families and communities. We argue, in other words, that colonial discourse is a "cause of causes" of health disparities, but one with a unique ability to account for the interplay of imaginative and material factors, and to tease out the multiple processes and practices that contribute to health. The integrative, multi-layered framework enabled by a discursive approach is particularly well-suited to understanding addictions and mental health concerns, moreover, because these health issues are themselves so complex and multifaceted.

Source: Extract from de Leeuw, S., M. Greenwood, and E. Cameron. 2010. "Deviant Constructions: How Governments Preserve Colonial Narratives of Addictions and Poor Mental Health to Intervene into the Lives of Indigenous Children and Families in Canada." *International Journal of Mental Health Addiction* 8: 282–295 (p. 292).

SUMMARY

The current struggles of Indigenous families are rooted in a history of domination and the attempts of colonial governments to assimilate them into Euro-Canadian society.

Common problems include discrimination and racism, language difficulties, constricted employment and housing choices, poverty, and social exclusion. Many of the parents, teachers, grandparents and leaders of today's Indigenous communities are residential school survivors. This means that in addition to an intergenerational effect, many descendants of the residential experience share the same burdens and health-related effects as their ancestors. These challenges include transmitted personal trauma and compromised family systems, in addition to the loss of Aboriginal communities of language, culture, and the teaching of tradition from one generation to another (Hanson, 2016).

Within this context, the role of government policy in shaping and constraining family life was reviewed, since it has played a significant role in creating the current conditions and experiences of Indigenous Peoples. Fortunately, government policies appear to be less racist and discriminatory than in the past, and victims of previous abuse are now stepping forward for compensation (for example, see the Assembly of First Nations' web site for the latest details on these claims). Yet, these past mistakes highlight the need for policy makers to carefully examine both the intended and unintended consequences of their assessments (a theme to be further explored in chapter 16), which may not be good for families in the long run. Researchers are also engaging with Indigenous Peoples in ways that directly involve their participation and ongoing concerns, as noted in chapter 2. Consequently, the relevance of research to Indigenous communities is increasingly a condition for this population's engagement in projects (Castellano, 2008). Yet, despite these seemingly successful developments, we have also learned how easy it is to mask moral, political, socio-cultural systemic issues and discourses, depending on who defines the "worth" of certain cultures and peoples.

Overall, Indigenous families are on a path to healing and are strengthening their families and communities by exercising their right to ethical treatment, self-determination and Nation re-building. Fair and equitable systems and supports for child welfare, education, health and well-ness, community safeness and justice issues are finally being taken seriously, given a long history of severe and extensive under-investments in essential services. There are also some signs that the federal budget is beginning to address decades of underfunding and neglect. Notably, the 2016 federal budget shows that the government is investing more in areas such as education, infrastructure on reserves, housing, health, and child and family services (Assembly of First Nations, 2016).

In closing, while important progress has been made, it is recognized that the process of reconciliation and efforts to reduce inequities will take time. As summarized by previous United Nations Special Rapporteur on the Rights of Indigenous Peoples, Anaya (2014) aptly noted:

> The well-being gap between Aboriginal and non-Aboriginal people in Canada has not narrowed over the last several years, treaty and Aboriginal claims remain persistently unresolved, Indigenous women and girls remain vulnerable to abuse, and overall there appears to be high levels of distrust among Indigenous peoples toward government ... It is necessary for Canada to arrive at a common understanding with Aboriginal peoples

of objectives and goals that are based on full respect for their constitutional, treaty, and internationally recognized rights.

QUESTIONS FOR CRITICAL REFLECTION AND DEBATE

1. Why is it important to consider the cultural, social, political, and historical realms of Indigenous communities with respect to better understanding challenges and opportunities in contemporary family life?
2. How might the lives of on-reserve Indigenous families be different than those of families living off-reserve? Consider issues related to geographical place and space, cultural preservation, language, identity, and sense of belonging.
3. How did the residential school experience of Indigenous children result in devastating consequences for children, their families, and communities and reverberate through successive generations?
4. Critically evaluate the following statement: "Professionals working with Indigenous families require a high degree of cultural literacy pertaining to traditional Indigenous parenting and extended family practices."
5. Is Indigenous self-government the answer to improving the lives of Indigenous Peoples in this country? What else can be done to address some of the ongoing challenges faced by this population?
6. To what extent should the federal government develop policies and programs to redress many of the problems created by earlier policies?

GLOSSARY

Acculturation is the transfer or transmission of values and customs from one cultural group to another, although some original customs and traditions may be retained.

Assimilation refers to the process of cultural absorption of a minority group into the main cultural body or society with the loss of original characteristics such as language, traditions, or self-identity.

Genocide is the deliberate intent or act of killing a particular ethnic or cultural group or nation.

The Indian Act of 1876 formalized the First Nations' dependency on the Canadian state and regulated almost every aspect of their social and economic life.

Indigenous Peoples or Aboriginals are defined as those persons who report identifying with at least one Indigenous group (First Nations, Métis or Inuit and/or those reported Registered or Treaty Indian Status).

Residential Schools are the school system set up by the government and administered by the churches in order to indoctrinate Indigenous children into a Euro-Canadian and Christian way of living.

Skip-Generation Family is a census family that consists of grandparents and grandchildren without the presence of parents in the home.

The "Sixties Scoop" refers to a large-scale removal of Indigenous babies and children from their families, usually without parental consent, into the child welfare system and into middle-class, European-Canadian families

FURTHER READING

Anderson, K. 2016. *A Recognition of Being: Reconstructing Native Womanhood,* 2nd ed. Toronto: Canadian Scholars' Press.
Anderson revisits her ground-breaking text to include recent work on Indigenous feminism and two-spirited theory. Focus is placed on documenting the efforts of Indigenous women to resist imposed roles and heteropatriarchy in order to reconstruct a powerful Native womanhood.

Cannon, M.J. and L. Sunseri (eds.). 2011. *Racism, Colonialism, and Indigeneity in Canada.* Toronto: Oxford University Press.
This collection of works by Indigenous scholars explores the interplay of racism and colonialism and how it has shaped the lives of Indigenous peoples in such areas as family relations, criminal justice, territorial rights, and relations with settler colonialists.

Furniss, E. 1995. *Victims of Benevolence: Discipline and Death at the Williams Lake Indian Residential School, 1981–1920.* Williams Lake: Cariboo Tribal Council.
Provides a deeply moving and troubling study of two tragic events that took place at a residential school.

Highway, T. 2008. *Kiss of the Fur Queen,* 3rd ed. Norman: University of Oklahoma Press.
This is a passionate story about the lives of two young Cree brothers from Northern Manitoba who are taken from their families and sent to a residential school, and follows the brothers as they become adults. It also explores issues around (homo)sexuality, relationships, and culture.

Jacobs, M.D. 2014. *A Generation Removed: The Fostering and Adoption of Indigenous Children in the Postwar World.* Lincoln: University of Nebraska Press.
Examines the post-WWII international phenomenon of governments legally removing Indigenous children from their primary families and placing them with adoptive parents in the US, Canada, and Australia.

Menzies, P. and L.F. Lavallée (eds.). 2014. *Journey to Healing: Aboriginal People with Addiction and Mental Health Issues: What Health, Social Service and Justice Workers Need to Know.* Toronto: CAHH.

A practical, comprehensive and evidence-based resource written to assist students and professionals providing counselling and social services to Aboriginal people in urban, rural, and isolated settings. It will also be of interest to prison, probation, parole, and police officers working with these communities.

Stote, K. 2015. *An Act of Genocide: Colonization and the Sterilization of Aboriginal Women.* Nova Scotia: Fernwood Publishing.

This book unpacks long-buried archival evidence to begin documenting the forced sterilization of Aboriginal women in Canada within the context of colonization. The author argues that sterilization should be understood as an act of genocide and explores the ways that Canada has managed to avoid this charge.

RELATED WEB SITES

Indigenous and Northern Affairs Canada supports Aboriginal people (First Nations, Inuit and Métis) and Northerners in their efforts to improve and sustain social and community well-being; it also offers information on the National Inquiry into Missing and Murdered Indigenous Women and Girls, www.ainc-inac.gc.ca/.

Assembly of First Nations provides links to other resources, as well as information on residential schools, legal claims, and other related material, www.afn.ca/Assembly_of_First_Nations.htm.

First Nations Child and Family Caring Society of Canada is a non-profit organization that provides research, policy, professional development and networking support caring for First Nations children, youth, and families, www.fncaringsociety.com.

Legacy of Hope Foundation is a national Aboriginal charitable organization whose purposes are to educate, raise awareness and understanding of the legacy of residential schools, including the effects and intergenerational impacts on First Nations, Inuit, and Métis; and to support the ongoing healing process of residential school survivors. www.legacyofhope.ca

Truth and Reconciliation Commission of Canada is a component of the Indian Residential Schools Settlement Agreement. Its mandate is to inform all Canadians about what happened in Indian Residential Schools (IRS). The Commission documented the truth of survivors, families, communities and anyone personally affected by the IRS experience, www.trc.ca/websites/trcinstitution/index.php?p=3

REFERENCES

Albanese, P. 2016. *Children in Canada Today,* 2nd ed. Toronto: Oxford University Press.

Ambert, A.M. 2012. *Changing Families: Relationships in Context,* 2nd ed. Toronto: Pearson Education Canada.

Anaya, J. 2014. "Report of the Special Rapporteur on the Rights of Indigenous Peoples." United Nations General Assembly: Human Rights Council. Retrieved April 12, 2016, from www. ohchr.org/Documents/Issues/IPeoples/SR/A.HRC.27.52.Add.2-MissionCanada_AUV.pdf.

Anderson, K. 2000. *A Recognition of Being: Reconstructing Native Womanhood.* Toronto: Second Story Press.

Assembly of First Nations. 2016. "AFN National Chief Says Federal Budget a Significant Step in Closing the Gap for First Nations." Retrieved April 12, 2016, from www.afn.ca/en/news-media/latest-news/16-3-22-afn-national-chief-says-federal-budget-a-significant-step-in-closing-the-gap-for-first-nations.

Canadian Council on Learning. 2009. *The State of Aboriginal Learning in Canada: A Holistic Approach to Measuring Success.* Ottawa, Ontario. Retrieved May 30, 2011, from www.ccl-cca. ca/sal2009.

Castellano, M.B. 2002. *Aboriginal Family Trends: Extended Families, Nuclear Families, Families of the Heart.* Ottawa: The Vanier Institute of the Family.

Castellano, M.B. 2008. "Indigenous Research." In L. Given (ed.), *The Sage Encyclopedia of Qualitative Research Methods* (pp. 1-6). Thousand Oaks, California: Sage Publications.

Das Gupta, T. 2000. "Families of Native People, Immigrants, and People of Colour." In N. Mandell and A. Duffy (eds.), *Canadian Families: Diversity, Conflict, and Change,* 2nd ed. (pp. 146–187). Toronto: Harcourt Brace.

Druke, M.A. 1986. "Iroquois and Iroquoian in Canada." In R. Bruce Morrison and C. Roderick Wilson (eds.), *Native Peoples: The Canadian Experience* (pp. 61–86). Toronto: McClelland & Stewart.

Elias, B., J. Mignone, M. Hall, S.P. Hong, L. Hart, and J. Sareen. 2012. "Trauma and Suicide Behaviour Histories among a Canadian Indigenous Population: An Empirical Exploration of the Potential Role of Canada's Residential School System." *Social Science and Medicine* 74: 1560-1569.

Errington, E.J. 1995. *Wives and Mothers, Schoolmistresses and Scullery Maids: Working Women in Upper Canada, 1790–1840.* Montreal: McGill-Queen's University Press.

Fuller-Thomson, E. 2005. "Canadian First Nations Grandparents Raising Grandchildren: A Portrait in Resilience." *International Journal of Aging and Human Development* 60: 331–342.

Furniss, E. 1995.*Victims of Benevolence: Discipline and Death at the Williams Lake Indian Residential School, 1981–1920.* Williams Lake: Cariboo Tribal Council.

Hansen, E. 2016. "The Residential School System." The University of British Columbia, Vancouver, BC: Indigenous Foundations.arts.ubc.ca. Retrieved February 29, 2016, from: www/indig-enousfoundations.arts.ubc.ca/home/government-policy/the-residential-school-system.html.

Johnson, P. 1983. *Native Children and the Child Welfare System.* Ottawa: The Canadian Council on Social Development.

Lafrance, J. and D. Collins. 2003. "Residential Schools and Aboriginal Parenting: Voices of Parents." *Native Social Work Journal* 4: 104-125.

Leacock, E. 1991. "Montagnais Women and the Jesuit Program of Colonization." In V. Strong-Boag and A. Clair Fellman (eds.), *Rethinking Canada: The Promise of Women's History*, 2nd ed. Toronto: Copp Clark Pitmam.

MacDonald, J. 2014. "The Osoyoos Indian Band Is Arguably the Most Business-Minded First Nation in Canada: So What's the Secret to Their Success?" *The Globe and Mail*, Thursday, May 29, 2014.

MacDonald, M.A. 1990. *Rebels and Loyalists: The Lives and Material Culture of New Brunswick's Early English-Speaking Settlers, 1758–1783*. Fredericton: New Ireland Press.

Mandell, N., and J. Momirov. 2005. "Family Histories." In N. Mandell and A. Duffy (eds.), *Canadian Families: Diversity, Conflict, and Change* (pp. 31–63). Toronto: Thomson Nelson.

Momirov, J., and K.M. Kilbride. 2005. "Family Lives of Native Peoples, Immigrants, and Visible Minorities." In N. Mandell and A. Duffy (eds.), *Canadian Families: Diversity, Conflict, and Change* (pp. 87–111). Toronto: Thomson Nelson.

Morrison, T., M.A. Morrison, and T. Borsa. 2014. "A Legacy of Derogation: Prejudice toward Aboriginal Persons in Canada." *Psychology* 5: 1001-1010.

Muir, N. and Y. Bohr. 2014. "Contemporary Practice of Traditional Aboriginal Child Rearing: A Review." *First Peoples Child and Family Review* 9: 66-79.

National Collaborating Centre for Aboriginal Health (NCCAH). 2011. "Access to Health Services as a Social Determinant of First Nations, Inuit and Metis Health." Prince George, BC: University of Northern British Columbia. Retrieved April 11, 2016, from www.NCCAH.ca.

Nett, E. 1993. *Canadian Families: Past and Present*, 3rd ed. Toronto: Butterworths.

Nett, E.M. 1988. *Canadian Families Past and Present*. Toronto: Butterworths.

Pediaa.com. 2017. "Difference between Assimilation and Acculturation." Retrieved January 1, 2017, from www.pediaa.com/difference-between-assimilation-and-acculturation.

The Royal Commission on Aboriginal Peoples. 2016. "Highlights from the Report of the Royal Commission on Aboriginal Peoples." Ottawa: Government of Canada. Retrieved April 12, 2016, from www.aadnc-ndc.gc.ca/eng/1100100014597/1100100014637.

Statistics Canada. 2015. "Aboriginal Statistics at a Glance," 2nd ed. Catalogue no. 89-645-x2015001. Ottawa: Minister of Industry.

Timpson, J. 1995. "Four Decades of Literature on Native Canadian Child Welfare: Changing Themes." *Child Welfare* 74, 3: 525–46.

Trocmé, N., D. Knoke, and C. Blackstock. 2004. "Pathways to the Overrepresentation of Aboriginal Children in Canada's Child Welfare System." *Social Service Review* (December): 577–600.

Unger, S. 1977. *The Destruction of American Indian Families*. New York: Association on American Indian Affairs.

CHAPTER 5

Immigration and the Changing Ethnic Mosaic of Canadian Families

LEARNING OBJECTIVES

In this chapter you will learn that ...

- the ethnocultural composition of Canadian families has changed over time
- our ethnic mosaic is influenced by changing government and immigration policies
- similar to Indigenous families, immigrants and refugees have not always had the right to live in a family context of their own choosing
- ethnic groups are diverse such that generalizations about ethnicity and visible minority status can be problematic and lead to racist outcomes
- despite diversity, there may be shared sources and experiences of generational conflict and solidarity among immigrant and refugee families
- the current Canadian ethnic mosaic is undergoing profound transformation

INTRODUCTION

Canada is internationally renowned not only for its beauty and rich natural resources, but also for its embrace of multiculturalism and its associated imagery of an **ethnic mosaic**. This term is used to denote a rich tapestry of families whose distinctive cultures give colour and texture to the whole. It also reflects a condition that symbolizes the reality of ethnic diversity, which has been increasingly characteristic of Canada over time. While Indigenous Peoples constitute the First Nations of our land, family life has increasingly become ethnically and culturally diverse as a growing number of immigrants and refugees arrive from Asia, Latin America, Africa, and the Middle East. The majority of these individuals belong to what is euphemistically and officially defined as the "**visible minority population**." While this term has been criticized for being artificial, unnecessary, and counterproductive, it is defined by the Federal Employment Equity Act as "persons, other than Aboriginal peoples, who are non-Caucasian in race or non-white in colour." However, critics charge that "there is something almost racist about the assumption that whites are the standard against which anyone else is noticeably, visibly different" (Woolley, 2013), in addition to other issues related to this type of categorization (also see box 5.1 for a critique of this term). Conversely, the Canadian government supports the use of this term, arguing that it is useful for the identification and the equalization of disadvantaged social groups in areas such as the labour market and its wage disparities.

Box 5.1: The Imperative of Minority Construction

Canadian official records refer to racialized peoples as visible minorities or racial minorities. This raises the obvious questions of what we mean by minorities, and why they are accorded that status. Minorities are socially constructed entities in societies, and the label implies the imposition of an inferior status. They are often set apart by the majority group as incompetent, abnormal, or dangerous because of differences pertaining to race, gender, culture, or religion. Majority or dominant groups use these differences to distance themselves from minorities for the purpose of acquiring or maintaining privilege and power. In the process, the minority group becomes the "other," an outsider, sometimes dangerous and sometimes a pariah. Although in the Canadian case, some argue that minority refers to the numerical status of the groups, the concept of minority is often extended to numerical majorities such as women, or the majority Black population in South Africa under the apartheid regime. In the case of race, as a determinant of minority status, imposing the label suggests that race is the most distinguishing feature in the experience of racialized people in Canada—not class or gender or religion. It also fixes their identity for all time within that imposed silo, suggesting that the racialized groups will always be the "other" in Canadian society.

Source: Galabuzi, G.E. 2006. *Canada's Economic Apartheid: The Social Exclusion of Racialized Groups in the New Century.* Toronto: Canadian Scholar's Press (p. 31).

In recognition of these complex issues, this chapter will focus on immigrant, refugee, and visible minority groups and provide an overview of how ethnicity, race, and government policy shape and constrain family life in Canada. Several emergent patterns will be identified, as well as some selected generational opportunities and challenges for selected ethnic groups. Although sociologists argue that "ethnicity" and "race" are social constructs that are historically specific, **ethnicity** can be defined as "cultural, organizational (tribe, nation), and ideational (religion) values, attitudes, and behaviours" that have to do with "social, socio-psychological, cultural, and organizational dimensions of human interaction" (Driedger, 2003: 9). In other words, ethnicity denotes social distinctions and relations among individuals and groups based on their cultural characteristics (e.g., language, religions, customs, and history). Although the term **race** is a social construct, it is often used to refer to people's assumed but socially significant physical or genetic characteristics (Liodakis, 2015). These assumptions can lead to racism and **racialization**, a topic that will be re-visited following a brief overview of historical and contemporary immigration patterns.

IMMIGRATION PATTERNS POST-CONFEDERACY

Boyd and Vickers (2000) document that record numbers of immigrants arrived in Canada during the early 1900s. These numbers plummeted during World War One and the Depression years, but by the end of the 20th century, they had again reached those levels documented almost a century earlier. The characteristics of immigrants have changed over time and reflect many factors, such as the displacement of people by wars; changes to government policies (e.g., the abolition of slavery); the cycle of economic booms and busts; and the growth of communication, transportation, and economic networks linking people globally. For example, at the turn of the 20th century, Canada's economy was rapidly expanding and immigrants were lured by the promise of good job prospects. Many found employment building the transcontinental railway, settling in the Prairies and in areas of industrial production. Men also greatly outnumbered women immigrants at this time, reflecting labour recruitment efforts targeted at men rather than women, although there was also strong demand for female domestic workers from England, Scotland, and Wales (see figure 5.1). Recruitment strategies included the production of posters and pamphlets (which advertised opportunities for work in every part of Canada) sent to targeted countries.

At the beginning of the 20th century, most immigrants originated in the United States or the United Kingdom. With the implementation of the Dominion Lands Act in 1872, people were offered the opportunity to secure 160 acres of free homestead land in the prairie provinces. This "pull" factor resulted in hundreds of thousands of migrants and immigrants moving to this area between 1867 and 1914. Yet, these people also faced many "push" factors that motivated them to leave their homelands, such as economic hardship, political and religious purges, class discrimination, and overpopulation. A world depression that occurred between 1873 and 1879 also pushed many individuals to leave many European countries and move their families to Canada in order to become homesteaders (Rollings-Magnusson, 2014).

CANADA

WANTS

| HIGH WAGES |
| GOOD HOMES |
| HEALTHY CLIMATE |

DOMESTIC

SERVANTS

TRANS-ATLANTIC   CABLEGRAM.

No   Time

Check

Route Via

JAS. KENT, Manager Telegraphs.

Ottawa, April 8 1908

Send the following Cablegram "Via Commercial Cables," subject to the terms and conditions printed on the back hereof, which are agreed to

To J. Obed Smith

Assistant Superintendent of Emigration.

London, England.

Canadian Government Employment Agents in Ontario alone, have situation for thirteen hundred domestics at once.

W. D. Scott

Superintendent of Immigration.

Please read the conditions on back and sign your name and address thereon for reference

Issued by the Authority of the
Minister of the Interior, Ottawa, Canada.

1908

Figure 5.1: "The Last Best West": Advertising for British Domestic Workers and Photo of British Immigrant Workers, 1900–1916

A bright future awaited British domestics in western Canada, this pamphlet suggested: "Canada has an ever growing excess of males over females of no less a number than 150,000 ... as a matter of fact, a very large percentage [of females] enter the matrimonial state shortly after their arrival, in turn become themselves mistresses requiring help in their household duties."

Source: Canadian Museum of History, Library and Archives Canada. n.d. "Advertising in Britain, 1900–1916." Retrieved from www.historymuseum.ca/cmc/exhibitions/hist/advertis/ads3-06e.shtml; Canadian Museum of History. n.d. "Presenting Newcomers to Canada, 1910–1911."

With World War One, immigration came to an abrupt stop. In the 1920s, large peasant families from the Ukraine were recruited to establish farms in western Canada, since these families had the labour power to acquire full title of the land (Satzewich, 1993). Families also began to arrive from other European countries, such as the Doukhobors and Jewish refugees from Russia. Immigration from Asia was relatively low at this time. During the Depression, most immigrants came from Great Britain, Germany, Austria, and the Ukraine, with only 6% having a non-European origin. After World War Two, the largest number of immigrants was from the United Kingdom, although the number of people from other European countries was increasing.

The time period from the 1970s through the turn of the 21st century represents an era in which immigration numbers fluctuated. The proportion of Canadian immigrants born in Asian countries (including the Middle East) and other regions of the world began to rise, especially during the 1980s, as shown in figure 5.2. Among all recent immigrants who arrived between 2006 and 2011, 56.9% came from Asia (including the Middle East). The second largest group of newcomers was European born, and accounted for 13.7% of all recent immigrants during this time period. The 2011 National Household Survey (NHS) also showed a slight increase in the share of immigration from Africa, the Caribbean, and Central and South America during those five years (Statistics Canada, 2013).

With regard to the top source countries for newcomers, the NHS revealed that the Philippines was the leading country of birth among those who immigrated to Canada between 2006 and 2010 (representing 13.1% of all newcomers), followed by China (at 10.5%), and India (10.4%). Completing the top 10 countries of birth were: the United States, Pakistan, the United Kingdom, Iran, South Korea, Colombia, and Mexico. Most of these immigrants, especially recent arrivals, live in the nation's largest urban centres—91%,

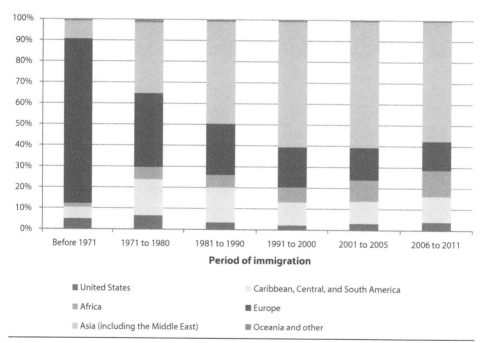

Figure 5.2: Region of Birth of Immigrants by Period of Immigration, Canada, 2011

Note: "Oceania and Other" includes immigrants born in Oceania, Canada, Saint Pierre and Miquelon, and responses not included elsewhere, such as "born at sea."

Source: Statistics Canada. 2013. "Immigration and Ethno-cultural Diversity in Canada." Catalogue no. 99-010-X2011001. Ottawa: Minister of Industry (figure 2). Retrieved June 25, 2016, from www12.statcan. gc.ca/nhs-enm/2011/as-sa/99-010-x/2011001/c-g/c-g02-eng.cfm.

compared with 63.3% of people who were born in Canada. Moreover, the vast majority (94.8%) of Canada's foreign-born population lived in four provinces: Ontario, British
Columbia, Quebec, and Alberta, in 2011 (Statistics Canada, 2013).

As a result of these immigration trends, the visible minority population—especially in
census metropolitan areas—has grown substantially in the last two decades. The three largest
visible minority groups in 2011 were South Asians, Chinese, and Blacks (representing 61.3%
of this population), followed by Filipinos, Latin Americans, Arabs, Southeast Asians, West
Asians, Koreans, and Japanese. As shown in table 5.1, these three largest groups comprise
the top three visible minority groups in the two largest urban areas (Toronto and Montreal),
while Vancouver's top three visible minority groups are Chinese, South Asians, and Filipinos.

Yet, it is important to keep in mind that while these data provide some interesting
and potentially useful information, these basic categories "lump" highly diverse groups into
one category, which is overly simplistic. For example, almost one-third of Blacks reported
multiple ethnic origins. The top ancestral origins were Caribbean and Africa and could include different countries of origin, such as Jamaica, Nigeria, Haiti, Somalia, and Trinidad/
Tobago. There were also Blacks who reported British Isles, Canadian, and French ethnic
origins (Statistics Canada, 2013).

Indeed, more than 200 ethnic origins were reported by all Canadian respondents in
the NHS. In 2011, 57.9% of the population reported one ethnic origin and the remaining
42.1percent reported more than one origin. The most common ethnic origin reported was
"Canadian" (10,563,800) followed by English (6,509,500), French (5,065,700), Scottish
(4,715,000), Irish (4,544,900), and German (3,203,300). Other ethnic groups that surpassed the 1 million mark were: Italian, Chinese, First Nations (North American Indian),
Ukrainian, East Indian, Dutch, and Polish (Statistics Canada, 2013).

STATE POLICIES, IMMIGRATION, AND FAMILY LIFE

Throughout Canadian history, we can find many other examples of how policies have created
both opportunities and difficulties for ethnic families. Historically, one of the major goals of
immigration policy has been to populate the country and contribute to our labour force and
economic production. This is because from the time of Confederation (1867), Canadian families have never been capable of maintaining population growth. However, in spite of efforts
to increase our population of workers, the government has often used specific recruitment
tactics and admission policies to keep out those deemed "undesirable" (Albanese, 2005).

When the supply of American and British immigrants was insufficient at the turn of
the 20th century, Canada began to recruit immigrants from "desirable" parts of Europe.
Oftentimes, the government employed a number of initiatives to recruit and maintain fit, permanent settlers to populate certain regions. For example, in order to attract
Mennonites, an Anabaptist sect committed to a simple life and pacifism, the government
promised them freedom from military service, the right to exercise their religious principles, and the right to avoid swearing the oath of allegiance. Conversely, certain equally

Table 5.1: Visible Minority Population and Top Three Visible Minority Groups, Selected Census Metropolitan Areas, Canada, 2011

	Total Population	Visible minority population		Top 3 visible minority groups
		Number	Percentage	
Canada	32,852,325	6,264,755	19.1	South Asian, Chinese, Black
Toronto	5,521,235	2,596,420	47.0	South Asian, Chinese, Black
Montreal	3,752,475	762,325	20.3	Black, Arab, Latin American
Vancouver	2,280,695	1,030,335	45.2	Chinese, South Asian, Filipino
Ottawa – Gatineau	1,215,735	234,015	19.2	Black, Arab, Chinese
Calgary	1,199,125	337,420	28.1	South Asian, Chinese, Filipino
Edmonton	1,139,585	254,990	22.4	South Asian, Chinese, Filipino
Winnipeg	714,635	140,770	19.7	Filipino, South Asian, Black
Hamilton	708,175	101,600	14.3	South Asian, Black, Chinese

Source: Statistics Canada. 2011. "Immigration and Ethnocultural Diversity in Canada." National Household Survey 2011, Catalogue no. 99-010-X2011001, Table 2. Ottawa: Minister of Industry.

necessary migrant labourers were deemed "undesirable" for permanent settlement, and others were deemed "unfit" (Albanese, 2005).

In this way, policies have often affected people's ability to form and live in family situations of their own choice. Many contend that from the earliest period, the government tried to exclude non-Whites from entering Canada. Yet, when visible minority migrants were needed as ready sources of labour, the government would create transitional "bachelor" communities, as formed among Chinese and East Indian male migrants. Women and families were discouraged from migrating in order to deter the creation of permanent communities. For example, thousands of young Chinese males were allowed to enter the country in the late 19th century, with the provision that they return to their homeland after working on the railway. Thus, the government's goal was to have an abundance of cheap labour to work in dangerous conditions, while also deterring mass migration from Chinese families. Indeed, the Canadian government levied a head tax of $50 per migrant, which was raised to $500 by 1903, such that it made it very difficult for Chinese men to bring their families to Canada. As a result, there were relatively few Chinese families in Canada before 1950 (Albanese, 2005; Satzewich, 1993). This gave rise to Chinese bachelor

Figure 5.3: "The Undesirables," 1910–1911

"Undesirable" immigrants were sent back to their departure points at the expense of the steamship company that brought them. Those barred included people suffering from a range of mental and physical afflictions, as well as prostitutes and their procurers.

Source: Canadian Museum of History. n.d. "Presenting Newcomers to Canada, 1910-1911." Retrieved January 1, 2017, from www.historymuseum.ca/cmc/exhibitions/hist/advertis/ads5-08e.shtml.

communities. These bachelors had to live without the wives, daughters, and mothers who normally animate Chinese communities, in addition to experiencing other challenges related to institutionalized racism and discrimination (Marshall, 2011).

Countless other examples of how government policy made large-scale restrictions in relation to colour, immigration, voting rights, and family life can be found throughout the last century (see Das Gupta, 2000; and Albanese, 2005, for a full overview). However, it should be recognized that overt discrimination against non-traditional, particularly non-White source countries and groups, has technically been abolished. Instead, the emphasis has been on filling gaps in the economy, resulting in the upsurge of immigration from Asian and developing countries. Notably, the point system established in 1967 opened the door for families from non-traditional countries, since it favoured immigrants with skills. As a result, those from middle- and upper middle-class backgrounds are now over-represented in the immigrant population, which has also facilitated the reunion of immigrants with their relatives (Satzewich, 1993).

Yet, research by McLaren and Black (2005) suggests that prevailing discourses that view family-class immigrants (versus economic-class immigrants), especially parents of immigrants, as undesirable burdens on society contribute to the recent decline of sponsored parents' immigration. They note that these discourses are legitimated by the growing influence of human capital theory on the immigration point system. This system establishes very specific criteria for selecting skilled workers and thereby sets up immigrant parents as antagonistic to taxpayer interests, to society, and to their own families. Thus, rather than being neutral, the point system reinforces and produces social exclusions and inequalities. As a result, officially inscribed distinctions between desirable and undesirable immigrants, and the resulting exclusionary policies, continue and have important consequences for families.

For example, McLaren and Black (2005) note that immigration policy does not consider parents and grandparents to be immediate family, despite the fact that they are often essential child-care providers and supports. This means that they need to be sponsored, despite an immigration policy that has dramatically reduced support for sponsorship over the past decade by setting low target levels. A preference for economic immigrants—that is, those who are highly educated and prepared for the labour market—gives priority to economic over family concerns and family traditions. Indeed, in 2012, the largest immigration class was that of economic immigrants, constituting almost half of all total immigration. Skilled workers (i.e., independent applicants admitted through the points system), constituted 29.6% of all economic immigrants (Liodakis, 2015).

Another interesting example of how policies encourage and/or facilitate the migration and reunification of families can be found in a study focused on discretion and decision-making in Canada's immigrant and temporary resident selection system. Based on site visits at 11 Canadian overseas visa offices throughout the world, Satzewich (2014) examines how visa officers make decisions about which spousal relationships are "real" and which ones are "fake" (see box 5.2). As argued by Satzewich, border control measures are as much about immigrant inclusion as they are about immigration exclusion. In short, these and other official and routine practices have far-reaching implications for individuals and for Canadian family life.

Box 5.2: Canadian Visa Officers and the Social Construction of Real Spousal Relationships

Examining how Canadian overseas visa officers make decisions about whether spousal relationships are real or fake offers a somewhat different approach to understanding the facilitation/enforcement paradox noted at the beginning of this paper. Rather than interpreting the paradox as a sign of a hidden anti-immigrant agenda of the state, or the result of racist individuals and/or bureaucratic cultures trying to keep certain categories of people out, this paper suggests that Canadian overseas visa officer decisions are about both immigrant exclusion *and* inclusion. Visa officers attempt to sort applicant pools into those who deserve and those who do not deserve a visa. In the case of spousal sponsorship cases, the former are defined as applicants in real relationships, while the latter are defined as applicants who have entered into relationships where the primary purpose is to gain permanent resident status in Canada.

This sorting process involves trying to decipher the motives for marriage using various flags and typifications of normality. Visa officers handle individual cases in light of a mix of understandings of what is normal or typical for any kind of relationship, for Canadian relationships, and for relationships that are formed and solemnized in culturally unique ways. These three overlapping cultural frameworks inform various typifications of how relationships normally develop. When assessing spousal and partner applications for permanent residence in Canada, visa officers deploy various typifications to assess credibility and socially construct real and fake relationships. These typifications work to both exclude and include applicants from the same national pool.

In the Canadian case, given the importance of processing targets, individual visa offices and officers cannot control the flow of immigrants from the region or country they are working in. Since visa offices and officers must meet processing targets, applicants from the same national pools are differentiated into "deserving" and "undeserving" categories. Rejection rates are undoubtedly higher in some offices than others. This should not necessarily be interpreted, however, to mean that visa officers racially discriminate against applicants, or treat applicants from some countries more harshly than others in order to keep racialized applicants out of Canada. For an individual visa officer, a high rejection rate means they have to work harder and process proportionately more applications in a year to find enough "deserving" cases.

Certainly, more research is needed on how the targets themselves are arrived at and how they are distributed across Canada's visa offices around the world (Simmons, 2010). But interpreting immigration policy or the decisions of visa officers by focusing solely on the mechanisms of exclusion is arguably a one-sided approach to understanding immigration policy and, with it, the job of a visa officer. In enforcing various control measures, these street-level bureaucrats also make decisions that allow individuals to migrate, and to be reunited with their families. Immigration policy and control measures are therefore about both exclusion and inclusion. Examining how visa officers negotiate the exclusion/inclusion dialectic offers an alternative perspective on the enforcement/facilitation paradox outlined above.

Source: Satzewich, V. 2014. "Canadian Visa Officers and the Social Construction of Real Spousal Relationships." *Canadian Review of Sociology* 51: 1–21 (pp. 18–19).

REFUGEE FAMILIES IN CANADA

Contrary to portrayals on media broadcasts and popular opinion, relatively few individuals are admitted to Canada as **refugees**. This term refers to individuals who have been judged by a refugee tribunal (according to the United Nations' definition of refugee) as having a well-grounded fear of persecution or danger on specified grounds. The most common grounds relate to ethnicity, race, religion, and gender. Many of these individuals are in refugee camps operated by the United Nations High Commissioner for Refugees (UNHCR). Canadian officials visit refugee camps and interview those who have applied for acceptance into Canada. It should also be noted that the laws affecting refugees are different from immigration laws.

Since 1979, approximately 20,000–25,000 people per year have been admitted to Canada as refugees. Other individuals arrive in Canada as refugee claimants or asylum seekers who have not yet been adjudged to be refugees, but who come claiming refugee status (Momirov and Kilbride, 2005). Most refugees (70%) originate from non-European countries, specifically conflict zones in Africa, the Middle East, and the Pacific region (Ali et al., 2003), and like other arrivals, they tend to settle in Canada's major urban centres.

Recently there has been considerable attention paid to the ongoing conflict in Syria, which has triggered the worst humanitarian crisis in the world today. As millions of Syrians continue to be displaced due to the conflict in their home country, the Canadian government has committed more than 1 billion dollars in humanitarianism, development, and security assistance in response to this crisis (Government of Canada, 2016). The majority of resettled Syrian refugees who have arrived in Canada are family units consisting of a couple with three or more children. Families tends to be extended in Syria and include not only parents and children, but also grandparents, aunts, uncles, and cousins. It is common for extended families to share a residence and many characterize Syrian society as patriarchal, with the family under the authority of the oldest man (Citizenship and Immigration Canada, 2015).

While numerous opportunities exist in Canada for these families (as illustrated in box 5.3), Syrians face many challenges during their resettlement process. The trauma of war and displacement can create mental health issues, in addition to many other obstacles. Therefore, it is essential that cultural considerations are acknowledged when providing support and services to these families. Notably, culturally appropriate health care; understanding of family dynamics, religious beliefs, and food and dietary restrictions; and language skills training are needed and are important factors in successful integration (Citizenship and Immigration Canada, 2015).

SELECTED ETHNO-CULTURAL FAMILY TRENDS AND ISSUES

It is well established that family patterns are influenced by norms, values, expectations and traditions, immigration history, and language, as well as processes of assimilation

Box 5.3: After Tumult of War, Deaf Syrian Family Finds Peace in Canada

Profoundly deaf, Mohamad al Kawarit did not hear the gun shot ring out as he made his way to prayers at the mosque in Al-Harra, his hometown in southern Syria.

But when he felt a jolt of pain and saw blood gushing from his neck, the 15-year-old knew he had been struck by a bullet. Clutching his neck, he waited for the flashing lights of the ambulance that took him to hospital in Dara'a province.

Mohamad's father and three of his siblings are also deaf. The war in Syria, and that stray round in particular, sent Mohamad and his family to Lebanon. The family ultimately found safety in Canada as government-assisted refugees, stepping off a plane in Calgary, a prairie city of 1.2 million people, in December 2014.

"If I say thank you to the Canadian Government and the Canadian people every day, it would not be enough," says Mohamad's mother, Souad Al Nouri, speaking through an interpreter in the tidy, sofa-lined living room of their new house.

As Souad shares her family's story, her husband and children quietly converse in sign language. Diana, 10, cradles the youngest brother, who has cerebral palsy, in her arms.

For the family of eight, life in Canada is a return to much-needed stability after years spent in mortal danger and flight. In Al-Harra, Souad and her husband, Hassan al Kawarit, ran successful businesses, including a construction company and several bakeries. The children had the support they needed for their disabilities. "Our life in Syria was very good," says Souad.

After the conflict erupted five years ago, the family hoped to remain in al-Harra. "For the first few months, everything was okay," says Souad. But peace did not last, and they fled to another village in Syria.

They tried returning to Al-Harra a few months later, after gathering from news stories that it was safe to go back, but they found their home had been partially destroyed by fire. "No doors, no windows, nothing," recalls Souad.

The family tried to make it habitable by putting plastic sheeting over the windows, but their return proved to be short lived. A few months later, Mohamad was shot, and then militants stormed the town, triggering a hurried evacuation. On the day they fled for the last time, in 2014, 15 people were killed in the melee, Souad recalls.

The family first sought refuge in the Bekaa Valley in Lebanon, where they stayed in a refugee settlement in the town of Saadnayel, before eventually moving into a decrepit apartment. "Our situation got turned upside down," says Souad.

The children were not in school, and the disruption took its toll. "They were like someone in the desert who doesn't know where to go," she said.

The family registered with UNHCR, the UN Refugee Agency, and sought resettlement. When the call came informing them that they had been selected for resettlement to Canada, Souad wept. "I cannot describe the feeling," she says. "I was so happy." Hassan and the children danced for joy. "It was like a birthday party."

Partnering with UNHCR, Canada has resettled more than 26,000 Syrian refugees since November [2014]. Like Souad's family, most are government-assisted refugees who have been initially resettled in 36 communities around the country, where they receive a one-time start-up allowance plus monthly support.

"Resettling refugees is a proud part of Canada's humanitarian tradition," says Nancy Caron, a spokesperson for the government agency Immigration, Refugees and Citizenship Canada. "It demonstrates to the world that we have a shared responsibility to help those who are displaced, persecuted and most in need of protection."

Once government-assisted refugees arrive in Canada, NGOs help them settle in. The Calgary Catholic Immigration Society, or CCIS, found a house for Souad and Hassan to rent on a quiet street in one of the city's most multicultural neighbourhoods. The agency also assisted with furnishing their new place, setting up bank accounts, and helping them enroll in services, including healthcare.

The agency stays in close contact with the family. "We follow up with them until they will be okay," says Ashour Esho, the family's resettlement counsellor with CCIS.

The Al Kawarit family stand on the balcony of their new home in Calgary, where they are starting over under a Canadian Government program to resettle Syrian refugees. © UNHCR/J. May

---

Source: Adapted from Klaszus, J. 2016. "After Tumult of War, Deaf Syrian Family Finds Peace in Canada." *UNHRC-The UN Refugee Agency*, March 21. Available at: unhcr.org/56efaf729.html.

and acculturation (two concepts that were covered in the previous chapter). As such, expectations of appropriate gender and family-related roles, responsibilities, living arrangements, and family practices often vary by ethnic group and immigrant generational status. Preferences for certain kinds of food, music, style of clothing, and the observance of certain religious holidays are commonly associated with specific ethnic groups (e.g., Chinese, Italian, or Indian food and restaurants) and are often passed down to younger generations. Food, for example, links people to one another and to the places where it grows. It also links individuals and families to the memories and countries from where they emigrated and plays an important role in nostalgia, collective memory, and in the creation of diaspora identities, as illustrated in box 5.4.

Box 5.4: Chinese Food and Identity

Just as there are diverse ways of being Chinese, so there are diverse ways of eating. What people eat and where they eat creates boundaries, such as the one around the Jewish and Ukrainian communities described above and also around Chinese and Ukrainian mixed families. What and where you eat signals degrees of taste and ethnic belonging. Joining that group takes time, as does changing from being perceived as a stranger to being someone who is welcomed into the back regions of cafes and other domains that characterize private life. Food is about relationships. Emile Ohnuki-Tierney puts it well:

> Food tells not only how people live but also how they think of themselves in relation to others. A people's cuisine, or a particular food, often marks the boundary between the collective self and the other, for example, as a basis of discrimination against other peoples.

While Ohnuki-Tierney emphasizes how taste discriminates, we can also extend her comments to show how recipes or menus that combine elements from two cultures bridges between those two cultures when the foods are eaten and shared. The "doing" of "authentic" food is amplified when it is produced, eaten, and shared in rural Manitoban settings, where there are usually only a few Chinese people. That hundreds and sometimes thousands of people went to one place to prepare, serve, and eat authentic meals demonstrates the creative power of such gatherings. Events like the annual Decoration Day created social heat and thus, become significant anchors to a shared past. Food—the way it looks, smells, and tastes—mediates memory, connecting people to earlier places and times. Elderly non-Chinese settlers remember the café owners' candy. Chinese Canadian settlers remember the Orange Crush and crispy pork served on Decoration Day. Chinese and Chinese Ukrainian Canadians remember the foods of their homeland through their mothers' recipes for latkes, roast duck, roast pork, and southern Chinese stir-fried beef.

In addition to its strong emotional power, authentic Chinese food is economically valuable. Some people travel long distances to obtain the ingredients to make such food; others have family members who bring the ingredients back from visits to China. People also often drive a half hour or more (which is considered to be quite a long time in rural communities) to privately consume authentic food or to attend community events at which it is served. The way one eats such food is also instructive. Newer immigrants consume rice a couple of times a day, use chopsticks at every meal, and if they drink anything, it is usually a kind of Chinese soup, or tea.

Source: Marshall, A.R. 2011. *The Way of the Bachelor: Early Chinese Settlement in Manitoba.* Vancouver: UBC Press (pp. 133-134).

Yet, as previously discussed in chapter 3, binaries of Western versus Eastern family lifestyles are overly simplistic and gloss over the tremendous diversity and complexity that can exist within each of these categories. Westernized family life styles cultures are often characterized as having a greater emphasis on individualistic pursuits and goals. Conversely, Eastern cultures are noted to have cultural histories and traditions that emphasize family-centredness, the collectivity, extended family, and holistic views of health. Respect for one's elders is based on the notion of filial piety, and can be traced to Confucian, Buddhist, or other religious principles of moral obligation, honour, and respect for one's ancestors.

However, the extent to which these values are embedded in culture (i.e., cultural traditions) and/or are tied to economic issues (e.g., the need for extended families to share a household) requires consideration. Therefore, in keeping with a life-course theoretical perspective and empirical studies, it is important not to over-generalize or to stereotype groups since there can be considerable heterogeneity (diversity in wealth or economic resources, for example) or "social capital" within social groups. Social capital is inherent in the structure of relationships and can be found in strong supportive families and in communities. Further, the quality of family relationships and level of contact are paramount, and they can transcend cultural traditions. There is also a need to consider immigration histories and age-related changes in family behaviours and support at particular transitional points in the lifespan, such as during childhood or old age.

Thus, although it may be fruitful to understand basic cultural differences or inequities across ethnic groups, it should not be assumed that all "ethnics" are the same. This can lead to prejudiced and misguided assumptions or even **racism**, an ideology that regards racial or ethnic categories as natural social or genetic groups. Accordingly, certain groups are associated with social or biological traits that are seen as either inferior or superior. Social groups that commonly report being victims of racism and discrimination are Indigenous, visible minority, and immigrant families. Fortunately, a **critical race theory** (CRT) has recently emerged that focuses on inequalities in the distribution of social goods, such as work, education, and training. These inequalities—in part created by systematic racism and discrimination—occur in the economy, the state, and in civil society. Another value of CRT is that methodically, personal stories and experiences of minorities are treated as facts rather than subjective or biased pieces of information (Liodakis, 2015, Pizarro, 1998).

Immigrant, Visible Minority, and Refugee Families

Many ethnic groups comprise the visible minority population and the immigrant population. Statistics Canada typically includes the following groups in the visible minority population: Blacks, South Asians, Chinese, Koreans, Japanese, Southeast Asians, Filipinos, Arabs and West Asians, Latin Americans, and Pacific Islanders, although members of some of these groups (e.g., Blacks) may originate from many different countries. Moreover, only two-thirds of visible minorities are foreign-born, and there is considerable diversity within this group, as well as the ethnic groups classified as visible minority. Yet, there are a number of worrisome trends with respect to current and future ethnic-related patterns of family life from Statistics Canada (2015) that show that racialized, immigrant, and Aboriginal children are more likely to live in poverty, a topic that will be further discussed in chapter 14. Living in households or families with poor economic resources is particularly likely for immigrant offspring whose ethnic origin is Arabic, Black/Caribbean, Latin/Central/South American, Spanish (born in the Americas), Vietnamese, and/or West Asian.

Recent visible minority immigrants are also more likely to experience a trajectory of long-term disadvantage over the life course, since they tend to leave home and school early, and experience disadvantage in the labour force compared to those born in Canada. There is also concern that many visible minority immigrants (especially women) face discrimination in the labour market, and that their educational qualifications from other countries are not given the recognition they deserve.

As previously mentioned, refugee families can encounter numerous challenges and barriers in their efforts to integrate into Canadian society. Similar to many newcomer families, some of these challenges include language problems, finding employment commensurate with their educational credentials (underemployment), securing affordable and safe housing, cultural loss, mental health problems, the loss of an extended family support system, and, for radicalized groups, racism (Este and Tachble, 2009). Refugees may also have the added challenge associated with having experienced tragedy and trauma including rape, torture, war, persecution, dangerous escapes, witnessing violence, and in some cases, serving as child soldiers (Beiser et al., 1999). Relationships within the family can also change, including situations where family members are absent or role reversal occurs between family members (e.g., between husband and wife, or parent and child).

Sources of Generational Conflict and Solidarity in Immigrant, Visible Minority, and Refugee Families

Generational conflict can occur in immigrant or visible minority families, especially when the older generation is foreign-born and holds traditional norms and values. Many studies find that older individuals (especially immigrant parents) tend to assimilate or acculturate to the new host society. However, they may do so less quickly than their children or grandchildren, which can create intergenerational conflict. Common reasons for disagreement between parents and children are clashing norms and values (e.g., religious differences), schoolwork, peer group influences, and dating (Mitchell, 2005).

Immigrant and visible minority groups can experience social exclusion due to the psychosocial stress of discrimination, which can also contribute to family and health problems. Visible minority youth can also encounter significant challenges coping with the school system. Factors underlying these problems include pressure from their parents to succeed in school (Momirov and Kilbride, 2005), school policies, and teachers' discriminatory attitudes. Moreover, recent studies also show that newcomer immigrant youth are twice as likely to suffer from depression as other individuals aged 35 and older (Beiser, 1999). As a result of some of these pressures, some young people may join peer groups that provide social support but that are destructive. For example, there has been growing concern that many visible minority youth are lured into gang and drug violence.

Furthermore, many elderly immigrant visible minority people experience poverty and do not qualify for pensions. Some must rely on other family members for food and shelter, which can potentially create strain, overcrowding, and dependency issues (Mitchell, 2005). Others may lack both financial and family support, particularly senior women, African men, and single mothers from Africa, Latin America, and the Caribbean. Also, while most visible minority families live in nuclear families, women from Latin America and the Caribbean are more likely to be single parents, which creates a different set of issues (Thomas, 2001).

With respect to refugee families, limited Canadian research has focused mainly on women or children. A notable exception is a study on refugee fathers conducted by Este and Tachble (2009) in Calgary. These researchers conducted in-depth interviews with Sudanese refugee men that focused on their perceptions and experiences as fathers. Major areas of concerns revolved around a perceived loss of cultural background for their children, underemployment, lack of social support, social isolation, gender role changes, the need for greater involvement in parenting, and the discipline of children. For example, one father in the study said he thought there was too much freedom given to children in Canada, "…too much freedom for somebody who does not know what is right and what is bad." This father also thought that this freedom contributed to young people in his community dropping out of school. This was echoed by another father who stated, "When we came to this country things began to change a bit because of the culture of Canadian freedom, and then children can be free, they can do whatever they want and children can even go against the regulations of their families" (quoted on p. 463).

Apart from refugees—who can also immigrate without their families—there are many instances in which nuclear families are forced to live separately across national borders. Ambert (2012) asserts that with more international trade and exchange fuelled by globalization, these kinds of families—often referred to as multi-local or transnational families—have become more commonplace. Consequently, many men and women now cross nation-state boundaries to live and work without their children (in addition to other family members) at the time of settlement, which can present unique family and inter-generational issues. For example, some parents and children may drift apart due to a long and/or unanticipated separation, or children may become resentful for having been left behind.

There is also a growing phenomenon of Asian "astronaut families" in which one or both parents spend much of their time abroad (in Hong Kong or China) while their young adult children are left to complete their education in Canada. Some children are considered "satellites," since they may return to their country of origin after immigration. These experiences can dramatically shape family interactions, identities, and relationships (Waters and Tse, 2013).

Yet, immigrant and visible minority families can also experience high levels of generational solidarity through fresh starts in a new country, the sharing of goals and resources, and the retention of their traditional culture. Sharing a new hope for the future, for instance, can promote family unity and widen a social life that spans borders (e.g., see Shik, 2015). Some ethnic groups may also have the opportunity to become even more institutionally complete, a term that refers to "parallel institutions that either inhibit or serve as alternatives to participation in the broader society" (Rosenberg and Jedwab, 1992). For example, living in a vibrant ethnic enclave or neighbourhood in an urban area with good social and economic opportunities, access to ethnic foods and newspapers, social networks, and religious institutions can help individuals and families to retain and reinforce their ethnic heritage and religious traditions. These conditions can also bridge bonds across generations, strengthen family solidarity, and provide opportunities to experience a familiar and high quality way of life.

FUTURE TRENDS: THE INVISIBILITY OF VISIBLE MINORITIES IN THE FUTURE?

In 2005, Statistics Canada produced a report with the main goal of projecting a portrait of Canadian diversity in 2017. This report produced estimates of the visible minority and immigrant populations and subgroups between 2001 and 2017, based on micro-simulation techniques. Five scenarios were produced based on differing assumptions of immigration, fertility, mortality, and internal migration.

1. The population of visible minority persons in Canada will increase from about 4 million in 2001 to between 6.3 and 8.5 million in 2017. This means that about one in five Canadians would be a visible minority in 2017 compared to one in eight in 2001.

Approximately one in four Canadians would be foreign-born (immigrants). In 2017, about half of all visible minority people will be South Asian or Chinese. Blacks will remain the third largest group. The fastest-growing groups are the West Asian, Korean, and Arab groups, which would more than double over that time period, as seen in figure 5.4.

2.   In 2017, the visible minority population will have a median age of 35.5, about eight years younger than the Canadian population.

3.   Recent immigrant women have higher fertility rates than others. In particular, Black, Arab, and Filipino groups have the highest fertility. Chinese, Korean, Japanese, and West Asian groups have the lowest.

4.   By 2017, between 21% and 25% of the total population of Canada will have mother tongues that are neither English nor French, compared to 17% in 2001. The religions with the fastest growth during this time period will be Islam (145% increase), Hinduism (92% increase), and Sikhism (72% increase).

5.   In 2017, Ontario will have 57% and BC will have 20% of the total visible minority population of Canada. Almost 75% of visible minority people will be living in

Table 5.2: Visible Minority Groups Could Comprise Half the Population of Toronto and Vancouver by 2017

	Number of Visible Minority Persons ('000)		Percent of Total Population	
	2001	2017	2001	2017
Canada	4,038	7,121	13	21
Census metro area				
Toronto	1,753	3,194	37	51
Vancouver	741	1,261	36	49
Montreal	454	749	13	19
Ottawa-Gatineau*	139	316	17	28
Calgary	166	295	17	24
Edmonton	136	211	14	18
Hamilton	64	125	9	15
Winnipeg	84	115	12	16
Windsor	40	97	13	23
Kitchener	45	79	10	15
Rest of Canada	418	679	3	4

*Ontario part only.

Note: Projections are based on the reference scenario, which uses assumptions based on trends observed in the 2001 Census and the preceding years.

Source: Belanger, A., and E.C. Malenfant. 2005. "Ethnocultural Diversity in Canada: Prospects for 2017." Canadian Social Trends, Catalogue no. 11-008-X, (p. 21).

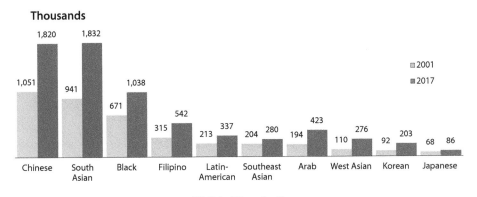

Visible Minority Groups

Figure 5.4: Chinese and South Asians Will Remain the Largest Visible Minority Groups in 2017

Note: Projections are based on the reference scenario, which uses assumptions based on trends observed in the 2001 Census and the preceding years.

Source: Statistics Canada, Catalogue no. 91-541-XIE, cited in Belanger A.and E.C. Malenfant. 2005. "Ethnocultural Diversity in Canada: Prospects for 2017." *Canadian Social Trends*, Catalogue no. 11-008. Ottawa: Minister of Industry (p. 20).

Toronto, Vancouver, and Montreal in 2017. More than half (51%) of the Toronto census metro area will belong to a visible minority group, followed by Vancouver (49%). More than half of Canada's South Asians will be living in Toronto. Montreal's minorities will include Blacks (27%) and Arabs (19%).

Overall, these projections point to a dramatic alteration of the composition of Canada's population as the visible minority population grows faster than the total population. These trends will undoubtedly have a major impact on Canadian family life in the future. They also raise a number of provocative questions about how family life will look, given the relationship between certain ethnic traditions and the adoption of family-related behaviours. A continued adherence to these practices could touch upon many realms such as gender roles, socialization, religious practices, living arrangements, and family support patterns over the life course. Further, an increasing tendency for families to adopt "traditional" behaviour could counter the general movement toward individualization and secularization in our society. It could also pressure governments to revisit the relationship between religion and state, such as occurred during the recent controversy over the use of *sharia* (a law used in some Muslim countries) in civil arbitrations in Ontario dealing with such matters as property, marriage, divorce, and custody, provided that both parties consent (Wente, 2004; see also box 10.4 in chapter 10 for more detail).

SUMMARY

This chapter explores the changing ethnic composition of the Canadian population, with a focus on themes of diversity, continuity, power relations, and social change. It is argued that ethnicity and race are social relations that are rooted in the history of colonialism and associated with the development of capitalism. Moreover, these concepts are not monolithic, but instead represent historically specific socially constructed relations. While many immigrant, visible minority, and refugee families have experienced Canada as a land of new opportunities and hope, barriers to equality have often occurred, and continue to persist. Many of these families have found it challenging to achieve a family of their own choosing as a result of government policies and other systemic barriers. Common problems include discrimination and racism, language difficulties, restrictive employment and housing choices, poverty, and social exclusion. Many non-White immigrant groups were also historically denied the right to vote in local or federal elections, a fundamental right if citizenship.

Within this context, the role of government policy in shaping and constraining family life was reviewed, since it has been critical in creating the ethnic composition of our population, as well as the lived experiences and everyday lives of families. Past mistakes highlight the need for policy makers to carefully examine both the intended and unintended consequences of their policies, a theme that we covered in chapter 3 and that will be further explored in chapter 16).

Government policies raise moral, political, social, and cultural issues about who defines the worth of immigrants and refugees and how policy reflects prevailing discourses. Yet, ironically, with the exception of Indigenous Peoples, everyone who lives in Canada is either an immigrant or a descendant of one. To conclude, future trends with respect to the changing ethnic mosaic of the Canadian family were presented, in recognition of projected patterns and the rapidly increasing "invisibility" of the visible minority population, especially in large urban areas.

QUESTIONS FOR CRITICAL REFLECTION AND DEBATE

1.   Is ethnic identity fluid over time and place? Provide examples from the immigrant and non-immigrant community.
2.   Debate the following: Ethnic youth join gangs as a result of racism and discrimination.
3.   Critically evaluate how immigration policy can marginalize "other" immigrant women and their extended families because of their skin colour, cultural and linguistic characteristics, age, and lack of human capital.
4.   What challenges do immigrant and refugee families face in trying to maintain and reproduce their traditional customs and mores upon their arrival to Canada? How might their area of settlement (i.e., community and neighbourhood) facilitate or hinder this process?
5.   To what extent should the federal government develop policies and programs to redress many of the problems created by earlier policies (e.g., the Chinese head tax)?

GLOSSARY

Critical race theory emphasizes racialized inequalities in the distribution of social goods such as work, education, housing, daycare, the legal system, policing, and other social services.

Ethnic mosaic denotes a rich tapestry of ethnically diverse families whose distinctive cultures give colour and texture to the whole.

Ethnicity refers to the cultural, organizational, and collective values, beliefs, attitudes, and behaviours of individuals who share or identify with a distinct culture or are descendants of those who have shared a distinct culture.

Race is a fluid, socially constructed concept that differentiates (racializes) people on the basis of assumed biological/genetic characteristics.

Racialization refers to a set of social processes and practices through which social relations among people based on biological traits are structured by dominant groups.

Racism is the practice of assuming that racial or ethnic categories are natural, social, or genetic groups associated with social or biological traits that are seen as either inferior or superior.

Refugees are individuals with a well-grounded fear of persecution or danger due to specified conditions related to ethnicity, race, religion, gender, and political affiliation.

Visible minority population is a Statistics Canada classification that refers to those Canadians who are not White, Caucasian, or Aboriginal in their descent and includes: Blacks, South Asians, Chinese, Koreans, Japanese, Southeast Asians, Filipinos, Arabs and West Asians, Latin Americans, and Pacific Islanders.

FURTHER READING

Bauder, H. and J. Shields, (eds.). 2015. *Immigrant Experiences in North America: Understanding Settlement and Integration.* Toronto: Canadian Scholars' Press.
From an interdisciplinary perspective, this original collection of essays explores major themes such as immigration policy; labour markets and the economy; gender, health, and well-being; and food security. Each chapter includes instructive case examples, resources, and questions for critical thought.

Beyer, P., and R. Ramji. 2013. *Growing Up Canadian: Muslims, Hindus, Buddhists.* Toronto: McGill-Queen's Press.

Based on interviews with over 200 young people aged 18 to 26, this book is the first comparative study of religion among young adults of Muslim, Hindu, and Buddhist immigrant families. It offers a fresh and critical approach to understanding religious diversity among second-generation Canadians.

Brewer, C.A., and M. McCabe (eds.). 2014. *Immigrant and Refugee Students in Canada*. Toronto: Brush Publishing.
This volume provides a thorough and wide-ranging analysis aimed at all levels of education. It draws upon the narratives of students and their families, educators, social workers, and other front-line workers. Focus is placed on the challenges that these students face, in addition to common aspects of successful intervention.

Epp, M. 2008. *Mennonite Women in Canada: A History*. Studies in Immigration and Culture 2. Winnipeg: University of Manitoba Press.
This book traces the multifaceted history of Mennonite women in Canada by documenting their experiences as migrants, mothers, missionaries, citizens, and workers. Using a variety of sources, from diaries and letters to memories and oral histories, Epps examines the rich diversity of their settlement experiences.

Man, G., and R. Cohen, (eds.). 2015. *Engendering Transnational Voices: Studies in Family, Work, and Identity*. Waterloo, Ont.: Wilfred Larrier Press.
This provides an examination of the transnational practices and identities of immigrant women, youth, and children in an era of global migration and neoliberalism. Many topics are explored, including: family relations, gender and work, school remittances, caring for children and the elderly, refugee discrimination, and social activism.

Tastsoglou, E., and P.S. Jaya. 2011. *Immigrant Women in Atlantic Canada*. Toronto: Canadian Scholars' Press.
This is an in-depth exploration of immigrant women's experiences in the labour force, the family, and the broader community in Atlantic Canada from a feminist, gender-based perspective that focuses on the intersection of gender with race, ethnicity, and class.

Wright, R.H., Jr., C.H. Mindel, T. Van Tran, and R.W. Habenstein. 2012. *Ethnic Families in America: Patterns and Variations*. Toronto: Pearson Canada.
This edited volume examines the multicultural diversity in the United States. Extensive coverage of historical background, family life styles, traditions, values, and adaptations of 17 ethnic groups is provided.

RELATED WEB SITES

Canadian Council of Refugees is a national, non-profit umbrella organization committed to the rights, protection, and settlement of refugees and other vulnerable migrants in Canada and around the world, www.ccrweb.ca/en/family-reunification.

Canadian Heritage provides information on multiculturalism programs, news releases, publications and links to various Canadian and international organizations, www.pch.gc.ca/eng/1266037002102/1265993639778.

Citizenship and Immigration Canada includes a number of useful resources such as government policies and regulations on immigration, www.cic.gc.ca/english.

Health Canada has a section that deals with immigrant and refugee health. It also provides research publications on numerous topics such as immigrant women, family violence, and older immigrants, www.hc-sc.gc.ca/index-eng.php.

Canadian Race Relations Foundation (CRRF) was established by an act of Parliament in 1991 and aims to eliminate racism in Canada. It provides publications, descriptions of programs, and useful links to other sites, www.crr.ca.

Metropolis is an international network for comparative research on public policy development on migration, diversity, and immigrant integration in cities in Canada and around the world, www.metropolis.net.

REFERENCES

Albanese, P. 2005. "Ethnic Families." In M. Baker (ed.), *Families: Changing Trends in Canada*, 5th ed. (pp. 121–142). Toronto: McGraw-Hill Ryerson.

Ali, M. 2003, with S. Taraban and J. Gill. 2003. "Unaccompanied/Separated Children Seeking Refugee Status in Ontario: A Review of Documented Policies and Practices." Toronto: Joint Centres of Excellence for Research on Immigration and Settlement, CERIS Working paper no. 27.

Ambert, A.M. 2012. *Changing Families: Relationships in Context*, 2nd ed. Toronto: Pearson Education Canada.

Beiser, M. 1999. *Strangers at the Gate: The "Boat People's" First Ten Years in Canada*. Toronto: University of Toronto Press.

Boyd, M., and M. Vickers. 2000. "One Hundred Years of Immigration." *Canadian Social Trends*, Catalogue no. 11-008, Autumn: 2–12. Ottawa: Statistics Canada.

Citizenship and Immigration Canada. 2015. "Population Profile: Syrian Refugees." Retrieved May 27, 2016, from www.cpa.ca/docs/File/Cultural/EN%20Syrian%20Population%20Profile.pdf.

Das Gupta, T. 2000. "Families of Native People, Immigrants, and People of Colour." In N. Mandell and A. Duffy (eds.), *Canadian Families: Diversity, Conflict, and Change*, 2nd ed. (pp. 146–187). Toronto: Harcourt Brace.

Driedger, L. 2003. *Race and Ethnicity: Finding Identities and Equalities*, 2nd ed. Don Mills: Oxford University Press.

Este, D.C. and A. Tachble. 2009. "Fatherhood in the Canadian Context: Perceptions and Experiences of Sudanese Refugee Men." *Sex Roles* 60: 456–466.

Government of Canada, Global Affairs. 2016. "Canada's Response to the Conflict in Syria." Retrieved May 27, 2016, from www.international.gc.ca/development-developpement/humanitarian_response-situations_crises/syria-syrie.aspx?lang=eng.

Liodakis, N. 2015. "Ethnic and Race Relations." In L. Tepperman and P. Albanese (eds.), *Sociology: A Canadian Perspective*, 4th ed., (pp. 260–285). Toronto: Oxford University Press.

Marshall, A.R. 2011. *The Way of the Bachelor: Early Chinese Settlement in Manitoba*. Vancouver: UBC Pres.

McLaren, A., and T. Lou Black. 2005. "Family Class and Immigration in Canada: Implications for Sponsored Elderly Women." Research on Immigration and Integration in the Metropolis, Working Paper Series, no. 05-26. Vancouver: Vancouver Centre of Excellence.

Mitchell, B.A. 2005. "Canada's Growing Visible Minority Population: Generational Challenges, Opportunities, and Federal Policy Considerations" (pp. 51–62). In *Canada 2017: Serving Canada's Multicultural Population for the Future*, Policy Forum Discussion Papers. Gatineau: The Multiculturalism Program, Department of Canadian Heritage.

Momirov, J., and K.M. Kilbride. 2005. "Family Lives of Native Peoples, Immigrants, and Visible Minorities." In N. Mandell and A. Duffy (eds.), *Canadian Families: Diversity, Conflict, and Change* (pp. 87–111). Toronto: Thomson Nelson.

Pizzaro, M. 1998. "Chicana/o Power! Epistemology and Methodology for Social Justice and Empowerment in Chicana/o Communities." *Qualitative Studies in Education* 11: 57–80.

Rollings-Magnusson, S. 2014. "Steerage, Cattle Cars, and Red River Carts: Travelling to the Canadian Western Prairies to Homestead, 1876–1914. *Journal of Family History* 39: 141–174.

Rosenberg, M.M., and J. Jedwab.1992. "Institutional Completeness, Ethnic Organizational Style and the Role of the State: The Jewish, Italian, and Greek Communities of Montreal." *Canadian Review of Sociology and Anthropology* 29: 266–287.

Satzewich, V. 2014. "Canadian Visa Officers and the Social Construction of "Real" Spousal Relationships." *Canadian Review of Sociology* 51: 1–21.

Satzewich, V. 1993. "Migrant and Immigrant Families in Canada: State Coercion and Legal Control in the Formation of Ethnic Families." *Journal of Comparative Family Studies* 24: 315–338.

Shik, A.W.Y. 2015. "Transnational Families: Chinese-Canadian Youth between Worlds." *Journal of Ethnic and Cultural Diversity in Social Work* 24: 71–86.

Statistics Canada. 2005. "Population Projections of Visible Minority Groups, Canada, Provinces, and Regions, 2001–2017." Catalogue no. 91-541-XIE. Ottawa: Minister of Industry.

Statistics Canada. 2013. "Immigration and Ethnocultural Diversity in Canada." Catalogue no. 99-010-X2011001. Ottawa: Minister of Industry.

Statistics Canada. 2015. "Aboriginal Statistics at a Glance," 2nd ed. Catalogue no. 89-645-x2015001. Ottawa: Minister of Industry.

Thomas, D. 2001. "Evolving Family Living Arrangements of Canada's Immigrants." *Canadian Social Trends* 61 (Summer): 16–22.

Waters, J.L., and J.K. Tse. 2013. "Transnational Youth Transitions: Becoming Adults in Vancouver and Hong Kong." *Global Networks* 13: 535–550.

Wente, M. 2004. "Life under Sharia in Canada? "Retrieved January 25, 2005, from www.youme-works.com/sharia_canada.html.

Woolley, F. 2013 (June 10). "'Visible Minority:' A Misleading Concept that Ought to Be Retired." The Globe and Mail, retrieved May 19, 2016 from www.theglobeandmail.com/opinion/visible-minority-a-misleading-concept-that-ought-to-be-retired/article12445364.

CHAPTER 6

More than a Labour of Love: Gender, Unpaid Work, and the Cult of Domesticity

LEARNING OBJECTIVES

In this chapter you will learn that ...

- contemporary patterns of work reflect transformations in the economy and the ideologies of motherhood and gender
- unpaid work, such as housework and child care, is a largely invisible, undervalued shadow economy, although critical to the functioning and well-being of society
- patterns of domestic work continue to be highly gendered despite technological advancements, increased male participation, and gains made by women
- the cult of domesticity, with related notions of ideal womanhood, continues to be powerful and pervasive throughout society and solidifies a gender-based power structure
- many families struggle with balancing their family and home life

INTRODUCTION

Imagine a situation in which a full-time housewife and mother attends a corporate social function with her husband. She is asked by one of his co-workers, "Do you work?" What do you think would be her most likely response? Many of us would assume that she would reply with some degree of ambivalence, such as, "Well, I stay at home with my children." Yet, in reality, she does work (and probably more hours than her partner), since when you actually detail what has to happen within any given household to make it run smoothly, it is striking just how much **family work** must actually be done. Indeed, work performed for wages, no matter how menial, is almost always regarded as "work," whereas work performed in the home is often not regarded as real work since it is generally taken for granted and invisible.

As you will learn in this chapter, domestic labour is "work" and more than "a labour of love" (Luxton, 1980). It is also highly valuable to families and society—so valuable that the economy would collapse in its absence (Wilson, 1986). It will also be shown that the people who perform most of the **unpaid work** are women and that they provide a crucial service to society by physically and emotionally nurturing the next generation of workers. In fact, Salary.com has valued the "Mom job" or "Mom's market value" at an annual salary of \$143,102, which is well over the average pay of a full-time male worker. This salary encompasses pay for the time that mothers spend performing 10 typical job functions for their families, such as child care, errands, cleaning, laundry, cooking, transportation, and bill paying (Mom.salary.com, 2016). In light of these issues, this chapter will explore the changing and ideological meanings, practices, and work roles of women and men in relation to paid and unpaid labour. Moreover, given men's increasing participation in unpaid work, we will examine the changing division of labour with respect to gendered processes.

PATTERNS IN LABOUR FORCE PARTICIPATION AND THE "NEW ECONOMY"

The changing economic role and decision-making power of women is one of the most significant changes in the lives of families over the past century. This transformation is reflected in popular culture and in changes in labour-force participation rates. For example, many of us have seen reruns of two very popular 1950s TV shows called "Leave It to Beaver" and "I Love Lucy," created in an era when it was not normative for married women to work outside the home. While "the Beav's" mother was a seemingly happy housewife, a repeated theme on "I Love Lucy" was Lucy trying to trick her husband, Ricky, into allowing her to work in the paid labour market, since she was totally dependent on him for money and status. In one episode, Ricky spanks her (he puts her over his knees and hits her on the buttocks) because she had bought some furniture without his permission. Afterwards, he promptly returns the furniture to the store. Ironically, Lucille Ball was the majority owner of and the power behind the company that produced the show she and her husband starred in (Liazos, 2004).

Although women have always worked and a proportion of them has always worked outside the home, female labour force participation has risen sharply over time. The greatest changes began to occur in the late 1970s, when, for the first time, large numbers of married women, including mothers, entered the paid labour force (see figure 6.1). In 1931, only 3.1% of married women had paid jobs, in contrast to 45% of those who were single, divorced, separated, or widowed. But since 1984, married women have been more likely than single women to be in the paid labour force (Crompton and Vickers, 2000). By 2003, 80% of married women worked outside the home, a pattern that has persisted over the past decade. Yet, variations in participation are found based on socio-economic factors such as family size, weekly wages of husbands, and immigrant status (Morissette and Galarneau, 2016).

Several reasons are cited for this striking socio-demographic shift. Economic growth in the post-war decades saw a rise in available jobs. The growth of the service sector and public service also expanded opportunities in "supportive" areas such as nursing, teaching, clerical, and secretarial work, jobs that conformed to the workplace and roles that were historically associated with the home (Ranson, 2005). Furthermore, Baker (2001a) notes that the cost of living increases of the 1960s necessitated two incomes. This was partly due to the economic growth that was accompanied by the availability of new products and the rise of a consumer-oriented culture. It was also a consequence of changes in thinking about how people should be rewarded for their work. Before World War Two, men's wages were usually based on their family status, with increases awarded following marriage and the birth of children. During the 1960s and 1970s, unions, professional associations, and feminist groups challenged the lack of pay scales based on individual merit. It was also

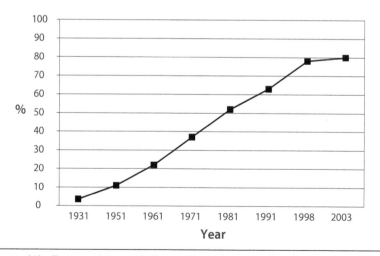

Figure 6.1: Percentage of Canadian Women in the Paid Labour Force, 1931–2003

Source: Statistics Canada. 2003. "Labour Force Historical Review." Catalogue no. 71F0004XCB. Ottawa: Minister of Industry.

argued that a "family wage" often needed to be earned by more than one person, given changes in the new global economy.

Changing ideas about women's roles in society also contributed to the rise in their labour force participation. Women continued to gain political rights throughout the 20th century (e.g., they were allowed to vote in a federal election for the first time in 1921). Also fuelled by the feminist movement, access to paid work, employment equity, and higher education became more available, as well as the right to take maternity leave and then return to paid work. Dramatic improvements in birth control also occurred when "the pill" was legalized in 1969, the year after Pierre Elliott Trudeau became prime minister (between 1961 and 1969, it could be prescribed legally only to regulate a woman's menstrual cycle). The increasing tendency for women to remain in paid employment after they had children also contributed to these new patterns (Baker, 2001a; McLaren and McLaren, 1997; Ranson, 2005).

The demands of the new economy also played a role in women's labour force participation. After the 1970s, the service sector expanded, a large segment of which offered jobs in the retail, hotel, and restaurant industry. Whereas in 1951, these jobs made up only 18% of the labour force, by 1995, they had grown to 37% (Glenday, 1997). While men were more likely to have **standard employment relationships** (that is, continuous full-time employment with the same on-site employer for most of their working lives), many of these positions were (and continue to be) held by women. However, these jobs tend to be less secure and well paid, be part-time, do not provide any health or pension benefits, and ultimately contribute to poverty. In 2011, approximately one out of five of all Canadian workers aged 15 and over were employed part-time—28% of employed women and 12.1% of employed men. Although some women tend to choose part-time work in order to accommodate family responsibilities, a significant proportion would prefer full-time jobs (Ambert, 2006). For example, in table 6.1 we see that among women aged 25 to 44 (those most likely to have young children), 34.4% report that they work part-time because they also care for children, compared to only 3.5% of men in the same age range.

Yet, statistics on unpaid work mask another important type of kin or domestic work termed "spousal career support" (Haas, 1999). This refers to a situation where a wife or partner is not formally employed but is very actively involved in supporting the career of her partner. For example, wives may be unpaid "support," "auxiliary," or "enabler" workers in their husbands' careers. This may entail doing some of the same work that the husband is doing or work that would otherwise be hired out by his business, such as bookkeeping, scheduling, or maintaining an office. Wives may also provide emotional support when times are tough, as well as other types of enabling assistance, such as volunteering or entertaining their husbands' colleagues in order to bring prestige to their work reputation (Seccombe and Warner, 2004). They may also run their own home businesses in order to better accommodate their family and work roles, including their husbands' careers.

Furthermore, some women may find themselves in complex marriage contracts in which they engage in heavy household labour or work that extends to a wide variety of activities. For example, Machum (2002) documents the situation of farm wives who

Table 6.1: Reasons for Part-Time Work by Sex, Ages 25 to 44, 2011

	Total	Males	Females
Own illness	2.8	4.5	2.2
Caring for children	26.5	3.6	34.4
Other personal/family responsibilities	3.5	1.9	4.1
Going to school	11.8	20.5	8.8
Personal preference	15.1	15.2	15.1
Other voluntary	3.4	5.3	2.7
Other*	36.9	49.0	32.6
Total employed part-time (thousands)	928.9	238.6	690.3
% Employed part-time**	12.4	6.1	19.5

*Includes business conditions and those unable to find full-time work

**Expressed as a percentage of total employed

Source: Adapted from Statistics Canada. 2011. *CANSIM Table 282-0014* and *CANSIM Table 282-0001*. Minister of Industry. Retrieved January 31, 2010, from www5.statcan.gc.ca/cansim/a26?lang=eng&retr Lang=eng&id=2820014&&pattern=&stByVal=1&p1=1&p2=-1&tabMode=dataTable&csid and from www. statcan.gc.ca/tables-tableaux/sum-som/l01/cst01/labor63a-eng.htm.

perform a triple day of work compared to their urban counterparts' double day. These wives work at jobs off the farm, directly on the farm for production, and do the reproductive work of child-bearing and child-rearing, as well as the domestic chores. These domestic activities might include growing, canning, and freezing vegetables, and raising animals such as chickens, tasks that subsidize the farm unit by reducing the cash needs of the family. Yet, state policy has tended to reinforce the inequity of their situation by treating this labour as if it's not "real work," since it has traditionally been considered a domestic service to the husbands.

UNPAID WORK, THE SHADOW ECONOMY, AND THE IDEOLOGY OF SEPARATE SPHERES

While paid work is easy to identify and define, Beaujot (2000) and Luxton (1997) observe that the concept of unpaid work involves a diversity of meanings and forms, making it difficult to measure (see box 6.1). The work that goes into creating a special family occasion—such as baking a birthday cake, for instance—can be seen as having no special monetary value because it comes with no monetary reward. It can also be viewed as a form of love, enjoyment, or caring work that has strong sentimental value. Or it can be perceived as a type of drudgery that is valued as part of the material that "makes family."

Although there is a lack of consensus as to what should constitute unpaid work, many individuals and organizations have tried to give it a monetary value by estimating its replacement or fair market value (i.e., what these services would cost to purchase if someone were

Box 6.1: Measuring Unpaid Work

Meg Luxton, author of the classic work *More than a Labour of Love: Three Generations of Women's Work in the Home* (Toronto: Women's Press, 1980), has examined the ways in which unpaid work is measured and valued, as well as the implications for women, families, and any social policies based on them. Below is an excerpt from a journal article based on Luxton's research that which highlights the difficulty in measuring unpaid work:

> In contrast to paid employment, where the division of labour and the hours of work are clearly (and usually contractually) known, domestic labour is task-oriented, and the tasks involved can vary significantly in the amount of time they take each time they are done and in the frequency with which they are done. Because it is an informal work process that is often done alone, with no standards regulated and enforced by an employer, and because it encompasses the activities of making a home and caring for the people who live there, domestic labour is difficult to measure. Where restaurant workers may be told exactly what motions to use and how much time to spend producing a drink for a customer…, making a cup of tea at home may vary quite a bit each time, so that a respondent may be unable to give anything more accurate than a rough guess … Because it is unregulated, people doing domestic labour have no reason to pay close attention to the amount of time tasks take, and they often underestimate time spent in familiar activities. They may be relatively unaware of even doing some tasks, either because they are so automatic, like locking the door at night, or because they do not really feel like work—for example, when a woman associates preparing a meal with time-consuming effort and so dismisses the act of preparing cereal, milk, and toast (Luxton, 1980, p. 142).

Source: Luxton, M. 1997. "The UN, Women, and Household Labour: Measuring and Valuing Unpaid Work." *Women's Studies International Forum* 20: 431–439 (p. 434).

hired to perform them). For example, it is estimated that in Canada, unpaid work is worth up to $319 million in the money economy, or 41% of the GDP (gross domestic product). Globally, the numbers skyrocket to $11 trillion US (Waring, 2006; OXFAM.org, 2016).

It has taken many years for governments to measure the hours dedicated to unpaid work. The 1996 Canadian Census was the first to collect data on unpaid work in response to mounting pressure that women's contributions to society were overlooked and devalued (see box 6.2). The collection of these data marked a major breakthrough for feminists across the country and provided an example for other countries around the world to follow. Statistics Canada now measures work that is not paid (not including volunteer work) by dividing it into three categories: housework, care of children, and care and assistance for seniors. Yet, although unpaid work is increasingly recognized as critical to the functioning and well-being of our society, many critical theorists and feminists argue that much unpaid work remains gendered and is taken for granted, invisible, and undervalued.

However, Doucet (2014) argues that we need to examine not only gender differences in paid and unpaid work, but also how ethnicity and class intersect with gender. Therefore, we must ask ourselves which women and which men are most affected. For example, Indigenous women and ethnic minority women are doubly disadvantaged because they are faced with inequalities in the labour market while still taking on extra shifts of unpaid work. Moreover, there is an increasing tendency for middle-class families with ample financial resources to rely on other lesser-paid women (e.g., nannies and housekeepers from countries such as the Philippines) for domestic work and child care. Paying others to perform these tasks ultimately passes on women's traditional domain from one group of women to another, thus complicating and hardening the boundaries that exist around gender and caring work.

It is further suggested that an **ideology of separate spheres** operates in the designation of paid activity in the public sphere of work or the formal economy, such that it is perceived as "real work." Whereas this work is highly valued (and enumerated), activities pursued in the private domestic sphere—activities that reproduce, support, and sustain others—are usually overlooked and not counted in labour force statistics or other economic indicators. As a result, patterns of normative thought or social ideology obscure the extent and value of these contributions. And since women perform most of these activities, they are particularly disadvantaged.

Box 6.2: The Canadian Census and Unpaid Work

Debate over the devalued perception of domestic work created quite a stir in Canada a few years back. In 1991, a Canadian housewife took issue with this item in the census questionnaire: "How many hours did you work in the last week, not including volunteer work, housework, [home] maintenance or repairs?" (Smith, 1996). She had run a household for 19 years, raising three children in the process, and she was furious that her hard work was considered irrelevant. So she refused to fill out the questionnaire—a crime, according to Canadian law. Under threat of prosecution, she embarked on a protest campaign, which eventually drew in women from all over the country. She formed a group called the Canadian Alliance for Home Managers, which threatened to boycott the next census if unpaid work remained uncounted. Five years later, Canada became the first country in the world to account in its national census for the hours spent performing household labour and child care without pay.

Source: Newman, D.M. and Grauerholz, L. 2002. *Sociology of Families*, 2nd ed. Thousand Oaks, California: Pine Forge Press (p. 310).

Box 6.3: Unpaid Domestic and Care Work

Across all countries, women carry out the majority of unpaid domestic and care work, on average 2.5 times the amount that men do. This includes activities such as cooking, cleaning, washing clothes, caring for dependents, and fetching water and firewood—work that is essential to the well-being and health of individuals, families, and economies, and for reproducing the labour force. However, it is not included in traditional measures of the economy, and often economic policies fail to recognize or invest in it, making inequalities worse. Research shows that poorer women tend to spend more of their time on unpaid care work than richer women, and in countries with higher levels of economic inequality, the difference is even wider. Even by conservative estimates, the time women spend on unpaid care work can be valued at $10 trillion a year.

Women's unequal responsibility for unpaid care work is a key determinant in the gendered nature of economic inequality. It creates "time poverty," limiting women's choices and the time they have available for other work, participation in public life, and rest or leisure time. It is also a strong contributory factor in women's lower rate of participation in the labour force, concentration in part-time work, and lower wages. In South Asia, the gender pay gap increases from 14% to 35% for women living in households with children. And yet, when unpaid care work is added to paid work, women consistently put in more hours than men or the same hours of total work that men do.

Inequalities in the share of unpaid care work are particularly stark in South Asia. In Bangladesh, for example, national time use surveys show that women spend on average 3.6 hours a day on unpaid care and domestic work, compared to 1.4 hours for men. In Pakistan, women spend 4.3 more hours per day than men on this work. Oxfam's research in Bangladesh has also shown that women spend less time on self-care and sleeping than men. In focus group studies, women reported an 84-hour work week, 16% more time spent working than men's 70 hours a week. The group estimated that women are paid for 31% of their work hours while men are paid for 90% of theirs. Although women are spending equal or more hours than men working, the majority of this time is not paid and goes unrecognized. As one participant noted:

> My daughter-in-law does most of the household chores with the assistance of [my] younger granddaughter, but we never asked my son to share household chores because it's our duty to take care of everyone.

Source: Oxfam International. 2016. "Underpaid and Undervalued: How Inequality Defines Women's Work in Asia." Retrieved June 16, 2016, from www.oxfam.org/sites/www.oxfam.org/files/file_attachments/ib-inequality-womens-work-asia-310516.pdf (pp. 7–8).

It is also asserted that women's greater participation in unpaid work results in a state of "lesser citizenship" or marginalization, such that they are more likely to live in poverty and have their own health compromised (Angus, 1994). For example, full-time stay-at-home mothers may suffer from low self-esteem because their tremendous social contributions are devalued. Also, since they receive no money for this work, many must also take on paid work, which can be highly stressful. However, it is also recognized that many benefits in unpaid work outweigh monetary gain. Taking time to raise one's own children, for instance, is an experience that many women find thoroughly rewarding and satisfying.

From the Washboard and Broom to Kenmore and Hoover: The Evolution of Housework over Time

The role of homemaker is commonly described as a woman's "traditional role" in society, yet this is a misperception, since it was only during a relatively short time period (from about 1920 to 1960) that most married women were, or wanted to be, full-time housewives. Indeed, it was not until the middle of the 20th century that the word "housework" came into existence. During this era, most households had some labour-saving appliances, such as washing machines, vacuum cleaners, and refrigerators. Prepared food, including canned food, was usually available, saving many hours of preparation time. For the first time in history, women could spend time on child care and household management (Eshleman and Wilson, 2001). Prior to the advent of labour-saving devices, housework was physically demanding and labour-intensive. For example, swollen joints, sprained wrists, skin rubbed raw, and eternally chapped hands were some of the "joys" of doing a heavy wash on washboards and in tubs and wringing clothes by hand (Horsfield, 1997).

At the turn of the 19th century, most Canadian families lived in rural areas and relied on farming or a combination of paid employment (e.g., lumbering or mining) and farming. A strong sense of interdependence characterized pre-industrial family life, and family members worked together to produce much of what they needed. During industrialization and urbanization, many families were drawn away from rural life and into cities. Women continued the time-consuming and physically taxing work of feeding, clothing, and caring for family members. However, whereas on the farm many of these activities, albeit still gendered, were shared, household jobs in the city increasingly became a woman's sole duty (Wilson, 1986). In short, industrialization minimized women's involvement in the market economy and "converted them into dependent homemakers, with their home-based work confined to the domestic realm" (McDaniel and Tepperman, 2004: 240).

"Housework" and "housewife" became synonymous by the middle of the 20th century, and cultural ideologies supported the view that women were naturally suited for housework and motherhood. This created a **cult of domesticity**. As Eshleman and Wilson (2001: 69) note, "these jobs became thought of as part of what women *were*, not what they *did*."

Advertising industries played an influential role in reinforcing a traditional division of labour in the home. Magazines were strongly affected by the growth of these industries and began to actively promote consumption; the model or Stepford housewife and the

Figure 6.2: Kellogg's Pep Cereal Ad, 1930s

Source: Miller, H. 2014. "Research Project." Milwaukee Institute of Art & Design. Retrieved June 16, 2016, from www.sites.google.com/site/haleymillermiad/home/ah213/research-project.

immaculate home, prominently featuring the latest in home appliances. These new devices also fed into the increasing paranoia about domestic cleanliness that emerged in the early decades of the 20th century. This "scientization" of housework also occurred in response to a better understanding of germs and disease, improved sanitation, and attention to hygiene (Horsfield, 1997; McDaniel and Tepperman, 2004; Wilson, 1986).

Ironically, the term "labour-saving device" turned out to be an oxymoron. Although these devices altered the nature of work and made it less physically taxing on some levels, many sources document that they have not dramatically reduced the overall amount of time spent on housework. It also caused housekeeping standards to go up. With respect to washing machines, some studies show that the time devoted to laundry actually increased over time. In many pioneer or pre-industrial households, for instance, laundry was done only four times per year (Eichler, 1983). It is purported that time usages have risen because machines make it possible to have clean sheets once (or twice) a week if we so choose, to do laundry daily, to wear clothes once—all practices that would have been unheard of in previous times.

Similarly, vacuum cleaners allow us to achieve dust-free wall-to-wall carpets, but when taken on regularly and seriously, vacuuming is just as time-consuming as sweeping floors and beating rugs was for earlier generations. According to an article in *Ladies' Home Journal* in 1930, "Because we housewives of today have the tools to reach it, we dig every day after the dust that grandmothers had left to a spring cataclysm" (cited in Horsfield, 1997: 136).

The Changing Nature and Perceptions of Child Care

Child care, which is often subsumed under the label "housework," has also changed in dramatic ways. Up until the 1970s, women had more children (and usually at an earlier age) at shorter intervals than they do now. In other words, we have moved from baby boom to baby bust. Moreover, an increasing number of preschool children receive some form of child care, defined by Statistics Canada as care not from their mother, father, or guardian. Slightly more than half (53%) of all Canadian children aged four and younger are in some form of child care, with the majority regularly using this care. Parents primarily rely on three types of arrangements: daycare centres (33%), home daycares (31%), or private arrangements (28%) such as care from a relative. Rates also differ by province; for example, rates of child care are highest in Quebec and lowest in Manitoba (Statistics Canada, 2014).

This trend represents a shift in social attitudes toward women's work, since there had been a long-standing assumption that children were "best off at home, looked after by their mothers." In fact, daycare centres were established only when they were seen to benefit society and to accommodate the need for mothers to join the paid workforce (Ward, 2002: 263).

Despite the greater need for and availability of child-care services, many Canadians complain that our current system of daycare is ineffective. Public concerns often focus on long waiting lists, a lack of regulation standards, few options for parents in non-standard employment (e.g., shift work) or with special-needs children, and inadequate government subsidization. Sitter care, for instance, is unregulated by any level of government, yet it remains the most prevalent type of care for employed parents. And while since the 1960s, governments have subsidized child-care spaces for low-income and single-parent families, there are often insufficient spaces for eligible families, and two-parent families with high incomes must pay the full cost. A notable exception is Quebec, which, unlike other provinces, offers heavily subsidized child care for all parents who need it. In 2016, the basic cost was only $7.55 per day for each child for a family whose net income was $50,545 or less.

Many advocacy groups and organizations (e.g., Code Blue) assert that we need a universal early-childhood education and care system that is available to all parents, regardless of their work status, income, ethnicity, or ability/disability. A national, universal system would entail federal leadership, and would be a central election issue. Legislation would be required to set out the principles of high-quality, affordable, public and non-profit services that meet both parents' and children's needs. Yet, other pro-family conservative groups (e.g., REAL Women of Canada) do not support the concept of a universally available, government-subsidized daycare, which they view as an imposed plan of institutional care for children. They argue that parents should be able to more freely choose the kind of care they need. In particular, they support the idea of direct payments to the family. This would provide the flexibility of using child-support monies for a parent to stay home, or spending it on daycare, whether government- or community-operated, private (such as a nanny or a relative), or a combination of both.

Box 6.4: REAL Women of Canada: What to Do about Childcare—REALity

Everybody knows that babies and toddlers are better cared for at home by their mothers. But what about mothers who have to work and have no family member to help them out? How can their child-care problem be solved?

This issue can be better understood by comparing Finland's approach to child care to that of Sweden. Finland provides financial support to parents, either through a home care allowance or a subsidized child-care system. About half of Finnish parents choose the home care allowance. This may explain why Finland is consistently one of the top nations in education in Europe.

Sweden, on the other hand, provides no choice—only a government-subsidized child-care system—i.e., institutional child care. A full 92% of all children in Sweden aged 18 months to five years are in daycare, which costs the government $20,000 annually per child. Swedish taxes are among the highest in the world, and the tax system is designed to make both parents seek employment in the paid workforce.

Providing Swedish parents with only one system may be contributing to long-term harm for children. In 2007, a Swedish study found that parenting ability decreased with the amount of time children spent in daycare. According to Jonas Himmelstrand, a business consultant and founder of the Swedish Mireja Institute, Sweden has some of the worst behaviour and discipline problems in European schools due to the decreasing psychological health of its youth. Girls aged 15 to 19 have experienced a 30% increase in mental health problems. Academic performance in Sweden has plummeted. This is ironic, since child care is supposed to produce academic achievers. Tragically, if children are kept for long hours in child care, parents do not develop the necessary confidence to raise them. According to Mr. Himmelstrand, people's parental instincts decrease, and parents lack the ability to set limits and sense their children's needs. Children and parents become alienated. Children do not develop a psychological attachment to their parents; instead, since they are being raised in large groups of their peers, they look to these peers for approval.

Mikhail Gorbachev was right in his book *Perestroika: New Thinking for Our Country and the World* (1988) when he stated that:

> Perhaps the breakdown in Russian society, with its prevalence of alcoholism, divorce, abortion, etc., may be due to the separation of young children from their mothers in daycare at too early an age.

WHAT SHOULD BE DONE?

We know that children do best in a family environment of warmth, love, and happiness. Only parents can judge how their children's needs can be understood and best provided for. Child-care decisions must be made by parents, without pressure from those with political agendas and ideological fantasies. Direct child-care payments to parents is the best and most positive solution. In Canada, this was the policy of the former Conservative government. Prime Minister Trudeau has promised to increase benefits for middle-class families, which he defines as those earning up to $150,000 annually. This indicates how little Mr. Trudeau, with his inherited wealth, knows or understands actual middle-class families and their financial situation. For example, according to Statistics Canada, in 2013 a family of two adults with or without children had an average annual income of only $84,080.00. Nevertheless, if Trudeau follows through on his child benefit policy and gives payments directly to parents, it will likely be one of the few sensible economic decisions he makes.

Source: REAL Women of Canada 2015. "What to Do about Childcare." *REALity*, XXXIV(12): 4–5. Retrieved June 17, 2016, from www.realwomenofcanada.ca/what-to-do-about-childcare-reality.

Furthermore, many would assume that the trend toward having fewer children and the growing popularity of daycare translate to a reduction in this type of domestic work. However, many studies find that the nature of child care has altered and the time spent on each child has expanded. This is partly because mothers have been increasingly advised by experts about the crucial and extensive nature of their parenting activities. Consequently, women spend more time keeping their children's teeth clean,

> **Box 6.5:** Code Blue: Child Care in Canada by 2020—A Vision and a Way Forward
>
> It's a May morning in 2020. High-quality early childhood education and child care (ECEC) has become a reality for most parents across Canada's six time zones. In Joe Batt's Arm on Fogo Island, Newfoundland, a nutritious lunch is being served to the toddlers at the new early childhood centre in the school. In the small town of Lac-Etchemin, Quebec, and in suburban Markham, Ontario, home child-care providers arrive at early childhood hubs to meet with their networks while the children enjoy outdoor activities. In Winnipeg, a stay-at-home mom with a new baby arrives at nursery school with her three-year-old daughter, while at Haida Gwaii's Skidegate Children's Centre, an educator greets the First Nations parents and children as they arrive.
>
> ECEC programs in each of these communities have unique features but they share many common characteristics. Although there are still waiting lists, parents across Canada know that a space will be available before too long. Substantial service expansion means that all parents—whether or not in the paid workforce—can now find a space. Sustained public operational/base funding to services means fees are much lower than before and affordable. Under the new Canada-wide policy framework, provinces, territories and Indigenous communities receive federal funds. Each has a well-worked-out long-term plan with expansion targets. To meet them, provincial/territorial officials work closely with the federal and local governments, school authorities, other service providers, early childhood educators, and parent/community groups.
>
> *Source:* Adapted from Child Care Advocacy Association of Canada (CCAAC). 2014. "Child Care in Canada by 2020: A Vision and a Way Forward." Retrieved June 17, 2016, from www.ccaacacpsge.files.wordpress.com/2014/11/visionchildcare2020nov3eng.pdf

driving their children around, making their beds and lunches, and worrying about the emotional consequences of their toilet-training techniques, reward systems, or sugar intake (Armstrong and Armstrong, 1984; Luxton, 1980). And in a consumer-oriented society, children are less likely to economically contribute to the household than in the past, which means more time spent trying to meet their needs (or wants) for a vast array of goods and services.

You've Come a Long Way, Baby? Contemporary Patterns of Domestic Work

Studies consistently establish that women continue to do most of the housework and child care, regardless of their increased labour force participation and the rise in dual-earner families (Doucet, 2014). In 2014, the majority (69.1%) of families that included a couple with at least one child under 16 were classified as dual earners. Of these dual earners, slightly over half (50.9%) were both working full-time, as shown in table 6.2. Only 2% of these couples comprised a wife working full time and a husband working part time. More common is the case where the husband works full time and the wife part time (15.3%) (Uppal, 2015).

Ironically, the shift toward maternal employment and dual-earner couples has occurred at a time when the care of small children has become more labour intensive and the pressure on women as mothers has risen (Hays, 1996). According to Ambert (2006), the net result of this trend is what sociologist Arlie Hochschild, with Machung (1989), calls the **second shift**. In other words, although society has become more liberal with respect to women's status and role in the workplace, this development has not been accompanied

Table 6.2: Employment Status of Couple Families with at Least One Child Under 16, 1976 and 2014

	1976	2014	1976	2014
	thousands		percentage	
Total couples	2,825	2,753	100.0	100.0
Dual earners[1]	1,014	1,901	35.9	69.1
Both working full time	673	1,402	23.8	50.9
Husband full time, Wife part time	329	422	11.7	15.3
Wife full time, Husband part time	7	55	0.2	2.0
Both part time	5	23	0.2	0.8
Single earners (SE)	1,657	736	58.6	26.7
SE working father	1,593	585	56.4	21.2
Mother unemployed	95	86	3.3	3.1
Mother not in the labour force	1,498	499	53.0	18.1
Permanently unable to work	3	12	0.1	0.4
Attending school	30	41	1.1	1.5
Staying home[2]	1,466	446	51.9	16.2
SE working mother	64	151	2.3	5.5
Father unemployed	33	70	1.2	2.5
Father not in the labour force	31	81	1.1	2.9
Permanently unable to work	6	11	0.2	0.4
Attending school	4	16	0.1	0.6
Staying home[2]	21	54	0.7	2.0
Non-earners	154	116	5.4	4.2

1. Excludes couples in the Armed Forces.

2. Defined as two-parent families with at least one child under 16 at home, with one non-working parent who is not in the labour force, excluding non-working parents who are unemployed, attending school, or unable to work due to a disability.

Source: Data from: Statistics Canada, Labour Force Survey, 1976 and 2014. Uppal, S. 2015. "Employment Patterns of Families with Children." Catalogue no. 75-006-X. Ottawa: Statistics Canada (Chart 4, p. 6).

by a similarly liberating one on the home front (also see box 6.6 for a discussion on beliefs versus feelings with respect to **gender ideology** and the second shift).

In the second shift, women arrive home from work only to continue to work, doing chores such as cooking, cleaning, laundry, and preparing school lunches for the next day. And while many women actively adopt strategies to change gender roles in the household by "supermoming," many men continue to alternate between periods of co-operation and resistance. For example, Hochschild, with Machung (1989: 211), illustrates how some men have used a resistance strategy of "needs reduction." This is shown in the case of a salesman and father of two who explained that he never shopped because "he didn't need

---

Box 6.6: The Second Shift, Gender Ideology, and Feeling Rules

When I began this research, I naively imagined that a person's gender ideology (a set of beliefs about men and women and marital or partnership roles) would cohere as a cognitive and emotional "piece." I imagined a man's gender ideology would "determine" how he wanted to divide the second shift. Couples with more egalitarian ideas about men and women would share more; those with less traditional ideas, less. But I discovered that the set of ideas a person has about gender are often fractured and incoherent. Peter Tanagawa supported his wife's career "a hundred percent," but grew red in the face at the idea that she would mow the lawn, or that his daughters, when teenagers, would drive a car to school. Many men like Evan Holt ideologically supported the idea of their wives working. They pointed out that they wanted their wives to work. It made them more interesting, and it gave the couple more in common. But when it came to the man's role in the work at home, the underlying principle changed. For Robert Myerson, the principle seemed to be that a man should share the work at home "if his wife asks him." Peter Tanagawa seemed to say a man should share the work at home if he's as good at it or as interested in it as his wife is.

More important than the surface fractures in gender ideology, however, were the contradictions between what a person said they believed about men and marital roles, and what they seemed to feel about them. Some people were egalitarian "on top" and traditional "underneath," like Seth Stein, or traditional on top and egalitarian underneath, like Frank Delacorte ... In each instance, what's involved is a person's gender ideology ... and the emotional meanings it evokes, which in turn reinforces or undermines that ideology ... All told, what John thought (his gender ideology) was only one small part of the explanation of why he divided the work at home as he did. His gender ideology gave coherence and reason to his biographically derived feelings and his social opportunities, even as it also cloaked these.

Source: Hochschild, A.R., with Machung, A. 1989. *The Second Shift.* New York: Avon (pp. 198–200).

anything." He also didn't need to take his clothes to the laundry to be ironed because he didn't mind wearing a wrinkled shirt. Through his reduction of needs, this man created a great void into which his wife stepped with her "greater need" to buy important items, see him wear an ironed shirt, and so on.

Although women generally perform more domestic labour than men, it is important to recognize that fathers have always been involved in certain domestic tasks, such as household and car maintenance and repairs, and mowing the lawn. Men are also participating more in non-traditional tasks than in the past, particularly in core household activities such as cooking, cleaning, and daily child care. As argued by Doucet (2014), in the area of child care, there has been somewhat of a "revolutionary" change in father involvement in Canada as well as in other Western countries.

Table 6.3: Average Time Spent per Day on Child Care Activities, Canada, 2010

Respondent's child's age group and employment status	Primary activities			Primary and simultaneous activities		
	Both sexes	Male	Female	Both sexes	Male	Female
	Hours and Minutes					
Children 12 years old or under	2:05	1:23	2:43	3:31	2:18	4:34
Full time work	1:38	1:20	2:04	2:44	2:14	3:28
Part time work	2:39	1:21 E	2:50	4:42	2:25 E	5:01
Other	3:23	1:58	3:45	5:38	3:10	6:16
Youngest child is less than 5 years old	2:49	1:51	3:35	4:52	3:07	6:33
Full time work	2:13	1:46	3:02	3:46	2:59	5:13
Part time work	3:20	F	3:38	6:09	2:41 E	6:43
Other	4:25	2:51	4:46	7:36	4:42 E	8:15
Youngest child is 5 to 12 years old	1:16	0:48	1:38	1:59	1:18	2:32
Full time work	1:00	0:46	1:17	1:37	1:16	2:02
Part time work	1:47	F	1:53	2:54	2:00 E	3:01
Other	2:01	1:04 E	2:18	2:59	1:37 E	3:25

E = use with caution; F = too unreliable to publish

Note: Refers to population aged 15 and over with children 12 years or under, by primary and simultaneous activities, sex, child's age group, and employment status. Average time spent is the average over a 7-day week.

Source: Statistics Canada. 2011. "Highlights, Paid Work and Related Activities." General Social Survey–2010: Overview of the Time Used by Canadians. Catalogue no. 89-647-X, Table 2. Retrieved from www.statcan.gc.ca/pub/89-647-x/2011001/tbl/tbl2-eng.htm.

One indication of fathers' increasing involvement in child care is the dramatic rise in stay-at-home fathers between 1976 and 2014, as seen in figure 6.3. And while the number of stay-at-home dads rose in all provinces/regions during this time period, the numbers increased at different rates and for different reasons. The relatively high proportion of stay-at-home fathers in the Atlantic provinces compared to Alberta, for instance, is attributed to men's greater seasonal work activities and higher unemployment rates in Atlantic Canada, making this a practical family choice. Local cultural attitudes toward the sharing of child care is also important. Notably, Quebec—a province that is known for its government and societal support of egalitarianism in gender roles—has consistently had higher rates of stay-at-home dads than other provinces/regions. Moreover, in 2006, Quebec introduced its own Parental Insurance Plan, which included higher benefit rates, no unpaid waiting period, and a five-week non-transferable leave for fathers.

Therefore, in addition to the role of labour market opportunities and cultural ideologies that support the feasibility of more equal sharing of unpaid work, the role of state supports and workplace policies (e.g., flexibility of work arrangements) are important to consider. Paid maternity and parental leave policies (which were not offered to women until 1971) have greatly assisted Canadians in balancing family and paid work. Because of broadened policies, men are increasingly likely to take parental leave, a change that has occurred in tandem with a societal shift in attitudes and expectations of fathers. Indeed, between 2001 and 2010, there was a nine-fold increase (from 3% to 29.7%) in recent fathers taking parental leave (Krull, 2014). Similarly, men are also increasingly likely to become custodial parents or to co-parent in the case of separation or divorce, a topic that will be explored in more depth in chapter 10.

"A Woman's Place Is in the Home": Gender Ideologies, Stepford Wives, and the Cult of Domesticity

Despite considerable change and functioning of Canadian families, certain ideas about women's domesticity remain entrenched in the public mind. These ideas are also reflected in the way that social scientists have theorized the gendered division of labour. Many classical theorists, such as Durkheim and Marx, generally ignored the interrelationship of the private and public spheres of work and women's contributions to society. For Marx, the sphere of economic production structured the totality of social relations. As a result, the reproductive or family sphere was the subordinate sphere, including the domestic or unpaid work that occurred in families (Beaujot, 2000).

Sociologists did not study unpaid work in the household systematically until the 1970s. This interest was also prompted by such books as Betty Friedan's *The Feminine Mystique* (1963). This classic work contributed to the second phase of the feminist movement, since it identified the isolation of the suburban housewife and her lack of meaningful work as major causes of women's malaise and oppression (Baker, 2001b).

Traditionally, sociologists assumed a sexual division of labour was a necessary feature of family life because it established a mutual dependency among family members.

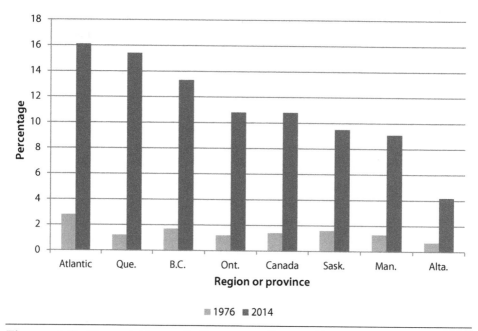

Figure 6.3: Stay-at-Home Fathers as a Proportion of Families with Stay-at-Home Parent, by Region or Province, 1976 and 2014

Note: Atlantic provinces have been grouped together because of sample size issues.

Source: Uppal, S. 2015. "Employment Patterns of Families with Children." Statistics Canada. Catalogue no. 75-006-X. (Chart 4, p. 6). Ottawa: Minister of Industry.

As covered in chapter 2, structural-functionalist Talcott Parsons was particularly influential in this regard, and his analysis of American middle-class family life had an enormous impact on the way that sociologists (who were predominantly men) thought about family interaction (Wilson, 1986). Parsons assumed that because of their early biological tie with children, women were better suited to provide affective support or the expressive function. Conversely, because men were more experienced in the public sphere, he thought they were better suited to perform the task of relating the family to society or the instrumental role.

There have been many variants of "anatomy-as-destiny"-type theories, all of which assume that sex differences are rooted in the biological tie between mothers and infants. Yet, many of these ideas have been strongly criticized by feminists, who argue that these explanations ignore the economic dependence of women on men and other dimensions of power relations and sexual inequality. Moreover, these "explanations" are ideological in the sense that they support a belief system that rationalizes women's secondary status in the paid labour force (Wilson, 1986). They also justify (rather than explain) men's resistance to do more unpaid work because women are deemed better suited to perform certain kinds of work (e.g., daycare, secretarial work) that also tend to be low paid.

Furthermore, these theories ignore how socialization processes, including systems of indoctrination and patriarchy, contribute to create a gendered division of labour and the cult of domesticity. The expectation that mothers willingly remain the primary caretakers of their children at all costs is an example of one societal-wide norm. According to Gustafson (2005), this deeply entrenched assumption advantages fathers by removing restrictions on their parental obligations, thus allowing them more flexibility, freedom, and control. Moreover, many structural barriers continue to exist that prevent men from equal parenting or splitting domestic work 50/50. For example, men who choose to take paternity leave, become stay-at-home dads, or do housework may be teased or ridiculed by co-workers, friends, or spouses, as commonly depicted in popular media. As a result, they may not feel competent enough to take on these responsibilities.

Finally, while it is critical to recognize women's disproportionate contributions to unpaid labour, it is also worthwhile to consider that "men's work" often comes with a high risk. Todd (2016) documents that men are 20 times as likely as women to die in the (paid) workplace. Occupations such as truck diving, construction work, carpentry, and firefighting have high rates of fatalities and men predominate in all of them. Moreover, there is also a social status element to workplace injuries in that men from lower socio-economic backgrounds are more vulnerable to taking jobs with unsafe working conditions. As suggested in "A Roadmap to Men's Health" (Bilsker, Goldenberg, and Davison, 2010), we almost subconsciously rely on these males to exhibit "masculine" traits such as risk-taking, qualities that are necessary for many hazardous jobs.

SUMMARY

This chapter has examined a fundamental feature of daily life for Canadians—work, and the paid and unpaid work that it takes to sustain families. Although unpaid work remains a shadow economy, it is necessary for the functioning of the rest of society. Although unpaid work is largely invisible, our monetary economy is dependent on this reproductive and caregiving work for the health, well-being, and very existence of the paid workforce. Moreover, these two categories of work entail both "earning and caring," and decisions about who does what are influenced by expectations of appropriate roles for men and women (Beaujot, 2000). These expectations about gender operate on many levels, beginning with the individual and ending with societal institutions (Ranson, 2005). In the words of one (anonymous) woman, "Society views domestic labour as women's responsibility and assumes that it is a donation they should make to the economy" (cited in Waring, 2006). Thus, work is more than the performance of basic tasks—it is also a symbolic expression of gendered relations in society.

It is shown that work roles are changing and becoming more demanding. They are also strongly influenced by opportunities (and constraints) for alternative behaviours, such as the pay structure of the formal labour market, workplace support, child care availability, and government programs and policies such as parental leave. This contributes to gendered inequities such as the **wage gap**, a term that refers to the lower overall earning power of women relative to men, resulting in the need for women to work longer hours than men to earn the same amount. Work-family problems and resultant imbalances can also lead to stress and guilt and can spill over into many aspects of our daily life.

Furthermore, during times of economic restructuring and cutbacks in globalizing Western democracies, privatization of care and primacy to intergenerational relations means that women do even more of the "dirty work" (as well as child care and emotional work). Ironically, this additional unpaid work further devalues paid caregiving. Consequently, women are serving as "ambulance attendants," picking up the bits and pieces of caring and intergenerational continuity as they "tumble out" of contemporary changes (McDaniel, 2002). Therefore, for women to move to full citizenship, the conditions by which men and women share responsibilities as social and political actors will need significant transformation (McDaniel, 2002; Voet, 1998).

In conclusion, thinking about how families divide their labour is a good way to understand the interrelationships among domestic life, ideologies, practices of "doing gender," caring, and the economy. Although women have made significant gains in the labour market and men are engaging in more domestic work, the division of work and the responsibility for "having it done" remains unequal and inequitable. Moreover, gendered paid and unpaid work patterns also intersect with class and ethnicity, highlighting the need to further connect inequities to larger structural and ideological forces and opportunities in society. Yet, this broader domain continues to reflect a "stalled revolution" (Hochschild, with Machung, 1989). The economy continues to rely heavily on women to devote and volunteer their time by "picking up the slack"—that is, by mopping floors; cooking; caring for children, husbands, and the elderly; and so on. And despite the tremendous significance of this caring work, these contributions keep many women "looking through the kitchen window" and on the margins of the public sphere.

QUESTIONS FOR CRITICAL REFLECTION AND DEBATE

1. Debate the following: Earnings outside the home should determine who does the housework and child care.
2. Critically analyze the popular notion that women are "naturally inclined" to cook, clean, and raise children with respect to how this ideology is used to justify gender inequality.
3. How are families portrayed on prime-time television with respect to the division of labour, and how has this changed over time? Do these portrayals influence gender role socialization and workplace inequality?
4. Discuss linkages among gendered patterns of family work and other societal institutions, such as religion, politics, and education.
5. Do you think that men and women will ever share paid and unpaid work equally? Outline barriers to "equal parenting," or the idea that couples should split child care and other household responsibilities 50/50.

GLOSSARY

Cult of domesticity developed as the family lost its function as an economic unit; it supports the ideology that a woman's place is in the home and she should therefore tend the "home, sweet home."

Family work includes all of the tasks and activities required to maintain and reproduce families, such as child-rearing, child care, and housework, as well as coordinating paid and unpaid work activities.

Gender ideology is a set of beliefs about men and women, and marital or partnership roles.

Ideology of separate spheres relates to the idea that paid activity in the public sphere is viewed as "work," whereas activity in the private sphere tends to remain invisible and undervalued.

Second shift refers to the household and child-care tasks that working women perform after a day of paid work.

Standard employment relationships occur when a worker (usually associated with the male model of employment) has continuous full-time employment with the same on-site employer for all or most of his/her working life.

Unpaid work, according to Statistics Canada, is work that is not paid (but does not include volunteer work), and is divided into three categories: housework, care of children, and care and assistance for seniors.

Wage gap is the lower overall earning power of women relative to men, resulting in the need for women to work longer hours to earn the same amount as men.

FURTHER READING

Addabbo, T., M.-P. Arrizabalaga, and A. Owens. 2016. *Gender Inequalities, Households and the Production of Well-Being in Modern Europe*. London: Routledge.
A set of interdisciplinary essays by feminist scholars that examines how care work and domestic labour continues to be largely unremunerated and unequally distributed by gender. Yet, this unpaid work sustains the well-being of the continent's population in significant ways.

Hochschild, A. 2012. *The Second Shift: Working Families and the Revolution at Home*. 3rd ed. New York: Penguin Books.
A newly revised version of Hochschild classical study on the challenges that women in dual-career households continue to face in combining paid work with unpaid work.

Meehan, K., and K. Strauss (eds.). 2015. *Precarious Worlds: Contested Geographies of Social Reproduction*. Athens, Georgia: University of Georgia Press.
This edited volume contributes to Marxist theorizing on the relationship between unpaid work and the paid labour market. Special focus is placed on how the social reproduction of domestic labour by women supports the formal economy.

Patton, E., and M. Choi (eds.). 2014. *Home, Sweat Home: Perspectives on Housework and Modern Relationships*. New York: Rowman & Littlefield Publishers.
An in-depth analysis of media images of housework from the mid-nineteenth century to the early twenty-first century. It reveals the widespread cultural image of "perfect" housewives.

Pearson, R. 2016. *Women, Work and Gender Justice in the Global Economy*. New York: Routledge.
Seeks to understand the role of women in the gendered expansion of the global economy since the 1970s by examining the different locations women have worked in both the paid formal economy as well as their less-visible labour in the family and care economy.

RELATED WEB SITES

Canadian Council on Social Development offers research and resources on policy aspects related to families and the economy, www.ccsd.ca.

Centre for Work, Families, and Well-Being is a research centre at the University of Guelph that offers statistics on work, family, and well-being, www.worklifecanada.ca.

Childcare Resource and Research Unit is at the University of Toronto, and provides national and international studies and resources on child care and family leave, in addition to other work-related material, www.childcarecanada.org. Facebook: Childcare Resource and Research Unit.

National Council of Women in Canada, founded in 1893, provides policy briefs and reports, and works to improve the conditions of life for women and families, www.ncwc.ca. Facebook: National Council of Women in Canada.

Statistics Canada's web site contains summary trends on labour force participation and unpaid work patterns by gender (search under "The People," Canada e-book), www.statcan.gc.ca.

REFERENCES

Ambert, A.-M. 2006. *Changing Families: Relationships in Context*, 2nd ed. Toronto: Pearson.
Angus, J. 1994. "Women's Paid/Unpaid Work and Health: Exploring the Social Context of Everyday Life." *Canadian Journal of Nursing Research* 26: 23–42.

Armstrong, P., and H. Armstrong. 1984. *Labour Pains: Women's Work in Crisis.* Toronto: The Women's Press.

Baker, M. 2001a. "Paid and Unpaid Work: How Do Families Divide Their Labour?" In M. Baker (ed.), *Families: Changing Trends in Canada*, 4th ed. (pp. 96–115). Whitby: McGraw-Hill Ryerson.

Baker, M. 2001b. *Families, Labour, and Love: Family Diversity in a Changing World.* Vancouver: University of British Columbia Press.

Beaujot, R. 2000. *Earning and Caring in Canadian Families.* Peterborough: Broadview Press.

Bilsker, D., L. Goldenberg, and J. Davison. 2010. *A Roadmap to Men's Health: Current Status, Research, Policy and Practice.* Vancouver: CARMHA.

Crompton, S., and M. Vickers. 2000. "One Hundred Years of Labour Force Participation." *Canadian Social Trends* (Spring): 2–13. Catalogue no. 11-008. Ottawa: Statistics Canada.

Doucet, A. 2014. "Families and Work: Connecting Households, Workplaces, State Policies, and Communities." In D. Cheal and P. Albanese (eds.), *Canadian Families Today: New Perspectives*, 3rd ed. (pp. 166–184). Toronto: Oxford University Press.

Eichler, M. 1983. *Families in Canada Today: Recent Changes and Their Policy Consequences.* Toronto: Gage Publishing.

Eshleman, J.R., and S.J. Wilson. 2001. *The Family*, 3rd Canadian ed. Toronto: Pearson Education.

Friedan, B. 1963. *The Feminine Mystique.* New York: W.W. Norton and Company.

Glenday, D. 1997. "Lost Horizons, Leisure Shock: Good Jobs, Bad Jobs, Uncertain Future." In A. Duffy, D. Glenday, and N. Pupo (eds.), *Good Jobs, Bad Jobs* (pp. 8–34). Toronto: Harcourt Brace.

Gustafson, D.L. (ed.). 2005. *Unbecoming Mothers: The Social Production of Maternal Absence.* New York: Haworth Press.

Haas, L. 1999. "Families and Work." In M.B. Sussman, S.K. Steinmetz, and G.W. Peterson (eds.), *Handbook of Marriage and Families*, 2nd ed. (pp. 571–612). New York: Plenum.

Hays, S. 1996. *The Cultural Contradictions of Motherhood.* New Haven: Yale University Press.

Hochschild, A.R., with A. Machung. 1989. *The Second Shift.* New York: Avon.

Horsfield, M. 1997. *Biting the Dust: The Joys of Housework.* London: Fourth Estate.

Krull, C. 2014. "Investing in Families and Children: Family Policies in Canada." In D. Cheal and P. Albanese (eds.), *Canadian Families Today: New Perspectives*, 3rd ed. (pp. 292–317). Toronto: Oxford University Press.

Liazos, A. 2004. *Families: Joys, Conflicts, and Changes.* Boulder: Paradigm Publishers.

Luxton, M. 1980. *More than a Labour of Love.* Toronto: The Women's Press.

Machum, S. 2002. "The Farmer Takes a Wife and the Wife Takes the Farm: Marriage and Farming." In G.M. MacDonald (ed.), *Social Context and Social Location in the Sociology of Law* (pp. 133–158). Peterborough: Broadview Press.

McDaniel, S.A. 2002. "Women's Changing Relations to the State and Citizenship: Caring and Intergenerational Relations in Globalizing Western Democracies." *Canadian Review of Sociology and Anthropology* 39: 125–151.

McDaniel, S.A., and L. Tepperman. 2004. *Close Relations: An Introduction to the Sociology of Families*, 3rd ed. Scarborough: Prentice-Hall.

McLaren, A., and A.T. McLaren. 1997. *The Bedroom and the State: The Changing Practices and Politics of Contraception and Abortion in Canada, 1880–1997*. Toronto: Oxford University Press.

Mom.salary.com. 2016. "What Is Your Mom Worth? Families Can Customize Mom's Job Description and Create a 'Mom Paycheck.'" Retrieved June 18, 2016, from www.swz.salary.com/momsalarywizard/htmls/mswl_momcenter.html.

Morissette, R., and D. Galarneau. 2016. "Labour Market Participation of Immigrant and Canadian-born Wives, 2006 to 2014." Economic Insights, Statistics Canada, released January 7, 2016. Retrieved June 18, 2016, from www.statcan.gc.ca/pub/11-626-x/11-626-x2016055-eng.htm.

Oxfam.org. 2016. "Underpaid and Undervalued: How Inequality Defines Women's Work in Asia. Retrieved June 16, 2016, from www.oxfam.org/sites/www.oxfam.org/files/file_attachments/ib-inequality-womens-work-asia-310516.pdf.

Ranson, G. 2005. "Paid and Unpaid Work: How Do Families Divide Their Labour?" In M. Baker (ed.), *Families: Changing Trends in Canada*, 5th ed. (pp. 99–121). Toronto: McGraw-Hill Ryerson.

Seccombe, K., and R.L. Warner. 2004. *Marriages and Families: Relationships in Social Context*. Toronto: Thomson Wadsworth.

Statistics Canada. 2014. "Child Care in Canada." Catalogue no. 89-652-X, No. 005. Ottawa: Minister of Industry.

Todd, D. 2016. "Men's Work Often Comes with High Risk." *The Vancouver Sun*, June 18.

Uppal, S. 2015. "Employment Patterns of Families with Children." Statistics Canada, Catalogue no. 75-006-X. Ottawa: Minister of Industry.

Voet, R. 1998. *Feminism and Citizenship*. London: Sage.

Ward, M. 2002. *The Family Dynamic: A Canadian Perspective*, 3rd ed. Toronto: Nelson Thomson Learning.

Waring, M. 2006. "Women and Unpaid Work." In *Women and the Economy*. Retrieved February 10, 2006, from www.unpac.ca/economy/unpaidwork.html.

Wilson, S.J. 1986. *Women, the Family, and the Economy*, 2nd ed. Toronto: McGraw-Hill Ryerson.

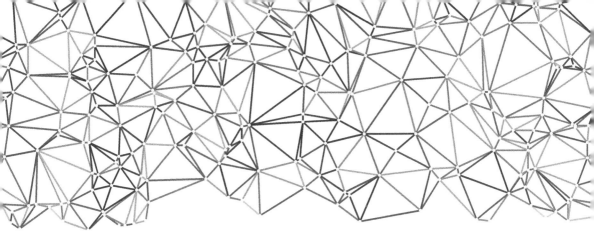

PART II

THE TIES THAT BIND: FAMILY FORMATION AND GENERATIONAL CONNECTIONS

From a life-course perspective, family transitional events or turning points often have a profound impact on our lives. These transitions are often key developmental phases that change as we age. For example, the transition to parenthood, which typically occurs in young adulthood, is a major developmental milestone that alters our day-to-day lives in significant ways as we care for and raise our children. Moreover, the timing and nature of these transitional events have important implications for family and kinship relations (e.g., our parents become grandparents), as well as support across the generations (e.g., grandparents may provide assistance with child care), which constitutes a secondary focus of this section. Beginning with the transition to adulthood, chapter 7 examines the family formation patterns of young people by considering the different ways in which they search for love and the changing nature of partnership formation and parenthood. In chapter 8, we consider families and children in the early years and the various agents of socialization (notably parents), including several theories used to explain how children become socialized. Chapter 9 explores fundamental text assumptions of both sameness and diversity amidst social change in family composition, and in family-related life-course patterns by examining the family lives of lesbian, gay, and transgender individuals.

Moreover, in recognition that transition events are not always permanent and are subject to reversibility—a theme found throughout many parts of this text—chapter 10 specifically focuses on family dissolution (divorce) and the transition to a "new" beginning (remarriage). In chapter 11, we examine how the transition to the empty nest is often reversed when young people return to parental nests as "boomerang kids." Finally, in chapter 12, attention will shift to transitions and intergenerational relations in later life by turning the spotlight on aging families, inequities in family caregiving, and other salient issues that are commonly experienced during the "sunset" years.

CHAPTER 7

Close Relations in Youth and Young Adulthood: Establishing Partnerships and Forming Families

LEARNING OBJECTIVES

In this chapter you will learn that ...

- a life-course perspective is invaluable for situating contemporary trends in intimate relations and family formation within the context of shifting gender roles and social change across the generations
- close relations are socially constructed and socially regulated and are shaped by political, socio-economic, and technological forces
- unmarried cohabitation is likely to be the first conjugal union of most Canadian young people, and is particularly prevalent in places like Quebec
- although marriage and parenthood occur at historically unprecedented older ages, these transitions are also characterized by diversity and fluctuations over time
- many young people increasingly choose to delay or reject marriage and parenthood and are having smaller families, yet the desire to form and create family ties remains as strong as ever

INTRODUCTION

The formation and maintenance of intimate partnerships and the development of one's own family—known as the **family of procreation**—are key markers of the transition to adulthood. The life-course perspective provides a dynamic and flexible framework for understanding the creation and changing nature of these close family ties. It also underscores the importance of situating family-related behaviours and transitions within their unique social contexts. Whereas the current generation of young people has grown up in an era of tumultuous social and economic change, the previous generation (known as the "baby boomers," born between 1946 and 1964), was raised in their own distinct historical location. The baby boomers were born during a time in which sexual expression was more constrained, young people left home relatively young to get married and have children, the nuclear "intact" family was pretty much the norm, men were the main breadwinners, and most marriages lasted a lifetime.

In this chapter, we will focus on patterns and changes in family-related transitions that occur primarily during the youth and young adult phase of the family life course. This time period covers the time of life described as "emerging adulthood" (Arnett, 2000), a topic that we will explore in more detail in chapter 11. This concept refers to a significant developmental phase that occurs between childhood and adulthood, a time in which many young people are experimenting with, and establishing, adult roles, statuses, and identities. Topics such as dating, romance, love, and sexuality will be explored, as well as shifting trends in the formation of committed couple relationships. The chapter will conclude with an overview of patterns in parenthood, including general trends in "making babies," or fertility behaviours.

DATING, ROMANCE, LOVE, AND SEXUALITY

Are you currently single or partnered? If you consider yourself to be single, is this by choice or by circumstance? Do you intend to get married some day? Or do you think that traditional, legal marriage is an outdated or antiquated institution? Regardless of your current relationship status and intentions, as young people navigate their way to adulthood, most will look for someone special with whom to share their private time and lives. Some of these relationships will be of a relatively short duration, while others may lead to a more long-term union, such as marriage. My only daughter, Kayzia, for example, recently married her boyfriend, Eric (as shown in the opening-chapter photo), following several years of serious dating.

The Search for Love and Intimacy: Dating Customs and the Role of Technology

Dating behaviours and customs in Canada have varied throughout history. In the years leading up to World War One, courtship took place mainly during community activities and in the parents' home, under adult supervision. Changes began to occur on university campuses among older young adults as they began to question these traditions, and this spread to the high school population, the media, and popular culture (Nett, 1988). The 1923 edition of Emily Post's etiquette book included a chapter called "Chaperones and Other Conventions." By the 1930s, this monitor of morals had been relegated to the past tense as "The Vanished Chaperone." Going out alone without parental surveillance was also made easier as cars became a more common means of transportation.

By the 1950s, new dating practices had become established, although they continued to be highly formalized. Dating typically involved a series of phases from casual to steady dating to engagement and marriage. Each of these stages was marked by an exchange or gift that symbolized the degree of seriousness in the relationship. Men and women usually developed distinct attitudes and roles towards these dates, reflecting a double standard; in most cases, men would initiate contact, pay for the cost of the date, and were socialized to emphasize sex, while women learned about love, romance, and marriage (Nett, 1988).

In our high-tech culture, methods and styles of dating and mate selection have undergone an incredible transformation. A growing number of people consider "traditional" dating styles to be out of date, time-consuming, and inefficient. One-on-one dating is becoming less popular among young people and there is a more egalitarian approach regarding who asks for and pays for "the date" (Ward, 2002). And although they are not the norm, there are other "novel" dating trends that are of sociological interest, including such innovative activities as "speed dating." Potential long-term partners may also be introduced through "mail order bride" services, as is further discussed in box 7.1.

Overall, modern youth romance culture is primarily informal, and this is reflected in language that frequently lacks a clear vocabulary to define relationship status or practices. In the 1990s, Miller and Benson observed the popularity of terms like "hanging out," "going out," and "talking to" instead of terms like "courtship" or "dating" (Miller and Benson, 1999). You only need to turn on the TV or surf the web to quickly get the idea that popular culture has undergone a huge transformation in how we approach intimacy and matchmaking. The proliferation of so-called reality shows devoted to helping people find mates is one example. Beginning with the 2000 Fox show "Who Wants to Marry a Millionaire?", in which 50 women competed to marry a wealthy man they had never met, a number of spin-off shows have since emerged. ABC's "The Bachelorette" and "The Bachelor," for instance, continue to be highly watched series.

Modern technology and modifications in dating customs have also contributed to an expansion of social network sites and chat rooms, as well as Internet dating services. These dating services cover a wide range of preferences and reflect shifting norms in dating behaviours and gender roles. For example, in 2007, Mark Penn documented the emergence of a new "micro trend" in dating where women (typically over the age of 40) seek younger men (Penn with Zalesne, 2007). These women were referred to as "cougars," a term popularized by the comedy series "Cougar Town." Subsequently, a number of web sites (such as the National Association of Prime Cougars) appeared that were geared toward professional older women who wanted to date younger men. Baker (2010a) provides

Box 7.1: From Russia, Maybe with Love: Mail-Order Brides a Booming Business

Three to six months' worth of e-mails, a 14-day visit to Russia, and a new wife. That's the promise of Mark Scrivener, a Martensville, Saskatchewan, man who on January 1st this year [2010] opened a Canadian branch of the Volga Girls Mail-Order Bride service. Though the service has been available for 10 years via its Kentucky-based head office, Scrivener is providing Canada-specific services to men looking for a wife who is a little bit more "out of the box."

Of the single men he's counselled, he says most of them are more interested in having their daily meals cooked and served to them than in earning a big paycheque. And the foreign women signed up for his service are willing to provide just that. "They are more traditional in a marriage. They still don't mind pulling up their roots and probably not pursuing their career and maybe pursuing a family, being a stay-at-home mother," Scrivener says. His company's web site provides a catalogue of such women who are looking for foreign husbands.

Take 22-year-old Natalia, who lists her interests as going to nightclubs, movies, and reading. She speaks no English, but has a college education and is the chief salesperson at a store in Togliatti, in Russia's western region. Prospective husbands can also learn about her height, weight, and bustline, all with the click of a mouse. According to her bio, Natalia hopes to travel around the world and have many children. For a fee, men can purchase her address, write her letters, send her gifts, and hope to win her affection.

The web site's main gallery lists more than 1,100 such profiles from women in and around Togliatti, a city of approximately 710,000. There are 60 men using the web site worldwide, and it results in approximately 14 engagements per year, says Scrivener. The process can take between nine months and one year and costs approximately $5,000, including flights, from initial correspondence "to the day you slide the ring on the lady's hand," Scrivener says. According to the company web site, the success rate is 75%, with clients who become engaged during their 10- to 14-day Russian visit. Once they become engaged, women can apply for a visa to come to Canada. "There's no reason for them not to be approved, unless they go absolutely stupid in their interview," Scrivener says.

His own quest for a foreign bride began in 2004. Everything in his life was good, he said, except for his inability to find a wife. The search culminated in his 2006 marriage to a Ukrainian woman. It didn't work out; she said she was returning home to take care of business and never came back. Scrivener decided to try a different agency, and to focus on Russia, where he said women outnumber men by 10 million. Women there are also subject to the label "old maid," says Scrivener. "If you're over the age of 26 there, you probably won't get married," he says. Scrivener believes he will be married again by August, as he plans to travel to Russia soon for business and to meet a couple of prospective brides.

But some critics say services such as this one are less about helping couples find love and more about exploiting a power imbalance between the First World and the Third World. "It becomes a way for men to access vulnerable women, women who ultimately have very high rates of turning up in battered women's shelters," says Norma Ramos, director of the New York City–based International Coalition Against Trafficking in Women.

Ramos says the mail-order bride phenomenon takes place all over the world, with men "helping themselves to women in vulnerable situations," and taking advantage of women who are desperately seeking better economic opportunities. For those women who enter a successful, loving relationship, coming to Canada as a bride is the culmination of a fantasy, a way out of old-world poverty. For those mail-order brides who end up in abusive, controlling relationships, the picture isn't so pretty. "The word is slavery for us," says Josephine Pallard, executive director of Changing Together, a centre for immigrant women in Edmonton.

In 2007, the group launched a web site called Canadian Law and Modern Foreign Brides, which aims to provide legal information for women who became victims of the mail-order bride system. Pallard says Canadian men are bringing over women from Latin America, Asia, and Eastern Europe, and she estimates up to 40% of these women end up in controlling, abusive relationships. In his defense, Scrivener says his clients are also often looking for women to provide the same life the men grew up with, with mothers and grandmothers who grew vegetables, baked, and raised children. "It's just a known fact that in North America a lot of women have wandered away from those traditional values," he says. "I think a lot of men really are looking for that. A woman who will stay at home and raise the kids." Pallard frames the situation differently. "It's the macho man," she says. "I am the king of the family so it has to be 'my word is all.' Of course, they see the Canadian women not tolerating that."

In some cases, mail-order brides are used to provide care to aging parents or children, or to perform labour on farms. In the worst situations, women are held as sex slaves and sold into prostitution. "It's men from developed nations who feel they can buy anything they want. They're not looking for equality in the marriage," says Ramos. "These mail-order, these Internet husbands, these buyers, they want someone who is not going to assert equality in the marriage. Someone who is going to look at this man as their ticket out."

Source: Adapted from Stewart, J. 2010. "From Russia, Maybe with Love: Mail Order Brides a Boom-ing Business." *Canwest News Service,* March 2. Retrieved July 29, 2011, from www.nationalpost.com/news/story.html?id=2634201.

a discourse analysis pertaining to the language use of the term "cougar" and concludes that it signifies important changes in gender relations and identities. As women become more economically independent and well educated, and gain more power to choose potential mates, they begin to adopt traditionally male dating behaviours, where the dating partner is considerably younger and less financially powerful in the relationship. Yet, at the same time there also appears to be a growth of "dating" web sites such as Seeking Arrangements. com, a controversial site widely reputed for facilitating encounters between rich older men ("sugar daddies") and young women who are often financially struggling college or university students.

Let's turn our attention to new media technologies such as cell phones, instant messaging, texting, and social network sites. Pascoe (2011) observes that these are now a central aspect of young people's social, romantic, and sexual lives, although most young people meet their partners "offline." These new media technologies provide a wider private sphere for youth dating practices, since they can expand the traditional habits of meeting, dating, and breaking up. They also can provide important resources about sexual health and identities. Yet, Pascoe argues, despite these possible benefits, use and access to these technologies often mirror the contemporary ordering of economic, racialized, and gendered power. For example, based on her multi-year, multi-site collaborative ethnographic research project, she finds that some marginalized young people (e.g., sexual minorities, homeless, and other disadvantaged youth) are more likely to experience online venues as riskier spaces than more advantaged youth (e.g., they worry about the risks of on-line sexual predators and cyber bullying).

Pascoe also critically evaluates the pervasiveness of cautionary tales (usually aimed at parents) about young people's sexuality and new media and how these stories are constantly turned into "moral panics" in the daily news cycle. The stories often feature teens posting risqué pictures of themselves on their social network sites, and sending semi-nude or nude self-portraits via their cell phones, known as "sexting." Pascoe recounts the tragic story of Jesse Logan, a high school student who sent nude photos of herself to her boyfriend. After they broke up, he forwarded the stored photos to other students. Sadly, Jesse was relentlessly harassed and eventually became so distraught she committed suicide. But Pascoe is quick to point out that while these kinds of stories are very real and troubling, they are relatively rare. She also argues that the tendency to focus on negative behaviours related to teen sexuality reinforces the societal stereotypes that adolescents are out of control and make poor decisions about their bodies, and that new media and sexuality are a dangerous mix.

Yet, there is growing concern about the increased exposure of children (and adults) to pornography—especially very explicit or what is known as "hard-core porn"—since it is so readily accessible over the Internet. With the click of a key (and despite porn site age restrictions), it is now possible to find thousands of sexualized photos that range from scantily clad bodies to highly violent and perverse sexual acts. Since this form of sexualized media is now a primary form of sex education for youth, critics warn that this exposure can be very detrimental to the formation of healthy relationships. Many research studies show that exposure to hard-core pornography (especially from a young age and in a repetitive or addictive manner) can reinforce harmful gender roles, create sexist attitudes, and contribute to violence against women and children (e.g., Stanley et al., 2016). Generally, critics contend that the rising availability and normalization of pornography creates unrealistic expectations and views about sex, bodies, and sexuality, and can significantly impact personal relationships and family life.

Love, Romance, and Sex among Singles

Whereas passion refers to the drive that leads to romance, physical attraction, and sexual consummation, love is a deep and vital emotion that involves caring and acceptance and satisfies certain needs (Reidmann et al., 2003). But the idea that romantic love is the basis for marriage is a relatively new social invention. Romantic love emerged gradually from the "courtly love" tradition practiced in the 12th century by feudal nobility and celebrated by poets, and developed even further during the Industrial Revolution. This was a time when there was a growing emphasis on individuality, such that young people began to demand the right to choose their own mates. The earliest settlers from Europe also brought their traditions of romantic love with them to North America (Ward, 2002).

Love relationships don't necessarily happen instantly, despite the well-known expression "love at first sight." Instead, love relationships "ebb and flow, with false starts and continual negotiations and renegotiations" (Kollock and Blumstein, 1988: 481). And since love and romance are somewhat elusive concepts that have been socially created, their meanings can vary according to the context in which they are expected or experienced. Indeed, what is desirable and sexually attractive varies from culture to culture, and from subculture to subculture. For example, some might view multiple body piercings and tattoos as sexy and erotic, while others might find this type of body adornment gross and disgusting. Some young adults from traditional ethnic backgrounds may not regard the pursuit of romantic love as the most important force behind a successful marriage. For example, in **arranged marriages** (discussed later in this chapter), love often grows during marriage as partners get to know one another.

As previously mentioned, sexuality is a critical aspect in the formation of intimate relationships. Castells (2004) has proposed that we are undergoing a sexual revolution unlike the sexual liberation of the 1960s and 1970s. The current revolution is characterized by the "de-linking of marriage, family, heterosexuality, and sexual repression (or desire)." In other words, sexuality and desire are increasingly separate from marriage and family. And, as always, this topic draws much public and personal attention, as well as considerable controversy.

A good illustration of the changing landscape of young adult relationships can be found in the phenomenon of "hooking up" among heterosexual university students. Despite the lack of consensus in defining the term (e.g., see Currier, 2013), it is often conceptualized as casual sexual activity in uncommitted relationships, ranging from kissing to intercourse.

It is apparently quite common in the contemporary university environment (Armstrong, Hamilton, and England, 2010). While some researchers assess these encounters as detrimental for women (Bogle, 2008), others frame them as offering women sexual freedom and agency apart from time-consuming relationships (Hamilton and Armstrong, 2009).

Consensual Non-monogamies and Plural Partners: From Swinging to Polyamory

Another contemporary trend that has garnered growing societal interest is the phenomenon of **consensual non-monogamies,** a term used to describe romantic relationships that are sexually and/or emotionally non-exclusive (Grunt-Mejer and Campbell, 2016). Examples of these include "swinging" (i.e., a couple engaging in extradyadic sex at parties), "open" relationships (partners are free to have extradyadic relationships), and "polyamorous" relationships (people are free to have not only sexual but also emotional relationships with multiple partners). Although polyamorous relationships have sometimes been lumped in with polygamy (a term that we covered in chapter 3), practitioners of both systems tend to see themselves as quite distinct (e.g., Shucart, 2016). Moreover, as you may recall, polygamy refers to a distinct (usually legalized) marriage type. While exact prevalence rates of those who participate in consensual non-monogamies are unknown, there appears to be a growing general tolerance for relationships and situations outside the bounds of traditional monogamous marriage. This greater acceptability may be partly due to a greater acceptance of non-traditional family forms, also spurred by recent legal changes in the recognition of same-sex partnerships. These changes have brought an increased awareness of alternatives to the standard model of heterosexual monogamy.

Despite not knowing how widespread these types of non-conforming relationships are, or whether they are actually on the rise, we can be certain that there is an increasing amount of academic research on the topic being conducted (e.g., see Barker and Langdridge, 2010, for a review). In one recent ground-breaking book, Scheff (2014) finds that polyamorous relationships are not that different from other family forms. In particular, she finds that they are relatively "normal" and resilient, despite common assumptions to the contrary. However, her gendered analysis seems to suggest that the division of labour remains stubbornly gendered and disadvantaged to women. She also found that polyamorous relationships involved other race- and class-based inequities.

Furthermore, studies seem to consistently suggest that social norms toward these kinds of relationships are not highly favorable. For example, in a recent study by Grunt-Mejer and Campbell (2016), 375 undergraduate students (with an average age of 21.6) were presented with hypothetical vignettes of different relationship styles and then asked to rate them on a number of different characteristics, including several moral components. Findings revealed that monogamy was still judged to be morally superior to consensual non-monogamy, and that the cheating couple was viewed the most negatively. Interestingly, the polyamorous relationship that included emotional connection was rated more positively than either the swinging or the open relationship. The authors conclude that although social norms of sexual and emotional monogamy are significant, the aspect that has the most effect on judgements is whether the relationship structure has been agreed to by all parties.

It is not surprising that there is controversy regarding these "new systems of courtship" and partnership formation (Heath, 2014). All societies have social norms that grant or withhold approval of certain sexual behaviours. For example, it is taboo in our culture for couples to engage in public sex, or to have sex with certain family members such as first cousins. Laws and customs have been established that punish certain sexual acts, and violators may face public shame, ridicule, fines, or imprisonment. In brief, sexual expression is highly regulated in a variety of ways. It also continues to both challenge and preserve components of hegemonic masculinity and societal notions of femininity (e.g., see Currier, 2013).

LIVING APART AND TOGETHER: TRENDS IN LAT RELATIONSHIPS AND COHABITATION

"Living together," "shacking up," "living in sin," and "trial marriage" are examples of expressions that describe the living arrangement demographers refer to as cohabitation or common-law union. Obviously, some of these terms are more value-laden than others, and their meanings reflect historical and cultural contexts (e.g., see Mitchell, 2001). For example, in Canada, "moving in together" no longer carries the same "immoral baggage" that it did prior to the 1970s, although some traditional ethnic groups continue to disapprove of this living arrangement for personal or religious reasons. And although cohabitation can refer to same-sex couples, most of the research to date has concentrated on opposite-sex partners.

As shown in table 7.1, an increasing proportion of couples are living together in common-law unions. This is particularly pronounced among those aged 20 to 34. In 2011, 18.4% of people in this age group reported this marital status, compared to only 4.8% of those 60 and older. Thus, in Canada, as in the US and many other countries (e.g., Sweden), it is not surprising that for young adults in their twenties, unmarried cohabitation is likely to be their first conjugal union.

It is also documented that the proportion of 20 to 24-year-olds that lived common-law slightly decreased from 13.1% in 2001 to 11.8% in 2011. It is likely that these young "emerging adults" may be concentrating more on educational, employment, or other goals beyond those related to being a spouse or partner (Milan, 2013). There has also been a rise in **Living Alone Together (LAT) relationships**, a topic that will be discussed later in the chapter.

Who Cohabits and Why

Cohabitation has become a normative part of the life course for many young people. The propensity to cohabit is influenced by a number of factors. In previous decades,

Table 7.1: Marital Status of People 20 and Over, by Age and Sex, 2001 and 2011

	Total		20 to 34		35 to 59		60 and over	
	2001	**2011**	**2001**	**2011**	**2001**	**2011**	**2001**	**2011**
	Percentage							
Total								
In a LAT couple	8.4	7.4*	19.6	17.9*	5.0	4.1*	1.8	2.3*
Living common law	10.6	12.6*	17.2	18.4	10.6	13.5*	2.0	4.8*
Married	57.3	55.5*	33.4	29.9*	68.4	66.3*	62.8	62.6
No partner	23.7	24.5	29.9	33.7*	16.1	16.1	33.5	30.3*
Men								
In a LAT couple	9.0	7.3*	20.2	17.5	5.3	3.7*	2.4	2.9
Living common law	11.0	13.2*	15.7	16.6	11.5	14.7*	2.7	6.3*
Married	58.8	58.0	29.7	27.0	68.9	67.3	75.4	74.9
No partner	21.2	21.5	34.4	38.9*	14.3	14.3	19.6	15.9*
Women								
In a LAT couple	7.8	7.5	19.0	18.4	4.7	4.6	1.3	1.8
Living common law	10.2	12.0*	18.6	20.3	9.7	12.3*	1.4	3.5*
Married	55.8	53.1*	37.1	32.8*	67.8	65.3*	52.3	52.0
No Partner	26.2	27.4*	25.2	28.5*	17.8	17.9	45.0	42.7

LAT = Living apart together.

*Difference statistically significant in relation to 2001.

Source: Turcotte, M. "Living Apart Together." 2013. *Insights on Canadian Society*, Catalogue no. 75-006-X, Table 1. Ottawa: Statistics Canada. Retrieved August 5, 2016, from www.statcan.gc.ca/pub/75-006-x/2013001/article/11771-eng.htm.

heterosexual cohabitation tended to be selective of people who are younger, more liberal, less religious, and more supportive of egalitarian gender roles and non-traditional family roles (Wu, 2000). For example, women in unmarried-partner households are less likely to be in a traditional homemaking role than their married counterparts. Furthermore, in Canada, the largest proportion of cohabiting relationships has been found in Quebec, where more than one-third of different sex unions are common-law. This pattern is attributed to the declining strength of the Roman Catholic Church, which historically upheld a traditional focus on marriage and families, as well as to support by successful provincial governments (Comacchio, 2014).

Why do people choose to live together rather than marry? The answer to this question will probably depend upon the couple you ask. However, many young people report that it is a convenient way to gain some of the benefits of marriage and to avoid the risk of divorce. If it doesn't work out, it is easy to dissolve the union, since the couple does not have to seek legal or religious permission. Conversely, macro-level explanations tend to focus more on the large-scale trend toward secularization and individualization, including an increasing rejection of traditional institutionalization and moral authority. And for same-sex couples, the choice to legally marry has only recently become an option.

Research indicates that many young people do not consciously plan to move in together or choose between cohabitation and marriage. Rather, the decision often seems to centre on whether to remain single or cohabit (although marriage is sometimes on the horizon in the future). A qualitative study on 115 young adults who are currently cohabiting or recently cohabited also found that the movement to cohabitation is often a gradual, unfolding process or a "general slide" (Manning and Smock, 2005). This makes it difficult to identify a clear beginning and ending and can raise issues of autonomy and independence, in addition to several legal/economic and relationship issues. For example, one respondent named Fiona stated, "Ah ... [when] we met, he was 19. I was 20. Within that next year, he basically moved in. There wasn't a definite date. He would stay one night a week, and then two nights, then ... it got to a point where he never left. And ... I wanted the control of saying, uh, go home, if need be. I didn't want him to pay the rent ... to have to be entitled to be here. That was at my discretion. It was kind of like my way of maintaining some control, independence, however you want to say it."

Studies also suggest that cohabiting women experience unique stressors and issues in these relationships because cohabitation is not a committed, "formalized" agreement identical to a legal marriage contract. Cohabiting men, for instance, tend to be less committed to the relationship and their partner than married men (Stanley et al., 2004). As a result, some of these men remain in a permanent state of availability and are still "playing the field" (Ambert, 2006), which can leave women feeling insecure and vulnerable.

Finally, another emergent trend in living arrangements in modern life that represents the flip side of living together without being legally married is the "commuter marriage" or **Living Apart Together (LAT)** relationship. This is defined by Statistics Canada as those who are not married or living common-law, but are in an intimate couple relationship and not living together (Turcotte, 2013). According to table 7.1, in 2011, 17.9% of those aged 20 to 34 lived as an LTA, a trend that has generally persisted since 2001.

It is also striking to observe that LAT relationships are the most common partnered relationships among those aged 20 to 24, as portrayed in figure 7.1. In 2011, nearly 1 in 3 of these young adults (31%) were part of an LAT couple. These LAT relationships—which are typically of a relatively short duration—may be necessary at this stage of life, given the many financial constraints associated with education and the high cost of housing in urban areas. Many of these young adults live with their parents, and the majority intend to move in with their partners in the future (Turcotte, 2013).

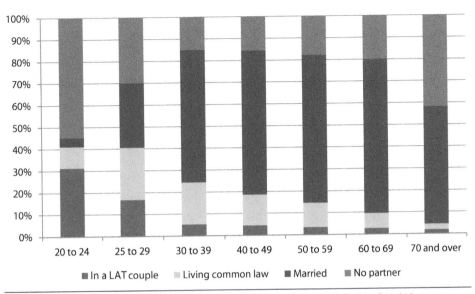

Figure 7.1: Close to 1 in 3 Young Adults Aged 20 to 24 Were Living Apart Together (LAT), 2011

Source: Turcotte, M. 2013. "Living Apart Together." *Insights on Canadian Society*, Catalogue no. 75-006-X. Ottawa: Statistics Canada (Chart 1). Retrieved June 23, 2016, from www.statcan.gc.ca/pub/75-006-x/2013001/article/11771-eng.htm.

Finally, a commuter marriage, another possible living arrangement for couples, refers to people who are married or living common-law but also live apart. Although Statistics Canada estimates that only a very tiny percentage of the Canadian population over the age of 20 fits this profile, the situation might happen if both partners are unable to find work in the same city. It may also be a lifestyle choice to accommodate education, professional career, or personal preference. For example, it could be a way for a couple to have autonomy and independence without sacrificing a committed relationship. Additionally, other economic, cultural, personal (e.g., health-related), or even policy pressures may also be at play in making some partnered couples choose this relationship. Notably, immigration laws and policies can make relocating to another country as a married couple very difficult (Turcotte, 2013).

"TYING THE KNOT": GOING TO THE CHAPEL … AND I'M GOING TO GET MARRIED

Marriage can broadly be defined as a socially and legally recognized relationship that includes sexual, economic, and social rights and responsibilities. This definition draws our attention to the fact that marriage is a matter of public concern and that society maintains norms and sanctions of appropriate behaviour related to marriage (Seccombe and Warner,

2004). Good illustrations of this are found in same-sex marriage debates and in the recent public outrage and controversy over the polygamous practices of the fundamental Mormons living in Bountiful, British Columbia (see box 7.2). In this secluded community that was formed over 50 years ago, plural marriage is practised such that some men have close to 30 wives, many of whom are underaged teenaged mothers, and have fathered up to 80 children.

On the one hand, many individuals and lobby groups have maintained that polygamy is a criminal offence, since it is illegal to have multiple wives in Canada. On the other hand, supporters say that the law banning polygamy is unconstitutional because it infringes on religious freedom. Despite this controversy, the BC Supreme Court recently upheld Canada's polygamy laws, arguing that while the law does infringe on religious freedom, it is justified, particularly given the substantial harm that it causes to children, women, and society, as well as the institution of monogamous marriage. As a result, this community is currently under investigation. Chief Justice Robert Bauman maintains, however, that minors who end up in polygamous marriages should be exempt from prosecution (CBC News, 2011).

McDaniel and Tepperman (2011) observe two trends in contemporary marriage: a decline in marriage rates and the continuing popularity of marriage. And although these trends appear contradictory, they actually are not. From a historical perspective, more people now marry at some point in their lives than they did in the 1910s. But at the same time there has been a decline in marriage rates since the 1970s. And despite the ever-increasing popularity of cohabitation, the institution of marriage remains highly valued in contemporary society. Indeed, the vast majority of young people in Western countries eventually legally marry, although this number will likely be smaller than in the past, largely due to more unmarried cohabitation (Milan, 2013).

Young people also tend to marry later now than they did in previous times, especially compared to the mid-20th century. This trend contributes to the dramatic rise in one-person households as young, independent singles delay marriage while focusing on their careers (Canadian Press, 2007). As revealed in table 7.1, being single was the most common status of young people aged 20 to 34 in 2011 (33.7%, an increase of about 3% since 2001). This table also shows that in 2011, 33.7% of young people in the same age group were legally married, representing a decrease of about 4% since 2001.

As you may recall from chapter 1, in 2008 women were about 29 years old on average at first marriage (due to cut-backs from Statistics Canada, this is the latest available data), and men about 31. Comparatively, in 1961, the average marriage age was much lower for both women (22.9) and men (25.8). Yet, this is only one historical benchmark—in some ways young adults are reverting to behaviours characteristic of earlier times. For example, during the Great Depression (1929–1939), marriage was often delayed because of great economic hardship.

In contemporary times, certain factors also lead to early marriage. Greater socio-economic resources generally slow down young adults' formation of intimate relationships. This is shown by the tendency for individuals from lower- and middle-class families to

Box 7.2: Polygamists Thrive Even though Polygamy Is Illegal

There's something so nutty about the polygamous, fundamentalist Mormon communities in Canada and the United States that it's easy to dismiss it all as a bad tabloid joke. It is incomprehensible to most of us that anyone—even Canada's best-known polygamist, Winston Blackmore—could have 145 children. But the 59-year-old does. The latest addition to the family was born earlier this month.

Siring so many offspring requires many wives, which he's had. There were 24 listed on the 2014 indictment on one count of polygamy. Some left him and the community of Bountiful, B.C., before he was charged. Others have taken their places. It bears repeating that polygamy is illegal in Canada and the United States. It was upheld here in 2011. This week [April 2016], a US federal appeal court upheld the American law in a decision ruling against Kody Brown and his wives, from the TV show "Sister Wives."

But it's not just the number of wives and children that's startling. In a Utah courtroom in 2014, Blackmore admitted under oath that 10 of his 24 "wives" were under the age of 18. Blackmore has also admitted that several of his wives were only 15 and 16 years old when they married in religious ceremonies, some of which took place at the polygamy summit he organized in 2005. There, Blackmore also said that one of his sons had married a 14-year-old.

Despite this, Blackmore has never been charged with sexual exploitation, even though at the time of those marriages he held several positions of trust and authority. He was the bishop, the head of the independent school's society, Bountiful's major employer, and de facto landlord for the many families living on property owned by the Fundamentalist Church of Jesus Christ of Latter Day Saints. Twice, he's been charged with a single count of polygamy. The first charge was dropped in 2009 after a judge agreed with Blackmore that the special prosecutor who recommended the charge had been improperly appointed.

Blackmore was charged again in 2014. He made the same argument about an improperly appointed special prosecutor and lost. He appealed and, four months after the B.C. Court of Appeal heard the case, there's still no decision. Three other people from Bountiful were also charged in 2014. [The trial is underway as of 2017.] on more serious offences. James Oler, another former FLDS bishop, is charged with one count of polygamy and one count of unlawful removal of a child from Canada. Oler is alleged to have taken one of his under-aged daughters to the United States to be "married" to another FLDS man.

Blackmore's brother Brandon and one of Brandon's wives, Emily Ruth Crossfield, were also charged with unlawful removal of one of their daughters. Aside from the price paid by the young women and children in the largely unfettered religious community, citizens are subsidizing these extraordinarily large and complicated families. Tens of thousands of dollars flow into the Blackmore family coffers in child benefits.

When the Conservative government sent out cheques for the universal child-care benefit last year [2015], a rough calculation of how much the Blackmore family might have been eligible for was $43,160. At that point, Blackmore had 133 children (124 of them are shown in the accompanying photo, which was taken around that time.)

Then there's the $637,607 the province provided to the Blackmore-run independent school called Mormon Hills, which has 132 students (mostly Blackmore's children, grandchildren, and other relatives). Blackmore founded Mormon Hills in 2003 after he was excommunicated from the FLDS, which split the Bountiful community of roughly 1,500 in two. In 2012, the FLDS school—Bountiful Elementary Secondary School, which had received $1.2 million in government support the previous year—abruptly closed. The order came from prophet Warren Jeffs, who is serving a life sentence in Texas for the rape of two of his child brides, aged 12 and 15. Since that school's closure, it's unclear whether any of the 257 students transferred to other schools, or what kind of home-schooling they might be receiving. So far, however, there's no evidence of the kind of money laundering and fraud alleged in the United States, where 11 FLDS members were arrested in in a scheme that investigators say involved more than $12 million dollars' worth of food stamps. Among those charged are two of Jeffs's brothers, one of whom heads the community in Pringle, South Dakota.

Nutty? Yes. But that doesn't explain why politicians and prosecutors here have been so slow to deal with it.

A Portrait of 124 of 145 of Winston Blackmore's Children

Source: Bramham, D. 2016. "Polygamists Thrive even Though Polygamy Is Illegal." *The Vancouver Sun,* April 13. Retrieved June 24, 2016, from www.vancouversun.com/opinion/columnists/daphne-bramham-polygamists-thrive-even-though-polygamy-is-illegal.

marry earlier than those from well-educated or privileged families. Also, the role models provided by mothers in professional occupations may reduce daughters' interest in early marriage and increase their labour force attachment (Amato and Booth, 2000). Moreover, young adults from urban areas tend to marry later than those from rural regions, and ethnic/cultural factors influence the timing of marriage.

Furthermore, although same-sex marriage is now legal in Canada, very little research has been conducted on this topic. This should not be surprising given that a federal law—Bill C-38, or the same-sex marriage bill—was signed only on July 20, 2005, putting an official end to two years of national debate. This occurred in 2003, when an Ontario court became the first to rule that the common-law restriction of marriage to the union between a man and a woman violated the Charter of Rights. Currently, most Canadians support the view that same-sex marriages should be recognized by the law as valid, with the same rights as traditional marriages.

The 2006 census was the first to provide data on same-sex marital and common-law partnerships. In this survey, a total of 43,345 same-sex couples fell into this category, representing 0.6% of all couples (married and unmarried). In 2011, the proportion of same-sex couples in Canada rose slightly to 0.8% of all couples, consistent with recent data from other countries such as Australia, the United Kingdom and the United States. Most same-sex couples are male, and they tend to be younger than opposite-sex couples (Milan, 2013).

Finally, some Canadian groups continue to practise arranged marriage, which is still common to many parts of Africa, Asia, and the Middle East. For example, many South Asian–Canadian young people report that their marriages were arranged (Netting, 2006). As a result, they recognize two family systems—the "love marriage" taken for granted by their Western peers, and the "arranged marriage" experienced and advocated by their parents. Contemporary arranged marriages vary with respect to the degree of parental or family input. Many religions (e.g., Muslim, Hindu) are becoming more understanding of what young people want and need from a life partner (Scott, 2016). In semi-arranged marriages, which are becoming increasingly common in many Canadian ethnic communities, young adults have more say in decisions and may be free to express preferences or to reject a match they consider unsuitable. Potential choices of mates are usually limited to people of the same race/ethnic group and socio-economic class, but some people will also consider the importance of love and compatibility.

Shazia, a Pakistani Muslim from Africa who comes from a privileged background, provides a good case study of how arranged marriages have changed over time. As she recounts, "I was in Toronto on vacation for a month, and my family had me meeting with men and their families almost every day. I went out with four or five different men, along with our siblings, before I even met my husband. I didn't really like any of them that much. Then I met my husband; he and his father came to my house and I thought he seemed really nice, and he made me laugh a lot," she says. Shazia's family had been looking for someone educated like her, so they chose a doctor from a respected family. The couple have now been married for 17 years and have two daughters. Shazia adds, "It's like somebody setting up a blind date, and if you like each other it can go further; if not, then it's over. The family won't introduce you to a loser; you meet people who meet your criteria of education and profession. It is a system to get similar people together" (Scott, 2016).

Generally, arranged marriages support collectivist rather than individualistic goals, since they preserve family resources, protect the economic well-being of the couple, and ensure family continuity from generation to generation (Ralston, 1997; Wilson, 2005). And despite euro-centric assumptions that these marriages cannot flourish or be happy, many couples report that "love grows over time." Conversely, forced marriages in which both partners don't fully agree or have much input into the arrangement, are often deemed to be abusive, coercive, and a violation of human rights. This viewpoint is illustrated by a lawyer's opinion that was published in a University of Toronto magazine in the summer of 2016 (see box 7.3).

Box 7.3: Against Their Will: Forced Marriage in Canada

Imagine a first-year law student waking from a recurring nightmare, heart racing, body drenched in sweat. What could be so terrifying? Being forced to marry against her wishes. Her control over her life stolen from her by her family and community. Her future decisions dependent on her husband's and her in-laws' permission. Her studies and her dreams for a career interrupted, if not ended permanently. This situation may seem difficult to believe, but forced marriage is a reality in Canada, even though many Canadians are unaware of it. As a lawyer practicing family law in the Greater Toronto Area and working with many diverse communities, I see the resulting impact on those affected. Yet, I am hopeful that Canada's new legislation against this type of abuse—passed in June—will be a powerful force for change.

A forced marriage occurs when one or both parties refuse to give full and free consent to be married to each other at that time. The pressure to marry may come from immediate or extended families and ethnic or religious communities, both here in Canada and abroad. Some women are taken to another country to visit family and forced into marriage there; some are coerced here at home. It happens to men too. Those who are forced to marry may be Canadian-born or more recent arrivals.

Forced marriage is sometimes confused with arranged marriage—even by those who have married against their will. The key distinction is that in an arranged marriage, while there may be the same level of involvement from family and community, both individuals are in full agreement with what is taking place and are looking forward to their lives together. In a forced marriage, the opposite is true for at least one party, whose consent may be assumed, given by others or coerced through extreme emotional pressure, threats, and even physical violence.

Patriarchal cultural traditions and communal definitions of honour and shame complicate and hide the very real human rights violations inherent in forced marriage. The individual loses agency over their life and is at greater risk of sexual assault, other forms of physical violence, emotional abuse, and financial control. These dangers are compounded because forced marriages are very hard to leave. Separation and divorce are still considered unacceptable in many communities and can lead to ostracism. I always find it difficult to help a woman who is experiencing family violence to understand that she can separate and leave the marriage to protect herself and her children from further abuse. She may have lacked choice then, but she can say no now.

These human rights violations need to be prevented, and this is where Canada's new legislation will be most helpful. Social service agencies have not been effective in working with the ethnic communities they are meant to serve because they lack the deep connections and understanding required for meaningful action. People mistrust them and believe they have vested interests, such as securing funding or furthering a political ideology. The agencies too often align with the very powerful and vocal within communities and end up functioning as cultural apologists.

Legislation helps to effect change in two key ways. It provides options for potential victims, such as peace bonds to place restrictions on potential abusers, and it gives the police the power to intervene when approached for assistance.

And clear laws with easily understood consequences will effect change through word-of-mouth. Criminal law serves an educational function; it delineates acceptable behaviour within society, especially when there are misperceptions regarding legality. This is why many countries, including the United Kingdom and Australia, have already enacted similar laws.

I am hopeful that this legislation and resulting awareness will empower the vulnerable and aid those who seek to assist them. Protecting the silent and powerless is fundamental to the very concept of the universality of human rights. For the powerless and the resilient, they too have dreams.

Source: Singh, N.K. 2015. "Against Their Will." *U of T Magazine* 43(1): 53. Retrieved June 24, 2016, from http://magazine.utoronto.ca/back_issues/autumn2015.pdf.

The Marriage Gradient

In celebrity news, media stories about rich or famous men marrying much younger women are plentiful. At 59, US President Donald Trump married 35-year-old former model Melania Knavs; numerous other examples can be seen among Hollywood couples. However, Canadian statistics do not show support for large age-discrepant marital unions, and recent data show a decline over time in the tendency for older men to partner with younger women. In 2011, almost 50% of all senior Canadian couples were 0 to 3 years apart, a proportion that has increased since 1981. Only about 12% of marriages between Canadian seniors involved a husband who was 10 years or more older than his wife. We are also seeing a rise in the percentage of women marrying men younger than themselves over the past several decades (Todd, 2015).

The phenomenon of women marrying older men is known as the **marriage gradient**, which was first documented by well-known sociologist Jessie Bernard in the 1970s. This gap declined steadily throughout the 20th century, such that the current gender disparity is fairly minimal. Yet, the fact that women continue to marry older men has important implications for women over the life course. The younger spouse (the wife) typically enters marriage with fewer assets, such as less schooling, less job experience, and a lower income.

Over time, this disadvantage accumulates, since the husband's job will be given priority because it is deemed more important to the overall economic situation of the family. A woman will also usually be the one who quits her job (which is usually lower paid) to care for young children. In this way, the initially small economic difference becomes a substantial gap. Therefore, women's "choice" to marry at a younger age, in addition to other existing structural economic inequities, contributes to their economic dependency. It also illustrates how gendered marital patterns have economic implications that operate in rather subtle but potent ways (Gee, 2000).

A PORTRAIT OF "MIXED" UNIONS

It has only been four and a half decades since Hollywood's first interracial kiss in the 1967 movie "Guess Who's Coming to Dinner?," starring Sidney Poitier, the first Black man to win an Academy Award. This groundbreaking comedy-drama featured a set of affluent parents whose attitudes are challenged when their daughter brings home a Black fiancé. La Rose (2008) recalls how this movie shocked mainstream America and that it reflected how North America used to have very different attitudes toward individuals partnering with someone of a different race or visible minority group. She documents that not only was this behaviour taboo; it could potentially land you in jail, particularly in the US, where up until 1967, 16 states had laws banning interracial marriage. At that time, the Supreme Court ruled that banning mixed-race marriages was unconstitutional. It ruled that the state of Virginia could not criminalize the marriage that Richard Loving, a White man, and his Black wife, Mildred, had entered into nine years earlier in Washington, D.C.

Fortunately, much has changed since then, and the latest census figures show that on both sides of the border, love is increasingly colour blind, since mixed unions are forming at unprecedented rates. In 2011, a relatively high percentage of certain Canadian visible minority groups were in mixed-race unions, reflecting shifting norms of **homogamy** (marriage between couples of the same race/ethnicity, religion, social class, and age group) and **endogamy** (the tendency to marry within one's group). Yet, overall only 4.6% of all couples in Canada were in mixed unions, suggesting that norms of endogamy were still strong, particularly within certain ethnocultural groups. Of those in mixed unions, Japanese-Canadians are the most apt to marry or live with a non-Japanese person (78.7%), followed by Latin Americans (48.2%), Blacks (40.2%) and Filipinos (29.8%). Chinese (19.4%) and South Asians (13.0%) are the least likely to form mixed unions

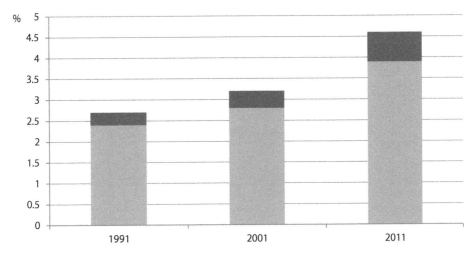

■ Mixed unions in which the two spouses or partners are members of different visible minorities

■ Mixed unions in which one spouse or partner is a visible minority member and the other is not

Figure 7.2: Proportion of Couples in Mixed Unions, Canada, 1991–2011

Source: Statistics Canada. 2011. "Mixed Unions in Canada." Catalogue no. 99-010-X2011003. Ottawa: Minister of Industry (figure 1). Retrieved June 23, 2016, from www12.statcan.gc.ca/nhs-enm/2011/as-sa/99-010-x/2011003/c-g/c-g3-01-eng.cfm.

(Statistics Canada, 2014). Further, other research establishes that well-educated, urban, and younger adults are the most likely to be in "mixed" unions. These factors are found to be related to the adoption of behaviours and attitudes that question the boundaries of prevailing social norms, as well as a greater tolerance and acceptance of diversity and social inclusion (Milan and Hamm, 2004).

Turning to other ethnocultural characteristics of Canadian couples in private households (see table 7.2), slightly over half (52.8%) of mixed unions share the same religious affiliation, whereas the majority (74.6%) of non-mixed unions do. Moreover, while relatively few *non-mixed* or *homogamous* couples include one spouse born in Canada and the other in another country (11.2%), almost half (49.2%) of mixed unions fit this situation. Mixed- union couples are also far less likely (54.6%) to share a common mother tongue, while this is only the case for 10.4% of non-mixed unions (Statistics Canada, 2014). Many mixed-union couples (54.6%) do not share a mother tongue, while only 10.4% of non-mixed couples are in this situation."

"ALONG COMES BABY": THE TRANSITION TO PARENTHOOD

As previously mentioned, the average age at which women become mothers has steadily climbed over the past several decades, but it has varied throughout history. During the

Table 7.2: Percentage Distribution of Couples by Various Ethno-cultural Characteristics, Canada, 2011

	All Couples	Mixed Unions	Non Mixed Unions
Number of couples in private households	7,888,100	360,045	7,528,050
Country of Birth			
Both spouses born in Canada	66.9	25.3	68.9
Both spouses born outside of Canada in the same country	18.2	6.0	18.8
Spouses born outside Canada in different countries	3.7	19.4	3.0
One spouse born in Canada, the other in a different country	11.2	49.2	9.3
Religion			
Same religious affiliation	73.6	52.8	74.6
No religious affiliation for either spouse	16.6	20.4	16.5
One spouse with religious affiliation, the other with no religious affiliation	8.6	17.3	8.2
Different religious affiliations*	1.2	9.5	0.8
Mother Tongue			
Having one or more common mother tongue(s)	87.6	45.4	89.6
No common mother tongue	12.4	54.6	10.4

*This category is composed of couples in which the spouses or partners reported an affiliation with two different broad religious groups (e.g., one person is Buddhist, the other Christian). Differences in affiliations within a broad religious group (e.g., Anglican and Roman Catholic) are not included in this category.

Source: Statistics Canada. 2014. "Mixed Unions in Canada." Catalogue no. 99-010-X2011003. Ottawa: Minister of Industry (Table 2, pg. 6). Retrieved December 31, 2016, from www12.statcan.gc.ca/nhs-enm/2011/as-sa/99-010-x/2011003/tbl/tbl2-eng.cfm.

1970s, the age of mothers at both marriage and childbirth began to rise, and by 2011, the average age at marriage had edged up to 30.2 years, the oldest on record. The average age at first birth in 2011 was 28.5, also the oldest recorded to date. Overall, unlike earlier time periods, the current time frame for childbearing has become increasingly concentrated around age 30. There are also some interesting regional/provincial differences. Ontario and British Columbia tend to have the oldest mothers on average, while Nunavut has the youngest. Overall, today almost half of all mothers are 30 and older, whereas two decades ago, three-quarters of mothers in Canada were under 30 (Statistics Canada, 2016).

Rates of teenage pregnancy have also been steadily declining and are at their lowest level in over 50 years. Notably, births to teenage mothers decreased from about 30 per 1,000 in 1974 to 12 per 1,000 in 2008. However, this overall rate masks some significant regional

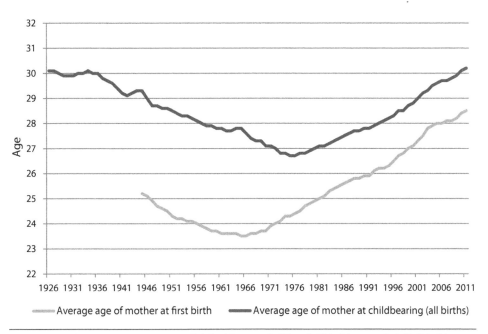

Figure 7.3: Average Age of Mother at First Birth and All Births, Canada, 1926–2011

Note: Births to mothers whose age was unknown were prorated.

Source: Statistics Canada. 2016. "Fertility: Fewer Children, Older Moms." *Canadian Megatrends*. Retrieved July 1 from www.statcan.gc.ca/pub/11-630-x/11-630-x2014002-eng.htm.

variations in the propensity to become a teenage mother. For example, in Nunavut, 94 out of every 1,000 women aged 14 to 19 are mothers (about one out of 10). Conversely, in Quebec, only about 9 out of 1,000 teens are mothers (about one out of 100). Additionally, more children are being born outside of traditional legal marital unions, with Canada's extramarital birth rate calculated at approximately 30% of all live births (Human Resources and Skills Development Canada, 2011).

Although most women are postponing having their first child and marrying, some women—particularly those from lower socio-economic status backgrounds—may have children at a relatively young age and out of wedlock. In an ethnographic study of poor families in the United States, Edin and Kefalas (2005) explore how girls from poor families conceptualize their active choices to have children while they are young and unmarried. They note that middle-class beliefs about the right way to start a family are conditioned by a social context that offers great economic rewards for those who are willing to wait to have children. For example, for a White, college-bound adolescent, postponed child-bearing will likely lead to higher lifetime earnings. And if she can hold out until her mid-thirties, she'll probably earn twice as much as if she'd had a child right out of college or university. Conversely, young people from impoverished communities do not share the same prospects. As concluded by these authors:

The centrality of children in this lower-class worldview of what is important and meaningful in life stands in striking contrast to their low priority in the view of more affluent teens and 20-something youth, who may want children at some point in the future, but only after educational, career, and other life goals have been achieved. Putting motherhood first makes sense in a social context where the achievements that middle-class youth see as their birthright are little more than pipe dreams: Children offer a tangible source of meaning, while other avenues for gaining self-esteem and personal satisfaction appear vague and tenuous. (Edin and Kefalas, 2005: p. 49)

Another rising trend that is occurring as people live longer, cohabit, divorce more, and increasingly have children outside of marriage is that of **multiple-partner fertility**. Also referred to as "multipartnered," this term refers to having biological children with more than one partner. For example, a woman might have three biological children from three different men whom she may or may not have married or cohabited with. While Canadian research in this area is virtually non-existent, some US studies (e.g., Guzzo and Furstenberg, 2007) suggest that the trend is more common among the poor and the unmarried; it is also more common if the father is Black, if he has been incarcerated, and if the parents were young when the first child was born. In sum, multiple-partner fertility appears to be most prevalent among the least advantaged in our society. It also underscores the increased complexity of kin relations and raises questions about stress and conflict stemming from this complexity (Smock and Greenland, 2010).

Moreover, biology alone does not determine parenthood—one can become a parent yet never give birth to a child; for example, by "inheriting" foster or stepchildren, through surrogacy, or via adoption. With regards to foster children, table 7.3 shows that in 2011, 17,410 private households had a least one foster child aged 14 and under. Almost half of these households had two or more foster children. Most of these children live in house-holds comprised of a married couple (56.9%), although some may be living with a lone parent (14%), or in "other" types of households. Moreover, there has been mounting criti-cism in recent years over our Canadian foster care system due to chronic underfunding, poor social work staffing, and the complexities of protecting children and youth as they age through, and out of, the current government system.

There has also been a rise in non-biological parenthood due to surrogacy through the development of the technology that enabled in vitro fertilization (IVF) in the late 1970s. This has increased the viability of gestational surrogacy, and ultimately commercial surrogacy, whereby a surrogate mother can reproduce a baby for another person. Transnational commercial surrogacy, for instance, represents a form of medical tourism undertaken by prospective parents who seek to hire women in other countries (e.g., Mexico, India). According to Lozanski (2015), while Canada "criminalizes" domestic surrogacy (i.e., it is illegal to pay for the service, although some out-of-pocket expenses can be reimbursed), it facilitates it transnationally. Therefore, this type of surrogacy is viewed as a contentious and controversial reproductive practice. For

Table 7.3: Distribution of Private Households with at Least One
Foster Child Aged 14 and Under, Canada, 2011

Private households with at least one foster child aged 14 and under	Number	Percentage
Number foster children		
One	7,845	45.1
Two	5,010	28.8
Three or more	4,555	26.2
Household type		
Married couple	9,910	56.9
Common-law couple	2,165	12.4
Lone-parent family	2,430	14.0
Multiple-family	990	5.7
Other	1,915	11.0
Total	**17,410**	**100.00**

Source: Statistics Canada. 2012. "Portrait of Families and Living Arrangements in Canada." Catalogue no. 98-312-X2011001. Ottawa: Minister of Industry. Retrieved July 22, 2016, from www12.statcan.gc.ca/census-recensement/2011/as-sa/98-312-x/98-312-x2011001-eng.pdf

instance, it is argued that it can reinforce transnational disparities and the exploitation of vulnerable women by middle and upper-class citizens through the commodification of "bioavailable" bodies.

Another pathway to non-blood parenthood is through adoption. Adoption Canada (2016) defines adoption as "the legal and permanent transfer of parental rights from a person or couple to another person or couple." Adoptive parents have the same legal rights and responsibilities as biological parents. The cost of adoption depends upon many different variables, such as the type of adoption (e.g., adopting a birth relative versus a child from another country), whether an agency is involved, the province the parents reside in, and associated travel costs. It is estimated by Adoption Canada.ca that the cost of adoption through the public child-welfare system in Canada is usually less than $3,000, whereas an international adoption can cost between $20,000 and $30,000.

Statistics show that in 2011, 537,000 people in Canada adopted children (Statistics Canada, 2015). Most adoptions involve adults who are already related to the child, such as a step-parent adopting a stepchild. It is also interesting to note that public perceptions of biological mothers who plan to put their child up for adoption vary according to gender and the circumstances of the mother. For example, men are more likely than women to consider the biological mother as uncaring (March and Miall, 2006). International adoptions are also on the rise, which raises a number of provocative sociological and political issues (e.g., see Dorrow, 2006). Many of these children are from China, with its preponderance of girls due to a one-child -per-family policy that favours boys (Adoption Council of Canada, 2016). Adoption as an alternative form of family formation has been socially

Box 7.4: Surrogacy in Canada: Tiffany's Story

It all started when I heard about a friend doing surrogacy and how amazing it was to be able to give the gift of life. We talked, and I started doing research to try and see how it worked and what I would need in order to become a surrogate. I found SCO (Surrogacy Canada Online) and applied; then I spoke to Sally, who was beyond words amazing at answering any questions or concerns I had while starting the process. I was young and very scared, but also very excited to start this amazing journey.

In 2012, I was put up as an available surrogate, and I received a couple of calls and some emails from couples desperately seeking a surrogate. I talked to a few but had a good feeling about one couple, and we decided to take it past emails and phone calls and met up for lunch. It was instant, we all felt so connected, and it was then I knew this was the couple for me. We matched that day and things started rolling.

Things happened pretty quickly, between meeting Dr. Del Valle and getting all my screening done to make sure everything was ready to go for a transfer. We got going right away on contracts and all the little things to get the ball rolling. Once everything was done and finalized it was time for our transfer. We were all very excited to have finally come.

[During] my first transfer, I had my Intended Mother and support from Karen and a SCO Support Worker. She made it so much less nerve-wracking on both me and my IM. It was filled with laughter and so much love from everyone. Everything went well at transfer, and now it was time for the two-week dreaded wait for our first Beta. [The] first and second Beta numbers were good and confirmed pregnancy. Unfortunately, a couple weeks later our first transfer failed.

We all had a hard time dealing with it, but we decided to try again for a second transfer. We started meds and went to try again. We had the dreaded two-week wait again and did the blood work and found out the transfer had worked and so far the numbers were good. Now we had to wait for the first ultrasound to confirm pregnancy!

Yes! Confirmation of pregnancy and things moved along amazing, I had more ultrasounds and later confirmed they were having a baby girl! I had a wonderful pregnancy and loved sharing all the moments with my Intended Parents. Other than the average problems, like heartburn and the horrible heat from summer, things went so perfect. I had Emelia on July 21st, 2013, weighing 7lbs, 9oz. She was so perfect, and the faces on her parents when they first got to see her and hold her was beyond words amazing for everyone around. We still talk once in a while, and I see her grow. She will be three in July, and such a beautiful little girl!

Source: Surrogacy in Canada Online. n.d. "Tiffany's Story." Retrieved June 26, 2016, from sur-rogacy.ca/tiffanys-story.html.

constructed as less "natural" than biological parenting. Regardless, studies reveal that the consequences of adoption tend to be divided between those adoptions that show no disadvantage and those that indicate small deficits. Ironically, if disadvantages do appear, they are most likely created by the less than optimal social climate surrounding adoption, particularly in children's peer groups (Ambert, 2006).

Cross-race and cross-cultural adoption is a sensitive issue that is often the source of debate and controversy. In 2006, there was a great deal of divided opinion with respect to popular singer/entertainer Madonna, who at age 48 had adopted a 13-month-old Malawi baby. Many individuals and the media questioned why she had adopted a Black child from a foreign country, especially given the high number of orphans and other "unwanted" children in her home country, the US. Similarly, in Canada, White parents who adopt babies from other countries (e.g., China, India, Russia) or Indigenous children are often the target of criticism. In the case of Indigenous children, White parents may be accused of being unable to provide them with the opportunity to learn about their ancestry and cultural traditions and to preserve their cultural identity (e.g., see Ambert, 2006).

Finally, similar to predictors of early and late marital timing, the age at which one becomes a parent is influenced by a number of factors, such as family background, gender, age, and educational attainment. Obviously, there are a number of benefits to delayed parenthood, such as maturity and improved economic resources. At the same time, some health professionals are concerned about the unprecedented number of women extending their reproductive years into their mid-thirties and beyond. They argue that there are a number of implications for the health care system, many of which relate to the increased demand and requirements for special services that assist pregnancy and birth. Overall, new reproductive technologies raise a number of concerns for sociologists, scientists, and ethicists and have many important ramifications for families.

The Shrinking Canadian Family and the Social Pressure to Reproduce

In demography, the crude birth rate of a population is an estimation of the number of live childbirths per 1,000 people per year. Another indicator of fertility frequently used is the total **fertility rate**, or the average number of live children born to each woman over the course of her life during her child-bearing years (ages 15 to 49). Generally, demographers prefer to use the total fertility rate rather than the crude birth rate because the former is not affected by the age distribution of the population. This also facilitates more accurate comparisons across countries. As a result, we are aware that fertility rates tend to be higher in less economically developed countries and lower in more economically developed countries.

From a historical perspective, the transition to low fertility (and reduced mortality rates) began around 1870 and is known as the **first demographic transition**. Since 1965, we have witnessed even more dramatic reductions in fertility; this is known as the second demographic transition. This means that the size of the Canadian family is shrinking and this affects the country's population growth and age structure. In figure 7.4, we see that over time the fertility rate has decreased substantially, a trend that is also occurring in many other industrialized countries. In 1851, the total fertility rate in Canada was 6.6; this declined to 1.53 in 2004 and remained fairly stable at 1.61 in 2011 (Statistics Canada, 2016). This is below the replacement level of 2.1, or the level of fertility at which a developed population exactly replaces itself from one generation to the next. In short, replacement-level fertility requires an average of 2.1 children per woman. Therefore, unless there is a radical shift in fertility, mortality, or immigration, our population will continue to get smaller and older during the next century.

It is also interesting to observe fluctuations or "blips" in fertility behaviour. In particular, the postwar baby boom (from 1946 to 1965) occurred when two decades of births were compressed into a decade and a half as a result of postponed fertility due to World War Two, as shown in figure 7.4. This blip clearly signifies how fertility is linked to various social and legislative changes that are discussed throughout this book.

Recent fertility intention studies (e.g., Edmonston et al., 2010) document that most Canadian young adults plan to have children, with one half reporting that they intend to have two children. Almost one-third plan to have three or four children, and only 7% report that they do not want any children. These statistics support actual trends in recent behaviour, which include the overall pattern of decreasing fertility rates and postponed births. Moreover, thoughts about intended fertility have not changed that much, and contemporary social norms about family size (around two children) are found to be remarkably resilient. Yet, at the same time, young people are now more likely to question whether they really want to have children, when they should start trying to conceive, and how many children they should ideally have (Vanier Institute of the Family, 2008).

Baker (2010b) points out that most parents see children as the natural outcome of adulthood and marriage rather than a conscious choice. Yet, sociological explanations—unlike biological ones, which may emphasize the role of "maternal instincts" in deciding

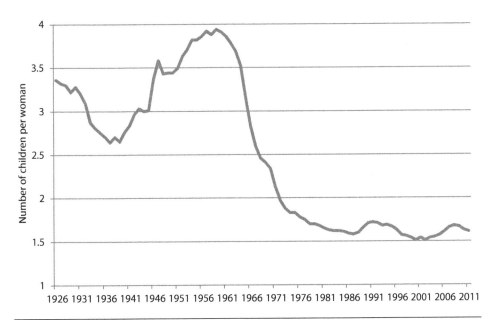

Figure 7.4: Total Fertility Rate per 1,000 Canadian Women, 1926 to 2011

Source: Statistics Canada. 2016. "Fertility: Fewer Children, Older Moms." *Canadian Megatrends.* Retrieved July 1 from www.statcan.gc.ca/pub/11-630-x/11-630-x2014002-eng.htm.

to reproduce—tend to focus on two reasons: social pressures, or costs and benefits. The social pressure to reproduce originates from many sources: religion, government officials, the media, family, friends, and even strangers. For example, churches have traditionally viewed the purpose of marriage as reproduction. After the wedding ceremony, friends and family often show this expectation by throwing symbols of fertility (such as rice or confetti) on the couple. Governments and community leaders see children as necessary because they become the future generation of taxpayers, voters, workers, and consumers. Individuals may also perceive that children provide benefits such as reduced stigma (i.e., the belief that the childless are selfish and immature), companionship, and personal fulfillment.

Turning to the topic of delayed family transitions, why are so many young adults postponing marriage and parenthood, and having fewer children? Numerous individual, socio-cultural, economic, and political factors are at play. Economic conditions, education, and career factors are reported as important in women's decision to delay marriage and parenthood. Contraceptive use and cohabitation have risen dramatically, and sex before marriage is less frowned upon. For example, as children increasingly remain at home and in school longer, and are thus consumers rather than producers (as was the case in pre-industrial society), it becomes very expensive to be parents and raise large families.

One can also remain unmarried or childless either for life or until one enters the older adult years. Childlessness is more prevalent now than in recent decades, and it is estimated that approximately 15% of Canadian women reach the age of 44 without having given birth (Mitchell, 2006). However, this is not a new trend, and rates have fluctuated over time. In fact, childlessness decreased from 15% among women born at the beginning of the century to a historic low of 7–8% among women born between 1927 and 1936—the very women who helped produce the baby boom (Rosenthal and Gladstone, 2000).

It is also important to distinguish between those who choose not to have children (the childless by choice) and those who are childless by circumstances, such as infertility (e.g., Clarke, Martin-Matthews, and Matthews, 2006; Veevers, 1980). Most young people intend, or want, to have at least one child. However, a minority of Canadians voluntarily intend not to become parents either because they do not want children (e.g., because of career demands) or because they are unable to have them due to medical problems (Stobert and Kemeny, 2003). Demographic characteristics of the voluntarily childless are relatively consistent, showing that these individuals tend to be well educated, live in urban areas, have little or no religious affiliation, and ascribe to non-traditional roles (Trella, 2007).

However, Trella (2007) asserts that research on childless couples relies not only on traditional conceptions of marriage and family, but also upon conceptions of femininity that she labels as **hegemonic motherhood**. This term refers to the perception that women are, by nature, maternal, and that they desire children. In other words, the research reflects a social discourse on motherhood that creates a taken-for-granted understanding of what is natural and indicative of healthy feminine identity.

In summary, research suggests that the decision to forego parenthood is linked to personal, economic, social, and political circumstances rather than selfish or immature personalities. A good example of how state policies can influence fertility decisions is the Chinese one-child policy, which was initiated for economic reasons in the 1970s to curb population growth. This policy began to be formally phased out in 2015, a policy that was highly effective in reducing the population. However, many have pointed out that this policy produced many negative side effects, such as a preference for boys, which led to a plethora of other problems. Moreover, social discourse on deciding whether to choose parenthood is restrictive in that it limits our understanding of why people want children in the first place. Indeed, Trella argues that the "invisible power of hegemonic parenthood operates in such a way that individuals are led to believe that they should want children, and will be unhappy and regretful if they choose not to have children" (Trella, 2007: 13).

SUMMARY

This chapter explores the changing nature of how young people form intimate and committed family relations. Many young people are choosing to stay single longer, cohabit, and marry and have children later, and they are more likely to have children outside of legal marriage. Canadian families are also shrinking and, while most young people will become parents someday, compared to recent decades, more are deciding to remain childless. However, a life-course perspective reminds us that many of the trends we witness in contemporary society were also witnessed in previous times. Rates of childlessness, for instance, have fluctuated over time due to changing social, medical, and economic opportunities and constraints. Our changing technological landscape has also played a significant role in shaping how, where, and when we form partnerships. Moreover, family structures and the acceptability of certain family behaviours as "legitimate" continue to broaden and evolve in relation to changing times.

What will become of intimate relations, marriage, and parenthood in the future, given these transformations? As discussed in chapter 1, many worry that families, in the traditional sense at least, will slowly disappear. Many researchers also emphasize that marriage generates numerous health and economic benefits (e.g., see Waite and Gallagher, 2000). For example, married individuals are more likely to maintain a healthy lifestyle and diet, and are less likely to use alcohol and drugs than non-married adults (Bachman et al., 1997). Conversely, some "radical" writers (e.g., Fineman, 1995) argue that marriage, as a legal category, ought to be abolished because it is an inherently conservative institution that places women in a subordinate position under patriarchal domination.

The recent federal law allowing same-sex couples to legally marry supports the idea that many Canadians continue to think that marriage provides greater equality and protection among citizens. It also shows that marriage remains a sacred institution. And with continuing high rates of immigration from countries in which marriage is the norm, in tandem with the growing strength of the wedding industry as big business, it is difficult to imagine that it will ever disappear. Whatever the future brings, there is little doubt that family ties will continue to be diverse, sought after, and highly valued by young people. However, our meanings and practices will undoubtedly undergo continued critical reflection and alteration in response to shifting socio-economic, political, cultural, and technological landscapes.

QUESTIONS FOR CRITICAL REFLECTION AND DEBATE

1. What advantages and disadvantages do you see with respect to meeting potential mates in non-traditional settings, such as through Internet dating services and chat rooms?
2. Why has cohabitation become so popular among young people? Do you think that it will eventually replace marriage?
3. Debate the following: Women who cohabit or marry men older than themselves experience a number of advantages over the course of their lives.
4. What factors do you think contribute to the decision for an individual or a couple to remain childless? To what extent is childlessness stigmatized in society?
5. Critically evaluate whether arranged marriages are more beneficial for individuals and families than free-choice marriages based on romantic love.
6. Same-sex and mixed unions are on the increase in Canada. Discuss the factors underlying these trends and consider other emergent patterns that will contribute to greater diversity in family life.

GLOSSARY

Arranged marriage involves an intermediary and occurs when families play a pivotal role in the choice of one's marital partner.

Consensual non-monogamy describes intimate romantic relationships (e.g., swinging, open relationships, polyamorous relationships) that are negotiated between two or more people and that are either sexually or emotionally exclusive or both.

Endogamy is the tendency to date and marry within one's social group or social class, race, religion, or language group.

Family of procreation refers to the family that we form when we mature, apart from our family of origin or the family that we are born into.

Fertility rate is an estimate of the average number of children that women will have in their lifetime.

First demographic transition is the shift from high mortality and fertility levels to low mortality and fertility levels that began around 1870 and lasted until about 1965.

Hegemonic motherhood refers to social discourse that creates the perception that women are, by nature, maternal, and that they desire children.

Homogamy refers to a non-random approach of selecting mates or spouses who have similar physical, intellectual, personality, and social class traits.

LAT relationships are defined as those partners who are neither married nor living common law, but who are in an intimate, committed couple relationship yet living apart together.

Marriage gradient is women's tendency to marry "up" with regards to age, education, occupation, and even height.

Multiple-partner fertility, a trend that is on the rise, refers to having biological children with more than one partner.

FURTHER READING

Crouse, J.S. 2016. *Marriage Matters: Perspectives on the Private and Public Importance of Marriage*. NJ: Transaction Publishers.
Argues that in a free society, our most vulnerable communities (especially minorities and the poor) suffer the most from a retreat from marriage. Therefore, since marriage advances the public interest, we should create laws and policies that support, rather than undermine, it.

DeLamater, J. and R.F. Plante (eds.). 2015. *Handbook of the Sociology of Sexualities*. New York: Springer.
Provides a broad overview of the contributions of sociology and psychology to the study of sexual relationships and sexual expression across the life course. Topics include dating, marriage, commercial sex work, sex education, embodiment, and trans-sexualities.

Edin, K., and M. Kefalas. 2007. *Promises I Can Keep: Why Poor Women Put Motherhood before Marriage*, 2nd ed. Berkeley: University of California Press.
Provides a classic ethnographic study on motherhood and marriage among 162 low-income urban women. Offers an intimate look at why these women put children ahead of marriage despite the daunting challenges they know lie ahead.

Fincham, F. and M. Cui. 2014. *Romantic Relationships in Emerging Adulthood*. New York: Cambridge University Press.

Presents a synthesis of cutting-edge theory and research that addresses the formation, nature, and significance of romantic relationships from an interdisciplinary perspective.

Gamson, J. 2015. *Modern Families: Stories of Extraordinary Journeys to Kinship*. New York: New York University Press.
Combining personal memoir and ethnographic storytelling, this book offers a variety of unconventional family-creation tales—adoption and assisted reproduction; gay and straight parents; coupled, single, and multi-parent families—set against the social, legal, and economic contexts in which they were made.

Greeley, H.T. 2016. *The End of Sex and the Future of Human Reproduction*. Cambridge: Harvard University Press.
This author argues that over the next several decades, most people in developed countries will stop having sex for the purpose of reproduction. Instead, prospective parents will be able to freely and legally choose "designer" babies through revolutionary biological technologies.

Sheff, E. 2014. *The Polyamorists Next Door: Inside Multiple-Partner Relationships and Families*. New York: Rowman & Littlefield.
Relying on 15 years of ethnographic research, interview data, and personal experience, the author provides a nuanced portrait of polyamorist families. This ground-breaking text on the family life of sexually non-conforming adults and their children is essential reading for anyone wanting to learn more about multi-partner families from a gender, race, and class-based analysis.

RELATED WEB SITES

Adoption Council of Canada, an umbrella organization, raises public awareness of adoption and provides services such as a resource library, a quarterly newsletter, referrals, and conference planning, www.adoption.ca.

Canadians for Equal Marriage adopts a nationwide, bilingual campaign for the rights of same-sex families and works at the grassroots level, in the media, and in Parliament. www.equal-marriage.ca.

Sex Information and Education Council of Canada is a non-profit organization (est. 1965) that fosters public and professional education about human sexuality, www.sieccan.org.

Quirky Alone explores issues of single living and cheerfully questions compulsory coupledom, www.quirkyalone.net.

Statistics Canada has a web site that provides some of the best information on family formation trends, including the latest figures on cohabitation, fertility, and marriage, www.
statcan.gc.ca.

REFERENCES

Adoption Council of Canada. 2016. "Adoption in Canada." Retrieved July 4, 2016, from www.
adoption.ca.

Amato, P.R., and A. Booth. 2000. *A Generation at Risk: Growing Up in an Era of Family Upheaval.*
Cambridge: Harvard University Press.

Ambert, A.M. 2006. *Changing Families: Relationships in Context.* Toronto: Pearson, Allyn and Bacon.

Armstrong, E.A., L. Hamilton, and P. England. 2010. "Is Hooking Up Bad for Young Women?"
Contexts 9: 22–27.

Arnett, J.J. 2000. "Emerging Adulthood: A Theory of Development from the Late Teens through
the Twenties." *American Psychologist* 55: 469–480.

Bachman, J.G., et al. 1997. *Smoking, Drinking, and Drug Use in Young Adulthood.* Mahwah, New
Jersey: Erbaum.

Baker, P. 2010a. "Discourse and Gender." In K. Hyland and B. Paltridge (eds.), *The Continuum
Companion to Discourse Analysis* (pp. 199–212). New York: Continuum International
Publishing Group.

Baker, M. 2010b. *Choices and Constraints in Family Life*, 2nd ed. Toronto: Oxford University Press.

Barker, M. and D. Landridge. 2010. "Whatever Happened to Non-Monogamies? Critical
Reflections on Recent Research and Theory." *Sexualities* 13: 748–772.

Bogle, K.A. 2008. *Hooking Up: Sex, Dating and Relationships On Campus.* New York: New York
University Press.

Canadian Press. 2007. "Solo-Dwellers on the Rise as Young, Independent Singles Delay Marriage"
Retrieved September 13, 2007, from www.canadianpress.google.com/article.

Castells, M. 2004. *The Power of Identity*, 2nd ed. Malden, M.A.: Blackwell Publisher.

CBC News. 2011. "Canada's Polygamy Laws Upheld in BC Supreme Court," November 23, retrieved January 17, 2011, from www.cbc.ca/news/canada/british-columbia/story/2011.

Clarke, L.H., A. Martin-Matthews, and R. Matthews. 2006. "The Continuity and Discontinuity
of the Embodied Self in Infertility." *Canadian Review of Sociology and Anthropology* 43: 95–113.

Comacchio, C. 2014. "Canada's Families: Historical and Contemporary Variations. In D. Cheal
and P. Albanese (eds.), *Canadian Families Today: New Perspectives*, 3rd ed. (pp. 22–44).
Toronto: Oxford University Press.

Currier, D.M. 2013. "Strategic Ambiguity: Protecting Emphasized Femininity and Hegemonic
Masculinity in the Hookup Culture." *Gender and Society* 27: 704–727.

Dorow, S. 2006. *Transnational Adoption: A Cultural Economy of Race, Gender, and Kinship.* New
York: New York Publishers.

Edin, K., and M. Kefalas. 2005. *Promises I Can Keep: Why Poor Women Put Motherhood before
Marriage.* Berkeley: University of California Press.

Edmonston, B., S. Lee, and W. Zheng. 2010. "Fertility Intentions in Canada: Change or No Change?" *Canadian Studies in Population* 37: 297–337.

Fineman, M.A. 1995. *The Neutered Mother, the Sexual Family, and Other Twentieth-Century Tragedies.* New York: Routledge.

Gee, E.M. 2000. "Contemporary Diversities." In N. Mandell and A. Duffy (eds.), *Canadian Families: Diversity, Conflict, and Change* (pp. 78–111). Toronto: Harcourt Canada.

Grunt-Mejer, K. and C. Campbell. 2016. "Around Consensus Non-Monogamies: Assessing Attitudes toward Non-Exclusive Relationships." *The Journal of Sex Research* 53: 45–53.

Guzzo, K.B. and F.F. Furstenberg. 2007. "Multipartnered Fertility among American Men." *Demography* 44: 583–601.

Hamilton, L. and E.A. Armstrong. 2009. "Gendered Sexuality in Young Adulthood: Double Binds and Flawed Options." *Gender and Society* 23: 589–616.

Heath, M. 2014. "Intimacy, Commitment, and Family Formation." In D. Cheal and P. Albanese (eds.), *Canadian Families Today: New Perspectives,* 3rd ed. (pp. 45–64). Toronto: Oxford University Press.

Human Resources and Skills Development Canada. 2011. "Family Life – Age of Mother at Childbirth." Retrieved January 28, 2012, from www4.hrsdc.gc.ca/.3ndic.1t.4r@-eng.jsp?iid=75.

Kollock, P., and P. Blumstein. 1988. "Personal Relationships." *Annual Review of Sociology* 14: 467–490.

La Rose, L. 2008. "Mixed-Race Marriages on the Rise," *The Star,* April 2, retrieved December 6, 2016, from www.thestar.com/printarticle/409104.

Lozanski, K. 2015. "Transnational Surrogacy: Canada's Contradictions." *Social Science and Medicine,* 124: 383–390.

Manning, W.D., and P.J. Smock. 2005. "Measuring and Modelling Cohabitation: New Perspectives from Qualitative Data." *Journal of Marriage and the Family* 67: 989–1002.

March, K., and C. Miall. 2006. "Reinforcing the Motherhood Ideal: Public Perceptions of Biological Mothers Who Make an Adoption Plan." *Canadian Review of Sociology and Anthropology* 43: 367–385.

McDaniel, S., and L. Tepperman. 2011. *Close Relations: An Introduction to the Sociology of Families,* 4th ed. Toronto: Pearson Prentice-Hall.

Milan, A. 2013. "Marital Status: Overview, 2011." Component of Statistics Canada, Report on the Demographic Situation in Canada, Catalogue no. 91-209-X. Ottawa: Minister of Industry.

Milan, A., and B. Hamm. 2004. "Mixed Unions." *Canadian Social Trends* 73: 2–6.

Miller, B.C. and B. Benson. 1999. "Romantic and Sexual Relationship Development during Adolescence. In W. Furman, B.B. Brown, and C. Feiring (eds.), *The Development of Romantic Relationships in Adolescence* (pp. 99–121). Cambridge: Cambridge University Press.

Mitchell, B.A. 2011. "Ethnocultural Reproduction and Attitudes toward Cohabiting Relationships." *The Canadian Review of Sociology and Anthropology* 38: 391–413.

Mitchell, B.A. 2006. *The Boomerang Age: Transitions to Adulthood in Families.* New Brunswick, New Jersey: Aldine Transaction.

Nett, E. 1988. *Canadian Families: Past and Present.* Toronto: Butterworths.

Netting, N. 2006. "Two Lives, One Partner: Indo-Canadian Youth between Love and Arranged Marriages." *Journal of Comparative Family Studies* 37: 129–146.

Pascoe, C.J. 2011. "Resource and Risk: Youth Sexuality and New-Media Use." *Sexuality Research and Social Policy* 8: 5–17.

Penn, M.J., with E.K. Zalesne. 2007. *Microtrends: The Small Forces behind Tomorrow's Big Changes.* New York: Hachette Book Group.

Ralston, H. 1997. "Arranged, Semi-arranged and 'Love' Marriages among South Asian Immigrant Women in the Diaspora and Their Non-Migrant Sisters in India and Fiji." *International Journal of Sociology of the Family* 27: 43–68.

Reidmann, A., M.A. Lamanna, and A. Nelson. 2003. *Marriages and Families.* Toronto: Thomson Nelson.

Rosenthal, C., and J. Gladstone. 2000. "Grandparenthood in Canada." Ottawa: Vanier Institute of the Family.

Seccombe, K., and R.L. Warner. 2004. *Marriages and Families: Relationships in Social Context.* Toronto: Wadsworth.

Scott, K. 2016. "Arranged Marriages: Are They So Different?" Retrieved June 30, 2016, from www.lisaliving.ca/love-relationships/venus-mars/arranged-marriages-are-they-so-different.

Sheff, E. 2014. *The Polyamorists Next Door: Inside Multiple Partner Relationships and Families.* New York: Rowman & Littlefield

Shucart, B. 2016 (January 8). "Polyamory by the Numbers." *The Advocate.* Retrieved December 23, 2016, from www.advocate.com/current-issue/2016/1/08/polyamory-numbers.

Smock, P.J., and F.R. Greenland. 2010. "Diversity in Pathways to Parenthood: Patterns, Implications, and Emerging Research Directions." *Journal of Marriage and the Family* 72: 576–593.

Stanley, S.M., S.W. Whitton, and H.J. Markman. 2004. "Maybe I Do: Interpersonal Commitment and Premarital or Nonmarital Cohabitation." *Journal of Family Issues* 25: 496–519.

Stanley, N., Barter, C., Wood, M., Aghtaie, N., Larkins, A.L., and Överlien, C. 2016. "Pornography, sexual coercion and abuse and sexting in young people's intimate relationships: A European Study. *Journal of Interpersonal Violence*, March 2016. Retrieved from www.jiv.sagepub.com/content/early/2016/03/04/0886260516633204.full.

Statistics Canada. 2014. "Mixed Unions in Canada." Catalogue no. 99-010-X2011003. Ottawa: Minister of Industry.

Statistics Canada. 2015. "Mother's Day by the Numbers: Adoptions." Retrieved July 22, 2016, from www.statcan.gc.ca/eng/dai/smr08/2015/smr08_199_2015.

Statistics Canada. 2016. "Fertility: Fewer Children, Older Moms." *Canadian Megatrends*, retrieved July 1 from www.statcan.gc.ca/pub/11-630-x/11-630-x2014002-eng.htm.

Stobert, S., and A. Kemeny. 2003. "Childfree by Choice." *Canadian Social Trends* (Summer): 7–10. Catalogue no. 11-008. Ottawa: Statistics Canada.

Todd, D. 2015. "Age Gap in Couples Declining." *The Vancouver Sun*, January 28. Retrieved July 1, 2016, from www.vancouversun.com/news/staff-blogs/couples-age-gaps-dropping.

Trella, D. 2007. "Hegemonic Motherhood: Reconceptualizing Femininity and Family through the Lens of Voluntary Childlessness." Paper presented at the annual meeting of the Population Association of America, New York, March 31.

Turcotte, M. 2013. "Living Apart Together." *Insights on Canadian Society*, catalogue no. 75-006-X. Ottawa: Statistics Canada.

Vanier Institute of the Family. 2008. *Profiling Canada's Families*. Ottawa: Vanier Institute of the Family.

Veevers, J.E. 1980. *Childless by Choice*. Toronto: Butterworths.

Waite, L.J., and M. Gallagher. 2000. *The Case for Marriage*. New York: Doubleday.

Ward, M. 2002. *The Family Dynamic: A Canadian Perspective*, 3rd ed. Toronto: Nelson Thomson Learning.

Wilson, S. 2005. "Partnering, Cohabitation, and Marriage." In M. Baker (ed.), *Families: Changing Trends in Canada*, 5th ed. (pp. 143–162). Toronto: McGraw-Hill Ryerson.

Wu, Z. 2000. *Cohabitation: An Alternative Form of Family Living*. Toronto: Oxford University Press.

CHAPTER 8

Families and Children in the Early Years: Childhood, Socialization, and Shifting Ideologies of Parenthood

LEARNING OBJECTIVES

In this chapter you will learn that ...

- childhood, similar to other life-course stages and categories, is a social construct embedded within a particular cultural time and place
- there are key agents of socialization, such as parents, daycare providers, siblings, the media, peer groups, and the educational system
- socialization is bi-directional or reciprocal, and lifelong
- theories on childhood socialization are not created in a vacuum; instead, they reflect changing assumptions about the nature and role of children in society
- gender-role socialization persists and continues over the life course in response to inequitable structural conditions and opportunities for alternative behaviour
- shifts in child-rearing advice and ideologies of parenthood have profound implications for how people interpret and do the work of parenting in their everyday lives

INTRODUCTION

From a life-course framework, childhood constitutes a distinct developmental phase of the life cycle associated with young family life. As such, childhood is conceived as a category strongly related to biology, since it is associated with our physical maturation. In other words, we are all young once, and with the passage of time, we will all become old. Yet, this empirical fact hides a much wider and more complex set of issues. Notably, there is not a precise definition of concepts like "childhood," and there is social significance of such concepts in relation to the social context in which they are created and applied. Therefore, in order to understand the sociological concept of "childhood," we need to appreciate how categorizations, interpretations, and attributions are socially constructed (e.g., see Livesey, 2005). That is, we need critical social understandings about what children experience and need, and what is expected of children, as well as children's place in the larger society and how it varies by culture and historical era (Wall, 2005).

Philippe Ariès (1962) highlighted the notion of **childhood as a social construct** in his classical work entitled *Centuries of Childhood*. This book ignited a great deal of controversy among historians because he argued that the concept of childhood did not exist in earlier times. Through an analysis of paintings and diaries in medieval Europe, Ariès offered a picture of society in which children were not considered a unique group. He observed that children were typically not represented in art and, if so, they were usually depicted as little or "miniature" adults. And although his ideas have been attacked by historians because of his methodology and interpretations, there is general agreement that conceptions of childhood have changed over time. For example, unlike today, children in the 17th and 18th centuries often left their families at a very early age to become wage earners. As a result, they entered the adult world much earlier than Canadian children do today (Bradbury, 2005).

In recognition that cultural conceptions of childhood vary according to time and place, this chapter will continue to pursue this theme by investigating a number of dimensions relevant to understanding contemporary childhood and families in the early years. Specifically, we will consider what socialization entails, as well as a number of theories on childhood socialization. And in recognition that socialization is lifelong and bi-directional—for instance, children can socialize parents just as parents socialize their young—we will examine a number of salient issues relevant to these processes. Finally, we will conclude with a review of how child-rearing advice and ideologies of parenthood have changed over time.

WHAT IS SOCIALIZATION? WHAT ARE THE KEY AGENTS OF SOCIALIZATION?

Socialization is the process by which a society passes on its behaviour patterns, attitudes, values, and knowledge to the next generation. This is a complex process that also allows an individual to develop a self-identity, including the skills needed to prepare for new roles and to function effectively in a given society. Hence, the emphasis is on social learning and learning the ways of a given society rather than predetermined inherited genetic traits. For example, most of us would agree that there is nothing in the genetic endowment of children to become racists or to commit to certain religions such as Christianity or Islam. Instead, these kinds of proclivities are generated or reproduced by differences in cultural and family background and in the structure of social relations. This does not mean that biological inheritance or genetic influences are irrelevant, since human beings are also biological organisms. Indeed, a certain degree of physiological ability (e.g., memory) is needed in order for socialization to occur or to be successful. Parents play one of the most significant roles in the socialization of their children. However, there are also many other important socializing agents and institutions, such as daycare and pre-school.

Over the last several decades, the need for child care has grown steadily. This demand has occurred in tandem with changing gender roles and family structures, the rise in women's employment, and the corresponding increase in dual-income earner families. Many parents are unable, or simply cannot afford, to stay at home to raise their children and must place them in some form of child care. Data from the 2011 General Social Survey show that almost half (46%) of parents reported using some type of care for a child 14 years old or younger in the previous year (Sinha, 2014). For children under age four, parents relied primarily on three types of arrangements: daycare centers (33%); home daycares (31%) and private arrangements, such as grandparents, other relatives, or nannies (28%). These types of arrangements differ by province/region, as revealed in table 8.1. Quebec stands out for having the greatest proportion of parents who use home daycares (50%), undoubtedly due to their generously subsidized child-care system. As well, the median cost of full-time child care also differed by province, ranging from a low of $152 per month in Quebec to a high of $677 in Ontario.

Table 8.1: Type of Child Care Arrangements among Parents Using Child Care for Children Aged 4 and Under, by Region

	Home Daycare	Daycare Centre	Private Care
		%	
Atlantic Provinces	16*	36	44
Quebec	50	38	10*
Ontario	19	36	32
Prairie Provinces	31	23	43
British Columbia	25*	20*	40
Canada	31	33	28

*Use with caution

Note: Responses of pre-school and other child care arrangements are included in the calculation of percentages, but are not shown in the table. Therefore, totals will not add to 100%.

Source: Sinha, M. 2014. "Child Care in Canada." Catalogue no. 89-652-X-No. 005, Table 1. Ottawa: Minister of Industry (p. 3).

Since daycare centres or home daycares can have differential staffing ratios, routines, and other resources, the effects of the daycare experience on children can vary tremendous-ly. In general, there is consensus that high-quality, stimulating daycare centres can have a number of positive benefits for children, such as improved social skills and cognitive development. But high-quality daycare typically comes with a higher financial cost. This means that better-off families have greater opportunity than their less-wealthy counterparts to provide "resource-rich" child-rearing experiences. These childhood experiences can also accumulate over the life course and reproduce and perpetuate class inequity through relative advantage or disadvantage.

As previously noted, delegating "mother-work" to paid child-care providers such as daycare workers, nannies, or au pairs is an increasingly common arrangement for working mothers. Arat-Koc (1989) notes how foreign domestic workers have historically been recruited as "a solution to the crisis in the domestic sphere in Canada," a topic to be further explored in chapter 16. These nannies and au pairs, usually hired only by wealthier families, are often characterized as "family-like" and "shadow labourers" because they play a significant role in the socialization of children, yet their work is often hidden in households and child-care centres. And while these child-care providers are "pseudo parents" and "like moms," and are often a part of the families they serve, they are also outside the dominant cultural ideology of what constitutes family (Murray, 1998). This means that these workers are continually engaged in emotional labour—that is, they must learn to mediate their emotional experiences of caregiving with others' expectations of them (Murray, 1998).

Domestic workers also experience a set of unique working conditions and interactions with the parents and children that they serve. For example, Macdonald (1998) finds that mothers and nannies "manufacture" a certain image and experience of motherhood that creates an idealized version of the mother-child relationship. As such, this "symbolic order re-defines the division of mother-work which magnifies a mother's significance and minimizes the nanny's," as depicted in box 8.1 (Macdonald, 1998: 37).

Other key socializing agents include siblings, the peer group, the educational system, religion, and the mass media. Siblings in particular can be a powerful source of influence on children and adolescents. Older siblings, for instance, can be important sources of information and can role model certain types of behaviour that younger children imitate. They may even play a large role in parenting or socializing younger children as babysitters and companions. Moreover, siblings can also be a source of conflict and competition over family resources, including parental time and attention.

Other institutions, such as religion and the media, are also key transmitters or shapers of knowledge, norms, values, and ultimately behaviour. It is well documented that attendance at formal religious services and religious affiliation among children has fallen dramatically over the past several decades, a trend that has many implications for family socialization processes. Notably, religious norms influence many facets of family life, such as gender roles, parent-child relations, attitudes toward moral issues (e.g., same-sex partnerships, abortion), and how families celebrate rituals such as births, weddings, and holidays. Yet, it is important to keep

Box 8.1: Manufacturing Motherhood: "Maximizing and Minimizing"

The mothers I interviewed simultaneously maximized and minimized the importance of their children's bonds with paid caregivers. On one hand, mothers frequently stressed the success of the nanny–child bond, stating that their nanny and child were "really attached" and the child "really loved" his or her caregiver. On the other hand, they defined nannies as out of the family by minimizing the importance of the nanny–child bond, particularly in discussions about nanny turnover. Although the need to feel good about her child-care arrangements can lead a mother to maximize the nanny–child bond and to state that her provider is "great" and that her children "love" the nanny, this same need can lead her to minimize the effects of nanny turnover on her children's emotional well-being.

For example, Jane, a corporate vice president, described the departure of various nannies as not being a problem for her sons. She said that because her older son (age eight) had been in daycare, "he deals with transitions incredibly well, so for him if a person is living here isn't that big an issue." She said that her younger son and his first nanny, who was with him from birth to 18 months, "adored each other," but at the same time described the nanny's departure as not a big deal:

"Well, he's young enough so that, you know, he talks about her all the time. I mean he understands and says that Andrea went home to be with her mommy and daddy. I think he missed her, but it doesn't seem to have had any huge impact on his overall well-being…I guess my sense has always been if family life is stable enough, that the transitions of child-care people, as long as they're not constant changes, aren't going to have any terrible effects."

Jane's distinction between "family life" and "child-care people" reveals how the nanny is situated in her child's life: although she spent more time with him than anyone else during the first year-and-a-half of his life, she is not an integral part of his family, psychologically or symbolically. This mother's strategy, therefore, was to simultaneously maximize the bond with the nanny in terms of how much her son benefited from it, and minimize the bond in terms of how much its loss affected him. Not surprisingly, mothers and nannies often disagreed in their appraisals of the effects of nanny turnover.

Source: Macdonald, C.L. 1998. "Manufacturing Motherhood: The Shadow Work of Nannies and Au Pairs." *Qualitative Sociology* 21: 25-53 (p. 37).

in mind that changing immigration patterns shape the ethnocultural mosaic of Canadian families. Therefore, there are diverse religious practices and customs in the general population (particularly in certain neighborhoods/geographical regions).

Turning to the socializing effects of the mass media, we see that studies reveal that children spend a large part of the day exposed to, and engaged in, various mediums, including TV, music, computers, and video games. In figure 8.1, we observe that on average, 8 to10- year-olds report almost one-third of the day (7:51 hours) is spent exposed to media, and almost one-quarter of the day (5:29 hours) using these media. Interestingly, this figure also shows that both exposure and use increase as children become teenagers. This high degree of media exposure and use, combined with new digital media (e.g., virtual world gaming), raises many controversial issues and concerns for parents and experts alike (e.g., see Willett, 2015). Indeed, Livingstone (2009) provides ample evidence that many families are navigating highly confusing and contested territory while trying to make "good" decisions about appropriate online content for their children.

On one hand, educational television shows such as *Teletubbies* and *Reading Rainbow* are deemed to positively mould socialization processes because they help children's imagination and mental skills to grow. Conversely, some television programming is shown to promote less desirable socialization by encouraging behaviours such as aggressiveness, or unhealthy eating habits, as well as consumerism through targeted advertising. The Campaign for a Commercial-Free Childhood (2016) estimates that children aged 2 to 11 view more than 25,000 advertisements on TV alone, a figure that does not include product placement. The campaign also shows evidence that marketing is linked to childhood obesity, eating disorders, precocious sexuality, youth violence, and family stress, as well a diminished capacity to play creatively.

The world of film and television also perpetuates gender roles, sexism, and racism, since it is largely a "White man's domain," with male characters far outnumbering non-White and female characters, particularly in more dominant roles. Also, male characters are often shown to be hypermasculine and violent, and are prominently featured as protagonists (Wooden and Gillam, 2016). Conversely, women tend to play roles that are "more ornamental" and in

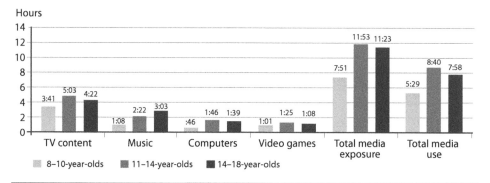

Figure 8.1: Average Amount of Time Spent with Each Medium in a Typical Day, 8- to 18-Year-Olds

Source: Rideout, V. J., U. G. Foehr, and D. F. Roberts. 2010. *Generation M²: Media in the Lives of 8- to 18-Year Olds: A Kaiser Family Foundation Study.* Menlo Park, California. Henry J. Kaiser Family Foundation (p. 5). Retrieved from: https://kaiserfamilyfoundation.files.wordpress.com/2013/01/8010.pdf.

which they are portrayed as young, attractive, and sexy. Disney movies (e.g., "Cinderella," "Beauty and the Beast," "The Little Mermaid") are often attacked for their negative, stereo-typical portrayal of female characters. And although characters have changed over time, it is still fairly common to see representations of women as submissive, feminine ideals of beauty who are often "damsels in distress" (Maity, 2014). Similarly, music videos and other types of media, such as movies, video games, Internet sites, and magazines, are also commonly criticized for sexualizing females and for presenting them as victims of violence.

Children can also participate in many social networks that can impact their learning, their sense of social connectedness, and their health and well-being. These social networks can also instill certain societal and sub-group values, such as cooperation and competition, as well as norms related to socially acceptable "masculine" and "feminine" behaviour. A good example is the popularity of sports participation. Many children regularly take part in sports, with soccer the most common activity for both boys and girls. Most children are first introduced to sports through the family, who strongly influence their children's involvement by investing time, emotional support, and financial resources in the sport. In short, "sporty parents" tend to have "sporty kids," with a majority of these parents being involved as participants, spectators, coaches, referees, and so on (Clark, 2011).

Therefore, it is not surprising to learn that parental and other family-related factors play a significant role in sports participation rates. Indeed, a major barrier that prevents 3- to 17-year-olds from participating in organized sports is the cost of enrolment fees (61%) and the cost of equipment (52%), as shown in figure 8.2. Clark (2011) also documents that cost, including the price of equipment, facility rentals, transportation to sports events, club memberships, and completion entry fees is strongly associated with household income. Not only is sports participation most prevalent among children from high-income households, it is also more common in two-parent families in which the father works full-time and the mother part-time. Boys are also more likely to participate in sports than girls the same age, although this gap is narrowing. Finally, children of recent immigrants are less likely to participate in sports due to financial barriers. This occurs even in sports like soccer, an internationally popular game that can offer a familiar place to integrate into Canadian society.

Furthermore, even though most books on socialization focus on the young child, socialization is a lifelong process that does not end in childhood (a theme to be further discussed later on in this chapter). A growing number of studies show that socialization is also very powerful during the adolescent and teen years, as is the influential role of the peer group in shaping these experiences. At this time, many adolescents become actively engaged in gender-role identification and learning the norms and expectations of the opposite sex. It is also during this developmental phase that many begin to separate from their parents and develop more self-reliance.

Overall, socialization is also a bi-directional or reciprocal process, a tenet that also helps to explain why children raised in the same family or in different historical locations can have very different experiences and outcomes. Indeed, children play a role in shaping

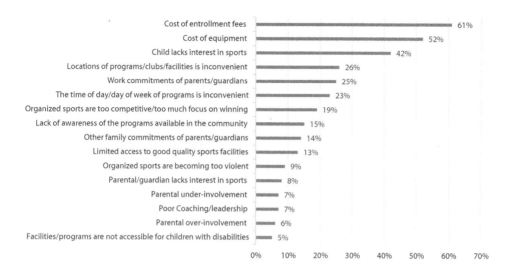

Figure 8.2: Barriers That Prevent 3- to 17-Year-Olds in Canada from Participating in Organized Sports, 2015

Source: ParticipACTION. 2015. *The Biggest Risk Is Keeping Kids Indoors: The 2015 ParticipACTION Report Card on Physical Activity for Children and Youth.* Toronto: ParticipACTION (pg. 19). Retrieved August 31, 2016, from www.exchange.youthrex.com/report/biggest-risk-keeping-kids-indoors-2015-participaction-report-card-physical-activity-children.

the behaviour of their parents just as parents can shape the behaviour of their children. An example of this is when adolescents (or "tweens" aged between 8 and 14) want to buy the latest consumer goods they have seen on television or that have been purchased by their peer group, such as iPods, cellphones, or trendy fashion accessories. Thanks to allowances, birthday money, and generous relatives, this demand influences parental and family spending patterns both subtly and directly. As a result, children are playing an increasingly powerful role in household purchases and as "agents of materialism" (see box 8.2). In short, our current generation of children and "tweens" have been raised and socialized as sophisticated, savvy, and influential consumers.

THEORIES ON CHILDHOOD SOCIALIZATION

Learning/Behaviourist Frame of Reference

Learning theory, which has its roots in behaviourism, assumes that the same concepts and principles that apply to animals apply to humans. Although there are many variations of this theory, learning or socialization as applied to the newborn infant involves changes resulting from maturation that may include classical or instrumental conditioning. **Classical conditioning,** for instance, links a response to a known stimulus. A common example is

---

Box 8.2: Parenting in a Culture of Consumption

Given the proliferation of goods on the marketplace, our almost constant exposure to commercial messages, and the energy we invest in acquiring consumer goods, one could argue that consumption activities dominate much of our everyday lives. Globalization, on-line shopping, and the proliferation of specialty stores have created a world of unlimited options...As advertising is increasingly directed at children, their needs and wants have also come to shape the organization of time and money in the household. As Schor (1989) has suggested, children are "agents of materialism," bringing their consumerist values into the home through their wants and shopping lists. In his work on the commodification of childhood, Cook (2014) argues that children's development is increasingly being defined by their stage of consumption (e.g., whether they are buying toys or clothes), and that rather than seeing children as in some way tangential to the culture of consumption, they are the very core of it. Many of our largest corporations (Nike, Sony, Nabisco) have found that the key to their success is marketing to children. Not only do children develop brand loyalty early on in their lives, but these loyalties last well into adulthood.

There are indications that children are playing an increasingly powerful role in family household purchases. Not only do children have an influence over small stuff that is brought into the home (e.g., cereal, games, clothing); they are influencing bigger consumer choices such as cars, computers, and holiday destinations. Smaller families, increased family income, and a shift from authority and obedience to negotiation and decision-making participation has meant that children are more market savvy and powerful than ever (Valkenburg and Cantor, 2002). The result, according to some, is that parents have become more indulgent with children, wanting to ensure that they do not lack for material goods (McNeal, 1992).

Source: Adapted from Daly, K. 2004. "The Changing Culture of Parenting." *Contemporary Family Trends*, May 2004. Ottawa: The Vanier Institute of the Family (pp. 15–17).

Pavlov's dog experiment. A hungry dog is placed in a soundproof room, where he hears the sound of a tuning fork (a conditioned stimulus) before receiving some meat. After this situation is repeated several times, the dog begins to salivate upon hearing the tuning fork. The same principles are assumed to hold true when an infant hears his or her mother's voice or approaching footsteps.

On the other hand, **operant or instrumental conditioning** focuses on a response that is not related to any known stimuli. Instead, it functions in an instrumental manner, whereby a person learns to use a certain response based on the outcome that response produces. According to Skinner, it is the response that correlates with positive reinforcement or a reward. For example, imagine that a baby is picked up after saying "da-da-da" because the father is convinced that the baby is saying "Daddy." Consequently, the baby begins to say "da-da-da" all day long because it may result in lots of rewards. As children grow older, different reinforcements (e.g., praise, candy, an allowance) are used as deliberate techniques to teach children approved forms of behaviour.

Some argue that while this theory can be useful, there may be limited applicability in generalizing animal behaviour to socialized humans. For instance, it is asserted that humans, unlike animals, have the capacity to share symbols and meanings in ways that animals cannot.

Psychoanalytic Frame of Reference

Developed by Sigmund Freud (1856–1939) and his followers, psychoanalytic theory stresses the importance of biological drives and unconscious processes. Beneath the surface of each individual's consciousness is the repressed unconscious, a storm of contradictory impulses controlled only by the individual's gradual internalization of societal restraints. Parents, therefore, play a key role and hold the main responsibility for their child's "impulse taming" (Strong and DeVault, 1992).

Socialization consists of a number of precise and overlapping stages of development. These stages, which occur between birth and age five or six, are called the *oral, anal,* and *phallic stages*; they are followed by a period of *latency* and then a *genital phase.* Three principal erogenous zones—the mouth, the anus, and the genitals—are of great importance in the socialization process because they are the first significant sources of irritating excitations a baby has to contend with and the zones in which the first pleasurable experiences occur. For example, during the oral stage, in the first year of life, the earliest erotic gratifications come from the mouth. As a result, the child forms a strong emotional attachment to the mother, who supplies the source of food, warmth, and sucking.

Overall, Freudian ideas have received mixed empirical support, and many of these ideas have been discredited. For instance, such practices as breastfeeding and bowel and bladder training (which have been so strongly emphasized in the psychoanalytic literature) have been found to be almost completely insignificant in terms of how they affect personality and psycho-social adjustment. Moreover, it should be noted that Freud's work was highly controversial at the time of his writings, particularly since he often focused on sexuality during a repressive Victorian era, when this topic was rarely discussed openly. Indeed, Freud thought that sexuality was the primary motivating force not only for adults, but also for children, an idea that sparked public outrage at the time.

Child Development Frames of Reference: Erikson and Piaget

Similar to Freud, both Erikson and Piaget emphasized the early stages of childhood development. But unlike Freud, they examined life stages beyond the early years and focused more attention on social structure and reasoning. Erikson, who was one of Freud's students, viewed socialization as a lifelong process that continues into old age. He developed the well-known theory that there are "eight stages of human development." These stages and related issues range from *trust versus mistrust* (first year of infancy) to *integrity versus despair* (old age). He believed that, as individuals create solutions to developmental concerns, those solutions become institutionalized in our culture. Swiss social psychologist Jean Piaget, who wrote during the 1920s, was also interested in maturational stages. However, his focus was more on cognitive development, which he characterized as the ability to reason abstractly, to think about hypothetical situations logically, and to organize rules into higher-order, complex operations or structures.

Piaget also believed there are four major cumulative stages of intellectual development, which include the sensorimotor period (birth to two years), the pre-operational period (two to seven years), the concrete-operational period (seven to 11 years), and the formal operational period (age 11 through adulthood). In Piaget's view, children develop their cognitive abilities through interaction with the world and adaptation to their environment. They adapt by assimilating, which means making new information compatible with their understanding of the world. In addition, they accommodate by adjusting their cognitive framework to incorporate new experiences as they become socialized into adults (Strong and DeVault, 1992).

So far, we have reviewed frames of reference that emphasize overt behaviour (the frame of reference of the behaviourists and the learning theorists); the unconscious role of motives and emotions (the frames of reference of the Freudians); and motor skills, thought, reasoning processes, and conflicts (the frames of reference of the child developmentalists). Next, we will review the symbolic interactionist frame of reference, a sociological perspective that shares many of the assumptions of Erikson and Piaget in relation to language, reasoning, and societal influences of behaviour.

Symbolic Interactionist Frame of Reference

From the symbolic interactionist perspective (e.g., Mead, Cooley, Blumer), socialization is viewed as a lifelong process. Central importance is placed on interactions with others and the internalized definitions and meanings of the work in which one interacts (Charon, 1979). Basic assumptions include:

1. *Humans must be studied on their own level.* This means we must be careful not to make inferences from non-human forms of life or animals. Social life involves sharing meanings and communicating symbolically via language, which enables humans alone to deal with events in terms of the past, present, or future. In other words, "lower animals" such as mice and dogs do not have a culture or a system of beliefs, moral codes, values, and ideas that is shared and symbolically transmitted.

2. *Analyzing society is the most valuable method in understanding it.* In order to best understand social behaviour, we need to contextualize individual behaviour within macro-level processes, or the structure of society. For example, when one is born into a given society, one learns the language, customs, and expectations of that culture. Thus,

behaviour that is appropriate in one culture (e.g., spanking a child) may not be appropriate in others.

3. *At birth, the human infant is asocial.* Newborns are born with impulses and needs, and with the potential for social development and to becoming a social being. For example, a newborn does not cry all night to punish parents, or sleep all day to please parents. Thus, behaviours and expectations do not begin to take on meaning until babies begin to learn to channel their behaviours in specific directions, via training and socialization from their parents.

4. *A socialized being is an actor as well as a reactor.* Humans do not simply react to one another in robotic fashion. Rather, humans are social beings, responding to a symbolic environment that involves responses to interpreted and anticipated stimuli. In this way, they can feel guilt over past behaviours, assess new ways of responding, and dream of future possibilities. This suggests that humans can take the role of others, or place themselves in someone else's shoes.

There are also a number of other key concepts. The first is the idea of the development of a social self, a self that is developed in interaction with others. For example, a young adult may occupy the status of child, student, sister, athlete, and many others. These statuses have expectations (roles) assigned to them, and are organized and integrated into the social self. In this way, the social self is never fixed, static, or in a final state. Family members play an important role not only in the child's development of the social self, but also in his feelings of self-worth, which do not exist at birth but are learned (e.g., Felson and Zielinski, 1989).

Also of central importance in understanding child development and modifications of the social self are the roles of **significant others** and reference groups. Although parents, particularly mothers, are usually the most significant socializers, other people or groups can also be important. These individuals can be other family members such as siblings, grandparents, aunts, or uncles, or even role models presented in the media, such as pop stars Justin Bieber or Miley Cyrus. These significant others influence children's behaviour through what they do and what they say. Reference groups, on the other hand, constitute a source of comparison that operates in a similar fashion. These groups serve as a point of reference and standard for conduct, and can include religious groups, hobby clubs, peer groups, or companies (e.g., Gap, Nintendo).

Finally, another central concept in the symbolic interactionist perspective is George Herbert Mead's notion of the **generalized other**. This concept signifies how individuals are often consistent and predictable in their behaviour, and how people learn to view themselves from the perspective of others who are either physically or symbolically present. As such, behaviour results less from drives and needs, unconscious processes, and biological forces and more from interaction processes and internalized meanings of self and others. Interactions are also situated within sociocultural contexts, including schools, peers, the mass media, and day-to-day living in particular social environments.

Gender-Role Socialization

Gender roles refer to the expectations associated with being masculine or feminine, which may or may not correspond with one's sex, whereas sex roles can be defined as the expectations related to being biologically of one sex or the other. Formation of these roles and one's identity (i.e., how one defines or perceives oneself in terms of these roles) is a developmental process that unfolds over time (Greenglass, 1982). There is also little doubt that males and females differ in these processes, and that gendered divisions are found in virtually all societies.

For many centuries, it was assumed that "anatomy is destiny" and gender and sex differences were largely innate or inborn. However, many feminists argue that this belief provides a major ideological justification for a system of stratification that privileges men and subordinates women. Instead, they argue, we must also consider **socialization** processes and the organization and practices of society. Fundamental differences in sex-role socialization and gender-role stereotypes continue to exist; these begin at birth and continue throughout one's life. This is illustrated in the media (as previously discussed) and the kinds of toys and games that continue to be manufactured, marketed, and bought for children. Gender-specific toys for girls are thought to perpetuate activities directed toward appearance, romance, and the home. Conversely, "rugged" and aggressive activities directed away from the home are encouraged for boys (Greenglass, 1982). Moreover, many studies show that little boys experience greater pressure than girls to behave in a gender-appropriate way, and that this pressure is enforced more harshly.

For example, traditionally, little girls are given dolls, sewing machines, and makeup, while little boys are often presented with toy guns, action figures, cars, and computer games that feature violent content. And while the ever-popular Barbie doll (introduced by Mattel in 1959) has been transformed over time to represent "career women," as well as non-White ethnic identities, many feminists continue to bemoan Barbie's unrealistic connotations and body measurements, cultural ideals that they claim are imposed on little girls by a patriarchal society. For example, in reality, the probability of a girl obtaining Barbie's body shape in adulthood is estimated at less than one in 100,000. Conversely, Ken—Barbie's "boyfriend"—has a body that is more realistic to achieve, with a probability of about one in 50 (Nortons, Old, Olive, and Dank, 1996).

Another example of how institutions are highly gendered is our educational system, which also plays an important role in the formation of gender identities through curriculum and its local culture. Connell (1996) maintains that each school has its own "gender regime," which contributes to the ongoing negotiation and renegotiation of femininity or masculinity. By way of illustration, a school's style of dress can act as a power signifier of social acceptability, an expression of identity, and a signifier of fashion that separates "the girls from the boys." For instance, at some schools, "the look for boys" is to appear somehow connected to sports, athleticism, strength, and power, and this becomes the hegemonic norm (Swain, 2004).

Box 8.3: What Do Little Girls Really Learn from "Career" Barbies?

Like a lot of moms, I faced the Barbie dilemma when my daughter was younger. Ultimately, I figured a little bit of Barbie would sate her appetite (and stop the nagging) without doing *too* much harm. Like a vaccination, or homeopathic inoculation against the Big Bad. I told myself my daughter didn't use her dolls for fashion play, anyway; her Barbie "funeral," for instance, was a tour-de-force of childhood imagination. I told myself I only got her "good" Barbies: ethnic Barbies, Wonder-Woman Barbie, Cleopatra Barbie. Now that she's 10 and long ago gave the dolls away (or "mummified" them and buried them in the backyard in a "time capsule"), I can't say whether they'll have any latent impact on her body image or self-perception. It would seem ludicrous, at any rate, to try to pinpoint the impact of *one* toy.

But now, according to a study published this week, it turns out that playing with Barbie, even career Barbie, may indeed limit girls' perception of their own future choices. Psychologists randomly assigned girls ages 4 to 7 to play with one of three dolls. Two were Barbies: a fashion Barbie (in a dress and high heels); and a career Barbie with a doctor's coat and stethoscope.

The third, "control" doll was a Mrs. Potato Head, who, although she comes with fashion accessories such as a purse and shoes, doesn't have Barbie's sexualized (and totally *unrealistic*) curves. So after just a few minutes of play, the girls were asked if they could do any of 10 occupations when they grew up. They were also asked if boys could do those jobs. Half of the careers, according to the authors, were male dominated and half were female dominated. The results: the girls who played with Barbie thought they could do fewer of the jobs than boys could do. But the girls who played with Mrs. Potato Head reported nearly the same number of possible careers for themselves as for boys.

More to the point: there were no differences in results between the girls who played with the Barbie wearing a dress and the ones who played with the career-focused, doctor version of the doll. Obviously, the study is not definitive. Obviously, one doll isn't going to make the critical difference in a young woman's life, blah blah blah. Still, it's interesting that it didn't matter whether the girls played with fashion Barbie or doctor Barbie; the dolls had the same effect and in only a few minutes.

That reminded me of a study in which college women who were enrolled in an advanced calculus class were asked to watch a series of four, 30-second TV commercials. The first group watched four neutral ads. The second group watched two neutral ads and two depicting stereotypes about women (a girl enraptured by acne medicine; a woman drooling over a brownie mix). Afterward, they completed a survey and—*bing!*—the group who'd seen the stereotyped ads expressed less interest in math- and science-related careers than the classmates who had watched only the neutral ads. Let me repeat: the effect was demonstrable after watching *two ads*. And guess who performed better on a math test—coeds who took it after being asked to try on a bathing suit, or those who took it after being asked to try on a sweater? (Answer: the latter group. Interestingly, the results for male students showed no such disparity.)

Now think about the culture girls are exposed to over and over and over and over and over, whether in toys or movies or TV or music videos, in which regardless of what else you are—smart, athletic, kind, even a feminist, even *old*—you must be "hot." Perhaps then, the issue is not "Well, one doll can't have that much of an impact," so much as "If playing with one doll for a few minutes has *that much impact*, what is the effect of the tsunami of sexualization that girls confront every day, year after year?"

Source: Orenstein, P. 2014. "What Do Little Girls Really Learn from "Career" Barbies?" *Sociological Images: The Society Pages*, March 12. Retrieved July 21, 2016, from www.thesocietypages.org/socimages/2014/03/12/what-do-little-girls-really-learn-from-career-barbies.

Fox (2001, 2009) reveals other structural sources of gender differences and how these can resurface beyond childhood (i.e., in young families). Her research uncovers how parenthood can produce a more conventional division of labour in the home. From this perspective, gender inequity and gender-role behaviour arise out of the gendered division of paid and unpaid work, and these conditions further shape and constrain women's options and behaviour. In contemporary society, a shortage of outside community supports and the privatization of parenthood mean that women continue to bear the ultimate responsibility for their babies' welfare. This creates women's dependence on men or other family members (e.g., their own mothers) and strengthens gendered divisions between men and women.

In short, gender socialization does not end in childhood; it is lifelong. It continues (and can even deepen) through certain institutional practices and discourses that produce gendered adults and identities. As a result, despite feminist efforts over the past 30 years to challenge gender-role socialization and conventional gender divisions, many inequities remain in families. And while many couples negotiate the changes in their lives, women in a materially strong position (those whose bargaining power tends to be relatively good before motherhood) may be better able to resist dynamics that place them in an unequal position within the family (Fox, 2009).

Furthermore, despite gender-role socialization, some scholars argue that empirical research actually shows more variation *within* genders than *between* them. For example, while many of us would imagine that, with respect to traits such as aggressiveness or math scores, there would be no overlap between a group of men and a group of women, in reality, the overlap between males and females is far greater than the difference, as depicted in figure 8.3. This means that two normal bell-shaped curves

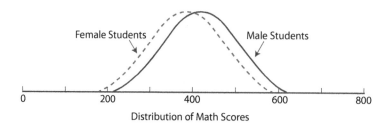

Figure 8.3: Overlapping Normal Curves and Gender: Distribution of Math Scores

Source: Travis, C. 1992. *Mismeasure of Woman: Why Women Are Not the Better Sex, the Inferior Sex, or the Opposite Sex.* New York: Touchstone (pg. 42).

on math scores would be virtually identical if we removed the tiny percentage of males who are prodigies from the sample (Travis, 1992). This finding calls into question popular conceptualizations such as "sugar and spice and everything nice, that's what little girls are made of." It also beckons us to move away from narrow and limited questions like "Do girls and boys differ, and if so, who's better?" and ask instead, "Why is everyone so interested in gender differences?" and "What functions does the belief in differences serve?" (Travis, 1992: 43).

Finally, although there have been some important changes in gender-role theorizing and socialization processes over time, it is interesting to note that some countries are making strong efforts to create gender-neutral learning environments for children. This is illustrated in Sweden, a country well known for its national focus on gender equality in the workplace and in society. For instance, Scandinavian toy retailer Top-Toy, a licensee of the Toys "R" Us brand, has tried to create a gender-neutral catalog, since it had been criticized by the government for depicting stereotypical scenes of girls with dollhouses and boys with weapons, among others. Recently, some pre-schools have also tried to eliminate gender-based pronouns due to the idea that attitudes about gender/sex roles are perpetuated and reflected in certain types of language. Therefore, they have introduced an alternative: a neutral–first pronoun, "hen," that applies to anyone, regardless of gender.

CULTURAL SHIFTS IN CHILD-REARING ADVICE AND IDEOLOGIES OF PARENTHOOD

It is also valuable to track changes in child-rearing advice and the culture of parenting, since these shifts also reflect changing conceptions of childhood as well as theoretical and hegemonic ideologies of childhood socialization. For example, Wall (2005) notes that child-rearing advice emerged in tandem with the growing authority of medical science in the late 19th and 20th centuries. At this time, advice in Canada focused on medical concerns over high rates of infant mortality. This was also an era of poor refrigeration and

Box 8.4: Should You Raise a Gender-Neutral Baby?

Blue is for boys and pink is for girls—that's what most of us were raised to believe. But some parents are taking the opposite approach by choosing to raise their children gender neutral. In fact, Sweden took a big step last year in addressing this trend by adding the gender-neutral personal pronoun "hen" to the country's vocabulary. A children's clothing company in Sweden has done away with its designated boys' and girls' sections to become a gender-neutral outlet, and a toy catalog in the same country featured a boy in a Spider-Man costume pushing a pink baby carriage.

Although the Swedes are embracing this parenting style, it's still a controversial topic in the United States. Although some think it's a great way to encourage a child to embrace his or her true identity, others believe it will confuse the child and alienate him socially. Following are some common questions and answers about this parenting style.

WHAT EXACTLY IS GENDER-NEUTRAL PARENTING?

There are different degrees of gender-neutral parenting. Some parents take an extreme approach. One couple from Toronto still hasn't revealed the gender of their 3-year-old, Storm. According to the *Toronto Star*, Storm's parents wrote an e-mail to family and friends explaining that their decision was "a tribute to freedom and choice in place of limitation, a standup to what the world could become in Storm's lifetime (a more progressive place?)."

Parents who want to practice a lesser form of gender-neutral parenting might simply encourage their children to play with both "boy" and "girl" toys, keep clothing and room décor neutral, and allow their children to pick their own clothes—even if that means their son goes to school in a tutu or their daughter goes out dressed as Spider-Man.

Lisa Cohn of Portland, Oregon, is raising her kids according to her family's version of gender-neutral parenting. "We definitely avoid stereotypes about Mom doing the dishes and Dad mowing the lawn. That's not what our kids see at all," Cohn says. "I generally let my youngest son wear pink if he wants to, and he often appears in public wearing a headband. And I'm very careful about how I talk about girls and boys—and don't choose books that stereotype men and women."

IS IT HEALTHY FOR THE CHILD?

It depends on whom you ask. "A major pro to raising a gender-neutral baby is that you will be allowing your child to develop without the artificially created limitations that society has placed around gender," says Israel Martinez, a licensed clinical social

Children engaging in gender-neutral play

Source: LightFieldStudios/iStock

worker. "As human beings, we crave to make life simpler and new information easier to digest. So we naturally want to establish categories, or boxes, that everything needs to fit into." Unfortunately, Martinez says, these gender norms are too limiting and can make kids feel like they have to be something they're not. This can keep kids from being as happy and healthy as possible.

For Jane Ward, an associate professor of Women's Studies at the University of California, Riverside, the decision to parent her son this way was an easy one. "Raising a child under these strict gender guidelines is denying them an entire world of colours—they become tracked into the characteristics of their biological sex." Ward's 4-year-old son has grown up wearing both jeans and dresses, plays with all types of toys, and until recently had long hair. He told his parents not long ago that although he identifies with being a boy, he doesn't want to give up wearing girls' clothes.

But other experts—like Fran Walfish, Psy.D., a psychotherapist based in Beverly Hills, California—disagree. "Every boy and girl child must make a strong identification as a male or female person. Without it, the child feels lost and confused about [his or her] own identity. Gender and sexuality are only aspects of a person's identification. The goal is for clarity. Without male or female gender clarity, the child is not a full person."

Source: Excerpts from DiProperzio, L. 2013. "Should You Raise a Gender-Neutral Baby?" *Parents.* Retrieved July 21, 2016, from www.parents.com/parenting/gender-neutral-parenting.

sewage/water systems, as well as high rates of contagious diseases. However, while a war was waged on infant mortality—a war that included government funding for milk depots, well-baby clinics, and a major educational campaign aimed at mothers—it did not include a battle against poverty or unsafe living conditions.

Rather, the target was mothers' behaviour and lack of knowledge, which spurred the growth of advice literature (Arnup, 1994; Wall, 2005). In particular, this advice, which shows the early influences of behaviourism, focused heavily on personal hygiene, breast-feeding, and proper food preparation. Mothers were expected to rely on "science" and "experts" for advice in all areas. Many of these experts (who, ironically, were often men) came from medicine and psychology backgrounds and strongly encouraged "scientific management" of children. As a result, they tried to promote self-discipline and good habits through behaviours such as rigid scheduling and early toilet training (Wall, 2005).

Many researchers (e.g., Coontz, 1992; Wall, 2005) observe that following World War Two, a distinct shift in child-rearing advice could be seen. Hay (1996: 9, 69) further notes that during this time, "the ideology of intensive mothering" became a widely accepted belief system. In other words, this set of child-rearing guidelines supported the view that child-rearing should be "child centered, expert guided, emotionally absorbing, labour intensive, and financially expensive." This was also an era in which many families wanted security and comfort. The favourable economic conditions of the time also allowed many families to live in middle-class, traditional family structures with distinct gender roles. In particular, mothers, who had been increasingly encouraged in the first part of the century by medical science to view motherhood as a full-time occupation (Arnup, 1994), now had the time and the means to make it so. As a result, child-rearing literature began to focus more on the social context of mother-child relationships and its role in psychological health, rather than on medical concerns such as children's physical health. In particular, Bowlby's theory of mother-child bonding, which inspired the subsequent **attachment theory**, strongly affected expert advice. This theory emphasized the importance of the continual presence of a warm, loving, and responsive mother from birth onward (Wall, 2005).

Wall (2005) also finds that there has been a wider expansion of educational material targeted at parents stressing the importance of secure attachment in addition to ample stimulation in a child's early years (usually ages three to five). This advice proliferated in the early 1990s based on the purportedly "new" brain science. This body of research "evidence" suggests that the amount and type of synaptic connections made in the young child's brain will affect the manner in which the child's brain will become wired. It is assumed that once the connections are made (or not made), brain wiring becomes almost impossible to undo. However, critics charge that there is very little evidence to prove that the years before five are as critical as the experts would suggest (e.g., see Brunner, 2000). Yet, despite this criticism, the new brain research has become part of the taken-for-granted discourse with respect to children's needs and "proper" parenting behaviour. Interestingly, this research has also spilled over into the pre-birth period, which focuses on how expectant mothers can give their children a competitive advantage by beginning to stimulate and educate them while they are still in the womb (Wall, 2005).

It is also important to note the legacy of Dr. Spock's pioneering book, *Baby and Child Care*, published in 1946. Advice in this book was very different from the kind of advice offered in earlier times, such as the 1920s (see example in box 8.5). As Wall (2005) notes, Spock's approach fit within, and helped to define, a more permissive and child-centred style of parenting. This is reflected in his opening words: "Trust yourself. You know more than you think you do." Spock saw children as more innocent than experts of the past did. Furthermore, the needs of the child took precedence over those of the mother. Therefore, by implication, mothers became more blameworthy when something went wrong.

Indeed, Gustafson (2005) asserts that "master discourses" about mothering continue in today's society. These discourses refer to those overarching social narratives that organize women's way of thinking about, interpreting, and performing motherwork, thereby creating social expectations for women's connection with their children. As elaborated in box 8.6, mothers continue to be blamed for children's negative experiences and behaviours, and a "good mother/bad mother" binary with oppositional categories is socially created.

Finally, it is also important to recognize how family life and the practice of mothering children has historically been monitored and regulated through government policy in

---

Box 8.5: Changing Advice on Children and Pacifiers

These excerpts illustrate interesting differences in child-rearing advice with respect to the use of pacifiers:

The "pacifier" habit—the habit of sucking a rubber nipple—is an inexcusable piece of folly for which the mother or nurse is directly responsible. The habit when formed is most difficult to give up. The use of the "pacifier," thumb-sucking, finger sucking, etc., make thick baggy lips, on account of the exercise to which the parts are subjected. They cause an outward bulging of the jaws, which is not conducive to personal attractiveness. (Toronto Department of Public Health, 1922)

A pacifier is helpful for fretfulness or to prevent thumb-sucking...A baby who has periods of mild irritability can often be entirely quieted by having a pacifier to suck. We don't know whether this is because the sucking soothes some vague discomfort or simply keep the baby's mouth busy...Most of the babies who use a pacifier freely for the first few months of life never become thumb suckers, even if they give up the pacifier at three or four months. (Spock, 1946)

Sources: Department of Public Health, City of Toronto. 1922. *The Care of the Infant and Young Child.* Toronto: City of Toronto; and Spock, B.M.D. 1946. *Baby and Child Care.* New York: Duell, Sloan and Pearce (p. 286).

Box 8.6: The "Bad Mother"

In the discourse of binary polarization, the opposite of the good mother is the bad mother. Marked as different, undeserving, and Other, the bad mother is the woman who fails to reproduce white, middle-class, Judeo-Christian family values in appearance, the espousal of beliefs, and the performance of motherwork. Poor women, Aboriginal women, immigrant women, lesbians, and other marginalized women tend to be positioned as Other mothers on a short downward slide to the embodiment of a bad mother.

The bad mother is imagined to ignore, trivialize, or reject her child's need for love, caring, and nurturance both as an intellectual understanding and as a lived practice. She is regarded as unloving and uncaring. The stereotypical image of the bad mother that springs to mind is the woman who neglects, abuses, or fails to protect her child. A woman who is unwilling or unable to perform her motherly duties is thought to be motivated by selfishness, self-absorption, and self-indulgence—all individual defects. Finally, and germane to this discussion, the bad mother is the absent mother—absent emotionally or absent physically from her children. Given these ways of thinking and talking about mothering, a woman who lives apart from her birth children would seem to be the epitome of the bad mother—an unnatural, aberrant woman.

In this passage drawn from the case study, the polarization of the good mother/ bad mother is evident in this woman's recollection of the day she told her work colleagues that her children were living with their birth father and his new wife:

> Colleagues who had not previously engaged me in discussions of a personal nature were intrigued by my decision. The questions were variously phrased, but the implications were clear. Why weren't the children living with me? Had the courts awarded custody to the father? Had I abused them? Had I neglected them? Was I unfit for some other reason? Did I have a "problem" with alcohol? Did I have a history of drug abuse? When I denied these causes for a change in custody, their questions took on a different tone. If there were no grounds for removing the children from my care, then why weren't they still with me? My simple answer was that the children wanted to live with their dad. Children want to do lots of things, I was told, but that doesn't mean that they get to decide where to live. Clearly I was abdicating my motherly duty to raise my children. Or perhaps, came the insinuation, there was a more ugly explanation. Was I using my children's feelings as a cover for my own deep-seated desires to be childless and carefree? Was I putting my own needs before those of my children? What other reasons could I have for downloading the care of my children to another woman? In any case, I was unfit to parent and the children were better off with their fathers.

Source: Gustafson, D.L. 2005. "The Social Construction of Maternal Absence," in D.L. Gustafson (ed.), *Unbecoming Mothers: The Social Production of Maternal Absence* (pp. 23-50). New York: Haworth Press (pp. 27–29).

tandem with the growth of other medical and social service institutional practices. For example, Donzelot (1979) draws upon data from European countries to show how governments deliberately set out to "police" mothers, and how this continues in contemporary social work practices. In the case of "the troubled child," the true locus of illness is seen as the family rather than certain conditions such as poverty or a lack of social support. Treatment, therefore, might consist of sending a child to a psychiatrist or to a foster home and by regulating his or her behaviour under juvenile law. In this way, the agency workers become "rivals" with the judicial system. In short, the politics of the family become, in fact, the business of official agencies such as psychiatry or social work. Similarly, Gubrium (1992) illustrates how parenting and domestic troubles are embedded in organizational activities and institutional images by focusing on a common venue of "domestic repair," the treatment facility. From this perspective, he highlights how family therapy workers come to see family troubles as they do, and how they get family members to accept their version of family troubles.

In sum, we have witnessed some significant changes in the type of expert advice presented to parents over the last century. We can also see the emergence of the **ideology of motherhood**. This set of beliefs highlights the powerful and persistent view that a woman's primary responsibility is to care for her biological offspring. Indeed, child-care labour, like all forms of caring labour, is highly gendered, yet change is slowly occurring in this area as fathers begin to participate more in child care and domestic life, as previously covered in chapter 6.

SUMMARY

This chapter underscores the problems inherent in viewing childhood as an essentially definable social position. Instead, childhood is a fluid social construct such that meanings of children and experiences of childhood and parenting change over time. For example, the emergence of adolescence as a "new" and separate developmental phase places new demands on parents and family consumption practices. From a life-course framework, this idea illuminates how life-course developmental stages are embedded within unique socio-historical, political, and geographical locations, and how they reciprocally influence "linked lives." Notably, conceptualizations of children and how they become socialized shift in tandem with the changing ideologies of childhood and the changing culture of parenting.

Socialization is defined as a lifelong, bi-directional process that teaches and prepares children to become functional members of society. The child's initial and most enduring social interactions are in the family, making parents one of the most significant agents of socialization. In addition to the family, other institutions also play important roles in moulding children's behaviour, such as daycare, the mass media, the educational system, the peer group, and religion. Several competing and complementary theories on childhood socialization were presented, and it was noted that these socialization processes are gendered and contribute to masculine or feminine identities.

And while childhood socialization theories often share some basic assumptions, like social constructions of childhood they are also created within a particular historical time and location and in reaction to the scientific and political thoughts of the day. Child-rearing advice has also been transformed in relation to these new developments, particularly in psychology and medicine, but also in relation to shifting and emergent ideologies of parenthood that occur at the societal and state level. In particular, the pervasive ideology of motherhood fosters discourse, practices, and the belief that mothers are most naturally suited to raising and socializing their children. This ideology has considerable consequence for child-rearing practices, gender socialization, and our day-to-day experiences of family life in Canada.

QUESTIONS FOR CRITICAL REFLECTIONS AND DEBATE

1. Debate the following: As life expectancy continues to increase, childhood as a social category will become extended.
2. Recall the last time that you visited a toy store. What kinds of toys and games seemed specifically targeted to little boys and girls? How might this affect the kinds of toys and games that parents buy for their children and how they are socialized into gender-specific roles?
3. Why are siblings raised in the same family environment often very different from one another? Consider the role of both genetics and socialization processes.
4. Present an argument for and against the following statement: Parental care is superior to daycare.
5. What kinds of challenges might a recent immigrant child face in trying to become socialized in Canadian society?
6. How do the popular media (e.g., films, TV, printed material) perpetuate specific ideologies of motherhood and fatherhood? Provide specific examples relative to other socialization agents (e.g., educational and religious institutions).

GLOSSARY

Attachment theory is based on the premise that a strong attachment to a warm, loving, and responsive mother is necessary for a child's emotional, psychological, and cognitive development.

Childhood as a social construct refers to how social understanding about what children experience, what they need, and what is expected of them in larger society varies by time and location.

Classical conditioning is rooted in learning theory and links a known response to a stimulus, as illustrated in Pavlov's dog experiment.

Generalized other is the internalized moral "self" and the social controls that the individual develops from interacting with significant others.

Ideology of motherhood is the belief system that women are "naturally" suited to take on the primary responsibility for the care and nurturance of children.

Operant or instrumental conditioning focuses on the response that is not related to any known stimuli. Instead, it functions in an instrumental manner in that one learns to make a certain response on the basis of the outcome the response produces.

Significant others are those individuals or role models who take on special importance to children, such as parents, other relatives, friends, or TV heroes.

Socialization is the lifelong process of learning to become a capable, functioning member of society and is shaped by institutions such as the family, peer groups, schools, religion, and the mass media.

FURTHER READING

Albanese, P. 2016. *Children in Canada Today*, 2nd ed. Toronto: Oxford University Press. The first in-depth work of childhood sociology in this country, it covers the key social theories and agents of socialization, as well as various social policies designed to improve children's lives. The latest edition includes a chapter on Aboriginal children, as well as expanded discussions on children with disabilities.

Bloch, M.N., B. Blue Swadener, and G.S. Cannella (eds.,). 2014. *Reconceptualizing Early Childhood Care and Education: Questions, Imaginaries and Social Activism*, 2nd ed. Bern, Switzerland: Peter Lang Publishing. Provides theories and debates about early childhood education and child care. It includes coverage of researchers who have been influential and inspirational in contesting the normalizing and universalizing discourses within the field to enact new imaginaries, policies, and curricula.

Cregan, K., and D. Cuthbert. 2014. *Global Childhoods: Issues and Debates*. Thousand Oaks, California: Sage Publications. Critically evaluates how the construction of childhood emerged unevenly, from the late 18th century to the time of the normative global child, as enshrined in the UN Convention on the Rights of the Child. Covers original research in the fields of embodiment, theorizations of childhood, children's policy, child placement and adoption, and family formation.

Fass, P.S. 2016. *The End of American Childhood: A History of Parenting from Life on the Frontiers to the Managed Child*. Princeton, NJ: Princeton University Press.

This book addresses a number of timely and provocative questions from a historical perspective, including: "Why have we reached the 'end of American childhood'?" and "What explains the surge in "helicopter parenting"?

Keel, S. 2016. *Socialization: Parent-Child Interaction in Everyday Life*. New York: Routledge. This research adopts a conversation-analytic approach based on audio-visual footage of families filmed extensively in their own homes. It focuses on how children use embodied resources such as talk, gaze, and gesture as they acquire communication skills and a sense of themselves as social actors.

Trier-Bieniek, A. (ed.). 2014. *Gender and Pop Culture: A Text-Reader*. New York: Springer. Provides an introductory-level theoretical, methodological, and historical foundation for studying gender and popular culture. Includes chapters on media and children, advertising, music, television, film, sports, and technology. Also offers ideas for activism and suggestions for further readings.

RELATED WEB SITES

Campaign for a Commercial-Free Childhood's mission is to support parents' efforts to raise healthy families by limiting commercial access to children and ending the exploitative practice of child-targeted marketing, www.commercialfreechildhood.org/resource/marketing-children-overview. Facebook: commercialfreechildhood, Twitter: commercialfree

Canadian Childcare Federation is a national organization dedicated to providing Canadians with information on early learning and child-care knowledge and its best practices, www.cccf-fcsge.ca

Kids' Health (est. 1995 by The Nemours Foundation's Centre for Children's Health Media), the largest and most visited site on the subject, provides health information about children from before birth and through adolescence, www.kidshealth.org

Mombian, a site for lesbian mothers and other LGBT parents, offers social support links on topics including starting a family, raising children, the law and politics, and other areas, www.mombian.com. Facebook: Mombian, Twitter: Mombian

The National Parenting Centre, founded in 1989, is America's leading parent advocacy organization. It dispenses valuable information and advice from some of the world's most respected authorities in the field of child-rearing and development, www.the-parenting-center.com, Facebook: NationalParentingCenter

REFERENCES

Arat-Koc, S. 1989. "In the Privacy of Our Own Home: Foreign Domestic Workers as a Solution to the Crisis in the Domestic Sphere in Canada." *Studies in Political Economy* 28: 33–55.

Ariès, P. 1962. *Centuries of Childhood: A Social History of Family Life.* New York: Vintage Books.

Arnup, K. 1994. *Education for Motherhood: Advice for Mothers in Twentieth-Century Canada.* Toronto: University of Toronto Press.

Bradbury, B. 2005. "Social, Economic, and Cultural Origins of Contemporary Families." In M. Baker (ed.). *Families: Changing Trends in Canada*, 5th ed. (pp. 71–98). Toronto: McGraw-Hill Ryerson.

Brunner, J. 2000. "Tot Thought. *The New York Review of Books* XLVII, no. 4: 27–30.

Campaign for a Commercial-Free Childhood. 2016. "Marketing to Children: Overview." Retrieved July 22, 2016, from www.commercialfreechildhood.org/resource/marketing-children-overview.

Charon, J.M. 1979. *Symbolic Interactionism: An Introduction, an Interpretation, an Integration.* Englewood Cliffs, NJ: Prentice-Hall.

Clark, W. 2011. "Kids' Sports." Retrieved January 24, 2011, from www.statcan.gc.ca/pub/11-008-x/2008001/article/10573-eng.htm#a3.

Connell, R.W. 1996. "Teaching the Boys: New Research on Masculinity and Gender Strategies for Schools." *Teachers College Record* 98: 206–235.

Coontz, S. 1992. *The Way We Never Were: American Families and the Nostalgia Trap.* New York: Basic Books.

Donzelot, J. 1979. *The Policing of Families.* New York: Random House.

Felson, R.B., and M.Z. Zielinski. 1989. "Children's Self-Esteem and Parental Support." *Journal of Marriage and the Family* 51: 727–735.

Fox, B. 2001. "The Formative Years: How Parenthood Creates Gender." *The Canadian Review of Sociology and Anthropology* 38: 373–390.

Fox, B. 2009. *When Couples Become Parents: The Creation of Gender in the Transition to Parenthood.* Toronto: University of Toronto Press.

Greenglass, E.R. 1982. *A World of Difference: Gender Roles in Perspective.* Toronto: John Wiley & Sons.

Gubrium, J. 1992. *Out of Control: Family Therapy and Domestic Order.* Thousand Oaks, California: Sage.

Gustafson, D.L. (ed.). 2005. *Unbecoming Mothers: The Social Production of Maternal Absence.* New York: Haworth Press.

Hay, M.S. 1996. *The Cultural Contradictions of Motherhood.* New Haven: Yale University Press.

Livesey, C. 2005. "Family Life: Childhood." Retrieved September 13, 2005, from Chris.Livesey: www.sociology.org.uk.

Livingstone, S. 2009. *Children and the Internet: Great Expectations, Challenging Realities.* Cambridge: Polity Press.

Macdonald, C.L. 1998. "Manufacturing Motherhood: The Shadow Work of Nannies and Au Pairs." *Qualitative Sociology* 21: 25–53.

Maity, N. 2014. "Damsels in Distress: A Textual Analysis of Gender Roles in Disney Princess Films." *IOSR Journal of Humanities and Social Sciences* 19: 28–31.

Murray, S.B. 1998. "Child-Care Work: Intimacy in the Shadows of Family Life." *Qualitative Sociology* 21: 149–168.

Nortons, K., T. Old, S. Olive, and S. Dank. 1996. "Ken and Barbie at Life Size." *Sex Roles: A Journal of Research* 34: 287–294.

Sinha, M. 2014. "Child Care in Canada." Statistics Canada Catalogue no. 89-652-X-No. 005. Ottawa: Minister of Industry.

Strong, B., and C. DeVault. 1992. *The Marriage and Family Experience*, 5th ed. New York: West Publishing Co.

Swain, J. 2004. "The Right Stuff: Fashioning an Identity through Clothing in a Junior School." In M. Webber and K. Bezanson (eds.), *Rethinking Society in the 21st Century: Critical Readings in Sociology* (pp. 81–92). Toronto: Canadian Scholars' Press Inc.

Travis, C. 1992. *Mismeasure of Woman: Why Women Are Not the Better Sex, the Inferior Sex, or the Opposite Sex*. New York: Touchstone.

Wall, G. 2005. "Childhood and Childrearing." In M. Baker (ed.), *Families: Changing Trends in Canada*, 5th ed. (pp. 163–180). Toronto: McGraw-Hill Ryerson.

Willett, R.J. 2015. "The Discursive Construction of 'Good Parenting' and Digital Media – the Case of Children's Virtual World Games." *Media, Culture, and Society* 37: 1060–1075.

Wooden, S.R., and K. Gillam. 2016. *Pixar's Boy Stories: Masculinity in a Postmodern Age*. New York: Rowman & Littlefield Publishers.

CHAPTER 9

All Our Families: Diversity, Challenge, and Continuity in Non-Conforming Coupled Relationships

LEARNING OBJECTIVES

In this chapter you will learn that ...

- heteronormative frameworks, the ideological use of "the family," and the assumption of difference in non-conforming couple families remain highly problematic
- it is difficult to arrive at accurate estimates of members of the LGBTQ2 community in the Canadian population
- there are both similarities and differences between conforming and non-conforming couples with respect to life-course patterns of support and family relationships
- children of non-conforming or non-heterosexual parents fare as well as children of "conventional" parents—socially, economically, and health-wise—despite assumptions to the contrary

- despite important progress, many challenges remain ahead with respect to the social and legal rights and acceptance of LGBTQ2 families

INTRODUCTION

We are all aware of the fact that not all intimate partnerships are "opposite sex," that is, comprised of one heterosexual man and one heterosexual woman. My own personal family experience involved my younger sister, Sally, partnering with her girlfriend, MacKenzie. They legally married in 2012 and are the proud parents of three beautiful, happy, and well-adjusted children—Ilya, August, and Abby—as shown in our opening chapter photograph.

Many Canadians identify themselves as lesbian, gay, bisexual, transgender, queer, or **two spirited** (as represented by the 2 in LGBTQ2). Although the groups comprising this umbrella acronym are diverse, and labels are social constructs, the terms gay and lesbian typically refer to male and female homosexuality. On the other hand, queer, or *transgender*, are blanket terms used to describe someone who feels that their body's biological sex does not match their socially ascribed gender status. These individuals may also consider themselves to be gender nonconforming, an even broader term used to describe someone who does not necessarily feel either "traditionally" male or female. Similarly, two-spirited denotes a North American indigenous tradition that historically recognized more than two genders. This term stems from the Ojibwe phrase *niizh manidoowag* and replaces the oversimplified term *berdache*, which appeared frequently in research and anthropological studies that tried to describe the place of gay men in Native society in the 18th and 19th centuries (Pullin, 2014).

Box 9.1: Two Spirit: The Story of a Movement Unfolds

The phrase "two spirit" began to gain traction across Native America after 1990, when 13 men, women, and transgendered people from various tribes met in Winnipeg, Canada, with the task of finding a term that could unite the LGBT Native community. Numerous terms in tribal languages identified third genders in their cultures that encompassed both masculine and feminine, and the challenge for those gathered in Winnipeg was to choose a contemporary term that would be embraced across all tribal cultures.

The attendees at the gathering settled on "two spirit." They wanted a term that "reflected the combination of masculinity and femininity which was attributed to males in a feminine role and females in a masculine role," says author Sabine Lang in the book *Men as Women, Women as Men: Changing Gender in Native American Cultures*. Many two spirit, historically, were keepers of traditions, tellers of the stories of creation, and healers.

One of the most well-known two spirits in history is We-wha, an honored Zuni cultural ambassador who lived in what is now New Mexico. In 1886, she travelled to Washington, D.C., and shared the stories and values of her people. Courtesy of TwoSpirit.org, as shown in Pullin (2014).

Source: Photograph and except from: Pullin, Z. 2014. "Two Spirit: The Story of a Movement Unfolds." *Native Peoples Magazine*, May-June. Retrieved July 31, 2016, from www.nativepeoples.com/Native-Peoples/May-June-2014/Two-Spirit-The-Story-of-a-Movement-Unfolds.

Yet, the family lives of the LGBTQ2 community have remained largely invisible until fairly recently. This partly stems from the methodological problems inherent in studying a sensitive topic. Gay and lesbian individuals, for instance, must be willing to disclose a status that is sometimes met with anti-homosexual prejudice, as conveyed in my sister Sally's story in box 9.2. Therefore, many of these individuals may not wish to share the intimate details of their lives with researchers for fear of being further victimized or categorized (Nelson, 1996: 10).

Box 9.2: Sally's Story

Growing up on a farm outside a small and largely Mennonite community in the 80s and 90s could be considered anything but a mecca for any person of a diverse nature. The only memories I have in respect to sexual diversity (pre-Ellen DeGeneres's coming out) were of the one single woman in a nearby town whom everyone referred to as "bull dyke" (while making disgusted faces); and the time on a field trip when a teacher referred to two gay men we saw as "filthy animals."

These early memories set the stage for deep repression, fear, and self-loathing when at the age of 12, while at horse camp, I laid eyes on my counselor and for the first time in my life had a legitimate crush. I lay awake trying to pray away my gay, to no avail. It did not feel safe to be anything but straight. It was a secret I had to push down as deep as it could go. I learned to play along, to flirt with the boys, to date (never wanting to go past first base), to hang up pictures of the boy bands, and to discuss crushes on all the "teen-beat" movie stars. And while I did experience legitimate crushes and attraction to males along the way, I never in my heart identified as straight. I told myself I was confused.

I know now that I was not confused. I was unsupported by my community, the media, the laws of our country, and so on. Not surprisingly, I developed terrible bouts of depression and anxiety in response to the stress of hiding myself and the years of guilt and self-rejection. These feelings would plague me for years to come.

When I was a young adult, I met and married a man and had a baby. I was living the dream, or at least I had materialized the expectations society had set for me. When that marriage did not work out and I found myself a single parent, I took a couple years, not committing to anything outside of mothering, just floating around life, trying to make myself the best me I could be for my daughter. But when the truth hit me, it hit me hard. I was examining my life in the middle of the night. I examined my past, wondering "How did I end up here?" Divorced by 24, no career, no relationship, utilizing the food bank and social services, living in a small, cramped, basement apartment with no sign of things ever turning around. It hit me like a ton of bricks. I had been hiding a major part of myself for years, denying my nature, denying myself, all the while wondering why things never "worked out for me."

I decided to "come out" very suddenly. I had so much time to make up for. My roommate bought me a rainbow balloon and hugged me. I was ready to live my authentic self, and I didn't care who knew it. I had tried living the life I felt society expected, and that did not work. Then I met McKenzie. The first time I made eye contact with McKenzie, it was love. We exchanged a few awkward sentences, and when I walked out of the store where she was working, I said to my friend, "I am going to marry that woman." It all happened so fast. I went back to that store an hour later, and by the end of the week we were basically inseparable. Nine months later we were engaged; a year later we were married in front of 200 of our friends and family. The love and support that I experienced that day will always be the single most important event of my life. Never downplay the important role you play when you accept and stand behind someone.

One of my fears as a young person that held me captive was the idea that if I were in a same sex relationship I could never have children. There were no role models, which is why it is important for me to be visible and out and proud. Taking a chance, we approached one of my brothers, asking him if he would donate sperm so my wife could carry a child and we could expand our family. Thanks to his selflessness, in the first three years of our marriage we added two more daughters to our family.

Living in Saskatchewan, we were allowed to put both of our names on the babies' birth certificates from day one. This has not always been the case in this province, and in some parts of our country it is still not the case. But the country is moving forward. In 2011, for the first time, the census recognized same-sex marriage. However, I actually have to legally adopt my children, which costs about 4 grand if I want full and equal rights under the law. To me this is silly and I won't do it, I refuse. Maybe this would be different if we had a sperm donor other than my brother, whom I trust fully. As it stands, I don't feel any threat to my parentage.

When I allowed myself the freedom to be myself, the world opened up for me, I was able to live up to my full potential. This is not to say it has always been easy; there will always be dirty looks, and people who do not accept us and do not think we should be raising children. There will always be small battles to be waged, but those battles are minor compared to the empty life you live when you are not true to yourself. We make a conscious effort to be involved in everything, coaching sports, parent councils, volunteering at the kids' schools. We have also been fortunate enough to have the support of most of our family members, and I do not possess the words to express how grateful I am for this support.

As an educator, I use my platform to teach everyone I can—from kindergarten students to pre-service teachers—the importance of acceptance (not tolerance), and inclusion. My goal in life is to make this world a safer, more loving place for everyone to live, regardless of their perceived differences. Nothing hurts more than the suggestion that my family is less than, or inferior to, any other family. It is important to me that people understand that while my family may seem different than the norm, it is built on the same foundations I believe all families strive for: unconditional love, respect, and support.

Source: Mitchell, S. 2016. Previously unpublished story, shared through personal correspondence, July 28, 2016.

While research on this topic continues to grow, much remains to be learned about vernacular and research, and how the very idea of assuming "difference" shapes our contemporary ideas and knowledge about diverse family lifestyles change and grow at a rapid pace (e.g., see 2014 work by Walks). A recent study identified ten of the most prominent journals that involve family issues (e.g., *Journal of Marriage and the Family; Family Relations; Journal of Family Psychology*). After a thorough content analysis of 6,003 articles, the authors found that LGBT scholarship made up only 2.2% of the total scholarship (Zrenchik and Craft, 2016). Furthermore, the fact that same-sex marriage became legal only in 2005 means that we do not know much about same-sex legal unions, or divorce, for that matter. Moreover, there is growing awareness of the pitfalls associated with characterizing non-heterosexual families as homogeneous and deviant relative to the "standard North American family" ideological code (or SNAF, as discussed in chapter 1). From this perspective, these families constitute a "social problem" rather than a legitimate family lifestyle, which is a bias against diverse family arrangements (Hicks, 2005; Kinsman, 2006—see boxes 9.3 and 9.4).

In light of these important research gaps and methodological issues, this chapter will explore a variety of trends and issues relevant to the lives of LGBTQ2 families. This will include a focus on the historical and ideological positioning of gay and lesbians in opposition to "the family." In addition, an overview of socio-demographic trends with respect to prevalence and partnership formation will be provided, as well as the wider network of kin and friendship relations. Finally, social and legal recognition in relation to rights, entitlements, and benefits; and challenges to reduce discrimination and homophobia, will be highlighted.

Box 9.3: Is Gay Parenting Bad for Kids? Responding to the Very Idea of Difference in Research on Lesbian and Gay Parents

I do not support the view that we live in a society in which lesbians and gay men are "just different." Instead, we live in one that organizes sexual discourse to produce hierarchies in which traditional and heteronormative family forms are dominant, and this is reinforced through a series of textual, legal, social, and cultural practices...if we start from the baseline that differences between gay and straight families exist, then such ideas can play into the hands of the Christian right because they do not question the very system of sexual knowledge that organizes contemporary ideas about sexuality. That is, the "idea of difference" shapes our practices of knowing (Seidman, 1997), so that we start to ask whether and how the children of lesbians and gay men turn out different, instead of asking how contemporary discourses organize "sexual identities" into discrete groupings.

Source: Hicks, S. 2005. "Is Gay Parenting Bad for Kids? Responding to the 'Very Idea of Difference' in Research on Lesbian and Gay Parents." *Sexualities* 8: 153–168. (pp. 164–165).

Box 9.4: Homosexuality as a "Social Problem"

Heterosexual hegemony is produced on many fronts—from family relations that often marginalize and sometimes exclude gays and lesbians to the violence we face on city streets; to state policies; to the medical profession; to sociology, sexology, and psychiatry; to the church, the school system, and the media. These forms of sexual regulation (which do not develop in a linear fashion) interact with the social relations we live to produce heterosexist "common sense." There also exist conflicts between and within various agencies over definitions of homosexuality, and jurisdictional disputes over who can best deal with the sexual deviant.

The entry of heterosexual hegemony into public "common sense" involves many variants of heterosexist discourse, each of which merits its own analysis... These include homosexuality as a sin (in religious discourse); as unnatural (in both religious and secular discourse); as an illness (in medicine and psychiatry and, in a new sense, with the current AIDS crisis); as a congenital disorder or inversion (in sex psychology and sexology); as deviance (in some sociological theory); homosexuals as child molesters, seducers, and corruptors (in certain sexological studies, the law, and the media); as a symptom of social or national degeneration (in Social Darwinist and eugenic discourse); homosexuals as communists, "pinkos," and a national security risk because of the potential for blackmail (rooted in McCarthyism, military organization, the Cold War, and 1950s/1960s security regime practices); homosexuality as tolerated only when practiced between consenting adults in "private" (the Wolfenden strategy of privatization); and as a criminal offence or a social menace (in police campaigns, "moral panics," and the media).

Source: Kinsman, G. 2006. "The Creation of Homosexuality as a 'Social Problem.'" In A. Glasbeek (ed.), *Moral Regulation and Governance in Canada: History, Context, and Critical Issues* (pp. 85–116). Toronto: Canadian Scholars' Press (pp. 103–104).

CHANGING ATTITUDES TOWARD SAME-SEX PARTNERSHIPS

Contemporary attitudes toward same-sex partnerships have religious, legal, and moral historical roots. Before the High Middle Ages, homosexual acts appear to have been widely tolerated or ignored by the Christian Church throughout Europe, although this had changed by the 13th century (Hereck, 2005). Negative sentiments continued into the 19th and early 20th centuries, such that public opinion was that all sex not intended to produce children could lead to "degeneration because precious bodily fluids were wasted" (Ward, 2002: 95). Yet, as previously mentioned, it is interesting to note that some Indigenous or Aboriginal peoples had complex systems of sex and gender in which some individuals were perceived to combine the spirits of male and female. These "two-spirited" people were thought to be very fortunate and blessed with power, generosity, and good luck (O'Brien and Goldberg, 2000; Williams, 1992).

By the mid-19th century, the notion that homosexuality was a mental illness came to be widely accepted in North American society, although homosexuality was not universally viewed as a "degenerative sickness." For example, Sigmund Freud's basic theory of human sexuality was that all individuals were innately bisexual and that they became heterosexual or homosexual as a result of their experiences with parents and others (Freud, 1905). Therefore, Freud argued that homosexuality should not be viewed as an unnatural form of pathology. It is also noteworthy that homosexuality was not removed from the American Psychiatric Association's *Diagnostic and Statistical Manual of Mental Illness* (DSM) until 1973 (Hereck, 2005), and transgenderism and transsexualism continued to be classified as "gender-identity disorders" by many professional organizations until fairly recently.

It was not until 1969 that the Canadian Criminal Code was reformed so that acts in private between consenting adults were no longer criminal. However, this change in law did not completely erase a (continuing) popular stereotype that homosexuality represents a deviant kind of "perversion" (Ward, 2002). Fortunately, at this point in the 21st century, attitudes are continuing to liberalize as the government, the scholars, and the general public are increasingly likely to recognize and accept non-heterosexual couples as "legitimate" and equally deserving of respect, rights, and entitlements. In 2016, federal legislation was introduced to protect transgendered rights and prevent discrimination based on **gender identity**. And since the Civil Marriage Act (introduced by Paul Martin's Liberal government as Bill C-38 and enacted on July 20, 2005), same-sex couples in Canada have been able to legally wed, as previously noted.

According to a new human rights report released by the International Lesbian, Gay, Bisexual, Trans and Intersex Association (ILGA), the number of countries banning same-sex relationships has declined over the last decade (Carroll and Mendos, 2017). This report was released following the wake of international outrage launched against the aggressive anti-gay campaign in Chechnya, an ultra-conservative Russian Republic. In 2016, more than 100 gay men were allegedly "rounded up and detained" for being gay, and many news sources continue to report horrific stories of abuse, torture, and death due to this mass persecution (e.g., see Walker, 2017). The ILGA report also found that same-sex relationships remain a crime in 72 countries around the world, although this is down from 96 in 2002. Eight United Nations member states issue the death penalty for same-sex activity, including Saudi Arabia, Iran, Yemen, and Sudan, while other countries enact "morality laws" to actively prohibit the public "promotion" of gay or transgender lifestyles (Mintz, 2017). There was some optimism in the ILGA report, however; 23 countries now legally recognize same-sex marriage. Worldwide, same-sex marriages are currently performed in many places, such as Canada, the United States, South Africa, and Belgium; and more recently, in Finland and Slovenia (see table 9.1 for a summary). A number of countries permit some type of same-sex civil union, contract, or domestic partnership. For example, since 2001, same-sex couples in Germany have been able to register for "lifetime partnerships," although they could not legally wed until June 2017. However, other European states (e.g., Italy) do not provide any legal recognition to same-sex couples, in spite of jurisprudence by the European Court of Human Rights (Dittrich, 2017).

Table 9.1: Examples of Gay Marriage Legalization around the Globe

Country	Year Recognized
Belgium	2003
Canada	2005
Columbia	2016
Finland	2017
France	2013
Scotland	2014
Slovenia	2017
South Africa	2006
Spain	2005
Sweden	2009
United States	2015

Source: Data extracted from Pew Research Centre. 2015. "Gay Marriage around the World." Retrieved June 20, 2016, from www.pewforum.org/2015/06/26/gay-marriage-around-the-world-2013; and Dittrich, B. 2017. "Finland to Allow Same-Sex Marriage: Other Council of Europe Countries Should Back LGBT Rights." Retrieved May 15, 2017, from https://www.hrw.org/news/2017/02/21/finland-allow-same-sex-marriage.

The Canadian Census recently began to collect data on same-sex couples, and researchers are also increasingly likely to include same-sex couples in studies of courtship, marriage, and other types of family matters. For example, Canadian researcher Humble (2016) has conducted extensive research on marriage among gay, lesbian, and bisexual Canadians aged 26 to 72. In her recently published paper on same-sex wedding planning and support from the wedding industry, she notes that this industry has been historically geared toward White, middle-class women, since they are the ones most likely to consume wedding-related products, attend wedding-related events (e.g., wedding or bridal shows), and respond to marketing messages. And while Humble recognizes that some wedding-related outlets (e.g., publications) have implemented gay-focused initiatives such as presenting same-sex images and stories, she asserts that heterosexism remains socially and ideologically constructed in weddings and marriage. Her research also finds that although many of her study participants reported receiving positive support from families, friends, and communities (including churches and religious leaders), the ideology of the wedding industry remains largely heteronormative. This idea is supported with regard to the wording on wedding forms and wedding registries; it is occasionally still heterosexist. Similarly, Humble found many instances in which businesses and store staff/personnel automatically assumed a heterosexual wedding. Dennis, for instance, describes his experiences in shopping for engagement rings (cited on pg. 291):

> Every time I went into the jewellers, I went into all five jewellers in the Shopping Centre, and every time I went in, and of course I'm in there with a suit and tie,

they're running around to help you 'cause you look like you have money. This is how this works. And so, a guy with a tie, they just assume you want to buy something for your girlfriend. So I said, I'm looking for engagement rings, and they never asked who I was marrying. They always brought me down to the women's section.

Overall, data and research focus almost exclusively on same-sex relationships such that we do not know much about bisexuality, transgenderism, or other nonconforming gendered identities. Therefore, most of this chapter focuses on the family lives of gays and lesbians, with the recognition that individuals do not always neatly fit into these categories.

IDEOLOGICAL POSITIONING OF GAYS AND LESBIANS AND "THE" FAMILY

The 1960s represents a decade distinguished by the formation of many social groups devoted to civil rights and greater equality for oppressed and disadvantaged groups. The Stonewall Riots (as shown in figure 9.1) are frequently cited as a defining moment in North American history, when people in the homosexual community fought back against what they perceived as a government-sponsored system that persecuted sexual minorities. Taking place in New York City, these spontaneous, violent demonstrations heralded the start of the gay rights movement in the United States and around the world. In Canada, many social activist groups began to form and numerous protests occurred (such as the one depicted in figure 9.1). For example, Pride Toronto came into existence in the 1970s; this group has been very active in many events (e.g., parades, picnics, marches), raising public awareness of queer issues.

Since the 1960s, gays and lesbians have formed a massive social movement aimed at improving their social recognition, as well as completely reorganizing gender, family, and sexuality. For example, some radical feminist lesbians and gays rejected traditional family values and motherhood because they saw these institutions as inherently patriarchal and oppressive. Indeed, some activists could be seen carrying banners that read "Smash the Family" and "Smash Monogamy" at public protests (Stacey, 1998). However, it is recognized that "lesbians and gays are not, and never have been, a unified group with one collective agenda for social change" (Clarke and Kitzinger, 2005: 139).

Many activists also fought against the tendency of heterosexual writers and researchers to characterize lesbian and gays as "outside relationships," and as unhappy, hedonistic, and alone, or as objects of pity and fear. Their concern was that as a result of this practice, homosexuality would come to mean the opposite of "family," with its presumed stability and as the natural source of happiness and caring. Yet, as argued by O'Brien and Goldberg (2000: 117), "this characterization of families is ridiculously wrong." In support of this assertion, they point to how heterosexual families are often sites of violence and abuse, as well as change, instability, and discomfort, themes that are also echoed throughout this textbook.

Figure 9.1: The Gay Rights Movement in North America

In 1969, during the final weekend in June, drag queens and queer street kids rioted at the Stonewall Inn, a gay club in New York City, as shown in the top photo. This event sparked a series of other riots and is commonly cited as the beginning of the gay liberation movement. Subsequently, many protests and demonstrations occurred throughout the rest of the world, including Canada, such as the one shown in the bottom photo, which took place at the Vancouver Courthouse on August 28, 1971.

Sources: Photo 1: New York Daily News Archive/Getty Images. Photo 2: Gay Alliance toward equality (Vancouver) demonstration. The Body Politic fonds, Canadian Lesbian and Gay Archives. Photo by Ron McLennan, August 28, 1971. Image #1986-032/18P(01).

In today's society, many social groups continue to denounce the gay and lesbian populations, which further sets up an ideological divide between lesbian/gay and heterosexual families. The so-called defenders of "family values" (e.g., Focus on the Family, REAL Women) tend to attack groups that supposedly menace and undermine "the family." Moreover, family sociology has traditionally displayed a **heterosexist bias** that reproduces an ideology that places gay men and lesbians outside of family relations and considers them hazardous to them. For example, many previous studies on lesbian/gay families have fallen into the category "sociology of deviance" or "social problems." Also, little original work has been done in a number of areas popular in sociology more generally, such as gender, social class, the effect of partner separation on children, ethnicity; and in areas of social policy and service delivery (Ambert, 2005). Notably, sociological research related to gender tends to assume that gender identity is a subjective and fixed sense of being either male or female, resulting in the usage of a binary with only two "legitimate" categories.

In sum, definitions and meanings given to "the family" by social groups and researchers have significant repercussions for the lives of lesbian/gay families. In particular, they can generate microaggressions and undermine claims for greater measures of social justice. Indeed, ideological usages of "the family" against gays and lesbians are homophobic since they spread an irrational fear and hatred of people who are not heterosexual. As a result, heterosexuality is politicized as the only valid form of sexual behaviour and as superior to any other family structure. Yet, as O'Brien and Goldberg further remind us, "there is no valid reason for refusing to call them families. They fall under every conceivable sociological criterion for identifying families" (2000: 133). Like all families, these individuals form close relations, pool material resources, socialize children, engage in emotional and physical support, and make up part of a larger kin network, topics that will be explored in further depth throughout this chapter.

FLUID AND DYNAMIC IDENTITIES AND THE PREVALENCE OF LGBTQ2 FAMILIES

There is not always a clear-cut distinction between sexual orientation and self-identity. Some homosexuals may self-identify only at certain points in their life, rather than throughout their entire adult years. Also, some individuals may have had a homosexual past, but may identify as heterosexual. And some individuals may identify as heterosexual, yet display or experiment with behaviours that do not conform to societal norms of what is considered "gender appropriate" (e.g., cross-dressing, having same-sex sexual fantasies). As Golden states, "Sexuality may be an aspect of identity that is fluid and dynamic as opposed to fixed and invariant" (1987: 19). Thus, due to this, along with a variety of other methodological issues, it is difficult to know exactly how many Canadians are gay, lesbian, bisexual, or **transgender**.

However, it is fairly well established that gays and lesbians constitute a significant but fairly small minority of the population. Using the concept of self-identity, a recent Statistics Canada survey found that among Canadians aged 18 to 59, 1.7% reported that they considered themselves to be homosexual, and 1.3% considered themselves bisexual, for a total of 3% of the population (Statistics Canada, 2015). Other carefully designed studies suggest that at the upper limit, approximately 5% of men identify as gay and fewer than 3.5% of women identify as lesbian, estimates that match other research studies (e.g., see Ambert, 2005, for review), although many would argue that under-reporting of non-heterosexual sexual orientation is pervasive.

Although previous national census surveys have not asked individuals about their sexual orientation, in Canada, the 2001 census was the first to provide data on same-sex partnerships. Since same-sex marriages were legalized in Canada in 2005, census data on legally married and same-sex couples are available for 2006 and 2011 only, as summarized below:

- 64,575 — the number of same-sex couple families in 2011, up 42.4% from 2006.
- 21,015 — the number of same-sex married couples.
- 43,560 — the number of same-sex common-law couples.
- 0.8% — the proportion of all couples in 2011 who were same-sex.
- 54.5% — the proportion of same-sex couples who were male.
- 45.5% — the proportion of same-sex couples who were female.
- 25.3% — the proportion of same-sex married spouses and common-law partners aged 15 to 34.
- 17.5% — the proportion of opposite-sex married spouses and common-law partners aged 15 to 34.
- 6.2% — the proportion of same-sex married spouses and common-law partners aged 65 and over.
- 17.8% — the proportion of opposite-sex married spouses and common-law partners aged 65 and over.
- 45.6% — the proportion of all same-sex couples in Canada living in Toronto, Montreal, and Vancouver.
- 33.4% — the proportion of all opposite-sex couples in Canada living in Toronto, Montreal, and Vancouver. (Statistics Canada, 2015)

According to the census, the number of same-sex married couples nearly tripled between 2006 and 2011, while the number of same-sex common-law couples rose 15%. As a result, married couples represented about 3 in 10 same-sex couples in 2011, nearly twice the share of 16.5% in 2006 (Statistics Canada, 2015).

GAY AND LESBIAN COUPLE RELATIONSHIPS AND PATTERNS OF SUPPORT

O'Brien and Goldberg (2000) argue that the ideological positioning of gay men and lesbians in opposition to "the family" leads to the stereotype that these individuals lead lonely lives characterized by casual sexual encounters. However, similar to heterosexual couples, lesbian/gay couples can form a variety of relationships, from casual dating to cohabitation to, more recently, legal marital unions. Breakup rates between lesbian/gay and heterosexual couples are also found to be relatively the same, and research on older gay men and lesbians indicates that relationships lasting 20 or more years are not uncommon (Peplau, 1991). Moreover, most gay men and lesbians are satisfied with their relationships and have similar relationship dynamics as heterosexual couples, despite the stresses of life in a heterosexist society (Moore and Stambolis-Ruhstorfer, 2013). And, as with heterosexual couples, partner abuse (covered in chapter 15) can also be a problem in some intimate homosexual relationships (O'Brien and Goldberg, 2000).

Lesbian and gay couples also tend to report a more egalitarian division of labour than married couples (Goldberg, Smith, and Perry-Jenkins, 2013). It is suggested that, unlike in heterosexual relationships, in which each gender is automatically given duties and rights, lesbian and gay couples negotiate a division of labour based upon skill, preference, and energy related to age and ability. Gay couples also often report more autonomy in terms of activities, friendships, and decision-making than heterosexual married couples. Lesbian partners also tend to state that they enjoy greater relationship satisfaction and more intimacy, autonomy, and equality than married couples (Ambert, 2005). It is suggested that the greater equality and satisfaction found in gay and lesbian partnerships may be related to the tendency for them to be dual-wage earners and therefore have a high level of "material self-sufficiency" (Weston, 1991).

LINKED LIVES: INTERGENERATIONAL RELATIONS, FRIENDSHIP NETWORKS, AND CHILDREN

The family of origin—the family that one is born into or grows up in—can also play an important role in the lives of LGBTQ2 individuals. D'Amico et al. (2015), for example, found that parents' struggles with their children's sexual orientations were significantly associated with dimensions of youth's identity and psychological adjustment. Relations between gays and lesbians and their families, similar to those in heterosexual families, can be fairly unproblematic, or they can be fraught with tensions and ambiguity. In particular, young people may struggle with **coming out** (that is, publicly acknowledging their sexuality) and try to challenge their family for acceptance (Gibson, 1989). Unfortunately, families can mirror societal **homophobia**; this can be particularly troublesome if youth are living at home and dependent on parents. And of those who decide to leave home to escape family- or school-related non-acceptance, many may find themselves caught in a vicious circle of homelessness and other social problems due to their young age, vulnerability, and lack of family support.

Research documents that members of the LGBTQ2 community commonly experience shame, self-hatred, social isolation, verbal and physical harassment, and rejection by their families and other societal institutions. A highly publicized recent example that shows some of these challenges is the case of transgendered Caitlyn Jenner, formerly known as Bruce Jenner, an American television personality and retired Olympic gold-medal winner. Other examples from popular culture include the Netflix production "Orange is the

New Black," about an incarcerated transgendered woman; and the Emmy award–winning reality television series "Transparent," which shows the struggles faced by a transitioning parent who is divorced and has three grown children. Similarly, the media has been showing greater representation of the LGBTQ2 community by trying to celebrate the diversity that exists within the broader "queer" experience. The Vancouver Queer Festival, for instance, has been lauded for showing films that portray multiple identities and the intersections of race and queer identities (Thorkelson, 2016).

Other research mirrors many of the same struggles that the LGBTQ2 population can experience. Suicide is commonly documented as a serious social problem among gay and lesbian youth, with family rejection and harassment at school cited as root causes. In addition, research establishes that members of this population are more likely to experience health care barriers and challenges. For example, in 2014, the Canadian Community Health Survey (Statistics Canada, 2015) found that homosexuals and bisexuals are more likely than heterosexuals to have unmet health care needs. They are also more likely to find daily life "quite a bit" or "extremely" stressful (33.4% and 26.7%). Moreover, youth not living in large urban centres may be particularly disadvantaged, since they may not have access to the same type of organizational support (e.g., in the educational system) and access to health and social services.

Yet, it is promising to observe that while most health research focuses on deficits, some researchers are beginning to take more of a "strength-based" approach that focuses on positives rather than negatives. For instance, one study found that bisexuals experienced many advantages because of their sexuality, such as freedom from social labels and the freedom to love whom they wanted without the restriction of gender (Rostosky, Riggle, Pascale-Hague, and McCants, 2010). This development of positive identity is clearly advantageous for generating positive mental health outcomes, as advocated by Rainbow Health Ontario.

With respect to family reactions to gay and lesbian cohabitation, in comparison with opposite-sex cohabitation, research suggests that parents can have problems with acceptance and ambivalence. For example, in one study a woman described being referred to in a joking manner by her partner's family as the "aunt" or "live-in-nanny" (Epstein, 2003). Indeed, the concept of **intergenerational ambivalence** (ambivalence is defined as the experience of contradictory emotions toward the same object) (Weigert, 1991: 21), has utility in furthering our understanding of "institutionally incomplete" (Cherlin, 1978: 634) family relationships, including lesbian/gay family relationships across the life course. This line of thinking suggests that contemporary family life is characterized by a multiplicity of forms yet to be "institutionalized," with well-established guidelines and norms for behaviours. This includes gay and lesbian unions, such that family relationships may be characterized by a polarization (i.e., a range from positive to negative) of simultaneous feelings (Luescher, 2000).

Generally, the concept of intergenerational ambivalence can be conceptualized as structurally created contradictions in relations between parents and adult offspring. This term also highlights how intergenerational solidarity is not a one-dimensional concept, because ambivalence is both a variable feature of structured sets of social relationships and a catalyst for social action, since actors can negotiate and renegotiate relationships over time. In this way, ambivalence represents a valuable "bridging concept" because it allows a conceptual link between social structure and individual agency (Connidis and McMullin, 2002; Lowenstein et al., 2003).

With regard to the impact of cohabitation and marriage among gay and lesbian partners on linked family lives, there is ample evidence to suggest that families can experience more ambivalence in their attitude toward same-sex cohabitation than heterosexual cohabitation (e.g., see Moore and Stambolis-Ruhstorfer, 2013; Reczek, 2016). This may be partly due to a general lack of social acceptance toward these types of unions (because of homophobia or fear of homosexuality), which in turn can make family acceptance more challenging. As a result, there may be more resistance from family members than in heterosexual partnerships (Nock, 1998). Some young adults may even be led to conceal the true nature of their partnership from their parents and other family members in an effort to avoid conflict and stress.

However, similar to the research on heterosexual cohabitation, the reactions and support from family members (particularly parents) are shown to vary according to a number of factors such as religion, race and ethnicity, parental education, and pre-existing relationship quality. For example, many religious orientations support only heterosexual unions, and some racial/ethnic groups are less supportive in their attitudes to same-sex unions (Miller and Chamberlain, 2016). Ambivalent or negative reactions are also more evident among older parents, those with less education, and parents who had strained relationships with their children prior to learning of their gay or lesbian identity (Savin-Williams, 2001).

Yet, research shows that over time, family members who initially showed disapproval often become more accepting and supportive of the relationship (Bernstein, 1995). This lends support to the idea that familial ties can involve more or less ambivalence at different points in the life course (Connidis and McMullin, 2002). However, in general, gay and lesbian individuals and cohabiting couples receive more social support than non-gay couples from friends and their subculture than from their parents and their family of origin (Kurdek, 1998).

Turning to the children of lesbian/gay couples, studies on family relationships in these households is relatively sparse but generally indicate more similarities than differences (Moore and Stambolis-Ruhstorfer, 2013). For example, home environments are as conducive to psycho-social growth among family members, including children, as are those of heterosexual couples. Also, the daily routine and family life cycle is largely similar for both same-sex and opposite-sex families—children arrive, need love and supervision, grow up, and parenting flows accordingly. Lesbian and gay parents may also create a network of fictive kin or chosen family (such as a mixture of gay and non-gay friends and relatives) for social and emotional support. This network can provide their children with social support to compensate for a lack of family-of-origin-support, or may constitute an additional network of supportive relations (Ambert, 2005).

With respect to the consequences of gay parenting, three main issues tend to surface at the societal level. These issues tend to be motivated by fears that: (1) children will grow up to be maladjusted because of social stigma; (2) offspring will be sexually molested by their parents or associates; and (3) children will grow up to become homosexual (because of a lack of proper role models). Yet, none of these concerns has received empirical support. For example, children of same-sex couples tend to show few psycho-social differences than other children, despite the existence of societal homophobia. Moreover, children are not at a higher risk of being molested; in short, homosexuality is not synonymous with pedophilia. In fact, the vast majority of child molesters are heterosexual men (Ambert, 2005; Epstein, 2003). Also, children of homosexual partners tend to develop heterosexual identities, although they may be more tolerant of same-sex experimentation than children of heterosexual parents (Stacey, 1998).

THE BATTLE CONTINUES: RIGHTS, ENTITLEMENTS, AND CHALLENGES AHEAD

LGBTQ2 social and legal rights, entitlements, and benefits continue to remain among the most hotly contested social and political issues, as illustrated in box 9.5. Among these issues is social recognition, since a lack of this can place unique stresses upon individuals and families. For example, some lesbian/gay individuals may not be able to come out in their families, workplaces, or communities. This can deny them the right to reveal their partner's existence, censor their conversations about their activities, and silence their pain and grief when a partner is ill or dies, or when a significant relationship has dissolved. And at social gatherings such as holidays or family events, they may have to bear the pain and stress of separation from their lovers, or have to downplay their verbal and physical expression of affection.

With respect to legal and other social issues, dramatic shifts in same-sex relationships and parenting rights have occurred between the late 1990s and today. Until relatively recently, for instance, homosexuality in a parent was sufficient "proof" to deem a person "unfit" to have custody of a child (Epstein, 2003). In fact, as recently as the early 1990s, a study conducted for the Royal Commission on New Reproductive Technologies revealed that 76% of medical practitioners would refuse donor insemination to women in a lesbian relationship even if it were stable (Rayside, 2002). Since that time, medical practitioners have become less discriminatory, and laws have broadened to allow lesbians and gays to adopt children.

Prime Minister Justin Trudeau has captured headlines and social media postings around the world through his promotion of LGBTQ2 causes such as Pink-Shirt Day (as shown in figure 9.2). However, some critics argue that much more remains to be done in terms of other legislative changes (e.g., see Salerno, 2016). It is argued that many members of the LGBTQ2 community continue to face barriers even though they have successfully fought for the inclusion of sexual orientation as a prohibited ground of discrimination in the human rights code. For example, some gays and lesbians continue to be ineligible for the same tax breaks and work-related benefits as heterosexuals, such as pensions, survivor's benefits, and

Box 9.5: Resisting Transnormativity: Challenging the Medicalization and Regulation of Trans Bodies

When Jenna Talackova entered the 2012 Miss Universe Canada competition, she did not disclose her history of being born and assigned male at birth (nor should she have to). When the competition's organizers, including business mogul Donald Trump, became aware that Talackova was a transsexual woman, she was disqualified from the competition as the incongruence between Talackova's sex assigned at birth and her current gender identity and presentation were grounds for dismissal. Talackova was the "normal" young woman she appeared to be. However, a month later she was told that if she could prove she meets the "legal gender recognition requirements of Canada and other international competitions," then she would be allowed to compete.

Following her initial ousting, Talackova gained media attention as she fought for the same opportunity to compete as other women. Her story included the narrative of cross-gender identification as a child: she knew she was a female by age four, she began hormone therapy at puberty, and she had undergone full sexual-reassignment surgery, which reconstructed her penis into a vagina. Jumping through all the right hoops to qualify for sexual reassignment surgery, Talackova upholds a society's standards of both beauty and femininity. Effectively, Talackova was presented as a normal heterosexual woman whose body (read: genitals) now matched her gender identity.

By wholly crossing from one side of the binary to the other, the sex-equals-gender model is upheld. Talackova "proved" she was a woman by conforming to traditional notions of gender. Consequently, Talackova was "rewarded" for subscribing to gender normative standards and was reinstated in the competition.

If Talackova had not been fortunate enough to undergo sexual reassignment surgery, it is likely that she would not have been allowed to compete as she would not have met the legal and competition requirements of being female. The incongruence between her gender and sex would have challenged the sex-equals-gender binary and would have been seen as a threat to normative gender standards.

Source: Vipond, E. 2015. "Resisting Transnormativity: Challenging the Medicalization and Regulation of Trans Bodies." *Theory in Action* 8: 21-44. (pp. 21-22).

parental leave. Yet, official forms of discrimination have been successfully challenged in a number of different ways, and recent changes to same-sex marriage legislation also show future progress. In short, with the rising acceptance of the "modern family," with its diverse meanings and family forms, and with specific laws and policies to support these families, it is hopeful that discriminatory behaviours and practices will continue to diminish.

Figure 9.2: Prime Minister Justin Trudeau Attending a Pink-Shirt Day Event

Source: Salerno, R. 2016. "Commentary: Justin Trudeau Still Has a Lot to Prove on LGBT Rights." *The Advocate*, April 8. Retrieved August 5, 2016, from www.advocate.com/commentary/2016/4/08/justin-trudeau-still-has-lot-prove-lgbt-rights.

SUMMARY

This chapter explores the lives of the LGBTQ2 individuals and their families, beginning with the recognition that a multitude of fluid, dynamic, and intersecting identities and communities fall under this umbrella acronym. We also learn that it is problematic to assume "difference" and that it is imperative to ask how our societal discourse organizes "sexual identity" into discrete groupings. A major theme is that traditional meanings and interpretations of "family" are non-inclusive and need to be challenged. These definitions tend to reflect **heteronormativity** and result in social, institutional, and legal practices that reinforce heterosexuality as the only "normal" sexuality (Kitzinger, 2005). This creates a bias against non-conforming family structures, since they are deemed not natural or legitimate and therefore not deserving of social recognition. Indeed, biology often becomes a more important component than emotional or social relationships in defining characteristics of a family (Epstein, 2003).

Studies have established that there are more similarities than differences between same-sex and heterosexual couples and families. This observation further highlights how treating gender and sexuality as measurable outcomes is problematic (Hicks, 2005). At the same time, conducting research on social processes and challenges (such as on unmet health-care needs) unique to gay/lesbian families has the potential to dispel homophobic stereotypes and improve lives (e.g., Benson, Silverstein, and Auerbach, 2005). For example, some research on how gay fathers work to challenge traditional cultural norms for fathers, families, and masculinity has helped to reconceptualize family and "de-gender" parenting. From this lens, gay fathers are shown to expand role norms in novel ways that may serve as alternative models for all families (Schacher, Auerbach, Silverstein, 2005). Similarly, a previous study on lesbian mothering in Alberta highlights the importance of a positive social milieu for successfully raising their children (e.g., see Nelson, 1996).

Several social and legal challenges are outlined with respect to individual and family rights, entitlements, and benefits. Overall, it is clear that, while progress has been made in reducing homophobia, we need to collectively address the systemic roots of oppression that is still faced by the LGBTQ2 community in the 21st century. These experiences and conditions of subordination and injustice continue to be supported by many of our dominant institutions, including our families, the educational system, religious organizations, the media, and the legal system. Thus, until widespread social and cultural transformation occurs within these key institutions, greater equality for all families—regardless of sexual orientation—will not be achieved.

QUESTIONS FOR CRITICAL REFLECTION AND DEBATE

1. Rates of youths' disclosure that they are lesbian, gay, or bisexual vary widely. Explore how ethnicity, religious orientation, and other factors might affect the propensity to disclose one's sexual orientation.
2. Public opinion remains divided on whether same-sex marriage should be legal. Provide arguments for and against this issue.
3. Research documents that lesbian and gay couples tend to report a more egalitarian division of labour than married couples. Explore some possible reasons for this finding.
4. Outline some strategies (national, local, community) for reducing homophobia and discrimination against lesbian/gay families in Canadian society.
5. Do you think that the Canadian government has the right to request that individuals reveal their sexual orientation in census surveys? What could be some possible uses and misuses of these data?
6. Imagine that you are a researcher studying transgender families. Which topic areas do you think require more attention? What challenges might you face in trying to collect these data?

GLOSSARY

Coming out is the public act of declaring oneself a gay man or a lesbian, as in "coming out of the closet."

Gender identity is the subjective sense of being, or the self-labelling as, either male or female.

Heteronormativity results in social, institutional, and legal practices that reinforce heterosexuality as the normal, natural, taken-for-granted sexuality.

Heterosexist bias is the tendency to assume that families and households consist of partnerships between men and women, and that heterosexuality is the only normal form of sexual expression.

Homophobia refers to the fear of homosexuality or homosexuals and the tendency to label certain kinds of sexual behaviours social problems.

Intergenerational ambivalence refers to the contradictory emotions or the coexistence of both positive and negative feelings within generational relationships.

Transgender is a term used to describe someone who does not conform to social roles based on his or her biological sex.

Two-spirited denotes an indigenous tribal term for a "third gender" that combines masculinity and femininity, attributed to males in a feminine role and females in a masculine role.

FURTHER READING

Bergstrom-Lynchj, C. 2015. *Lesbians, Gays, and Bisexuals Becoming Parents or Remaining Childfree: Confronting Social Inequalities.* New York: Rowman & Littlefield.
Recognizes the intense public battles waged in the US over the rights of LGB people to form legally and culturally recognized families. Based on in-depth qualitative interviews with 61 self-identified LGB people regarding how they came to have children or remain childless.

Chacaby, M.-N., and M. Plumer. 2016. *A Two-Spirited Journal: The Autobiography of a Lesbian Ojibwa-Cree Elder.* Winnipeg, Manitoba: University of Manitoba Press.
An inspirational and emotional account of Chacaby's life as a lesbian and how she overcame the social, economic, and health legacies of colonialism. Includes heartwarming stories of childhood friendships and the powerful relationship between the author and her grandmother.

DeVries, B., and E.F. Croghan (eds.). 2015. *Community-Based Research on LGBT Aging*. New York: Routledge.
Originally published as a special issue of the *Journal of Homosexuality*, this compilation of eight papers addresses a wide variety of topics such as social care networks and older LGBT adults; friends, families, and caregiving among midlife and older lesbians; service use among older adults with HIV; and aging African American lesbians and gay men.

Goldberg, A.E. (ed.). 2016. *The SAGE Encyclopedia of LGBTQ Studies*, 3 volume set. Thousand Oaks, California: Sage Publications.
Examines and explores the lives and experiences of LGBTQ individuals through a multidisciplinary lens. Covers theories, the transition to parenthood, intersections with other social locations (e.g., race), and the issue of marriage equality.

Mezey, N.J. 2015. *LGBT Families*. Thousand Oaks, California: Sage Publications.
Provides a historical, cross-cultural review of how structures of race, class, gender, sexuality, and age shape LGBT families. Helps us to understand the challenges and strengths of LGBT families and why newer family forms are so threatening to certain groups of people in society.

Newton, I.E. 2014. *LGBT Youth Issues Today: A Reference Handbook*. Santa Barbara, California: ABC-CLIO Publishing.
Provides information that will help LGBT youth overcome their challenges and give non-LGBT youth a better understanding of sexual identities different from their own. Also presents a historical background on the topic and up-to-date examinations of the issues of concern to LGBT young people, in addition to an extensive list of resources.

Schippers, M. 2016. *Beyond Monogamy: Polyamory and the Future of Polyqueer Sexualities*. New York: New York University Press.
Through an investigation of sexual interactions and relationship forms that include more than two people, from polyamory to threesomes, the author explores the queer, feminist, and anti-racist potential of non-dyadic sex and relationships.

RELATED WEB SITES

Canadian Lesbian and Gay Archives was established in 1973 and preserves lesbian and gay history in Canada and other parts of the world. It offers public access to collected records, photographic collections, posters, and artifacts, www.clga.ca.

Children of Lesbians and Gays Everywhere (COLAGE) is a support and advocacy organization for daughters and sons of lesbian, gay, bisexual, and transgender parents, www.colage.org. Facebook: COLAGE Twitter: COLAGEnational

Family Equality Council is a national online resource centre (i.e., searchable library) related to lesbian, gay, bisexual, and transgender families, www.familyequality.org/site/PageServer. Facebook: Family Equality Council, Twitter: familyequality

Lesbian and Gay Immigration Task Force—Canada (LEGIT/ICGL) is an all-volunteer organization that provides Canadian immigration information and support for same-sex partners, www.legit.ca/. Facebook: LEGIT: Canadian Immigration for Same-Sex Partners

Parents, Families, and Friends of Lesbians and Gays (PFLAG) has several chapters across Canada, www.pflagcanada.ca.

REFERENCES

Ambert, A.M. 2005. *Same-Sex Couples and Same-Sex Parent Families: Relationships, Parenting, and Issues of Marriage*. Ottawa: The Vanier Institute of the Family.

Benson, A.L., L.B. Silverstein, and C.F. Auerbach. 2005. "From the Margins to the Center: Gay Fathers Reconstruct the Fathering Role." *Journal of GLBT Family Studies* 1: 1–29.

Bernstein, R.A. 1995. *Straight Parents, Gay Children: Keeping Families Together*. New York: Thunder's Mouth Press.

Carroll, A., and Mendos, L.R. 2017. *State-Sponsored Homophobia 2017: A World Survey of Sexual Orientation Laws: Criminalisation, Protection and Recognition*. Geneva: ILGA. Retrieved May 15, 2017, from http://ilga.org/what-we-do/state-sponsored-homophobia-report.

Cherlin, A. 1978. "Remarriage as an Incomplete Institution." *American Journal of Sociology* 84: 634–650.

Clarke, V., and C. Kitzinger. 2005. "We're Not Living on Planet Lesbian: Constructions of Male Role Models in Debates about Lesbian Families." *Sexualities* 8: 137–152.

Connidis, I.A., and J. McMullin. 2002. "Sociological Ambivalence and Family Ties: A Critical Perspective." *Journal of Marriage and the Family* 64: 558–568.

D'Amico, E., D. Julien, N. Tremblay, and E. Chartrand. 2015. "Gay, Lesbian, and Bisexual Youths Coming Out to the Parents: Parental Reactions and Youths' Outcomes." *Journal of GLBT Family Studies* 11: 411–437.

Dittrich, B. 2017. "Finland to Allow Same-Sex Marriage: Other Council of Europe Countries Should Back LGBT Rights." Retrieved May 15, 2017, from https://www.hrw.org/news/2017/02/21/finland-allow-same-sex-marriage.

Epstein, R. 2003. "Lesbian Families." In M. Lynn (ed.), *Voices: Essays on Canadian Families*, 2nd ed. (pp. 76–102). Scarborough: Thomson Nelson.

Freud, S. 1905. "Three Essays on the Theory of Sexuality." In J. Strachey (ed. and trans.), *The Standard Edition of the Complete Psychological Works of Sigmund Freud* (vol. 7, pp. 123–245). London: Hogarth Press.

Gibson, P. 1989. "Gay Male and Lesbian Youth Suicide." In M.R. Feinleib (ed.), *Report of the Secretary's Task Force on Youth Suicide* (vol. 3, pp. 109–142). Washington: US Dept. of Health and Human Services.

Goldberg, A.E., J. Smith, and M. Perry-Jenkins. 2013. "The Division of Labor in Lesbian, Gay, and Heterosexual New Adoptive Parents." *Journal of Marriage and the Family* 74: 812–828.

Golden, C. 1987. "Diversity and Variability in Women's Sexual Identities." In Boston Lesbian Psychologies Collective (ed.), *Lesbian Psychologies* (pp. 18–34). Urbana, IL: University of Illinois Press.

Hereck, G. 2005. "Facts about Homosexuality and Mental Illness." Retrieved December 6, 2005, from www.psychology.ucdavis.edu/rainbow/html/facts_mentalhealth.

Hicks, S. 2005. "Is Gay Parenting Bad for Kids? Responding to the 'Very Idea of Difference' in Research on Lesbian and Gay Parents." *Sexualities* 8: 153–168.

Humble, A.M. 2016. "She Didn't Bat an Eye": Canadian Same-Sex Wedding Planning and Support from the Wedding Industry." *Journal of GLBT Family Studies* 12: 277–299.

Kinsman, G. 2006. "The Creation of Homosexuality as a 'Social Problem.'" In A. Glasbeek (ed.), *Moral Regulation and Governance in Canada: History, Context, and Critical Issues* (pp. 85-116). Toronto: Canadian Scholars' Press Inc.

Kitzinger, C. 2005. "Heteronormativity in Action: Reproducing the Heterosexual Nuclear Family in After-Hours Medical Calls." *Social Problems* 52: 477–498.

Kurdek, L.A. 1998. "Relationship Outcomes and Their Predictors: Longitudinal Evidence from Heterosexual Married, Gay Cohabiting, and Lesbian Cohabiting Couples." *Journal of Marriage and the Family* 60: 553–568.

Lowenstein, A., R. Katz, D. Prilutzky, and D. Melhousen-Hassoen. 2003. "A Comparative Cross-National Perspective on Intergenerational Solidarity." *Retraite et Societe* 38: 52–80.

Luescher, K. 2000. "A Heuristic Model for the Study of Intergenerational Ambivalence." *Arbeitspapier* no. 29. Konstanz: University of Konstanz.

Miller, M.K., and J. Chamberlain. 2013. "How Religious Characteristics are Related to Attitudes toward GLB Individuals and GLB Rights." *Journal of GLT Family Studies* 9: 449–473.

Mintz, L. 2017. "It Is Illegal to Be Gay in 72 Countries, New Human Rights Report Finds." Retrieved May 15, 2017, from http://www.pinknews.co.uk/2017/05/15/still-illegal-to-be-gay-in-72-countries-new-human-rights-report-finds.

Moore, M.R., and M. Stambolis-Ruhstorfer. 2013. "LGBT Sexuality and Families at the Start of the Twenty-First Century." *Annual Review of Sociology* 39: 491–507.

Nelson, F. 1996. *Lesbian Motherhood*. Toronto: University of Toronto Press.

Nock, S.L. 1998. *Marriage in Men's Lives*. New York: Oxford University Press.

O'Brien, C.A., and A. Goldberg. 2000. "Lesbians and Gay Men Inside and Outside Families" In N. Mandell and A. Duffy (eds.), *Canadian Families: Diversity, Conflict, and Change*, 2nd ed. (pp. 115–145). Toronto: Harcourt Canada.

Peplau, L.A. 1991. "Lesbian and Gay Relationships." In J.C. Gonsiorek and J.D. Weinrich (eds.), *Homosexuality: Research Implications for Public Policy* (pp. 177–196). Newbury Park: Sage.

Pullin, Z. 2014. "Two Spirit: The Story of a Movement Unfolds." *Native Peoples Magazine*, May-June, retrieved July 31, 2016, from www.nativepeoples.com/Native-Peoples/May-June-2014/Two-Spirit-The-Story-of-a-Movement-Unfolds.

Rayside, D. 2002. "The Politics of Lesbian and Gay Parenting in Canada and the United States." Paper presented at the 2002 Annual Meeting of the Canadian Political Science Association.

Reczek, C. 2016. "Ambivalence in Gay and Lesbian Family Relationships." *Journal of Marriage and the Family* 78, 644–659.

Rostosky, S.S., E.B. Riggle, D. Pascale-Hague, and L.E. McCants. 2010. "The Positive Aspects of a Bisexual Self-Identification." *Psychology and Sexuality* 1: 131–144.

Salerno, R. 2016. "Commentary: Justin Trudeau Still Has a Lot to Prove on LGBT Rights." *The Advocate*, April 8. Retrieved August 5, 2016, from www.advocate.com/commentary/2016/4/08/justin-trudeau-still-has-lot-prove-lgbt-rightsom.

Savin-Williams, R.C. 2001. *Mom, Dad, I'm Gay: How Families Negotiate Coming Out*. Washington: American Psychological Association.

Schacher, S.J., C.F. Auerbach, and L.B. Silverstein. 2005. "Gay Fathers Expanding the Possibilities for Us All." *Journal of GLBT Family Studies* 1: 31–52.

Stacey, J. 1998. "Gay and Lesbian Families: Queer Like Us." In M.A. Mason, A. Skolnick, and S.D. Sugarman (eds.), *All Our Families: New Policies for a New Century* (pp. 117–143). New York: Oxford University Press.

Statistics Canada. 2015. "Same-Sex Couples and Sexual Orientation…by the Numbers." Retrieved August 3, 2016, from www.statcan.gc.ca/eng/dai/smr08/2015/smr08_203_2015.

Thorkelson, E. 2016. "A Wide Focus on Queer Film: Festival Offers a Celebration of Diversity." *The Vancouver Sun*, Friday, August 2, B6.

Walker, S. 2017. "Chechens Tell of Prison Beatings and Electric Shocks in Anti-Gay Purse: 'They Called Us Animals.'" *The Guardian*, Thursday, June 13.

Walks, M. 2014. "'We're Here and We're Queer!' An Introduction to Studies in Queer Anthropology." *Anthropologica* 56: 13–16.

Ward, M. 2002. *The Family Dynamic: A Canadian Perspective*, 3rd ed. Toronto: Nelson Thomson.

Weigert, J. 1991. *Mixed Emotions: Certain Steps toward Understanding Ambivalence.*

Albany, New York: State University of New York Press.

Weston, K. 1991. *Families We Choose: Lesbians, Gays, Kinship*. New York: Columbia University Press.

Williams, W.L. 1992. "Benefits for Nonhomophobic Societies: An Anthropological Perspective." In W.J. Blumenfield (ed.), *Homophobia* (pp. 509–517). Boston: Beacon.

Zrenchick, K., and S.M. Craft. 2016. "The State of GLBT Family Research: An Opportunity to Critically Reflect." *Journal of GLBT Family Studies* 12: 138–59.

CHAPTER 10

Family Dissolution and the Brady Bunch: Separation, Divorce, and Remarriage

LEARNING OBJECTIVES

In this chapter you will learn that ...

- there are shifting trends in divorce and remarriage
- there are important predictors of divorce and remarriage at individual, family background, and societal levels
- divorce and custody laws have changed over time, and changes are proposed to the Divorce Act highlighting the "best interests of the child"
- there are consequences of divorce and remarriage for adults in areas such as socio-economic status and social-psychological well-being
- it is necessary to critically evaluate popular perceptions of the consequences of divorce and remarriage for children, such as the cultural stereotype of the "wicked stepmother"

INTRODUCTION

For most us, marriage symbolizes a relationship that should ideally last a lifetime or until "death do us part." Realistically, many of us know that not all marriages will last forever, and that many Canadian families will experience marital disruption and possibly remarriage. More than one-third or approximately 40% of Canadian first marriages end in divorce (Vanier Institute of the Family, 2011). Although this rate is relatively high, it is lower than the common assumption that 50% of all marriages will end in divorce, a statistic that has been based on American trends and perpetuated by sensationalistic media reports. Given that many divorced individuals will eventually re-partner, numerous opportunities and challenges arise for families "the next time around." And while many will go on to experience successful and positive relationships, others will face stress and strain. Indeed, the sociological conceptualization of **remarriage as an incomplete institution** (Cherlin, 1978) reflects the idea that remarriage is often characterized by ambiguity and confusion in role and status boundaries as well as by divided loyalties.

From a life-course perspective, a family member's decision to separate, divorce, or remarry carries significant implications for their life, as well as for other transitional behaviours and for "linked lives." This is because the effects of experiences that occur at a later point in the life course often depend on earlier events. For example, children who experience parental divorce while growing up are more likely to see their own marriages dissolve than children from intact families (Mitchell, 2006). Also, divorcing at a relatively young age may carry different short- and long-term consequences compared to divorcing in later life. For example, it may be more difficult to remarry in mid- or later life because of a narrowing pool of eligible mates.

It is also recognized that transitions to divorce or remarriage are "long-term processes that result in a qualitative reorganization of inner life and external behaviour" (Cowan, 1991: 5). These transitions can also create a **counter-transition**—that is, a transition produced by the life changes of others—that can add or remove social roles and relationships. For example, in the case of remarriage, previous in-laws may be replaced with new ones. Furthermore, if children are involved, divorce creates a counter-transition for at least two generations—the parents and the children of the divorcing couple (Downs, Coleman, and Ganong, 2000).

In this chapter, we will consider how formal relationship dissolution and remarriage affect the lives of both adults and children in a number of realms. Before we consider the aftermath of divorce and remarriage for families, an overview of socio-demographic trends in divorce and remarriage will be presented. Explanations of why divorce rates have generally risen over time and research on who is likely to divorce and remarry will also be reviewed. Finally, selected issues with respect to divorce law and the division of property, as well as custody and the notion of the "best interests" of children, will also be highlighted.

TRENDS IN SEPARATION, DIVORCE, AND REMARRIAGE

There are many means that couples can use to try to get out of an unsatisfactory marriage, such as desertion, **legal separation**, informally agreed-upon separation, and annulment. Desertion can be defined as the willful abandonment of one's spouse, children, or both, while a legal separation means that people are living apart with the intention of obtaining a divorce. In an informal separation, on the other hand, the couple is separated but still legally married. It is an arrangement that has been called "the poor man's divorce," since it occurs mostly among low-income families who cannot afford a divorce. An annulment occurs when the marriage contract is considered void due to a particular cause that existed before the marriage, such as a partner who is underage, a partner who is already married, or a couple that is involved in an incestuous relationship. And while most of these situations are stepping stones to divorce, it is possible (particularly in the case of marital separation) that some couples will use this time to work out a reconciliation in order to end their marital difficulties.

Divorce can be defined as the formal dissolution of a valid marriage by judicial decree. Prior to 1867, divorce was not allowed in Canada, with the exception of the Maritimes. Throughout that era, marriage was viewed as "a divine institution ordained by God." As a result, divorce in Canada was very rare before 1900, at fewer than 2 per million population. By 1921, divorce rates had climbed up to 6.4 per 100,000 population (Eshleman and Wilson, 2001). These rates have steadily increased over time, particularly following the liberalization of divorce laws in 1968 and 1985. Before 1968, adultery, cruelty, and desertion of 10 years were the only grounds for obtaining a divorce. After 1968, it became possible to get a divorce following a separation of three years. The Divorce Act of 1985 further amended these changes. Notably, parties to the divorce no longer had to show fault, and the waiting period on the grounds of marriage breakdown was reduced to one year (Ward, 2002).

Crude divorce rates, calculated as the number of divorces in a given year divided by the mid-year population, also show that divorce has generally risen over time. And although this method of reporting is often criticized (one reason given is that the populations surveyed have not aged enough to face the risk of divorce), some interesting patterns are worth highlighting, both nationally and internationally. In figure 10.1, we observe that in 1921 the divorce rate was relatively low, but it rose steadily to 54.8 divorces per 100,000 population in 1968. In 1969, following reforms to the divorce laws, the rate almost doubled to 124.2, which is relatively low in comparison to the more recent 2003 rate (approximately 224 divorces per 100,000). Since that time (and as you will note in table 10.1), divorce rates have remained fairly stable at 220 divorces per 100,000 in 2008.

However, there are striking fluctuations over time, or peaks and valleys, in divorce rates. Contrary to public opinion that divorce is at an all-time high, the peak year for divorce was in 1987, when the rate was 362.3 divorces per 100,000 population. Moreover, in 2008, women and men were, on average, 41.9 and 44.5 years old, respectively, when they divorced, although divorce is most likely to happen after four or five years of marriage. Also, the average duration of a marriage before divorce (for marriages that ended in divorce in 2008) was 14.5 years.

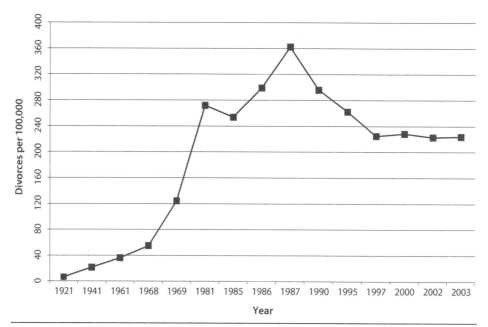

Figure 10.1: Divorce in Historical Perspective, Canada, per 100,000 Population, 1921–2003

Source: Statistics Canada data, adapted from Ambert, A.M. 2005. *Divorce: Facts, Causes, and Consequences.* Ottawa: The Vanier Institute of the Family (p. 4).

Crude Canadian divorce rates are also similar to those observed in other Western industrialized countries, such as the United Kingdom, France, and Germany, as shown in table 10.1. Yet, these rates are relatively low compared to those of the United States. Canadian rates are also much higher than those in countries such as Chile, Mexico, and Italy. In general, worldwide divorce rates tend to be associated with factors such as socio-economic development. For instance, although not shown in this table, other developing countries of Latin America (e.g., Nicaragua, Peru) and Asia (e.g., Thailand, Sri Lanka) typically have substantially lower divorce rates than more developed countries. Strong traditional or religious forces (e.g., Catholicism) in some countries can also influence divorce laws, attitudes, and behaviours; such is the case in Italy or in Ireland, where divorce was not legal until relatively recently.

The overall trend toward increased divorce is typically explained by fundamental social, cultural, and legal shifts, as well as changes in the ties that bind family members to one another. The possibility of same-sex marriage and divorce (as discussed in chapter 9) is but one more step in the same direction, although we know little about causes of divorce among this population, given its recent arrival (McKie, 2014). Whereas family bonds once rested on strong economic interdependence, today they rest more often on voluntary emotional ties. Economic development also stimulates individualism and secularization by changing the values, norms, and preferences in the larger society. Women's economic independence, for instance, makes them less dependent on a male breadwinner. Sociologists also focus on how laws governing

Table 10.1: Selected International Divorce Rates per 1,000 Population, 2010–2014

Country	Rates Per 1,000 Population
Australia	2.21
Canada	1.80
China	1.80
Chile	.10
Cuba	2.90
France	1.90
Germany	2.10
Japan	1.80
Italy	.90
Iran	2.00
Mexico	.80
Russian Federation	4.50
Singapore	1.80
Spain	2.00
Sweden	2.80
Turkey	1.60
United Kingdom	2.00
United States	2.80

Note: Rates are the number of final divorce decrees granted under civil law per 1,000 mid-year population for the latest data available between 2010 and 2014, with the exception of Canada.

Sources: United Nations, 2015. *Demographic Year Book.* New York: UN Publications (Table 24, pp. 639–645). Retrieved August 5, 2016, from www.unstats.un.org/unsd/demographic/products/dyb/dybsets/2014.pdf, except for Canadian data, which are from: Statistics Canada. 2006. *CANSIM Table 101-6501 – Divorce and Crude Divorce Rates, Canada, Provinces and Territories.* Retrieved August 5, 2016, from www5.statcan.gc.ca/cansim/a01?lang=eng.

divorce have liberalized over time, making divorce relatively simple to obtain. Indeed, rates quickly rose after the liberalization of divorce laws in 1968 and 1985. Yet, many researchers are quick to point out that laws only reflect ideological change. In this vein, liberal divorce laws have been described as "merely tools for the ready user" (McDaniel and Tepperman, 2004).

The Second (or Third) Time around: Patterns in Repartnering and Remarriage

Following divorce, many individuals will find another partner to date, cohabit with, or remarry. Among Canadians aged 15 to 64, recent data show that cohabitation is the predominant repartnering choice following a divorce. Within 10 years of marital dissolution, 47% of women are cohabiting, but only 12% are married. For men, the comparable figures are 56% and 15%, respectively (Schimmele and Wu, 2016).

Overall, with respect to remarriage, the rate of this behaviour among divorced men and women has fallen, particularly for men. Most of this can be explained by the corresponding increase in cohabitation. As previously discussed in chapter 7, cohabitation is increasingly viewed as providing the benefits of marriage without its legal obligations, economic consolidation, or traditional gender roles. Yet, approximately 70% of divorced men and 58% of divorced women in Canada eventually remarry, with the exception of Quebec, probably due to a preference for cohabitation in this province (Ambert, 2009).

Divorced individuals who repartner, either through cohabitation or remarriage, often bring their previous children into their new family environment. Surprisingly, stepfamilies were counted for the first time only in the 2011 Canadian census. According to these data, approximately 1 in 8 (12.6%) Canadian couples with children was a stepfamily, defined as a couple with children where the birth or adoption of at least one of the children preceded the current relationship. Statistics Canada (2012) also further distinguishes among different types and sub-types of stepfamilies, including simple stepfamilies and complex ones, as shown and defined in table 10.2.

While many step-parents have previously been married at least once or twice (Statistics Canada, 2012), it is extremely rare for someone in the general population to marry three or more times. Although recent data are unavailable, in 2001, 137,500 Canadian adults had been married more than twice. This represents less than 1% of the ever-married population aged 25 and over, and virtually all of them had tied the knot three times (Clark and Crompton, 2006). In other words, it would be very difficult to locate someone who has experienced

Table 10.2: Distribution of Couple Families with Children by Step-family Status, Canada, 2011

Couple family with children*	Number	Percentage
All couple families with children	13,684,675	100.0
Intact families**	3,220,340	87.4
Stepfamilies	464,335	12.6
Simple stepfamilies	271,930	7.4
Complex stepfamilies	192,410	5.2
Families with child(ren) of both parents and child(ren) of one parent only	149,365	4.1
Families with child(ren) of each parent only and no children of both parents	35,765	1.0
Families with child(ren) of both parents and child(ren) of each parent only	7,275	0.2

*Refers to couples with at least one child aged 24 and under.

**Couple families with at least one child aged 24 and under for whom it cannot be determined if there are stepchildren present are considered intact families.

Source: Statistics Canada. 2016. Canadian Demographics at a Glance, 2nd ed. Catalogue no. 91-003-X. Ottawa: Minister of Industry. Retrieved July 28, 2016, from www.statcan.gc.ca/pub/91-003-x/91-003-x2014001-eng.pdf.

more than three marriages, contrary to the well-publicized remarriage behaviour found among celebrities like the late movie-star legend Elizabeth Taylor (married eight times to seven husbands) and previous CNN talk-show host Larry King (seven times to six wives).

Studies also establish that remarriages are more likely than first marriages to end in divorce. This may be due to several factors. "Serial" brides and grooms may be more accepting of divorce. They may also have more "emotional baggage" due to the unfulfilled expectations of the prior relationship, which can strain remarriages. Also, the presence of stepchildren, ex-spouses, and ex-in-laws, along with a general lack of social support, can create forces that divert the couple's task of building their relationship (Ambert, 2009).

The Divorcing and Remarrying Kind: Who Is Likely to Divorce and Remarry?

Age at marriage is consistently found to be the strongest predictor of divorce in the first five years of marriage. People who enter marriage at the youngest ages, particularly during their teenage years, do so with the greatest risk for marital dissolution. Also, people with less than a high school education are more at risk for marital dissolution than those with a university degree. People who cohabit prior to marriage are also more likely to divorce, possibly due to adverse selectivity; that is, cohabitation may attract some who are less keen on commitment and stability, although as cohabitation becomes more normative, this effect may be diminishing (Mitchell, 2006).

People who attend religious services have a lower risk of dissolution than those who do not attend at all, showing that religious belief can be a protective factor. As far as children are concerned, the relationship between premarital child-bearing and the likelihood of divorce is overwhelming. Yet, couples who divorce often have no children, or fewer than the average, a phenomenon that is found across most societies and cultures. In addition, the longer a couple has been married, the greater the likelihood of staying together.

The attitudes and religiosity of serial marriers are different than those of couples who have not married multiple times. For example, research shows that serial marriers are less likely to believe that in order to be happy it is very important to have a lasting relationship, or that married couples facing problems should stay together for the sake of the children. They are also more likely to report no religious affiliation and less likely to attend religious services (Clark and Crompton, 2006).

With regard to family background factors, researchers have found that children who experience the disruption of their parents' marriage are more likely to see their own marriages dissolve (Amato, 1996; Wolfinger, 2000). It is postulated that parental divorce affects the risk of offspring divorce through three mediating mechanisms: life-course and socio-economic variables (e.g., early marriage, lower socio-economic origins); commitment and attitudes toward divorce; and patterns of interpersonal behaviour that are detrimental to marital stability (Amato, 1996). Children born out of wedlock (and who did not experience parental divorce or death) are as likely, if not more likely, to have their own marriages dissolve (Teachman, 2002). Cultural background or ethnicity can also affect the probability of divorce. For example, divorce is less common among people from certain ethnic backgrounds, such as Chinese and South Asian Canadians.

Figure 10.2 shows that geographical locale and regional factors are also related to the risk of divorce. The lowest divorce rates are found in the Maritimes and the highest rates in the Yukon Territories and Quebec. In 2008, the Yukon had the highest proportion (59.7%) of marriages expected to end in divorce before the 30th wedding anniversary, while Newfoundland and Labrador had the lowest (25%). Lower rates in the Maritimes may be due to the fact that, despite economic pressure, there may be a higher level of social integration, or demographic factors such as fewer married couples or an older population. Conversely, higher divorce rates may reflect less "traditional" family values, or regional conditions that prevent marital stability. For example, in Quebec, more divorces may occur due to a combination of variables such as widespread cohabitation before marriage, lower religiosity, and more individualistic or liberal attitudes (Ambert, 2005).

Finally, it is also important to consider the personal reasons people give for divorce. These include such problems as different values and interests, domestic abuse/violence, drug or alcohol abuse, adultery, career-related conflict, and money issues (Ambert, 2009). Regarding individual perceptions of divorce, we can refer to a study of 274 divorcees who were asked, "What do you think caused the divorce?" Their responses showed some general tendencies. The three most common answers were: infidelity (18.4%), incompatibility

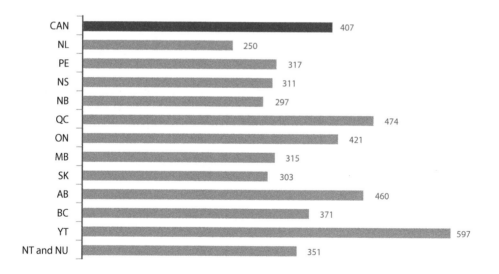

Figure 10.2: Thirty-Year Total Divorce Rate, by Province and Region, 2008 (per 1,000 marriages)

Note: The total divorce rate represents the proportion of new marriages that can be expected to end in divorce before the 30th wedding anniversary if the divorce rates by marriage duration observed in a given year are repeated in the future.

Source: Canadian Vital Statistics, Divorce Database and Marriage Database. Ottawa: Statistics Canada, 2011.

(16.4%), and drinking or drug use (9%). Gender differences were also found, with women more likely than men to cite infidelity or drinking or drug use as the major reason. And in general, former wives were more likely than former husbands to cite a cluster of negative partner behaviours including physical and mental abuse, substance use, going out with "the boys," and neglect of the home and children (e.g., see Amato and Previti, 2003).

With respect to motivation for remarriage from a historical perspective, in earlier times this typically involved widows or widowers. Due to lower life expectancies, men and women often died at a relatively young age, and the surviving spouse often needed a new partner. Now, with increased divorce, remarriages are more prevalent and usually involve younger people. And, as previously noted, men are more likely to remarry than women. It is postulated that men may have more advantages in their chances to remarry than women, partly due to age factors (e.g., see Sweeney, 1997). Also, men may have a greater need to remarry and a greater interest in remarrying than women, who generally have stronger support networks and domestic skills that can support independent living.

CONSEQUENCES OF DIVORCE AND REMARRIAGE FOR ADULTS

There is little doubt that divorce can be an emotionally painful and devastating experience for individuals and families and that remarriage introduces a new layer of complexity into family life (e.g., see box 10.1 for Patti Posner's story). Consequently, in an effort to reduce pressure on the family court system and encourage mediation over litigation, some provinces, such as Ontario, have introduced mandatory pre-divorce information sessions for couples (see box 10.2). These sessions are attended by couples before they take the step of ending their marriage in court. From a symbolic interactionist perspective, family members must now renegotiate new relationships and meanings in their daily lives. Some of these relationships will deteriorate or vanish, and this can affect relationships between other extended-family members, such as former in-laws or friends with whom the couple shared time together. Also, immediate and extended family networks may be placed under new strains; for example, the divorcing couple's parents may have a greater need for assistance.

Box 10.1: Family Narratives: One Family's Journey to Healing

I was divorced in 1986, when my daughter was eight years old. When I started dating and realized that one day I would remarry, I remember thinking that I would like to marry a man who already had children. I never thought about what it would mean to be a part of a step or blended family, and just how that would impact my life.

In 1990 I married a man who had two children. My husband also has an ex-wife, ex-in-laws, plus his ex-wife's live-in significant other. The coming together of my daughter and myself, my husband, his children, his ex-wife, her significant other, and her parents has been a very difficult task.

It is very difficult to form a blended and extended family. Part of the dilemma of blending families is that there are few, if any, cultural guidelines to follow. For example, we know how to behave and what is expected of us when we become in-laws. But we really do not know what our role is with our spouse or ex-spouse. There is no language for these new members of our extended family, nor do we think of them as friends. They may actually be seen as intruders, and a relationship built on this type of foundation can be very draining.

My own story is probably not all that different from [that of] the many other women who have married men who have previously been married. It took over eight years for the adults to come together. For years I felt in the midst of an angry tug of war. My husband's relationship with Jane ([his] ex-spouse) was based on anger and fighting. I was hurt when my husband was unable to set boundaries for himself and for letting [sic] Jane manipulate him. I felt that Jane was trying to control her children in ways that were interfering with my life with my new husband. It seemed that no matter what my husband and Jane did, I had to enter into the picture and would become angry and frustrated as well. The two main issues that I was confronted with were control and anger. And then I had to learn to deal with issues of jealousy. I had no role model, and I was very confused by all the emotions because of having Jane in my life....There were no road maps for any of us to follow. The difficulties between the three of us kept growing, and none of us were capable at the time to make the necessary adjustments. I could no longer take having Jane call our home, because most times an argument would ensue. I did not know how to pull myself out of the turmoil. I did something that may sound radical; I sent a note to Jane asking her not to call our home and explained that I could no longer deal with the arguing.

A year later I came to a halting revelation: I can choose to be married to my husband, and if I do, then his ex-wife must be part of the picture. I sent another note [to Jane], this time asking her to simply put the past aside and to begin again as friends. I give Jane much credit because she has been able to do this with dignity.

Our first meeting was for her son's college graduation. The whole family went— myself, my husband, all our children, Jane and her boyfriend, and her parents. Our first few minutes were a bit awkward, and then we eased into a relationship. Her boyfriend and I have an inside take on "our family," as we share the sense of being "the in-laws." In the past two years we have shared several family events. Having been able to succeed at this relationship has been and continues to be a very gratifying experience.

Source: Extract from Posner, P. 2007. "One Family's Journey to Healing." *Stepfamily Network Inc.* Retrieved January 1, 2010, from www.stepfamily.net.

Box 10.2: Pre-Divorce Talks Mandatory in Ontario

All Ontario couples seeking a divorce will now be required to attend a mandatory information session before ending their marriage in court, ushering in a program aimed at unclogging the family court system and encouraging mediation over litigation.

Divorcing couples must attend a two-hour session run by volunteer lawyers and social workers whose goal is to educate parents about the effects of divorce on both their bank accounts and their children.

"We're trying to take some of the emotional and financial cost out of separation and divorce," Attorney General Chris Bentley said. "We want to help them resolve their issues so they can get on with the rest of their lives as quickly as possible."

Although the concept is not new in Ontario—as part of a pilot program, 17 courts already offer the mandatory information session—the latest move expands the requirement to more than 50 provincial courts at a total cost of $7.2 million per year. The province, which is paying for the program through savings elsewhere, will also fund on-site mediation for couples who are willing to forego litigation.

Grant Gold, immediate past chair of the Canadian Bar Association's family law branch, which launched its program within the Superior Court system several years ago, has led mandatory information sessions for both applicants and respondents in Toronto and runs the evening sessions each week.

"On applicants' night, they're all kind of gung-ho because they started the whole thing and they want the divorce," Gold said. "On respondents' night, you see people who are all uptight and cranky that they have to be there. But by the end of the two-hour session, you can see people's shoulders go down. You hear people saying their eyes were opened to different processes."

Bentley said the program will make the family justice system more affordable, more efficient, and less confrontational. "Some cases involve a long court fight," he said, adding that spouses will ideally attend the session before they even file for divorce.

But while family lawyers and mediators say they welcome the new rules, some among the divorce community feel the regulations do not go far enough. "There might be some people who say, 'I didn't know those services were available,' or 'They're putting it right in my face so I'll spend the time and try to settle some of the issues of the case,'" Toronto-based divorce lawyer Brian Ludmer said.

Source: Carlson, K., and Postmedia News Ontario. 2011. "Pre-Divorce Talks Mandatory." *The Vancouver Sun*, Tuesday, July 19 (p. B3).

Most of us would agree that making a valiant attempt to save a marriage is a worthwhile effort, especially when children are involved. However, if these efforts are not successful, many of us would also agree that divorce may be the best decision, since it can provide the opportunity to build a healthier life. Indeed, recently there has been a plethora of books published that focus more on some of the positive experiences that individuals have following their marital breakdown. In her book *Happily Ever After Divorce: Notes of a Joyful Journey*, radio commentator Jessica Bram (2009) shares with readers how she maintained a sense of self and humour during a most difficult time and emerged triumphant. She also discusses how she handled everything—from everyday tasks to earning a living with newly discovered talents, from the delightful aspects of single-parenthood to eventually finding love all over again. Overall, her story is consistent with that of others who maintain that, all things considered, their divorce was the right decision for them and they have few regrets.

Yet other studies establish that divorce can also have a strong negative effect on adults' social-psychological well-being, particularly in the short term. Some degree of anger toward the ex-spouse is a relatively common sentiment, and this hostility can last for 10 or more years (Seccombe and Warner, 2004). Moreover, other research shows that there may be a gender difference in the experience of divorce; people (especially men) who are divorced tend to be less happy and healthy than people who are married (Waite and Gallagher, 2000).

In addition to emotional or social-psychological effects and changes to social networks, there are usually economic repercussions to divorce. Virtually all studies report a decline in economic well-being for women (and children) in the immediate post-divorce period. In particular, women's economic standing is altered, usually because their spouses earned more money in the paid labour force. Women also tend to take primary responsibility for children, if they are involved. One obvious outcome of divorce that involves children is single-parent households. Although there is more than one path to single parenthood (the parent may have never married), we have witnessed a general rise in the number of single parents over the past several decades. As noted in chapter 1, by 2011, approximately 16% of Canadian children were living in single-parent families, with the vast majority of these parents being female.

Many single parents (particularly mothers) live well below the poverty line, a topic that will be explored in further depth in chapter 14. Single parents can also face many difficulties in relation to child care (expenses, availability) and the adequacy and affordability of housing. Achieving a good social life can also be problematic, particularly if there is a lack of support systems to help out with child care, or if cost is an issue. This is easy to understand if we calculate the total cost of going to dinner and a movie—which would include paying for the meal, movie admission, snacks, transportation, and babysitting.

In summary, it is obviously too simplistic to picture the aftermath of divorce for individuals in completely positive or negative terms. It is also misleading to emphasize either negative outcomes or greater personal-growth opportunities following divorce because it "places the onus for adaptability solely on the individual" (Gorlick, 2005). In particular, this practice overlooks the complexity of the process and the differing concerns, resources, and capacities of individual family members, and how these can change over time. When women leave a physically or emotionally abusive relationship, for instance, many simultaneously experience more challenges with respect to their economic standing and finding affordable housing. At the same time, these women can experience relief and improved mental and physical functioning as well as enhanced self-worth.

THE BRADY BUNCH OR WICKED STEPMOTHER? CONSEQUENCES OF DIVORCE AND REMARRIAGE FOR CHILDREN

Previous research on this topic has generally assumed a host of negative consequences for children, contrary to the popular 1970s sitcom "The Brady Bunch," which depicted a happy suburban stepfamily with six precocious and well-adjusted children from previous marriages. Many of these outcomes centred on finding short- and long-term behavioural problems and emotional trauma, problems that were purported to be due to the missing father or "deadbeat dad" and the "emotionally overwrought mother." Generally, it is assumed that children are living in an "aberrant" single-parent family or a troublesome "blended" or remarriage family (Gorlick, 2005). In the case of single parents, it has been especially common for sociologists and other professionals in the past to refer to these families as "broken," as if something were missing or faulty.

Children living in single-parent homes are often found to be at risk for developing certain kinds of problems. On average, children from single-parent homes tend not to do as well in school as children in two-parent families. They are also more likely to marry and cohabit at an earlier age, both of which are connected to higher chances of divorce. Moreover, many young adults are more likely to have long-term emotional difficulties (particularly if their parents separated before they were five)—known as the **sleeper effect**—as well as more likely to commit serious crimes, or to have children outside of marriage (Ward, 2002).

Many of these problems can be traced to a lack of financial resources and a lack of outside supports rather than the family structure per se. Moreover, some research shows that many single parents and their children develop very strong, supportive, and close-knit relationships to compensate for the lack of an additional adult in the home (Seccombe and Warner, 2004). However, in light of the fact that stepfather-stepchild relationships are more common than stepmother-stepchild relationships (because children typically remain with their mother), the "wicked stepmother" myth remains strong (Cheal, 1996). But this cultural stereotype of the wicked stepmother, which emerged from folk tales and children's stories such as "Cinderella" and "Snow White," has not been supported empirically. For example, Cheal (1996) found that stepmothers were not harsher or more inconsistent in their interactions with their stepchildren than were biological/adoptive mothers with their biological/adopted children.

Yet, children exposed to stepfamily environments are found to leave home earlier due to conflict at home (e.g., Mitchell, 2006) than those raised in intact families, and these children are faced with more complex relationship structures and processes (e.g., Ferri and Smith, 1998). For example, if the child has stepsiblings, there may be tension if they now have to share a bedroom or other possessions. Problems can also result if the "baby of the family" suddenly has to contend with younger stepsiblings and reduced time and attention from a parent.

Research generally supports the view that it is important to consider a number of characteristics and circumstances that can influence the aftermath of divorce and remarriage, such as who the child lives with, the age and gender of the child, the level of parental conflict, visitation patterns and parental involvement, socio-economic status, and outside support networks. For example, sometimes parents use the children as a weapon to hurt the ex-partner or try to get children to take sides in a dispute. They may also communicate their anger and hurt toward each other to their children and demean or ridicule their ex-spouses. As a result, children experience tremendous stress. Conversely, if parents can co-operate or at least try to minimize overt conflict in front of them, children tend to have fewer emotional and behavioural problems (Seccombe and Warner, 2004).

Demo and Fine (2010) further demonstrate the highly dynamic nature of the divorce process and the complex set of factors that affect adult and child adjustment. Their integrated model (as shown in figure 10.3) outlines the key processes influencing outcomes. In particular, this conceptual model highlights the importance of marital and family relationship trajectories beginning in the pre-divorce years and evolving through the post-divorce period. This includes consideration of individual and interpersonal skills and resources, socioeconomic changes accompanying and following divorce, reconfigurations in family structure over time, and alterations in family processes following divorce. Overall, this model is consistent with a life-course approach in that it situates adjustments within a variety of contexts (e.g., socio-historical, economic) and considers the highly fluid and variable nature of individual adjustment.

Finally, it is important to acknowledge the limitations of divorce and stepfamily research. Notably, many researchers argue that the literature on single or stepfamilies uses a nuclear "intact" measuring stick to compare blended family experiences. This tendency assumes that non-intact families—a commonly used but value-laden term—are "deviant," which glosses over the tremendous variability that can occur within categories of family structure, as well as changes over time. For instance, research documents that children who grow up in "intact" but conflict-ridden families may suffer more than children whose parents divorce but maintain a friendly family relationship. In addition, some family environments are transitional (e.g., single-parent homes), such that remarriage may improve the financial well-being of children whose parents divorced, and provide the children with an additional caretaker.

SELECTED ISSUES IN DIVORCE: THE LAW, PROPERTY DIVISION, AND CUSTODY

Divorce entails the division of property and assets, as well as the responsibilities and care of children, if children are involved. However, many feminists argue that since legislatures and courts have historically been dominated by men, family law has been more protective of men's than women's interests. A good example of this argument can be found in the *Murdock vs. Murdock* case (see box 10.3). This case rested on the assumption that the wife had no claim on matrimonial property (property acquired during marriage), even though she worked very hard to acquire it.

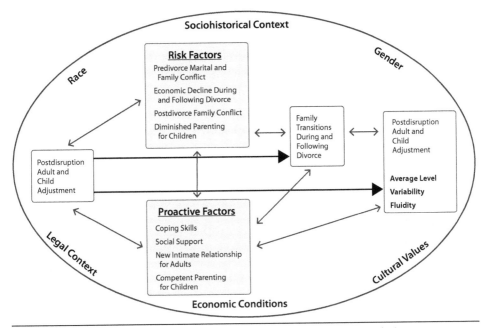

Figure 10.3: The Divorce Variation and Fluidity Model

Source: Demo, D.H., and M.A. Fine. 2010. *Beyond the Average Divorce.* Thousand Oaks, California: Sage Publications (pg. 17).

Box 10.3: Murdock vs. Murdock

The Murdocks were Alberta ranchers who separated in 1968 after 25 years of marriage, during which time Irene Murdock had worked alongside her husband to the extent that he did not have to hire a hand. However, when she sued for half-interest in their property, cattle, and other assets, the Alberta courts and, ultimately, the Supreme Court of Canada, decided that Mrs. Murdock was entitled to alimony but had no claim on the value of the property because she had not made "a direct financial contribution" to the ranch; the work she had carried out for 25 years was "the work done by any ranch wife." In short, Mr. Murdock held the title to the property, and Irene Murdock "was expected to hoe, mow, dehorn, brand (and cook, clean, and bear and raise children)" with no hope of a share of it when the marriage ended.

Sources: Kieran, 1986; Morton, 1988 (cited in Chunn, 2005: 288); Kieran, S. 1986. *The Family Matters: Two Centuries of Family Law and Life in Ontario.* Toronto: Key Porter (p. 142); Morton, M.E. 1988. "Dividing the Wealth, Sharing the Property: The (Re)formation of 'Family' in Law in Ontario." *Canadian Review of Sociology and Anthropology* 25: 254–75; and Chunn, D.E. 2005. "Politicizing the Personal: Feminism, Law and Public Policy." In N. Mandell and A. Duffy (eds.), *Canadian Families: Diversity, Conflict and Change,* 3rd ed. (pp. 276–310). Toronto: Thomson Nelson.

The obvious injustice of this case led to revisions in matrimonial property laws in all of the provinces by the early 1980s. Both federal and provincial family laws now stipulate that the division of property will be governed by the principle of equalization. As a general rule, all family assets are to be shared equitably, although not necessarily equally (e.g., see Chunn, 2005). There also remain variations in provincial laws, particularly with respect to guidelines specifying the conditions under which the court may order an unequal division of business assets. And, as discussed in box 10.4, increased immigration to Canada from other countries presents new challenges to the Canadian legal system. This is illustrated by the emergence of Islamic law (*sharia*) in Canadian legal institutions.

Box 10.4: The Emergence of Sharia Law in Canadian Legal Institutions

Because Canadian society now consists of individuals from many places and cultures, it is not possible to generalize about how Canadians actually live out their pair bonding and dissolution experiences. What we all experience in common is the law. Whether or not religious rules apply is now strictly a matter of individual choice, in striking contrast to earlier periods, when the demands of religious edicts were sometimes harsh and imposed with considerable force. Some cultural practices that newcomers to Canada might otherwise be inclined to follow are ruled out by law, as is multiple marriage, or are granted not standing in law, as is religious divorce. One striking departure from this pattern has begun to emerge, however.

The gradual and subtle introduction of Islamic law (sharia) in Canada has raised some difficult and troubling questions. In the normal course of events, countries have one universal system of civil and criminal codes. Indeed, it is one of the elemental aspects of democracy that all citizens be accorded the same rights and privileges under law. Canada has always been an exception to this rule by the acceptance of the Civil Code system in Quebec, an integral part of the historic bargain that brought Quebec into Confederation. Other slight departures of a purely optional nature have existed for some time. Among these are the orthodox Jewish requirement for a religious *get* or divorce before remarriage can occur, and a similar Roman Catholic requirement for a religious annulment. The *get* has been an especially vexing problem for some divorcing wives because it is granted (or not) exclusively by the husband of the failed marriage. Lawsuits of the common civil variety to compel the delivery of a *get* are not unknown.

But the introduction of sharia principles in recent years is a qualitatively different initiative. In reflection of the growing diversity of cultural origins present in Canadian society, disputes involving Muslim women's dowries, divorce, inheritance, and property ownership have actually been arriving in civil court.

In Ontario until 2006, judges might choose to refer such cases to an Islamic tribunal for binding arbitration, provided the parties were willing. However, the matter of parallel justice systems in Ontario came to a head in early 2006 when the government of Ontario ultimately decided against continuing this practice. The Family Statute Law Amendment Act, passed 14 February 2006, ensures that only Ontario family law can be used in binding arbitrations in Ontario. According to Attorney General Michael Bryant, "the bill reaffirms the principle that there ought to be one law for all Ontarians."

But in British Columbia, courts have on occasion upheld a Muslim woman's *maher*, a form of prenuptial agreement that defines in advance the amount of payment to be made upon subsequent marriage termination. Acknowledging that a maher has force and effect in Canadian courts as a contract (even though it has purely religious legitimacy) is a step in the direction of parallel legal systems, which is completely alien to the Canadian legal context. Although it does have some resonance with sentencing circles and restorative justice initiatives carried out in Aboriginal communities across Canada with the blessing of the courts, the fact remains that some few separation and divorce proceedings in Canada are now taking place in purely religious context, with judgments only subsequently confirmed (as in "rubber-stamped") in a conventional civil law document. Actions such as that of the province of Ontario in disallowing the use of religious-based tribunals in the settlement of civil disputes may simply drive these activities underground, with judgements officially registered with an Islamic court in another country, for instance.

Source: McKie, C. 2014. "Separation and Divorce: Fragmentation and Renewal of Families." In D. Cheal and P. Albanese (eds.), *Canadian Families Today: New Perspectives,* 3rd ed. (pp. 83–100). Toronto: Oxford University Press. (pp. 94–95).

Apart from the division of property, another significant consequence of divorce is children's custody and child support, which is under federal control. While a separation or divorce can involve multiple children 18 and under, the majority (57%) of separated or divorced parents had only one child together in 2011 (Sinha, 2014). In Canada, the governing principle is that custody awards should be based on the "best interests of the child," regardless of the wishes of the parents. Since most children have two parents and the child's welfare is strongly affected by the conditions of access, a number of issues can arise with respect to legal custody (the authority to make long-term decisions about how the child is to be raised), physical custody (who is responsible for the child on a daily basis), and **joint custody** (legal custody is shared equally, although it may not necessarily mean sharing physical custody).

Children in joint custody are now in a **bi-nuclear family** (see figure 10.4), since they continue to have two parents, but in two separate residences. Based on the 2011 General Social Survey, approximately 70% of separated or divorced parents indicated that the child lived primarily with his/her mother and 15% with the father, while only 9% reported equal living time between the two parents (Sinha, 2014).

A recent meta-analysis of research compared the adjustment of children in joint and sole custody (Baude, Pearson and Drapeau, 2016). Joint custody was defined as a proportion of time spent by children in each home ranging from a one-third time division to an equal share. The overall results of the 19 selected studies revealed better outcomes for children in joint custody, despite some individual studies suggesting that joint custody can produce negative results concerning children's emotional adjustment. Repeatedly moving from one home to another and having to follow two sets of rules, for instance, has been found to create stress and confusion for some children. As described by Marschall (2017), in many ways the everyday lives of children who commute between two households are "double looped." This is because these children have to be attentive to the routines, expectations, and demands of each separate household.

While mothers continue to mainly have primary custody of children (and children of recently divorced or separated parents are most likely to live in lone-mother households compared to lone-father households men are increasingly likely to apply for either sole or joint custody. We have also seen a movement toward an ideal of co-operative co-parenting, although it is recognized that not all situations lend themselves to this type of parenting arrangement (BC Council for Families, 2012). This model is compatible with the emergence of the notion of a "good divorce," a term popularized by Ahrons in her 1994 book by the same title (Ahrons, 1994). From this perspective, family bonds from both parents are collaboratively maintained, hostilities are pushed aside, and children's needs are the priority.

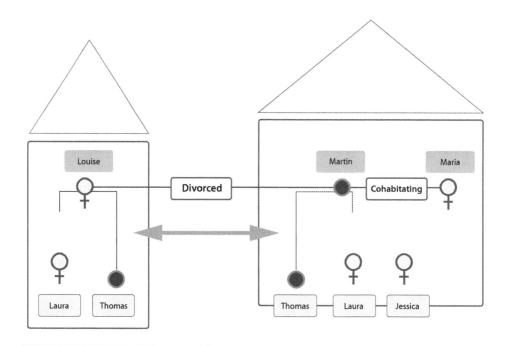

Figure 10.4: The Bi-Nuclear Family

Source: Juby, H.D. 2003. "Canada's Stepfamilies." Transition Magazine *33, no. 4. Ottawa: Vanier Institute of the Family.*

These trends toward greater father involvement also reflect a change in the norms and ideologies that a mother's care is necessarily "best." Yet, there is concern that with the increasing emphasis on the "best interests" of children and the increasing political strength of the fathers' rights movements, mothers' rights will become less visible. This appears to be particularly pronounced for women dealing with substance abuse, mental health issues, and family violence (Greaves et al., 2002).

Given the impact of various custody, guardianship, access, and support issues on children and families, many local governments and organizations have created programs and support materials to assist parents who have recently separated, as well as for those working directly with families. For example, in British Columbia, the BC Council for Families has produced many resource guides, including "Kids: The Heart of Co-Parenting: An Introductory Guide to Issues of Separation and Divorce for Family Professionals." This guidebook offers foundational theories and concepts to better understand the separation/divorce experience (e.g., child development, loss and grief, and attachment theory), in addition to checklists and tips for promoting effective parenting and co-parenting.

With regard to child support, determining the parent or parents responsible for this is based on the living arrangements of the child. A parent will usually pay child support if their children primarily reside with the other parent, while they will receive support if the children live mostly with them. Monthly payments are the most common schedule, and the payer's personal income and number of children influence these amounts. For example, in 2011, payers earning $100,000 or more a year paid a median amount of $8,000 per year, double the amount paid by parents earning less than $40,000 annually (Sinha, 2014).

Although the programs are relatively recent, most jurisdictions and ministries in Canada have created family maintenance and enforcement programs to ensure that child and spousal support payments are made on time and in full. If enforcement is necessary, federal and provincial laws are used, such as the Family Responsibility and Support Arrears Enforcement Act, passed in 1996 in Ontario. Under this legal authority, measures such as garnishing wages, tax returns, and bank accounts; making liens against real estate or personal property; and/or withholding driver's licenses can be taken to monitor and enforce court-ordered support payments.

Despite statistics showing that the majority of support recipients reported receiving their full child-support payment amounts in 2011 (Sinha, 2014, Statistics Canada, 2012), the "deadbeat dad" stereotype is a common figure in news media and public discourse. These fathers are often pictured as cold and heartless, living the high life, while their former families live on welfare and visit food banks. There are even web sites dedicated to assisting families in the recovery of unpaid court-ordered child support. For example, the non-profit site "Deadbeat Dads," which is operated and maintained by an army of "concerned citizens" (i.e., parents, bill collectors, lawyers) features "most-wanted" posters in their hall of shame. A "web detective" helps individuals locate "deadbeat" family members. Yet, some critics charge that it should not be assumed that these "deadbeats" are uncaring or unsupportive in principle. Some of these parents in arrears may be members of the working poor, whose low incomes may be based on seasonal or part-time employment (Gorlick, 2005).

SUMMARY

This chapter explores family relationships following separation, divorce, and remarriage. Contrary to popular perception, it is noted that although divorce rates have generally risen over time, they are not at an all-time high, nor are Canadian rates the same as the 50-per-cent failure rate found in the United States, although more than one in three first marriages in Canada will end in divorce. Macro- and micro-level factors associated with divorce are also considered, such as the effects of secularization, individualization, divorce law reform, and the changing role of women in families. Several consequences of the effects of divorce on individuals and children are also discussed. In particular, given the low pay structure for many women, divorced single mothers often face poverty and struggle financially to support and raise their families. A lack of economic resources, community, and state supports can produce stress and vulnerability for parents and children alike. It is also interesting to note that many studies indicate that a sizable proportion of divorces are salvageable, and that some ex-spouses are not happier or better off after the divorce (Ambert, 2009).

Trends in serial marriage are reviewed, as well as the consequences for both adults and children. While remarriages can be highly successful, like in the 1970s TV sitcom *The Brady Bunch*, remarried couples face a higher probability of divorce than first-married couples. Stepfamilies also often face vague, ambiguous, and confusing expectations, obligations, and rules because remarriage is an "incomplete institution." As a result, family members may face additional complexity and unique challenges.

Despite these general tendencies, it is important to acknowledge that stepfamilies—similar to all families—are diverse, and that not all parents and children will face major problems. After divorce, it is very possible for individuals to experience a fresh start and go on to lead a happy, well-adjusted, and successful life in a new family setting. Finally, it is important to challenge and critically reflect upon the language and terms that we use to identify and describe various family forms (e.g., the terms non-intact or broken families), since labels can carry enormous weight and powerful connotations.

Box 10.5: Family Labels Gloss Over Diverse Experiences

While many texts claim that being raised in a home by single parents may predispose children to negative outcomes, some research challenges the causal relationship between growing up in a single-parent family and detrimental outcomes. As researchers Don Kerr and Roderic Beaujot point out, "Studies that do not take into account the pre-existing difficulties of children and their families have a tendency to overstate the effect of growing up in a single-parent family." There are many circumstances in which mothers have created healthier environments for themselves and their children precisely *because* they ended a negative relationship to become single mothers.

Often, it seems that *resources* such as money, time, and community supports (i.e., extended family, friends, and other community members) have a more significant impact on child and parent experience and/or outcome than a parent's relationship status. As Jon Bernardes states in *Family Studies: An Introduction*, "Whilst Queen Victoria was a single parent for many years, she is not thought of as a 'problem parent.'"

However, what is perhaps most important to note is that children tend not to care about how the census categorizes their parents, nor do they tend to repeatedly quantify any kind of relationship status distinction when speaking about their parents. While they may initially share their familial status with friends—for example, "It's just me and my dad," or "My dad doesn't live with us"—there's most likely an informal, colloquial tone to this statement. It's highly unlikely that, once this personal information is shared, any future descriptions of an event or an issue linked to their parent/s includes determining terminology such as "my single father" or "my lone-parent mother." They most likely simply say "my mom" or "my dad" or "my whomever" with a sense of confident, unconditional, personal belonging and attachment marking the initial, and perhaps most crucial, signifier in that type of statement: "my."

Source: Bailey, V. 2016. "Languages, Labels and 'Lone Parents.'" Ottawa: VanierInstitute of the Family. Retrieved July 27, 2016, from www.vanierinstitute.ca/language-labels-lone-parents.

QUESTIONS FOR CRITICAL REFLECTION AND DEBATE

1. Debate the following: Despite difficulties, married couples with children should remain together for the sake of the children.
2. Why are remarriages less stable than first marriages? Do you think this will change in the future as remarriage becomes a more complete institution?
3. What are some of the ways in which gender, ethnicity, sexual orientation, and social class can affect the divorce experience of individuals and families?
4. From a life-course perspective, discuss fundamental similarities and differences between newly separating and divorcing families with young children, and divorcing families with teenaged children.
5. Why are power and control issues often at the root of many of the problems following divorce? Discuss this issue in the context of property division, using the *Murdock vs. Murdock* case as an example (box 10.3).
6. Following divorce, some couples may opt for joint custody of the children. What are the advantages and disadvantages of this arrangement, from the perspective of both generations? Also, what is your opinion of "parallel parenting" (as described in box 10.1)?

GLOSSARY

Bi-nuclear family is created when both the mother and the father act as parents to their children following divorce, although they maintain separate residences.

Counter-transition is a transition produced by the life changes of others (e.g., remarriage creates new in-laws).

Crude divorce rate is calculated as the number of divorces in a given year divided by the mid-year population.

Joint custody is defined as the legal right and responsibility of both parents to make decisions and care for their child(ren) following a divorce.

Legal separation occurs when married couples separate with the intention of obtaining a divorce.

Remarriage as an incomplete institution refers to a lack of normative guidelines for solving problems and can result in disagreement, division, and conflict among family members.

Sleeper effect is manifested as a problem or a set of problems that emerge long after a stressful or traumatic event (such as divorce) is experienced.

FURTHER READING

Allan, G., G. Crow, and S. Hawker. 2011. *Stepfamilies*. New York: Palgrave Macmillan. Combining published studies with original fieldwork, this book provides a sociological review of stepfamily life and the internal dynamics of stepfamily households and relationships.

Demo, D.H., and M.A. Fine. 2010. *Beyond the Average Divorce*. Thousand Oaks, California: Sage.
Provides a rich depiction of how children and adults of all ages respond to the divorce experience, rather than "average" or typical outcomes. Also offers a dynamic theoretical model and discusses policy implications.

Emery, R.E. (ed.). 2013. *Cultural Sociology of Divorce: An Encyclopedia*. Thousand Oaks, California.: Sage.
Covers curricular subjects related to divorce as studies by disciplines, ranging from marriage and the family to anthropology, social and legal history, developmental and clinical psychology, and religion, all through the lens of cultural sociology.

Kruk, E. 2013. *The Equal Parent Presumption: Social Justice in the Legal Determination of Parenting after Divorce*. Montreal: McGill-Queen's University Press.

The author challenges existing ideas and critiques the existing system of determining parental rights and responsibilities. He proposes a child-focused approach that considers the best interests of the child from the perspective of the child.

Moore, E. 2016. *Divorce, Families, and Emotion Work: "Only Death Will Make Us Part."* New York: Palgrave McMillan.

Focuses on the often neglected emotional, relational, and familial aspects of post-divorce, everyday family practices based on a 10-year longitudinal study. The book also examines the gendered responsibilities for sustaining family lives post-separation and how these reflect inequalities in family practices.

Singh, K. 2013. *Separated and Divorced Women in India: Economic Rights and Entitlements*. Thousand Oaks, California: Sage.

Explores all of the laws and policies relating to financial support for a wife or child in India post-separation/divorce, based on a survey of more than 400 women in four different regions across the country. Also discusses how women seldom recover their dowry and *stridhan* through the law.

Sportel, I. 2016. *Divorce in Transnational Families: Marriage, Migration, and Family Law*. New York: Springer.

This book emphasizes the role of family law in transnational marriages, based on extensive field research in Morocco, Egypt, and the Netherlands. It also addresses the interactions of European and Islamic family law within the highly politicized debates on gender, Islam, migration, and the family.

RELATED WEB SITES

Canadian Children's Rights Council provides information on a child's right to equal parenting and "parental alienation syndrome" (i.e., brainwashing a child to hate one parent following a divorce), www.canadiancrc.com/default.aspx

Canada Focus on the Family is a charitable organization that provides care, advice, support, and encouragement to families at every stage of life (e.g., the step-parenting stage), www.focusonthefamily.ca.

Canadian Equal Parenting Groups Directory is a not-for-profit definitive directory of Canadian groups concerned with the continued support of children's relationships with both parents after divorce or separation, and for children's relationships with fathers and mothers who never lived married or in a common-law relationship, www.canadianequal-parentinggroups.ca/default.aspx.

Department of Justice Canada offers questions and answers on divorce law, www.cana-da.justice.gc.ca/eng/index.html.

Duhaime's Canadian Family Law Centre offers a wealth of information on separation and divorce in Canada, including an informative section on the treatment of matrimonial property and spousal support, www.duhaime.org/family/default.aspx.

Supporting Families is an initiative by the Department of Justice of Canada that pro-vides information to adults and children experiencing family dissolution. Notable are the documents providing information and guidance to children, www.justice.gc.ca/eng/rp-pr/fl-lf/divorce/vcsdm-pvem/pdf/vcsdm-pvem.pdf.

REFERENCES

Ahrons, C. 1994. *The Good Divorce: Keeping Your Family Together When Your Marriage Comes Apart.* New York: HarperCollins.

Amato, P.R. 1996. "Explaining the Intergenerational Transmission of Divorce." *Journal of Marriage and the Family* 58: 628–640.

Amato, P.R., and D. Previti. 2003. "People's Reasons for Divorcing: Gender, Social Class, the Life Course, and Adjustment." *Journal of Family Issues* 24: 602–626.

Ambert, A.M. 2006. *Changing Families: Relationships in Context.* Toronto: Pearson.

Ambert, A.M. 2009. Divorce: *Facts, Causes, and Consequences,* 3rd ed. Ottawa: The Vanier Institute of the Family.

Baude, A., J. Pearson, and S. Drapeau. 2016. "Child Adjustment in Joint Physical Custody Versus Sole Custody: A Meta-Analytic Review. *Journal of Divorce and Remarriage* 57: 338–360.

BC Council for Families. 2012. *Kids: The Heart of Co-Parenting: An Introductory Guide to Issues of Separation and Divorce for Family Professionals.* Retrieved July 28, 2016, from www.bccf.ca/static/media/uploads/Tip%20Sheets/kids-heart-coparenting_workbook.pd.

Bram, J. 2009. *Happily Ever After Divorce: Notes of a Joyful Journey.* Deerfield Beach, Florida: Health Communications.

Cheal, D. 1996. *Growing Up in Canada.* National Longitudinal Survey of Children and Youth, no. 1. Ottawa: Statistics Canada and Human Resources Development Canada.

Cherlin, A.J. 1978. "Remarriage as an Incomplete Institution." *American Journal of Sociology* 84: 634–651.

Chunn, D.E. 2005. "Politicizing the Personal: Feminism, Law, and Public Policy." In N. Mandell and A. Duffy (eds.), *Canadian Families: Diversity, Conflict, and Change,* 3rd ed. (pp. 276–310). Toronto: Thomson Nelson.

Clark, W., and S. Crompton. 2006. "Till Death Do Us Part? The Risk of First and Second Marriage Dissolution." *Canadian Social Trends*, Catalogue no. 11-008, 81: 25–31.

Cowan, P.A. 1991. "Individual and Family Life Transitions: A Proposal for a New Definition." In P.A. Cowan and M. Hetherington (eds.), *Family Transitions*, 3rd ed. (pp. 3–30). Hillsdale, New Jersey: Erlbaum.

Demo, D.H., and M.A. Fine. 2010. *Beyond the Average Divorce*. Thousand Oaks, California: Sage.

Downs, J.M., M. Coleman, and L. Ganong. 2000. "Divorced Families Over the Life Course." In S. Prince, P.C. McKenry, and M.J. Murphy (eds.), *Families Across Time: A Life Course Perspective* (pp. 24–36). Los Angeles: Roxbury Publishing.

Eshleman, J.R., and S.J. Wilson. 2001. *The Family*, 3rd Canadian ed. Toronto: Pearson.

Ferri, E., and K. Smith. 1998. *Step-Parenting in the 1990s*. Family and Parenthood. Policy and Practice Series. London: Family Policy Studies Centre.

Gorlick, C.A. 2005. "Divorce: Options Available, Constraints Forced, Pathways Taken." In N. Mandell and A. Duffy (eds.), *Canadian Families: Diversity, Conflict, and Change*, 3rd ed. (pp. 210–238). Toronto: Harcourt.

Greaves, L., C. Varcoe, N. Poole, M. Marrow, J. Johnson, A. Pederson, and I. Irwin. 2002. *A Motherhood Issue: Discourses on Mothering under Duress*. Ottawa: Status of Women Canada.

Marschall, A. 2017. "When Everyday Life Is Double Looped. Exploring Children's (and Parents') Perspectives on Post-Divorce Family Life with Two Households." *Children and Society*. Published online first. Retrieved January 7, 2017, from www.onlinelibrary.wiley.com/doi/10.1111/chso.12202/full.

McDaniel, S., and L. Tepperman. 2004. *Close Relations: An Introduction to the Sociology of Families*, 2nd ed. Scarborough: Prentice-Hall.

McKie, C. 2014. "Separation and Divorce: Fragmentation and Renewal of Families." In D. Cheal and P. Albanese (eds.), *Canadian Families Today: New Perspectives*, 3rd ed. (pp.85–108). Toronto: Oxford University Press.

Mitchell, B.A. 2006. *The Boomerang Age: Transitions to Adulthood in Families*. New Brunswick, New Jersey: Aldine Transaction.

Schimmele, C., and Z. Wu. 2016. "Repartnering after Union Dissolution in Later Life." *Journal of Marriage and the Family* 78: 1013–1031.

Seccombe, K., and R.L. Warner. 2004. *Marriages and Families: Relationships in Social Context*. Toronto: Nelson.

Sinha, M. 2014. "Parenting and Child Support after Separation or Divorce. Catalogue no. 89-652-X-No 001. Ottawa: Minister of Industry.

Statistics Canada. 2012. "Study: Profile of Parents in Stepfamilies, 2011." *The Daily* (Oct. 18). Retrieved July 25, 2016, from www.statcan.gc.ca/daily-quotidien/121018/dq121018d-eng.pdf.

Sweeney, M.M. 1997. "Remarriage of Women and Men and Divorce: The Role of Socioeconomic Prospects." *Journal of Family Issues* 1: 479–502.

Teachman, J.D. 2002. "Childhood Living Arrangements and the Intergenerational Transmission of Divorce." *Journal of Marriage and the Family* 64: 717–729.

Vanier Institute of the Family. 2011 (October 26). "Four in Ten Marriages End in Divorce." *Fascinating Families*, Issue 41.

Waite, L.J., and M. Gallagher. 2000. *The Case for Marriage*. New York: Doubleday.

Ward, M. 2002. *The Family Dynamic: A Canadian Perspective*, 3rd ed. Toronto: Nelson.

Wolfinger, N. 2000. "Beyond the Intergenerational Transmission of Divorce: Do People Replicate the Pattern of Marital Instability They Grew Up With?" *Journal of Family Issues* 21: 1061–1086.

CHAPTER 11

Families in the Middle and the Launching of Children: Home-Leaving, Boomerang Kids, and the Empty Nest

LEARNING OBJECTIVES

In this chapter you will learn ...

- to situate contemporary patterns of transitions to adulthood and child launching within the context of social and economic change
- that there is not one singular institutionalized life course with respect to mid-life family development
- how mid-life family living arrangements are diverse and socially structured by factors such as gender, ethnicity, region, and social capital
- to understand the reciprocal effects of mid-life family co-residence on "linked lives"
- to critically evaluate popular stereotypes of co-resident adult children who are "too close for comfort" and the "empty nest syndrome"

INTRODUCTION

What is your current living arrangement? Have you left your parental household to go to school? Are you living alone, or with a roommate or a partner, or in a dorm? Or, like many other Canadian post-secondary students, are you still living at home with your parents while you attend school? And if you have left the "parental nest," do you plan to return home as a boomerang kid once you complete your studies? Leaving the parental home and establishing a separate residence is obviously a significant and meaningful milestone for most Canadian mid-life parents and their children. As previously noted, dramatic transformations have occurred in the child-launching phase of family development. And, unlike in previous times—particularly prior to World War Two, when there was an absence of state supports to assist the older generation—young people today continue to live at home for economic and housing support, rather than to provide such assistance to their aging parents.

Table 11.1 presents a comparison of three generations—late baby boomers (born between 1957 and 1966), Generation X (born between 1969 and 1978), and Generation Y (born between 1981 and 1990). This table highlights how Generation Y (often referred to as "millennials") grew up during a period of rapidly changing family dynamics and family formation. Notably, their baby-boomer parents were predominantly dual-wage earners, and a substantial number of mothers were primary earners. Moreover, during Generation Y's childhood, some of the fathers were likely to have taken parental leave, a program that was introduced and offered to fathers for the first time in 1990.

Overall, this profile shows that several socio-economic and socio-demographic characteristics have changed considerably from one generation to the next, a theme that appears throughout many other chapters of this book. Yet, more recent data show that Generation Z—a popular term used by demographers, cultural observers, and marketers to describe those born anywhere from the early 90s to the mid-2000s—are also living at home with their parents, staying in school longer, and forming families of their own later in life (Williams, 2015).

Thus, if you have remained at home, have returned home, or plan to return at some future time, you are certainly not alone; you are characteristic of the generation that follows the footsteps of Generation Y. And not only are Gen Zers postponing the final departure from the parental home, they are increasingly likely to refill parental households, similar to Generation Y. This trend has led to the popular conceptualization of **boomerang kids**, who are viewed as members of the "boomerang age" (Mitchell, 2006). Therefore, once today's children leave home, they are not necessarily gone for good, which suggests a number of emergent trends and issues for family sociologists and mid-life family development. This phenomenon also sensitizes us to the fact that life-course and living arrangement transitions are diverse, retractable, and flexible in modern society.

In light of these important patterns, this chapter evaluates contemporary research on the child-launching phase of mid-life family development, with an emphasis on extended

Table 11.1: Profile of Late Baby Boomers and Generations X and Y at Ages 20 to 29

	Late baby boomers (born 1957 to 1966)	Generation X (born 1969 to 1978)	Generation Y (born 1981 to 1990)
	thousands		
Total population	4,552	4,186	4,663
	percentage		
Sex			
Men	51	50	51
Women	49	50	49
Age			
20 to 24 years	50	48	49
25 to 29 years	50	52	51
Marital Status			
Married/ common-law	48	37	33
Single	50	61	67
Other	F	F	F
Has children	29	22	19
Employment rate			
Both sexes	73	72	74
Men	78	76	75
Women	68	69	72
Student			
Both sexes	15	18	19
Men	16	20	19
Women	13	17	20
Lives at home with one or both parents			
All ages (20 to 29 years)	28	31	51
20 to 24 years	43	46	73
25 to 29 years	12	17	30
Immigrant	11	16	18
Reports no religion	14	25	35

F = too unreliable to be published

Source: Statistics Canada, General Social Survey and Labour Force Survey, 1986, 1998 and 2010. Cited in: Marshall, K. 2011. "Generational Change in Paid and Unpaid Work." *Canadian Social Trends*, Catalogue no. 11-008-X, Table 1. Ottawa: Statistics Canada (p. 16).

home-leaving processes. The focus will be on macro-level factors (e.g., changing economic and cultural conditions) and micro-level ones (e.g., gender, family background, parent-child relationships) that are shaping this transition. Moreover, since patterns of home-leaving and intergenerational co-residence have profound implications for mid-life family experiences, attention will also be paid to examining the effects of these trends on intergenerational relations.

WHO IS A HOME-LEAVER? A MATURE CO-RESIDER? A BOOMERANG KID?

Child launching is a mid-life developmental phase in which young adult children leave home, which usually entails a process of separation. Young adults can physically separate from the parental home, although they can continue to be financially or social-psychologically dependent on their families and/or on parental household resources. This illustrates Goldscheider and DaVanzo's (1985) concept of **semi-autonomous living arrangements**. For example, a young adult may move into a dorm or an apartment with a roommate but continue to have daily emotional contact and support from one or both parents; receive food, money, or gifts; and continue to rely on many of their parents' household utilities (e.g., laundry facilities, use of the family car).

Box 11.1: The Process of Leaving Home

A recent Canadian study examined the first-person accounts of the process of leaving home of 30 university students aged 21 to 26. These young adults attended a large commuter school (with virtually no on-campus housing) in a Canadian city and were interviewed individually. Sixteen had already left home to live on their own, while fourteen lived with their families and anticipated leaving home.

The findings show that home-leaving was a gradual process typically spanning months or years. It was also perceived as a significant transition, and adaptation was either facilitated or impeded by external supports, as well as by personal attitudes and abilities. Parents played an important role in how confidently young people experienced the transitions, and peers also exerted a unique and important influence as sources of information and reassurance.

Six general themes emerged from the interviews conducted with the 14 participants living at home. Below you will find examples that illustrate each of these themes.

1. **Anticipation** (making plans to leave): Leaving home is "kind of the next move... like the natural flow of life."
2. **Prerequisites** (elements required for moving out): "If you're preparing yourself to move out, you know, think positive...start saving money and be more responsible."

3. **Benefits of home** (sources of support): Practical and financial benefits, but also a need to establish personal space; leaving home would mean being "free from family."
4. **Parents** (need to disengage from parents): "I want my parents to slowly step away from being in charge and [start] letting me do things."
5. **Peers** (as potential roommates and sources of information): "They were telling me to wait. Like they were, 'Oh, you're so lucky you are still at home.'"
6. **Modelling** (other roles of peers and siblings): "Well, my sister moved out a couple of years ago, so I kind of saw the transition and what she needed. It kind of prepared me for what I needed."

Similarly, six general themes characterized the narratives of the 16 home-leavers.

*   **Motivation** (reasons for wanting to leave home): "A lot of people I was meeting in school were already self-sufficient and I wanted that too."
*   **Catalyst** (an opportunity or an event that triggered the leave): "I think what really prompted my move out was also speaking with my cousin. She was in the same mind set as me."
*   **Transition** (adjustment to independent living): "It was a mixture of excitement, of nerves and excitement at the same time."
*   **Stabilizers** (those who contributed to a successful move): "That feelings of trust (from my parents) helped me...like, okay they trust me, so I can do this. I didn't have a second thought and just left."
*   **Destabilizers** (factors that contributed to stress during the transition): "You are tired from your long day and papers to write and sleeping late...I didn't spend as much time with friends. So I felt as if there was a negative feeling attached to being at home."
*   **Adaptation** (a calmer time during the settlement phase): "I forced myself to learn how to cook and like, do healthy food...so all these changes. It might be the simple things, but it matters."

Source: Mann-Fedder, V.R., Eades, A., Sobel, E., and DeStegfano, J. 2014. "Leaving Home: A Qualitative Study." *Canadian Journal of Family and Youth* 6: 1–28.

Ideally, home-leaving should be conceptualized as a multidimensional behaviour and process that entails physical as well as non-physical dimensions of separation and autonomy. However, researchers usually measure home-leaving as a discrete transitional event in the form of a physical residential move from the parental home of at least four months. Remaining at home past the usual age of approximately 19 to 20 is generally conceptualized as "home staying" or intergenerational co-residence, while co-residing past the age of 25 has been coined "**mature co-residency**" (e.g., see Mitchell, Wister, and Gee, 2002). Similarly, in order to be considered a boomerang kid, the young adult who leaves is usually required to return for at least four months, since shorter stays have very different causes and consequences. For example, returning home after travelling abroad for two months is qualitatively very different than a longer and more definitive leave related to partnership formation and employment.

THE TIMING OF HOME-LEAVING AND PATHWAYS OUT OF THE PARENTAL HOME

A large proportion of young adults over-reside in the parental home, and there is an increasing propensity for older young adults to live at home as "mature co-residers." In 2011, 59.3% of Canadian young adults aged 20 to 24 and 25.2% of those aged 25 to 29 were living in a parental home, rates that are higher than those of the previous few decades but are similar to those seen in 2006. For instance, in that year, 43.5% of Canadian young adults aged 20 to 29 lived with their parents, a jump from 32% in 1986 (Statistics Canada, 2007; 2012). An uncertain labour market and the increasing need for a higher education have contributed to these trends. For example, in 2011, 52% of young adults who attended school lived with their parents, compared to only 29% of students with other living arrangements." (Milan, 2016).

Although these trends highlight some important reasons for remaining at home, more detailed analyses find that specific characteristics of young people and their families shape these processes. Females tend to leave home earlier than males in all industrialized

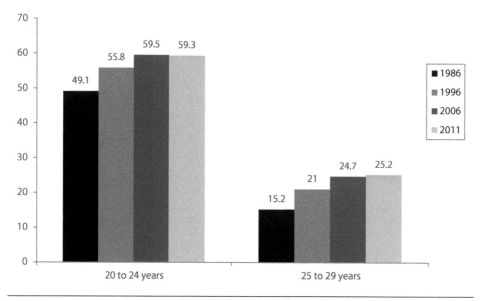

Figure 11.1: Young Adults Living in the Parental Home, 1986–2011

Source: Milan, A. 2016. "Diversity of Young Adults Living with Their Parents." Statistics Canada, Catalogue no. 75-006-X (modified from Chart 1, pg. 18). Ottawa: Minister of Industry. Retrieved January 2, 2017, from www.statcan.gc.ca/pub/75-006-x/2016001/article/14639-eng.htm.

countries, although the overall timing conceals wide gender differences in the reasons for moving out. Women tend to marry at a younger age than men and are also more likely to begin a non-traditional family, either through cohabitation or single parenthood. It is also speculated that young women leave earlier because they are subjected to higher levels of parental supervision and monitoring while living at home. They also tend to have better domestic skills that facilitate independent living.

A variety of family background factors also affect home-leaving. Living in a non-biological two-parent households has been found to lead to early home-leaving. In particular, living in a stepfamily has been found to lead to early and frequent home-leaving due to conflict. (Mitchell, 1994; Turcotte, 2006; Zhao, Fernando, and Ravanera, 1995). It is also interesting to note that children are more likely to leave home later when their parents left home after the age of 21 (Turcotte, 2006). Moreover, there may be a positive selection factor in the propensity to remain at home until a later age; that is, adult children who get along better with their parents are more likely to stay at home (Mitchell, Wister, and Gee, 2004). Thus, **social capital**—an "intangible" resource inherent in the structure of relational bonds such as close, supportive parental relations—can make the family home a very comfortable "feathered nest" and decrease the probability of early home-leaving.

With respect to parental socio-economic status, previous research has found that social class makes a difference in the timing of home-leaving; more highly educated parents can purchase privacy and independence, thus reducing the probability of later home-leaving (e.g., see Goldscheider and Goldscheider, 1999). However, Turcotte (2006) finds that overall, the effects of socio-economic status are no longer influential per se. Instead, what matters most is the type of dwelling the parents live in. Generally for parents, having more space (e.g., living in a detached home versus an apartment) increases the likelihood that their children will leave home later. Having more siblings in the home also promotes earlier home-leaving for children because of household crowding (Mitchell, 2006).

Milan (2016) also documents that certain ethnocultural characteristics are associated with the prevalence of young people living with their parents. Immigrants in their 20s are more likely to live with their parents (50%) than non-immigrants (42%). With regard to other characteristics, more than one-half of West Asian (57%), Filipino (55%), Korean (55%), South Asian (54%), Chinese (53%), and Southeast Asian (52%) young adults in their 20s lived at home in 2011. By comparison, 42% of Latin American and 40% of Japanese young adults lived with their parents, rates that are close to the national average. Gender differences are also more apparent among visible minority groups; the proportion of young men who co-resided was higher than that of young women (47% and 38%, respectively).

Strong differences by mother tongue are also revealed, as shown in figure 11.2. It is interesting to note that in 2011, the highest proportion of young adults living with their parents were those whose non-official mother tongue was either Greek or Italian (72% and 68%, respectively). The proportions were also relatively high for young adults whose mother tongue was Persian (57%) or Urdu (56%). Conversely, only 28% of young adults whose mother tongue was German co-resided with their parents. These trends may be partly explained by the tendency for young adults from certain ethnic backgrounds to live in urban areas and remain at home until they have completed school. Gender differentials are most pronounced among those with a Punjabi mother tongue. While 46% of these young adults lived with their parents, the proportion was higher for men (57%) than women (37%). Cultural reasons may partly explain these trends; daughters commonly leave home to get married rather than to seek independence, while sons who marry remain at home in a multi-generational household.

Youths with greater financial resources and those who are employed generally leave home earlier than those with less income and the unemployed (Boyd and Norris, 1999; South and Lei, 2015). Conversely, young adults who are looking for work have a tendency to remain at home longer than those who are attending post-secondary school or who are in the paid labour force (Goldscheider and Goldscheider, 1999; Mitchell, Wister, and Gee,

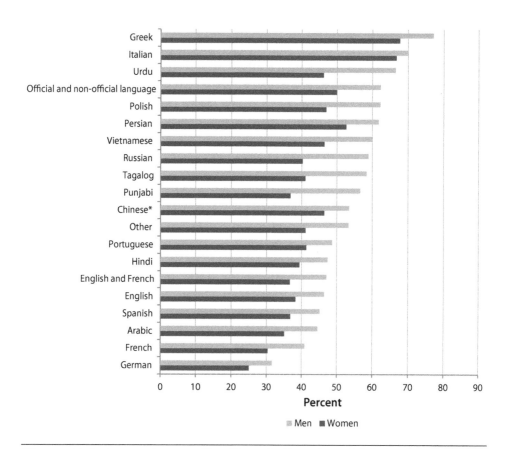

Figure 11.2: Proportion of the Population Aged 20 to 29 Living with Their Parents, by Mother Tongue and Sex, 2011

Chinese refers to Cantonese, Mandarin, Hakka, Taiwanese, Chaochow, Fukien, Shanghainese, and Chinese, n.o.s. (not otherwise specified).

Source: Milan, A. 2016. "Diversity of Young Adults Living with Their Parents." Statistics Canada, Catalogue 75-006-X (Chart 5, pg. 10). Ottawa: Minister of Industry. Retrieved January 2, 2017, from www.statcan. gc.ca/pub/75-006-x/2016001/article/14639-eng.htm.

2004). The place of residence can also greatly affect opportunities related to employment and the location of educational institutions. For example, remaining at home to attend college or university may not be an option for rural youth who live far away from the school. "Local culture" can also affect family-related norms and preferences, as well as expectations related to dependency and autonomy. In short, regional variations can be viewed as an important social or community context that can shape family relationships and family behaviours.

In Canada there are striking differences by region, especially by province/territory, in the propensity of young adults aged 20 to 29 to live in parental homes. As you will notice from the map shown in figure 11.3, there was a large share of young adults in the parental home in the Atlantic provinces (particularly Nova Scotia) and southern Ontario. Lower proportions are found in the Prairie provinces and southeastern Quebec. Moreover, the proportion of young adults in the parental home is highest in metropolitan areas such as Toronto (56.3%) and Vancouver (46.7%), but relatively low in cities such as Saskatoon (27.6%) and Sherbrooke (25.5%). In general, living in the parental home is more common in places where the price of housing, the cost of living, and the proportion of immigrants are all high (Statistics Canada, 2012).

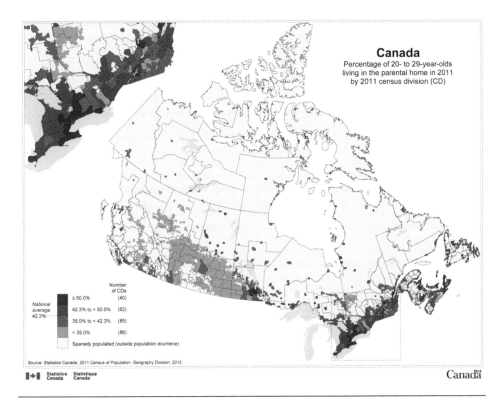

Figure 11.3: Percentage of 20- to 29-Year-Olds Living in the Parental Home in 2011 by Census Division

Source: Statistics Canada. 2012. "Living Arrangements of Young Adults Aged 20 to 29, Families, Households and Marital Status, 2011 Census of Population." Catalogue no. 98-312-X2011003. Ottawa: Minister of Industry.

LEAVING THE NEST "EARLY" OR "LATE": FACTORS CONTRIBUTING TO PREMATURE OR POSTPONED HOME-LEAVING

A life-course perspective emphasizes how the age at which someone leaves home can set up a chain reaction of consequences that reverberate over their life. Early home-leaving (leaving when under the age of 18), particularly when not in conjunction with attending school away from home, has been shown to create a host of negative repercussions for young people's trajectory into successful career patterns and stable families (Goldscheider and Goldscheider, 1999). Many early leavers (especially "runaways") have lower educational attainment and are at a higher risk of poverty, homelessness, street prostitution, drug addiction, and other problems (e.g., see Schmitz and Tyler, 2016). This can seriously limit their life chances and opportunities, as well as their health and well-being. Moreover, many of these young people do not have the option of returning home because of a history of problematic family relations. As a result, intergenerational ties and family relations can be compromised or severed, in both the short- and the long-term.

At the other end of this age spectrum, living at home well past the "normal" age of emancipation (past age 25, and particularly during the 30s) as a "mature co-resider" also has important consequences for both adult children and their parents. Late home-leaving can delay the empty-nest period for parents, which can affect mid-life marriages, plans to downsize, retirement planning, leisure activities, or other post-parental plans. Yet, the benefits of "home" can provide a myriad of benefits and make the transition to adulthood much easier. For example, young adults can use parental and household resources to expand their educational training, travel abroad, save money, and acquire consumer goods while continuing to live in a supportive family setting.

What factors promote early or late home-leaving? One of the strongest sets of findings is that family disruption in the parental household can promote premature home-leaving. Children who experienced a great deal of household change while growing up or are exposed to stepfamilies have a higher risk of early home-leaving, as previously noted (Goldscheider and Goldscheider, 1999; Mitchell, 1994; Zhao, Fernando, and Ravanera, 1995). As a result of conflict at home, young people will often try to escape these stressful environments or move to another place. Research on mature co-residency also shows there are factors that increase the likelihood of young people remaining at home until they are older. Not surprisingly, those with more social capital in the form of supportive intergenerational ties (especially with moms) are more likely to remain at home past the age of 25.

BACK HOME AGAIN: CONTEMPORARY PATTERNS OF HOME RETURNING

The trend of adult children moving back to the parental home has been rising since the 1970s and contributes to the dramatic increase in the number of young adults who live with their parents. Although recent Canadian statistics are unavailable, data from 2006 found that approximately 1 out of 3 Canadian young adults between the ages of 20 and 29 returned home to live at least once. From an international perspective, home returning is also very popular in many industrialized countries, such as Britain, Japan, Australia, France, and Germany, in addition to the United States (Davis, Kim, and Fingerman, 2016; Mitchell, 2006; Sandberg-Thomas, Snyder and Jang, 2015). In the United States, high rates of home returning are due to a broad range of "push" and "pull" factors similar to the Canadian context (South and Lei, 2015), and also to higher rates of military service among young people (Goldscheider and Goldscheider, 1999).

Why are young adults increasingly likely to flock back to the parental nest? It has been argued that the rise in the homeward bound signifies not only the changing transition to adulthood, but also a fundamental shift in how parents and adult children view their roles and identities within the family. Prior to the mid- to late 1990s, having an adult child back at home was not generally perceived as a desirable living arrangement because it was assumed to violate parental (and Western cultural) expectations for independence and autonomy. This theme was reflected by the North American media and the scholarly literature on the subject in books such as *Boomerang Kids: How to Live with Adult Children Who Return Home*

"I'm here to update your census form. Since you mailed the form in, have any of your children moved back in with you?"

Figure 11.4: Boomerang Kids: A Popular Trend in Today's Families

Source: Bacall, A. 2010. "Kids Living at Home." Retrieved January 1, 2107, from Cartoon Stock.com. (ID: aban689).

(Okimoto and Stegall, 1987). This book counselled parents about thorny issues like charging children rent, the move toward eventual eviction, and negotiating household chores. Its general advice was that parents should work hard to "let the children move on."

However, with changing times, parental roles have shifted, and some people point the finger at the older generation for facilitating children's longer periods of residential stays and the "bouncing back and forth" to and from the parental home. For example, a controversial article in *Psychology Today* entitled "The PermaParent Trap" (Paul, 2003) discusses how many parents today are unable to "let go when they ought to," and says that this is partly to blame for the high numbers of boomerang kids. Whereas previous generations emphasized educational and financial independence, baby boomer parents are the first generation for whom their children's emotional fulfillment is a primary goal. As a result, some suggest that there is more of a tendency to "hyper-invest" in children; one example of this behaviour is the reluctance of some parents to want to empty the nest during mid-life.

A related manifestation is the phenomenon of **helicopter parenting**, as described in box 11.2. This term, which has been popularized through various media outlets, refers to parents' unique habit of hovering or becoming overly involved in the lives of their emerging-adult children. As you may recall from chapter 7, emerging adulthood is often described as the years between 18 and 25, and is characterized as a period when young people delay assuming the adult role while they explore the areas of education, love, and work. These changing developmental trends have occurred in tandem with parallel shifts in parental dynamics between parents and their emerging adult children (Arnett, 2000; Willoughby, Padilla-Walker, and Nelson, 2016).

Although the concept of emerging adulthood has been criticized as a flawed developmental theory and for being biased toward White, middle-class experiences (e.g., see Côté, 2014), there is ample evidence that adulthood has become an ambiguous milestone for both parents and their children. It is also clear that some parents are a lot more involved in the lives of their children than others. Indeed, many college administrators across North America have expressed concern over what they claim is a growing trend of "over-involved" baby boomer parents. These parents are unable to "let go," and administrators claim that this interferes with campus life and student learning, and does not facilitate the transition to independence. And while popular media typically describe the adverse effects of high levels of parental involvement and assume that they exist, a recent study finds that grown children who receive intense support from their parents report greater psychological adjustment and life satisfaction than children who do not receive this level of support (Fingerman et al., 2012).

Yet, another recent study suggests that overinvolved helicopter parents may cause emerging adults to feel less freedom to explore new activities and roles that could create some negative health outcomes (Willoughby, Padilla-Walker, and Nelson, 2016). For example, although most helicopter parents want to protect their children, high levels of parental control can produce maladaptive behaviours (e.g., dependency and extended singleness) that further delay the transition to adulthood.

Box 11.2: Helicopter Parents

Source: Skow, J. 2015. "Helicopter Parenting." Retrieved September 5, 2016, from www.lmhcny.com/helicopter-parenting.

The term "helicopter parenting" emerged in the popular press in the early 2000s following its initial use in a parenting book by Cline and Fay (1990) more than a decade earlier. Helicopter parenting occurs when well-meaning but misguided parents provide excessive support characterized by over-involvement in, and micromanagement of, their children's daily affairs. Most popular accounts and empirical studies focus on emerging adults, though the term is applied to both young and grown children. Though the term is typically used pejoratively in media outlets, social scientists have demonstrated that helicopter parenting produces positive and negative consequences for parents and children.

Psychological theory and research on parenting identify three broad dimensions of parenting—support, control, and autonomy-granting—that alone and in combination shape well-being. Helicopter parenting is marked by high levels of age-inappropriate support and control and low levels of autonomy-granting (Padilla-Walker and Nelson, 2012). Conceptualizing helicopter parenting as frequent, excessive parental support, researchers find that one-sixth to one-fifth of young adults are "landing-pad kids," and that one-fourth of parents report intensive support of at least one grown child.

Prolonged intensive parenting has its basis in the extended adolescence of post-industrial society. In the mid-twentieth century, most men and women achieved the hallmarks of adulthood—finishing schooling, leaving home, joining the labour force—by their mid-20s. Changes in the global economy have since delayed the onset of adulthood. The necessity of a college education coupled with rising costs of living have left many young people dependent on their parents. Sociologists contend that structural barriers to autonomy contribute to a rise in "accordion families," in which adult children move back into or fail to leave the parental household (Newman, 2012). Though the roots of intensive parental support of young adults are structural in nature, cultural commentators often blame parents and contemporary parenting culture for being overly indulgent.

Source: Zito, R. 2016. "Helicopter Parents." In C.L. Shehan (ed.), *The Wiley Blackwell Encyclopedia of Family Studies* (pp. 1–2). New York: John Wiley and Sons, Inc.

At a more macro-economic level, researchers usually emphasize factors that in turn affect opportunity structures and delay adult transitions and statuses. In this way, family-related change in union formation among young adults has also helped to fuel the trend of home returning. Transitions out of the parental home have become increasingly unstable since the 1950s, when leaving home to marry during an era of low divorce was generally fairly permanent. As you will recall from chapter 7, marriage has become increasingly delayed, and cohabitation is a popular living arrangement for many young adults. Yet cohabitation is considerably more fragile than legal marriage. The need for a post-secondary degree has also increased; enrolment levels skyrocketed in the 1990s in North America and many European countries. This can make the parental home a convenient "base" when one is single and during "transitional periods."

Moreover, returning home has become a popular and expected lifestyle choice for many young adults, especially after college or university. Low starting salaries in expensive housing markets, fewer career jobs, and high student-loan debt, in conjunction with rising tuition fees, are common reasons for deciding to move back home. Indeed, neo-liberal government policies that treat post-secondary education as a private consumer good enormously impact Canadian families. These policies do more than affect young people's lives; they shift responsibility for financial support back onto the shoulders of the families of post-secondary students and recent graduates.

Moreover, recent research based on a sample of almost 500 parents living in the greater Vancouver area (a region with very expensive housing) shows that, unlike cohorts who experienced the severe recessions of the early 1980s and early 1990s, many young people do not return home due to dire economic circumstances (Mitchell, 2011). Instead, they often move home as a means to save money and pay off debts while living in a comfortable and familiar setting. Thus, many young people are willing to sacrifice some independence to maintain their parents' standard of living. This has been called an **intergenerational taste effect**, whereby the luxuries of one generation become the necessities of the next (Crimmins et al., 1991). Moreover, a more recent study on family transitions and intergenerational relationships (Mitchell, 2017) also reveals increasing de-stigmatization and acceptance of intergenerational co-residence, which helps to fuel its popularity.

Other personal-level and family background factors affect the propensity to return home in North America. Generally, sons are slightly more likely to return than daughters (Milan, 2016). This phenomenon is partly explained by the fact that females tend to marry at a younger age. Marital status also affects the propensity of young adults to return. Generally, the vast majority of returnees are single, although a small percentage are divorced/separated or married. Only a small minority return with children, and race/ethnicity is not found to strongly affect the likelihood of returning home (Goldscheider and Goldscheider, 1999; Mitchell, Wister, and Gee, 2004).

LINKED LIVES: IMPLICATIONS OF LEAVING HOME AND CO-RESIDENCE FOR INTERGENERATIONAL RELATIONS

There is a growing body of literature that documents how nest-leaving and intergenerational co-residence affects mid-life parental experiences and parent-child relations. Recent research suggests that parents (particularly moms) do not seem to experience the **empty nest syndrome**, although there may be gender and cultural differences in how this event is perceived and experienced (Mitchell and Lovegreen, 2009). Furthermore, it should be recognized that relationships with parents usually continue long past the time when children leave home, and most young adults find that parents are a continuing source of companionship and support. Yet some young people, after leaving home, have little contact with their parents; others harbour feelings of resentment toward parents because of childhoods that were less than idyllic (Amato and Booth, 2000). Thus, the nature of these relationships has important implications over the life course, as feelings of affection facilitate exchanges of assistance between parents and adult children.

Box 11.3: The Empty Nest

Based on the story of a young bird that has the strength and maturity to fly away from its mother's nest, the term "empty nest" refers to the composition of the parental home after young adult "fledgling" children have moved out. This expression, which gained particular prominence during the 1970s, is often associated with related concepts such as "empty nesters" (parents who live without their children) and the "empty-nest syndrome" (the sadness and grief some parents experience when their children leave home). From a historical perspective, the empty nest phenomenon is unique and relatively new, and it constitutes an important phase in the family life-course development. Family scholars and researchers (notably sociologists, gerontologists, and social demographers) often apply a life-course perspective or framework to this topic, since it emphasizes transitional changes and linkages within the life trajectories and living arrangements of family members. Psychologists tend to focus more on the cognitive and emotional effects of this transition, including the theoretical and applied issues of role loss, depression, attachment, and identity change.

Although household composition and children's home-leaving patterns have shown diversity and fluctuations throughout time (e.g., see Goldscheider and Goldscheider, 1999), the possibility of a distinct and prolonged empty nest phase was not possible until the 21st century. Relatively low life expectancy and larger families (coupled with a lack of reliable contraception) meant that most parents spent their entire lives raising and co-residing with at least one child (Chudacoff and Hareven, 1979). For example, given the age-specific mortality rates in 1900, the average American could not expect to live much longer than 50 years. Over time, life spans have continually expanded and family sizes have shrunk, and in this century most childbearing takes place in the early stages of a couple's partnership.

Increased economic affluence and a shift to a more formalized labour market economy have also contributed to the ability of parents to retire from family roles and paid work. Thus, because more people live to middle and old age, more and more couples experience a period of time together after their children have left home. Another distinct feature of contemporary life is that the family life-cycle has become less linear or fixed in terms of static and discrete stages. Family-related transitional events, such as child launching, have become subject to greater reversibility and are therefore less permanent. This is because young adult children are increasingly likely to return home as "boomerang kids," a phenomenon that has been documented in virtually all industrialized societies.

It is estimated that one-third to half of young adult children in Canada and the United States aged 19 to 35 have returned home at least once to live with their parents for a period of four months or more. This counter-trend began in the recessionary periods of the early 1980s and early 1990s and became particularly evident at the beginning of the 21st century. It is largely attributed to economic factors, including educational inflation (i.e., the need for increased levels of post-secondary education), the rising costs of living and housing, and transformations in the labour market (e.g., fewer well-paying jobs after graduation). In addition, changes in family formation, such as marrying and having children later, and higher rates of single parenthood and/ or partnership dissolution, have contributed to the increasing propensity of young people to refill parental nests. As well, a smaller proportion of adult children continue to live with their parents because of the older generation's needs rather than their own. For example, some adult children co-reside with a parent to help with aging- or health-related issues. Others do so to provide companionship or financial assistance to a parent who may be unemployed, divorced, or widowed. Consequently, many parents today know that the nest will not necessarily remain empty as they transition to retirement and/or other family roles, such as caregivers of their elderly parents.

Source: Adapted from Mitchell, B.A. 2016. "Empty Nest." In C.L. Shehan (ed.), *The Wiley Blackwell Encyclopedia of Family Studies* (pp. 1–4). New York: John Wiley and Sons, Inc.

Box 11.4: The Midlife Parenting Project: Cultural and Gendered Aspects of the Empty Nest Syndrome

A recent Social Sciences and Humanities Research Council (SSHRC)-funded study entitled "The Parenting Project" (2006-2009), conducted by Principal Investigator Barbara Mitchell from Simon Fraser University, surveyed 490 metro Vancouver parents of children aged 18 to 35. The parents self-identified as belonging to one of four primary Canadian cultural groups: Chinese, South Asian, Southern European or British. In-depth telephone interviews (35 to 55 minutes long) were conducted with the respondents primarily using random sampling techniques in the language of their choice. Parents were asked many questions (both open- and closed-ended) about the relationships they had with their children, their spouses, and other family members, as well as questions about their health and well-being. Follow-up face-to-face interviews (1.5 hours long) were also conducted with a sub-sample of 40 parents who agreed to be re-interviewed.

In the survey, parents (whose mean age was 59) were asked, "Generally speaking, do you feel that this [the empty nest syndrome (ENS), previously defined as a situation whereby parents become very depressed when their children leave home] is something you experienced when your child left home?" Parents were also asked, "How difficult was it for you on an emotional level to see your child leave home (for the first time, if he/she left more than once)?" and were given the opportunity to elaborate on their answers.

The results of this mixed-methods study reveal some interesting findings. The quantitative analyses (conducted with a sub-sample of 316 parents who had at least one home-leaver) show that only a minority of parents reported experiencing the empty nest syndrome. Most parents experienced positive psychological consequences after their children left, such as increased personal growth, improved marital relations, more leisure time, and feelings of mastery in successfully raising and launching their children.

However, particular cultural backgrounds, along with other socio-demographic and relational processes were found to increase the likelihood of reporting ENS, which was mainly of a temporary duration. Below, find the emergent themes based on the qualitative analysis of why parents reported ENS:

1. ATTACHMENTS MATTER IN CULTURAL AND SOCIAL CONTEXTS

Certain parents tended to report difficulties over their child's departure because they perceived a loss of cultural tradition or a severed relationship. This was particularly pronounced in the South Asian community and among parents with ambiguous attachment ties to their child. For example, in the South Asian community, some parents expected that their oldest son would remain at home, and that the son's future wife would provide an important source of help in a multigenerational or extended household. As one father (aged 59) states, "I'm not used to the son's leaving home." Other parents, especially mothers (regardless of ethnic background), had difficulty because they mourned the loss of their parental identity or the day-to-day contact with and companionship of their child and experienced great loneliness.

2. UNFINISHED BUSINESS: OFF-TIME LAUNCHES AND VIOLATIONS OF SOCIAL SCHEDULING EXPECTATIONS

Some parents experienced ENS because they felt that the child's departure had occurred too early or too late, based on their cultural and social lens. For example, one Southern European (Italian) mother reported, "I thought he could have stayed with us, that being 25, it was pretty early for him to leave." Conversely, a British mother (aged 64) was depressed because of her son's reluctance to "launch on time": "I bloody well had to get a team of oxen to pull him out of the house. I had to move to a one-bedroom apartment to force him out. This was hard on me." Parental personal experiences of their own home-leaving timing also influenced normative expectations with respect to their children's timing of home-leaving.

3. PARENTAL ANXIETY OR WORRY AND THE REAL WORLD: FLYING THE COOP AND UNFEATHERED LANDINGS

Many parents expressed ENS because they had deep-seated worries about their child's health and well-being and their ability to maintain independence. These concerns were less likely to be tied to cultural background or gender, although some cases supported a cultural interpretation, and mothers generally worried more than fathers. For instance, in the South Asian community, parents of daughters who left home because of an arranged marriage sometimes experienced ENS. Conversely, when children were perceived to be "looked after," the emotional difficulty was less prevalent. As one Chinese mother (aged 58) stated, "My eldest son had gone to Hong Kong for work before my other child left. I thought they could take good care of each other, if needed."

Perhaps these concerns over safety, security, and well-being are not surprising, given our culture of fear. Today's parents must face the media's constant barrage of possible threats, ranging from terrorism, road rage, health epidemics, environmental disasters, and predatory behaviour from strangers.

Source: Adapted from Mitchell, B.A. 2010. "The Empty Nest Syndrome in Mid-life Families: A Multimethod Exploration of Parental Gender Differences and Cultural Dynamics." *Journal of Family Issues* 30: 1651–1670.

The Effects of Delayed Home-Leaving on Intergenerational Relations: Feathered Nest or Gilded Cage?

On a broad level, the trend toward delayed home-leaving suggests that the roles and responsibilities of mid-life and aging parents have become restructured in modern society. Today, many parents must modify prior expectations and resume their day-to-day "in-house" parental roles to facilitate their children's transition to adulthood. This has led researchers to comment that parenthood has become a more unpredictable and complex role and experience (Ambert, 1994). This issue is particularly salient for mothers, since they are generally more bound to caregiving and domestic roles than fathers.

However, there are fundamental differences in caregiving experiences among women linked to their time and their economic, socio-political, cultural, and physical locations, as well as to their health and their abilities (Armstrong and Armstrong, 2002). Therefore, the effects of extended co-residence on mothers will depend on the unique circumstances and resources of each particular family. For example, "sandwich-generation" mothers (those who are faced with demands from competing generations; this topic will be addressed in the next chapter), who are trying to juggle work and family roles with few economic and social supports, are more vulnerable to adverse consequences (Kobayashi, 2014).

In a similar vein, the trend of home staying has several distinct implications for family socialization over the life-course. When adult children remain at home, mid-life and aging parents are confronted with carrying out extended or "additional" socialization. This occurs, in part, because parents must continue to impart to their children the expertise, skills, and knowledge necessary to become independent adults. Young people living at home may also adopt their parents' behaviour more thoroughly (Boyd and Pryor, 1989). Since co-residency is an experience lived through a network of family relationships, it follows that unique processes of reciprocal socialization occur. One outcome of mutual influence may be greater intergenerational monitoring, whereby parents monitor adult children and children monitor middle-aged and elderly parents (Boyd and Pryor, 1989). It is also possible that parents and children develop more peer-like orientations toward each other at this time.

Moreover, staying at home until a later age has the potential to either increase intergenerational solidarity or weaken it by creating intergenerational conflict. While traditional life-course theory predicts general dissatisfaction with "mature co-residence" or the return of an adult child, Elder (1994) emphasizes the interplay of human lives and socio-historical context. During the postwar period between the 1950s and the 1990s, social scientists and the popular press usually portrayed extended home-leaving as something aberrant or abnormal. Home-returning was assumed to signal family dysfunction or individual pathology, and social scientists frequently offered conceptualizations fraught with negative connotations such as "the returning-adult syndrome" and the "cluttered nest." Indeed, it was not uncommon for researchers to assume that when young adults live at home, "everybody loses" (Bibby and Posterski, 1992: 221).

Yet media images of families with co-resident children continue to be sympathetic to a White, middle-aged, middle-class readership. In particular, adult children (especially men over 25) living with their parents continue to be portrayed in movies, newspapers, magazines, or on daytime talk shows as "adultescents" and their parents as victims of greedy or lazy children. Afflicted with what has been termed the "Peter Pan syndrome" (Goldscheider, 1997), these adult children living at home continue to be stereotyped as immature adults or "mamma's boys" who are unable or unwilling to let go of the apron strings. Indeed, a series of "Doctor Phil" shows featured the theme "The New Generation of Moochers," while in 2006 Paramount released the movie *Failure to Launch* with the tagline, "To leave the nest, some men just need a little push." This movie portrayed a White, middle-class family with a 30-something co-resident son who is a successful boat salesman and drives a Porsche. Since their "slacker son" refuses to leave the comfort of home, the parents resort to hiring an attractive private detective to lure him out of the nest. While this movie is obviously an extreme version of real life, it does represent a popular cultural stereotype that continues to persist.

Studies generally find that the vast majority of parents and their children are relatively satisfied with their living arrangement, although a minority report significant stress and conflict. This is possibly due to "positive selection factors" that support family co-residence during young adulthood. Close families tend to stick together; therefore unhappy living arrangements would likely dissolve before the typical four-month period after which the child is considered a home returner. This positive selection process can also inhibit the formation of co-resident living arrangements among less compatible family members (Mitchell, 2006; South and Lei, 2015).

What are some of the direct effects on intergenerational relations when young adults live with their parents? As previously noted, in the past, it was assumed that the presence of adult kids in the household was problematic because it could create intra-familial conflict and tensions. It was thought that mid-life parents, faced with the day-to-day presence of returnee children, experienced disruption and thought the situation reflected badly on their parenting skills. Similarly, it was assumed that children felt like social and economic failures due to their inability to maintain residential independence and adult roles and responsibilities. As a result, many speculated that the stress associated with a mutual intergenerational mindset of "Where did I go wrong?" combined with the extra dependency and responsibility, created a host of negative side effects that threatened family functioning and well-being.

Despite these alleged negative effects, research shows that overall, intergenerational relations tend to be characterized by mutual interdependence and reciprocity. Although children generally receive more instrumental and financial support than parents, they attempt to reciprocate by exchanging a variety of helping behaviours. Some of these exchanges are non-tangible yet may be perceived as an adequate reward for instrumental and financial contributions. For example, parents whose adult children live at home commonly report that they receive benefits such as companionship and the satisfaction of helping their children become more successful adults. However, parents are the most satisfied when their children reciprocate support and show definitive signs of moving toward adult roles and statuses (Mitchell, 1998). Young adults also reveal that they enjoy the day-to-day companionship and emotional support of their parents, in addition to the comforts of home. However, children are more likely than parents to report economic benefits such as "It is cheaper to live at home to save money."

Table 11.2: Parental Appraisals of "Boomerang Kid" Living Arrangements by Gender

	Fathers		Mothers	
	Percent	**N**	**Percent**	**N**
Aspects Like				
Companionships/friendship	47.5	29	72.5	108
Having family together	36.1	22	17.4	26
Child helps out/emotional support	6.6	4	4.7	7
Other	9.8	6	5.4	8
Total	100.0	61	100.0	149
Chi Square = 11.9, 3df, p.<.01				
Missing observations = 7				
Aspects Don't Like				
Child messy/does not help	6.5	4	11.9	18
Lack privacy/independence	17.7	11	24.5	37
Child's personality/attitude	16.1	10	9.9	15
Child's lifestyle	8.1	5	10.6	16
Fights/arguments/stress	6.5	4	6.6	10
Child's dependence	1.6	1	8.6	13
Other	11.3	7	8.6	13
No answer	32.3	20	19.2	29
Total	100.0	62	100.0	151
Chi Square = 11.57, 7df, Not statistically significant				
Missing observations = 4				

Source: Mitchell, B.A. 1998. "Too Close for Comfort? Parental Assessments of 'Boomerang Kid' Living Arrangements." *Canadian Journal of Sociology* 23: 21–46 (p.36).

It is also not surprising that while both generations report mainly positive experiences, they are also able to cite several things they don't like about living together under one roof. From the parents' perspective, the most commonly cited problem with boomerang kids is the lack of privacy and independence. This finding is hardly surprising, given the long-standing Western cultural ideal of "intimacy at a distance." That is, most aging parents want to maintain close contact with their adult children, but they generally do not want to live with them. Parents also often complain that their child is messy or doesn't help out around the house. And they have issues with the child's personality, attitude, or lifestyle, and their dependence. Additional research on this topic also finds that while home-returners do not negatively affect mid-life marriages, returning home multiple times can negatively affect parental relationships (Mitchell and Gee, 1996). Notably, the child's "bouncing back and forth" can create frustration and spill over to the marital relationship by creating problems such as divided loyalties and financial stress. And when grandchildren are present (although this is relatively rare), this can add more complexity with respect to child-care issues and financial expenses.

Similarly, adult children commonly cite a number of positive and negative aspects about living with their parents after the age of 19. Advantages mentioned often include the ability to save money, and the experience of emotional and social support, whereas a lack of privacy and independence is a frequently cited drawback. Other disadvantages of co-residence commonly reported by young people include conflict and stress, feelings of dependency, and parental rules and regulations, including the popular dictum "As long as you are under my roof, you'll do what I say." This can be particularly difficult for those young people who have returned home after living on their own.

SUMMARY

This chapter highlights one important aspect of mid-life family development by focusing on the process of child launching. Generally, this rite of passage has become delayed in most Westernized countries due to significant transformations in economic, educational and state policies, and family-related realms. As a result, middle-generational parents are increasingly responsible for providing housing, economic, and social support for their children. This prolongation of adult transitions has a number of important implications for contemporary families, society, and economic policy, as discussed by two prominent sociologists in boxes 11.5 and 11.6.

From a historical or cross-cultural perspective, however, parent-child co-residence is not something new. For example, high rates of co-residence between aging parents and unmarried adult children were observed in earlier parts of the 21st century, particularly during recessionary periods (White, 1994), as well as during the economic recessions of the early 1980s and early 1990s. Moreover, many cultures in Canada and throughout the world prefer and continue to practice some form of extended family living for economic or practical reasons.

Box 11.5: On a New Schedule: Transitions to Adulthood and Family Change

That the passage to adulthood has become more protracted and the sequence of transitions less orderly and predictable is well documented...Social scientists, having relied for too long on anecdotal reports from the mass media about the direct effects of the later transition to adulthood, are now conducting their own independent research. So far, though, researchers still know far more about the demography and economics of the change than about its implications for family life and practices. Recent evidence from the General Social Survey shows that families generally accept that it now takes their children longer to pass the milestones that mark economic independence and social maturity. How parents and their young-adult offspring are managing this longer period of co-residence and economic dependency remains less well understood. More fine-grained information on daily routines, rules, and understandings; and exchanges of time, money, and support among co-resident parents and children should make it possible to chart how this new timetable for growing up affects the family. It also remains to be seen whether and how this period of semi-autonomy (or semi-dependency, if the glass is seen as half empty) changes the path of psychosocial development. Using new and more discriminating measures of development during the early-adult years, analysts will be able to examine more directly whether and how the experience of adult transitions fosters psychological development, a topic that has remained largely unexplored.

The new schedule of adulthood has complicated family formation itself, particularly for the less-advantaged members of American society. Moving out of the natal household has become precarious for those with limited means. Unlike the not-so-distant past, when marriage provided an easy (though not always a successful) route out, fewer young adults today are willing to commit to a permanent union, in part because they lack the resources and the mind-set to settle down and in part because they lack confidence that marriage provides the security that it once did. These conditions help to explain why parenthood now often precedes marriage for many young adults growing up in disadvantaged households. By contrast, for youth from advantaged families who are able to complete college, the extended period of growing up brings few costs and many benefits. The longer educational process provides greater opportunities for self-exploration, including the search for stable life partners. Delaying marriage and parenthood, it appears, results in wiser marriage choices and consequently more stable family situations and more positive environments for childbearing and childrearing. This class divide in the early-adult transition risks reinforcing social advantage and disadvantage in family formation in the next generation.

The body of research on the connections between young adults and their parents across households is growing. Clearly, parents continue to channel support and economic assistance to their adult children after they leave home. But exactly how, when, and why do parents extend help, and how is it reciprocated in both the short term and the long term? Much also remains to be learned about how such family assistance affects both the givers and the receivers of help. How intergenerational exchange is affected by the distribution of resources in the larger society also requires more investigation. I have argued that the United States, with its relatively underdeveloped welfare system, relies more on the family to invest in young adults than do many nations in Europe. The heavy burden placed on families may come at a price if young adults begin to regard childbearing as too onerous and perhaps not sufficiently rewarding. Although there may be no immediate policy prescription for addressing this problem, it is essential to recognize the importance of strengthening the family nest and reducing the immense and competing demands that are being placed on today's parents.

Source: Furstenberg, F.F. 2010. "On a New Schedule: Transitions to Adulthood and Family Change." *The Future of Children* 20(1): 67–68. *The Future of Children* is a collaboration of the Woodrow Wilson School of Pulic and International Affairs at Princeton University and the Brookings Institute.

Box 11.6: Delayed Life Transitions: Trends and Implications

The delay in early life-course transitions cannot be separated from the rest of the life course, which means that there are significant implications for individuals and societies. As with other changes that are central to life, there are both positives and negatives, and significant adjustments are necessary....In many regards, the implications of these delays are positive. By leaving home later, children are receiving more transfers from the parents; by staying in education longer, youth is better prepared for a world where the labour force is growing much more slowly and we need to depend on the quality of workers. Two-worker families reduce the dependence of women on men and reduce the exposure of women and children to the risks associated with family instability.

At the individual level, the most negative implication is that people will not have saved enough during a shorter work life, partly because they entered full-time work later, partly because children have spent more time in education and have been slow at establishing their financial independence and leaving home. The accommodations here are obvious: to work longer while one is still healthy and productive, turning at least part of what we have called the troisième age (60–79) into a longer period of post-reproductive productivity. The stronger negatives are at the societal level, because delayed early-life transitions bring lower fertility and population aging.

Source: Beaujot, R. 2006. "Delayed Life Transitions: Trends and Implications." In K. McQuillan and Z.R. Ravanera (eds.), *Canada's Changing Families: Implications for Individual and Society* (pp. 105–132). Toronto: University of Toronto Press (pp. 123–124).

Leaving home is also not necessarily a one-time event; it is often a "circular" process. The current high rate of home-returning (which is unprecedented from a historical perspective) is a trend that may be here to stay. Refilling parental nests has become increasingly normative and a popular strategy for many young adults and their families to maximize their economic and social well-being during the transition to adulthood (Mitchell, 2017). Implications of the timing and nature of home-leaving and intergenerational co-residence also have considerable consequences for young adults and their linked lives. Generally, research on parent-child co-residence reveals positive experiences for mid-life families, contrary to popular media discourse and associated stereotypes. These stereotypes are shown to be ideological in the sense that they tend to reflect an ethnocentric view of how families ought to live, rather than embracing ideas of cultural or family diversity and incorporating the changing social and economic realities of youth.

This chapter also considers how intergenerational "doubling-up" adds new roles and responsibilities for mid-life families. Notably, many Canadian mid-life parents are increasingly confronted with additional (unpaid) caregiving and financial responsibilities, and a delay in their own transition to retirement and the empty nest. And while this extra caring work may not seem a huge burden for Canada's wealthier families, there is little doubt that it creates more challenges for families that struggle in weaker economic, social, or physical positions.

QUESTIONS FOR CRITICAL REFLECTION AND DEBATE

1. Debate the following: Leaving home is strictly an individual decision.
2. Critically evaluate the advantages and disadvantages of prolonged home-leaving for parent-child relations from a life-course perspective.
3. Returning to the parental home most commonly occurs during young adulthood. Do you think that the reasons for returning would be different at later ages? Consider the changing needs of both generations in your answer.
4. Do you agree or disagree that today's parents are unable to let go compared to parents in previous generations? Evaluate how changing socio-demographic, economic, political, and technological advances influence changing patterns of middle-generation parenting styles.
5. Further consider how cultural background, gender, and socio-economic status can influence parental reactions to empty nest transitions.
6. Discuss how globalization, technological change, and population aging will affect mid-life families, household living arrangements, and intergenerational relations in the future.

GLOSSARY

Boomerang kids are young adults who return to live in the parental home, usually after an absence of four or more months, for a stay of at least four months.

Child launching is the mid-life developmental process of children leaving parental homes, which typically takes place during young adulthood.

Empty nest syndrome refers to the grief that many parents feel when their children move out of the home, and is more common in women since they are more likely to have had the role of primary caregiver.

Helicopter parenting is a term popularized by the media that refers to parents who hover over, or become overly involved in the lives of their emerging adult children.

Intergenerational taste effect is the phenomenon whereby the luxuries of one generation become the necessity of the next generation.

Mature co-residency refers to adult children, usually over the age of 25, who continue to live in the parental home.

Semi-autonomous living arrangements occur when young adults physically leave the parental home, but continue to live in family-like settings (e.g., dorms) and draw upon parental resources.

Social capital is a non-tangible resource that inheres in the quality of relationships. It can be found in strong, supportive families or other social networks and facilitates certain goals or objectives (e.g., the opportunity to remain at home during a transitional period).

FURTHER READING

Farris, D.N. 2016. *Boomerang Kids: The Demography of Previously Launched Adults*. New York: Springer.
Explores the phenomenon of adult children in the United States who have moved back into their family homes. Features quantitative analyses that describe the large scale trends and implications. Includes cross-country comparisons that offers another perspective on the issue.

Krauss-Whitbourne, S., M.J. Sliwinki, and M.M. Sliwinski, (eds.). 2012. *The Wiley-Blackwell Handbook of Adulthood and Aging*. West Sussex, UK: Wiley.
From a human development perspective, this collection of papers covers a wide range of topics relevant to aging families, including transitions to the empty nest and retirement.

Mitchell, B.A. 2006. *The Boomerang Age: Transitions to Adulthood in Families*. New Brunswick, New Jersey: Aldine Transaction.

Reviews the literature on patterns of home-leaving and intergenerational co-residence (including the "boomerang kid" phenomenon) from a life course, historical, and international perspective. Implications for intergenerational relations, midlife/aging families, and social policy are also discussed.

Newman, K. 2012. *The Accordion Family*. Boston: Beacon Press.
From a social, economic, and political lens, this book explores relationships between parents and their adult children, with a particular focus on boomerang kids.

Seemiller, C., and M. Grace. 2016. *Generation Z Goes to College*. San Francisco, California: Jossey-Bass Education.
Showcases findings from an in-depth study of over 1,100 Generation Z college students from vastly different US higher educational institutions, as well as additional studies from youth, market and education research. Recommendations (e.g., curriculum changes) to maximize the educational impact on Generation Z students are also offered.

Settersten, R., and B. Ray. 2010. *Not Quite Adults: Why 20-Somethings are Choosing a Slower Path to Adulthood, and Why It's Good for Everyone*. New York: Bantam Books.
Offers a fresh and compelling view of why it is taking this generation longer to make career and family decisions. Draws upon a decade of research and nearly 500 interviews with young people.

RELATED WEB SITES

AARP (American Association for Retired Persons) provides a webpage on how parents cope with the empty nest in addition to other issues that aging parents face in relation to child launching (e.g., retirement and family caregiving). www.aarp.org.

Aging Hipsters: The Baby Boom Generation offers a humorous look at many of the issues that aging parents currently face and provides a source for trends, research, comment, and discussion of, and by, people born from 1946–1964. www.aginghipsters.com/blog

Empty Nest Advice, from the Berkeley Parents Network, illustrates the stories and experiences of parents faced with the empty nest, www.berkeleyparentsnetwork.org/advice/parents/emptynest.

Older Women's (Ontario) Network presents the voices of midlife and older women and an executive summary and recommendations of this network. It also reports challenges that women face with respect to challenges such as economic security, www.olderwomensnetwork.org/whoweare

Women and Children's Health Network provides advice, information and resources for families on children's leaving home, www.cyh.com/HealthTopics/HealthTopicDetails. aspx?p=114&np=122&id=1535

REFERENCES

Amato, P.R., and A. Booth. 2000. *A Generation at Risk: Growing up in an Era of Family Upheaval.* Cambridge: Harvard University Press.

Ambert, A.M. 1994. "An International Perspective on Parenting: Social Change and Social Constructs." *Journal of Marriage and the Family* 56: 529–544.

Armstrong, P., and H. Armstrong. 2002. *Thinking It through: Women, Work, and Caring in the New Millennium.* Halifax: Nova Scotia Advisory Council on the Status of Women.

Bibby, R.W., and D.C. Posterski. 1992. *Teen Trends: A Nation in Motion.* Toronto: Stoddart.

Boyd, M., and D. Norris. 1999. "The Crowded Nest: Young Adults at Home." *Canadian Social Trends* (Spring): 2–5. Catalogue no. 11-008. Ottawa: Statistics Canada.

Boyd, M., and E. Pryor. 1989. "The Cluttered Nest: The Living Arrangements of Young Canadian Adults." *Canadian Journal of Sociology* 15: 462–479.

Côté, J. 2014. "The Dangerous Myth of Emerging Adulthood: An Evidence-Based Critique of a Flawed Developmental Theory." *Applied Developmental Science* 18: 177–188.

Crimmins, E.M., R.A. Easterlin, and Y. Saito. 1991. "Preference Changes among American Youth: Family, Work, and Goods Aspiration, 1976–86." *Population and Development Review* 17: 115–133.

Davis, E.M., K. Kim, and K.L. Fingerman. 2016. "Is an Empty Nest Best?: Coresidence with Adult Children and Parental Marital Quality Before and After the Great Recession." *Journals of Gerontology: Psychological Sciences*, Advance Publication. Retrieved December 26, 2016 from www.psychsocgerontology.oxfordjournals.org/content/early/2016/05/20/geronb.gbw022.

Elder, G.H., Jr. 1994. "Time, Human Agency, and Social Change: Perspectives on the Life Course." *Social Psychology Quarterly* 57: 4–15.

Fingerman, K.L., Y.-P. Cheng, E.D. Wesselmann, S. Zarit, F. Furstenberg, and K.S. Birditt. 2012. "Helicopter Parents and Landing Pad Kids: Intense Parental Support of Grown Children." *Journal of Marriage and the Family* 74: 880–896.

Goldscheider, F. 1997. "Recent Changes in US Young Adult Living Arrangements in Comparative Perspective." *Journal of Family Issues* 18: 708–724.

Goldscheider, F., and J. DaVanzo. 1985. "Semiautonomy and Leaving Home in Early Adulthood." *Social Forces* 65: 187–201.

Goldscheider, F., and C. Goldscheider. 1999. *The Changing Transition to Adulthood: Leaving and Returning Home.* Thousand Oaks, California: Sage.

Kobayashi, K. 2014. "'Mid-life Crises': Understanding the Changing Nature of Relationships in Middle-Age Canadian Families." In D. Cheal (ed.), *Canadian Families Today: New Perspectives,* 3rd ed. (pp. 109–124). Toronto: Oxford University Press.

Milan, A. 2016. "Diversity of Young Adults Living with Their Parents." Statistics Canada, Catalogue 75-006-X retrieved January 2, 2017 from http://www.statcan.gc.ca/pub/75-006-x/2016001/article/14639-eng.htm.

Mitchell, B.A. 1994. "Family Structure and Leaving Home: A Social Resource Perspective." *Sociological Perspectives* 37: 651–671.

Mitchell, B.A. 1998. "Too Close for Comfort? Parental Assessments of Boomerang Kid Living Arrangements." *Canadian Journal of Sociology* 23: 21–46.

Mitchell, B.A. 2006. *The Boomerang Age: Transitions to Adulthood in Families.* New Brunswick, New Jersey: Aldine Transaction Publishers.

Mitchell, B.A. 2011. "Preliminary Findings: The Midlife Parenting Project." Unpublished findings based on SSHRC-funded project #31-635133, Simon Fraser University.

Mitchell, B.A. 2017. "Preliminary Findings: The Families and Retirement Project." Unpublished research findings based on SSHRC-funded #32-639971 project, Simon Fraser University.

Mitchell, B. A., and E.M. Gee. 1996. "Boomerang Kids and Midlife Parental Marital Satisfaction." *Family Relations* 45: 442–448.

Mitchell, B.A., and L.D. Lovegreen. 2009. "The Empty Nest Syndrome in Midlife Families: A Multimethod Exploration of Parental Gender Differences and Cultural Dynamics." *Journal of Family Issues* 30: 1651–1670.

Mitchell, B.A. and A.V. Wister. 2016. "Midlife Challenge or Welcome Departure? Cultural and Family-Related Expectations of Empty Nest Transitions." *International Journal of Aging and Human Development* 81: 260–280.

Mitchell, B.A., A.V. Wister, and E.M. Gee. 2002. "There's No Place like Home: An Analysis of Young Adults' Mature Coresidency in Canada." *International Journal of Aging and Human Development* 54: 1–28.

Mitchell, B.A., A.V. Wister, and E.M. Gee. 2004. "The Family and Ethnic Nexus of Homeleaving and Returning among Canadian Young Adults." *Canadian Journal of Sociology* 29: 543–575.

Okimoto, J.D., and P.J. Stegall. 1987. *Boomerang Kids: How to Live with Adult Children Who Return Home.* Boston: Little, Brown and Co.

Paul, P. 2003. "The PermaParent Trap." *Psychology Today,* September 1. Retrieved October 11, 2003, from www.psychologytoday.com/thdoscs/prod/PTOArticle/Pto-2003.

Sandberg-Thoma, S.E., A.R. Snyder, B.J. and Jang. 2015. "Exiting and Returning to the Parental Home for Boomerang Kids." *Journal of Marriage and Family* 77: 806–818.

Schmitz, R.R, and K.A. Tyler. 2016. "Growing up Before Their Time: The Early Adultification Experiences of Homeless Young People." *Children and Youth Services Review* 64: 15–22.

South, S.J., and L. Lei. 2015. "Failures-to-Launch and Boomerang Kids: Contemporary Determinants of Leaving and Returning to the Parental Home." *Social Forces* 94: 863–890.

Statistics Canada. 2007. "2006 Census: Families, Marital Status, Households and Dwelling Characteristics." *The Daily* (September 12, 2007).

Statistics Canada, 2012. "Living Arrangements of Young Adults Aged 20 to 29, Families, Households and Marital Status, 2011 Census of Population." Catalogue no. 98-312-X2011003. Ottawa: Minister of Industry.

Turcotte, M. 2006. "Parents with Adult Children Living at Home." *Canadian Social Trends* 80: 2–9. Catalogue no. 11–008.

White, L. 1994. "Coresidence and Leaving Home: Young Adults and Their Parents." *Annual Review of Sociology* 20: 81–102.

Williams, A. 2015. "Move over, Millennials, Here Comes Generation Z." *The New York Times*, September 18. Retrieved September 10, 2016 from www.nytimes.com/2015/09/20/fashion/move-over-millennials-here-comes-generation-z.html?_r=0.

Willoughby, B., J. Hersh, L. Padilla-Walker, and L. Nelson. 2016. "'Back Off'! Helicopter Parenting and a Retreat from Marriage among Emerging Adults." *Journal of Family Issues* 36: 669–692.

Zhao, J.Z., R. Fernando, and Z.R. Ravanera. 1995. "Leaving Parental Homes in Canada: Effects of Family Structure, Gender, and Culture." *Canadian Journal of Sociology* 20: 31–50.

CHAPTER 12

Aging Families and the Sunset Years: Caregiving and Support across the Generations

LEARNING OBJECTIVES

In this chapter you will learn that ...

- many inaccurate stereotypes and myths about aging families and the elderly exist
- there are many difficulties inherent in defining aging families and the elderly
- key socio-demographic patterns shape generational relations and aging families
- elder care is predominantly provided by women in the form of unpaid work
- exchanges of support across the generations tend to be reciprocal and are influenced by a number of factors
- given rapid population aging and changes to our economic systems, there are many pressing issues facing aging families

INTRODUCTION

What images come to your mind when you think of aging families and the elderly? Some of you may conjure up warm, fuzzy memories of nostalgia based upon your own childhood family experiences with your older relatives at family gatherings or during visits. Others may envision grey-haired grandparents with mobility or cognitive problems that require constant care. And while our conceptions often arise from our personal experiences, the media and other socializing agents are also highly influential in the formation of many images and stereotypes. Fortunately, many favourable gains in this area have been made—in particular, we are seeing a growing number of positive age-related images portrayed in society and the media, such as movies and print sources. The Canadian lifestyle magazine *Zoomer*, which targets "baby boomers with zip" is a great example of changing trends and attitudes toward aging. Affiliated with the Canadian Association of Retired Persons (CARP), this relatively new magazine is directed at older adults and regularly features photos and articles that show the positive side of aging. In the October 2016 issue, the magazine profiled the remarkable Dinnie Greenway from London, Ontario, a very spry and athletic 96-year-old woman who has absolutely no plans to stop horseback riding.

Unfortunately, however, other scholarly and popular media continue to exaggerate and negatively depict aging individuals and family-related experiences. A study by Blakeborough (2008) published in the *Canadian Journal on Aging*, about representations of aging, for example, shows that cultural stereotypes portraying elderly people as senile, feeble, and useless abound. Blakeborough illustrates this point through a critical analysis and deconstruction of the dialogue and scenes between some of the main characters of the highly popular show "The Simpsons":

> HOMER: Hmmm....sorry, Dad. You're too old.
> ABE: [Stammers] Too old? Why, that just means I have experience. Who chased the Irish out of Springfield village in aught four [sic]? Me, that's who!
> IRISH MAN: And a fine job you did too.
> HOMER: Aw, Dad. You've done a lot of great things, but you're a very old man now, and old people are useless. [Tickles Abe]. Aren't they? Aren't they? Huh? Yes they are! Tee hee—
> ABE: Stop it! That's a form of abuse.
> (Swartzwelder, 1994, cited in Blakeborogh, 2008, p. 57)

Blakeborough cites additional instances of how the show uses irony, parody, and satire, and makes overt references to negative portrayals of aging and the stereotypes associated by the elderly. For example, he describes how the family drops Grampa off at the retirement home where he lives. The sign out front reads, "Springfield Retirement Castle—Where the Elderly Can Hide from the Inevitable." After dropping off Grampa, the family speeds off, and the discussion turns to what Grandpa smells like. Bart feels that he smells "like that trunk in the garage where the bottom's all wet," while Lisa thinks he smells more like a photo lab.

Many critics contend that these negative stereotypes originate from a culture that worships youth and ableness and has a growing and powerful anti-aging industry. Hence, aging is seen as something undesirable yet easily reversed or fixed by buying the proper products and services, such as expensive skin creams, facial fillers, and Botox. Demographically, there is also widespread focus on the problem of population aging (the growing proportion of people over the age of 65) and its associated and assumed disability and dependency. These concerns have given rise to popular discourse framed in unflattering terms as "the silver tsunami" and its projected escalating rates of caregiver burden. Yet, in reality, the majority of older adults are healthy, and only a relatively small percentage suffers from serious health problems such as Alzheimer's disease. Yet, prejudicial practices, as well as alarmist views, perpetuate ageism and institutionalized ageism (e.g., see Gee and Gutman, 2000; Chappell, 2014; Nelson, 2016).

Moreover, imagery of older adults as frail, unproductive, and dependent are often accompanied by an equally disturbing, contradictory, and inaccurate societal stereotype: the wealthy, jet-setting "snowbirds" or "greedy geezers." From this viewpoint, the elderly are seen to be taking a disproportionate share of society's resources (including paid jobs from the younger generation) and disrupting intergenerational relations in the process (Zimmerman, 2000). In reality, many elderly provide large amounts of support to their families, their communities and in particular, "down the generational ladder." Also, there is also a great deal of diversity in the economic standing and resources of older adults.

Some critics also argue that, in part, many of these images are overstated because they sell services and products like newspapers, or because they are politically motivated. It has been asserted that **apocalyptic demography**, which forecasts a number of dismal scenarios based on rapid population aging, is used by policy makers to justify or rationalize a retreat from the welfare state. Escalating health care and pension costs can be blamed on population aging and deemed too expensive for the state to sustain. As a result, this ideological stance justifies family care and individual responsibility—rather than social responsibility—for looking after seniors. Indeed, many of these premises are speculative and gloss over the real systemic challenges such as poverty, sexism, racism, or lack of family support.

Further, there is much more to aging family life than caregiving and dependency, and we must adopt a more balanced view by considering both positive and negative aspects of aging-related social processes. It is also critical that we carefully evaluate what changes in structure over time actually mean to families and their lives. Indeed, there are a number of reasons why the study of aging processes and the social world of aging families is important (see box 12.1). In recognition of these issues, this chapter will explore a number of facets relevant to aging families and the elderly.

Box 12.1: Why Study Aging and Older Adults?

- To challenge, refute, and eliminate myths about aging and older people
- To question popular, automatic assumptions about aging
- To know yourself and others by examining personal journeys across the life course
- To assist and support older family members as they move through the later stages of life
- To prepare for a job or a career (as a practitioner, policy-maker, or researcher) where the mandate is to address aging issues or serve an older population
- To understand inter-generational relations and the status of older adults in a multicultural society
- To evaluate policies and practices for an aging population and identify areas where the needs of older adults are not being met
- To enhance the quality and quantity of interactions with older people in your personal and professional life

Source: McPherson, B. 2004. *Aging as a Social Process: Canadian Perspectives.* Toronto: Oxford University Press (p. 5).

DEFINING AGING FAMILIES AND THE ELDERLY

Although, technically, we all live in aging families, it is important to define what we mean by aging families and the elderly. In keeping with our life-course perspective, aging families and the elderly experience particular age-related changes or developmental transitions relevant to certain phases of the life span. These relatively unique transitional events and experiences are important to consider because they can affect family functioning and well-being and the availability of resources and social support. For example, taking care of an widowed elderly parent can bring many joys and rewards, but it can also produce financial or social-psychological hardship for those with limited means or little social support. Moreover, social hierarchies within aging families create differential experiences both within and between families. Clearly, aging families and older people's lives and relationships are affected by power relations and inequities (e.g., gendered, racialized, and social class) that generate different views and experiences of social reality and day-to-day life (Walker et al., 2001).

For the purpose of this chapter, aging families are conceptualized as mid- to later-life families that confront a number of shared transitions despite diversity in the timing, prevalence, and nature of these events. These transitions include child launching (covered in the previous chapter), retirement, becoming a grandparent, taking care of an elderly parent, and the death of a family member. It is also interesting to note that with changing times and longer life expectancies, the entire life cycle has shifted upwards (people retire or become grandparents later than they did in the past), raising the age of "on time" transitions.

Gerontologists (professionals who study aging from a multidisciplinary perspective) usually regard an individual over the age of 65 as elderly. Historically, this has been the age at which people become eligible for pension and income-security benefits and has long been associated with retirement from the paid labour force. The problem with this somewhat arbitrary definition is that it artificially categorizes the aged, implying that all people over 65 are the same. Moreover, some researchers note that inequalities in younger life may become more pronounced in the later years due to a chain reaction of cumulative advantage or disadvantage over the life course, which can result in increasing inequality over time (O'Rand, 1996).

FAMILIES OF THE PAST: GOLDEN AGE OR ROSE-COLOURED GLASSES?

Many myths and stereotypes abound with respect to aging families of the past. It is commonly thought that the family life of older people was better in the past; this is known as the **golden age myth**. This myth presents images of a time in which Grandma and Grandpa's house was a multigenerational hub comprised of a large, happy, and harmonious family of children and grandchildren. This stereotype often serves as a standard with which to gauge today's families. Obviously, contemporary images do not measure up, since families now purportedly abandon elderly members in the embrace of materialistic consumption and individualistic pursuits (Gee, 2002: 282).

Yet contrary to popular belief, Canadian families of the past did not usually reside in three-generation households, nor were relationships necessarily better. Most families throughout the Western world, including the United States, Canada, and Europe, were nuclear in structure. High mortality rates and lower life expectancies also made the probability of multiple generations living together a rarity. As a result, grandparents often did not get to see their grandchildren grow up, and other intimate ties were of a relatively short duration compared to today's.

Furthermore, the idea that the elderly had more status and respect in previous times is controversial, given a lack of data and relatively low life expectancies in the past. However, North American culture is often viewed as less reverent of the elderly relative to past cultures and to other societies, such as Asian and Latin American countries (see box 12.2). And although this idea does receive some empirical support, it is important not to homogenize North American culture and to acknowledge that some attitudes are changing among younger Asian youth as they become more Westernized (ICGI, 2006).

Box 12.2: How the Elderly Are Treated throughout the World

KOREA: CELEBRATING OLD AGE

Not only do Koreans respect the elderly, they also celebrate them. For Koreans, the 60th and 70th birthdays are prominent life events that are commemorated with large-scale family parties and feasts. As in China, the universal expectation in Korea is that roles reverse once parents become old, and it is an adult child's duty—and an honorable one at that—to care for his or her parents.

JAPAN: AN ELDERLY PREDICAMENT

Like the Chinese and the Koreans, the Japanese prize filial piety and expect children to dutifully tend to their parents. But Japan also faces the unique problem of an increasingly elderly population. According to *Social Gerontology: A Multidisciplinary Perspective,* 7.2% of the Japanese population will be 80 or older by 2020 (compared to 4.1% in the US), which will likely lead to a host of new problems for the country. Adult diapers are already outselling baby diapers, and the pension system is on course to dry up.

THE US AND THE UK: PROTESTANTISM AT PLAY

Western cultures tend to be youth-centric, emphasizing attributes like individualism and independence. This relates back to the Protestant work ethic, which ties an individual's value to their ability to work—something that diminishes in old age. Anthropologist Jared Diamond, who has studied the treatment of the elderly across cultures, has said that the geriatric in places like the UK and the US live "lonely lives separated from their children and lifelong friends." As their health deteriorates, they often move to retirement communities, assisted living facilities, and nursing homes.

FRANCE: PARENTS ALSO PROTECTED BY LAW

It's difficult to imagine an elderly rights law as a legislative priority in many Western cultures. But France passed a decree in 2004 (Article 207 of the Civil Code) requiring its citizens to keep in touch with their geriatric parents. However, this was enacted as a result of two disturbing events: the revelation that France had the highest rate of pensioner suicide in Europe; and a heat wave that killed 15,000 people, most of them elderly, and many of whom had been dead for weeks before they were found.

THE MEDITERRANEAN AND LATIN CULTURES: ONE BIG, HAPPY FAMILY

Mediterranean and Latin cultures place a similar priority on the family. In both cultures, it's commonplace for multiple generations to live under one roof, (à la "My Big Fat Greek Wedding") sharing all the duties that come with maintaining a home. In the contemporary iteration of this living arrangement, the oldest generation is often relied on to assist with caring for the youngest, while the breadwinners labour outside the home. In this way, the aged remain thoroughly integrated well into their last days.

Source: Martinez-Carter, K. 2013. "How the Elderly Are Treated throughout the World." *The Week,* July 23. Retrieved October 18, 2016, from theweek.com/articles/462230/how-elderly-are-treated-around-world.

THE LONGEVITY REVOLUTION AND OTHER SOCIO-DEMOGRAPHIC PATTERNS

As you may recall from chapter 1, three major factors contribute to the longevity revolution phenomenon: increased life expectancy or decreased mortality, immigration patterns (which lower the relative age of the population), and declining fertility (including smaller family sizes). As a result, the population of Canada will progressively contain larger proportions of people in older age groups. This process is projected to have a significant impact on society and family life over the next 40 years.

The United Nations defines an aged population as one in which more than 7% of the population is over 65. In 2015, nearly 1 in 6 Canadians (16.1%) were at least 65 years old (Statistics Canada, 2016). This number is expected to double within the next 25 years to reach over 10.4 million by 2036. It is also interesting to note that people 80 and over constitute the fastest-growing segment of the elderly, and the number of centenarians is also quickly rising. As shown in figure 12.1, an increasing number of Canadians are reaching the age of 100. Recent population projections show that by 2031, the number of centenarians could reach more than 17,000, and by 2061, close to 80,000. More women than men reach the age of 100 because women's probability of dying is lower than men's at all ages.

It is also noteworthy that the population of children aged 14 and under has significantly declined, and people 65 and over now slightly outnumber that group of children at 16% of the population. Overall, the growth of Canada's older population started to accelerate in 2011 when the front edge of the baby boomers (those born between 1946 and 1965) reached age 65. In 2015, 18.2% of baby boomers were 65 and older (Statistics Canada, 2016). Currently, the baby boom generation comprises approximately 30% of the population in Canada.

Life expectancy, or the average number of years a person is expected to live, has increased substantially over the last century. In the early 1800s, average life expectancy was

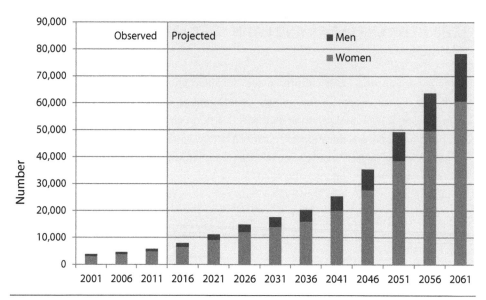

Figure 12.1: Centenarians in Canada: Number of Centenarians by Sex, Canada, 2001 to 2061

Note: Data based on Statistics Canada, Censuses of population, 2001, 2006, and 2011, and Statistics Canada, 2010, *Population Projections for Canada, Provinces and Territories, 2009 to 2036*, Statistics Canada Catalogue no. 91-520 (medium-growth scenario). Projection scenarios for Canada are available up to 2061.

Source: Statistics Canada. 2012. "Centenarians in Canada, Age and Sex, 2011 Census." Catalogue no. 98-311-X2011003. Ottawa: Minister of Industry.

only about 40 years. This increased to 50–55 by the late 1800s. Put another way, in 1900 a 20-year-old had only a 52% probability of surviving to age 65 (Wister and McPherson, 2014). Based on averaging data between 2010 and 2012 (see table 12.1), Canadian women can expect to reach close to age 84, while men can anticipate living to about 79. However, life expectancy varies by geographic region, gender, ethnicity, race, education, and lifestyle (which includes habits of diet, exercise, smoking, and drinking). For example, among Indigenous peoples, life expectancy is, on average, several years lower for both men and women than it is for non-Indigenous peoples.

Other important socio-demographic patterns need to be considered. As Gee (2002: 287) notes, "who lives (or does not) with whom is an important dimension of family life—even though we must remember that families and households are not necessarily the same thing." Statistics Canada (2012) reports that 92.1% of seniors lived in private dwellings in 2011, while 7.9% lived in collective dwellings (e.g., nursing homes, residences for seniors, or long term–care hospitals). Of those living in private dwellings, 56.4% lived with a spouse or partner, including same-sex partners. About one-quarter (24.6%) lived alone; this is more common for women (31.5%) than men (16%). This is in part due to women's higher life expectancy and their tendency to form unions with spouses/partners who are slightly older than they are, as well as the desire to remain single after divorce or widowhood.

Table 12.1: Life Expectancy at Birth, by Sex and Province, 2010–2012

Region	Males	Females
Canada	79.4	83.6
Newfoundland and Labrador	77.3	82.1
Prince Edward Island	78.6	83.2
Nova Scotia	78.1	82.5
New Brunswick	78.5	83.2
Quebec	79.4	83.6
Ontario	79.8	84.0
Manitoba	77.7	82.1
Saskatchewan	77.5	82.3
Alberta	79.1	83.5
British Columbia	80.2	84.2
Yukon	75.9	81.4
Northwest Territories	75.3	80.4
Nunavut	69.3	74.7

Note: Data on deaths over a three-year period, taken from Canada's Vital Statistics (3233), are used to calculate the life tables. The above table covers the 2010–2012 reference period and is based on the deaths that occurred in 2010, 2011, and 2012.

Source: Statistics Canada, Demography Division. 2016. *Life Tables, Canada, Provinces, and Territories, 2010–2012,* Catalogue no. 84-537-X, Summary Table. Retrieved October 7, 2016, from www.statcan. gc.ca/pub/84-537-x/84-537-x2016006-eng.htm.

And although common-law unions were previously unusual for older couples compared to those in younger age groups, this trend appears to be reversing. Common-law unions at older ages are rising due to several reasons. These include: more social acceptance of this living arrangement, more aging in place of common-law partners (that is, older partners who formed their union while they were younger), a cohort effect, and all of the above. In general, older adults may still want to be part of a couple but perhaps with fewer perceived obligations or complexities than marriage (Milan, 2013).

Statistics Canada (2012) data also show that in recent years, common-law unions have increased most rapidly among older age groups, specifically among people in their late 40s and over. The number of individuals aged 65 to 69 in common-law unions grew 66.5% between 2006 and 2011, representing the fastest rise of all age groups. Conversely, growth occurred at a much slower pace among younger individuals, and there were declines in some cases.

Connidis (2010) suggests that the trend toward cohabitation in later life usually follows rather than leads to marriage, unlike the pattern observed among younger cohabitors. This pattern may also reflect an adaptive, contemporary alternative to marriage rather than indicative of a declining commitment to intimate relationships. For example, cohabitation

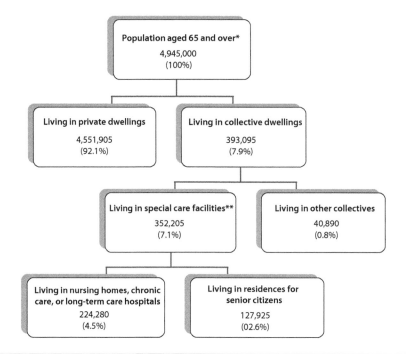

Figure 12.2: Living Arrangements of Seniors in Canada, 2011

*Includes all individuals living in private or collective dwellings in Canada. Persons outside of Canada on government, military, or diplomatic postings are not included.

**Nursing homes, chronic care, long-term care hospitals, and residences for senior citizens.

Note: Since some collectives are classified by the types and levels of services offered, rather than by their names or official status from a business perspective, caution should be taken when comparing census collective dwelling types with classifications used in other data sources.

Source: Statistics Canada. 2012. "Living Arrangements of Seniors: Families, Households, and Marital Status, Structural Type of Dwelling and Collectives." Ottawa: Minister of Industry.

is shown to offer a more egalitarian relationship than marriage, and it better protects the interests of adult children (for example, financial interests related to inheritance). Living together later in life can also provide a financial cushion for the less economic secure, particularly women, through the sharing of expenses. It may also be an attractive alternative to being alone, single, or facing a second or third marriage.

Another notable trend in living arrangements among older adults is the increase in LAT relationships (a term introduced in chapter 7) and multigenerational households. LAT relationships may be attractive to seniors who are widowed or divorced but want to keep and maintain their own homes while being part of a committed couple. Multi-generational living is defined as living in a household that contains three or more generations. In 2011, the total population of these households numbered 362,600 across Canada and represented 2.7% of the population. Not surprisingly, a significant number of elderly live in this family structure as grandparents (Battams, 2016). Fewer than 1% of co-residing grandparents lived with only their grandchildren in "skip generation" households (Statistics Canada, 2011).

The number of multi-generational households has risen over the last several decades due to advances in home care, public transportation, assistive technologies, and increased mobility (Battams, 2016). Moreover, increased immigration from societies in which extended living and **filial piety** (respect, obligation, and reverence for aged parents) have been part of a cultural tradition has added to these households. Cultural reasons, economic factors (e.g., sharing resources makes financial sense), and other issues (e.g., language barriers) are also fuelling this trend.

Overall, multi-generational living has a number of important implications for facilitating exchanges of support and care across the generations, for family bonding, and family continuity. For example, grandparents often play an important role in socializing grandchildren and help out with domestic tasks, and the middle generation can provide daily care for elderly parents requiring assistance (Gee and Mitchell, 2002). In **skip-generation households**, grandparents may assume parental roles due to parents' absence (due to substance abuse problems or incarceration) and can provide a valuable emotional and/or financial resource for their grandchildren. According to Statistics Canada (2011), the highest share of skip-generation families in 2011 was found in Nunavut (2.2%), the Northwest Territories (1.8%), and the province of Saskatchewan (1.4%).

THE TIES THAT BIND: PATTERNS OF SUPPORT ACROSS THE GENERATIONS

The majority of support (over 80%) provided to older adults comes from non-paid or informal sources such as families and friends (Connidis, 2010). Indeed, many older people report that they receive informal "family" support not only from their immediate family, but also from community ties in places ranging from RV (recreational vehicle) networks to retirement homes (see box 12.3). This assistance may be in the form of emotional support, companionship, help with daily activities, and a wide range of other help.

However, older adults are not passive recipients of support; reciprocal support is often provided. For example, they "often provide financial or emotional support for other family members and for friends during illness or other crises. In this way, many families tend to be engaged in exchange relations involving **global reciprocity**. These exchanges are balanced over time, rather than at one specific point in the life course" (Norris and Tindale, 1994).

Recent research by McDaniel and Gazso (2016: 405) suggests that meanings and patterns of reciprocity in support networks can be class- and ethnic-based and should be expanded to include non-kin or "fictive kin" (a term introduced in chapter 1). For example, their qualitative interview data from 20 diverse families in the Greater Toronto Area reveal that low-income aging families may be less concerned about give and take while aging and more concerned with enjoying relations and the long-term security in familial networks. This is illustrated through one of their findings, which showed how low-income immigrants constructed new families after their arrival in Canada in order to preserve and create new family traditions through the sharing of experiences and supportive networks:

> I am really close to one family, we are really close, and so they can be considered as an extension to my family…I have known them and their parents for more than 30 years…we got to know each other in China…We arrived in Canada before them… They were extremely happy, because they have friends in Canada, who they can rely on. We helped them a lot when they first got there… they were unfamiliar with the new environment, so I took them around with me and showed them the bank, the marketplace, the schools, etc. (Lan, age 83, mother of five, married, immigrated to Canada in 1997, cited in McDaniel and Gazso, 2016).

Box 12.3: Metaphors of Community: They're My Family Now

"Home is Where I Park It"

—Bumper sticker on a recreational vehicle

RVers frequently use the metaphor of family to describe their feeling of community. To describe the family feeling they use words such as "friendship," "love," "trust," and "caring," and recount times when other RVers helped and supported them in a crisis. Some, like Polly Neuhaus, use sibling terms to describe their relationship with other RVers. A fellow Skip [or SKP, an acronym for Sharing, Karing People] helped her when she was in hospital. She says of her friend, "I could not have received better or more loving care from my family, and take her as my 'chosen' sister." Judy Parrack, who was widowed in 1988, describes a similar experience. Her letter is an eloquent testament to the community feeling among Escapees [an RV club]: "Family was with me for a week after Ernie died, but it is the continuing support of my SKP [Co-op] Family, who write and drop by to visit, that keeps me going. I don't think I'd have made it without SKPs! You'll never know how grateful I am."

The founders of Escapees consciously used the metaphor of family to describe and shape the relationships they hoped to foster among other club members:

> Our main goal has always been to unite SKPs into an RV "family" that cares about each other. Chapters, Co-ops, and BOF groups provide a close family feeling in the same way that it works with any large family. The family unit consisting of parents and children is closer than the extended family that includes aunts, uncles, and cousins. Yet when the small units come together, they are all parts of the larger family unit.

RVers also create community by sharing activities—work as well as play. They play games of all kinds, from bridge, to bingo, to washer toss. People gather to learn line-dancing and square dancing. They meet to share knowledge with one another: how to use computers, how to do crafts. They volunteer to build and maintain their parks, organize holiday feasts, and clean park trails and buildings.

The most common food-sharing ritual among RVers is the pot-luck dinner. Pot-luck dinners are a regular event at RV resort parks, at many state parks during the winter, in boondocking areas, and at RV parks of all sorts at Thanksgiving and Christmas. RVers who are away from their families during the holidays may pool their funds to buy a turkey and share a holiday meal. Some RVers travel year after year to the same park, where they meet friends to share Christmas or Thanksgiving dinner. Finally, any important celebration—such as a wedding—includes a pot-luck dinner.

Source: Counts, D.A., and D.R. Counts. 2001. *Over the Next Hill: An Ethnography of RVing Seniors in North America.* Toronto: University of Toronto Press (pp. 228–234).

Types, Sources, and Exchanges of Support

Assistance being given or received usually falls into five categories of instrumental help: home maintenance, transportation, household help, personal care, and financial support. This represents a wide range of activities that can entail relatively low duration or intensity (e.g., driving an elderly parent to the shopping mall) or relatively high duration or intensity (e.g., providing daily personal care such as help with bathing). Support may also be affective or emotional, such as companionship or giving advice.

The **hierarchical-compensatory model** (Cantor, 1979) assumes that older people have a hierarchy of favoured relationships from whom all forms of support are sought. Spouses and children typically top the list, but if these are not available, substitutes can be found, such as other relatives or friends. However, Connidis (2010) argues that this model does not offer a dynamic view of social support with its fixed notions of support networks, which are subject to change over time. In fact, the average middle-aged caregiver is 54 years old and is looking after a parent or parent-in-law with a long-term disability or physical limitation. In contrast, the typical older caregiver is 73 years old and is looking after a spouse, close friend, or neighbour. Also, women devote more time to personal and emotional caregiving tasks than men, regardless of age. Siblings also represent an important source of support for older adults. Their assistance is related to factors such as gender, marital status, age, proximity, relationship history, and availability of other family members (Connidis, 2010). For example, siblings, especially if they are widowed or childless, may be the only source of support for each other in their later years (Wister and McPherson, 2014).

Life course trajectories are relevant when considering the capacity of families to provide informal social support for older people. Given falling fertility rates, one concern that is commonly voiced is that there will be a shortage of family members (i.e., adult children) to provide care for these seniors. However, many counter this view by noting that one critical distinction in provisions of support from adult children is whether a parent has no children versus one or more (e.g., Rosenthal, 2000). And since most women who entered old age at the beginning of the 21st century were less likely to be childless than those in preceding cohorts, researchers argue that concern about the shortage of adult children to provide care to the elderly is a fallacious contention. Furthermore, three-quarters of people over the age of 80 also have at least one living sibling, and siblings (as well as other family members or friends) also constitute a potential source of support (Connidis, 2010).

Moreover, it is important to consider the positive effects of population aging on family life. For example, in chapter 1 we considered the family decline hypothesis, which purports that many families are at risk in contemporary times due to high rates of divorce and remarriage. However, a more optimistic scenario emphasizes expansion of the family as well as increasing availability of extended kin, such as grandparents, great-grandparents, uncles, and aunts. Also, due to increased generational overlap, many grandparents can experience longer and richer relationships with their grandchildren. Given increased life expectancy, we can also expect to see more generations alive at the same time, and there is the possibility that children will get to know their great-grandparents.

In summary, the provision of assistance between parents and children is affected by a number of factors such as age, ethnicity, gender, availability, and life-course stage. Parents typically receive the most help when they are at advanced ages, reflecting the changing needs of the generations over time. And parents tend to give more help to children than they receive from them until very old age. Moreover, Connidis (2010) asserts that a useful way to understand social support within families is to combine the influences of social structure, culture, and family history, as well as individual preferences. For example, in certain cultures, daughters-in-law are traditionally expected to care for their husbands' aging parents, therefore these women may have little option but to fulfill this obligation. Moreover, as noted, many elderly people creatively develop strong and diverse social networks with fictive kin (a concept introduced in chapter 1). These family-like supports can include friends, neighbours, health care providers, home care workers, and people met through other voluntary associations.

SELECTED ISSUES FACING TODAY'S AGING FAMILIES

In this section we will briefly highlight a number of additional topics that are particularly salient for aging families and the elderly. These include: (1) increased cultural diversity; (2) caregiving; (3) dating, cohabitation, remarriage, and sexuality; (4) the transition to retirement; (5) grandparenthood; and (6) institutionalization and end-of-life issues. Other important issues, such as poverty, elder abuse and neglect, and Alzheimer's disease are covered in more detail in other chapters.

Increased Cultural Diversity

Canada's elderly population is more ethnically diverse than the Canadian population as a whole. While 17% of the total Canadian population is foreign-born, 27% of residents 65 and over were born outside Canada (Statistics Canada, 2010). Continuing high rates of immigration contribute to the increased cultural diversity of the population. And since ethnic groups may exhibit distinctive norms, values, and traditions, it is important to consider them in relation to such aspects as filial obligation and patterns of support (e.g., see Kobayashi, 2000; Kobayashi and Funk, 2010). Certain cultural groups, such as Italians and Asians, for instance, have historically held strong beliefs about not "abandoning" relatives to nursing homes (Maurier and Northcott, 2000). Moreover, ethnic seniors may also face unique barriers in their communities due to a lack of culturally sensitive programs and services and language barriers.

As Canada's aged population becomes more ethnically diverse, we need to revisit many of our assumptions about ethnic family life and family ties. For instance, many people assume that daughters are a strong and supportive tie for elderly widowed women. However, "it is rather ethnocentric for [North] Americans to assume that the mother-daughter tie is inevitably the closest one, since that is not the case for many societies" (Lopata, 1995: 121–122). Throughout much of Asia and the Middle East, for example, it is the son rather than the daughter who has the closest relationship with an elderly mother (Martin-Matthews, 2005).

Koehn et al. (2013) also argue that we need to adopt an intersectionality theoretical lens when considering health care and other related issues of ethno cultural minority older adults in Canada. Yet, theoretical perspectives and studies that specifically incorporate race/ethnicity/culture and other spheres of social location are not well developed in the ageing literature. Given that Canada can be defined as a land of immigrants, in tandem with the challenges/barriers that senior immigrants can experience as they age, ongoing research requires "a conscientious effort by researchers to consider multiple dimensions of difference and the influence of their intersections for which appropriate raw data are needed" (Koehn et al., 2013: 458). Thus, while there is some usefulness to studying variations among distinct ethnic groups, these researchers rightfully acknowledge the limitations inherent in reducing ethnic seniors to a single, fixed, and often stereotypical category or identity.

Providing Care

Nearly half of all Canadians from coast to coast (13 million) have at some point in their lives provided care to a family member or a friend who had a long-term health condition, a disability, or who was aged (Vanier Institute of the Family, 2016). It has also been estimated that family/friend caregivers provide 70–80% of care to persons with a chronic health problem or disability at an estimated value of $25–26 billion annually (Fast et al., 2010). Although not all these care recipients are seniors, strong gendered differences emerge in unpaid elder care similar to caregiving trends in other age groups. According to the General Social Survey, fewer than 3% of Canadians were providing care to a senior in their household. Instead, care of seniors outside the home was more common, with 14%

of women and 9% of men providing elder care. Women also spent more time than men providing care; 49% of women compared to 25% of men spent more than 10 hours per week on this activity (Milan, Keown, and Robles Urquijo, 2011).

Many of these caregivers are aged 45–64 and are members of the so-called sandwich generation, since they are wedged between the responsibilities of raising children and caring for seniors. Approximately 75% of these individuals are also engaged in paid work. Fifteen percent of these people found that in caring for a senior, they had to reduce their paid work hours to provide caregiving. Many also felt burdened in terms of their health and social life (Fast et al., 2010).

Another recent study by Statistics Canada shows that many other people, such as friends, neighbours, and other relatives, also provide care to seniors, as discussed and highlighted in figure 12.3. Research also shows that while most caregivers effectively cope with their responsibilities, and although caregiving may bring many rewards, physical and emotional health can be compromised by these responsibilities. In particular, caregivers can find the work stressful, and may experience fatigue or irritability, feel overwhelmed, and have disturbed sleep (e.g., see Sinha, 2012). These feelings increase with the number of hours and the intensity of care.

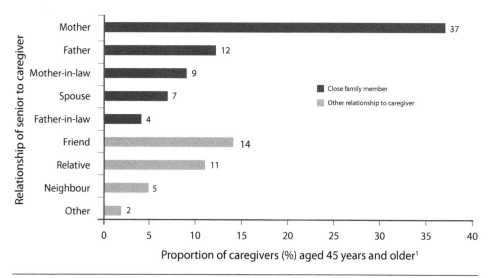

Figure 12.3: Caregivers Most Often Provide Care for a Family Member, but Friends Provide Care as Well

1. Due to rounding, totals might not add up to 100.

Note: Close family members (mother, father, mother-in-law, spouse, father-in-law) made up 69% of those seniors who received care from caregivers 45 and older.

Source: Cranswick, K.A, and D. Dosman. 2008. "Eldercare: What We Know Today." *Canadian Social Trends,* Catalogue no. 11-008. Ottawa: Statistics Canada. (Chart 1, p. 50, based on General Social Survey 2007). Retrieved August 15, 2011 from www.statcan.gc.ca/pub/11-008-x/2008002/article/10689-eng.htm.

The most common type of help wanted by those who provided sandwiched care and those who provided only elder care was respite care, or occasional relief or sharing of responsibilities (see caregiver's wish list in table 12.2). Other types of help, such as information to help improve their skills, information about the nature of long-term illnesses, more flexible work arrangements, and financial compensation, were also suggested by a substantial portion of caregivers.

Table 12.2: Caregivers' Wish List

	Employed (%)	
	Sandwiched	**Elder Care Only**
Respite care	52	46*
Flexible work or study arrangements	46	36*
Information on long-term disabilities	43	39
Information on caregiving	42	37
Financial compensation or tax breaks	36	35
Counselling	28	24
Other	12	10

*Indicates statistically significant difference from sandwiched group (those who provided elder care to someone over 65 and had single children younger than 25 living at home; sandwiched workers had a paid job or business as their main activity in the past 12 months).

Source: Williams, C. 2005. "The Sandwich Generation." *Canadian Social Trends*, Catalogue no. 11-008. Ottawa: Statistics Canada (p. 20).

Seniors living in rural areas can also face greater challenges in receiving care than their urban counterparts. For example, their family members may live in a different town or city. Rural areas also often lack adequate transportation and many of the health-related services and organizations found in more urban areas. Since many rural and remote communities have a shrinking population base, it is challenging to develop a sufficient and efficient health care system for them. While more than 20% of older Canadians reside in rural areas, many public policies overlook this sector when allocating health care resources (Keating 2008; Keating et al., 2011). The situation has deteriorated in recent years with the fragmentation of services, the closing of small rural hospitals, the restructuring and regionalization of health services, and the continuing difficulty that rural communities encounter in attracting and retaining physicians and other health care and social service workers.

Dating, Cohabitation, Remarriage, and Sexuality

Since the majority of older men have partners, whereas the majority of older women do not, gendered differences are important to consider in understanding intimate ties in later life. As previously noted, this difference is partly due to the fact that women tend to outlive their spouses and fewer eligible men are available, but also because of societal and individual-level attitudes. For example, many older women report that although they are still attracted to men, they do not want to marry. Many report that they enjoy the freedom of being single after divorce or widowhood. As one older woman stated in a study on this topic, "For the first time in my life, I have no responsibilities except for myself.... In other words, I'm just learning to fly a little bit. And I love it. Selfish, huh?" (cited in Talbott, 1998). Men, on the other hand, are seven times more likely to remarry than women (Connidis, 2010).

Generally, the decision to date, cohabit, or remarry in later life is a complex decision that is influenced by economic, social, legal, religious, and demographic factors. Other family members can also create barriers through disapproval or by being unsupportive of a particular relationship. Nonetheless, many older adults are using introduction or dating agencies, placing personal ads in local newspapers or in magazines for retired people, or using Internet dating sites (i.e., "Silver Singles") to meet potential partners. Divorce rates among older adults, although historically quite low, are also rising and, combined with longer life expectancy, will probably create more demand for these kinds of services.

With regard to research on sexuality and intimacy in later-life couples, Lodge and Umberson (2016) observe that most studies on this topic have been from a medical perspective and that it has been largely atheoretical. There is also little consensus in the literature on how to define sexual behaviour since aging adults often redefine the meaning of sexuality to include other physically intimate experiences such as kissing, holding hands, and cuddling beyond sexual intercourse. Yet, research is fairly definitive in concluding that sexual behaviour is positively related to relationship quality and to mental/physical health.

It is also important to recognize the link between sexuality and ageism, which can also act as a barrier to the formation of intimate relations (Thompson et al., 2014). In their book entitled, *Sex May Be Wasted on the Young*, Stones and Stones (1996) argue that ageist views of sexuality are still prevalent in today's society. They note that young people in their teens and twenties often think of their grandparents as "way past it." Indeed, "the idea of their own relatives making love with passion evoked reactions from giggles at the improbable to horror at the unimaginable" (Stones and Stones, 1996). Older people in institutional settings may also face unique challenges when they try to express their sexuality. For example, attitudes of staff and facility policies (e.g., no locks on doors) can limit sexual activity, and even married couples who share a room may feel inhibited. Yet, studies consistently show that, provided both partners are in good health, many desire and can enjoy active sex lives well into their sunset years. Further, drugs (such as Viagra) now exist to restore or enhance sexual performance in older adults and are sometimes used to overcome impotence.

Turning to gay/lesbian seniors, unique challenges may occur if these older adults are estranged from or rejected by family members. However, as Laird (1996) (who is a mother, grandmother, and lesbian) claims, many gays and lesbians have good, although complicated, family relationships. They also may create a surrogate family comprising a network of gay, lesbian, and heterosexual friends. Yet, gay and lesbian seniors (especially gay men because of AIDS) can face problems in accessing medical care, home care, and community services. Partners may also have limited legal rights and may be denied access to employer drug and health benefit plans. Administrators of rental housing or long-term care facilities may reject their applications, and there are very few retirement or nursing facilities available to serve this community.

The Transition to Retirement

Szinovacz (2006) asserts that retirement processes and experiences are usually examined from an "individualistic" perspective. In other words, they are viewed almost exclusively in relation to individual characteristics such as health, work history, or social security and pension coverage. He argues that this perspective glosses over the intricate linkages between family and retirement experiences and their relationship to policies. It also underplays the significance of life-course transitions and how they are contextually embedded in the planning of, and adjustment to this process. As such, retirement transitions are often related to past work experiences, yet family contexts (e.g., rules regarding benefits of spouses) also play a significant role.

Figure 12.4 summarizes Szinovacz's model of family-retirement linkages, which is grounded in life-course theoretical concepts of linked lives, interdependence, timing and sequencing of transitions, and contextual embeddedness. Family contexts consist of marital and family characteristics that precede the retirement transition and can impinge on decisions and adaptation processes. They include family-related statuses, spouse characteristics, activities, the quality of the relationship, and norms/attitudes. Statuses are the family positions held by workers, such as marital and grandparent status. The influence of these contexts may be direct (e.g., wives tend to retire at the same time as their husbands) or indirect (e.g., if a sibling cares for an elderly parent, the worker can remain in the workforce). The impact of family statuses will be further conditioned by the type of activities involved in each role, the quality of each relationship and pertinent attitudes and norms. For example, the "push" effect of a husband's' retirement on that of his wife may depend on the couple's gender role attitudes. Notably, if spouses follow traditions that stress the husband's role as main family provider, it may be problematic for the wife to continue to work after her husband retires.

Szinovacz (2006) also observes that increases in the labour force participation of women in general, and middle-aged women in particular, suggests that retirement is becoming a "couple phenomenon." Studies indicate, for example, that retired husbands' attitudes toward their wives' continued employment proved to be one of the most potent predictors of the wives' retirement. Other reasons include spouses' preference for joint leisure activities, similarities in their background (age, education), or shared economic restrictions. Yet, couples are not always able to implement these preferred timing patterns, since their decisions may also depend on the benefit eligibility and pensions of both spouses. Another factor is a spouse's health or disability; for example, one spouse may have to retire to care for the other.

Overall, it is expected that the transition to retirement will continue to transform as people live longer and gender roles, economic conditions, and the labour force continue to

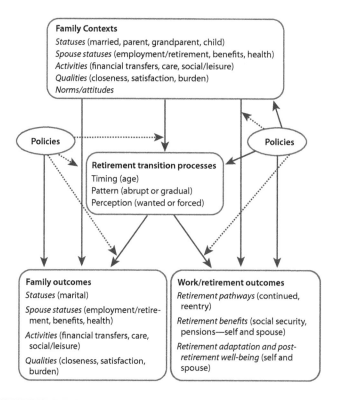

Figure 12.4: Linkages between Family and Retirement
Experiences

Source: Statistics Canada. 2008. "New Frontiers of Research on Retirement." Catalogue no. 75-511-XWE.
Ottawa: Minister of Industry (figure 11.1). Retrieved August 12, 2011 from www.statcan.gc.ca/pub/75-
511-x/2006001/figures/5203436-eng.htm.

change. The abolishment of mandatory retirement at age 65 (with the exception of New
Brunswick) means that many people can choose to retire or not, based on their own need,
lifestyle preferences, circumstances, and priorities. Yet, it is also expected that the number
of retirement-aged Canadians in the workforce will continue to increase over the next
ten years, a trend that has again sparked apocalyptic fears of increased pressure on public
pensions and raised issues of intergenerational inequity (Hill, 2010).

The financial meltdown in 2008 and the subsequent global recession also exposed
a number of weaknesses in pension plans, such as underfunding of corporate pension
plans and the need to restructure C/QPP (McDonald and Donahue, 2011). While the
proportion of workers in Registered or Employment Programs provided by companies or
the public sector has diminished, and there has been a shift to defined contribution over
defined-benefit plans, the proportion of workers with private pension plans (e.g., RRSPs)
has risen. A significant implication of these patterns is that more responsibility for economic security in retirement will fall on the shoulders of individuals and their families
during a period of increasing economic instability.

The Modernization of Grandparenthood

The vast majority of Canadian women (80%) and men (74%) over 65 are grandparents. At birth, approximately 66% of children have four living grandparents (including stepgrandparents), and by age 30, three-quarters have at least one grandparent (Connidis, 2010). Because of socio-demographic change, it is also not surprising that grandparenthood—as a distinct and nearly universal stage of family life—is largely a post–World War Two phenomenon. According to Cherlin and Furstenberg (1992), we have witnessed the **modernization of grandparenthood**. This is due to several factors: declines in mortality, falling birth rates, technological advances in travel and long-distance communication (e.g., e-mail, webcams), retirement and increased affluence (e.g., pensions), and more leisure time. In other words, grandparents are living long enough to enjoy a lengthy life as grandparents, they can keep in touch more easily with grandchildren, they have more time to devote to them, and they have more money to spend on them. They are also less likely to still be raising their own children.

To further illustrate this concept, many families did not own cars before World War Two, and long trips could take quite some time. As one grandchild recounts (as cited by Cherlin and Furstenberg, 1992: 3):

> Well, I didn't see my grandmother that often. They just lived one hundred miles from us, but back then one hundred miles was like four hundred now, it's the

"Can you believe we got married, raised a family and retired, all without the help of a hand-held computer?"

Figure 12.5: Technology and Aging Families

Source: Brown, D. 2004. "Old Age, Technology, and Retirement." Retrieved January 1, 2017 from Cartoon Stock.com (ID: dbrn168).

truth. It just seemed like clear across the country. It'd take us five hours to get there, it's the truth. It was an all-day trip.

Grandparents today generally play an active role in the lives of their grandchildren, although there is diversity with respect to grandparenting styles. For example, grandmothers tend to be more involved in matters related to family relationships and caregiving, while grandfathers tend to be more involved in instrumental or practical matters, such as giving advice. However, in keeping with our theme of heterogeneity in family life and in gendered processes, it should be recognized that grandfathers are increasingly being recognized for their ability to adopt caring, supportive, and mentoring roles that appear to become more pronounced in later life. Indeed, Mann (2007) argues that one of the pitfalls of the previously dominant feminist perspective in this area of study is that it underestimated or ignored the experiences, contributions, and capacities of older men to provide emotional care to family members.

Some grandparents can also play a particularly active role as family "watchdogs," arbitrators, or historians, or in practising family traditions. These grandparents often look out for the well-being of younger relatives, help them when they can, and try to mediate or create linkages between family members and across the generations. As such, some grandparents play an important role in passing down important family memories through the retelling of family stories as well as by reproducing long-standing family traditions. For example, in a qualitative study by Kemp based on life-history interviews (2004: 512), one grandfather, age 88, states, "I think story telling is perhaps one of the main roles ... true stories too that could give you a sense of history that a lot of families lose." Conversely, some grandparents are more detached, and tend to see or contact their grandchildren less often. These grandparents take a more "hands-off" approach, which might be because of age, health status, distance, or because their children obstruct visits (Novak and Campbell, 2010).

Institutionalization and End-of-Life Issues

Contrary to popular belief, only a minority of elderly live their last years in nursing homes or other institutionalized settings, as previously noted. Declines in health are associated with moves to institutions. For example, many elderly with Alzheimer's disease ultimately require 24-hour care, such that families have little option but to move an older person into a residential-care facility. This relocation is necessary for their care and safety, and for the relief of family caregivers who cannot manage the behavioural problems, such as agitation, aggressiveness, and wandering.

Further, even though older people usually want to die in their own home, the vast majority end their life journey in a hospital or long-term care facility. As a result, new models and practices for end-of-life care are being offered and recommended. Some of these newer proposals include **palliative care**—a term that refers to a program of active compassionate care primarily directed toward improving the quality of life for the dying—in other primary health-care facilities and support systems or groups for family and paid caregivers. Many palliative care programs also try to account for cultural, religious, and spiritual diversity associated with death and dying among Canadians.

While there is considerable diversity with respect to institutionalized care for the elderly, profit motives can undermine the delivery of care. In *Making Gray Gold*, Diamond (1995) uses personal narratives to describe how the work of nurses and other caregivers in a nursing home is set powerfully in the context of wider political, economic, and cultural forces that shape and constrain the quality of care for the elderly. Overall, this study of what it's like to work in and live in a nursing home shows the price that business policies extract from the elderly and their families as well as those whose work it is to care for them.

Finally, the ethical issue of physician-assisted suicide and euthanasia, which is sometimes referred to as "mercy killing," is likely to become more hotly debated as our population ages. "Euthanasia" is a term that comes from the Greek word for "good death" and means helping someone end his or her life. A distinction is often made between passive euthanasia (which means withholding or ceasing treatment for someone, such as turning off a life-support system), or active euthanasia (which means intervening actively to end a person's life, such as by administering a lethal dosage of sedatives). Until recently, euthanasia was illegal in Canada, although the law did not require doctors to take heroic measures to keep a terminally ill patient alive. And given that family members and physicians sometimes differ in their judgment of the person's will to live and of the person's end-of-life preferences, increasing numbers of individuals are drafting living wills. An advance directive, for instance, allows a person to think about his or her preference while in a sound state of mind.

Box 12.4: Medical Assistance in Dying in Canada

In Canada, physician-assisted suicide and euthanasia are termed medical assistance in dying.

In February 2015, the Supreme Court of Canada ruled in Carter v. Canada that parts of the Criminal Code would need to change to satisfy the Canadian Charter of Rights and Freedoms. The parts that prohibited medical assistance in dying would no longer be valid. Bill C-14, legislation on medical assistance in dying in Canada, received royal assent on June 17, 2016. This legislation allows eligible Canadian adults to request medical assistance in dying.

In order to be eligible for medical assistance in dying, a person must be at least 18 years old and fully capable of making health care decisions, have a serious and irreversible medical condition, experience unbearable physical or mental suffering from the medical condition, make a voluntary request for medical assistance in dying that is not the result of outside pressure or influence, and give informed consent to receive medical assistance in dying.

There are two types of medical assistance in dying available to Canadians. In the first type, a physician or nurse practitioner directly administers a substance that causes death, such as an injection of a drug. This is becoming known as clinician-assisted medical assistance in dying and was previously known as voluntary euthanasia.

In the second type, a physician or nurse practitioner provides or prescribes a drug that the eligible person takes themselves, in order to bring about their own death. The patient is responsible for taking the prescription to a pharmacy to have it filled and for deciding if or when to take the medication to end their life. The doctor does not administer the drug. This is becoming known as self-administered medical assistance in dying and was previously known as physician-assisted suicide.

JEAN'S STORY: DECREASING QUALITY OF LIFE

Jean has advancing amyotrophic lateral sclerosis (ALS) or Lou Gehrig's disease. It is a progressive disease that affects the nervous system and eventually decreases mobility, communication, swallowing and breathing, and independent functioning. Jean has been married for 45 years and her husband also has health problems. Jean is now having trouble walking because of leg weakness. Her arms are getting weaker also, and she now needs help with bathing, dressing and preparing meals. She gets daily support from community services and from her children, but she sees that this is causing her children hardship and stress. This weighs on her mind, because she knows that the burden on her children will only get heavier as she and her husband become even more dependent. The loss of independence and the knowledge that she is a source of difficulty and stress makes Jean feel her quality of life is decreasing and everything is over.

Jean talks at length with her family about this distress and how it leads her to seek physician-assisted suicide. The family is upset about this, but try hard to understand her reasons. Jean researches the process with her physician and submits a request to be considered for the program. After a thorough investigation, she is found to be eligible, and she gets a prescription for a lethal dose of drug. While she may still have had many more months to live, she decides to take the drug and dies.

Source: Adapted from Government of Canada. 2017. "Medical Assistance in Dying." Retrieved October 31, 2017 from https://www.canada.ca/en/health-canada/services/medical-assistance-dying.html; and Gallagher, R. 2016. "Physician-Assisted Suicide and Euthanasia: Introduction." *Canadian Virtual Hospice*, August 21. Retrieved October 21, 2016 from www.virtualhospice.ca/en_US/Main+Site+Navigation/Home/Topics/Topics/Decisions/Physician_Assisted+Suicide+and+Euthanasia_+Introduction.aspx.

Box 12.5: Insights on Death and Dying

Since 1987, Joy Ufema has written her popular column, "Insights on Death and Dying," for *Nursing* journal in which she focuses on the emotional well-being of everyone involved. Below find one of Joy's favourite firsthand accounts of how she helped families, patients, and co-workers through stressful times.

SOMEONE'S WAITING FOR HER

I believe that all patients live or die in spite of our care. (That's rather humbling to those of us in nursing and medicine).

Many times I've seen patients choose to finish their own lives rather than go to a nursing home, endure another amputation, or continue with futile chemotherapy. We all need a reason or purpose to wake up every morning. No one can give that to another.

Last week, one of my favourite physicians shared a story with me. As an intensivist, Dr. Peters was caring for a 91-year-old woman who'd had an episode of heart failure. As she typically does with ICU patients, Dr. Peters spoke to Mrs. Dobbs about her wishes regarding heroic measures.

"Oh, don't worry about that, dear," said Mrs. Dobbs. "I signed my living will and all that business is taken care of."

Dr. Peters assured her patient that her wishes would be honoured. Then she added, "I want to tell you that you're doing better, so we really don't need to dwell on that."

"Oh, but you see, dear, I have someone waiting for me," replied Mrs.Dobbs. "Mr. Dobbs has been gone for years. I miss him and I want to see him."

Dr. Peters nodded respectfully but again reassured Mrs. Dobbs that her condition was improving.

Later that evening, Mrs. Dobbs began singing "Amazing Grace." She asked her nurse to join in, which she did. As another physician entered her ICU cubicle to assess her, Mrs. Dobbs waved him away. "Don't come in now," she said. "I'm focusing."

A few hours later she complained of "pain all over" and the nurse administered morphine. A short time later, Mrs. Dobbs left this world. She'd already explained why: She had someone waiting for her. —Joy Ufema, R.N., M.S.

Source: Ufema, J. 2007. *Insights on Death and Dying.* New York: Lippincott Williams and Wilkins (pp. 176-177).

SUMMARY

This chapter explores a broad range of issues relevant to family ties in the context of social change and rapid population aging. Many stereotypical assumptions about aging families and the elderly are critically evaluated in conjunction with an overview of structural socio-demographic change and its implication for patterns of support across the generations. Overall, the tendency to view aging families of the past with "rose-coloured glasses" is problematic. Instead, a life-course perspective allows us to appreciate that not only has family life always been diverse, but aging families have always faced unique challenges relative to their socio-historical and geographical location.

This chapter also considers both the challenges and opportunities created by the longevity revolution. For the first time in history, many grandparents can now watch their children and grandchildren grow up. However, increased life expectancy also means that many elderly—particularly women—are often living alone, poor, and with chronic health problems. Women are also more likely to provide care to seniors, although we should not overlook the fact that many men are providing significant amounts of care as well. And while caregiving is often viewed as a "labour of love," a theme we covered in chapter 6, caring work can be very difficult for those who are trying to juggling multiple work demands with limited resources. Care provision is also not always predictable and does not always arise outside of regular working hours.

Reconciling family caregiving as a human right and paid work in a harmonious manner requires respect and recognition from employers. Workplace policies also need to be both inclusive and flexible (Vanier Institute of the Family, 2016). It is also imperative that the state improves caregiver and care recipient policies, community programs and services, despite ideological claims that "they are just too expensive to fund." This ongoing discourse about the purported fiscal "crisis" facing the Canadian government negatively impacts our most economically and socially vulnerable seniors, all in the name of deficit reduction (McDonald, 2000). For example, studies show that when home care needs are not met, seniors are more likely to become institutionalized, which is a much more costly and less humane strategy than allowing seniors to "age in place" (Turcotte, 2014).

The phenomenon of population aging also raises many ethical issues with respect to end-of-life issues such as physician-assisted suicide, euthanasia, death and dying, and palliative care. It is also recognized that we need to consider family issues beyond caregiving, including such topics as increased cultural and ethnic diversity in aging families and geographical mobility, friendships and fictive kin, siblings, sexuality and intimacy, and advances in medical and information technology. Clearly, all of these topics will gain added significance in the future as they become increasingly salient to more and more members of the Canadian population.

QUESTIONS FOR CRITICAL REFLECTION AND DEBATE

1. Critically evaluate the popular viewpoint that the elderly in Canadian society have been abandoned by their families.
2. Why are older men more likely to remarry than older women? Also discuss how families can help or hinder the formation of intimate relations among older adults following divorce or widowhood.

3. To what extent do the media (e.g., films, TV commercials, print) promote positive images of sexuality and the elderly?
4. How can a cross-cultural study of aging families help us to better understand Canadian aging family life and the role of seniors in families?
5. Debate the following: Euthanasia and assisted-suicide should remain legal in Canada to help families end the suffering of elderly, frail family members.
6. Evaluate the common "apocalyptic" statement that, "As the population ages, social policy will be challenged."

GLOSSARY

Apocalyptic demography is the tendency to equate rapid population aging with a number of negative implications for society and for the family, especially with respect to escalating health care and pension costs and associated caregiving issues.

Filial piety is rooted in the idea that the core of moral behaviour lies in several obligations that children owe to parents (e.g., respect and caregiving).

Global reciprocity refers to the tendency of families to balance exchanges of support over the course of their lives rather than at one particular point in time.

Golden age myth is the tendency to assume that, historically, elderly people tended to reside in multigenerational households with strong ties across the generations, and that they enjoyed more status and respect than they do today.

Hierarchical-compensatory model suggests that people choose their supports initially from their inner family circle and then outward to receive assistance from less intimate sources as they need more help.

Modernization of grandparenthood is the phrase used to describe the phenomenon of contemporary grandparenthood due to increased longevity, technology, affluence, and leisure time.

Palliative care is a program of active compassionate care primarily directed toward improving the quality of life for the dying.

Skip-generation households are those households in which grandparents live with at least one grandchild without the presence of the middle (parent) generation.

FURTHER READING

Carr, D.S., K.F. Ferraro, L.K., George, J.M. Wilmoth, and D. Wolf. 2016. *Handbook of Aging and the Social Sciences,* 8th ed. London, UK: Elsevier Academic Press.
Comprehensive synthesis and review of the latest theory, methods, and research findings. Covers the key areas in sociological gerontology research and well as new topics such as: families, immigration, caregiving, neighborhoods, natural disasters, religion and health, and sexual behavior.

Cheng, S. 2015. *Successful Aging: Asian Perspectives.* Springer: Dordrecht.
Examines the differences between the Asian and Western contexts in which the aging process unfolds, including cultural values, lifestyles, physical environments and family structures.

Connidis, I.A. 2010. *Family Ties and Aging,* 2nd ed. Thousand Oaks, California: Sage Publications.
This book provides a comprehensive overview of research and issues on aging families in North America. Particular attention is paid to diverse family relationships and how they are structured by gender, ethnicity, socio-economic status, and sexual orientation.

Novak, M., and L. Campbell. 2010. *Aging and Society: A Canadian Perspective,* 6th ed. Toronto: Thomson Nelson.
Presents a positive look at issues relating to aging within the context of Canada's history, family, and social life.

Ramirez-Valles, J. 2016. *Queer Aging. The Gayby Boomers and a New Frontier in Gerontology.* Toronto: Oxford University Press.
Framed by Queer Theory and an interdisciplinary approach, this book examines aging amongst older gay men from various economically and racially diverse backgrounds. Candid, first-person narratives reflect a variety of life experiences.

Wister, A.V. and B. McPherson. 2014. *Aging as a Social Process,* 6th ed. Toronto: Oxford University Press.
The most comprehensive and up to date overview of topics relevant to aging Canadians. Topics include many issues relevant to aging families, such as life-course issues, social networks and participation, the health contexts of aging, social inequality, and social change, and work, retirement, and economic security.

RELATED WEB SITES

Canadian Association of Gerontology offers information on the organization in addition to sources about publications and research from a multidisciplinary perspective, www.cagacg.ca. Facebook: http://www.facebook.com/CdnAssocGero/ Twitter: www. twitter.com/cagacg

CANGRADS is a Canadian not-for-profit organization that provides support for grandparents and others who are raising grandchildren or other kin, www.cangrands.com.

Canadian Association of Retired Persons (CARP) is a national, non-partisan, non-profit organization committed to a "New Vision of Aging for Canada" promoting social change that will bring financial security, equitable access to health care, and freedom from discrimination, www.carp.ca/. Facebook: www.facebook.com/CARP. Twitter: www.com/CARPNews

Seniors Canada is Government of Canada resource that offers information for seniors, their families, their caregivers and supporting service organizations on federal, provincial, territorial and some municipal government benefits and services. www.seniors.gc.ca/eng/index.shtml.

Facebook: www.facebook.com/SeniorsinCanadaAineauCanada.

Twitter: www.twitter.com/socdevsoc

Gerontological Society of America is a large non-profit professional organization that provides researchers, educators, practitioners, and policy makers the opportunity to share information on aging to improve the quality of life for seniors and their families, http://www.geron.org.

Facebook: www.facebook.com/geronsociety

Twitter: www.twitter.com/geronsociety

REFERENCES

Battams, N. 2016. "Sharing a Roof: Multi-generational Homes in Canada." Ottawa: The Vanier Institute of the Family. Retrieved October 11, 2016 from www. vanierinstitute.ca/multigenerational-homes-canada/?print=print

Blakeborough, D. 2008. "'Old People are Useless': Representations of Aging on the Simpsons." *Canadian Journal on Aging* 27: 57-67.

Cantor, M.H. 1979. "Neighbours and Friends: An Overlooked Resource in the Informal Support System." *Research on Aging* 1: 434–463.

Chappell, N. 2014. "Aging in Canadian Families Today." In D. Cheal and P. Albanese (eds.), *Canadian Families Today: New Perspectives*, 3rd ed. (pp. 125-143). Toronto: Oxford University Press.

Cherlin, A.J., and F.F. Furstenberg, Jr. 1992. "The Modernization of Grandparenthood." In A.S. Skolnick and J.H. Skolnick (eds.), *Family in Transition*, 7th ed. (pp. 105–111). New York: HarperCollins.

Connidis, I.A. 2010. *Family Ties and Aging*, 2nd ed. Thousand Oaks, California: Sage.

Diamond, T. 1995. *Making Gray Gold: Narratives of Nursing Home Care*. Chicago: University of Chicago Press.

Fast. J., K. Duncan, C. Dunlop, J. Eales, N. Keating, D. Lero, and S. Yoshino. 2010. "Gender Differences in Family/Friend Caregiving in Canada. *"Research on Aging Policies and Practices*. December Issue: 1–4. Edmonton: University of Alberta.

Gee, E.M. 2002. "Families and Aging." In N. Chappell, E. Gee, L. McDonald, and M. Stones (eds.), *Aging in Contemporary Canada* (pp. 278–308). Toronto: Prentice-Hall.

Gee, E.M. and G.M. Gutman (eds.). 2000. *The Overselling of Population Aging: Apocalyptic Demography, Intergenerational Challenges, and Social Policy*. Toronto: Oxford University Press.

Gee, and B.A. Mitchell. 2002. "One Roof: Exploring Multi-generational Households in Canada." In M. Lynn (ed.), *Voices: Essays on Canadian Families* (pp. 291–311). Toronto: Thomson Nelson.

Hill, J. 2010. "In-Depth, Aging Population: Mandatory Retirement Fades in Canada," *CBC News*, Monday, October 18. Retrieved August 15, 2011 from www.cbc.ca/news/canda/story/2009/08/20/mandatory-retirement.

ICGI (Ithaca College Gerontology Institute). 2006. *A Comparison of Japan and the United States on Issues of Aging*. Retrieved July 4, 2006, from www.ithca.ed/aging/schools.

Keating, N. (ed.). 2008. *Rural Ageing: A Good Place to Grow Old?* London, UK: Policy Press.

Keating, N., J. Swindle, and S. Fletcher. 2011. "Aging in Rural Canada: A Retrospective and Review" *Canadian Journal on Aging* 30: 323-338.

Kemp, C. 2004. "'Grand' Expectations: The Experiences of Grandparents and Adult Grandchildren." *Canadian Journal of Sociology* 29: 499–525.

Kobayashi, K.M. 2000. "The Nature of Support from Adult Children to Older Parents in Japanese Canadian Families." *Journal of Cross-cultural Gerontology* 15: 185–205.

Kobayashi, K.M., and L. Funk 2010. "Of the Family Tree: Congruence on Filial Obligation and its Implications for Social Support among Older Parents and Adult Children in Japanese Canadian Families." *Canadian Journal on Aging* 29: 85–96.

Koehn, S., S. Neysmith, K. Kobayashi, and H. Khamisa. 2013. "Revealing the Shape of Knowledge using an Intersectionality Lens: Results of a Scoping Review on the Health and HealthCare of Ethnocultural Minority Older Adults." *Ageing and Society* 33: 437-464.

Laird, J. 1996. "Invisible Ties: Lesbians and Their Families of Origin." In J. Laird and R. Green (eds.), *Lesbians and Gays in Couples and Families: A Handbook for Therapists* (pp. 89–122). San Francisco: Jossey-Bass.

Lodge, A.C., and D. Umberson. 2016. "Sexual Intimacy in Mid- and Late-Life Couples." In J. Bookwala (ed.), *Couple Relationships in the Middle and Later Years: Their Nature, Complexity, and Role in Health and Illness* (pp. 115-134). Washington, DC: American Psychological Association.

Lopata, H.Z. 1995. "Feminist Perspectives on Social Gerontology." In R. Bleiszner and V.H. Bedford (eds.), *Handbook of Aging and the Family* (pp.114-131). Westport: Greenwood Press.

Mann, R. 2007. "Out of the Shadows? Grandfatherhood, Age, and Masculinities." *Journal of Aging Studies* 21: 281–91.

Martin-Matthews, A. 2005. "Aging and Families: Ties over Time and Generation." In N. Mandell and A. Duffy (eds.), *Canadian Families: Diversity, Conflict, and Change* (pp. 311–345). Toronto: Thomson Nelson.

Maurier, W.L., and H.C. Northcott. 2000. *Aging in Ontario: Diversity in the New Millennium.* Calgary: Detselig Enterprises.

McDonald, L. 2000. "Alarmist Economics and Women's Pensions: A Case of 'Semanticide.'" In E.M. Gee and G.M. Gutman (eds.), *The Overselling of Population Aging: Apocalyptic Demography, Intergenerational Challenges and Social Policy* (pp. 114–128). Toronto: Oxford University Press.

McDonald, L., and P. Donahue. 2011. "Retirement Lost?" *Canadian Journal on Aging* 30: 401–422.

McDaniel, S.A., and A. Gazso. 2016. "Liminality and Low-Income Aging Families by Choice: Meanings of Family and Support." *Canadian Journal on Aging* 33: 400-412.

Milan, A. 2013. "Marital Status: Overview, 2011." Component of Statistics Canada Catalogue no. 91-209-X. Ottawa: Minister of Industry.

Milan, A., L.A. Keown, and C. Robles Urquijo. 2011. "Families, Living Arrangements, and Unpaid Work." Statistics Canada Catalogue no. 89-503-X. Ottawa: Minister of Industry.

Nelson, T.D. 2016. "Promoting Healthy Aging by Confronting Ageism." *American Psychologist,* 71: 276-282.

Norris, J.E., and J.A. Tindale. 1994. *Among Generations: The Cycle of Adult Relationships.* Toronto: W.H. Freeman and Company.

Novak, M., and L. Campbell. 2010. *Aging and Society: A Canadian Perspective,* 6th ed. Toronto: Thomson Nelson.

O'Rand, A.M. 1996. "The Precious and the Precocious: Understanding Cumulative Advantage and Cumulative Disadvantage over the Life Course." *The Gerontologist* 36: 230–238.

Rosenthal, C. 2000. "Aging Families: Have Current Challenges Been 'Oversold'?" In E.M. Gee and G.M. Gutman (eds.), *The Overselling of Population Aging: Apocalyptic Demography, Intergenerational Challenges, and Social Policy* (pp. 45–65). Toronto: Oxford University Press.

Sinha, M. 2013. "Portrait of Caregivers, 2012." Retrieved October 8, 2016 from www.statcan. gc.ca/pub/89-652-x/89-652-x2013001-eng.htm.

Swartzwelder, J. (Writer), and J. Reardon (Director). 1994, January 6. "Homer the Vigilante." In J.L. Brooks, M. Groening, and S. Simon (Executive Producers), *The Simpsons.* New York: Twentieth Century Fox.

Statistics Canada. 2010. *"Population Projections for Canada, Provinces and Territories (2009-2036),* Statistics Canada catalogue number 91-520 XIE, table 052-0005. Ottawa: Minister of Industry.

Statistics Canada. 2011. "Study: Grandparents Living with Their Grandchildren 2011." *The Daily,* April 14, 2015.

Statistics Canada. 2012. "Living Arrangements of Seniors: Families, Households and Marital Status, Structural Type of Dwelling and Collectives, 2011 Census of Population." Ottawa: Minister of Industry.

Statistics Canada. 2016. "Canada's Population Estimates: Age and Sex, July 1, 2015." Retrieved October 11, 2016 from www.statcan.gc.ca/daily-quotidien/150929/dq150929b-eng.htm

Stones, L., and M. Stones. 1996. *Sex May Be Wasted on the Young*. North York: Captus.

Szinovacz, M.E. 2006. "Families and Retirement." In L. Stone (editor in chief), *New Frontiers of Research on Retirement*, Statistics Canada catalogue number 75-511-XWE pp. 165–187. Ottawa: Minister of Industry.

Talbott, M.M. 1998. "Older Widows' Attitudes towards Men and Remarriage." *Journal of Aging Studies* 12: 429–440.

Thompson, A.E., L.F. O'Sullivan, S. Byers, and K. Shaughnessy. 2014. "Young Adults' Implicit and Explicit Attitudes towards the Sexuality of Older Adults." *Canadian Journal on Aging* 33: 259-270.

Turcotte, M. 2014. "Canadians with Unmet Home Care Needs." Statistics Canada Catalogue no. 75-006-X. Ottawa: Minister of Industry.

Vanier Institute of the Family. 2016. *Family Caregiving in Canada: A Fact of Life and a Human Right*. Retrieved October 8, 2016 from www.vanierinstitute.ca.

Wister, A.V., and B. McPherson. 2014. *Aging as a Social Process*, 6th ed. Toronto: Oxford University Press.

Zimmerman, L. 2000. "Foreword." In E.M. Gee and G.M. Gutman (eds.), *The Overselling of Population Aging: Apocalyptic Demography, Intergenerational Challenges, and Social Policy* (p. ix). Toronto: Oxford University Press.

Zoomer Magazine. 2016 (October). "Watch: Dinnie Greenway, 96, Has No Plans to Stop Horseback Riding." Retrieved October 21, 2016 from www.everythingzoomer.com/dinnie-greenway-96-has-no-plans-to-stop-horseback-riding/

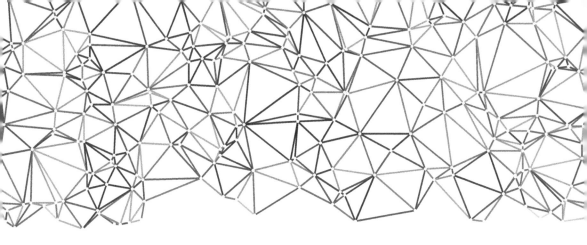

PART III

FAMILIES ON THE FAULT LINE AND SOCIAL POLICY ISSUES

While life for many Canadians is relatively comfortable and trouble free, a significant number of families face considerable hardship and challenge. Some of these problems may be relatively short term with relatively modest consequences, such as temporary unemployment or a brief illness. Or, these challenges can be chronic or long term (e.g., having a child with special needs) or occur at certain points in the life course (e.g., Alzheimer's disease in old age). Although previous parts of this text have also highlighted some critical issues facing families, in this section, we focus on a number of particularly problematic areas for families, with continued emphasis on how many of life's challenges are socially structured over the life course. In other words, social problems and what we often view as "private troubles" are often related to access to key social and economic resources. They therefore vary according to such aspects as gender, ethnicity, social class, and geographical locale. We will also consider how these inequities and challenges affect, and are affected by, family relationships and shape family interactions.

In chapter 13, for instance, we will learn that many serious health problems are more likely to occur among individuals who live in poverty than those who are wealthier. Health problems can also impact the entire family system, such as when a family member has physical or mental health issues. And poverty and financial hardship (which will be covered in chapter 14) are more likely to occur within certain social groups, such as among women, recent immigrants, the disabled, and Indigenous populations. Similarly, certain social groups are more likely to experience violence, stress, and abuse (the focus of chapter 15) because they are more vulnerable and dependent. They may also not have access to important community resources and programs. As such, social policy can play an important role in the distribution of societal resources and can play a pivotal role in the overall general health and well-being of Canadian families. Thus, in chapter 16, we will examine some key social and family policy issues as well as some salient policy concerns for the present and future. These "critical" issues will be reviewed in light of many of the key family-related life-course patterns uncovered throughout this book.

CHAPTER 13

In Sickness and in Health: Families Facing Health Challenges and the Creation of Healthy Lifestyles

LEARNING OBJECTIVES

In this chapter you will learn that ...

- experiences of health and well-being in families are embedded in socio-cultural, economic, and political contexts
- definitions of health and "ableness" are multifaceted, and there are multiple social determinants of health
- health challenges can significantly affect family roles and relationships, presenting unique challenges, particularly for low-income families and those without social support
- health policies and promotion strategies need to target families and social conditions early in life
- healthy public policy can improve population health and reduce structural barriers for those experiencing problems, thereby reducing social and economic costs in the future

INTRODUCTION

Our **health and well-being** are shaped by many factors and social contexts, such as where we live, our income and education level, the quality of our home environment, genetics, and our relationships with our friends and family. Fortunately, most Canadians report being in good to excellent health, which is defined by the World Health Organization as "a state of complete physical, mental, and social well-being and not merely the absence of disease or infirmity" (WHO, 1946). The widespread use of this over-arching definition reflects how our perception of health has shifted beyond the traditional Western biomedical model that was prevalent in our society for most of the last century. This definition also suggests that health encompasses more than the absence of illness and disease—it is multidimensional, multidetermined, and also incorporates a subjective component.

Although Canadians are among the healthiest people in the world, "good health" is not enjoyed equally by everyone, as is consistently shown through our Canadian Community Health Surveys. Indeed, not all social groups and individuals are healthy. Families living in poverty, for example, are particularly vulnerable to health problems, and this raises a number of implications for families, society, and the Canadian health care system. In this chapter we will review key social determinants of health. Selected health and well-being issues and how they affect, and are affected by, our family environments will also be examined. Focus will be placed on families and disabilities, special needs children, substance abuse, mental health, caregiving for the elderly, and the death of a family member. Finally, we will consider **health promotion** initiatives and state supports in the context of healthy public policy and community programs.

THE SOCIAL DETERMINANTS OF HEALTH: WHY ARE SOME FAMILIES HEALTHIER THAN OTHERS?

As previously noted, our health and well-being are influenced by factors that extend beyond genetic endowment or biological realms. This has led Health Canada and researchers to develop the social determinants of health framework, which refers to "the economic and social conditions that influence the health of individuals, communities, and jurisdictions as a whole" (Raphael, 2004: 1). In 2001, the organizers of a York University conference on health identified 11 social determinants of health, as shown in box 13.1 All of these determinants interact with gender and other important contexts (e.g., geographical place of residence).

Generally, a social determinant of health framework highlights how structured inequality produces inequality of health conditions, and the way health is profoundly influenced by governments' social policy decisions. For example, we see in figure 13.1 that Canadians are more likely to report having unmet health care needs when they are living in poverty and in certain provinces. Poor Canadians are also less likely to report unmet health care needs than poor Americans. The cost of health care, (regardless of health insurance

Box 13.1: What Are the Social Determinants of Health?

The 11 social determinants of health are:

- Aboriginal status
- early life
- education
- employment and working conditions
- food security
- health care services
- housing
- income and its distribution
- social safety net
- social exclusion
- unemployment and employment security

Source: Raphael, D. 2004. "Introduction to the Social Determinants of Health," in D. Raphael (ed.), *Social Determinants of Health: Canadian Perspectives.* Toronto: Canadian Scholars' Press (p. 6).

status) is the primary barrier cited in the United States. Indeed, **social epidemiology**, the study of the socio-cultural, economic, and political forces that shape patterns of disease and death in human populations, differentiates the health status of populations by inequities such as socio-economic status.

The health gap between the rich and poor continues to exist, and upper-income Canadians live longer, are healthier, and have fewer disabilities on average than lower-income Canadians. Poor material and social conditions, such as inadequate housing and poor nutrition, contribute to high mortality in the low-income population. Figure 13.2 highlights how housing affects other health determinants.

Research also documents that people with higher socio-economic status, particularly those with a greater education, have better access to resources that are conducive to better health habits and lifestyles than people with lower socio-economic status (e.g., see Gulati and Ray, 2016). For instance, people with a higher education tend to engage in healthy behaviours such as exercising, avoiding smoking and overeating, and moderate drinking, and are more likely to seek preventative health checkups. They also tend to have a greater sense of control and autonomy in their work lives, which increases their general health and well-being (Mirowsky and Ross, 1998; Mirowsky, Ross, and Reynolds, 2000).

The life-course perspective, synthesized with the concept of "social capital" (covered in chapter 2), is particularly useful when considering the **social determinants of health**. As stated by Raphael (2004: 16):

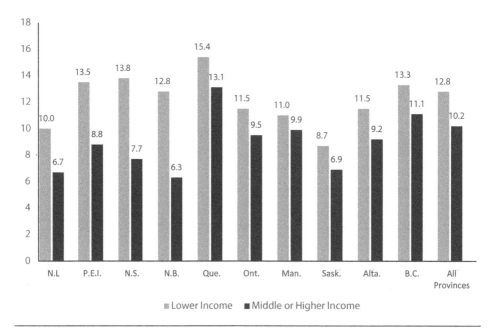

Figure 13.1: Individuals Reporting an Unmet Health Care Need by Household Income and Province of Residence, in Percentages, 2014

Note: Data are based on the Canadian Community Health Survey 2014; a survey of household population aged 12 or older in Canada. The rate of unmet health care needs in Nunavut had a coefficient of variation (CV) between 16.6 and 33.3%; this should be interpreted with caution. Statistically significant differences are noted only in Nova Scotia (NS), New Brunswick (NB), Quebec (Que.), and Ontario (Ont.), where those with lower incomes were more likely to report an unmet health care need ($p < 0.05$).

Source: Statistics Canada. 2016. "Health Fact Sheets, Unmet Health Care Needs, 2014." Catalogue 82-625-X. Ottawa: Minister of Industry. Retrieved August 31, 2016 from www.statcan.gc.ca/pub/82-625-x/2016001/article/14310-eng.htm.

Adopting a life-course perspective directs attention to how social determinants of health operate at every level of development … to both immediately influence health as well as provide the basis for health or illness during following stages of the life course.

Human capital (education in the form of skills and knowledge) combined with social capital (strong social support from family, friends, and community earlier in life can help buffer the effects of stress; this can positively affect health later in life. An example of this is illustrated in box 13.2, which summarizes key findings of The Nun Study. This highly cited research uncovers links among supportive networks of relations, stress, education, and a positive attitude, demonstrating how these factors contribute to health outcomes in later life. This study also illuminates how social support is not the sole domain of blood or formal kinship ties, since it can be found in other kinds of close relationships.

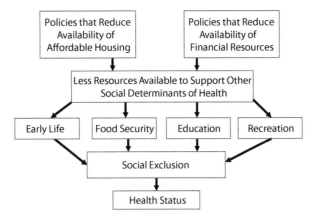

Figure 13.2: How Housing Affects Other Health Determinants

Source: Bryant, T. 2004. "Housing and Health." In D. Raphael (ed.), *Social Determinants of Health: Canadian Perspectives.* Toronto: Canadian Scholars' Press Inc. (p.223).

Box 13.2: Nuns' Story of Aging Study Links Sharp Minds to a Positive Mindset

....In *Aging with Grace: What the Nun Study Teaches Us About Leading Longer, Healthier, and More Meaningful Lives* (New York: Bantam), Snowdon (2002) yields some startling, often encouraging discoveries...not the least of which is that an educated mind, healthy habits and, maybe most important, a sense of joy in living can lead to a long, vibrant and productive life, and may even block the effects of Alzheimer's disease. "Those who are hopeful, happy, optimistic in attitudes live much longer," Snowdon says. "That happy state is probably also a healthy state." The nuns involved in the study range in age from 75 to 106, and they are members of the School Sisters of Notre Dame congregation... Because the sisters share similar lifestyles and can be followed for so many years, "it's as close as you can get to a laboratory-pure environment, a unique model of aging in a population," Snowdon says...."You don't have to join a convent to learn from these sisters...Buckle your seat belt, watch your blood pressure, eat a prudent diet, and be good at what humans are good at—language and social intercourse."... The nuns in the study aren't representative of American society. They're better educated...and their overall health reflects a life without tobacco, alcohol, or excesses of any kind... "They're very mellow," Snowdon says. He attributes that to a life of prayer and community ..."Part of it is the social support they have, and I think the spiritual part is the way they get through some of the ups and downs of life." The sisters remain interested in each other and in life around them. "They're always looking forward," he says.

Source: Manning, A. 2001 (May 14). "Nuns' Story of Aging Study Links Sharp Minds to a Positive Mindset." USA TODAY.com, USA Today Information Network, Anita Manning, May 14, 2001. Retrieved October 29, 2001, from www.pqasb.pqarchiver.com/USAToday.

SELECTED HEALTH CHALLENGES AND IMPLICATIONS FOR FAMILY RELATIONSHIPS

Families with Disabilities and Special Needs Children

Disability is a fluid and elastic concept; conceptions of disability have changed dramatically over time. Prior to the 20th century, many definitions involved religious and supernatural explanations, ranging from karma (a destiny or fate based on one's previous actions) to God's will. Today in Canada, disability is defined as having difficulty performing certain kinds of "normal" daily activities, such as hearing, seeing, walking, or climbing stairs; or as having certain conditions that limit participation in these activities. According to a Statistics Canada (2015) report, in 2012 approximately 3.8 million Canadians aged 15 and over—13.7% of the population (one in seven)—reported that they had one or more disabilities.

Owen (2014) further emphasizes how self-identification is critical to a disability perspective because it shifts the power of naming disability away from those in authority and toward the subjective identities of those who are imposed with disability labels. Against this backdrop, it is easy to understand how definitions of disability and the usage of this terminology have been hotly debated by disability activists and in the literature. In this regard, defining words is a political act, as feminists and critical race theorists have struggled to emphasize. Disability connotes a lack of ability, carrying the label of inferiority and dependency. Similarly, there are differing ideological and historical perspectives on disability, as previously noted by the Office for Disability Issues (2001: 42).

> The biomedical perspective sees disability as a disease, disorder, medical condition, or biological 'abnormality' within the individual. The functional perspective understands disability as a restriction in ability to perform certain standard tasks in a way that is considered 'normal.' The social/environmental perspective presents disability as the result of barriers in the social environment that prevent persons with disabilities from participating fully in community, work, and learning. Finally, the human rights perspective focuses on respect for human dignity and protection against discrimination and exclusionary practices in the private and public spheres.

Overall, the emphasis on defining disability has moved away from a medical model of (ab)normality to a focus on social structure. As observed by Owen (2014), this shift has been a significant move in the rethinking of disability and the beginning of political action. Previously, disability was centred on individual impairments, and people with disabilities were 'othered' because of their difference from the ableist norm. Alternatively, from a **social model of disability** lens, it is the external obstacles that limit 'ableness' rather than individual characteristics per se. For example, the lack of a ramp in a public place is the problem, not the condition that someone uses a wheelchair.

Cognizant of these important issues, a significant number of Canadian families are confronted with the associated health and economic challenges that result from disability. These challenges can be chronic or temporary, and they can occur at any point in the family life course and at any age, although generally, the prevalence of disability tends to increase with age. Yet a common theme echoed across many different kinds of family circumstances —for example, from having a child with cerebral palsy, to being a parent with a learning disability, to having a grandparent with Parkinson's disease—is how a lack of support and the obstacles that prevent a full life are the problem, rather than the disability itself.

By way of example, Owen (2014) finds that many parents of children with disabilities experience significant frustration, largely rooted in a lack of support, rather than in the child's disability. In some cases, children may be placed in residential or foster care because of this lack of support, and family breakdown, poverty, and unemployment can result. There are also reciprocal effects between disability and poverty, as well as ripple effects for the health and well-being of all family members. For instance, low-income parents with a disabled child may have less access to good housing and certain health or educational services, which in turn can lead to further family health problems. Also, disabled individuals of working age may not be able to find employment; the lack of resources can exacerbate their health and functioning. Indeed, chronic poverty is an everyday reality for many people with disabilities, and recent data (e.g., see Statistics Canada, 2015) clearly highlights the need for more attention to poverty reduction.

Although not all special needs children are necessarily considered disabled, it is estimated that between 5 and 20% of children have special needs because of physical or intellectual disabilities, behavioural problems, or giftedness (Child and Family Canada, 2005). These children and their families can face unique challenges. Haaf (2015) notes that while many Canadians enjoy free health care, many parents of kids with special needs struggle to cover these costs. Many of these children need equipment, services, and care that may not be covered by provincial health plans or other programs, including extended health coverage. For example, autistic children often require specialized care and educational programs; some provinces are more generous than others as far as subsidies for therapies, programs, tools, and parent training.

And while many parents of special needs children report that the experience of parenting such a child has enriched their lives in a magnitude of ways, they can also simultaneously face frustration and stress. In particular, there is growing concern that special needs often go unaddressed in schools and communities, which can create additional challenges for families and society. Of notable concern is children born with fetal alcohol syndrome (FAS), which is caused by alcohol abuse during pregnancy. FAS can cut across all socio-economic groups, but it has been observed to be particularly prevalent in certain Indigenous communities in Canada. Deemed one of the leading causes of learning and behavioural difficulties, FAS can put youth at increased risk of developing a number of other problems. For example, research shows that 30–70% of young offenders and inmates have experienced learning problems (Boland et al., 1998). Moreover, almost 50% of adolescents

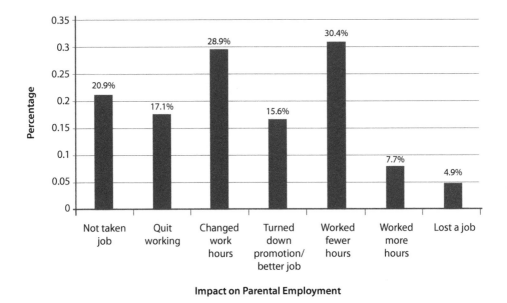

Impact on Parental Employment

Figure 13.3: Impact of Child's Condition on Parental Employment for Parents of Children with Disabilities Aged 0 to 14, Canada, 2006

Source: Human Resources and Skills Development Canada. 2006. *Disability in Canada: A 2006 Profile* (Chart 3.1). Retrieved January 1, 2010 from http://www.hrsdc.gc.ca/eng/disability_issues/reports/disability_profile/2011/page03.shtml.

who committed suicide had previously been diagnosed with learning disabilities (Child and Family Canada, 2005).

Another type of special needs children are those with attention deficit hyperactive disorder (ADHD). This neurologically based developmental disorder (also viewed as a mental health disorder) is accompanied by symptoms of hyperactivity, impulsivity, and distractibility. These symptoms, which begin in infancy, are estimated to affect between 5 and 12% of school-aged children, usually boys. The condition sometimes continues into adulthood, affecting academic progress, social skills development, and, later on, job performance. The impact is felt at home, at school, on the job, and within the community (Centre for ADHD Awareness Canada, 2016). While caring for these children presents a number of challenges, deep-rooted inequalities means that low-income mothers face unique demands relative to more privileged mothers.

Overall, low-income mothers have fewer personal resources and are confronted with dwindling government support services for poor disabled children or children with special needs. Based on qualitative interview data, Litt (2004: 640) shows how these mothers are caught within "inflexible and punitive environments," and how "notions of disability disregard the lived experiences of the care needs of these children." In particular, these women must experience and negotiate a system that expects them to financially support their children while also providing care for them. As a result, these mothers face unrealistic work demands and inadequate public supports. Unfortunately, this undermines their employment and education options as well as their long-term prospects for financial stability. Visible minority women face additional burdens, since limited access to health care continues to be a problem in these communities.

Alcohol and Substance Abuse

The Canadian Centre on Substance Use and Addiction (CCSA) documents the extensive toll that alcohol and substance abuse can take on individuals and their families. The CCSA's Substance Use in Canada series publishes reports on key contemporary issues around problematic substance use and highlights areas for action in both policy and practice. For example, the first report examines alcohol policy, cannabis sanctions, drug-impaired driving, and prescription medication misuse. In other reports, they focused on the co-occurrence of mental health and substance abuse problems, in addition to licit and illicit drug dependency in pregnant women (e.g., Leyton and Stewart, 2014).

Although all forms of addiction, along with alcohol and substance abuse, are potentially problematic for families and society and contribute to the global burden of adult ill-health (e.g., see Orford et al., 2013), growing public attention has been paid to the dangers of prescription and recreational drug use. This is displayed in recent sensationalistic and alarming media headlines like "Fentanyl Deaths Are a Canada-Wide Disaster" (Sagan, 2015), and "Overdose Deaths Continue to Climb in B.C. as Fentanyl Use Spreads" (Canadian Press, 2016). The CCSA documents that between 2009 and 2014, there were at least 655 fentanyl-implicated deaths in Canada (fentanyl is an opioid-based pain killer much stronger than morphine), and that this figure is likely an underestimate (CCSA, 2015). Many of the people who died thought they were taking other drugs, such as heroin, oxycodone, or cocaine. In addition to overdose mortality, other significant harms associated with fentanyl include non-fatal overdoses and substance use disorders, which can affect almost every facet of daily life.

Moreover, the CCSA also presents compelling evidence that while genetics can play an important role in someone's vulnerability, propensity to use drugs, and develop substance abuse problems, there is a powerful interplay between genes and environmental factors (see figure 13.4). This finding is consistent with a growing body of literature that establishes the importance of incorporating social and cultural contexts in understanding how/why macro and interpersonal factors (e.g., media, economic stressors, neighborhood, parental role modelling, peer groups) intersect with individual characteristics and biology (e.g., Adams, 2016; Sudhinaraset, Wigglesworth, and Takeuchi, 2016).

Moreover, an emergent **epigenetic** approach provides an important key to understanding how family and social environment can "get under the skin" to affect gene expression and brain function. This kind of thinking also has enormous implications for prevention,

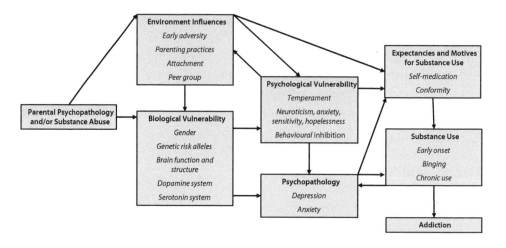

Figure 13.4: A Developmental Model of Internalizing Problems and Addiction

Source: O'Leary-Barrett, M. 2014. "The Internalizing Developmental Pathway to Substance Use Disorders." In M. Leyton and S. Stewart (eds.), *Substance Abuse in Canada: Childhood and Adolescent Pathways to Substance Abuse Disorders.* (pp. 46–67). Ottawa: Canadian Centre on Substance Abuse (p. 62).

intervention, and treatment. In particular, it directs complete attention away from the individual, as opposed to the common "blaming" or rehabilitation approach. It also encourages family-inclusive practices for addressing root causes and treatment strategies. Accordingly, complex intimate relationships are seen as the vehicle for long-term change and as critical for good health and successful outcomes. Moreover, this kind of perspective considers how other social networks (e.g., friends, who often report similar family backgrounds) can serve as bridges to unhealthy parental influences. Thus, attention can be also be placed on how persons outside of the immediate family can exert social control over individual behaviours (e.g., see Ragan, Osgood, and Feinberg, 2014).

Mental Health Issues

Mental illness refers to a broad classification for many disorders such as anxiety, depression, bipolar disease, schizophrenia, and eating disorders, and it accounts for a large percentage of hospital stays every year (CMHA, 2016). It is also relatively common—statistics indicate that one in every five Canadians will have a mental health problem at some point in their lives. However, there is considerable variation in the duration and intensity of the illness, as well as its actual and perceived root causes. Table 13.1 shows that while many Canadians believe the primary cause of stress, anxiety, or major depression (apart from work) stems from money problems, others believe that it can be the result of family or health problems, or daily life in general.

Table 13.1: Perceived Causes of Stress, Anxiety, or Major Depression, Apart from Work

"In your opinion, what are the primary causes of stress, anxiety, or major depression in your personal and family life, apart from work?"

Cause	Percentage Reporting
Money problems	44
Illness of someone close to you	13
Conflicts or disputes with children	11
Conflicts or disputes with spouse	10
Family matters/family problems	10
Staying healthy/personal health problems	9
Interpersonal relations/interactions with people	7
Death of someone close to you	6
Everything/life in general/daily life/the future	6
Parenting/concern for children/meet children's needs	5
Don't know/didn't answer	6

Note: Based on a 2006 telephone survey about health and financial security, conducted on 1,501 randomly selected Canadian adults by research firm SOM .

Source: "Desjardins Financial Security Survey on Health and the Desjardins National Financial Security Index," report posted by the Canadian Mental Health Association, 2006, p. 25, retrieved August 11, 2006, from www.cmha.ca (research reports: 2006 Survey on Canadian Attitudes towards Physical and Mental Health at Work and at Play).

Families can be devastated and torn apart by mental illness. Fear, frustration, embarrassment, ambivalence, and social stigma can create significant emotional repercussions for families. Jones (2004) documents that those families with a family member who suffers from serious mental illness often experience complex loss. This loss is complicated by the continuing presence of the person who is felt to have been "lost," and by feelings of anger, subsequent guilt, and shame. Some families may be hesitant to seek professional help. And even if that help is solicited, there may be problems with denial and the patient's adherence to medication and therapy. And from a legal standpoint, there may be barriers in forcing a mentally ill individual to comply with doctor's recommendations. It is common for a person suffering from severe psychosis or delusional behaviour to believe that others are the enemy, that the medication is part of a conspiracy to poison them, and that they are not the ones who really need the help. And although far from the norm, the result of mental illness can be dangerous or deadly consequences such as violent behaviour, suicide, or the death of innocent family members. A well-publicized example is the case of Andrea Yates, a mother who, suffering from severe postpartum depression and psychosis, drowned her five children in the bathtub (see box 13.3).

Finally, while mental illness can strike any family, poverty can contribute to mental health problems, although the majority of poor people are not mentally ill. This makes it

---

Box 13.3: Andrea Yates

Andrea Pia Yates (born July 2, 1964) is a woman from Houston, Texas, who is currently serving a life sentence for methodically drowning her five children (ages six months to seven years) in a bathtub on June 20, 2001. She was suffering from a severe case of psychotic depression, recurring, after having her last baby. She immediately called 911 after the murders and was arrested shortly thereafter.

....Some believe or believed that her husband, Russell "Rusty" Yates, an employee of the Johnson Space Center, was responsible for creating the conditions that culminated in the tragedy. Andrea's psychiatrist, Dr. Eileen Starbranch, testified that she urged the couple not to get pregnant again to avert future psychotic depression, but the procreative plan taught by the Yates' preacher, Michael Peter Woroniecki, a doctrine to which Rusty Yates subscribed, insisted she should continue to have "as many children as nature allows."

Andrea Yates told her jail psychiatrist, "It was the seventh deadly sin. My children weren't righteous. They stumbled because I was evil. The way I was raising them they could never be saved. They were doomed to perish in the fires of hell."

Source: Wikepedia. n.d. "Andrea Yates." Retrieved October 31, 2005, from http://en.wikipedia.org/wiki/Andrea_Yates.

---

very difficult for individuals and families with mental health problems to rise above the poverty line. Recent studies on homelessness, for example, show that a large proportion of homeless people suffer from mental illness and a lack of family support (e.g., CMHA, 2016). Also, alcohol and drug abuse are often used by the homeless in an attempt to self-medicate, which can lead to other health and social risks. These circumstances make it very difficult to achieve social connectedness and stability, including steady employment. Unfortunately, this perpetuates a vicious cycle of poverty, vulnerability, and other related problems.

Caregiving for the Elderly and Those with Dementia and Alzheimer's Disease

Although as discussed in the last chapter, most seniors are relatively healthy and generational support tends to be reciprocal, a significant proportion of families provide informal support to a physically disabled or cognitively impaired older person. As shown in figure 13.5, over one-quarter of Canadian caregivers aged 15 and older provide care specifically for age-related needs, although providing some type of care to a family member or friend with a long-term health condition or disability is also relatively common.

Caregiving assistance may encompass a wide array of activities, varying in levels of intensity and degree. Assistance may be emotional or instrumental, such as helping with personal care, rides to the doctor or the shopping centre, and daily activities. Spouses, adult children, siblings, and friends are the most common sources of support for the elderly. Married people, in particular, have a built-in caregiving system. This may keep many old people with serious functional disabilities out of institutions. Indeed, older married people have half the institutionalization rate of elderly unmarried people (Novak, Campbell, and Northcott, 2014).

Caregiving can bring many joys and rewards, such as the opportunity to reciprocate for previous care. However, it can also lead to **caregiver burden**. This refers to stress and problems such as depression, psychological distress, and negative feelings about caregiving. Some studies also show that spouses suffer a greater burden from caregiving than adult children. This strain may be particularly acute as caregivers watch their partners decline, both mentally and physically. They may also be experiencing health problems of their own, which adds to the burden. Older caregivers may also have fewer financial and social resources than middle-aged caregivers (Novak, Campbell, and Northcott, 2014). However, this should not downplay the considerable toll that can be placed on the minority of families that are in the "sandwich generation," particularly those with few social and economic supports.

Dementia is a particularly challenging health problem for families. The current global focus on dementia is increasing, as is the demand on health, social, legal, and financial services (WHO, 2012). The syndrome consists of a number of symptoms including loss of memory, judgment, and reasoning, as well as changes in mood, behaviour, and

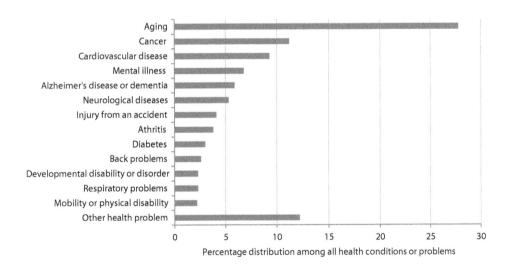

Percentage distribution among all health conditions or problems

Figure 13.5: Over a Quarter of Caregivers Provided Care for Age-Related Needs

Source: Sinha, M. 2013. "Portrait of Caregivers, 2012." Ottawa: Minister of Industry (Chart 1, p. 2). Retrieved September 2, 2016, from www.statcan.gc.ca/pub/89-652-x/89-652-x2013001-eng.htm.

communication abilities. For example, an elderly family member might be unable to start a conversation, have difficulty in planning and making decisions, become unusually aggressive, or engage in dangerous, inappropriate, or repetitive behaviours such as wandering. Alzheimer's disease (AD), the most common form of dementia, accounts for 64% of all dementias in Canada. An estimated 564,600 of Canadians are living with dementia, and 25,000 new cases are diagnosed each year. Women account for over two-thirds of all cases. Some projections indicate that this number might reach 1,125,200 (2.8% of the population) by 2038, with the economic cost of caregiving rising from approximately $15 billion in 2008 to $153 billion in 2038 (Alzheimer Society of Canada, 2010; 2016). Unfortunately, there is no known cause or cure for AD, and its prevalence is expected to grow rapidly as our population ages.

A diagnosis of early-onset dementia (under the age of 65) can be particularly troublesome for families since it comes "out of time," and it can lead to a disrupted family social clock. This non-normative or disrupted social timetable is experienced not only by the person who has dementia, but also by those who make up the constructed family unit. These relational changes and disrupted biographical continuity can impact people's coping abilities and quality of life (Roach, Drummond, and Keady, 2016). As one study participant stated, "Seeing the changes in my dad—that's what made it a lot harder to deal with. Even at family get-togethers he used to always be like the life of the party and talking to everyone. And now he kinda like sits to himself...." (p. 29).

From a symbolic interactionist perspective, MacRae (2002) studied how family members help a parent or a spouse cope with the loss of self that the disease causes. She found that family members use a number of strategies to help their relative preserve some of his or her former identity. One strategy is to conceal the diagnosis from others to avoid the label of dementia. Another strategy is to interpret inappropriate behaviour as something caused by the disease rather than the "real person." A third strategy is to assist the relative with dressing and grooming so he or she will present an unchanged image of self to others.

Death of a Family Member

At some point, all families must confront death and dying and a process of bereavement. These experiences are shaped by cultural contexts, religious beliefs, support systems, and family relationship history, as well as by the circumstances surrounding the death. Life course researchers find that deaths that occur "off time" or "too early," such as the death of a child, may be particularly difficult to cope with. A recent study by Song et. al (2010) examined the long-term effects of a child's death on the bereaved parents' health-related quality of life (HRQoL). Bereaved parents were found to have significantly worse HRQoL than parents in a comparison group. While gender differences, the age of the child, or the amount of time since their death did not significantly predict health outcomes, bereaved parents whose child died in violent circumstances had particularly low levels of HRQoL. The authors suggest that this finding provides evidence that having an opportunity to say goodbye to a loved one before they die is related to better adaptation after bereavement and possibly to better outcomes in later life. In addition, the researchers find that marital closeness plays a critical role as a source of social support for spouses and is also a significant predictor of better health for bereaved couples.

Generally, death typically takes place in old age homes or hospitals, even though most people want to die at home surrounded by their loved ones. Palliative care, which was introduced in chapter 12, can be very helpful for family members. It refers not only to the care and management of patients approaching the end of life but also to the reduction of suffering for the patient throughout the course of illness, and for the family into bereavement. A complete program would include symptom control and spiritual support, as well as bereavement support and education (Novak, Campbell, and Northcott, 2014). Culturally and spiritually sensitive care is also needed to empower both patients and their families (Fang, Sixsmith, Sinclair, and Horst, 2016). Palliative care and other approaches to the treatment of dying raise many moral and ethical questions. For example, how much information should family members give a dying person about his or her condition?

LIFESTYLES, FAMILIES, AND COMMUNITIES: A POLITICAL ECONOMY PERSPECTIVE

The study of lifestyles, health, and the interplay among families, communities, and social-structural conditions has received considerable attention in the literature. The term **lifestyle** denotes certain behaviours—such as poor diet, smoking, drinking, drug abuse, or inactivity—that are often considered sources of illness and diseases such as FAS, cancer, and obesity. And although it is individuals who engage in these behaviours, lifestyle choices are not made in a vacuum. Lifestyles are structured by social situation and constrained by life chances. These life chances are influenced by factors such as family background, socio-economic status, age, gender, race, ethnicity, and geographical locale. They are also shaped by government policies and community programs that can facilitate or hinder the formation of certain behaviours.

Let us consider the health issue of addictive behaviours such as smoking. Tobacco use is the single most preventable cause of morbidity and mortality in most developed nations. Smoking also kills more people in this country than HIV/AIDS, car accidents, murder, suicide, and illicit drug use combined (BC Ministry of Health Services, 2016). Yet, despite a significant decline in tobacco smoking over the past several decades, there are striking regional variations in daily or occasional smoking behaviour in those aged 12 and older. According to a recent Canadian Community Health Survey (2015), the lowest rates of smoking are reported in British Columbia (14.3%) and Ontario (17.4%). Yet, in the territories, the rates are well above the national average of 18.1% (e.g., Nunavut's is 62%).

Why do such disparities in smoking rates exist? Part of the explanation lies in the social conditions that can encourage/discourage this kind of addictive behaviour. British Columbia is a leader in tobacco control nationally and internationally and has introduced some of the most progressive anti-smoking programs in the country. Strongly supported by the provincial government, these programs have placed a strong emphasis on youth issues, with many school and community resources dedicated to ensuring that youth never start smoking. BC has also initiated programs to increase awareness of tobacco issues and to support smokers who want to quit.

Alexander (2008) offers another provocative perspective on addictions more generally, examining a broad range of unhealthy and destructive behaviours that range from smoking and alcohol to porn, compulsive shopping, and dysfunctional social relationships. His central thesis is that addiction is particularly endemic in a Western free-market society. Drug abuse, for instance, is found to be particularly high among certain socially dislocated groups, such as Indigenous people. This is because free markets inevitably dislocate people from traditional sources of psychological, social, and spiritual support and meaning. In this way, a lack of social integration in this broad sense becomes the precursor of addiction. Overall, Alexander's social theory on addiction provides added weight to the argument that individualizing unhealthy conditions or behaviours can be problematic. Hence, he argues that recognition of the social determinants of health, along with social-environmental and political responses to health problems, are critical. This topic will be examined in further detail in the next section.

HEALTH PROMOTION AND HEALTHY PUBLIC POLICY: SHOULD WE TARGET INDIVIDUALS, FAMILIES, OR SOCIAL CONDITIONS?

A central goal of health policy is to improve the health status of our population. How society should achieve this objective, however, is subject to a great deal of controversy. We all tend to agree that Canadians are very fortunate to have universal health coverage and that the health care system is one of the better ones in the world. It is also recognized that the health care system needs reform, but there is no consensus as to what those changes should be. For example, some analysts argue that we need to move away from a medically dominated, hospital-based health care system and toward more community care, community programs, and prevention/health promotion approaches. Others believe that we require improved medical care and hospital services, including more hospital beds (e.g., see Bolaria and Dickinson, 2002).

Despite this controversy, there are a number of issues highlighted in this chapter that are worthy of further consideration. The first is that health-promotion policies need to target not only individuals and their families but also the underlying conditions that contribute to, or further exacerbate, health inequities and health problems. For example, it may be difficult for an individual to quit smoking if other family members smoke, and if he or she lives, works, or socializes in smoker-friendly environments. There is also growing concern over the advertising of junk food and the fast-food industry, given that fast-food diets are generally low in nutrition and high in fat (Wister, 2005). This type of diet contributes to many health conditions, such as obesity, which is related to diabetes and other health problems. Indeed, obesity rates have skyrocketed over the past two decades, especially among lower-income individuals and children, in tandem with the proliferation of fast-food chains in shopping malls, schools, and even hospitals. This observation calls into question theories that obesity is usually the direct result of genetics, since it is highly improbable that our genes have changed so much in such a short time frame (Wister, 2005).

In Schlosser's well-known and still timely book (later made into a movie) *Fast Food Nation* (2002), we learn how the fast-food industry has been driven by fundamental changes in American society and how it has dramatically altered the diets of families (see box 13.4) The searing portrayal of this industry also shows an almost complete lack of government regulation that manipulates and exploits workers at every point of the production process. Overall, this history of the development of the fast-food industry—similar to that of the tobacco industry—reveals the power and greed of corporate capitalists and governments. In short, by illuminating the role of corporate giants in fostering unhealthy lifestyle choices and a variety of health problems, Schlosser exposes "what really lurks between those sesame-seed buns" (Schlosser, 2002: 10).

Box 13.4: Fast–Food Nation: The Dark Side of the All-American Meal

The extraordinary growth of the fast food industry has been driven by fundamental changes in American society. Adjusted for inflation, the hourly wage of the average US worker peaked in 1973 and then steadily declined for the next 25 years. During that period, women entered the workplace in record numbers, often motivated less by a feminist perspective than by a need to pay the bills. In 1975, about one-third of American mothers with young children worked outside the home; today almost two-thirds of such mothers are employed. As the sociologists Cameron Lynne Macdonald and Carmen Sirianni have noted, the entry of so many women into the workforce has greatly increased demand for the types of services that housewives traditionally perform: cooking, cleaning, and child care. A generation ago, three-quarters of the money used to buy food in the United States was spent to prepare meals at home. Today about half of the money used to buy food is spent at restaurants—mainly at fast food restaurants.

The McDonald's Corporation has become a powerful symbol of America's service economy, which is now responsible for 90% of the country's new jobs. In 1968, McDonald's operated about one thousand restaurants. Today it has about 30,000 restaurants worldwide and opens almost two thousand new ones each year. An estimated one out of every eight workers in the United States has at some point been employed by McDonald's. The company annually hires about one million people, more than any other American organization, public or private. McDonald's is the nation's largest purchaser of beef, pork, and potatoes—and the second largest purchaser of chicken. The McDonald Corporation is the largest owner of retail property in the world. Indeed, the company earns the majority of its profits not from selling food but from collecting rent. McDonald's spends more money on advertising and marketing than any other brand. McDonald's operates more playgrounds than any other private entity in the United States. It is responsible for the nation's bestselling line of children's clothing (McKids) and is one of the largest distributors of toys. A survey of American schoolchildren found that 96% could identify Ronald McDonald. The only fictional character with a higher degree of recognition was Santa Claus. The impact of McDonald's on the way we live today is hard to overstate.

Source: Schlosser, E. 2002. *Fast Food Nation: The Dark Side of the All-American Meal.* New York: Houghton Mifflin (p. 4).

In times of economic constraint, the government tends to provide most support to individual-level approaches for solving health problems, although it is beginning to play a role in regulating the quality of food sold by fast-food chains (e.g., through mandating the reduction of trans fats). However, generally, it is argued that the government adopts a **victim-blaming epidemiology**. From this ideological stance, individuals are to blame for their own problems and it is up to them to adopt a healthier lifestyle (Doyal and Pennell, 1979). Similar to the Victorian notion of "the undeserving poor" (also discussed in chapter 14), this stance applies the equally inappropriate notion of "the undeserving sick," which has strong implications for health care policy (Bolaria and Bolaria, 2002).

Yet, as we have seen throughout this chapter, strategies aimed solely at individuals mask the social production of inequality and the social variability in health. A focus on factory workers' individual lifestyles, for instance, diverts attention from unhealthy and unsafe work environments and a lack of family-friendly work policies. The end result is that health policies are neither comprehensive nor holistic, since they do not treat individuals' illnesses in the context of their everyday lives. Nor do they address the systematic root cause of people's behaviour (e.g., not having enough money to buy a high-quality family dinner in a restaurant) or illness (e.g., poverty and a lack of resources, exploitation). And since earlier health problems contribute to later ones, these strategies are not an investment in long-term solutions.

Moreover, there is concern over the growing power of the pharmaceutical industry and adjacent growth industries (e.g., psychiatry) in our capitalist economy to manufacture and treat health problems once they occur because their primary motivation is making drugs or selling treatments for profit. Consequently, many people are highly critical of these industries and how they treat purported disorders. For example, in her *New York Review of Books* article titled "The Illusions of Psychiatry," Angell (2011) critically examines the

American Psychiatric Association's *Diagnostic and Statistical Manual of Mental Disorders* (DSM), often referred to as the bible of psychiatry, and its enormous influence within American society. She also discusses a book by D. Carlat entitled *Unhinged* (2010) that provides a disillusioned insider's view of the psychiatric profession and the widespread use of psychoactive drugs on children, which she views as "the baleful influence of the pharmaceutical industry on the practice of psychiatry" (Angell, 2011: 2).

In her article, Angell further notes that, while the 1980 edition of the DSM contains 265 diagnoses (up from 182 in the previous edition), the DSM-IV-TR, revised in 2000, contains 365 diagnoses, and a forthcoming edition is expected to be even larger and more expansive. She also documents how the manual came into nearly universal use, not only by psychiatrists, but by insurance companies, hospitals, courts, prisons, schools, researchers, government agencies, and the rest of the medical professions. As psychiatry became a drug-intensive specialty, the pharmaceutical industry was eager to forge bonds with the psychiatric profession. As a result, drug companies began to lavish attention and gifts on psychiatrists, and even began to subsidize meetings of the American Psychological Association and other related conferences. In addition, drug companies began to heavily support many related patient advocacy groups and educational organizations. Yet, according to many outspoken critics of these practices, the use of these drugs is often ineffective and inappropriate, and can have dangerous side effects.

Angell also writes that "there seem to be fashions in childhood psychiatric diagnoses, with one disorder giving way to the next," providing the example of how juvenile bipolar disorder quickly came to replace ADHD to become one of the fastest-growing diagnoses. Arguing that one "would be hard pressed to find a two-year-old who is not sometimes irritable, a boy in fifth grade who is not sometimes inattentive, or a girl in middle school who is not anxious," she observes that whether such children are labelled as having a mental disorder and treated with prescription drugs depends a lot on who they are and the pressures their parents face (Angell, 2011: 5).

Notably, as low-income (American) families experience growing economic hardship, many are finding that one strategy for survival is to apply for Supplemental Security Income (SSI) payments on the basis of mental disability. Hospitals and state welfare agencies also have incentives to encourage uninsured families to apply for SSI, since hospitals will get paid and states will save money. Citing a Rutgers University study that showed that children from low-income families are four times as likely as children with private insurance to receive antipsychotic medicines, Angell concludes that "we need to rethink the care of troubled children. Here the problem is often troubled families in troubled circumstances....Our reliance on psychiatric drugs, seemingly for all of life's discontent, tends to close off other options. In view of the risks and questionable long-term effectiveness of drugs, we need to do better. Above all, we should remember the time-honoured medical dictum: first, do not harm (*primum non nocere*)" (Angell, 2011: 10).

SUMMARY

In this chapter, health and well-being are recognized as more than the absence of disease and illness. An overarching theme of this chapter is that experiences of health and well-being need to be understood within the context of social, cultural, economic, and political environments. For example, government policies and the enormous power of corporations (e.g., pharmaceutical, tobacco, fast food) shape the ability of families to adopt healthy lifestyles. Several key social determinants of health are also identified (such as education and income), since these factors play an influential role in the health status of Canadians. However, it is recognized that complex processes underlie structural conditions, such as access to health care and the availability of personal and public supports. Selected serious health problems and their implications for family relationships are also highlighted. These conditions illustrate how health status and behaviour reciprocally shape family experiences that are embedded within unique ecological or community contexts.

Another central theme of this chapter is the need to create and implement health promotion (the process of improving knowledge and the capacity to improve health) strategies and health policies that target macro-level conditions and families rather than place the responsibility on individuals. For instance, it is noted that low-income families are vulnerable to special risks and conflicts with health-related caregiving demands. In short, they can face "triple jeopardy," with no paid sick leave, no paid vacation leave, and no scheduling flexibility (Heymann, 2000). This creates conditions that place unique strains on caregivers and makes it very difficult to maintain paid employment and achieve financial stability. Also, in an increasingly ethnically diverse society, we require a culturally sensitive health care system that addresses the unique needs of Canadian families in addition to the significant health challenges faced by various cultural groups, in particular, Indigenous families. For example, some recent immigrant groups and refugees have language difficulties and financial barriers, and their cultures' views of health and illness can affect their access and utilization of health care programs.

Finally, given the link between poor health in early life and later life, it is critical to adopt a life-course lens in the development of health policies. In particular, policies and programs need to invest in preventing and reducing inequities early in life rather than Band-aid solutions, a theme that will be revisited in chapter 16. These kinds of efforts will collectively improve our family and collective health and well-being and save health dollars in the future.

QUESTIONS FOR CRITICAL REFLECTION AND DEBATE

1. Discuss the limitations of the persistence of a biomedical clinical framework in the understanding of health and illness and disability.

2. Szasz (1972) argues that mental illness is a myth and that the issues being diagnosed and treated as medical problems by psychiatry are really "psychosocial problems with living." Do you agree or disagree with this viewpoint?
3. To what extent is the media responsible for the health and well-being of young adult men and women? To what extent can our families mitigate these influences, if at all?
4. What are some key ideological and health policy implications of focusing on individual lifestyles and self-imposed risky behaviours such as smoking, unprotected sex, and heavy drinking?
5. Identify some vulnerable populations and their respective challenges in accessing health services and programs.
6. Adopting a life-course perspective, highlight how poor health while in the womb, during infancy, and during childhood shapes life chances and health status in old age.

GLOSSARY

Caregiver burden refers to problems and stress due to caregiving, such as depression and psychological distress.

Epigenetics is the study of how our environment modifies and influences our genetic make-up and its expression over time to create health and illness.

Health and well-being is a state of complete physical, mental, and social wellness, not merely the absence of disease and illness.

Health promotion is the process of increasing the knowledge of health and the capacity to improve it among individuals, groups, and communities.

Lifestyle or style of life denotes individual behaviours, such as smoking and drinking, that are structured by one's social situation.

Social determinants of health are the socio-economic, political, cultural, and environmental forces and factors that influence our health status.

Social epidemiology is the empirical study of the socio-cultural, economic, and political forces that shape patterns of disease and death in human populations.

Social model of disability emphasizes the external obstacles that limit "ableness" rather than individual characteristics per se.

Victim-blaming epidemiology is the tendency to shift the responsibility for illness and disease onto the individual rather than blaming social conditions.

FURTHER READING

Alexander, B.K. 2008.*The Globalization of Addiction: A Study in Poverty of the Spirit.* Toronto: Oxford University Press.
Presents an intriguing social theory on the nature of addictions (ranging from drugs and alcohol to relationship problems, internet porn, and compulsive shopping) from a global perspective by considering the role of social dislocation in a free-market society.

Greenwood, M., S. De Leeuw, N.M. Lindsay, and C. Reading. 2015. *Determinants of Indigenous Peoples' Health in Canada: Beyond the Social.* Toronto: Canadian Scholars' Press.
Covers Indigenous perspectives on health and offers an in-depth focus on the realities of health and health care in Indigenous communities. Written by Indigenous people and relating their perspectives on health, it features an eclectic compilation of research papers and reflective essays from First Nations, Inuit, and Métis writers.

Swain, J., S. French, C. Barnes, and C. Thomas. 2014. *Disabling Barriers, Enabling Environments,* 3rd ed. Los Angeles: Sage.
The authors—many of whom are disabled—provide a multidisciplinary and international approach. This edition features many new topics, including death and dying, sports, hate crimes, and the criminal justice system.

Strohschein, L., and R. Weitz. 2014. *The Sociology of Health, Illness, and Health Care in Canada: A Critical Approach.* Toronto: Nelson Education.
This first Canadian edition challenges students to use their 'sociological imagination' to question aspects of health, illness, and health care that were previously taken for granted. It introduces students to a variety of theories, including Foucaultian theory, Bourdiesian theory, postmodernism, and sociology of the body.

Taylor, D., and G. Filax. 2014. *Disabled Mothers: Stories and Scholarship by and about Mothers with Disabilities.* Bradford: Demeter Press.
Mothers with a variety of physical and mental disabilities explore parenting issues in this collection of 18 scholarly works and personal accounts from Canada, the US, and Australia. The book delves into pregnancy, birth, adoption, child custody, discrimination, and disability politics, combining perspectives of disability studies with the lived experiences of mothering and being mothered.

Weitz, R. 2017. *The Sociology of Health, Illness, and Health Care: A Critical Approach.* 7th ed. Boston: Cengage Learning.

Challenges readers to think creatively and analytically about health and health care. Explores the social forces affecting who gets ill and how we think about illness, including the ethical dilemmas that underlie modern health care as well as the politics behind those dilemmas. Covers topics such as big data in health care and research, the underlying causes of Ebola Virus Disease, and the rise in mobile digital health devices.

RELATED WEB SITES

Canadian Institute of Child Health is dedicated to promoting and protecting the health, well-being, and rights of all children and youth through monitoring, education, and advocacy, http://www.cich.ca/about.html. Facebook: www.facebook.com/Canadian-Institute-of-Child-Health-313427342097626/ Twitter: www.twitter.com/CICH_ICSI

Canadian Institute for Health Information (CIHI) is an independent, not- for- profit organization providing comprehensive information on health of Canadians and Canada's health system. It combines information from variety of databases, evidence based reports, and analyses. CIHI focus is on evaluation of the existing health system and spending but also on other factors influencing health. www.cihi.ca/en. Facebook: www.facebook.com/CIHI.ICIS/ Twitter: www.twitter.com/CIHI_ICIS

Canadian Mental Health Association was founded in 1918 and is one of the oldest voluntary organizations in Canada. It provides research and information, services, workshops, seminars, pamphlets, newsletters, and resource centres, www.cmha.ca. Facebook: www.facebook.com/CANMentalHealth Twitter: www.twitter.com/CMHA_NTL

Canadian Public Health Association is a national, independent association representing public health in Canada with links to the international public health community. Its members believe in universal and equitable access to basic conditions. www.cpha.ca/en/default.aspx. Facebook: www.facebook.com/cpha.acsp Twitter: www.twitter.com/CPHA_ACSP

DisAbled Women's Network Canada (DAWN Canada) is a national feminist organization controlled by and comprised of women who self-identify as women with disabilities and provides personal profiles, a chat room, and related links. www.dawncanada.net/en. Facebook: www.facebook.com/DawnRafhCanada Twitter: www.twitter.com/DAWN-RAFHCanada

Health Canada is the federal government department that encourages the health of Canadians through promotion, prevention activities and such initiatives as DrugsNot4Me.ca Prevention Campaign, the Children's Health and Safety Campaign, as well as Healthy First Nations and Inuit initiative. It also produces publications such as Schizophrenia:

A Handbook for Families, in co-operation with the Schizophrenia Society of Canada. www.hc-sc.gc.ca/index-eng.php.

World Health Organization (WHO) is the United Nation's specialized agency that began in 1948. Its primary goal is to coordinate international health, to address non-communicable and communicable diseases and to ensure survival and promote health throughout the life-course. www.who.int/en. Facebook: www.facebook.com/WHO Twitter: www.twitter.com/who YouTube channel: www.youtube.com/user/who/videos.

REFERENCES

Adams, P.J. 2016. "Switching to a Social Approach to Addiction: Implications for Theory and Practice." *International Journal of Mental Health and Addiction*. 14: 86-94.

Alexander, B.K. 2008.*The Globalization of Addiction: A Study in Poverty of the Spirit*. Toronto: Oxford University Press.

Alzheimer Society of Canada. 2010. *Rising Tide: The Impact of Dementia on Canadian Society*. Toronto: Alzheimer Society of Canada.

Alzheimer Society of Canada. 2016. "Dementia Numbers in Canada." Retrieved September 2, 2016 from www.alzheimer.ca/en/About-dementia/What-is-dementia/Dementia-numbers.

Angell, M. 2011 (July 14). "The Illusions of Psychiatry." *The New York Review of Books*. Retrieved January 16, 2011 from www.nybooks.com/articles/archives/2011/jul/14/illusions-of-psychiatry.

BC Ministry of Health Services. 2016. "Quitting Tobacco and Tobacco Use." Retrieved September 2, 2106 from www2.gov.bc.ca/gov/content/health/managing-your-health/mental-health-substance-use/quitting-smoking-tobacco-use.

Boland, F.J., R. Burrill, M. Duwyn, and J. Karp. 1998. *Fetal Alcohol Syndrome: Implications for the Corrections Service*. Ottawa: Correctional Service Canada.

Bolaria, B.S., and R. Bolaria. 2002. "Personal and Structural Determinants of Health and Illness: Lifestyle and Life Chances." In B.S. Bolaria and H.D. Dickinson (eds.), *Health and Illness and Health Care in Canada,* 3rd ed. (pp. 445–459). Toronto: Nelson-Thomson Learning.

Bolaria, B.S., and H.D. Dickinson (eds.). 2002. *Health, Illness, and Health Care in Canada,* 3rd ed. Toronto: Nelson Thomson.

Canadian Centre on Substance Abuse (CCSA). 2015. "Deaths Involving Fentanyl in Canada, 2009-2014." CCENDU Bulletin, August 2015. Retrieved September 1, 2016 from www.ccsa.ca/Resource%20Library/CCSA-CCENDU-Fentanyl-Deaths-Canada-Bulletin-2015-en.pdf.

Canadian Community Health Survey. 2015. "Smoking on the Decline." Retrieved September 1, 2016 from www.statcan.gc.ca/daily-quotidien/150617/dq150617b-eng.htm.

Canadian Press. 2016 (August 18). "Overdose Deaths Continue to Climb in BC as Fentanyl Use Spreads." Retrieved September 1, 2016 from www.thestar.com/news/canada/2016/08/18/overdose-deaths-continue-to-climb-in-bc-as-fentanyl-use-spreads.html

Centre for ADHD Awareness, Canada. 2016. "What is Attention Deficit Hyperactivity Disorder?" Retrieved August 30, 2016 from www.caddac.ca/cms/page.php?67.

Child and Family Canada. 2005. *Fact Sheet #18—Children with Special Needs.* Retrieved October 20, 2005, from www.cfc-efc.ca/docs/vocfc/00018_en.htm.

CMHA (Canadian Mental Health Association). 2016. "Homelessness." Retrieved September 9, 2016 from www.cmha.ca/public-policy/subject/homelessness.

Doyal, L., and I. Pennell. 1979. *The Political Economy of Health.* London: Pluto Press.

Fang, M.L., Sixsmith, J., Sinclair, S., and G. Horst. 2016. "A Knowledge Synthesis of Culturally- and Spiritually-Sensitive End-of-Life Care: Findings from a Scoping Review." *BMC Geriatrics* 16. Retrieved September 1, 2016 from www.bmcgeriatr.biomedcentral.com/articles/10.1186/s12877-016-0282-6.

Gulati, N., and T. Ray. 2016. "Inequality, Neighborhoods and Welfare of the Poor." *Journal of Development Economics* 122: 214-228.

Haaf, W. 2015 (September 10). "The Cost of Raising a Special needs Child." *Today's Parent.* Retrieved August 30, 2016 from www.todaysparent.com/family/family-budget/the-cost-of-raising-a-special-needs-child.

Heymann, J. 2000. *The Widening Gap: Why America's Working Families Are in Jeopardy and What Can Be Done about It.* New York: Basic Books.

Jones, D.W. 2004. "Families and Serious Mental Illness: Working with Loss and Ambivalence." *British Journal of Social Work* 34: 961–979.

Leyton, M. and S. Stewart. 2014. *Substance Abuse in Canada: Childhood and Adolescent Pathways to Substance Use Disorders.* Ottawa, ON: Canadian Centre on Substance Abuse.

Litt, J. 2004. "Women's Carework in Low-Income Households: The Special Case of Children with Attention Deficit Hyperactivity Disorder." *Gender and Society* 18: 625–644.

MacRae, H. 2002. "The Identity Maintenance Work of Family Members of Persons with Alzheimer's Disease." *Canadian Journal on Aging* 21: 405–415.

Mirowsky, J., and C.E. Ross. 1998. "Education, Personal Control, Lifestyle, and Health: A Human Capital Hypothesis." *Research on Aging* 20: 415–449.

Mirowsky, J., C.E. Ross, and J. Reynolds. 2000. "Links between Social Status and Health Status." In C.E. Bird, P. Conrad, and A.M. Fremon (eds.), *Handbook of Medical Sociology,* 5th ed. (pp. 47–67). Upper Saddle River: Prentice-Hall.

Novak, M., L. Campbell, and H. Northcott. 2014. *Aging and Society: Canadian Perspectives,* 7th ed. Toronto: Nelson.

Office for Disability Issues, 2001. Disability in Canada: A 2001 Profile. Gatineau, Quebec: Human Resources Development Canada.

Orford, J., R. Velleman, G. Natera, L. Templeton, and A. Copello. 2013. "Addiction in the Family as a Major but Neglected Contributor to the Global Burden of Adult Ill-Health." *Social Science and Medicine* 78: 70-77.

Owen, M. 2014. "Lack of Support: Canadian Families and Disabilities." In D. Cheal and P. Albanese, (eds.), *Canadian Families Today: New Perspectives,* 3rd ed. (pp. 248-269). Toronto: Oxford University Press.

Ragan, D.T., W. Osgood, and M.E. Feinberg. 2014. "Friends as a Bridge to Parental Influence: Implications for Adolescent Alcohol Use." *Social Forces* 92: 1061-1085.

Raphael, D. (ed.). 2004. *Social Determinants of Health: Canadian Perspectives.* Toronto: Canadian Scholars' Press Inc.

Roach, P., N. Drummond, and J. Keady. 2016. "'Nobody would say that it is Alzheimer's or Dementia at this Age': Family Adjustment Following a Diagnosis of Early-Onset Dementia." *Journal of Aging Studies* 36: 26-32.

Sagan, Aleksandra. 2015. "Fentanyl deaths are a Canada-wide 'disaster.'" *CBC News*, 10 August.

Schlosser, E. 2002. *Fast Food Nation: The Dark Side of the All-American Meal.* New York: Perennial.

Song, J., F.J. Floyd, M. Seltzer, J.S. Greenberg, and J. Hong. 2010. "Long-term Effects of Child Death on Parents' Health-Related Quality of Life: A Dyadic Analysis." *Family Relations* 59: 269–282.

Statistics Canada. 2015. "Canadian Survey on Disability, 2012." Retrieved August 30, 2016 from www5.statcan.gc.ca/olc-cel/olc.action?objId=89-654-X&objType=2&lang=en&limit=0.

Szasz, T.S. 1972. *The Myth of Mental Illness: Foundations of a Theory of Personal Conduct.* Frogmore: Paladin.

Sudhinaraset, M., C. Wigglesworth, and D.T. Takeuchi. 2016. "Social and Cultural Contexts of Alcohol Use: Influences in a Social-Ecological Framework." *Alcohol Research: Current Reviews* 38: 35-45.

WHO. 2012. *Dementia: A Public Health Priority.* Geneva: World Health Organization.

WHO. 1946. *Preamble to the Constitution of the World Health Organization.* New York: International Health Conference

Wister, A.V. 2005. *Baby Boomer Health Dynamics: How Are We Aging?* Toronto: University of Toronto Press.

CHAPTER 14

Trying to Make Ends Meet:
Family Poverty, Living on the Margins,
and Financial Struggle

LEARNING OBJECTIVES

In this chapter you will learn that ...

- Canada is a stratified society in which some families and children experience extensive poverty
- definitions and meanings of poverty vary across time and place
- it is common for the general public and the media to blame the individual for their financial condition
- many families, such as the working poor, experience great economic hardship despite living above or close to the poverty line
- certain social groups (e.g., women, people with disabilities, Indigenous people) are more vulnerable to poverty than others
- an increasing proportion of families, including middle-class ones, is being squeezed financially
- studies establish a link between economic hardship and a number of negative outcomes that reverberate over the life course and among generations

INTRODUCTION

Many of us associate poverty with malnourished children with sunken eyes and bloated bellies living in drought-ridden regions of the world. We might picture poverty in our own country as homeless people who sleep in back alleys, push shopping carts with all their belongings, and hold out cups to strangers on city streets for money. And while the latter image certainly portrays poverty in Canada, it is not typical of the average poor person. Indeed, poverty in Canada is not necessarily a matter of starving or begging on a street corner, but rather of asking for food at shelters and food banks. It is also a matter of barely being able to make ends meet and struggling to pay for life's basic necessities, such as shelter, transportation, clothing, and food. Moreover, poverty is not just a lack of riches, but rather an unequal distribution of them.

Recent statistics that summarize how Canada is doing in addressing child and family poverty shows a relatively dismal assessment. Based on 2014 statistics, 1 in 7 (4.9 million) people in Canada live in poverty. Marginalized groups are particularly vulnerable to poverty, including those living with disabilities, Aboriginal people, the elderly, and racialized communities (Canada Without Poverty, 2016). And from an international perspective on poverty, Canada is not far behind many other industrialized countries such as the United States. This may be surprising to many of us, since we often assume there are significantly higher rates of poverty to the south or farther outside our borders. The sad reality is that poverty and economic hardship are a significant social problem for many Canadian families and their children, with consequences that entail struggle and hardship in everyday life as well as over the life course.

MEASURING POVERTY

There are two basic definitions and measures of poverty in Canada—absolute and relative (see table 14.1 for definitions and examples of different measures). The idea behind **absolute poverty** is that an absolute measure can be determined by examining an essential basket of goods and services deemed necessary for survival. In other words, what bare necessities are sufficient to keep the human body alive? A basic basket would include food provided by a food bank, shelter provided by a community hostel, second-hand clothing from a thrift shop, and access to basic remedial health care. The poverty line implied by such a budget would obviously be very low, such that an annual income of mere thousands of dollars would probably cover it.

Fortunately, prevailing definitions of absolute poverty tend to be more generous, taking into consideration such factors as social well-being, cost of living, region size, and family size. One of the most commonly used definitions is Statistics Canada's low-income cut-off point (LICO) after tax (Kerr and Michalski, 2014). This definition is more conservative than others, such as that offered by the Canadian Council of Social Development (which therefore calculates higher rates of poverty). Statistics Canada LICOs, which are

Table 14.1: Examples of Absolute and Relative Poverty and Low-Income Cut-Off Concepts and Definitions: What Are We Measuring?

Absolute Poverty	Who Uses?	Applicability
$1.90 US per day (minimum survival budget, effective in October 2015)	World Bank	international/global poverty line only useful for some developing countries
Basic Needs Poverty Line (BNL) Meeting basic needs	Fraser Institute	Advanced industrialized allowance societies; no allowance for recreation and culture
Market Basket Measure (MBM) Basket concept, meeting modest needs	Statistics Canada	Canada; includes necessities and some social amenities; takes into consideration a nutritious diet and regional/geographic differences
Relative Poverty	**Who Uses?**	**Applicability**
Exclusion from mainstream resources, opportunities, and sources of well-being	Canadian Council on Social Development	Advanced industrialized societies
Exclusion from the standards of living broadly available to others in same society	Organization for Economic Co-operation and Development (OECD)	Advanced industrialized societies
Low Income Measure (LIM); falling below a threshold relative to changing income of population	Statistics Canada	Canada; relative to annual national household incomes, set at one-half of the median income in a given year
Low-Income Cut-off	**Who Uses?**	**Applicability**
Higher percentage of income than average spent on necessities of life (food, shelter, clothing)	Statistics Canada	Canada; considers family and community size and changes in household spending patterns

Sources: Adapted from: Lammam, C., and H. MacIntyre. 2016. "An Introduction to the State of Poverty in Canada". Vancouver: Fraser Institute. Retrieved August 9, 2016, from www.fraserinstitute.org/studies/an-introduction-to-the-state-of-poverty-in-canada; Statistics Canada. 2016. "Low Income Lines: What They Are and How They Are Created." *Income Research Paper Series*, Catalogue no. 75F0002M-No.002, Ottawa: Minister of Industry; and The World Bank. 2016. Poverty Overview-Context (updated April 13, 2016). Retrieved August 9, 2016, from www.worldbank.org/en/topic/poverty/overview.

updated periodically, account for community and family size (see table 14.2 for Statistics Canada LICOs, and the poverty lines are set at a level where a family spends significantly more of its income on food, clothing, and housing than the average. The MBM (Market Basket Measure), in use since 2002, includes allowances for food, household expenses, clothing, personal needs, furniture, telephone, and entertainment.

However, as argued by Ward (2002), these cut-off points are somewhat arbitrary or artificial, since a family with an income 10% above the poverty line could afford only a

Table 14.2: Fact Sheet: 2014 Poverty Lines, after Tax

Family Size	Community Size				
	Cities of 500,000+	**100,000– 499,000**	**30,000– 99,000**	**Less than 30,000**	**Rural areas**
1	$20,160	$17,050	$16,836	$15,093	$13,188
2	$24,536	$20,750	$20,493	$18,370	$16,051
3	$30,553	$25,839	$25,517	$22,873	$19,987
4	$38,117	$32,236	$31,835	$28,537	$24,934
5	$43,404	$36,707	$36,251	$32,495	$28,394
6	$48,136	$40,709	$40,204	$36,038	$31,489
7+	$52,869	$44,711	$44,155	$39,581	$34,585

*Low Income cut-offs after tax (LICO-AT) are based on the 1992 Family Expenditures Survey

Source: Statistics Canada. 2016. CANSIM Table 206-0094-Low Income Cut-offs (LICOs) before and after Tax by Community and Family Size in Current Dollars. Ottawa: Minister of Industry. Retrieved August 15, 2016, from www5.statcan.gc.ca/cansim/a26?lang=eng&retrLang=eng&id=2060094&tabMode=da taTable&srchLan=-1&p1=-1&p2=9.

couple of cups a coffee per day more than a family at the poverty line. Other critics of this approach also ask "Who defines what is essential to keep a family out of poverty?" pointing out that what is really being measured is **relative poverty** (Harman, 2005; Jackson, 2000).

Relative poverty is what is considered poor relative to what the contemporary social standards are for normal and wealthy. It can also have a subjective component. For example, most of us probably feel poor compared to Donald Trump or Paris Hilton, yet we might feel wealthy relative to people living in drought-ridden parts of Africa or on Canadian streets. However, these reference points are obviously not fair comparisons, since we are more likely to compare ourselves to our neighbours (keeping up with the Joneses) or to our peer groups in our community. Moreover, these standards are not permanent; they can change according to economic fluctuations, technological developments, and varying definitions of the "good life" (Harman, 2005). They can also fluctuate over the course of our lives in response to expectations we might hold at certain points in time. For example, as a university student, you might feel relatively well off if you live at home and have access to your parents' car, some cash in your pockets, and a small savings account to meet your basic monthly expenses. However, if at the age of 40 (now married with two kids) you are in the same situation, you might feel relatively poor, since you probably expected to own your own home and car, and to have more financial resources.

Moreover, factors that influence the impact of poverty on families are its duration and depth. Duration refers to how long the experience of poverty lasts; its repercussions will probably be very different depending on how long the family remains poor. When poverty is experienced in childhood and adulthood, chances are good that its effects will be felt into old age. This is because disadvantages that begin in childhood (e.g., lack of a good education, malnutrition, stress) accumulate over time to produce deficits in employment and health in mid- and later life. Also, when poverty is prolonged, everyday resources are eventually depleted, making it difficult to get ahead. Depth of poverty, on the other hand, is how far below the poverty line a family or an individual income is. The deeper the level of poverty, the more difficult it is to provide basic needs (Ward, 2002). Furthermore, the experience of poverty can also be affected by the availability and quality of durable support networks like family, community, and government, which are found to be malleable and in flux over the life course (Gazso, McDaniel, and Waldron, 2016).

Finally, while there are numerous definitions of economic vulnerability, its opposite, **economic security**, has been defined by the Canadian Council on Social Development (CCSD) as follows:

> Economic security refers to an assured and stable standard of living that provides individuals and families with a level of resources and benefits necessary to participate economically, politically, socially, culturally, and with dignity in their community's activities. Security goes beyond mere physical survival to encompass a level of resources that promotes social inclusion. (Jackson et al., 2002: 7)

WHY ARE SOME FAMILIES POORER THAN OTHERS? BLAMING THE VICTIM AND SOCIAL REPRODUCTION OF POVERTY ARGUMENTS

What are the origins of poverty? Obviously, the answer is not simple, since most of the conditions people find themselves in are not the result of one causal factor. Yet, it is common to hear one of two common explanations for this phenomenon. The first, which we will call the "blame the victim" argument, focuses on personal sources and places blame squarely on the shoulders of the individual. Early sociologists such as Herbert Spencer considered poverty a marker of human genetic fitness (or rather, "unfitness"). In other words, people are poor because they lack the abilities, such as the IQ or the creativity, to become anything else. In a similar vein, the **culture of poverty** thesis (Lewis, 1966) holds that certain types of cultures restrict people from reaching their potential. It is argued that poor families tend to develop fatalistic values and attitudes and low aspirations; they are politically apathetic, devalue education, and reject middle-class definitions of success. Once this culture is in place, it develops mechanisms that perpetuate it, even if structural conditions change. This creates a self-fulfilling prophecy in which failure is inevitable and poverty perpetuates poverty (Harman, 2005).

Not surprisingly, this theory is not without controversy, and critics maintain that it contains many problems. Notably, it assumes that an individual's behaviours are caused by their values, rather than their conditions or their constraints in life. The theory also leads to a circular or tautological argument in relating values to behaviour, such as "individuals have little interest in success because they have a culture characterized by low success." Conversely, research shows that most poor people do not want to be poor and actually value middle-class lifestyles (e.g., see Liebow, 2003). However, they are unable to attain the opportunities (e.g., good jobs) needed to be able to afford these lifestyles. The culture of poverty theory also assumes that people's culture is fixed or static, and that it cannot change. Moreover, the idea that people in certain racial or ethnic groups have a culture is not very compelling when trying to understand the disparities in poverty in these groups. Indeed, as noted in chapter 3, a single culture can represent very diverse families. There are more intra-group differences (differences between individuals in a group) than inter-group differences (differences between groups).

A second explanation locates the source of poverty in systems or structures. According to this belief, it is social conditions such as discrimination and unequal opportunities that generate poverty, especially in the educational and occupational realms. Major causes of poverty are also linked to macro fluctuations in the economy (i.e., the global recession; restructuring of the labour market resulting in fewer permanent career jobs), the decline of well-paid, unionized, entry-level manufacturing jobs, and pay inequity due to gender. These causes are also associated with the **social reproduction of poverty**, the tendency for social stratification to reproduce itself generationally. As a result, a child born into poverty inherits similar social and economic conditions and opportunities as his or her parents, resulting in a relatively similar socio-economic status later in life.

The general public, the media, and public policy makers tend to favour and present personal, rather than structural explanations. Media targeted at adults and children (e.g., movies), for instance, are found to portray poverty and class inequality as the result of individual merit and moral worth. This idea is supported and expanded upon in a recent study by Streib, Ayala, and Wixted (2016) that focuses on the framing of poverty and social class inequality in children's movies. Based on the content analysis of the highest grossing G-rated movies (ones that earned more than $100 million, such as "Aladdin," "The Jungle Book," and "Toy Story") and the proportional representations of characters, the researchers found that benign (unproblematic) metaframes are more common than malevolent ones, and they appear through that which is visible and invisible. For example, in Aladdin, the main character is homeless and hungry. And although he views his life as difficult, Jasmine, who is a princess, views her life as equally hard. These researchers conclude that, "Overall, the sampled movies repeatedly downplay and sanitize poverty and social class inequality, while less often highlighting and justifying them. The benign metaframe legitimizes poverty and social class inequality by suggesting that they create so few problems that they are not worth changing" (Streib, Ayala, and Wixted, 2016: 16).

However, most individuals born into poverty do not have opportunities to become wealthy adults, just as most people born into wealth do not become poor adults. This is particularly evident at the extreme ends of the social class spectrum. Despite this, there may be some movement in upward (or downward) social or economic mobility. Indeed, many social demographers note that living in Canada relative to other countries (e.g., the United States) provides more advantages with regard to upward economic mobility (e.g., Kerr and Michalski, 2014). In Canada, generous public transfers and a strong public education system help reduce the incidence of poverty. Therefore, a child raised in a working-class family could more easily obtain a university degree (which is an important predictor of economic success in establishing oneself in the workplace) here than in other countries.

Yet, poverty in Canada is socially structured to the extent that social classes tend to reproduce themselves. For instance, young adults whose parents attended university are far more likely to pursue that education than those whose parents did not go to university. The fact that poverty tends to be socially structured also means that certain groups are more vulnerable to poverty than others. This idea is also supported by the latest studies in intergenerational mobility, as documented by Statistics Canada (2016). They measured intergenerational mobility by comparing the income of parents with the income of their children. The study found that a child's future income level in Canada is more strongly determined by his/her father's income than previously thought. This is especially evident in sons with high-earning fathers, since these fathers pass their economic advantage on to their sons. This advantage was also passed along to daughters, but the effect was somewhat weaker.

TRENDS IN POVERTY AND SOCIAL GROUPS VULNERABLE TO POVERTY

It is estimated that about 2 out of 10 Canadian children live in poverty, and it is well documented that some children are at a greater risk of poverty than others. For example, some children may be poorer than others by virtue of where they were born or where they grew up. Data consistently document these regional and other subgroup variations in child poverty, as well as the average amount required in order to reach the poverty line in these areas. These regional differences provide a good example of how poverty is socially structured, and they reflect differences in such aspects as employment and economic opportunities and conditions. Rural, remote, and smaller resource-rich communities, in particular, often face unique challenges and disadvantages with respect to viability and sustainability, making families particularly vulnerable to poverty (Ryser and Halseth, 2016). Additionally, subgroup variations in child poverty rates show how persistent social and economic inequality lead to a stronger likelihood of experiencing poverty. In figure 14.1, we can see how immigrants, racialized groups, people with an Indigenous identity, and those with a disability are clearly at a higher risk for poverty than others.

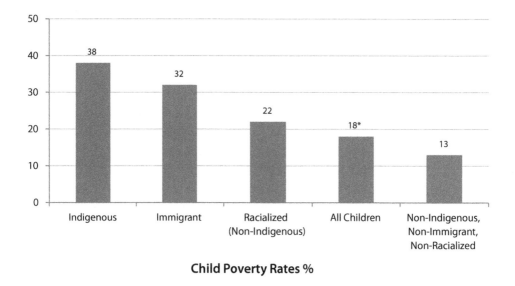

Child Poverty Rates %

Figure 14.1: Child Poverty Rates (in Percentages) for Selected Social Groups in Canada: Children 0–14 Years

Note: Child poverty rate for 2013 is estimated at 19% by both Raising the Roof, "Putting an End to Child & Family Homelessness in Canada" (2016), and by Campaign 2000, "2015 Report Card on Child and Family Poverty in Canada." This 2013 estimate is based on the LIM-AT measure using Statistics Canada annual T1 Family File, based on the 2011 National Household Survey, updated from Census 2006.

Source: MacDonald, D., and D. Wilson. 2016. *Shameful Neglect. Indigenous Child Poverty in Canada.* Ottawa: Canada Centre for Policy Alternatives. Retrieved August 8, 2016, from www.policyalternatives.ca/publications/reports/shameful-neglect.

Furthermore, there has been little progress in narrowing the gap between rich and poor families. Many have argued that the distribution of income between classes has remained remarkably intransigent over the past 50 years (e.g., Harman, 2005). Statistics also reveal that the average income of the wealthiest share of families with children increased more than twice as much over the past several decades. The slow growth of the average income of all families with children also shows why middle-income families experience economic insecurity. Furthermore, it is observed that since the early 1990s, tax changes at all levels of government have rendered a somewhat progressive tax system less progressive. The result of these trends show that high-income Canadians gained the most, and that inequality among the classes was aggravated (Campaign 2000, 2011).

Moreover, using a feminist political economy lens, Gazso (2007) argues that the retrenchment of the welfare state and changes to social policy have made it increasingly difficult for many of the poorest parents to get ahead. As far as social assistance, it is documented that entitlement to state-based income support is increasingly contingent on employability efforts (e.g., mandatory job searches, participation in welfare-to-work programs). She states that "this entitlement relationship is implicated by simultaneous and contradictory processes embedded in neo-liberal restructuring—gendering and familization—that problematically affect parents' ability to balance their actual or potential employability expectations with family caregiving demands" (Gazso, 2007: 32).

Consequently, it is argued that welfare reform threatens feminist gains and social justice goals. It also undermines family and financial stability, since parents are forced to adopt survival strategies to manage these competing demands just to stay afloat. Hence, living on social assistance in neo-liberal times is "analogous to trying to stay afloat in a leaking life raft that keeps changing course, and at times, appears more or less buoyant" (Gazso, 2007: 55). Thus, this research reveals growing obstacles for vulnerable families to make ends meet. It also dispels the popular idea that most of these parents are using and abusing the system, getting a free ride. Not only it is very difficult for individuals to access and understand all of the complicated policy rules and regulations, but maintaining eligibility for such meagre benefits can hardly be considered a pleasant or lucrative financial experience.

The Working Poor

Many people who live in poverty have jobs; they are called the **working poor**. Although there are numerous definitions, The Metcalf Foundation—a private family organization established in 1960 that helps Canadians to imagine and build a just, healthy, and creative society—defines a member of the working poor as someone between 18 and 64 who is not a student, lives independently, earns at least $3,000 a year, and whose after-tax income is below the Low-Income Measure. Despite being employed, these individuals may be earning only minimum wage. These rates have not kept pace with inflation. In 2016, the minimum wage ranged from a low of $10.85 in British Columbia to a high of $13.00 in Nunavut; these amounts are deemed by many to be inadequate to cover basic living costs. Since housing is particularly expensive, families have to cut back in other areas, one of which is food. Food insecurity is the uncertainty of being able to buy enough nutritious food (see figure 14.2 for prevalence of food insecurity by household income). To fill this need, families turn for help to food banks, soup kitchens, and friends or relatives.

The first food bank in Canada opened in Edmonton in 1981, at the height of a deepening recession, in order to assist poor individuals and families on an emergency basis. The number of food banks continued to grow throughout the 1980s and they have become well entrenched in our communities as a common response to hunger (Kerr and Michalski, 2014). However, many critics charge that while food banks help the needy to cope, they do not directly address root causes of hunger and thereby do not create long-term, stable solutions (see box 14.1).

According to a report by Food Banks Canada (2016), 850,000 people turn to food banks each month and more than one-third of these are children and youth. However,

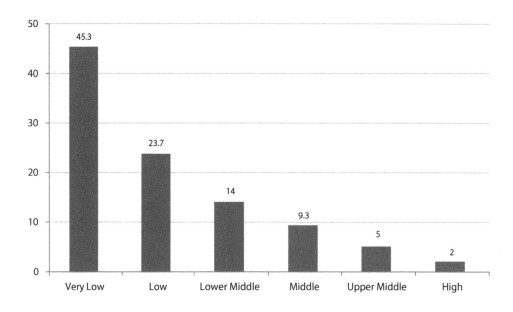

Figure 14.2: Prevalence of Food Insecurity (in Percentages), by Household Income, 2012

Source: Data based on the 2012 Canadian Community Health Survey. Cited in: Tarasuk, V., A. Mitchell, and N. Dachner. 2014. "Household Food Insecurity in Canada, 2012." Toronto: Research to Identify Policy Options to Reduce Food Insecurity (PROOF). Retrieved August 9, 2016, from www.nutritionalsciences.lamp. utoronto.ca.

food bank users are diverse and come from many different backgrounds. Typical users include families with children, employed people whose low wages do not cover basic living essentials, individuals on social assistance, and those on a fixed income, including seniors and people with disabilities. These findings show how some social groups are disproportionately affected by poverty and economic hardship, further revealing how social stratification has its roots in structured inequities rather than being simply the result of individual failure. For example, among all ages and social groups, women tend to be more vulnerable to poverty than men.

Moreover, Hatcher (2016), a law professor, argues that a highly lucrative poverty industry has emerged and grown over time. This industry offers many benefits to the government and related businesses. Although Hatcher applies his ideas to American society, which has a very different kind of social safety net, his analysis offers some provocative ideas. His compelling analysis shows how the guise of helping out our most vulnerable populations may be illusionary. For instance, foster care agencies can team up with companies to take away disability and survivor benefits from abused and neglected children. Additionally, other forms of social assistance (e.g., welfare payments) are often turned into highly profitable sources of revenue for other capitalists in realms ranging from payday loan centres, casinos, and lotteries, to rent-to-own centres and pawnshops.

Box 14.1: The Problem with Food Banks

There's something horribly wrong when Canada produces plenty of food for everyone, yet there are many people who depend on food banks to get enough to eat, says Graham Riches, the co-editor of a new book that examines how wealthy countries around the world address hunger.

A retired director of the school of social work at the University of British Columbia, Riches co-edited *First World Hunger Revisited: Food Charity or the Right to Food?* with Tiina Silvasti, a social and public policy professor from Finland.

"Hunger has successfully been socially constructed as a matter for charity and not an issue requiring the priority attention of the state and public policy," says a chapter, co-authored by Riches and Valerie Tarasuk at the University of Toronto, that deals with Canada's response to hunger.

The writers look at food insecurity and the rise of food banks in a dozen countries including the United States, Australia, Spain, Brazil, and South Africa. They find common patterns that Riches attributes to the spread of global neo-liberalism, with its reduced role for governments and lack of support for people left outside the labour market.

"The ineffectiveness of charitable food banks is masked by their high degree of public legitimacy," Riches and Tarasuk write. "Increasingly they have become embedded within popular and now corporate culture as practical compassion and a common-sense response to household food insecurity and the country's broken social safety net."

The Greater Vancouver Food Bank Warehouse on Prior Street. Photo: Colleen Kimmett

Source: McLeod, A. 2015. "How Hunger Became a First-World Problem: Food Needs to Be Recognized as a Right." *The Tyee,* February 24. Retrieved August 9, 2016, from www.thetyee.ca/Culture/2015/02/24/Hunger-First-World-Problem.

Box 14.2: Working Poor: Stuck between Getting Ahead and Losing It All

Unaccustomed to hosting guests at her tiny, dilapidated Hespeler apartment, Marjorie Knight politely apologizes as she sets out two mismatched chairs in hopes of creating a comfortable place for conversation. "I never, ever expected I would be in this kind of situation," she soon confessed. "I never expected to be poor."

Still struggling to reconcile her current reality with the life she had always envisioned, Knight ponders out lout. She's not looking for luck, merely for an opportunity to prove what she's capable of doing if given the chance. "When you sit with me, what do you see...when you speak with me, what do you hear? I'm an intelligent person. I work. I have a good work ethic. Why did I end up where I am?"

Born in Canada but raised in Jamaica, Knight served as an executive manager of a popular Jamaican vacation resort. As an educated administrator who possessed resourceful thinking and problem-solving skills, Knight earned a solid living for her family. But after she came to Cambridge 11 years ago she could not secure a full-time job in the hospitability field. A lack of Canadian experience appeared as a red flag on her resume. Desperately worried about providing for her two daughters, still young at the time, Knight finally found work through a temp agency at a local energy company's call centre. The pay wasn't substantial, but the hours were regular. She kept her family afloat and was even able to buy a home.

The thin layer on which she had hoped to build a foundation for her family shattered when the call centre closed. Unable to find a job quickly, Knight depleted her savings and her pension, and ultimately couldn't fend off bankruptcy. She had little choice but to swap a permanent address for temporary residence in a local homeless shelter. Eventually, after finding work as a data entry clerk at a Kitchener furniture store, where she still works six years later, Knight can afford a $700 a-month rental unit in a second-storey apartment in Hespeler.

Despite the fact that she works between 40 and 44 hours per week, Knight's life barely hovers above the poverty line. During our conversation, she revealed that she had only an extra loonie to last until payday, still five days away. By the time rent is paid and bus passes are purchased—to get to work and back—there's little left but spare change. "It's literally month to month," she said. "You're paycheque to paycheque. I've had days where I sat there and tried to figure out whether I'm going to buy food or I'm going to buy a bus pass."

Knight is not alone in living in such tenuous circumstances. She is part of a disturbing and rapidly growing socio-economic class known as the working poor. This working class may put in the equivalent of full time hours, yet their low-income wages are barely enough to survive, let alone thrive. Benefits are a rarity.

According to a report by the Worker's Action Centre, *Still Working on the Edge*, Ontario is developing a low-wage economy populated by workers who are trapped in part-time jobs that pay minimum wage. Research conducted by the centre maintains that since the recession, many full-time, well-paying jobs have vanished and been replaced by part-time, temporary and contract jobs that pay lower wages and often don't come with benefits. Those caught in this low-wage trap aren't there because they're lazy, emphasizes Knight. It's not for lack of trying. "When you talk about the working poor, and people who are economically disadvantaged, there's a whole new set of us out there," she explained. While there are those who grew up poor and are well-versed in navigating government social assistance, there are also those who have fallen due to circumstances beyond their control. According to its report, the number of part-time jobs available is growing faster than that of full-time jobs. In 2014, 33% of employees worked in low-wage jobs, compared to 22% 10 years ago. For Knight, life is a daily walk across a tightrope with no safety net.

Those living like this are also fighting a stigma that paints them as lazy. It's a myth that Knight would like to break. And she walks that talk. The Cambridge woman has done recent mission work in Kenya. She often volunteers at a food bank in the region, yet refuses to bring any items home with her. "There are so many people worse off than me; how can I just go into a food bank?"

Knight is currently studying for her Bachelor of Social Work at the University of Waterloo to become a personal support worker. Her tuition is paid by a relative.

Source: Adapted from Rutledge, L. 2015. "Working Poor: Stuck between Getting Ahead and Losing It All." *Cambridge Times*, June 12. Retrieved October 1, 2017, from https://www.cambridgetimes.ca/news-story/5673990-working-poor-stuck-between-getting-ahead-and-losing-it-all/

Women

It is well established that poverty tends to affect women more than men. This has led researchers to call the growth of poverty among women the **feminization of poverty**, a term coined by Diana Pearce in 1978. The women with the highest risk of living in poverty are single mothers. Poverty rates are about 10% for two-parent families and 22.2% for families headed by a single parent, but the rate for single mothers with children under six is 52.1% (Campaign 2000, 2011). Finding affordable housing is a particularly difficult challenge for single-parent families, particularly in large urban centres.

Moreover, although the percentage of women in the paid labour market is higher than before and women are increasingly becoming the primary bread-winners, they still earn less than men and are more likely to be in part-time or non-standard employment that pays low wages or minimum wage. Women are more likely to be employed as low paid, non-unionized, part-time workers in clerical, sales, and service jobs (pink-collar jobs).

Men's work, conversely, has been compartmentalized into more highly paid, high-status white-collar jobs and relatively well-paid blue-collar sectors (Campaign 2000, 2011).

Disabled Individuals

The World Health Organization defines disability as "any restriction or lack (resulting from impairment) of ability to perform an activity in the manner or within the range considered normal for a human being" (WHO, 1976). This definition suggests the essence of the experience of being in a disabled body in the sense that the world of work, family, and life in general is the privileged sphere of non-disabled people, or the "normals." It was not that long ago that those who did not conform to the category of normal were regarded as freaks, not entitled to work in the public sphere, or to have love, happiness, and family in the private sphere (Goffman, 1963; Harman, 2005).

Fortunately, times have changed and opportunities for disabled individuals have broadened on many levels, yet previous and continuing discrimination have left disabled people vulnerable to poverty. When Statistics Canada (2014) asked persons with disabilities whether they had perceived employment discrimination in the past five years, 12% reported having been refused a job as a result of their condition. Moreover, they also found that the employment rate of Canadians with disabilities aged 25 to 64 was 49% in 2011, compared with 79% for those without a disability. While it is recognized that some disabilities can be more limiting than others, among those with a severe disability the employment rate was 26%.

Moreover, the prevalence rate of working-age people with disabilities who are living below Statistics Canada's LICO is 15%, compared to 6.5% for those who do not have a disability. Rates also vary widely depending upon the type of disability. For example, people with any cognitive or psychological disability have a poverty rate of 22.3%, while those with a hearing disability have a poverty rate of 10.3% (Council of Canadians with Disabilities, 2010). Moreover, when gender, ethnic or Indigenous status, and disability are combined, individuals can be doubly or triply disadvantaged. Finally, it should also be noted that many people with disabilities who are not in the workforce rely on various forms of state support such as disability pensions, and these pensions are relatively meagre (Council of Canadians with Disabilities, 2010).

Indigienous Families, Visible Minorities, and Recent Immigrants

As previously noted, Indigenous, visible minority, and immigrant families are more likely to experience poverty and economic vulnerability than other groups, and as just noted, child poverty rates are very high among these groups. As discussed in chapter 4, Indigenous families faced a history of systemic discrimination at the hands of an imperialistic state. Indigenous children, for example, are more than twice as likely to live in poverty as non-Indigenous. Indigenous women and single parents are particularly prone to poverty, especially those with a large number of children and large households. Moreover, adult Indigenous peoples are more likely to be young, have lower education levels, face racial discrimination, and be unemployed compared to the Canadian average (Kerr and Michalski, 2014).

Recent immigrant families (the majority of which are classified as visible minorities or racialized individuals) are also highly vulnerable to living in poverty. Approximately 90% of racialized individuals living in poverty are newcomers to Canada or first-generation immigrants (National Council of Welfare, 2012). Many find themselves among the low-wage poor compared to Canadian-born people or more established immigrants (as shown in figure 14.3), or to those working full-year, full-time for low wages. Moreover, some visible minority families (e.g., Arabic, Black/Caribbean, Latin American) are at a greater risk of unemployment, underemployment, and low income. Issues of education and work experience from another country (among the foreign-born), language barriers, and general **marginalization** play a role in these patterns. Marginalization occurs when individuals are systematically excluded from meaningful participation in social, political, and economic activities in their communities.

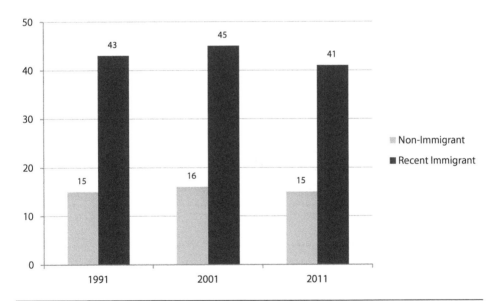

Figure 14.3: Percentage in Low Wage by Immigrant Status, Canadian- and Non-Canadian Born, 2011

Notes: Recent immigrants are defined as foreign-born residents who arrived in Canada within 5 years prior to the census date; Low Wage is based on Statistics Canada's low-income cut-off based on family size and composition.

Source: Data are based on the 2011 National Household Survey and for the earlier years on the Canadian Census, as shown in Table 1, in Edmonston, B. 2016. "Canada's Immigration Trends and Patterns." *Canadian Studies in Population* 43: 78-116. Retrieved August 9, 2016, from www.ejournals.library.ualberta.ca/index.php/csp/article/view/25395/20365.

The Senior Situation

Over the past several decades, there has been a significant decline in poverty among seniors (defined as persons aged 65 and over) as a result of improved pensions and government benefits. Currently, the number of seniors living in poverty is lower than that of children and working-age people. As shown in table 14.3, seniors are the least vulnerable to poverty, with only 3.9% classified as living under the LICO in 2014. Most elderly receive their income from public programs rather than paid employment. Yet, there is an overall trend toward delayed retirement for both financial and personal reasons, a topic that was covered in chapter 12.

If the individual was employed, the Canada Pension Plan or the Quebec Pension Plan supply an income. Old Age Security (OAS) is paid to all seniors, although it is subject to clawback at higher income levels. Those with low incomes can receive additional benefits through the Guaranteed Income Supplement (GIS). However, there is some concern that seniors' poverty may be on the rise again because OAS and GIS payments have not risen at the same rate as the incomes of Canadian households as a whole (Madden, 2016).

Table 14.3: Percentage of Persons in Low Income, after Tax, 2010, 2012, and 2014

	2010	2012	2014
All persons (in economic and non-economic families)	9.6%	10%	8.8%
Persons under 18 years (in economic families)	8.6%	10.6%	8.3%
Persons under 18 years (in couple families with children)	6.3%	8.2%	5.5%
Persons under 18 years in female lone-parent families	23.6%	30.1%	29.6%
Persons 18 to 64 years old (in economic and non-economic families)	10.6%	11%	10%
Persons 65 years and over (in economic and non-economic families)	6%	4.6%	3.9%
Persons 65 years and over (in non-economic family	15.7%	12.6%	11.3%
Persons less than 65 years old (in non-economic family)	31.9%	31.9%	31.2%

Notes: An economic family refers to a group of two or more persons who live in the same dwelling and are related to each other by blood, marriage, common-law, adoption, or a foster relationship; low income measures (LIMs) are relative measures of low income, set at 50% of the adjusted median household income. These measures are categorized according to the number of persons present in the household, reflecting the economies of scale inherent in household size.

Source: Statistics Canada. 2015. CANSIM Table 206-0041- *Low Income Statistics by Age, Sex and Economic Family Type, Canada.* Retrieved July 29, 2016, from www5.statcan.gc.ca/cansim/a26?lang=eng&id=2060041.

The combination of these benefits keep many seniors above the poverty line, although a large number are among the near-poor. Unfortunately, many elderly poor are single women who live alone, Aboriginals, immigrants, seniors with disabilities, and gays and lesbians (Madden, 2016). And since many elderly women and immigrants do not qualify for certain pensions, this makes them especially vulnerable to poverty. As a result, many seniors must rely on other family members for food and shelter, which can create strain, overcrowding, and dependency issues.

Under Pressure: The Shrinking Middle Class and the Financial Squeeze

Although middle-class families are generally able to afford the basic necessities of life and enjoy a fairly decent standard of living relative to poorer families, it should not be assumed that they never have to struggle financially to make ends meet. Middle-class families are usually defined as the 60% of families who are neither the poorest 20% nor the richest 20%. These families are also diverse, with a relatively wide range of after-tax incomes. And although median family income in Canada is higher today than it was three decades ago, it is well documented that the middle class is facing considerable financial pressure, despite the fact that their working hours have dramatically increased. Moreover, the overall proportion of middle-income families has been reduced, while the share of low- and high-income families has grown. These trends are largely attributed to rising inequalities in income distribution (Vanier Institute of the Family, 2010).

As a result, many average Canadian households increasingly carry a large debt load and find it difficult to get ahead. Yalnizyan (2010) reports that not only do Canadians have one of the worst debt-to-income ratios of 20 OECD nations, but their rate of savings ($2.80 on every $100 of household income) is less than half that of Americans. Overall, a rising number of middle-class families report financial difficulties related to paying bills and heavy debt (e.g., credit cards, mortgages) due to the high costs associated with daily living, especially in urban areas with high food and housing costs. Middle-class parents are also increasingly relied upon by their older children for housing assistance, rising educational costs, transportation, and other expenses (e.g., consumer goods) because of changing socio-demographic and labour market conditions, as discussed in chapter 11.

POVERTY, NEGATIVE OUTCOMES, AND THE LIFE COURSE

As presented in box 14.3, the potentially adverse consequences of poverty and economic hardship on families are numerous and often persist over the life course. These consequences are well documented and are intensified the longer an individual is impoverished. However, poverty can strike at any time due to circumstances like unemployment, sickness, divorce, or addiction. However, although most research focuses on negative consequences, it should not be assumed that being poor translates into a wretched existence, devoid of happiness, love, and close-knit family relations. In fact, economic hardship might bring some family members closer together since there is a greater need to pool resources and rely on one another for various types of support.

Box 14.3: Pathways to Poverty

There is clustering of advantage and disadvantage among Canadians. Individuals who are advantaged as children by way of parents' income and wealth are more likely to achieve higher education levels, better paying work, and more secure employment. The availability of greater amounts of income and wealth also facilitate access to a variety of other commodities that shape health and quality of life (Bryant, 2004). These include quality daycare, cultural and educational activities, leisure opportunities, and food and housing security. These material living conditions shape psychological understandings of the world and promote a sense of control over life, feelings of self-efficacy, and a belief that the world is understandable. Those living in poverty are likely to experience the opposite conditions and develop little sense of control, self-efficacy, and a belief that the world is understandable.

Together, these positive or negative life experiences and the psychological concomitants of these conditions shape an individual's trajectories over time. Material and social disadvantage associated with poverty contributes to lower educational achievement and employment that provides less compensation and security, which then contributes to continuing material and social disadvantage.

Similarly, policies that reduce the availability and affordability of housing and the amount of financial resources available to people affect resources available to Canadians. This is because low social assistance rates and minimum wages and the lack of affordable housing reduce the resources that support other social determinants of health such as food security, education, and recreation. These issues come together to have direct effects upon health and quality of life.

Source: Raphael, D. 2007. "Pathways to Poverty." In D. Raphael, *Poverty and Policy in Canada: Implications for Health and Quality of Life.* Toronto: Canadian Scholars' Press (p. 21).

Compared to other children, those who are exposed to poverty (especially over a long time period) or suffer severe economic loss generally have poorer physical health and more chronic health problems. They are more likely to have a low birth weight and be born with nutritional deficiencies, which are linked to developmental processes. In general, poor children tend to have more socio-emotional mental health and behavioural problems (e.g., depression, attention deficit disorder) than more affluent children (see Hubler et al., 2016, for review). They also have more frequent accidents because their surroundings are less safe (Ambert, 2006).

There are also strong associations between poverty and later educational outcomes; poor children typically have fewer resources and chances for educational achievement.

This decreases their stock of cultural capital or knowledge of middle-class or high culture. It is argued that access to cultural capital results in behaviours, lifestyle preferences, and predispositions that help children do better in school. For example, poor children may have limited vocabularies and less frequent participation in high-society cultural activities, such as travelling or going to museums and libraries. As a result, teachers (who are predominantly middle-class) tend to give these children less attention and assistance and perceive them less favourably. In turn, poor children typically receive lower grades and are less likely to graduate from high school and attend college or university. And since educational attainment is associated with adult socio-economic status, poor children often grow up to be poor adults.

Based on Statistics Canada data, in 2013, youth, women and persons with a low level of education were the groups most likely to be paid at minimum wage (Galarneau and Fecteau, 2014). Notably, 50% of employees aged 15 to 19 and 13% of those aged 20 to 24 were paid at minimum wage, although many of these employees might be students and will receive higher pay in the future. Among women, the rate was 8% (compared with 6% of men). Of particular relevance to this discussion is the finding that among the least educated, specifically those with less than a high school diploma, the proportion was 20%, compared with fewer than 3% among university graduates. In this way, a lack of human and cultural capital, as well as social capital (which creates opportunities through social networks or connections) contributes to the reproduction of the structure of power relationships and symbolic relationships between classes (Bellamy, 1994).

Overall, poor adults have significantly higher morbidity (sickness), in addition to lower rates of life expectancy than other adults. This is because income is highly correlated with health and disease, including both objective and subjective diseases, as outlined in chapter 13. Poor adults are also more likely to work in dangerous occupations and live in unsafe or crime-ridden neighbourhoods. Housing problems are more common, which results in a higher likelihood of becoming homeless or living in crowded or substandard conditions. In fact, homelessness is a serious problem in Canada, and the situation does not seem to be improving.

Poverty can also affect the formation and quality of intimate relationships. This is because financial struggle often creates stress and strain, which can spill over into family relationships. For example, the chronic unemployment of one spouse can undermine marital stability and happiness. One recent study found that finances are often a hot button issue for many couples, such that disagreements overs finances predicted divorce more strongly than other potential problem area, such as household tasks or spending time together as a couple (Drew, Britt, and Huston, 2012). Poor families are also more likely to move than wealthier families, which can disrupt the formation of friendships and social networks in the community (Ward, 2002). This trajectory contributes to isolating people socially and deprives families of social capital. Indeed, low-income Canadians are less likely to report that they trust other people or to participate in community activities (Statistics Canada, 2004).

SUMMARY

Many people think of our society as a meritocracy with a fair and level playing field. They contend that we all have an equal chance of success, such that those at the top are those who work the hardest and have the most merit and talent. In other words, it is often assumed that because we live in a liberal democracy, everyone has the same opportunity for upward mobility, regardless of family background or wealth, if they have the corresponding talent and ambition. This line of reasoning is reflected in the belief that people on welfare are lazy bums, and it receives additional support from anecdotal stories of individuals with rags to riches stories about making it big through hard work.

In reality, contrary to the perception that it is a relatively egalitarian society with a fair distribution of income across social groups, Canada is a deeply stratified, class-based nation where some families experience great economic struggles on a daily basis. Regardless of the fact that Canada is one of the wealthiest countries in the world and has experienced continued economic growth, rising employment, and record job creation, poverty remains a rampant and serious problem.

Moreover, despite a political landscape "littered with political rhetoric about children," (National Council of Welfare, 1999), Canada has had only modest success in reducing child poverty. Certain social groups are more vulnerable to poverty than others, such as women, Indigenous peoples, people with disabilities, and visible minorities. For example, at every stage of their lives, women are more vulnerable to poverty than men, more prone to be trapped, and to die in poverty. And for a significant number of older Canadians, the prospect of a golden retirement simply does not exist.

While it is common to blame the victim for their situation, it is clear that some families simply do not have access to the same types of opportunities, resources, and privileges. Indeed, there is a tendency for social classes to reproduce themselves; this can be seen in the extent to which individuals from poor family backgrounds are underrepresented in higher education and professional or managerial occupational sectors. In short, available evidence shows that it is the economy and the class system that usually create these conditions, rather than personality traits such as lack of motivation, rejection of middle-class values, or poor parental socialization.

In closing, blaming the victim for their poverty does little to improve the situation. Instead, it is more fruitful to examine the interaction between individuals and society and the intersections that work to create even greater vulnerability to poverty. Therefore, we need to address the multiple and systematic roots causes of poverty and the processes by which people struggle to overcome their challenges and obstacles. This idea beckons us to dig deeper beyond mere stereotypes and labels of poverty and behooves us to contemplate how this social problem costs us all (also refer to Box 14.4). Hence, it prompts us to think critically about ways to reduce these conditions and negative consequences in order to finally break the vicious cycle of economic and related hardships in both families and the economy.

Box 14.4: How Paying People's Way Out of Poverty Can Help Us All

[...] When people are poor, out of work, or homeless, it hurts the bottom line of all Canadians. And as the country struggles to maintain a shaky recovery amid growing global economic uncertainty, that's not a hit they can afford to take.

If Ottawa and the provinces fail to make this a priority, Tory Senator Hugh Segal predicts, "over time, we will begin to run out of the money that we need to deal with the demographic bulge because it will be consumed in the health care requirements of the poor, which will increase. It will be consumed in the costs of the illiteracy and unemployment which relate to poverty. ... And it'll be unsustainable."

It's not just Canada's problem; income inequality is sparking social unrest in the Middle East, North Africa, and China. It rang alarm bells at the Organization for Economic Co-operation and Development's conference in Paris this week, where the think-tank warned that if a slew of countries—from Sweden to Canada to the United Kingdom—don't take drastic action by raising taxes for the richest, they risk runaway increases in inequality.

[...] Calgary's business community crunched the numbers: It costs four times more to pay for a year's worth of emergency shelter, emergency-room medical care, and law-enforcement for one homeless person than it costs to fund that person's supportive housing for a year.

More recent figures have backed this up: a 2010 study from St. Michael's Hospital in Toronto found that homeless patients cost hospitals an average of $2,559 more than their housed counterparts.

BY THE NUMBERS

$134,000
Estimated amount for emergency shelter, emergency hospital care, law enforcement, and other social services for one homeless person in Calgary for one year
$34,000
Estimated cost to provide supportive housing for one person in Calgary for one year
$12,555
Average cost of hospital stay for one non-homeless patient at St. Michael's Hospital in Toronto
$15,114
Average cost of hospital stay for one homeless patient at St. Michael's Hospital in Toronto

At the same time, research into projects that guarantee people a minimum annual income indicated savings in everything from social services and health care to law enforcement. The philosophy behind this is simple: people making a decent living are more likely to stay in school, out of emergency rooms, and out of jail; they contribute to their economy through purchases; they are more likely to eventually rise above the poverty line and pay taxes.

Source: Excerpt taken from Paperny Mehler, A., and T. Grant. "How Paying People's Way Out of Poverty Can Help Us All." *The Globe and Mail*, May 5. Retrieved August 1, 2016, from www. theglobeandmail.com/news/politics/how-paying-peoples-way-out-of-poverty-can-help-us-all/ article2011940.

QUESTIONS FOR CRITICAL REFLECTION AND DEBATE

1. Debate the following: If people work hard enough in life, they will not have to experience poverty.
2. How might poverty affect the kinds of intimate relationships or unions that people form?
3. Do you think that processes of globalization and future technological advances will deepen or decrease the prevalence of poverty in Canada and other societies?
4. Critically outline strategies to reduce poverty and its effects at the government and community level. Why have previous strategies failed?
5. Studies show that homeless children suffer high rates of developmental, mental, and behavioural problems and that many of these persist into adulthood. Discuss possible reasons for these outcomes.
6. Analyze the following statement: financial wealth broadens families' social and cultural capital.

GLOSSARY

Absolute poverty is a condition of mere physical survival.

Culture of poverty refers to a fatalistic set of values, behaviours, and attitudes that is not conducive to middle-class standards of financial or material success.

Economic security refers to a standard of living that provides resources and benefits necessary for social and economic participation and social inclusion.

Feminization of poverty is the tendency for women to be more poor than men.

Marginalization occurs when individuals are systematically excluded from meaningful participation in social, political, and economic activities in their communities.

Relative poverty is what is considered poor relative to contemporary social standards for normal and wealthy.

Social reproduction of poverty is the tendency for individuals born into poor families to become poor later in life.

Working poor are those individuals who experience poverty while working in the paid labour force.

FURTHER READING

Béland, D., P. Daigneault, and Scholars Portal. 2015. *Welfare Reform in Canada: Provincial Social Assistance in Comparative Perspective.* Toronto: University of Toronto Press. Offers a comparative and historical review of social assistance policies and practices in each Canadian province. Addresses challenges and issues such as aging and welfare, homelessness, and immigrants on social assistance.

Brady, D., and L. Burton. 2016. *The Oxford Handbook of the Social Science of Poverty.* New York: Oxford University Press. Brings together inter-disciplinary perspectives on the issue of poverty both in the United States and globally. Contains an overview and a discussion of leading theories, concepts, and debates in poverty research. Incorporates many methodological perspectives.

Green, D.A., W.C. Riddell, and F. St-Hilaire, (eds.). 2016. *Income Inequality: The Canadian Story.* Montreal: Institute for Research on Public Policy. Comprehensive review of Canadian income inequality aimed at policy-makers and the general public. It contributes to our understanding of many trends and issues such as income distribution, provincial polarization of jobs and wages, immigrant earnings, re-distributive policies, and the persistence of poverty.

Page-Reeves, J. 2014. *Women Redefining the Experience of Food Insecurity: Life Off the Edge of the Table.* Lanham, Maryland: Lexington Books. Problematizes how women procure food and survive in a context of food scarcity and larger patriarchal and hegemonic systems. Examines the relationship between food insecurity and women's agency, with a special focus on immigrant women and their strategies of obtaining food for their families.

Sumner, A. 2016. *Global Poverty: Deprivation, Distribution, and Development since the Cold War.* London: Oxford University Press.
Examines the changing patterns of global poverty. Includes question-led chapters addressing such issues as the new middle-income poverty trap and global changes that have occurred since the Cold War.

Wallis, M.A., and S. Kwok. (eds.). 2011. *Daily Struggles.* Toronto: Canadian Scholars' Press.
Offers a critical perspective on poverty with an emphasis on gender and race in a Canadian context. Also connects issues of human rights, political economy perspectives, and citizenship issues to other areas of social exclusion such as class, sexuality, and disability.

RELATED WEB SITES

Campaign 2000 is a non-partisan, cross-Canada network of over 90 national, provincial, and community partner organizations committed to working together to end child and family poverty in Canada, www.campaign2000.ca. Facebook: www.facebook.com/Campaign2000/ Twitter: www.twitter.com/Campaign2000.

Canada Without Poverty is a non-partisan, not-for-profit and charitable organization dedicated to the elimination of poverty in Canada using human rights approach. www.cwp-csp.ca. Facebook: www.facebook.com/CanadaWithoutPoverty. Twitter: www.twitter.com/CWP_CSP

Canadian Centre for Policy Alternatives (CCPA) is an independent and non-partisan research institute; respected voice on the issues of justice and inequality, www.policyalternatives.ca. Facebook: www.facebook.com/policyalternatives Twitter: www.twitter.com/ccpa. YouTube channel: www.youtube.com/user/policyalternatives

Canadian Council on Social Development has been in existence since 1920 and focuses on nation building and social development (improving the well-being of every person in society). This not-for-profit organization collaborates with all sectors to help with current challenges. Poverty and income inequality are among the prevalent topics. www.ccsd.ca/index.php. Facebook: www.facebook.com/CanadianCouncilonSocialDevelopment Twitter: www.twitter.com/the_ccsd.

Food Banks Canada is a charitable organization aimed at ending hunger in Canada. Their web site contains personal stories, research studies, position papers, and information on advocacy and community action, as well as a link to Hunger Count 2015. www.foodbankscanada.ca. Facebook: www.facebook.com/FoodBanksCanada YouTube: www.youtube.com/channel/UClX59tkVpqjAsSA7tGZVhCQ.

Global Call to Action against Poverty (GCAP) is associated with the Make Poverty History campaign. GCAP is defined as an alliance of trade unions, INGOs, women's and youth movements to call for action from the global North and South. It aims to promote human rights, challenge institutions, and create all-inclusive national platforms. It addresses global issues of poverty and inequality. www.whiteband.org. Facebook: www.facebook.com/GlobalCalltoActionAgainstPoverty, Twitter: twitter.com/whiteband.

People First of Canada is an organization and movement that directed by people who have been labelled as poor. It promotes citizenship and equality for everyone. www.peoplefirstofcanada.ca/. Facebook: www.facebook.com/PeopleFirstofCanada. Twitter: www.twitter.com/PeopleFirstCA.

Raising the Roof is an advocacy-oriented organization devoted to eliminating homelessness. www.raisingtheroof.org. Facebook: www.facebook.com/RaisingtheRoof/ Twitter: twitter.com/RaisingtheRoof. YouTube: www.youtube.com/user/RaisingtheRoofCanada.

REFERENCES

Ambert, A.M. 2006. *Changing Families: Relationships in Context*. Toronto: Pearson Education.

Bellamy, L. 1994. "Capital, Habitus, Field, and Practice: An Introduction to the Work of Pierre Bourdieu." In L. Erwin and D. MacLennan (eds.), *Sociology of Education in Canada: Critical Perspectives on Theory, Research, and Practice* (pp. 120–136). Toronto: Copp Clark Pitman, Ltd.

Campaign 2000. 2011. *Revisiting Family Security in Insecure Times: 2011 Report Card on Child and Family Poverty in Canada*. Toronto: Family Services Toronto.

Canada without Poverty. 2016. "Basic Statistics about the Realities of Poverty faced by Canadians." Retrieved August 11, 2016, from www.cwp-csp.ca/poverty/just-the-facts.

Council of Canadians with Disabilities. 2010. "A Call to Combat Poverty and Exclusion of Canadians with Disabilities by Investing in Disability Supports." Retrieved February 3, 2006, from www.ccdonline.ca/ccpe.htm.

Drew, J., S Britt, and S. Huston. 2012. "Examining the Relationship between Financial Issues and Divorce." *Family Relations* 61: 615–628.

Food Banks Canada. 2016. "About Hunger in Canada: Facts about Food Insecurity." Retrieved August 14, 2016, from www.foodbankscanada.ca/Hunger-in-Canada/About-Hunger-in-Canada.aspx.

Galarneu, D., and E. Fecteau. 2014. "The Ups and Downs of Minimum Wage." *Insights on Canadian Society*. Catalogue no. 75-006-X. Ottawa: Statistics Canada.

Gazso, A. 2007. "Staying Afloat on Social Assistance: Parents' Strategies of Balancing Employability Expectations and Caregiving Demands." *Socialist Studies* 3: 31–57.

Gazso, A., S.A. McDaniel, and I. Waldron. 2016. "Networks of Social Support to Manage Poverty: More Changeable than Durable." *Journal of Poverty* 20: 441–463.

Goffman, E. 1963. *Stigma: Notes on the Management of Spoiled Identity*. New York: Simon and Schuster.

Harman, L.D. 2005. "Family Poverty and Economic Struggles." In N. Mandell and A. Duffy (eds.), *Canadian Families: Diversity, Conflict, and Change*, 3rd ed. (pp. 241–275). Toronto: Thomson Nelson.

Hatcher, D.L. 2016. *The Poverty Industry: The Exploitation of America's Most Vulnerable Citizens.* New York: New York University Press.

Hubler, D.S., B.K. Burr, B.C. Gardner, R.E. Larzelere, and D.M. Busby. 2016. "The Intergenerational Transmission of Financial Stress and Relationship Outcomes." *Marriage and Family Review* 52: 373–391.

Jackson, A. 2000. "Defining and Redefining Poverty." *Perception: Canada's Social Development Magazine* 25: 3–6.

Jackson, A., S. Tsoukalas, L. Buckland, and S. Schetagne. 2002. "The Personal Security Index 2002: After September 11." Ottawa: Canadian Council on Social Development.

Kerr, D., and J. Michalski. 2014. "Family Poverty in Canada: Correlates, Coping Strategies, and Consequences." In D. Cheal and P. Albanese, (eds.), *Canadian Families Today: New Perspectives*, 3rd ed. (pp. 185–207). Toronto: Oxford University Press.

Lewis, O. 1966. "The Culture of Poverty." *Scientific American* 2: 19–25.

Liebow, E. 2003. *Tally's Corner: A Study of Negro Streetcorner Men.* New York: Rowman and Littlefield.

Madden, T. 2016. "Seniors' Poverty Rates on the Rise in Canada." London, Ontario: London Poverty Research Centre at Kings College.

Mitchell, B.A. 2005. "Canada's Growing Visible Minority Population: Generational Challenges, Opportunities, and Federal Policy Considerations." In *Canada 2017: Serving Canada's Multicultural Population for the Future* (pp. 51–62), Policy Forum Discussion Papers. Gatineau: The Multiculturalism Program, Department of Canadian Heritage.

National Advisory Council on Aging. 2005. *Seniors on the Margins: Aging in Poverty in Canada.* Ottawa: Minister of Public Works and Government Services.

National Council of Welfare. 1999. *Children First: A Pre-Budget Report by the National Council of Welfare.* Ottawa: National Council of Welfare.

National Council of Welfare. 2012. *Snapshot of Racialized Poverty in Canada. Poverty Profile: Special Edition.* Ottawa. National Council of Welfare.

Ryser, L. and G. Halseth. 2016. "Opportunities and Challenges to Address Poverty in Rural Regions: A Case Study from Northern BC." *Journal of Poverty* 23: 1–22.

Statistics Canada. 2004. "General Social Survey: Social Engagement." *The Daily* (July 6).

Statistics Canada. 2014. "Study: Persons with Disabilities and Employment." *The Daily* (December 3).

Statistics Canada. 2016. "Study: Intergenerational Income Mobility: New Evidence from Canada." *The Daily* (June 17).

Streib, J., M. Ayala, and C. Wixted. 2016. "Benign Inequality: Frames of Poverty and Social Class Inequality in Children's Movies." *Journal of Poverty*, published online first. Retrieved August 11, 2016, from www.tandfonline.com/doi/abs/10.1080/10875549.2015.1112870.

Vanier Institute of the Family. 2010. *Families Count: Profiling Canada's Families IV.* Ottawa: Vanier Institute of the Family.

Ward, M. 2002. *The Family Dynamic: A Canadian Perspective*, 3rd ed. Toronto: Nelson Thomson Learning.

WHO. 1976. *WHO Document A29/INFDOCI/*. Geneva, Switzerland.

Yalnizyan, A. 2011. "Canadian Households: Among Highest Debt to Income Ratios in the World." Ottawa: Canadian Centres for Policy Alternatives.

CHAPTER 15

Families in Crisis:
Family Violence, Abuse, and Stress

LEARNING OBJECTIVES

In this chapter you will learn that ...

- there is a dark side to family life, and certain individuals are more vulnerable to violence, abuse, and stress
- there are many definitions and various forms of violence, abuse, and stress
- this area of study is fraught with definitional and methodological challenges
- there are short- and long-term consequences of violence and abuse
- a life course, ecological perspective is important and helps us to critically evaluate explanations for violence, abuse, and stress
- there are several issues relevant to prevention and intervention

There was an old woman who lived in a shoe,
She had so many children she didn't know what to do.
She gave them some broth without any bread,
And whipped them all soundly and sent them to bed.

—Mother Goose rhyme (cited in Engelbreit, 2005: 29)

INTRODUCTION

For most us of, the family represents a sacred institution that provides "a haven in a heartless world" (Lasch, 1979). As such, the family home symbolizes a cozy and safe retreat from a violent world with its legacy and repertoire of conflict, war, and terrible human atrocities. Yet for many people, especially women and children, there is a dark side to family life. In fact, families may be some of the most violent and cruel groups in which to belong. According to one study, a significant proportion of all violent crimes reported to a sample of police services involved cases of family violence, including dating violence (Statistics Canada, 2016). Moreover, despite fears to the contrary, it is not a stranger but a so-called loved one who is more likely to assault, rape, or murder us (DeKeseredy, 2005).

Unfortunately, many of us do not reveal these private troubles to others, and this topic has only recently been discussed in public domains. The popular daytime talk show *The Oprah Winfrey Show* was one of the first mass media forums to openly discuss familial child abuse in 1985. This landmark show included Oprah's own personal account of her childhood sexual molestation by a family member. Similarly, violence in intimate relations was kept hushed in scholarly realms until relatively recently. A review of the table of contents of *The Journal of Marriage and the Family*, the leading international journal in the field of family studies from its inception in 1939 through 1969, shows a complete absence of the word "violence." A survey by Eichler (1983) in the 1970s further documented that violence in the family continued to be ignored by social scientists. Out of 18 textbooks on the family published or reprinted in the 1970s, only three mentioned family violence. Norms of family privacy, coupled with the sensitive nature of the issue and the assumption that it rarely happened, contributed to this "blind eye to reality" (Drakich and Guberman, 1987). Fortunately, over the last several decades, studies and public awareness of this significant social problem have grown considerably.

In light of these issues, the purpose of this chapter is to examine family violence, abuse, and stress across the life course. We will begin by defining key terms and various forms of family violence, as well as giving an analysis of their consequences and explanations. Sources of family stress are also highlighted. The chapter concludes with recommendations for prevention and intervention.

WHAT IS FAMILY VIOLENCE AND NEGLECT? DEFINITIONS, FORMS, AND PREVALENCE

Directly or indirectly, virtually all of us have experienced some form of **family violence** or neglect in our lives. But what is family violence and neglect? Defining and measuring family violence is not an easy task, since there is seldom consensus as to what constitutes a violent act. Therefore, most controversies centre on how broad (or narrow) these definitions should be. These definitions are significant, since they can affect the collection of data and prevalence rates, which can have enormous social and legal implications. Definitions can influence the quality and quantity of policies and social support services implemented by official agencies to deal with the issue. This can be problematic if narrow definitions are used. For example, if spousal abuse is defined only as extreme acts of violence (i.e., broken bones, murder), then government officials may be led to believe that violence against women is not a pressing social problem. As a result, they may channel fewer resources into programs and services designed to prevent and control the phenomenon.

Violence is defined by the World Health Organization (2005: 1) as "the intentional use of physical force or power, threatened or actual, against oneself, another person, or against a group or community that either results in or has a high likelihood of resulting in injury, death, psychological harm, maldevelopment, or deprivation." Three broad types of violence can be identified: self-directed, interpersonal, and collective. Each is further divided to reflect more specific types of violence. Interpersonal violence (depicted in figure 15.1) distinguishes family violence, which occurs largely between family members and intimate partners. Usually, this type of violence takes place in the home. Community violence, on the other hand, generally takes place outside the home and occurs between individuals who are not related and who may not know each other.

This typology also illustrates that the nature of violence can be physical (including sexual assault) or psychological, or it can involve deprivation or neglect. Abuse can also entail financial exploitation, as shown in table 15.1. Additionally, recent research on **polyvictimization** establishes the need to theorize and study the connections between various types of violence, since they often do not occur in isolation from one another. It is increasingly recognized that it is common for multiple types of abuse to co-occur in the lives of victims, a finding that helps us to better understand the effects of abuse on victims (Anderson, 2010). For example, some children can experience repeated victimizations and several forms of abuse while they are growing up. These acts of violence can also occur in multiple settings, including inside and outside of the family home (e.g., at school, the neighbourhood, a friend's house) and can feature more than one perpetrator. Consequently, these children may be at much greater risk for complex traumatic experiences, as well as lifetime adversities such as chronic distress (Slowikowski et al., 2011).

Seen through this lens, family violence and abuse is as an umbrella term covering a range of different types and experiences of violence among different sets of family members. From a life-course perspective, certain types of violence may be inflicted on certain

Table 15.1: What Is Abuse and Neglect?

Type	Definition and Examples across the Life Course
Physical	Inflicting discomfort, pain, or injury by slapping, punching, rough handling, sexual assault, over- or undermedicating, or excessive use of physical restraint.
	Example: Father straps son with belt because son had slapped brother.
Psychological	Diminishing dignity and self-worth by name-calling, insulting, threatening, ignoring, isolating, excluding from meaningful events.
	Example: Uncle cannot accept gay niece and calls her a "freak of nature" and "stupid dyke," among other insulting names.
Financial	Misuse of money or property, stealing money or possessions, forging signatures or legal documents.
	Example: Adult grandson tricks elderly grandmother into signing cheques to cover his personal expenses and money for drugs.
Neglect	Failing to meet the needs of family members, unable to meet those needs alone. Denial of food, water, medication, treatment, health aids, clothing, visitors.
	Example: Mother and father keep young child locked up in room while they work and provide inadequate diet and social interaction.

Source: Adapted from The National Advisory Council on Aging. 2003–2004. "Hidden Harm: The Abuse of Seniors." *Expression: Bulletin of the National Advisory Council on Aging* 17, no. 1. Ottawa: Government of Canada (p. 2).

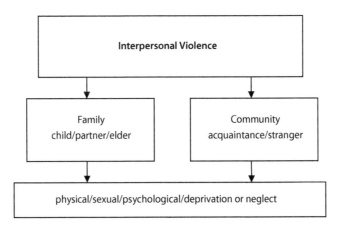

Figure 15.1: Typology of Violence

Source: Adapted from World Health Organization (WHO). 2005. "Violence Prevention Alliance: Building Global Commitment for Violence Prevention. *Global Campaign for Violence Prevention.* Geneva: WHO Press. Retrieved December 2, 2007, from www.whqlibdoc.who.int/publications/2005/924159313X_eng.pdf.

family members at particular stages of the family life cycle, such as childhood (child abuse, including sibling abuse), young adulthood and adulthood, and the elderly years. This is because age is interrelated with conditions connected to vulnerability, dependency, and access to resources that can influence the risk of being injured. In the next section, we will focus on common kinds of violence that occur in families, using a life-course organizational framework.

Child Abuse and Neglect

From a historical perspective, children have often been considered the property of their parents, especially their father. As a result, children have had few rights and have been vulnerable to abuse and neglect. Moreover, it was common in the past for both parents and teachers to condone physical discipline, often quoting the biblical phrase "Spare the rod and spoil the child" to justify this behaviour. Sexual abuse was also prevalent. In both a historical and a global perspective, various types of child abuse, such as trafficking, sexual exploitation, and genital mutilation of young girls, has been and continues to be commonplace.

In Canada, the first Children's Aid Society was formed in Toronto in 1891. Yet, the initial concern of reforms focused on child employment and substitute caregivers, not on neglect and abuse by parents (although the latter was covered by the legislation). For many years, Canadian concerns and legislation changed little. Following the popularization of the phrase "battered child syndrome" (coined by Kempe in the early 1960s), laws on mandatory reporting were passed. By the late 1970s, nine of the 12 provincial and territorial jurisdictions had passed such laws and the rest had implemented monitoring programs (Wachtel, 1989; Ward, 2002).

There is much controversy over the definition and manifestation of child abuse. For example, while many Canadians today view spanking as an aggressive act intended to harm or injure, in the past, many did not see it as abuse since it was the norm rather than the exception (Flynn, 1998). Part of the reason is that spanking is legal, albeit only under certain conditions (see box 15.1). It is also interesting to note that while spanking is relatively common throughout the world, it is illegal in many countries, including Sweden, Germany, Greece, Brazil, and Kenya.

Box 15.1: Spanking Laws and the Use of Force on Children in Canada

A few years ago, the Supreme Court of Canada made a decision about section 43 that helps to understand the law on assault today. It said that the use of force on a child is only allowed to help the child learn. The parent, caregiver, or teacher using force must be correcting a behaviour at the time it is happening, and the person must not use force on a child in anger.

The Supreme Court of Canada found it is not appropriate to use force on a very young child or a teenager. The use of force would be allowed under the exception in section 43 only if the child was between 2 and 12 years old. The

Court declared that using force to punish a child under two is not appropriate because a child that young cannot learn from the situation. Using force on a teenager is not appropriate because there are better and more effective ways to respond to their behaviour.

Section 43 says that the force used on a 2 to 12-year-old child must be "reasonable under the circumstances". The Supreme Court defined "reasonable" as force that would have a "transitory and trifling" impact on the child. For example, spanking or slapping a child so hard that it leaves a mark that lasts for several hours would not be considered transitory and trifling.

The Supreme Court also said that the method used must not be degrading, inhumane, or harmful. The person must not use an object, such as a ruler or a belt, and must not hit or slap the child's head. Finally, the Court declared that the seriousness of the child's misbehaviour is not relevant. The force used must be minor, no matter what the child has done.

THE USE OF FORCE WHEN MANAGING CHILDREN'S BEHAVIOUR

There are times when parents, caregivers, and teachers may have to use force to control a child and keep him, or other children, safe. Grabbing a child to keep her child from running across the street, carrying a screaming three-year-old out of a store, or separating two young students who are fighting may require a parent, caregiver, or teacher to touch or restrain the child. Without section 43, parents, caregivers, and teachers could face criminal charges and have to go to court to defend their actions whenever they used force to respond to a child's behaviour.

SUMMARY

The use of force to correct a child is only allowed to help the child learn and can never be used in anger.

- The child must be between 2 and 12 years old.
- The force used must be reasonable and its impact only "transitory and trifling".
- The person must not use an object, such as a ruler or a belt, when applying the force.
- The person must not hit or slap the child's head.
- The seriousness of what happened or what the child did is not relevant.

Using reasonable force to restrain a child may be acceptable in some circumstances. Hitting a child in anger or in retaliation for something they did is not considered reasonable and is against the law.

Source: Department of Justice. n.d. "Criminal Law and Managing Children's Behaviour." Retrieved October 28, 2016, from www.justice.gc.ca/eng/rp-pr/cj-jp/fv-vf/mcb-cce/index.html.

It is virtually impossible to know the full extent of child abuse and neglect in Canada. This is because only the most extreme cases come to the attention of the professional community, and there are no Canadian national representative sample survey data. Also, many people do not disclose abuse due to fear of reprisal, shame, or denial. Based on a recent government report (see table 15.2), most substantiated reports of child maltreatment (34%) relate to neglect (failure to meet the emotional or physical needs); followed by exposure to domestic violence (34%); physical abuse (20%), emotional maltreatment (9%), and sexual abuse (3%).

Who is most likely to mistreat a child? Figure 15.2 shows that at every age from birth to age 17, children are most likely to be victimized by their parents, as reported to the police in 2014. Siblings are also common perpetrators, especially when they are older. Extended family members (e.g., uncles, cousins, grandparents) are also responsible for child mistreatment (Public Health Agency of Canada, 2016).

While any of these types of abuse is inexcusable and unacceptable, one particularly traumatizing crime committed in families—falling under the category of sexual abuse—is incest. The Criminal Code of Canada defines incest in section 155(1): "Everyone commits incest who, knowing that another person by blood relationship is his or her parent, child, brother, sister, grandparent, or grandchild, as the case may be, has sexual intercourse with that person." However, this definition does not include touching, fondling, oral sex, or masturbating, which can be considered forms of sexual abuse. Nor does it encompass sexual acts between people with non-biological family ties, although these individuals can be charged under different criminal codes (e.g., having sex with a minor). Victims of Violence (a federally registered charitable organization devoted to providing victim support and general promotion of public

Table 15.2: Primary Categories of Substantiated Child Maltreatment Investigations in Canada

Primary category of maltreatment	Number of investigations	Rate per 1,000 children	%
Physical abuse	17,212	2.86	20%
Sexual abuse	2,607	0.43	3%
Neglect	28,939	4.81	34%
Emotional maltreatment	7,423	1.23	9%
Exposure to intimate partner violence	29,259	4.86	34%
Total substantiated investigations	**85,440**	**14.19**	**100%**

Note: Based on a sample of 6,163 substantiated investigations. Percentages are columnpecentages.

Source: Public Health Agency of Canada. 2011. *Canadian Incidence Study of Reported Child Abuse and Neglect - 2008*, Table 4-1. Retrieved August 10, 2011, from www.phac-aspc.gc.ca/ncfv-cnivf/pdfs/nfnts-cis-2008-fact-feuil-eng.pdf.

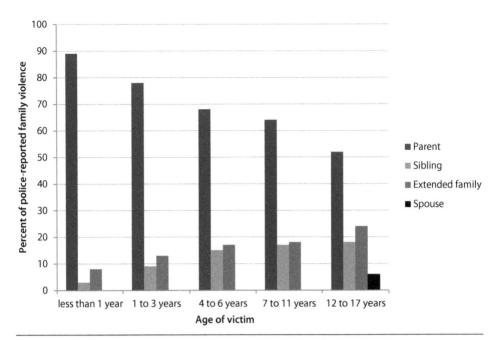

Figure 15.2: Relationship to the Child Victim in Police-Reported Family Violence, 2014

Notes: Parent includes biological, step-, adoptive and foster parents. Sibling includes biological, step-, half-, adoptive, and foster brothers and sisters. Extended family includes all family members related by blood, marriage, or adoption. Spouse includes current or former legally married and common-law spouses.

Source: Public Health Agency of Canada. 2016. *Report on the State of Public Health in Canada 2016: A Focus on Family Violence in Canada.* Ottawa: Government of Canada (figure 9). Retrieved October 28, 2016, from www.healthycanadians.gc.ca/publications/department-ministere/state-public-health-family-violence-2016-etat-sante-publique-violence-familiale/index-eng.

safety), argues that a more appropriate definition of incest would take into account those other acts.

Victims of Violence (2011) report that incest can happen at any age, although most children are victimized between the ages of 8 and 12. Incest is also found to be more likely to occur in families of low socio-economic status, or those in which substance abuse is a factor, although it can occur in many diverse settings and contexts. And although victims can be either male or female, statistics show that female victims outnumber male victims 10 to 1. Perpetrators of incest tend to be male and are usually considerably older than their victims. Seventy-five percent of cases are stepfather/stepdaughter relations.

Similar to incest, the intentional killing of a child (known as filicide) prompts reactions of shock and horror from most members of society, especially when the accused is the child's mother or father. During the past two centuries, filicide rates have declined in Westernized countries. However, the true rate of filicide is unknown because perpetrators often successfully conceal their crime, particularly when infants are involved (Dawson, 2015).

Generally, researchers caution against a complete reliance on statistics of violence and abuse to produce a profile of victim and perpetrator, since certain individuals may be more (or less) likely to report the crime to authorities such as the police. For example, boys may be more reluctant to report the abuse than girls due to the pressures that stem from societal norms of masculine behaviour, such as the idea that "all boys want sex" or "big boys don't cry." Biological children may also be less likely to report sexual abuse (categorized as "consanguine" since it involves blood relatives) than stepchildren or children of "quasi-relatives" (live-in parental partners or foster parents).

Furthermore, it should be recognized that children can also abuse, or, in extremely rare cases, murder their own parents. This is illustrated in the case of 26-year-old Gregory White, who lived with his parents in a single-storey house northwest of Barrie, Ontario. He was charged with the first-degree murder of his parents, aged 53 and 51, in addition to indecent interference with human bodies (CBC News, 2011). Estimates suggest that 7 to 13% of children attack their parents. Most of these are between the ages of 10 and 24, with a peak in the late teens. Older children tend to be more violent than younger ones, and substance abuse, delinquency, and a lack of interest in school is common among these. Moreover, some researchers theorize that parent abuse is an attempt to retaliate for earlier abuse by a parent ("what goes around comes around"), although this aggression tends to be targeted at the less powerful parent rather than the one who committed the abuse. Generally, children who abuse their parents use assault to gain power and control in the family (e.g., see Ward, 2002).

Sibling Abuse

Sibling violence can be defined as any form of intentional harm inflicted by one child in a family unit on another (children can be blood siblings or stepsiblings). It includes highly injurious physical, psychological, or sexual behaviour. Unfortunately, researchers as well as parents often regard violence between siblings (with the exception of incest) as a normal part of sibling rivalry and growing up. Most parents rarely discourage their children from engaging in aggressive behaviours such as slapping, shoving, and hair pulling, and intervene only when minor events are seen as escalating into major conflict (DeKeseredy, 2004; Perozynski and Kramer, 1999).

Although Canadian research is limited, sibling violence is considered the most common form of violence in the family (DeKeseredy, 2004). Indeed, many siblings (especially younger ones) behave like those depicted on reality shows such as *Nanny 911* or *Supernanny*, which often show siblings engaged in behaviours like hitting and pushing. Older children tend to use language instead of physical aggression to resolve conflict. Research also shows that girls are not always "sugar and spice and everything nice." Contrary to stereotypes, girls are often as violent as boys (e.g., see Duffy and Momirov, 1997), although the highest levels of sibling violence is seen in pairs of brothers (Hoffman, Kiecolt, and Edwards, 2005).

Abuse between Partners

There are many different forms of abuse between partners, from emotional abuse to murder. Abuse can occur in dating relationships, cohabiting and marital unions, and between same-sex couples. Some researchers are also beginning to include coercive controlling violence (or intimate terrorism) as a type of abuse, since it is aimed at maintaining dominance over the other partner. This can include a wide array of abusive tactics such as restricting the use of the partner's personal time or their use of the phone, or constantly accusing the other of having an affair (e.g., see Hardesty et al., 2015). Most of this research has focused on abuse against women. Like child abuse, abuse against women is rooted in history, since they have long been viewed as possessions of men. In England, for instance, women and children were considered property of the husband and father, and courts were often reluctant to interfere in domestic disputes without a third-party witness. As women's rights and feminism grew during the 1970s, the Canadian Criminal Code included wife battering as a separate offence. However, the victim often had to show a greater level of harm than what was required in cases of assaults by strangers. Moreover, it was not until 1983 that a man could be charged with raping his wife (Ward, 2002).

With respect to spousal violence (violence committed by a spouse or an ex-spouse) reported to police, rates increased for both men and women from 1995 to 2001 but have remained relatively stable since then (Statistics Canada, 2011). However, this does not mean that spousal violence was less common prior to 2001; victims may be more willing to recognize and report these experiences than in the past. It is also estimated that fewer than one in five victims of spousal violence report abuse to the police (Statistics Canada, 2016). While it appears that the vast majority of victims are female, research more generally shows that many assaults and other types of abuse (e.g., emotional) also occur against husbands. It may be that men are more reluctant than women to report abuse to authorities for fear of shame or ridicule.

Despite the fact that women do abuse men, it is well documented that women are more likely to suffer sexual assault, more serious injuries, and death than men (see figure 15.3). Women are three times more likely to be killed by husbands than vice versa. The highest incidence for spousal homicide is of women aged 15 to 24; the risk of spousal homicide declines with age. According to Statistics Canada (2011), while most male victims (66%) were killed by a common-law partner, female victims were more likely to be killed by their legally married spouse (39%) than by a common-law partner (33%). In addition, it is more common for men than women to hunt down and kill a partner who has moved out or been unfaithful, and to kill their children along with their spouse. Furthermore, women who kill their partners usually do this as a defensive action following years of abuse, and often because they see no other way out.

We are also learning more about the high prevalence of dating violence, in addition to high rates of sexual assaults on Canadian university and college campuses. In 2014, 15% of police-reported incidents of violent crime were committed by a dating partner, and

Box 15.2: Male Victims of Family Violence and Abuse: Duncan's Personal Story

I lived with a violent female. We were both 30 at the time. She had a problem. I noticed at first how everything had to be in its place, the house looked like no one lived there and she kept it spotless. My first mistake was to leave some beer bottles by the chair. I did not live there all the time. She waited till everybody left and then verbally abused me about it. That was an insight of what was to come. No. I did not have a drinking problem—it was a party.

I tried to be all the things that she wanted but drew the line at having to mow the lawn every week whether it needed it or not. In her head it had to be done regardless.

You dare not put any condiments on her cooking or you are toast. She would start a fight about nothing. She did not need a reason. One day I heard her say from the kitchen, "Why is it so fucking quiet in here?" One of her antics was to open the car door at any speed and put her foot on the road as if she was going to jump. I always pulled up. She got out of the car, came around to my side, punched me fair in the mouth, grabbed the keys out of the ignition, threw them into the bush and stormed off. Her abuse was mental as well as physical.

I can honestly say I never hit her, but she would hit me and send my teeth through my lip on a number of occasions. Because I would not hit her back she had to feel pain, so she would stand there after it and pull her own hair as hard as she could.

I lasted a year. Don't you always think it will get better? I moved out and finished the relationship. I never went out with anybody for 2 years after that and I still think it affects my view of women. I am 56.

Source: One in Three Campaign. 2016. "Personal Stories from Male Victims of Family Violence and Abuse," posted September 23. Retrieved October 28, 2016, from www.oneinthree.com.au/stories.

80% of these victims were female. Many of these victims were teenagers, adolescents, and young adults. This is a highly troubling social problem, since this time of life is a significant developmental period and an important time for establishing good relationship skills and patterns (Public Health Agency of Canada, 2016).

Finally, although spousal or woman abuse cuts across all socio-economic groups, some individuals are more vulnerable than others. For example, Papp (2010) argues that culturally driven violence against women is a growing problem in Canada's immigrant communities. Data also show that certain ethnic groups, such as Black and Indigenous women, are over-represented as clients in women's shelters (Sev'er, 2014). Moreover, Indigenous women report a higher prevalence rate of violence than non-Indigenous ones. According to the Public Health Agency of Canada (2016), Aboriginal women were more than three times as likely as Non-Aboriginal women to report that they experienced

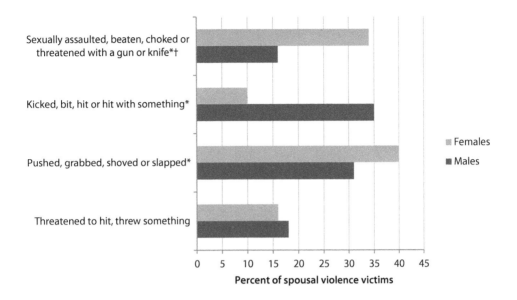

Figure 15.3: Victims of Self-Reported Spousal Violence, by Most Serious Form of Violence and by Sex, 2014

Statistically significant difference between males and females (*p* < 0.05).

†*Use* with caution.

Note: Includes legally married, common-law, same-sex, separated, and divorced spouses who reported having experienced violence within the five-year period preceding the survey.

Source: Statistics Canada. 2016. "Family Violence in Canada: A Statistical Profile." Catalogue no. 85-002-X. Ottawa: Canadian Centre for Justice Statistics.

unhealthy conflict, abuse, or violence committed by a spouse or a common-law partner in the previous five years. They were also more likely to report more severe types of violence and a more severe impact on their health. Overall, the high rates of violence and abuse witnessed in Indigenous communities should be understood within historical and political contexts. Notably, the destructive impact of colonization, including the legacy of the Residential School experience, along with deficiencies in health and social services (covered in chapter 4) have undoubtedly contributed to these unhealthy relationship patterns.

Although gender or patriarchal ideologies may not be as much of an issue in same-sex relationships, violence is as much a matter of power and control here as it is in heterosexual violence. Although we lack reliable data, the rate of violence between heterosexual and homosexual partners appears to be similar, albeit claims are usually based on findings from separate studies, rather than theoretically informed comparative studies (Anderson, 2010). As Lewin (2004: 5) argues, most research does not apply a structuralist theoretical framework that recognizes sexual orientation as a location within a structure of inequality: "Rarely do researchers consider the real institutional differences

Box 15.3: Crimes of "Honour" in Immigrant Communities

South Asians determined to maintain the oppression of women and reject assimilation into the host society use religious and cultural values as a pretext to control female chastity. This effectively places the maintenance of traditional values and family honour on the woman alone. Sons are rarely punished for their lack of chastity. Because the stakes are so high, punishment for perceived rejection or disobedience of the cultural code can be severe. The reasons for honour killings—usually offered by those perpetrating the crimes—are diverse: wearing makeup, socializing with unacceptable friends, wearing unacceptable clothes, staying out late, dating, lack of sex in the marriage, extramarital sex, gossip, or challenging the authority of the dominant male in the family.

As vital as legal and human rights policies are, more individuals and agencies that provide services to abused women are starting to identify the magnitude of domestic violence by recognizing that children are being brainwashed in the service of maintaining male power over females, and by understanding how respect for culture and religion is being exploited to sustain this control. While legal sanctions are needed, third parties cannot establish the conditions for reform. The leaders of South Asian immigrant communities must take responsibility for breaking the silence, to borrow a much-used locution from campaigns against Western paradigms of domestic violence. They must challenge the deep-rooted cultural thinking and traditional structures that lie at the root of abuse against in South Asian homes.

Community mobilization and outreach programs are important in generating dialogue within this community and developing partnerships and networks. While there are legal options for supporting women and providing safety for them, it is imperative that we generate an open dialogue within the community that is not threatening in order to guarantee the security of all immigrant women and to ensure their right to live without fear of violence from those who, according to Canadian values, should be their most trustworthy companions and protectors.

Source: Papp, A. 2010. *Culturally Driven Violence against Women: A Growing Problem in Canada's Immigrant Communities.* Winnipeg: Canada Frontier Centre for Public Policy (p. 16).

that affect, for example, homosexual and heterosexual couples differently; nor do they question the strategy of directly comparing gay and straight couples without regard for their distinct circumstances." Notably, an additional level of intimidation can exist between same-sex partners if one of them threatens to expose the sexual orientation of the other, and this other has not informed family members or co-workers. Additionally, gay and lesbian victims of violence and abuse may also be less likely than straight victims to report it to authorities because of fear of shame or ridicule (Public Health Agency of Canada, 2016).

Seniors

Seniors are vulnerable to the same types of abuse as younger family members. In fact, some researchers believe that some seniors are more vulnerable to victimization than younger members. As we age, the likelihood of disability rises, and may include mobility, hearing, vision, and speech problems as well as cognitive disabilities such as Alzheimer's disease. According to some studies, people with disabilities are 50% more likely to be victims of violence or abuse (Roeher Institute, 1995). In short, some seniors are more at risk than others. This includes not only seniors with disabilities who are dependent on others, but older seniors, women, those who are socially isolated and have reduced cognitive capacity, and seniors cared for by people with an alcohol or drug problem (NACA, 2003–2004). Risk factors for elder abuse can also be linked to situations at the individual, relationship, community, and society level as shown in table 15.3.

Table 15.3: Risk Factors for Elder Abuse Perpetration

Individual Level	• Current diagnosis of mental illness • Current abuse of alcohol • High levels of hostility • Poor or inadequate preparation or training for care giving responsibilities • Assumption of caregiving responsibilities at an early age • Inadequate coping skills • Exposure to abuse as a child
Relationship Level	• High financial and emotional dependence upon a vulnerable elder • Past experience of disruptive behavior • Lack of social support • Lack of formal support
Community Level	• Formal services, such as respite care for those providing care to elders, are limited, inaccessible, or unavailable
Societal Level	A culture where: • there is high tolerance and acceptance of aggressive behavior; • health care personnel, guardians, and other agents are given greater freedom in routine care provision and decision making; • family members are expected to care for elders without seeking help from others; • persons are encouraged to endure suffering or remain silent regarding their pains; or • there are negative beliefs about aging and elders.

In addition to the above factors, there are also specific characteristics of institutional settings that may increase the risk for perpetration of vulnerable elders in these settings, including: unsympathetic or negative attitudes toward residents, chronic staffing problems, lack of administrative oversight, staff burnout, and stressful working conditions.

Source: Centers for Disease Control and Prevention. 2014. "Elder Abuse: Risk and Protective Factors." Retrieved October 28, 2016, from www.cdc.gov/violenceprevention/elderabuse/riskprotectivefactors.html.

It is estimated that 4 to 10% of seniors experience some form of abuse, although it is difficult to arrive at accurate statistics given that many seniors do not want to report abuse to the authorities due to embarrassment, shame, or fear of ridicule or further abuse. Many elderly victims may even be unaware that they are being abused. Common types of abuse include financial abuse (e.g., misuse of money or property; forgery), physical or psychological abuse, and neglect. Neglect occurs when a caregiver fails to meet the needs of a charge who is unable to look after him or herself, such as the denial of food or visitors (Spencer, 2005). In addition, older people may be vulnerable to medication abuse, such as purposeful overdosing of drugs (which can leave the victim almost comatose), or a reluctance/refusal to give medications when needed.

There may also be cultural-specific forms of elder abuse that often remain hidden. Seniors who are recent immigrants may be isolated and completely dependent upon their families. They also commonly have language and other issues (e.g., transportation, financial) that make them particularly vulnerable to abuse and seeking outside help. Families may also hold certain cultural values regarding aging and the care of the elderly that can affect the experience of, and risk for, abuse. Based on a qualitative study of home care workers, Tam and Neysmith (2006), found that disrespect is the key form of elder abuse in the Chinese community. The concept of disrespect can be defined in many ways, but it was often described by the study participants as abusive, unnecessary scolding and nagging. It also included rude treatment (e.g., bossy and controlling behaviour), deprivation (e.g., not allowing Chinese television and radio), and space/mobility restrictions (e.g., being forced to stay in their rooms). Researchers further note that this type of emotional violence remains invisible from a Western cultural perspective, such that a social exclusion framework is needed to understand the experiences of particular immigrant populations.

Furthermore, most abuse is perpetrated by someone the senior knows. According to NACA (2003–2004), in cases of family violence, adult children and spouses account for 71% of the abusers. Older women are as likely to be abused by a spouse (36%) as by an adult child (37%), while men are more likely to be abused by an adult child (43%). Generally, these patterns have remained relatively similar over time (Public Health Agency of Canada, 2016).

CONSEQUENCES OF ABUSE: THE RIPPLE EFFECT

Victims of abuse can experience a host of negative consequences in both the short- and long-term. In particular, we are becoming increasingly aware of linkages among abuse, neglect, maltreatment, and health outcomes. One report places family violence among contributing or causal factors for a wide range of illnesses and diseases such as sleep and eating disorders, thyroid malfunction, and irritable bowel syndrome (e.g., see BCIF, 2005). Victims of serious spousal violence are also known to experience PTSD (Post-Traumatic Stress Disorder). Symptoms might include feelings of detachment, being constantly on guard, nightmares, and avoidance behaviours (Public Health Agency of Canada, 2016).

The reactions of children who witness domestic violence can include emotional, social, cognitive, physical, and behavioural maladjustment problems (e.g., see Moss,

2004). These children also tend to exhibit lower levels of social competence and higher rates of depression, worry, and frustration. They are also more likely than other children to develop stress-related disorders and to show lower levels of empathy (Dauvergne and Johnson, 2001). Polyvictims (those who have experienced multiple victimizations of different kinds rather than just multiple episodes of the same type), in particular, appear to suffer greater trauma than victims who suffered from multiple incidents of a single type of violence (Anderson, 2010).

Other studies also highlight the ripple effect of early abuse on life. For example, various forms of child maltreatment negatively affect the victim's development physically, intellectually, and psycho-socially. Moreover, victims are more likely to experience anxiety and depression, eating disorders, attachment difficulties, and low self-esteem (Kolko, 1996). A recent Canadian study also showed that a history of child abuse and maltreatment was one of the leading predictors of psychological problems in adulthood (Public Health Agency of Canada, 2016).

Abuse in childhood is also shown to be related to the risk of later victimization. For example, Laporte et al. (2011) found that female adolescents who had been victimized by either of their parents were at a greater risk for revictimization within their dating relationships. High-risk adolescent males who reported childhood victimization were at a significantly higher risk of being aggressive toward their girlfriends, especially if they had been harshly disciplined by their fathers. Also, using a longitudinal study of college women, Smith et al. (2003) found that the risk of physical and sexual assault in college was greater among respondents who reported both childhood and adolescent abuse.

Additionally, children raised in violent or conflict-ridden homes are also more likely to run away or leave home at an early age to escape an unhappy home environment (Mitchell, Wister, and Burch, 1989). This places them at risk for dropping out of high school, homelessness, and a number of social problems such as engaging in risky behaviours like prostitution, drug addiction, and criminal activities. Thus, there is a broader harm or cost to society as a whole. Not only are abuse/neglect victims more likely to engage in illegal and delinquent behaviours as teenagers and adults, but they may also create a host of additional public costs to the health care system and the economy. For example, many adult victims of violence may often skip work or arrive late, have trouble concentrating at work, or be unable to keep a job.

WHAT HAS LOVE GOT TO DO WITH IT? WHY DO PEOPLE ABUSE AND NEGLECT THEIR FAMILY MEMBERS?

There are many theories as to why people abuse their family members. They vary according to the type of abuse inflicted. For example, theories of wife abuse often focus on patriarchal structures, power, and gender inequality. On a general level, theories range from blaming the perpetrator to placing responsibility on our social structure. They fall into one of three categories: (1) violence as individual pathology; (2) violence as learned behaviour; (3) violence as a by-product of environmental stressors.

Violence as Individual Pathology

Violence is often studied from both the biological and psychological disciplines, and the treatment of family violence has been the focus of medical and mental health professionals. Analyses have therefore been directed towards the biological and psychological anomalies that produce and characterize perpetrators of violence. The medical model, also termed the pathological model, asserts that individuals who assault or abuse members of their family possess distinguishing personality characteristics that reflect some form of mental illness or pathology. This viewpoint fits in neatly with the general diagnostic framework of practitioners and the beliefs held by the general public that abusers are sick. For example, from a biological perspective, bad behaviour is the effect of a person's physiological makeup as a result of such causes as bad genes or hormonal imbalances.

In the psychological framework, defective personality structures result in individuals who are impulsive, immature, depressed, and insecure. Thus, violence and abuse occur because these individuals are incapable of loving or forming empathic attachments. However, research establishes that personality disorders occur no more often in perpetrators of violence than in the general population. Moreover, many criticize this explanation because it oversimplifies behaviour and provides an easy excuse for the perpetrator. It also fails to consider the context in which the abusive behaviour unfolds, such as opportunity structures and stressful environments.

Violence as Learned Behaviour

Social learning theory, which was covered in chapter 2, argues that violent or abusive behaviour is learned in interaction through others. For example, children who witness violence between their parents may learn that this is an acceptable means for achieving goals or resolving problems. And since the family is a primary agent of socialization, it is assumed to be a potential **cradle of violence**. For example, if small children are disciplined with physical punishment, they will imitate the behaviour and internalize the belief that violence and the use of power is a legitimate form of interpersonal control and behaviour. In this way, violence breeds violence, which perpetuates a cycle of violence (Drakich and Guberman, 1987).

This **intergenerational transmission of violence** or social learning theory viewpoint has been extensively studied. Generally, most research concludes that children who experience or are exposed to family violence do not inevitably grow up to become perpetrators of violence. However, there is only partial support for this theory. Indeed, some studies show a carry-over effect of violence from one generation to the next, which perpetuates a cycle of violence, neglect, and maltreatment (Zuravin et al., 1996). Therefore, several other social and cultural factors must also be taken into account.

Violence as a By-product of Environmental Stressors

From this perspective, the perpetrator is considered the primary source of violence, but he or she has been pushed to it by environmental triggers or stressors such as alcohol, drugs, or stress. Stress is defined as "a state which arises from an actual or perceived imbalance between demand (e.g., challenge, threat) and capacity (e.g., resources, coping) in the family's functioning" (Huang, 1991: 289). Indeed, stress as an explanation for family violence is pervasive in the literature, and the family is seen as a receptacle for both inside and outside stresses (Drakich and Guberman, 1987). This has led researchers to the famous ABCX family crisis model, devised by Hill in 1949. Simply put, A (the stressor event) interacts with B (the family's crisis-meeting resources), and C (the definition the family makes of the event), which in turn produces X (the crisis).

Possible environmental stressors include new members added to the family structure, the death of a family member, divorce, war, and natural catastrophes such as earthquakes or hurricanes. Recently, this model has been expanded to the **Double ABCX crisis model of stress**. This revised model takes into account the idea that the ability to cope depends on family circumstances when the stressor is experienced. It also emphasizes family wellness and strengths rather than a pathological or deficient model of families (e.g., see Price, Bush, and Price, 2017). Also, since all families experience prior strains and hardships, there can be a pile-up of stresses (the AA in the model). New resources, such as social support (BB in the model), may help the family to cope. Coping is also influenced by the family's perception of the demand pile-up (the CC in the model). Generally, strong and resilient families adapt more successfully to stresses. Weak families have less flexibility and fewer resources for dealing with stresses, and therefore handle stress less effectively.

The fact that stress exists both inside and outside the family cannot be denied. Lack of social support, unemployment, relationship and health problems, workplace and child-care challenges, and other demands can create considerable stress and anxiety. This can place individuals at risk of making poor decisions, as depicted in box 15.4, where an elderly man accidentally kills his wife, who suffers from dementia. Moreover, there is a link between stress, violence, and alcohol/drug abuse. However, not all individuals who experience stress or abuse alcohol or drugs harm their family members. Indeed, alcohol abuse is considered a "disavowal technique" that releases the individual from feeling responsibility for violent behaviour. Therefore, attention must extend beyond the precipitating factors of stress to social structural conditions and institutional practices that can trigger or contribute to abuse and neglect.

An Ecological and Dialectical Perspective: Social Location and Context, Contradictions, and Institutional Practices

A critical evaluation of the previous theories suggests that it is fruitful to consider various levels of risk factors from an **ecological perspective**, a conceptual framework that was

Box 15.4: Domestic Abuse Walk Returns

Sherwood Park residents can once again take a stand against domestic abuse by participating in Wednesday's Regional Walk Against Domestic Abuse. The walk will take place on Oct. 5 at 6:30 p.m. at the Rotary Clock in front of the Strathcona County Library at 401 Festival Lane. The event is free, but organizers will accept donations to A Safe Place, a shelter for abused women and their children.

Rugby Orvis got the idea for the walk from seeing women from her mother's group defend women who had been killed as a result of domestic abuse from nasty comments online. "We're all trying to show support for these families and the people that have been lost, so why don't we have a walk?" Orvis said. "Let's do something positive, let's bring some awareness and show some support rather than everybody following these comments on newsfeeds."

Strathcona County RCMP and Enforcement Services said the number of domestic violence calls in the county has increased by 18% since 2014. A survey by the Alberta Council of Women's Shelters found three in five men in Alberta said they don't understand why women stay in abusive relationships, and half believe women could leave a violent relationship if they really wanted to.

This belief has proven to be false. Almost 60% of all dating violence happens after the relationship has ended, according to Statistics Canada. One American study found women are 70 times more likely to be killed in the two weeks after making an attempt to leave than at any other time in the relationship.

Domestic abuse hurts more than the women involved. Justice Canada estimates family violence costs taxpayers $7.4 billion every year. A study by the University of Toronto found children who witness chronic parental domestic violence before the age of 16 are at least twice as likely to attempt suicide. "It is a quiet topic that not a lot of people talk about," Orvis said. "[By having the walk], we're trying to make it a topic that people are more likely to speak about."

Source: Grace-Dacosta, M. 2016. "Domestic Abuse Walk Returns." *Sherwood Park News*, September 29. Retrieved October 28, 2016, from www.sherwoodparknews.com/2016/09/29/domestic-abuse-walk-returns.

introduced in chapter 2. This perspective is based on evidence that no single factor can explain why some individuals or groups are at a higher risk of interpersonal violence while others are more protected from it (World Health Organization, 2005). As articulated by leading proponent Bronfenbrenner (1979: 3), "the ecological model environment is conceived as a set of nested structures, each inside the other like a set of Russian dolls." This model is applied in figure 15.4, where violence is conceptualized as the outcome of interaction among many factors at four levels: the individual, the relationship, the community, and

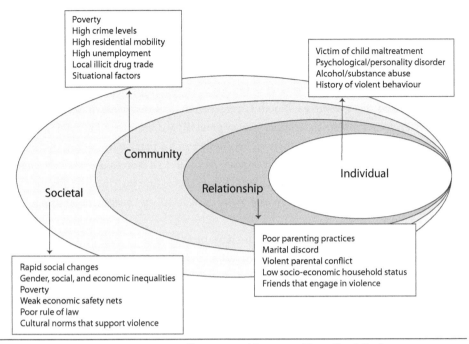

Poverty
High crime levels
High residential mobility
High unemployment
Local illicit drug trade
Situational factors

Victim of child maltreatment
Psychological/personality disorder
Alcohol/substance abuse
History of violent behaviour

Community

Individual

Societal

Relationship

Rapid social changes
Gender, social, and economic inequalities
Poverty
Weak economic safety nets
Poor rule of law
Cultural norms that support violence

Poor parenting practices
Marital discord
Violent parental conflict
Low socio-economic household status
Friends that engage in violence

Figure 15.4: An Ecological Perspective on Family Violence:
Examples of Risk Factors at Each Level

Source: Adapted from World Health Organization (WHO). 2005. "Violence Prevention Alliance: Building
Global Commitment for Violence Prevention. *Global Campaign for Violence Prevention.* Geneva: WHO Press.
Retrieved December 2, 2007, from www.whqlibdoc.who.int/publications/2005/924159313X_eng.pdf.

the societal. These factors range from macro-societal structures in a patriarchal capitalist
society (e.g., laws, ageism, sexism, racism) to meso/exo-level factors (e.g., social networks
and community resources available, work-related elements, relationship history) to micro-
level individual factors (e.g., gender, age, drug abuse history, personality).

A focus on these nested structures and processes illuminates how certain social
structural conditions (e.g., poverty and a lack of community supports), combined with institutional practices in a variety of realms (e.g., law, policing, and social work), contribute to
individual acts of violence, abuse, or neglect. For example, Swift (1995) provides a powerful
critique of how many organizational practices obscure social injustices and place the blame
for neglectful mothers back onto poor mothers for failing to cope. Similarly, McKendy
(1997) shows how certain ideological practices work to keep "class seen but unnoticed" in
cases of wife abuse. In particular, these practices obscure the issues of inequality and the
conditions faced by poor men in a patriarchal capitalist society that place them at a greater
risk for wife abuse.

Moreover, institutional practices and responses can impinge on an individual's ability
to deal with abuse and neglect and prevent further abuse or neglect from occurring. For

example, Renzetti (2005) offers a **dialectical approach to intimate aggression** (which dates back to such classical theorists such as Karl Marx) that is congruent with a life-course and ecological perspective. This dialectical approach emphasizes how social location (e.g., age, gender, class, race/ethnicity, sexuality, disability, and geography) intersects with structural and institutional contexts. It is dialectical in that it considers contradictions and tensions between these domains. Notably, perpetrators and recipients of aggression react to, understand, and act on aggression within prevailing discourses of gender, intimacy, sexuality, and violence that are deeply rooted in hierarchy, patriarchy, racism, heteronormativity, and inequity. Intimate violence is paradoxical in that it often occurs in the context of a loving or supportive relationship that is also shocking and hurtful. The violence may also be preceded and followed by everyday acts of care, hostility, concern, or control (Olsen, Fine, and Lloyd, 2005).

Examining the scenario of women who have been abused by their partners, Renzetti (2005) notes that they often reject arrest and jailing of their partner because they fear negative consequences for their children. These women may rely on their partner for child care or financial support and may be unable to pay for child care in the public sector. Jailing a partner, therefore, might mean having to travel several hours a day by public transportation to a low-paying job, which further limits their ability to care for their children. As a result, certain institutional practices (which, ironically, were created to protect women and hold men accountable for their actions) can impede some women's agency in dealing with abuse as well as other aspects of their lives, particularly in the absence of alternative resources.

Overall, an ecological and dialectical perspective does not excuse the individual for violent or abusive behaviour. Rather, it provides a contextual social location explanation that anchors acts of abuse and neglect in relation to issues of vulnerability, dependency, and access to resources and ideological and institutional practices. This emphasis on deeply-rooted or systemic contributors to social problems helps us to improve action-oriented solutions (e.g., eradicating poverty, changing norms) to a very serious social problem. Unfortunately, however, these solutions tend not to be implemented because this would require a significant restructuring and more equal distribution of societal resources, in addition to changing dominant societal discourse and systemic institutional practices. Nonetheless, we will briefly review some of the commonly used approaches to prevention and intervention.

PREVENTION AND INTERVENTION

Preventing family violence and stress before they occur is an obvious way to reduce or eradicate these problems. Three basic approaches to prevention include: (1) primary prevention; (2) secondary prevention; and (3) tertiary prevention.

Primary prevention is the attempt to keep abuse from occurring at all. This is done mainly through education. An example is the widespread "No means no" campaign launched by the Canadian Federation of Students on university campuses during the 1980s. This campaign was designed to prevent date rape and dating violence against young women by educating young men. Courses in marriage preparation, prenatal care, parental education, and caregiving for the elderly can also include the discussion of abuse. These courses can also provide individuals with strategies and resources to prevent stress and abuse such as the tragic scenario depicted in box 15.4. Visits by public health nurses to new mothers, recent immigrants, and isolated elderly people can also play an important role. These professionals are trained to spot early signs of stress, dependency, and abuse. As a result, they can refer stressed individuals to the appropriate educational, health, and support programs (Wachtel, 1999).

Secondary prevention programs entail working with groups deemed to be at risk for abuse. For instance, in the case of preventing child abuse, programs geared at prenatal nutrition, fetal alcohol syndrome support programs, and remedial schools (e.g., for children diagnosed with attention deficit disorder) could be helpful. Providing poor families with adequate income and housing assistance can also help to alleviate stress. With respect to elder abuse, outreach programs can reduce isolation, and educational programs can teach elders how to avoid physical and financial exploitation. For example, seniors can be taught the importance of having accurate knowledge of their finances and being alert to unusual withdrawals from their bank accounts (NACA, 2003–2004).

The third approach, **tertiary prevention**, is one of the most common, and it entails treatment or some other intervention to keep abuse from recurring. For example, services for battered women, such as help lines, shelters and temporary housing, counselling, and skills training can help them to leave an abusive situation. Other types of intervention include counselling and anger-management courses for perpetrators, and educational programs to teach effective parenting skills to abusive parents (e.g., Wachtel, 1999; Ward, 2002). This approach is generally viewed as less costly (at least in the short term) than the first two, which are more broad-based. However, it is often criticized for being a Band-aid solution, since it usually does not address systemic factors that can often be traced to deeper root issues of poverty, racism, sexism, and ageism.

Although these common "cookie cutter" approaches have addressed issues of violence and have offered some strategies for interventions and prevention, a growing number of scholars and activists argue that we must critique the role of the state's engagement in violence in general. In particular, it is highly problematic to reduce domestic violence to a criminal justice and social service issue without addressing broader institutionalized social, economic, and political vulnerabilities of certain individuals. For example, a more long-term solution should provide a more comprehensive, coordinated response that does not slot and compartmentalize various forms of violence. This kind of approach would also invest in non-paternalistic state policy instruments such as education, affordable and safe housing, health care, and pathways to economic independence in order to provide people with the ability to escape abuse (Abraham and Tastsoglou, 2016).

SUMMARY

In this chapter, the dark side of family life is brought to light through an exploration of what can occur behind closed doors. Tragically, violence, abuse, and stress exist in many families, and some people, such as women, children, and seniors, are more vulnerable to these problems. Indeed, we may have more reason to fear a member of our own family than someone we don't know. Thus, our intense fears of "stranger danger" are not well founded. An examination of various definitional and methodological issues also shows that violence, abuse, and neglect are difficult to measure and probably seriously underreported. In fact, many question the use of generic terms such as family violence or domestic abuse because they can fail to identity the most likely perpetrators or targets (e.g., see Sev'er, 2014).

A critical analysis of general theories of violence, abuse, and stress reveal that searching for a singular cause is futile. Instead, these problems are multifactorial and can fruitfully be viewed from a life-course ecological perspective that considers social location and the dialectical nature of violence, abuse, and neglect. This holistic framework incorporates a multitude of risk factors and addresses the interactions between persons, socio-cultural contexts, and institutional practices. For example, inadequate financial resources and a lack of social supports for caring for a dependent elderly family member can foster caregiver resentment against the elderly member and an inability to provide proper care. And when cultural values like ageism are included in the picture, older adults may be seen as less worthy than younger individuals, further contributing to a family climate conducive to elder abuse.

Moreover, a dialectical approach reminds us that while family life has a darker and more malevolent connotation, it is also filled with contradictions and tensions, including an odd, paradoxical mixture of aggression and tenderness (Olsen, Fine, and Lloyd, 2005). This observation suggests that family violence, abuse, and neglect are complex and multifaceted.

While domestic violence and abuse cuts across communities, its damage is compounded by historical, structural, and cultural factors. Therefore, when it comes to issues of law and social policy, intersections of gender with such aspects as ethnicity/race and Indigenous status, class, immigration, and citizenship status, region, ableness, and sexuality must be taken into account. And despite our awareness that family violence has an impact on health beyond immediate physical injury and an increasing risk for many health-related problems, it remains a significant social problem that is in many cases highly preventable. In short, it is critical for policy makers to make more long-term investments in addressing and eradicating this serious social problem, with its significant health and economic costs to individuals, families, and society.

QUESTIONS FOR CRITICAL REFLECTION AND DEBATE

1. Discuss some key methodological barriers to collecting data on the prevalence of violence and abuse within the family. What strategies might help researchers to collect more accurate data?

2. Many people believe that family life was better in "the good old days" and that violence and abuse in families is a relatively recent phenomenon. Do you agree or disagree with this assertion?

3. Why are family members often reluctant to report abuse to the authorities? Do these reasons vary by gender, age, socio-economic status, or location?

4. Identify some major sources of family stress that could trigger violence and abuse and relate these examples to the Double ABCX model.

5. Debate the following: Victims of child abuse are more likely to become abusers when they are adults than those who were not victimized as children.

6. What do you think the community's role should be in providing services to families and individuals under stress and at risk of inflicting violence and abuse? Should the focus be placed on prevention programs or assistance programs?

GLOSSARY

Cradle of violence refers to how the family environment is a potential birthplace of violence, since it is the key agent of socialization.

Dialectical approach to intimate aggression offers theoretical integration and a focus on paradox, contradictions, and tensions in close relations that are intertwined with social, historical, and environmental contexts.

Double ABCX crisis model of stress extends the ABCX model of stress, with its focus on pile-up events and the family's access to resources during crisis events.

Ecological perspective applied to family violence contextualizes risk factors at four nested levels: macro (societal), meso (community), exo (relationship), and micro (individual).

Family violence occurs largely between family members and intimate partners and usually takes place in the home. It can involve physical, sexual, or psychological force or power, as well as deprivation or neglect.

Intergenerational transmission of violence refers to how violence is transmitted from one generation to the next.

Polyvictimization is exposure to multiple types of violence, crime, or abuse.

Primary prevention is geared toward preventing family violence and abuse in the first place and can be distinguished from intervention strategies.

Secondary prevention entails working with groups that are at risk for violence and abuse.

Tertiary prevention refers to treatments or interventions that keep abuse from recurring.

FURTHER READING

Asay, S.M., J.D. DeFrain, M. Metzger, and B. Moyer (eds.). 2014. *Family Violence from a Global Perspective: A Strengths-Based Approach,* Thousand Oaks, California: Sage.
This collection of essays outlines and follows a strengths-based conceptual framework for understanding family violence worldwide. Focusing on the lived experiences of victims, the book draws on the expertise of authors from 16 countries representing 17 cultures to tell the story of domestic violence in their respective parts of the world.

Cook, P.W., and T.L. Hodo. 2013. *When Women Sexually Abuse Men: The Hidden Side of Rape, Stalking, Harassment, and Sexual Assault.* Santa Barbara, CA: Praeger.
This companion and follow up to the 2009 *Abused Men* is intended for general readership. It provides a comprehensive overview of research, news account, and personal stories of adult men who were sexually assaulted or harassed by women.

DeKeseredy, W.S., M. Dragiewicz, and M.A. Schwartz. 2017. *Abusive Endings: Separation and Divorce Violence against Women.* Los Angeles: University of California Press.
Part of the Gender and Justice Series. Based on many years of fieldwork, this book is punctuated with the stories and voices of both perpetrators and survivors of abuse. This highly readable book will be a useful resource for researchers, practitioners, activists, and policy makers.

González-López, G. 2015. *Family Secrets: Stories of Incest and Sexual Violence in Mexico.* New York: New York University Press.
This gripping, emotional narrative brings the unspoken issues of incest and sexual violence in families to light. Through a feminist and sociological lens, it tells the life stories of 60 men and women in Mexico whose lives were irrevocably changed in the wake of childhood and adolescent incest.

LaViolette, A.D., and O.W. Barnett. 2014. *It Could Happen to Anyone: Why Battered Women Stay.* 3rd ed. Los Angeles: Sage.
Completely revised and expanded, this book addresses cross-cultural issues in partner violence, immigrant and racialized women, and violence and abuse in same-sex partnerships.

Pelzer, D. 2014. *Too Close to Me: The Middle-Aged Consequences of Revealing a Child Called "It."* New York: Rosetta Books.
This book provides an honest and courageous examination of the difficulties inherent in marriage, parenthood, work, and life from the perspective of someone who survived horrific physical and emotional terrors as a child.

RELATED WEB SITES

Child Welfare League of Canada is a national organization dedicated to promoting the well-being and protection of vulnerable young people in Canada. It promotes best practices for those who work in the field of child welfare, children's mental health, and youth justice and contains links to research and policy initiatives. www.cwlc.ca.

Family Violence in Canada: A Statistical Profile 2014 (released January 21, 2016) is available as free, downloadable copy of a recent Statistics Canada report, www.statcan.gc.ca/pub/85-002-x/2016001/article/14303-eng.pdf.

Stop Family Violence provides a one-stop source of information on family violence for those affected and also for professionals that are involved in prevention. This part of the Family Violence Prevention initiative falls under the umbrella of **Public Health Agency of Canada,** combines pages from **National Clearinghouse on Family Violence, Child Maltreatment Division** and those listed previously under **Health Canada** directory section on violence. Stop Family Violence. Links to supports and services in a given geographic area are provided, in addition to a section specific to people with disabilities. www.phac-aspc.gc.ca/sfv-avf/index-eng.php.

International Network for the Prevention of Elder Abuse is dedicated to global dissemination of information on the prevention of abuse against older people, www.inpea.net.

Status of Women Canada is a federal government organization that promotes equality for women and their full participation in the economic, social and democratic life of Canada. Amongst other issues it focuses on ending violence against women and girls, and gender-based violence. Status of Women Canada is responsible for providing strategic policy advice, gender-based analysis support, and administration of the Women's Program. www.swc-cfc.gc.ca/index-en.html; Facebook: www.facebook.com/womencanada Twitter: www.twitter.com/Women_Canada

REFERENCES

Abraham, M., and E. Tastsoglou. 2016. "Addressing Domestic Violence in Canada and the United States: The Uneasy Co-Habitation of Women and the State." *Current Sociology* 64: 568-585.

Anderson, K.L. 2010. "Conflict, Power, and Violence in Families." *Journal of Marriage and the Family* 72: 726–742.

BCIF (BC Institute against Family Violence). 2005. "The Health-Care Costs of Family Violence." *Aware Newsletter* 12, no. 1 (Summer).

Bronfenbrenner, U. 1979. *The Ecology of Human Development: Experiments by Nature and Design.* Cambridge: Harvard University Press.

CBC News 2011 (March 28). "Son Charged in Killing of Barrie-Area Couple." Retrieved August 10, 2011, from cbc.ca.news/Canada/Toronto/story/2011/03/28/barrie-rem.

Dauvergne, M., and H. Johnson. 2001. "Children Witnessing Family Violence." *Juristat* 21, no. 6. Catalogue no. 85-002-XPE. Ottawa: Statistics Canada.

Dawson, M. 2015. "Canadian Trends in Filicide by Gender of the Accused, 1961–2011." *Child Abuse and Neglect* 47: 162-174.

DeKeseredy, W. 2005. "Patterns of Family Violence." In M. Baker (ed.), *Families: Changing Trends in Canada*, 5th ed., (pp. 229–257). Toronto: McGraw-Hill Ryerson.

Drakich, J., and C. Guberman. 1987. "Violence in the Family." In K.L. Anderson et al. (eds.), *Family Matters: Sociology and Contemporary Canadian Family Patterns* (pp. 201–335). Toronto: Methuen.

Duffy, A., and J. Momirov. 1997. *Family Violence: A Canadian Introduction.* Toronto: James Lorimer.

Eichler, M. 1983. *Families in Canada Today: Recent Changes and Their Policy Consequences.* Toronto: Gage Publishing.

Engelbreit, M. 2005. *Mary Engelbreit's Mother Goose: One Hundred Best-Loved Verses.* New York: HarperCollins.

Slowikowski, J., D. Finkelhor, H. Turner, S. Hamby, and R. Ormrod. 2011. "Polyvictimization: Children's Exposure to Multiple Types of Violence, Crime, and Abuse." US Department of Justice, Office of Juvenile Justice and Delinquency Prevention. Rockville, MD: Juvenile Justice Clearinghouse.

Flynn, C.P. 1998. "To Spank or Not to Spank: The Effect of Situation and Age of Child on Support for Corporal Punishment." *Journal of Family Violence* 13: 21–37.

Hardesty, J., K.A. Crossman, M. Haselschwerdt, M. Raffaelli, B.G. Ogolsky, and M.P. Johnson. 2015. "Toward a Standard Approach to Operationalizing Coercive Control and Classifying Violence Types. *Journal of Marriage and the Family* 77: 833-843.

Hoffman, K.L., K.J. Kiecolt, and J.N. Edwards. 2005. "Physical Violence between Siblings: A Theoretical and Empirical Analysis." *Journal of Family Issues* 26: 1103–1130.

Huang, I.-C.1991. "Family Stress and Coping." In S.J. Bahr (ed.), *Family Research: A Sixty-Year Review, 1930–1990.* Vol. 1. New York: Lexington Books, Maxwell MacMillan International.

Kolko, D. 1996. "Child Physical Abuse." In J. Briere, L. Berliner, J.A. Bulkley, C. Jenny, and T. Reid (eds.), *The APSAC Handbook on Child Maltreatment.* Thousand Oaks, California: Sage Publications.

Kolko, D. 2002. "Child Physical Abuse." In J.E.B. Myers, L. Berliner, J. Briere, C.T. Hendrix, C. Jenny, and T. Reid (eds.), *The APSAC Handbook on Child Maltreatment.* 2nd ed. (pp.21–54). Thousand Oaks, California: Sage Publications.

Lasch, C. 1979. *Haven in a Heartless World: The Family Besieged.* New York: Basic Books.

Laporte, L., D. Jiang, D.J. Pepler, and C. Chamberland. 2011. "The Relationship between Adolescents' Experience of Family Violence and Dating Violence." *Youth and Society* 43: 3–27.

Lewin, E. 2004. "Does Marriage Have a Future?" *Journal of Marriage and the Family* 66: 1000–1006.

McKendy, J.P. 1997. "The Class Politics of Domestic Violence." *Journal of Sociology and Social Welfare* 24: 135–155.

Mitchell, B.A., A.V. Wister, and T.K. Burch. 1989. "The Family Environment and Leaving the Parental Home." *Journal of Marriage and the Family* 51: 605–613.

Moss, K. 2004. "Kids Witnessing Family Violence." *Canadian Social Trends* 73: 12–16.

NACA (National Advisory Council on Aging). 2003–2004. "Hidden Harm: The Abuse of Seniors." *Expressions: Bulletin of the NACA* 17, no. 1. Ottawa: Government of Canada.

Olsen, L.N., M.A. Fine, and S.A. Lloyd. 2005. "Theorizing about Aggression between Intimates." In V.L. Bengtson, A.C. Acock, K.R. Allen, P. Dilworth-Anderson, and D.M. Klein (eds.), *Sourcebook of Family Theory and Research* (pp. 315–331). Thousand Oaks, California: Sage.

Papp, A. 2010. "Culturally Driven Violence against Women. A Growing Problem in Canada's Immigrant Communities." *FCPP Policy Series, July 2010.* Winnipeg: Frontier Centre for Public Policy.

Perozynski, L., and L. Kramer. 1999. "Parental Beliefs about Managing Sibling Conflict." *Developmental Psychology* 35: 489–499.

Price, C., K. Bush, and S. Price. 2017. *Families and Change: Coping with Stressful Events and Transitions,* 5th ed. Thousand Oaks, California: Sage Publications.

Public Health Agency of Canada. 2016. *Report on the State of Public Health in Canada 2016: A Focus on Family Violence in Canada.* Ottawa: Government of Canada.

Renzetti, C.M. 2005. "The Challenges and Promise of a Dialectical Approach to Theorizing about Intimate Violence." In V.L. Bengtson, A.C. Acock, K.R. Allen, P. Dilworth-Anderson, and D.M. Klein (eds.), *Sourcebook of Family Theory and Research* (pp. 335–337). Thousand Oaks, California: Sage.

Roeher Institute. 1995. *Harm's Way: The Many Faces of Violence and Abuse against Persons with Disabilities.* North York: Roeher Institute.

Sev'er, A. 2014. "All in the Family: Violence against Women, Children, and the Aged." In D. Cheal and P. Albanese (eds.), *Canadian Families Today: New Perspectives,* 3rd ed. (pp. 273–291). Toronto: Oxford University Press.

Slowikowski, J., D. Finkelhor, H. Turner, S. Hamby, and R. Ormrod. 2011. "Polyvictimization: Children's Exposure to Multiple Types of Violence, Crime, and Abuse." US Department of Justice, Office of Juvenile Justice and Delinquency Prevention. Rockville, MD: Juvenile Justice Clearinghouse.

Smith, P.H., White, J.W., and L.J. Holland. 2003. "A Longitudinal Perspective on Dating Violence among Adolescent and College-Age Women." *Journal of American Public Health Associations* 93: 1104–1109.

Spencer, C. 2005. "Abuse in Institutions." In A. Soden (ed.), *Advising the Older Client* (pp. 235–246). Markham: LexisNexis Butterworths.

Statistics Canada. 2011. *Family Violence in Canada: A Statistical Profile, 2011.* Canadian Centre for Justice Statistics. Retrieved August 3, 2011, from www.statcan.gc.ca/pub/85-244-x/2010000/ct016-eng.htm.

Statistics Canada, Canadian Centre for Justice Statistics. 2016. *Family Violence in Canada: A Statistical Profile, 2014.* Canadian Centre for Justice Statistics. Catalogue no. 85-002-X. Ottawa: Minister of Industry.

Swift, K.J. 1995. *Manufacturing "Bad" Mothers: A Critical Perspective on Child Neglect.* Toronto: University of Toronto Press.

Tam, S., and S. Neysmith. 2006. "Disrespect and Isolation: Elder Abuse in Chinese Communities." *Canadian Journal on Aging* 25: 141–151.

Victims of Violence. 2011. "Incest: Introduction, Definition, Victims, and Perpetrators." Retrieved August 10, 2011, from www.victimsofviolence.on.ca/rev2/index.php.

Wachtel, A. 1989. *Discussion Paper: Child Abuse.* Ottawa: Health and Welfare Canada.

Wachtel, A. 1999. *The "State of Art" in Child Abuse Prevention, 1977.* Ottawa: Health Canada.

Ward, M. 2002. *The Family Dynamic: A Canadian Perspective*, 3rd ed. Toronto: Nelson Thomson Learning.

World Health Organization. 2005. *Violence Prevention Alliance.* Retrieved October 11, 2005, from www.who.int/violenceprevention.

Zuravin, S., C. McMillan, D. DePantilis, and C. Risley-Curtis. 1996. "The Intergenerational Cycle of Child Maltreatment: Continuity versus Discontinuity." *Journal of Interpersonal Violence* 7: 471–489.

CHAPTER 16

Families and the State:
Family Policy in an Era of Globalization
and Economic Uncertainty

LEARNING OBJECTIVES

In this chapter you will learn that ...

- family policy within the context of broader social policy is influenced by political environments, processes of globalization, and economic restructuring
- a critical perspective on family policy is needed
- key policy issues face Canadian families at all phases of the life course
- there are distinctions between policy advocacy, research, and evaluation
- many recommendations for forward-looking family policy have been made
- there are numerous policy challenges for future family life

INTRODUCTION

Many of us have heard former Prime Minister Pierre Trudeau's highly quoted 1967 statement that "There's no place for the state in the bedrooms of the nation" (e.g., CBC News, 1976). And while most of us would support this general principle with respect to the sexual behaviour of consenting adults, many of us would also agree that there will always be a need for governments to support and regulate other aspects of family life. Indeed, for over a century, the state has regulated many domains of family life by enforcing government legislation and regulations.

The **welfare state** has been a defining feature of advanced capitalist societies, especially since the end of World War Two. It refers to government-sponsored programs designed to improve the social and economic well-being of families and individuals, and is comprised of an intricate web of supports. These supports include income and security payments, social insurance, universal and targeted cash transfers, and a wide range of social services (including housing, education, and health care), as well as several related laws and regulatory measures (Evans and Wekerle, 1997; Olsen, 2002).

As social programs (most of which were developed between the 1950s and 1970s) became more costly, governments began to question their ability to improve them or even to maintain them (Baker, 2005). Between the late 1970s and the 1990s, economic growth was generally slow. Spurred by factors such as **globalization** and world trade production, this was a period punctuated by severe worldwide recessions and rapidly escalating rates of unemployment (Olsen, 2002). As a result of these and other social, economic, and political transformations, the welfare state was dramatically restructured and reshaped. A notable outcome of this retrenchment has been massive cutbacks in state supports and a heavier reliance on family and community resources. High levels of inequality and disparities both across and within countries have also deepened. Taken together, these trends have introduced a number of new challenges for Canadian families.

Along with these points, a number of family policy issues from a critical, life-course perspective will be examined in this chapter. First, we will define what we mean by social and family policy. This will be followed by an identification of some important policy issues relevant to the life courses of Canadian families. A brief overview of policy advocacy and research will be provided, as well as a number of forward-looking policy recommendations. Finally, salient policy issues likely to affect families in the near future will be identified, in recognition of the major trends, themes, and issues covered throughout this book.

WHAT IS SOCIAL AND FAMILY POLICY?

Broadly speaking, social policies and programs are those social arrangements aimed at the distribution of social resources and the promotion of the welfare of the individual and society. They are formed out of competing values (Gee and McDaniel, 1994). **Family policy**, therefore, is a subfield of social policy concerned with the problems of families in relation to society and whose goal is the advancement of family well-being. It can be defined as "a coherent set of principles about the state's role in family life which is implemented through legislation or a plan of action" (Baker, 1995: 5). Yet, it is important to recognize that numerous definitions of family policy have been advanced, and these are characterized by differences in scope, content, and target audience. For example, Kamerman and Kahn (1978: 3) conceptualize the scope of family policy as "everything that government does to and for the family."

Moreover, as summarized in box 16.1, Baker (1995) states that family policy can be divided into three categories: (1) laws relating to family issues (e.g., marriage, adoption, divorce, child support); (2) policies to help family income (e.g., tax concessions, maternity leave); and (3) the provision of direct services (e.g., child care, home care health services, subsidized housing). Family policies are objectives and goals that are more or less deliberate, intended, and desirable, while programs are the practical applications used to achieve or fulfill those goals. Thus, the range of policies and programs affecting families is very broad; some support a nurturance or social function, while others support economic ones.

Box 16.1: Families, the State, and Family Policies

The government of Canada has never developed explicit family policies, in part because it lacks the jurisdiction to intervene in many areas of family life. In addition, there is little consensus about how to create more explicit and cohesive family policies. In fact, two broad views are prevalent among the lobby groups pressuring government. One is that family structure and practices reflect pressures and changes in the broader society as well as personal preferences. Therefore, governments cannot easily modify them through legislation or regulation. Nevertheless, parents make an important contribution to society by raising children, and they deserve ongoing state supports to combine paid work with child care and to raise children under difficult circumstances. The contrasting view is that the family is deteriorating and declining as the major institution in society. The state has an obligation to fight against unhealthy influences and the intrusion and growing acceptance of alternative lifestyles. One way of doing this is to tighten welfare rules, ensure that the family remains a legal and heterosexual unit, and strictly enforce parental and spousal obligations.

In recent years, governments have tried to strengthen families but have found that new policies are difficult to create, costly to enforce, and often have unintended results. Any new initiative is fraught with controversy and opposition from various lobby groups. Interest groups from the political left and those who applaud new family forms are suspicious of the call for a family policy because they fear it could represent a conservative agenda opposing greater equality for women and families of choice. Groups on the political right often argue that new programs are too expensive and reward the "undeserving" poor. Creating social policies and programs that integrate these two opposing viewpoints has been challenging, both for Canada and other countries.

Source: Baker, M. 2005. "Families, the State, and Family Policies." In M. Baker, *Families: Changing Trends in Canada*, 5th ed. (pp. 258–276). Toronto: McGraw-Hill Ryerson (pp. 275–276).

It is also important to recognize that, unlike many European countries, Canada (with the exception of Quebec) has never developed explicit family policies in which the state's role is very clear (see table 16.1). This is because it lacks the jurisdiction to intervene in many areas of family life. Instead, most governments have an array of policies and practices that affect families either directly or indirectly. These implicit policies establish general legislation and social programs that contain a particular ideological view of family and the role of the state in family life. **Family ideologies** can be found within laws, social policies, and regulations, rather than within one specific document.

Despite the absence of an explicit family policy in Canada, Eichler (1987) argues that two different models have directed most family-oriented policies (see table 16.2 for a chronology of selected family-support policies in Canada). These are: (1) the Patriarchal Model of the Family; and (2) the Individual Responsibility Model of the Family. These models can be distinguished by a number of both shared and unique characteristics. In both models, the household and the family are treated as identical. However, in the first model, the husband/father is viewed as responsible for the economic well-being of the family, while the wife/mother is seen as responsible for the household and the personal care of family members, especially children. This model is premised on the notion of gender inequality, which expresses itself in a rather strict gendered division of labour. Women are largely viewed as dependents. Conversely, the second model assumes that each partner is responsible for his or her own support. Also, both father and mother are seen as responsible for the household and personal care of family members, especially children.

Although Canadian social policies largely reflect the Individual Responsibility Model (especially since the late 1970s), a good example of policy based on patriarchal assumptions

Table 16.1: Defining Social and Family Policy

Term	Definition and Examples
Social Policy	Social arrangements aimed at the distribution of social resources and the promotion of the welfare of the individual and society; formed out of competing values at three levels of government (federal, provincial, and municipal); impacts all families
Family Policy	A subfield of social policy; addresses family-related conditions and problems; refers to a coherent set of generally agreed-upon (explicit or implicit) principles about the state's role in family life; implemented through legislation or a plan of action; can be divided into three categories: (1) laws relating to family issues (e.g., marriage, adoption, divorce, child support); (2) policies to help family income (e.g., tax concessions, maternity leave); (3) the provision of direct services (e.g., child welfare, home care health services, subsidized housing)

Table 16.2: Chronology of Selected Social Policies and Reforms in Canada

Social Benefit	Descriptions and Reforms
Family Tax Benefits (1918-1993)	Tax deductions for taxpayers with dependants began with first Income Tax Act; tax credits added 1972
Mothers/Widows Pensions (1920+)	Started around 1920; date varies by province
Old Age Pension	Established in 1926 as a pension for those with low incomes; became a universal pension in 1951
Family Allowance	Paid to all mothers for each child (replaced by the Child Tax Benefit in 1993)
(Un)employment Insurance (1940)	Established as a federal social insurance program; other insurance benefits added over time (e.g., maternity in 1971)
Medicare (1966)	Public insurance established for hospitals and diagnostic services in 1958 and for visits to physicians in 1966
Spouses Allowance (1975)	Created as an income-tested pension for spouses aged 60–64 of old age pensioners, mainly women
Resolution to end "Child Poverty" (1989)	An all-party agreement in Parliament
Canada Child Tax Benefit (1998)	Prior Child Tax Benefit (1993–1998) merged with Working Income Supplement
Choice in Child Care Allowance (2006)	$100 per month direct payment per child under the age of six in addition to current Canada Child Tax Benefit, National Child Benefit Supplement, and Child Care Expenses Deduction (although these amounts will decrease in certain households)
Canada Child Benefit Program (2016)	Combines the previous Canada Child Tax Benefit and the Universal Child Care Benefit into one benefit that is entirely income-tested

Sources: Derived from information presented in Baker, M. 2005. "Families, the State, and Family Policies," in M. Baker (ed.), *Families: Changing Trends in Canada*, 5th ed. (pp.258–276). Toronto: McGraw-Hill Ryerson (Table 12.1, p. 270); and updated from The Conservative Party of Canada. 2006. "A New $1,200 Choice in Childcare Allowance for Pre-School Kids." Retrieved August 14, 2006, from www.conservative.ca/EN/1091/33693; and Canada Revenue Agency. 2016. *Canada Child Benefit–Overview.* Retrieved November 5, 2016, from www.cra-arc.gc.ca/bnfts/ccb/menu-eng.html.

can be found in Ontario during the 1980s when the "Spouse in the House" social welfare rule was in existence. The regulation at the time was that a mother was eligible for welfare only if she did not live with a man. It was assumed that a man would take over the function of breadwinner, even if in reality he was unemployed or did not contribute any income to the household. To illustrate the effects of this policy, an article from *The Toronto Star* is reproduced below. On January 19, 1984, *The Toronto Star* featured on its front page the headline "Mom's Welfare Fraud Blamed on 'System'" (see box 16.2). The story concerned a mother who allegedly defrauded welfare of more than $37,000 because she was afraid of losing her children. For 10 years, this woman had received about $270 per month to support herself and her three children.

Box 16.2: Mom's Welfare Fraud Blamed on "System"

The following excerpt shows an example of a controversial government welfare policy implemented during the 1980s known as the "Spouse in the House Rule."

A 37-year-old Brampton mother of four defrauded welfare of more than $37,000 because she was afraid of losing her children, a Peel County Court has been told. She was put on probation for two years and ordered to repay part of the money. But she might never have committed the crime had she received proper child support, Judge Francis McDonald said yesterday. "Our system could not pay her so she found one that would, it is as simple as that," he said. For 10 years Patricia Geall told authorities that she lived alone and was given about $270 a month to support herself and her three children, although she was living with a man. Her former husband never paid her child support, which now adds up to $19,500, despite a court order. Warrants for his arrest were never executed, the court was told. "If [the husband] had been forced to pay, she might never have been pressed into the situation she has found herself in," McDonald said. Geall had been told that if she had no way of supporting her children, she could lose them to the Children's Aid Society, the court was told.

Source: Excerpted from Moore, L. 1984. "Mom's Welfare Fraud Blamed on 'System.'" *The Toronto Star*, January 19 (p. A1).

Interestingly, her husband had been court-ordered to pay child support (which added up to arrears of $19,500) but had never paid any, and warrants for his arrest were never executed. The woman had been informed that if she had no way of supporting her children, they would be turned over to the Children's Aid Society. The reason she was accused of defrauding welfare was that she was living common-law with another man, rather than as a single woman, yet there was no evidence that this man was able or willing to support her or her children. As a result, the woman was ordered to repay the money she had received minus the amount owed by her husband over six years. However, she earned only $200 a week as a manual labourer, which made it very difficult to repay the money. As she logically argued, "The system sold us out.... You took my children's rights. You didn't protect them. If they were in Children's Aid, you'd be paying $550 a month to protect them" (as quoted in *The Toronto Star*, January 19, 1984: 1). It is also ironic to note that this rule may have produced another unintended outcome—some single mothers may have avoided forming live-in partnerships, unions that might have had a number of positive consequences for both the mothers and their children.

Many of these implicit policies have been developed over the years and have been influenced by the ideology of the party in power, the concerns of the day, and the pressure of powerful advocacy groups. From a historical perspective, Canada has been characterized by two fundamentally opposed value positions: conservatism and liberalism. Conservatives tend to be opposed to intervention in family affairs when it takes the form of income transfers to the less well-off, yet are often more in favour of it with respect to sexual matters. Generally, conservative governments have been supportive of traditional family values and opposed to same-sex marriage and abortion. In contrast, liberal governments tend to press for aid to disadvantaged families but have less interest in regulating intimate relationships between consenting adults. Thus, these underlying values are especially prevalent within labour market and social welfare programs, and relate to notions of how families are defined with respect to their responsibilities and values, and under what circumstances the state will assist or intervene in family life. As such, it may be necessary to review a wide variety of laws or to read between the lines of these laws (Baker, 1995).

SELECTED POLICY ISSUES FACING CANADIAN FAMILIES OVER THE LIFE COURSE

Based upon the current trends and issues reviewed previously throughout this text, several suggestions for policy reform and community programs can be identified. These will include a focus on the following five areas: (1) parenthood and child care; (2) education, income, and work; (3) partnership formation and dissolution; (4) seniors and caregiving; and (5) health care and social services. It is recognized that many of these areas intersect, but they do allow for a brief identification of key family-related policy issues relevant to the diverse and changing needs of families over the life course.

Parenthood and Child Care

Although many parents with preschool children would prefer to stay home and raise them, the reality, of course, is that most parents cannot achieve this ideal situation. In today's economy, most families need two incomes in order to be financially stable. As a result, a major policy challenge is child care. This issue is particularly salient for women, since they continue to perform most of this work while participating in the labour force in record numbers. Child care is also crucial to gender equality, since without access to affordable child care, some mothers are forced to restrict themselves to part-time work or lower-paying jobs. Furthermore, structural and ideological barriers impede many men from taking paternity leave or time off work to care for children, which further perpetuates gender inequities. This also disadvantages men in terms of the time they have to be with their children.

Families need a variety of options to meet their specific child-care needs, such as corporate on site–based daycares and after-school programs. Yet, the availability and provision of quality daycare is minimal, with the exception of Quebec, which provides a stellar example of government initiatives that prioritize the family (Krull, 2014). The province recognizes three types of subsidized daycare services (child care and daycare centres and home care providers) at a reasonable cost of $7.55 per child per day (for those who meet the eligibility criteria), as previously covered in this text. Access to affordable daycare is also an enormous problem for single parents or for parents who work untraditional hours, such as night shifts, weekends, or part-time. Indeed, access to high-quality daycare should be available to all Canadians, regardless of race, ethnic background, level of competence, or ability to pay. Some groups (e.g., recent immigrants) may not have access to these programs, or to other tax credits and exceptions.

Only a wealthy few can hire live-in-caregivers or nannies to provide at-home child care. CanadianNanny.ca, for instance, calculates the total out-of-pocket cost for a live-in nanny in Ontario in 2016 (with all tax credits deducted) at $1,053.50 per month. In addition, it is often only affluent women and couples who can take advantage of many government programs, such as maternity and parental leave, because of employment eligibility criteria.

In summary, Canada needs a national standard of high-quality child care, with universal access for those families who require or choose to use them. A social-based, centralized policy is multi-beneficial; not only will it further women's equality, but it will also promote good population health and encourage positive child development (e.g., see Telford, 2016). This means that the government should establish consistent training, education, and licensing requirement for day care providers. Greater effort is also needed to implement and monitor programs, as well as to collect information on child-care options in a collaborative and coordinated manner across the provinces.

Education, Income, and Work Issues

It is well documented that individuals from higher socio-economic families are more likely to attend post-secondary institutions and marry and have children at a later age. Similarly, they are less likely to experience poverty, drop out of school, become teenaged or young parents, or divorce. A recent study by Seabrook and Avison (2015) shows that parental education and family income is a stronger determinant of status attainment than family structure (the kind of families in which children grow up; e.g., single parent versus two-parent). Overall, educational qualifications are a key determinant of life chances in industrial societies and are generally strong correlated to making a higher income. In short, higher income enables individuals to have more choices and fewer constraints in decision-making. It is also well documented that less-educated workers have become increasingly disadvantaged in the labour market during the past two decades, and that income inequality has grown in many countries.

As discussed in chapter 14, we should all be very concerned about the high levels of poverty in Canada, especially with regard to Indigenous children. Close to 1 in 5 Canadian children live below the poverty line, and these rates are easily doubled for Indigenous children. Our overall rate of relative child poverty puts Canada at the top of the bottom third percentile of all industrialized countries. The Scandinavian countries, as well as

Switzerland, Austria, and the Netherlands, have the least amount of child inequality, according to a recent UNICEF (2016) report. These countries top the list with rates that often fall below 5%. Indeed, UNICEF argues that children in Canada are not made a top priority in budget allocations in any jurisdiction, including the federal government. Therefore, governments need to be more child-sensitive in order to eradicate poverty and improve educational opportunities for all young people.

It is also recognized that not all individuals are willing or able to complete high school or attend college or university. Thus, it might be useful to devise support mechanisms or incentives to assist at-risk adolescents during secondary school. For example, it might be beneficial to have an expanded system of apprenticeship and vocational education as other options to formal college attendance. In addition, greater attention should be given to the likely impact of government policies on the economic well-being of families and children, especially those living at or near the poverty line, such as the working poor.

Moreover, there are rural/urban and regional variations in the access to post-secondary institutions, as well as in the availability of good jobs. As revealed in figure 16.1, unemployment rates are the highest in the Atlantic or eastern provinces, and generally decline as you move west; a trend that has been relatively long term. Thus, families living in economically depressed areas or regions with fewer opportunities can have different life-course trajectories and require unique supports and policies. For example, in the Atlantic region, seasonal labour (e.g., in the fishing, mining, forestry, and produce industry) is common. This means that these families face unique challenges in maintaining household income and balancing work and family demands; they require supports tailored to their unique conditions and problems. In other areas, high unemployment in single-industry, small community areas (e.g., as experienced in Nova Scotia) can force families to migrate to urban areas in search of a better life, which then further impacts the local community. For example, as families and young people leave their home communities for jobs in urban areas, schools may begin to close and local businesses can suffer, which creates a ripple effect impact on the lives of those who remain in the community.

Researchers often characterize the tension caused by work/family challenges as the "double squeeze," since there is often pressure on economic resources and a simultaneous squeeze on the time and energy needed for family, work, and community commitments (Skocpol, 1997). And although many policies have emerged that provide more flexibility for employees with family responsibilities, many argue that, in comparison with Europeans, North Americans have significant policy deficits in work/family and other policy supports. For example, social-democratic regimes have vastly more generous paid maternity and parenting leave policies and paid leave to care for sick children. Sweden is a notable early innovator in this regard, having established the gold standard for these kinds of progressive policies (Mahon, Bergqvist, and Brennan, 2016). Thus, the major concern voiced most often by North American parents is conflict between work and family. This issue is also exacerbated by intersections with class, gender, race, ethnicity, and family structure.

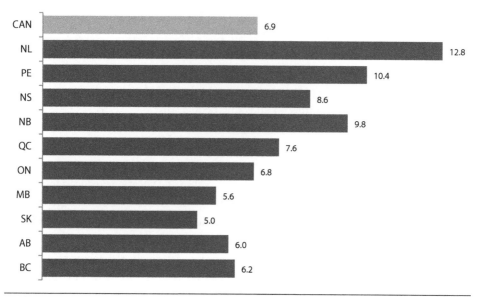

Figure 16.1: Annual Average Unemployment Rate by Province/ Region, 2015, Canada (in Percentages)

Note: Unemployment rate for those 15 years and older

Source: Statistics Canada. 2016. CANSIM Table 282-0086-Labour Force Survey Estimates (LFS), Supplementary Unemployment Rates by Sex and Age Group Annual (Rate). Ottawa: Minister of Industry. Retrieved June 1, 2016, from www5.statcan.gc.ca/cansim/pick-choisir?lang=eng&p2=33&id=2820086.

Therefore, a major challenge for many people is trying to balance the competing demands of family and work responsibilities. As a result, many families are chronically overworked and overwhelmed in their daily lives. It is well documented that a significant proportion of those in the workforce feel chronically overworked. One study showed that 38% of working mothers are severely time stressed, averaging 74 hours of paid and unpaid work each week. Single mothers are particularly prone to stressful lives, since they often do not have a partner to rely on for emotional and financial support. Furthermore, women who do primarily unpaid work can be prone to isolation and are at greater risk of physical, emotional, and or/sexual abuse (Women and the Economy, 2006).

Other emergent economic and socio-demographic trends contribute to the need for more unpaid work within the family and have significant consequences for families and the labour market. As noted in chapter 11, children tend to remain at home longer than in recent decades, thus prolonging the transition to the empty nest and retirement. Extended domestic responsibilities are largely borne by mothers, who continue to provide domestic labour in the form of day-to-day caring, cooking, and cleaning services for their young adult children. This caregiving may also occur at a time when elderly parents or other aging family members and friends require help as well.

Partnership Formation and Dissolution

Many Canadians still believe that legal marriage is the ideal, that children should be raised by both biological parents, and that marriage should last a lifetime. Yet, there appears to be growing consensus that we also need policy reform and community programs to support healthy families and close relationships more generally, with a focus that extends beyond legal, heterosexual marital relationships. These kinds of policies and programs could also prevent teenagers from engaging in risky behaviours, such as drug abuse or sexual practices that lead to sexually transmitted diseases or pregnancy. Also, although some partnerships and marriages cannot be salvaged, the argument has been made that future generations would be well served if some of the couples considering separation remained together. This is particularly germane to those relationships that could be saved with appropriate social and economic supports.

Overall, community resources are needed to support the diverse relationships of young people. In chapter 9, it was noted that gays and lesbians experience more resistance than heterosexuals to their choice of partners and their decision to cohabit or marry. Generally, gay and lesbian young adults receive more support from non-family members than from their families of origin. This suggests that this group of individuals and their families require specific community resources (e.g., information and public education to overcome homophobic ideologies). Also, as Canada continues to experience high rates of immigration from countries that are more traditional, we need to provide culturally sensitive community programs and services to deal with the unique issues that these families face as they try to assimilate into a new country. For example some traditional ethnic groups disapprove of same-sex unions, unmarried cohabitation, and single parenthood.

Seniors, Caregiving, and Dependency Issues

As previously mentioned in this text, Canada is aging, and it is expected that approximately 25% of the population will be over 65 by the year 2031. Therefore, policy in a number of realms (e.g. health care, pension, housing) will need to be revised in order to meet the needs of this growing and diverse group. And as Canada's aged population becomes more ethnically diverse, we may need to devise new policies and programs. Elderly members of ethnocultural communities experience language barriers, religious and cultural differences, and economic dependency, which can reduce their access to community-based health and social services. Elderly ethnic minority women, in particular, are found to have high rates of poverty and are often not eligible for pensions. Thus they may face "triple jeopardy" (Brotman, 1998).

It is important to reiterate that most elderly people receive support from informal caregivers (family and friends), such that aging population will have important implications for Canadian families. And while some argue that the purported "caregiving crunch" has been exaggerated to justify cutbacks in programs and services, many assert that the challenges for the sandwich generation will increase in the future. Thus, more supports (e.g., respite care) are needed to help alleviate caregiver burden and dependency among the elderly. Moreover, while caregiving may be perceived as a labour of love, it can also generate numerous financial, psychological, health, and social costs. As a result, many recommendations for policy/program reform are necessary, such as a federal program of home care and increasing tax credits for caregivers who incur financial loss. At the community level, programs to alleviate caregiver burden, assist with respite care, and provide recreation and transportation will need renewed attention.

Despite the fact that Canada is currently undergoing rapid population aging, with more of the population over 65 than under 14, Employment Standards legislation place significantly greater value on infant care than on care of the aged. This means that some kinds of caregiving relationships are privileged over others. Similarly, Compassionate Care Leave Policy requires that the family member have a serious medical condition with a significant risk of death within 26 weeks. The caregiver must also produce a certificate from a medical practitioner to certify this condition. Generally, current government policies tend to be highly restrictive and ageist, and they leave little room for caring work that is often unpredictable, fluctuating, and episodic (Canadian Centre for Elder Law, 2016).

Health Care and Social Services

The Canadian welfare state has developed a wide range of health and social services to promote health and well-being. These services range from preventative, community-based programs and primary health care to acute care in the case of accident or illness. Social services encompass such areas as child protection, social work interventions, settlement services for refugees and immigrants, and residential services for those unable to live independently. Yet, although Canadians enjoy relatively good health and universal coverage for most health and social services, financial and other barriers exist for many individuals. Many products and services are only partially insured (or not at all), including dental care, eyeglasses, prescription drugs, and fees for ambulance and ancillary services.

Geographical isolation also makes it difficult for some families to access appropriate services. This is particularly problematic for Indigenous families living in remote areas. Moreover, the priorities set by Indigenous peoples are often at variance with those developed by the government. In part, this is because Indigenous peoples define health in terms of balance, holism, harmony, and spirituality rather than Western concepts of physical dysfunction and disease within the individual. Fortunately, in recent years many Indigenous communities have assumed the administration and management of their own health care. And with more land claims settlements, self-determination, and political autonomy for these families, it is hoped that their health situation (e.g., high mortality and chronic conditions), in addition to other challenges (e.g., the high number of children in the social welfare system), will continue to improve.

Furthermore, alternatives to conventional drug therapy are required, given the growing strength of the pharmaceutical industry and concerns that we are headed toward an over-medicalized society (a topic discussed in chapter 13). These issues may also be gendered; for example, women are more likely than men to be prescribed central nervous system depressants as well as sleeping pills, and for longer periods of time. They are also more likely to be prescribed medication for non-medical reasons—to help them cope with work or family stress, grief, or natural life events such as childbirth and menopause, as well as chronic illness and pain. Yet, no comprehensive policy or intervention strategy exists to address this serious health issue (Currie, 2003).

And with continuing retrenchment of the welfare state, many programs and services have also been reduced or cut, such as women's crisis centres and other social services. This means that important services are simply no longer available. Governments also often change the eligibility criteria with respect to who is deserving of such assistance in order to generate cost savings. Moreover, many researchers and delivery providers recognize the need to enhance the cultural competence and gender-sensitivity of health care service provisions. For example, some immigrants seeking care experience outright racism and may have to endure a waiting period before they are eligible for provincial health insurance.

Rioux (2006) argues that we need a human rights–based approach to health and social well-being, given that this is influenced by a variety of social, economic, and environmental factors, and not just access to health care. This rights-based approach uses human rights as a framework for health development. In this way, basic principles of human rights become integral to the design, implementation, and evaluation of policies and programs. This approach can also be used to assess the human rights implications of policy, programs, and legislation. In this way, social policy can enhance rather than diminish the well-being of families. As illustrated in figure 16.2, these fundamental human rights include political and civil rights (such as the right to life), freedom of opinion, a fair trial, and protection from torture and violence. They also include economic, social, and cultural rights, such as the right to work, social protection, an adequate standard of living, the highest possible standards of physical and mental health, education, and enjoyment of the benefits of cultural freedom and scientific progress (Rioux, 2006). Additionally, it is argued that we must consider family caregiving as a human right, a perspective that is discussed in box 16.3.

Policy development and implementation is a complicated and multi-faceted political process, as is depicted in figure 16.3. The general policy research process (which can take place in a variety of government and non-government settings)typically begins with a general statement that some kind of social action may be desirable. Individuals can play important roles in affecting family-related policy as advocates, community organizers and protestors, and researchers. For instance, researchers can seek to examine whether recommendations need to be made to change laws, develop programs, or take action to fulfill specific needs. (e.g., see Patterson, McIntyre, Anderson, and Mah, 2016).

Generally, the advocate endorses and actively works for a course of action that improves community and family life and the well-being of its members. This kind of advocacy typically requires some type of leadership and group mobilization—for example, at the local or

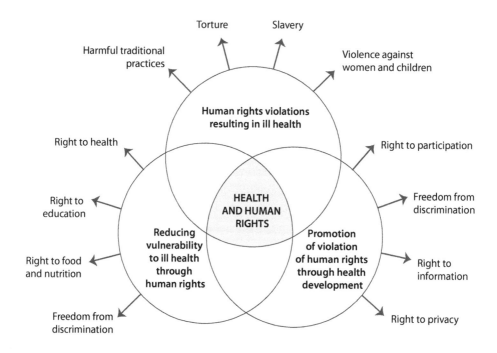

Figure 16.2: Linkages between Health and Human Rights

Source: World Health Organization (WHO). 2016. "Health and Human Rights." *Health and Human Rights Publication Series.* Geneva: WHO Press. Retrieved November 4, 2016, from www.who.int/hhr/HHR%20link-ages.pdf.

Box 16.3: Family Caregiving in Canada: A Fact of Life and a Human Right

At some point in our lives, there is a high likelihood that each of us will provide care to someone we know—and receive care ourselves—at least once. Family members are typically the first to step up to provide, manage, and sometimes pay for this care. The forms of family care we provide and receive are so diverse, not to mention second nature, that we may not even think of them as caregiving: driving a sibling to a medical appointment, preparing a meal for a grandparent, picking up a sick child from school—these are all a part of the "landscape of care" in which we live.

Families are highly adaptable and most of the time people find ways to manage their multiple work *and* family responsibilities, obligations, and commitments. However, this can be challenging for some working caregivers, since most who juggle work and caregiving are employed full-time. When working people who are protected by the *Canadian Human Rights Act* find themselves torn between providing necessary care for a family member and fulfilling their work obligations—and if they have exhausted other reasonable options to arrange for this care—employers may be obligated under human rights law to accommodate them on the basis of *family status*.

Human rights are intended to provide a framework of rights and flexibility so that workers can fulfill both their work and their caregiving obligations.

ACCOMMODATION UNDER HUMAN RIGHTS REQUIRES FLEXIBILITY FROM EMPLOYEES AND EMPLOYERS

Reconciling care and work in a harmonious manner requires employers to recognize that sometimes family circumstances require *focused attention*. Ideally, employers have in place policies that are inclusive, providing both flexible workplaces (which can reduce the number of individual requests for accommodation) and a process for handling individual requests when flexibility may not be enough.

Individual requests for accommodation based on family status require that the employee show a *substantial caregiving obligation;* it cannot simply be a personal choice to do something for a family member. For example, leaving work to drive a child to extracurricular activities would be a personal choice, whereas leaving work to drive them to the hospital if a caregiver was not available would be an obligation.

Obligation alone, however, is not enough. The employee must demonstrate that they have attempted to reconcile work-care conflicts and explored all realistic alternatives accessible to them. When individual requests arise, the employer must examine whether the choice between caregiving obligations and workplace practices or rules will have a negative impact on the employee. If this is the case, the employer must allow time for the employee to explore options, discuss the issue with them, do an individual assessment of the specific circumstances, and consider flexible workplace arrangements (FWAs).

Employers can refuse to accommodate a request, but only if they can provide evidence that doing so would create undue hardship for the organization resulting from adjusting policies, practices, bylaws, or physical space. Undue hardship has no strict legal definition; each case must be treated within the specific context, taking into account various workplace and operational requirements. Human rights law also requires requests for accommodation to be considered *individually*, taking into account diverse family roles and expectations. Employers must provide evidence as to the nature and extent of the hardship.

Johnstone v. Canada was a landmark family status case that helped to clarify the types of circumstances in which an employer has a duty to accommodate an employee with parental child-care obligations. Fiona Johnstone and her husband worked full-time on rotating, unpredictable shifts for the Canada Border Service

Agency (CBSA) while raising two toddlers. The husband also travelled for business. Johnstone requested a full-time, fixed-shift schedule so she could fulfill her child-care obligations. While the CBSA permitted fixed shifts, they were granted only on a part-time basis, so they refused to accommodate the request. The CBSA argued that child-care responsibilities are the result of *personal choice* and did not trigger a duty to accommodate.

The Canadian Human Rights Tribunal sided with Johnstone, ruling that she had been discriminated against, and the Federal Court dismissed the Attorney General's application for a judicial review of the case, confirming that parental child-care obligations fall within the scope and meaning of the ground "family status" in the *Canadian Human Rights Act*. Honourable Mr. Justice Mandamin, dismissing the Attorney General's application for a judicial review in *Canada v. Johnstone*, stated,

> ...it is difficult to have regard to family without giving thought to children in the family and the relationship between parents and children. The singular most important aspect of that relationship is the parents' care for children. It seems to me that if Parliament intended to exclude parental child-care obligations, it would have chosen language that clearly said so.

In 2014, this decision was upheld at the Federal Court of Appeal, and it has since been cited in a number of cases in jurisdictions in Canada. But the laws on this matter still vary slightly across the country. For example, in New Brunswick, family status is not a protected ground, and in Ontario it covers only parent-child relationships, although it applies to those who provide care to an elderly parent.

Source: Battams, N. 2016. "Family Caregiving in Canada: A Fact of Life and a Human Right." Ottawa: Vanier Institute of the Family. Retrieved November 4, 2016, from www.vanierinstitute.ca/family-caregiving-in-canada.

community level. Community organizing can be defined as "a search for social power and an effort to combat perceived helplessness through learning that what appears personal is often political." It creates a capacity for democracy and sustained social change (Shragge, 2003: 41). And while certain kinds of activism and protest can be risky, provided they are lawful, they can be an important part of Canadian democracy and the right to free expression. For example, anti-gentrification activists in the Downtown Eastside of Vancouver (also known as Canada's poorest postal code) have brought public awareness to the perils of gentrification, with its many related implications and issues for local individuals and their families.

Researchers also have a variety of ways to propose and establish family policy, as is illustrated in box 16.4. The proposed policy changes entitled "A New Deal for Families," recommended by researchers at the University of British Columbia, focus on families raising young children. The researchers call for change in the areas of parental benefits, child

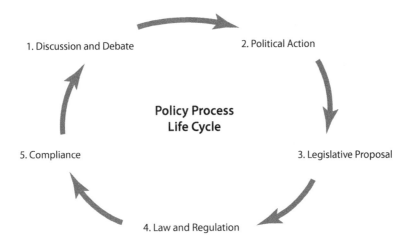

Figure 16.3: The Policy Process

Source: Petersen, R.J. 2009. "The Policy Process Lifecycle." *EDUCAUSE Review* 44: 74–75. Retrieved January 28, 2012, from www.educause.edu/EDUCAUSE+Review/EDUCAUSEReviewMagazineVolume44/ThePolicyProcessLifeCycle/16380.

Figure 16.4: Vancouver's Vision for Downtown Eastside Stokes Anti-Gentrification Protest

Source: "Anti-gentrification activists converge on gentrifying restaurant in the downtown eastside of Vancouver," 2013. Photo courtesy of Tami Starlight, Cree/Norwegian intersectional community organizer.

care services, and work-family balance, issues that have been previously identified as in need of critical evaluation and reform. Think tanks such as the Vanier Institute of the Family in Ottawa (established in 1965) are also actively involved in both family research and policy advocacy. Members of these types of institutes and foundations typically publish books, special reports and position papers, and press releases, and convey this information to elected policy officials, policy makers, educators, researchers, and the general public.

Box 16.4: A New Deal for Families

There is a silent generational crisis occurring in homes across Canada. The generation raising young children today struggles with less time, stagnant household incomes, and skyrocketing housing costs compared to those of the 1970s. The failure to invest in the generation raising young children is not consistent with Canada's proud tradition of building and adapting.

Canada has become a country in which it is far harder to raise a young family. The country's economy has doubled in size since the mid-1970s, yet the reality for parents with pre-school children is a decline in the standard of living. Compared to the previous generation, the average household income (after adjusting for inflation) for young Canadian couples has flat-lined, even though the share of young women's contributions to household incomes today is up 53%. Meanwhile, housing prices have increased 76% across the country since the mid-1970s.

The generation raising young children today is squeezed for time at home, squeezed for income because of the high cost of housing, and squeezed for services like child care that would help them balance earning a living with raising a family.

A PRACTICAL SOLUTION IS PROPOSED: A NEW DEAL FOR FAMILIES WITH YOUNG CHILDREN

The New Deal will provide a time dividend to families to ensure that the generation raising young children accesses 2.8% of the economic prosperity produced today compared to the mid-1970s. The Time Dividend will...put the family back into Canadian values, while acknowledging the diversity of households, and recognizing the very different circumstances facing parents compared to the Baby Boomers; ....provide choices for women and men to contribute at home and on the job, while enabling personal responsibility for moms and dads alike as they have enough time to raise their kids, and enough time to earn a living.

THE NEW DEAL IS CENTRED ON THREE CORE POLICY CHANGES:

New mom and new dad benefits: WHY? To transform the uneven access to parental leave into a benefit system that ensures all parents, including the self-employed, have the time and resources to be home with their newborns. **HOW?** Extend parental leave from 12 months to 18 months, generally reserving the extra six months for dads (with exceptions for lone parents and same-sex couples). Introduce a healthy child check-in and parenting support program during a child's first 18 months to monitor for early development delays and to answer parents' questions regarding children's feeding, sleeping, crying, etc. **DETAILS:** Benefits would be available to ALL single- and dual-earner households (including the self-employed) regardless of parents' attachment to the labour market. Moms and dads who currently do not qualify for leave would see their after-tax income increase by at least $11,000 in the 12 months following the birth of their child. Leave would be made affordable by insuring 80% of parents' income up to $60,000 a year. This increase will double the existing maximum benefit. The minimum benefit will be $440 weekly, enough to eradicate child and family poverty for this age group.

Ten-dollar-a-day child-care services: **WHY?** To remedy the current system of unregulated, unaffordable child-care services, thus ensuring that parents can spend enough time in employment to manage the rising cost of housing and stalled household incomes. **HOW?** Reduce child-care service fees to no more than $10/day (full-time) and $7/day (part-time), making it free for families earning less than $40,000 a year. Ensure quality services by providing funding for ample caregivers on site so that children (including those with extra support needs) spend their time in developmentally stimulating activities and play. Caregivers will have appropriate training in child development and will be paid pay equity wages. **DETAILS:** Universal, affordable child-care services would support healthy child development by supplementing, but never replacing, the care that families provide directly. Families could choose to use the services regardless of parental employment. Families could also choose to access parenting support even if they do not use child-care services. Programs will reflect the diverse cultures in local communities. Where numbers permit, families could choose programs that feature a language other than English or French, in recognition that Canadian families speak many languages at home. For Indigenous citizens, funding is allocated to enrich services that prioritize exposure to the languages and cultures of First Nations, Métis, and Inuit, as part of Canada's commitments to Truth and Reconciliation.

Flex-time for employees and employers: **WHY?** To remedy workplace standards that ignore the family by ensuring all employees can choose to combine work and family successfully. **HOW?** Adapt overtime, Employment Insurance, and Canada Public Pension premiums paid by employers to make it less costly for businesses to use employees up to 35 hours per week, and more costly for hours thereafter. Overtime will kick in at 35 hours a week (average over a year). Overtime premiums will be paid either as cash or earned time away from home. **DETAILS:** With new incentives, employers would reduce the work week by 3–5 hours on average for the half of men and the third of women who work more than 40 hours a week. These employees would trade some after-tax wages (or future wage increases) in order to gain four more weeks of time per year. In negotiation with employers, this time could be taken in chunks, or as earned hours away from work each week through the year. Changes to the National Child Benefit Supplement will ensure any reduction in employment hours does not reduce income for low-earning families. This may be especially important for some lone-parent households. Employees who currently work part-time hours would gain opportunities for more employment. Within two-parent homes, flex-time may not change the total hours that parents work, but will redistribute them more evenly between dads and moms.

Source: Kershaw, P., and L. Anderson. 2011. "Fact Sheet: A New Deal for Families." Human Early Learning Partnership, University of British Columbia. Retrieved January 25, 2011, from earlylearning.ubc.ca.

Another type of policy research is aimed at policy evaluation. As previously noted, many policies, although created with good intentions, can actually be harmful to individuals or families. Basically, policy evaluation is done at a programmatic level to determine the extent to which social programs have achieved or are achieving their stated goals. Evaluation can also determine the actual impact social programs have on families. For instance, what is the impact of a program such as Head Start on mothers as well as children? What is the consequence of not allowing dependent, co-resident young adults to be eligible for welfare benefits? It is also interesting to note that evaluation research may demonstrate that intended goals are being met, while the impact analysis may show that the goals are counterproductive, producing **unintended family policy consequences** for families.

One example of a government policy that came under fire for creating unintended consequences is the Choices in Child Care Allowance, introduced by the Harper government in 2006. Parents were given this allowance to spend "as they choose," on formal child care, babysitting, or helping one parent stay at home. According to critics, this allowance—direct payments of $100 a month for each child under the age of six—provided the least benefit to the working poor and the modest-income families who need help the most. Indeed, this allowance paid more to most one-earner families than it did to two-earner and one-parent families, and more to higher-income families than to modest-income families earning $30,000. This is because the true value of the allowance was not the same as the face value families received. Because the allowance in the hands of lower-income parents counted as taxable income, these families had to pay higher federal and provincial/territorial income taxes, while receiving fewer benefits than they had with the previous federal Canada Child Tax Benefit and other credits.

As a result, it was argued that one-earner families with a parent who stays home would do better than lone-parent and two-earner families (Child Care Advocacy Association of Canada, 2006). Other critics charged that this program had another high cost, since it cut the federal and provincial investments designed to increase the number of regulated child-care spaces. As a result, it did little to attract and retain qualified child-care workers, who are the most underpaid workers relative to their qualifications in Canada (Jacobs, 2006).

Another benefit of policy evaluation is that it can uncover improved methods of policy implementation, delivery, and cost reduction, which can provide a number of long-term advantages to both families and the state. For example, extensive research by Browne et al. (2001; 2011) shows that our current system of service delivery is inadequate because of its short-sighted, piecemeal approach. These researchers assert that we need policies and programs that are comprehensive, holistic, and investment oriented. However, this is difficult to achieve because governments change, many sectors receive their funding separately, and there is little coordination of services across ministries and portfolios. This approach also often fails to identify the root cause(s) of the problem, which is often the source of a chain reaction of other problems across the life course. It may also be difficult for one trained professional to ascertain the links among a person's condition (e.g., chronic depression), the context in which they live (e.g., poverty), and the set of circumstances that led to the problem (e.g., a lifetime of little family support or social capital, abuse and neglect, low education, and so forth).

Instead, researchers argue that a more effective and proactive approach would be to provide individuals (particularly vulnerable ones) with coordinated service packages. For example, in one pilot project (Browne et al., 2001; Browne, 2011), single mothers living on social assistance were provided with a tailored package of services, such as help with child care, access to recreational facilities, job training, mental health counselling, and visits by public health nurses. At the end of the study, these parents and children experienced a multitude of benefits. The single mothers were more likely to give up welfare and had improved mental health. Also, there was a savings of $300,000 in social assistance within the first year for every 100 mothers.

SUMMARY

Although it is difficult to forecast how families will look in the future, it is certain that the one institution in which the majority of people spend their lives will not remain unchanged. It is impossible to predict what we will face in our environmental future (e.g., climate change, epidemics, wars, natural disasters), although some researchers (e.g., Eichler, 2014) predict that we will undoubtedly experience some troubling times. Similarly, we do not know the economic and social challenges that families will face. Yet, we do know that policies and programs will need to be continually revised or developed in response to the changing life-course needs and conditions of Canadian families. Socio-demographic and technological transformations will occur and will undoubtedly affect patterns of support within families, family structure, and lifestyles in profound ways. Notable trends likely to persist (or rise) in the near future include delays in family formation, low fertility, non-marital cohabitation, same-sex and mixed-race unions, "commuter" unions/marriages

(LAT couples living apart for job-related reasons), divorce and remarriage, labour force participation of women, population aging, continuing high rates of immigration, and geographical dispersion and mobility. It is also expected that new technologies (e.g., medical, reproductive, electronic/digital) will continue to dramatically transform family patterns, including relationships and means of communication.

Therefore, issues germane to child care, intimate ties, household living arrangements, work-family balance, elder care, and population health more generally are expected to become even more salient. Rising rates of immigration will also create pressure on the government to address many inequities in policies, programs, and services. For example, some argue that family reunification policies are highly restrictive and gender-biased, and ultimately impact immigrant integration, a sense of belonging, and family caregiving (Bragg and Wong, 2016).

Moreover, with more economic opportunities for women and continued secularization, it is expected that relationship dissolution rates will continue to be relatively high, particularly as non-marital cohabitation (both heterosexual and homosexual) will continue to grow in popularity. Overall, these transformations in family life will necessitate associated changes such as availability and access to programs and services, and examination of legal issues relevant to common-law relationships and child custody.

Finally, given the trend toward **neo-liberalism** and growing social inequality, many critics of current social policy assert that we need to develop a new model of the family that emphasizes social responsibility and promotes full citizenship (e.g., see Eichler, 1987; McDaniel, 2002) rather than economic gain and competition. In this way, personal troubles can be treated as public issues, since most events and circumstances have elements of both (Mills, 1959). For example, policies based on this model could facilitate greater involvement of fathers in child care as well as constructive solutions to workplace-family dilemmas. Policies should also more fairly support gender equality and lower-income earners rather than socially reproducing and further preserving gendered behaviours and class inequalities (McKay, 2016; Neilson and Stanfors, 2014). Most importantly, implementing policies that start with the notion that care for people is a social responsibility rather than a private one, can help to create a more humane, sustainable, and healthier society. In short, these social policies can help to build a better Canadian society in which diverse families of all shapes, sizes, and ages can thrive and flourish.

QUESTIONS FOR CRITICAL REFLECTION AND DEBATE

1. Should Canadian family policy be value-free? Also, can or should family research be separated from family advocacy?
2. Debate the following: The state should not interfere with family life. Consider family issues such as adoption, marriage, reproductive technology, sexual relations, and dependency between family members.

3. Provide an argument for and against the following statement: Family policy should be established at the federal as opposed to the provincial level. Is a national family policy feasible?
4. Should policies be age-based? Consider how policies target particular age groups and identify their key limitations and advantages.
5. Do you think it is more effective to develop policies and programs that target individuals or interpersonal relations (micro level) or at a systems level (macro level)? Also consider issues of prevention and intervention (e.g., poverty, alcoholism and substance abuse, family violence).
6. What predictions would you make with respect to family life and changes in family policy for the year 2050? Consider some of the following areas: daycare, parental roles, same-sex unions, changing parent-child relationships, and the aging of the population.

GLOSSARY

Family ideologies incorporate a set of family-related values and beliefs that reflect the interests and beliefs of a social group or society and form the basis of political action.

Family policy can be defined as a coherent set of principles about the state's role in family life that is implemented through legislation or a plan of action.

Globalization refers to the world scale of economic and other market activity facilitated by the expansion of telecommunications technology.

Neo-liberalism supports the restructuring of welfare societies to better meet the demands of a global market economy. This political rationality stresses competition and personal responsibility.

Unintended family policy consequences are the negative effects on family life that result from well-intentioned government policy.

Welfare state refers to a wide range of government-sponsored programs and legislations designed to improve the social and economic well-being of families and individuals, particularly in times of need.

FURTHER READING

Baker, M. 2014. *Choices and Constraints in Family Life*, 3rd ed. Toronto: Oxford University Press.

Focuses on Canada within a global context and contextualizes family life within broader structural concerns, such as the economy and government policy.

Banting, K.G. and J. Myles. 2013. (eds.). *Inequality and the Fading of Redistributive Politics*. Vancouver: UBC Press.
Mixing sociological, economic, and political science perspective this interdisciplinary overview addresses the decline in redistributive politics in Canada. Contains chapters devoted to various public and social policies that impact families and critically examines such policies as tax-transfer, seniors' income security, child care, health care and labour market income transfers.

Bonoli, G. 2013. *The Origins of Active Social Policy: Labour Market and Childcare Policies in a Comparative Perspective*. Oxford: Oxford University Press.
Investigates labour market and child-care policy trajectories in seven European countries post 1990. It outlines the origins of active social policy in Europe and offers quantitative evidence on public spending.

Eichler, M. 1997. *Family Shifts: Families, Policies, and Gender Equality*. Toronto: Oxford University Press.
A seminal piece of work outlining various ideological models of the family and how they have affected policy development and implementation.

Lin Chang, M. 2010. *Shortchanged: Why Women Have Less Wealth and What Can Be Done About It*. Oxford, New York: Oxford University Press.
Using national data and in-depth interviews, this book addresses the gender-wealth gap and its relationship to policies on equal pay, caregiving, and family-friendly workplaces.

Robila, M. 2014. *Handbook of Family Policies across the Globe*. New York: Springer.
Through a cross-comparison of countries such as Canada, Russia, Japan, and Colombia, this book provides comprehensive coverage of explicit and implicit family policies. Issues such as family-friendly work practices, work-life balance, child care, poverty, domestic violence, social exclusion/inclusion, immigration, and disability are covered.

RELATED WEB SITES

Caledon Institute of Social Policy is a centre-left think tank based in Ottawa and offers many discussion papers on social policy issues affecting families, www.caledoninst.org. Twitter: https://twitter.com/CaledonINST.

Campaign 2000 was founded in 1989 to monitor child poverty in Canada. It produces an annual report card, www.campaign2000.ca. Facebook: www.facebook.com/Campaign2000. Twitter: www.twitter.com/Campaign2000.

Canadian Centre for Policy Alternatives (CCPA) is an independent and non-partisan research institute; respected voice on the issues of justice and inequality, www.policy-alternatives.ca. https://www.policyalternatives.ca/Facebook: www.facebook.com/policy-alternatives. Twitter: www.twitter.com/ccpa YouTube channel: www.youtube.com/user/policyalternatives.

Childcare Resource and Research Unit publishes Canadian and cross-national research on child-care policy issues. Its mandate is to further early childhood education and child-care policies in Canada, www.childcarecanada.org.

Vanier Institute of the Family is a family-oriented think tank national organization (established in 1965) dedicated to promoting the well-being of Canadian families through advocacy, research, and policy, www.vanierinstitute.ca. Facebook: www.facebook.com/vanierinstitute Twitter: www.twitter.com/VanierInstitute.

REFERENCES

Baker, M. 1995. *Canadian Family Policies: Cross-national Comparisons.* Toronto: University of Toronto Press.

Baker, M. (ed). 2005. *Families in Canadian Society,* 5th ed. Toronto: McGraw-Hill Ryerson.

Bragg, B., and L. Wong. 2016. "Cancelled Dreams: Family Reunification and Shifting Canadian Immigration Policy." *Journal of Immigrant and Refugee Studies* 14: 46–65.

Brotman, S. 1998. "The Incidence of Poverty among Seniors in Canada: Exploring the Impact of Gender, Ethnicity, and Race." *Canadian Journal on Aging* 17: 166–185.

Browne, G., J. Roberts, C. Byrne, A. Gafni, R. Weir, and B. Majumdar. 2001. "The Costs and Effects of Addressing the Needs of Vulnerable Populations: Results of 10 Years of Research." *Canadian Journal of Nursing Research* 33: 65–76.

Browne G. 2011. "More Effective/Less Expensive Health Services also Address the Social Determinants of Health." *The Journal of the Ontario Association of Social Workers* 37 (March, number 1). Retrieved November 7, 2016, from www.oasw.org/media/186627/NewsmagMarch2011.pdf.

Canadian Centre for Elder Law. 2016. "Employment Leave for Family Caregiving." Retrieved November 7, 2016, from www.bcli.org/elder-law-resources/execsum/chapter3.

Canadian Nanny.ca. 2016. "Nanny Rates in Canada." Retrieved November 28, 2016, from www.canadiannanny.ca/how-much-does-a-nanny-cost.

CBC News. 1967 (December 21). "Omnibus Bill: 'There's no place for the state in the bedrooms of the nation.'" Toronto: CBC Digital Archives.

Child Care Advocacy Association of Canada. 2006. "The Harper Child Care Plan: Buyer Beware." Retrieved August 13, 2006, from www.childcareadvocacy.ca.

Currie, J.C. 2003. *Manufacturing Addiction: The Over-prescription of Benzodiazepines and Sleeping Pills to Women in Canada.* British Columbia Centre of Excellence for Women's Health Policy Series, Vancouver. Retrieved January 2, 2011, at www.bccewh.bc.ca.

Eichler, M. 1987. "Family Change and Social Policies." In K.L. Anderson et al. (eds.), *Family Matters: Sociology and Contemporary Canadian Families* (pp. 63–85). Toronto: Methuen.

Eichler, M. 2014. "The Past of the Future and the Future of the Family." In D. Cheal and P. Albanese (eds.), *Canadian Families Today: New Perspectives*, 3rd ed. (pp. 318–338). Toronto: Oxford University Press.

Evans, P.M., and G.R. Wekerle. 1997. "The Shifting Terrain of Women's Welfare: Theory, Discourse, and Activism." In P.M. Evans and G.R. Wekerle (eds.), *Women and the Canadian Welfare State* (pp. 1–27). Toronto: University of Toronto Press.

Gee, E.M., and S.A. McDaniel. 1994. "Social Policy for an Aging Society." In V. Marshall and B. McPherson (eds.), *Aging: Canadian Perspectives* (pp. 219–231). Peterborough: Broadview Press.

Jacobs, J. 2006. "Editorial: Conservative Child-Care Plan Comes at High Price" (February 21). Ottawa: Canadian Centre for Policy Alternatives.

Kamerman, S.B., and A.J. Kahn. 1978. "Families and the Idea of Family Policy." In S.B. Kamerman and A.J. Kahn (eds.), *Family Policy: Government and Families in Fourteen Countries* (pp. 1–16). New York: Columbia University Press.

Krull, C. 2014. "Investing in Families and Children: Family Policies in Canada." In D. Cheal and P. Albanese (eds.), *Canadian Families Today: New Perspectives*, 3rd ed. (pp. 292-317). Toronto: Oxford University Press.

Mahon, R., C. Bergqvist, and D. Brennan. 2016. "Social Policy Change: Work-Family Tensions in Sweden, Australia and Canada." *Social Policy and Administration* 50: 165-182.

McDaniel, S.A. 2002. "Women's Changing Relations to the State and Citizenship: Caring and Intergenerational Relations in Globalizing Western Democracies." *Canadian Review of Sociology and Anthropology* 39: 1–26.

McKay, L. 2016. "Parental-Leave Rich and Parental-Leave Poor: Inequality in Canadian Labour Market–Based Leave Policies." *Journal of Industrial Relations*, 58: 543–562.

Mills, C.W. 1959. *The Sociological Imagination*. New York: Oxford University Press.

Neilson, J., and M. Stanfors. 2014. "It's about Time! Gender, Parenthood, and Household Divisions of Labor under Different Welfare Regimes." *Journal of Family Issues* 35: 1066–1088.

Olsen, G.M. 2002. *The Politics of the Welfare State: Canada, Sweden, and the United States*. Toronto: Oxford University Press.

Patterson, P., L. McIntyre, L. Anderson, and C. Mah. 2016. "Political Rhetoric from Canada Can Inform Healthy Public Policy Argumentation." *Health Promotion International*, published online first, March 22. Retrieved December 29, 2016, from www. heapro.oxfordjournals.org/content/early/2016/03/21/heapro.daw019.abstract?sid=ae0980c4-f8dd-4d01-aacd-9ec83476027c.

Rioux, M. 2006. "The Right to Health: Human Rights Approaches to Health." In D. Raphael, T. Bryant, and M. Rioux (eds.), *Staying Alive: Critical Perspectives on Health, Illness, and Health Care* (pp. 85–114). Toronto: Canadian Scholars' Press Inc.

Seabrook, J.A., and W. Avison. 2015. "Family Structure and Children's Socioeconomic Attainment: A Canadian Sample." *Canadian Review of Sociology* 52: 66–88.

Shragge, E. 2003. *Activism and Social Change: Lessons for Community and Local Organizing*. Peterborough: Broadview Press.

Skocpol, T. 1997. "A Partnership with American Families." In S.B. Greenberg and T. Skocpol (eds.), *The New Majority: Toward a Popular Progressive Politics* (pp. 104–129). New Haven: Yale University Press.

Telford, N. 2016. "Can Canadian Women Have It All? How Limited Access to Affordable Child Care Restricts Freedom and Choice." *Canadian Journal of Family and Youth* 8: 153-172.

UNICEF. 2016. "Fairness for Children: Canada's Challenge." UNICEF Report Card 13. Toronto: UNICEF Canada. Retrieved November 7, 2016 from www.unicef.ca/sites/default/files/legacy/imce_uploads/images/advocacy/rc/rc13_infographen_media.pdf.

Women and the Economy. 2006. "Women and Unpaid Work." Retrieved February 10, 2006, from www.unpac.ca/economy/unpaidwork.html.

Copyright Acknowledgements

ethics in Aboriginal health research." *Paediatrics & Child Health* 19(2): 64. Used by permission of Oxford University Press, on behalf of the Canadian Paediatric Society.

Box 4.4: Cram, S. 2016. "5 Recommendations for National MMIW Inquiry: Native Women's Association of Canada." *CBC News*, February 23. Retrieved February 26, 2016, from www.cbc.ca/news/aboriginal/5-recommendations-for-national-mmiw-inquiry-1.3458993. Used with permission of CBC Licensing.

Box 4.6: de Leeuw, S., M. Greenwood, and E. Cameron. 2010. "Deviant Constructions: How Governments Preserve Colonial Narratives of Addictions and Poor Mental Health to Intervene into the Lives of Indigenous Children and Families in Canada." *International Journal of Mental Health Addiction* 8: 282–295. With kind permission of Springer.

CHAPTER 5

Opening photo: Sergei Bachlakov / Shutterstock

Box 5.2: Republished with permission of John Wiley and Sons Inc., from Satzewich, V. 2014. "Canadian Visa Officers and the Social Construction of Real Spousal Relationships." *Canadian Review of Sociology* 51: 1–21; permission conveyed through Copyright Clearance Center, Inc.

Box 5.3: Klaszus, J. 2016. "After Tumult of War, Deaf Syrian Family Finds Peace in Canada." UNHCR-The UN Refugee Agency, March 21. Available at: unhcr.org/56efaf729.html. Used by permission of the author.

Box 5.4: Reprinted with kind permission of the Publisher from *The Way of the Bachelor* by Alison R. Marshall © University of British Columbia Press 2011. All rights reserved by the Publisher.

CHAPTER 6

Opening photo: vgajic / iStock

Box 6.3: Courtesy of Oxfam International. 2016. "Underpaid and Undervalued: How Inequality Defines Women's Work in Asia." Retrieved June 16, 2016, from www.oxfam.org/sites/www.oxfam.org/files/file_attachments/ib-inequality-womens-work-asia-310516.pdf.

Box 6.4: REAL Women of Canada. 2015. "What to Do about Childcare." *REALity*, XXXIV(12): 4–5. Retrieved June 17, 2016, from www.realwomenofcanada.ca/what-to-do-about-childcare-reality. Used by kind permission of REAL Women of Canada.

CHAPTER 7

Opening photo: Barbara A. Mitchell

Box 7.1: Stewart, J. 2010. "From Russia, Maybe with Love: Mail Order Brides a Booming Business." *Canwest News Service*, March 2. Retrieved July 29, 2011, from www.na-

CHAPTER 8

CHAPTER 9

Figure 9.1, Photo 2: Gay Alliance toward equality (Vancouver) demonstration. The Body Politic fonds, Canadian Lesbian and Gay Archives. Photo by Ron McLennan, August 28, 1971. Image #1986-032/18P(01). Used by permission of the CLGA.

Figure 9.2: Salerno, R. 2016. "Commentary: Justin Trudeau Still Has a Lot to Prove on LGBT Rights." *The Advocate*, April 8. Retrieved August 5, 2016, from www.advocate.com/commentary/2016/4/08/justin-trudeau-still-has-lot-prove-lgbt-rights. Photo used by permission of Rob Salerno.

CHAPTER 10

Opening photo: GOLFX / Shutterstock

Box 10.2: Carlson, K., and Postmedia News Ontario. 2011. "Pre-Divorce Talks Mandatory." *The Vancouver Sun*, July 19 (p. B3). Material republished with the express permission of Postmedia Network Inc.

Box 10.4: McKie, C. 2014 "Separation and Divorce: Fragmentation and Renewal of Families," from Cheal, David, and Albanese, Patricia, *Canadian Families Today* 3e © 2014 Oxford University Press Canada. Reprinted by permission of the publisher.

Figure 10.3: Demo, D.H., and M.A. Fine. 2010. "The Divorce Variation and Fluidity Model," from *Beyond the Average Divorce*. Thousand Oaks, California: Sage Publications. Reproduced with permission of Sage Publications via Copyright Clearance Center.

Figure 10.4: H.D. Juby, "Yours, Mine and Ours: New Boundaries for the Modern Stepfamily," *Transition*. © Vanier Institute of the Family, 2003. Reprinted with permission of the publisher.

CHAPTER 11

Opening photo: YinYang / iStock

Figure 11.4: Bacall, A. 2010. "Kids Living at Home." aban689, from www.CartoonStock.com.

CHAPTER 12

Opening photo: espies / Shutterstock

Box 12.2: Martinez-Carter, K. 2013. "How the Elderly Are Treated throughout the World." *The Week*, July 23. Retrieved October 18, 2016, from theweek.com/articles/462230/how-elderly-are-treated-around-world. Used by permission of the publisher.

Box 12.3: Counts, D.A., and D.R. Counts. 2001. *Over the Next Hill: An Ethnography of RVing Seniors in North America*. Toronto: University of Toronto Press. Reprinted with permission of the publisher.

Figure 12.5: David Brown, "Old Age, Technology, and Retirement." dbrn168, from www. CartoonStock.com.

CHAPTER 13

Opening photo: Jaren Jai Wicklund / Shutterstock

Box 13.4: Excerpt from FAST FOOD NATION by Eric Schlosser. Copyright © 2001 by Eric Schlosser. Reprinted by permission of Houghton Mifflin Harcourt Publishing Company. All rights reserved.

Figure 13.4: O'Leary-Barrett, M. 2014. "The Internalizing Developmental Pathway to Substance Use Disorders." In M. Leyton and S. Stewart (eds.), *Substance Abuse in Canada: Childhood and Adolescent Pathways to Substance Abuse Disorders* (pp. 46–67). Ottawa: Canadian Centre on Substance Abuse (p. 62, Figure 14). Used by permission of the Canadian Centre on Substance Use and Addiction.

CHAPTER 14

Opening photo: Sean_Warren / iStock

Box 14.2: Rutledge, L. 2015. "Working Poor: Stuck between Getting Ahead and Losing It All." *Cambridge Times*, June 12. Retrieved October 1, 2017, from https://www. cambridgetimes.ca/news-story/5673990-working-poor-stuck-between-getting-ahead-and-losing-it-all/. Used by permission of the *Cambridge Times*.

Box 14.4: Paperny Mehler, A., and T. Grant. 2011. "How Paying People's Way Out of Poverty Can Help Us All." *The Globe and Mail*, May 5. Retrieved August 1, 2016, from www.theglobeandmail.com/news/politics/how-paying-peoples-way-out-of-poverty-can-help-us-all/article2011940. © 2011 The Globe and Mail Inc. All Rights Reserved.

Figure B14.1: Photo used by permission of Colleen Kimmett.

CHAPTER 15

Opening photo: Lisa S. / Shutterstock

Box 15.1: The Criminal Law and Managing Children's Behaviour. http://www.justice.gc. ca/eng/rp-pr/cj-jp/fv-vf/mcb-cce/index.html. Department of Justice Canada, 2016. Reproduced with the permission of the Department of Justice Canada, 2018.

Box 15.4: Grace-Dacosta, M. 2016. "Domestic Abuse Walk Returns." *Sherwood Park News*, September 29. Retrieved October 28, 2016, from www.sherwoodparknews. com/2016/09/29/domestic-abuse-walk-returns. Material republished with the express permission of Postmedia Network Inc.

CHAPTER 16

Opening photo: DONOT6_STUDIO / Shutterstock

Box 16.3: Battams, N. 2016. "Family Caregiving in Canada: A Fact of Life and a Human Right." Ottawa: Vanier Institute of the Family. Retrieved November 4, 2016, from www.vanierinstitute.ca/family-caregiving-in-canada. Used by kind permission of Nathan Battams.

Box 16.4: Kershaw, P., and L. Anderson. 2011. "Fact Sheet: A New Deal for Families." Human Early Learning Partnership, University of British Columbia. Retrieved January 25, 2011, from http://earlylearning.ubc.ca/documents/159/. Used by kind permission of Paul Kershaw.

Figure 16.4: Photo used by permission of Tami Starlight, Cree/Norwegian intersectional community organizer

Index